American Casebook Series
Hornbook Series and Basic Legal Texts
Nutshell Series

of

WEST PUBLISHING COMPANY
P.O. Box 64526
St. Paul, Minnesota 55164–0526

ACCOUNTING

Faris' Accounting and Law in a Nutshell, 377 pages, 1984 (Text)

Fiflis, Kripke and Foster's Teaching Materials on Accounting for Business Lawyers, 3rd Ed., 838 pages, 1984 (Casebook)

Siegel and Siegel's Accounting and Financial Disclosure: A Guide to Basic Concepts, 259 pages, 1983 (Text)

ADMINISTRATIVE LAW

Davis' Cases, Text and Problems on Administrative Law, 6th Ed., 683 pages, 1977 (Casebook)

Davis' Basic Text on Administrative Law, 3rd Ed., 617 pages, 1972 (Text)

Davis' Police Discretion, 176 pages, 1975 (Text)

Gellhorn and Boyer's Administrative Law and Process in a Nutshell, 2nd Ed., 445 pages, 1981 (Text)

Mashaw and Merrill's Cases and Materials on Administrative Law–The American Public Law System, 2nd Ed., approximately 1125 pages, 1985 (Casebook)

Robinson, Gellhorn and Bruff's The Administrative Process, 2nd Ed., 959 pages, 1980, with 1983 Supplement (Casebook)

ADMIRALTY

Healy and Sharpe's Cases and Materials on Admiralty, 875 pages, 1974 (Casebook)

Maraist's Admiralty in a Nutshell, 390 pages, 1983 (Text)

Sohn and Gustafson's Law of the Sea in a Nutshell, 264 pages, 1984 (Text)

AGENCY—PARTNERSHIP

Fessler's Alternatives to Incorporation for Persons in Quest of Profit, 258 pages, 1980 (Casebook)

AGENCY—PARTNERSHIP—Continued

Henn's Cases and Materials on Agency, Partnership and Other Unincorporated Business Enterprises, 2nd Ed., 733 pages, 1985 (Casebook)

Reuschlein and Gregory's Hornbook on the Law of Agency and Partnership, 625 pages, 1979, with 1981 pocket part (Text)

Seavey, Reuschlein and Hall's Cases on Agency and Partnership, 599 pages, 1962 (Casebook)

Selected Corporation and Partnership Statutes and Forms, approximately 560 pages, 1985

Steffen and Kerr's Cases and Materials on Agency-Partnership, 4th Ed., 859 pages, 1980 (Casebook)

Steffen's Agency-Partnership in a Nutshell, 364 pages, 1977 (Text)

AGRICULTURAL LAW

Meyer, Pedersen, Thorson and Davidson's Agricultural Law: Cases and Materials, approximately 925 pages, 1985 (Casebook)

AMERICAN INDIAN LAW

Canby's American Indian Law in a Nutshell, 288 pages, 1981 (Text)

Getches, Rosenfelt and Wilkinson's Cases on Federal Indian Law, 660 pages, 1979, with 1983 Supplement (Casebook)

ANTITRUST LAW

Gellhorn's Antitrust Law and Economics in a Nutshell, 2nd Ed., 425 pages, 1981 (Text)

Gifford and Raskind's Cases and Materials on Antitrust, 694 pages, 1983 with 1985 Supplement (Casebook)

Hovenkamp's Economics and Federal Antitrust Law, Student Ed., approximately 375 pages, 1985 (Text)

LAW SCHOOL PUBLICATIONS—Continued

ANTITRUST LAW—Continued

Oppenheim, Weston and McCarthy's Cases and Comments on Federal Antitrust Laws, 4th Ed., 1168 pages, 1981 with 1985 Supplement (Casebook)

Posner and Easterbrook's Cases and Economic Notes on Antitrust, 2nd Ed., 1077 pages, 1981, with 1984–85 Supplement (Casebook)

Sullivan's Hornbook of the Law of Antitrust, 886 pages, 1977 (Text)

See also Regulated Industries, Trade Regulation

ART LAW

DuBoff's Art Law in a Nutshell, 335 pages, 1984 (Text)

BANKING LAW

Lovett's Banking and Financial Institutions in a Nutshell, 409 pages, 1984 (Text)

Symons and White's Teaching Materials on Banking Law, 2nd Ed., 993 pages, 1984 (Casebook)

BUSINESS PLANNING

Epstein and Scheinfeld's Teaching Materials on Business Reorganization Under the Bankruptcy Code, 216 pages, 1980 (Casebook)

Painter's Problems and Materials in Business Planning, 2nd Ed., 1008 pages, 1984 (Casebook)

Selected Securities and Business Planning Statutes, Rules and Forms, 470 pages, 1985

CIVIL PROCEDURE

Casad's Res Judicata in a Nutshell, 310 pages, 1976 (text)

Cound, Friedenthal, Miller and Sexton's Cases and Materials on Civil Procedure, 4th Ed., approximately 1147 pages, 1985 with 1985 Supplement (Casebook)

Ehrenzweig, Louisell and Hazard's Jurisdiction in a Nutshell, 4th Ed., 232 pages, 1980 (Text)

Federal Rules of Civil-Appellate-Criminal Procedure—West Law School Edition, approximately 457 pages, 1984

Friedenthal, Kane and Miller's Hornbook on Civil Procedure, Student Edition, approximately 750 pages, 1985 (Text)

Hodges, Jones and Elliott's Cases and Materials on Texas Trial and Appellate Procedure, 2nd Ed., 745 pages, 1974 (Casebook)

Hodges, Jones and Elliott's Cases and Materials on the Judicial Process Prior to Trial in Texas, 2nd Ed., 871 pages, 1977 (Casebook)

Kane's Civil Procedure in a Nutshell, 271 pages, 1979 (Text)

CIVIL PROCEDURE—Continued

Karlen's Procedure Before Trial in a Nutshell, 258 pages, 1972 (Text)

Karlen, Meisenholder, Stevens and Vestal's Cases on Civil Procedure, 923 pages, 1975 (Casebook)

Koffler and Reppy's Hornbook on Common Law Pleading, 663 pages, 1969 (Text)

Park's Computer-Aided Exercises on Civil Procedure, 2nd Ed., 167 pages, 1983 (Coursebook)

Siegel's Hornbook on New York Practice, 1011 pages, 1978 with 1981–82 Pocket Part (Text)

See also Federal Jurisdiction and Procedure

CIVIL RIGHTS

Abernathy's Cases and Materials on Civil Rights, 660 pages, 1980 (Casebook)

Cohen's Cases on the Law of Deprivation of Liberty: A Study in Social Control, 755 pages, 1980 (Casebook)

Lockhart, Kamisar and Choper's Cases on Constitutional Rights and Liberties, 5th Ed., 1298 pages plus Appendix, 1981, with 1984 Supplement (Casebook)—reprint from Lockhart, et al. Cases on Constitutional Law, 5th Ed., 1980

Vieira's Civil Rights in a Nutshell, 279 pages, 1978 (Text)

COMMERCIAL LAW

Bailey's Secured Transactions in a Nutshell, 2nd Ed., 391 pages, 1981 (Text)

Epstein and Martin's Basic Uniform Commercial Code Teaching Materials, 2nd Ed., 667 pages, 1983 (Casebook)

Henson's Hornbook on Secured Transactions Under the U.C.C., 2nd Ed., 504 pages, 1979 with 1979 P.P. (Text)

Murray's Commercial Law, Problems and Materials, 366 pages, 1975 (Coursebook)

Nordstrom and Clovis' Problems and Materials on Commercial Paper, 458 pages, 1972 (Casebook)

Nordstrom and Lattin's Problems and Materials on Sales and Secured Transactions, 809 pages, 1968 (Casebook)

Nordstrom, Murray and Clovis' Problems and Materials on Sales, 515 pages, 1982 (Casebook)

Selected Commercial Statutes, approximately 1379 pages, 1985

Speidel, Summers and White's Teaching Materials on Commercial and Consumer Law, 3rd Ed., 1490 pages, 1981 (Casebook)

Stockton's Sales in a Nutshell, 2nd Ed., 370 pages, 1981 (Text)

Stone's Uniform Commercial Code in a Nutshell, 2nd Ed., 516 pages, 1984 (Text)

Uniform Commercial Code, Official Text with Comments, 994 pages, 1978

LAW SCHOOL PUBLICATIONS—Continued

COMMERCIAL LAW—Continued

UCC Article 9, Reprint from 1962 Code, 128 pages, 1976

UCC Article 9, 1972 Amendments, 304 pages, 1978

Weber and Speidel's Commercial Paper in a Nutshell, 3rd Ed., 404 pages, 1982 (Text)

White and Summers' Hornbook on the Uniform Commercial Code, 2nd Ed., 1250 pages, 1980 (Text)

COMMUNITY PROPERTY

Mennell's Community Property in a Nutshell, 447 pages, 1982 (Text)

Verrall and Bird's Cases and Materials on California Community Property, 4th Ed., 549 pages, 1983 (Casebook)

COMPARATIVE LAW

Barton, Gibbs, Li and Merryman's Law in Radically Different Cultures, 960 pages, 1983 (Casebook)

Glendon, Gordon, and Osakwe's Comparative Legal Traditions in a Nutshell, 402 pages, 1982 (Text)

Langbein's Comparative Criminal Procedure: Germany, 172 pages, 1977 (Casebook)

COMPUTERS AND LAW

Mason's An Introduction to the Use of Computers in Law, 223 pages, 1984 (Text)

CONFLICT OF LAWS

Cramton, Currie and Kay's Cases-Comments-Questions on Conflict of Laws, 3rd Ed., 1026 pages, 1981 (Casebook)

Scoles and Hay's Hornbook on Conflict of Laws, Student Ed., 1085 pages, 1982 (Text)

Scoles and Weintraub's Cases and Materials on Conflict of Laws, 2nd Ed., 966 pages, 1972, with 1978 Supplement (Casebook)

Siegel's Conflicts in a Nutshell, 469 pages, 1982 (Text)

Engdahl's Constitutional Power in a Nutshell: Federal and State, 411 pages, 1974 (Text)

Lockhart, Kamisar and Choper's Cases-Comments-Questions on Constitutional Law, 5th Ed., 1705 pages plus Appendix, 1980, with 1984 Supplement (Casebook)

Lockhart, Kamisar and Choper's Cases-Comments-Questions on the American Constitution, 5th Ed., 1185 pages plus Appendix, 1981, with 1984 Supplement (Casebook)—reprint from Lockhart, et al. Cases on Constitutional Law, 5th Ed., 1980

Manning's The Law of Church-State Relations in a Nutshell, 305 pages, 1981 (Text)

CONFLICT OF LAWS—Continued

Miller's Presidential Power in a Nutshell, 328 pages, 1977 (Text)

CONSTITUTIONAL LAW

Nowak, Rotunda and Young's Hornbook on Constitutional Law, 2nd Ed., Student Ed., 1172 pages, 1983 (Text)

Rotunda's Modern Constitutional Law: Cases and Notes, 2nd Ed., approximately 1055 pages, 1985 (Casebook)

Williams' Constitutional Analysis in a Nutshell, 388 pages, 1979 (Text)

See also Civil Rights

CONSUMER LAW

Epstein and Nickles' Consumer Law in a Nutshell, 2nd Ed., 418 pages, 1981 (Text)

McCall's Consumer Protection, Cases, Notes and Materials, 594 pages, 1977, with 1977 Statutory Supplement (Casebook)

Selected Commercial Statutes, approximately 1379 pages, 1985

Spanogle and Rohner's Cases and Materials on Consumer Law, 693 pages, 1979, with 1982 Supplement (Casebook)

See also Commercial Law

CONTRACTS

Calamari & Perillo's Cases and Problems on Contracts, 1061 pages, 1978 (Casebook)

Calamari and Perillo's Hornbook on Contracts, 2nd Ed., 878 pages, 1977 (Text)

Corbin's Text on Contracts, One Volume Student Edition, 1224 pages, 1952 (Text)

Fessler and Loiseaux's Cases and Materials on Contracts, 837 pages, 1982 (Casebook)

Freedman's Cases and Materials on Contracts, 658 pages, 1973 (Casebook)

Friedman's Contract Remedies in a Nutshell, 323 pages, 1981 (Text)

Fuller and Eisenberg's Cases on Basic Contract Law, 4th Ed., 1203 pages, 1981 (Casebook)

Hamilton, Rau and Weintraub's Cases and Materials on Contracts, 830 pages, 1984 (Casebook)

Jackson and Bollinger's Cases on Contract Law in Modern Society, 2nd Ed., 1329 pages, 1980 (Casebook)

Keyes' Government Contracts in a Nutshell, 423 pages, 1979 (Text)

Reitz's Cases on Contracts as Basic Commercial Law, 763 pages, 1975 (Casebook)

Schaber and Rohwer's Contracts in a Nutshell, 2nd Ed., 425 pages, 1984 (Text)

COPYRIGHT

See Patent and Copyright Law

LAW SCHOOL PUBLICATIONS—Continued

CORPORATIONS

Hamilton's Cases on Corporations—Including Partnerships and Limited Partnerships, 2nd Ed., 1108 pages, 1981, with 1981 Statutory Supplement and 1984 Supplement (Casebook)

Hamilton's Law of Corporations in a Nutshell, 379 pages, 1980 (Text)

Henn's Cases on Corporations, 1279 pages, 1974, with 1980 Supplement (Casebook)

Henn and Alexander's Hornbook on Corporations, 3rd Ed., Student Ed., 1371 pages, 1983 (Text)

Jennings and Buxbaum's Cases and Materials on Corporations, 5th Ed., 1180 pages, 1979 (Casebook)

Selected Corporation and Partnership Statutes, Regulations and Forms, approximately 560 pages, 1985

Solomon, Stevenson and Schwartz' Materials and Problems on Corporations: Law and Policy, 1172 pages, 1982 with 1984 Supplement (Casebook)

CORPORATE FINANCE

Hamilton's Cases and Materials on Corporate Finance, 895 pages, 1984 (Casebook)

CORRECTIONS

Krantz's Cases and Materials on the Law of Corrections and Prisoners' Rights, 2nd Ed., 735 pages, 1981, with 1982 Supplement (Casebook)

Krantz's Law of Corrections and Prisoners' Rights in a Nutshell, 2nd Ed., 384 pages, 1983 (Text)

Popper's Post-Conviction Remedies in a Nutshell, 360 pages, 1978 (Text)

Robbins' Cases and Materials on Post Conviction Remedies, 506 pages, 1982 (Casebook)

Rubin's Law of Criminal Corrections, 2nd Ed., 873 pages, 1973, with 1978 Supplement (Text)

CREDITOR'S RIGHTS

Bankruptcy Code, Rules and Forms, Law School Ed., 602 pages, 1984

Epstein's Debtor-Creditor Law in a Nutshell, 2nd Ed., 324 pages, 1980 (Text)

Epstein and Landers' Debtors and Creditors: Cases and Materials, 2nd Ed., 689 pages, 1982 (Casebook)

Epstein and Sheinfeld's Teaching Materials on Business Reorganization Under the Bankruptcy Code, 216 pages, 1980 (Casebook)

LoPucki's Player's Manual for the Debtor-Creditor Game, 123 pages, 1985 (Coursebook)

CREDITOR'S RIGHT'S—Continued

Riesenfeld's Cases and Materials on Creditors' Remedies and Debtors' Protection, 3rd Ed., 810 pages, 1979 with 1979 Statutory Supplement and 1981 Case Supplement (Casebook)

White's Bankruptcy and Creditor's Rights: Cases and Materials, approximately 820 pages, 1985 (Casebook)

CRIMINAL LAW AND CRIMINAL PROCEDURE

Cohen and Gobert's Problems in Criminal Law, 297 pages, 1976 (Problem book)

Davis' Police Discretion, 176 pages, 1975 (Text)

Dix and Sharlot's Cases and Materials on Criminal Law, 2nd Ed., 771 pages, 1979 (Casebook)

Federal Rules of Civil-Appellate-Criminal Procedure—West Law School Edition, 457 pages, 1984

Grano's Problems in Criminal Procedure, 2nd Ed., 176 pages, 1981 (Problem book)

Israel and LaFave's Criminal Procedure in a Nutshell, 3rd Ed., 438 pages, 1980 (Text)

Johnson's Cases, Materials and Text on Substantive Criminal Law in its Procedural Context, 3rd Ed., approximately 750 pages, 1985 (Casebook)

Kamisar, LaFave and Israel's Cases, Comments and Questions on Modern Criminal Procedure, 5th ed., 1635 pages plus Appendix, 1980 with 1984 Supplement (Casebook)

Kamisar, LaFave and Israel's Cases, Comments and Questions on Basic Criminal Procedure, 5th Ed., 869 pages, 1980 with 1984 Supplement (Casebook)—reprint from Kamisar, et al. Modern Criminal Procedure, 5th ed., 1980

LaFave's Modern Criminal Law: Cases, Comments and Questions, 789 pages, 1978 (Casebook)

LaFave and Israel's Hornbook on Criminal Procedure, Student Ed., approximately 1100 pages, 1985 (Text)

LaFave and Scott's Hornbook on Criminal Law, 763 pages, 1972 (Text)

Langbein's Comparative Criminal Procedure: Germany, 172 pages, 1977 (Casebook)

Loewy's Criminal Law in a Nutshell, 302 pages, 1975 (Text)

Saltzburg's American Criminal Procedure, Cases and Commentary, 2nd Ed., 1193 pages, 1984 with 1984 Supplement (Casebook)

LAW SCHOOL PUBLICATIONS—Continued

CRIMINAL LAW AND CRIMINAL PRO-CEDURE—Continued

Uviller's The Processes of Criminal Justice: Investigation and Adjudication, 2nd Ed., 1384 pages, 1979 with 1979 Statutory Supplement and 1983 Update (Casebook)

Uviller's The Processes of Criminal Justice: Adjudication, 2nd Ed., 730 pages, 1979. Soft-cover reprint from Uviller's The Processes of Criminal Justice: Investigation and Adjudication, 2nd Ed. (Casebook)

Uviller's The Processes of Criminal Justice: Investigation, 2nd Ed., 655 pages, 1979. Soft-cover reprint from Uviller's The Processes of Criminal Justice: Investigation and Adjudication, 2nd Ed. (Casebook)

Vorenberg's Cases on Criminal Law and Procedure, 2nd Ed., 1088 pages, 1981 with 1985 Supplement (Casebook)

See also Corrections, Juvenile Justice

DECEDENTS ESTATES

See Trusts and Estates

DOMESTIC RELATIONS

Clark's Cases and Problems on Domestic Relations, 3rd Ed., 1153 pages, 1980 (Casebook)

Clark's Hornbook on Domestic Relations, 754 pages, 1968 (Text)

Krause's Cases and Materials on Family Law, 2nd Ed., 1221 pages, 1983 (Casebook)

Krause's Family Law in a Nutshell, 400 pages, 1977 (Text)

Krauskopf's Cases on Property Division at Marriage Dissolution, 250 pages, 1984 (Casebook)

ECONOMICS, LAW AND

Goetz' Cases and Materials on Law and Economics, 547 pages, 1984 (Casebook)

Manne's The Economics of Legal Relationships—Readings in the Theory of Property Rights, 660 pages, 1975 (Text)

See also Antitrust, Regulated Industries

EDUCATION LAW

Alexander and Alexander's The Law of Schools, Students and Teachers in a Nutshell, 409 pages, 1984 (Text)

Morris' The Constitution and American Education, 2nd Ed., 992 pages, 1980 (Casebook)

EMPLOYMENT DISCRIMINATION

Player's Cases and Materials on Employment Discrimination Law, 2nd Ed., 782 pages, 1984 (Casebook)

EMPLOYMENT DISCRIMINATION—Continued

Player's Federal Law of Employment Discrimination in a Nutshell, 2nd Ed., 402 pages, 1981 (Text)

See also Women and the Law

ENERGY LAW

Rodgers' Cases and Materials on Energy and Natural Resources Law, 2nd Ed., 877 pages, 1983 (Casebook)

Selected Environmental Law Statutes, 758 pages, 1984

Tomain's Energy Law in a Nutshell, 338 pages, 1981 (Text)

See also Natural Resources Law, Environmental Law, Oil and Gas, Water Law

ENVIRONMENTAL LAW

Bonine and McGarity's Cases and Materials on the Law of Environment and Pollution, 1076 pages, 1984 (Casebook)

Findley and Farber's Cases and Materials on Environmental Law, 2nd Ed., approximately 800 pages, 1985 (Casebook)

Findley and Farber's Environmental Law in a Nutshell, 343 pages, 1983 (Text)

Rodgers' Hornbook on Environmental Law, 956 pages, 1977 with 1984 pocket part (Text)

Selected Environmental Law Statutes, 758 pages, 1984

See also Energy Law, Natural Resources Law, Water Law

EQUITY

See Remedies

ESTATES

See Trusts and Estates

ESTATE PLANNING

Kurtz' Cases, Materials and Problems on Family Estate Planning, 853 pages, 1983 (Casebook)

Lynn's Introduction to Estate Planning, in a Nutshell, 3rd Ed., 370 pages, 1983 (Text)

See also Taxation

EVIDENCE

Broun and Meisenholder's Problems in Evidence, 2nd Ed., 304 pages, 1981 (Problem book)

Cleary and Strong's Cases, Materials and Problems on Evidence, 3rd Ed., 1143 pages, 1981 (Casebook)

Federal Rules of Evidence for United States Courts and Magistrates, 337 pages, 1984

Graham's Federal Rules of Evidence in a Nutshell, 429 pages, 1981 (Text)

Kimball's Programmed Materials on Problems in Evidence, 380 pages, 1978 (Problem book)

LAW SCHOOL PUBLICATIONS—Continued

EVIDENCE—Continued

Lempert and Saltzburg's A Modern Approach to Evidence: Text, Problems, Transcripts and Cases, 2nd Ed., 1296 pages, 1983 (Casebook)

Lilly's Introduction to the Law of Evidence, 486 pages, 1978 (Text)

McCormick, Elliott and Sutton's Cases and Materials on Evidence, 5th Ed., 1212 pages, 1981 (Casebook)

McCormick's Hornbook on Evidence, 3rd Ed., Student Ed., 1155 pages, 1984 (Text)

Rothstein's Evidence, State and Federal Rules in a Nutshell, 2nd Ed., 514 pages, 1981 (Text)

Saltzburg's Evidence Supplement: Rules, Statutes, Commentary, 245 pages, 1980 (Casebook Supplement)

FEDERAL JURISDICTION AND PROCEDURE

Currie's Cases and Materials on Federal Courts, 3rd Ed., 1042 pages, 1982 (Casebook)

Currie's Federal Jurisdiction in a Nutshell, 2nd Ed., 258 pages, 1981 (Text)

Federal Rules of Civil-Appellate-Criminal Procedure—West Law School Edition, 457 pages, 1984

Forrester and Moye's Cases and Materials on Federal Jurisdiction and Procedure, 3rd Ed., 917 pages, 1977 with 1981 Supplement (Casebook)

Redish's Cases, Comments and Questions on Federal Courts, 878 pages, 1983 (Casebook)

Vetri and Merrill's Federal Courts, Problems and Materials, 2nd Ed., 232 pages, 1984 (Problem Book)

Wright's Hornbook on Federal Courts, 4th Ed., Student Ed., 870 pages, 1983 (Text)

FUTURE INTERESTS

See Trusts and Estates

IMMIGRATION LAW

Aleinikoff and Martin's Immigration Process and Policy, approximately 800 pages, 1985 (Casebook)

Weissbrodt's Immigration Law and Procedure in a Nutshell, 345 pages, 1984 (Text)

INDIAN LAW

See American Indian Law

INSURANCE

Dobbyn's Insurance Law in a Nutshell, 281 pages, 1981 (Text)

INSURANCE—Continued

Keeton's Cases on Basic Insurance Law, 2nd Ed., 1086 pages, 1977

Keeton's Basic Text on Insurance Law, 712 pages, 1971 (Text)

Keeton's Case Supplement to Keeton's Basic Text on Insurance Law, 334 pages, 1978 (Casebook)

Keeton's Programmed Problems in Insurance Law, 243 pages, 1972 (Text Supplement)

York and Whelan's Cases, Materials and Problems on Insurance Law, 715 pages, 1982 (Casebook)

INTERNATIONAL LAW

Henkin, Pugh, Schachter and Smit's Cases and Materials on International Law, 2nd Ed., 1152 pages, 1980, with Documents Supplement (Casebook)

Jackson's Legal Problems of International Economic Relations, 1097 pages, 1977, with Documents Supplement (Casebook)

Kirgis' International Organizations in Their Legal Setting, 1016 pages, 1977, with 1981 Supplement (Casebook)

Weston, Falk and D'Amato's International Law and World Order—A Problem Oriented Coursebook, 1195 pages, 1980, with Documents Supplement (Casebook)

Wilson's International Business Transactions in a Nutshell, 2nd Ed., 476 pages, 1984 (Text)

INTERVIEWING AND COUNSELING

Binder and Price's Interviewing and Counseling, 232 pages, 1977 (Text)

Shaffer's Interviewing and Counseling in a Nutshell, 353 pages, 1976 (Text)

INTRODUCTION TO LAW

Dobbyn's So You Want to go to Law School, Revised First Edition, 206 pages, 1976 (Text)

Hegland's Introduction to the Study and Practice of Law in a Nutshell, 418 pages, 1983 (Text)

Kinyon's Introduction to Law Study and Law Examinations in a Nutshell, 389 pages, 1971 (Text)

See also Legal Method and Legal System

JUDICIAL ADMINISTRATION

Carrington, Meador and Rosenberg's Justice on Appeal, 263 pages, 1976 (Casebook)

Nelson's Cases and Materials on Judicial Administration and the Administration of Justice, 1032 pages, 1974 (Casebook)

LAW SCHOOL PUBLICATIONS—Continued

JURISPRUDENCE

Christie's Text and Readings on Jurisprudence—The Philosophy of Law, 1056 pages, 1973 (Casebook)

JUVENILE JUSTICE

Fox's Cases and Materials on Modern Juvenile Justice, 2nd Ed., 960 pages, 1981 (Casebook)

Fox's Juvenile Courts in a Nutshell, 3rd Ed., 291 pages, 1984 (Text)

LABOR LAW

Gorman's Basic Text on Labor Law—Unionization and Collective Bargaining, 914 pages, 1976 (Text)

Leslie's Labor Law in a Nutshell, 403 pages, 1979 (Text)

Nolan's Labor Arbitration Law and Practice in a Nutshell, 358 pages, 1979 (Text)

Oberer, Hanslowe and Andersen's Cases and Materials on Labor Law—Collective Bargaining in a Free Society, 2nd Ed., 1168 pages, 1979, with 1979 Statutory Supplement and 1982 Case Supplement (Casebook)

See also Employment Discrimination, Social Legislation

LAND FINANCE

See Real Estate Transactions

LAND USE

Hagman's Cases on Public Planning and Control of Urban and Land Development, 2nd Ed., 1301 pages, 1980 (Casebook)

Hagman's Hornbook on Urban Planning and Land Development Control Law, 706 pages, 1971 (Text)

Wright and Gitelman's Cases and Materials on Land Use, 3rd Ed., 1300 pages, 1982 (Casebook)

Wright and Webber's Land Use in a Nutshell, 316 pages, 1978 (Text)

LEGAL HISTORY

Presser and Zainaldin's Cases on Law and American History, 855 pages, 1980 (Casebook)

See also Legal Method and Legal System

LEGAL METHOD AND LEGAL SYSTEM

Aldisert's Readings, Materials and Cases in the Judicial Process, 948 pages, 1976 (Casebook)

Berch and Berch's Introduction to Legal Method and Process, approximately 460 pages, 1985 (Casebook)

Bodenheimer, Oakley and Love's Readings and Cases on an Introduction to the Anglo-American Legal System, 161 pages, 1980 (Casebook)

LEGAL METHOD AND LEGAL SYSTEM—Continued

Davies and Lawry's Institutions and Methods of the Law—Introductory Teaching Materials, 547 pages, 1982 (Casebook)

Dvorkin, Himmelstein and Lesnick's Becoming a Lawyer: A Humanistic Perspective on Legal Education and Professionalism, 211 pages, 1981 (Text)

Fryer and Orentlicher's Cases and Materials on Legal Method and Legal System, 1043 pages, 1967 (Casebook)

Greenberg's Judicial Process and Social Change, 666 pages, 1977 (Coursebook)

Kelso and Kelso's Studying Law: An Introduction, 587 pages, 1984 (Coursebook)

Kempin's Historical Introduction to Anglo-American Law in a Nutshell, 2nd Ed., 280 pages, 1973 (Text)

Kimball's Historical Introduction to the Legal System, 610 pages, 1966 (Casebook)

Murphy's Cases and Materials on Introduction to Law—Legal Process and Procedure, 772 pages, 1977 (Casebook)

Reynolds' Judicial Process in a Nutshell, 292 pages, 1980 (Text)

See also Legal Research and Writing

LEGAL PROFESSION

Aronson, Devine and Fisch's Problems, Cases and Materials on Professional Responsibility, approximately 710 pages, 1985 (Casebook)

Aronson and Weckstein's Professional Responsibility in a Nutshell, 399 pages, 1980 (Text)

Mellinkoff's The Conscience of a Lawyer, 304 pages, 1973 (Text)

Mellinkoff's Lawyers and the System of Justice, 983 pages, 1976 (Casebook)

Pirsig and Kirwin's Cases and Materials on Professional Responsibility, 4th Ed., 603 pages, 1984 (Casebook)

Schwartz and Wydick's Problems in Legal Ethics, 285 pages, 1983 (Casebook)

Selected Statutes, Rules and Standards on the Legal Profession, 276 pages, Revised 1984

Smith's Preventing Legal Malpractice, 142 pages, 1981 (Text)

Wolfram's Hornbook on Professional Responsibility, Student Edition, approximately 700 pages (Text)

LEGAL RESEARCH AND WRITING

Cohen's Legal Research in a Nutshell, 4th Ed., approximately 425 pages, 1985 (Text)

Cohen and Berring's How to Find the Law, 8th Ed., 790 pages, 1983. Problem book by Foster and Kelly available (Casebook)

Cohen and Berring's Finding the Law, 8th Ed., Abridged Ed., 556 pages, 1984 (Casebook)

LAW SCHOOL PUBLICATIONS—Continued

LEGAL RESEARCH AND WRITING—
Continued

Dickerson's Materials on Legal Drafting, 425 pages, 1981 (Casebook)

Felsenfeld and Siegel's Writing Contracts in Plain English, 290 pages, 1981 (Text)

Gopen's Writing From a Legal Perspective, 225 pages, 1981 (Text)

Mellinkoff's Legal Writing—Sense and Non-sense, 242 pages, 1982 (Text)

Rombauer's Legal Problem Solving—Analysis, Research and Writing, 4th Ed., 424 pages, 1983 (Coursebook)

Squires and Rombauer's Legal Writing in a Nutshell, 294 pages, 1982 (Text)

Statsky's Legal Research, Writing and Analysis, 2nd Ed., 167 pages, 1982 (Coursebook)

Statsky's Legislative Analysis: How to Use Statutes and Regulations, 2nd Ed., 217 pages, 1984 (Text)

Statsky and Wernet's Case Analysis and Fundamentals of Legal Writing, 2nd Ed., 441 pages, 1984 (Text)

Teply's Programmed Materials on Legal Research and Citation, 334 pages, 1982. Student Library Exercises available (Coursebook)

Weihofen's Legal Writing Style, 2nd Ed., 332 pages, 1980 (Text)

LEGISLATION

Davies' Legislative Law and Process in a Nutshell, 279 pages, 1975 (Text)

Nutting and Dickerson's Cases and Materials on Legislation, 5th Ed., 744 pages, 1978 (Casebook)

Statsky's Legislative Analysis: How to Use Statutes and Regulations, 2nd Ed., 217 pages, 1984 (Text)

LOCAL GOVERNMENT

McCarthy's Local Government Law in a Nutshell, 2nd Ed., 404 pages, 1983 (Text)

Michelman and Sandalow's Cases-Comments-Questions on Government in Urban Areas, 1216 pages, 1970, with 1972 Supplement (Casebook)

Reynolds' Hornbook on Local Government Law, 860 pages, 1982 (Text)

Valente's Cases and Materials on Local Government Law, 2nd Ed., 980 pages, 1980 with 1982 Supplement (Casebook)

MASS COMMUNICATION LAW

Gillmor and Barron's Cases and Comment on Mass Communication Law, 4th Ed., 1076 pages, 1984 (Casebook)

Ginsburg's Regulation of Broadcasting: Law and Policy Towards Radio, Television and Cable Communications, 741 pages, 1979, with 1983 Supplement (Casebook)

MASS COMMUNICATION LAW—
Continued

Zuckman and Gayne's Mass Communications Law in a Nutshell, 2nd Ed., 473 pages, 1983 (Text)

MEDICINE, LAW AND

King's The Law of Medical Malpractice in a Nutshell, 340 pages, 1977 (Text)

Shapiro and Spece's Problems, Cases and Materials on Bioethics and Law, 892 pages, 1981 (Casebook)

Sharpe, Fiscina and Head's Cases on Law and Medicine, 882 pages, 1978 (Casebook)

MILITARY LAW

Shanor and Terrell's Military Law in a Nutshell, 378 pages, 1980 (Text)

MORTGAGES

See Real Estate Transactions

NATURAL RESOURCES LAW

Laito's Cases and Materials on Natural Resources Law, approximately 900 pages, 1985 (Casebook)

See also Energy Law, Environmental Law, Oil and Gas, Water Law

NEGOTIATION

Edwards and White's Problems, Readings and Materials on the Lawyer as a Negotiator, 484 pages, 1977 (Casebook)

Williams' Legal Negotiation and Settlement, 207 pages, 1983 (Coursebook)

OFFICE PRACTICE

Hegland's Trial and Practice Skills in a Nutshell, 346 pages, 1978 (Text)

Strong and Clark's Law Office Management, 424 pages, 1974 (Casebook)

See also Computers and Law, Interviewing and Counseling, Negotiation

OIL AND GAS

Hemingway's Hornbook on Oil and Gas, 2nd Ed., Student Ed., 543 pages, 1983 (Text)

Huie, Woodward and Smith's Cases and Materials on Oil and Gas, 2nd Ed., 955 pages, 1972 (Casebook)

Lowe's Oil and Gas Law in a Nutshell, 443 pages, 1983 (Text)

See also Energy and Natural Resources Law

PARTNERSHIP

See Agency—Partnership

LAW SCHOOL PUBLICATIONS—Continued

PATENT AND COPYRIGHT LAW

Choate and Francis' Cases and Materials on Patent Law, 2nd Ed., 1110 pages, 1981 (Casebook)

Miller and Davis' Intellectual Property—Patents, Trademarks and Copyright in a Nutshell, 428 pages, 1983 (Text)

Nimmer's Cases on Copyright and Other Aspects of Entertainment Litigation, 3rd Ed., approximately 1000 pages, 1985 (Casebook)

POVERTY LAW

Brudno's Poverty, Inequality, and the Law: Cases-Commentary-Analysis, 934 pages, 1976 (Casebook)

LaFrance, Schroeder, Bennett and Boyd's Hornbook on Law of the Poor, 558 pages, 1973 (Text)

See also Social Legislation

PRODUCTS LIABILITY

Noel and Phillips' Cases on Products Liability, 2nd Ed., 821 pages, 1982 (Casebook)

Noel and Phillips' Products Liability in a Nutshell, 2nd Ed., 341 pages, 1981 (Text)

PROPERTY

Aigler, Smith and Tefft's Cases on Property, 2 volumes, 1339 pages, 1960 (Casebook)

Bernhardt's Real Property in a Nutshell, 2nd Ed., 448 pages, 1981 (Text)

Boyer's Survey of the Law of Property, 766 pages, 1981 (Text)

Browder, Cunningham and Smith's Cases on Basic Property Law, 4th Ed., 1431 pages, 1984 (Casebook)

Bruce, Ely and Bostick's Cases and Materials on Modern Property Law, 1004 pages, 1984 (Casebook)

Burby's Hornbook on Real Property, 3rd Ed., 490 pages, 1965 (Text)

Burke's Personal Property in a Nutshell, 322 pages, 1983 (Text)

Chused's A Modern Approach to Property: Cases-Notes-Materials, 1069 pages, 1978 with 1980 Supplement (Casebook)

Cohen's Materials for a Basic Course in Property, 526 pages, 1978 (Casebook)

Cunningham, Stoebuck and Whitman's Hornbook on the Law of Property, Student Ed., 916 pages, 1984 (Text)

Donahue, Kauper and Martin's Cases on Property, 2nd Ed., 1362 pages, 1983 (Casebook)

Hill's Landlord and Tenant Law in a Nutshell, 319 pages, 1979 (Text)

Moynihan's Introduction to Real Property, 254 pages, 1962 (Text)

Phipps' Titles in a Nutshell, 277 pages, 1968 (Text)

PROPERTY—Continued

Uniform Land Transactions Act, Uniform Simplification of Land Transfers Act, Uniform Condominium Act, 1977 Official Text with Comments, 462 pages, 1978

See also Real Estate Transactions, Land Use

PSYCHIATRY, LAW AND

Reisner's Law and the Mental Health System, Civil and Criminal Aspects, approximately 700 pages, 1985 (Casebooks)

REAL ESTATE TRANSACTIONS

Bruce's Real Estate Finance in a Nutshell, 2nd Ed., approximately 300 pages, 1985 (Text)

Maxwell, Riesenfeld, Hetland and Warren's Cases on California Security Transactions in Land, 3rd Ed., 728 pages, 1984 (Casebook)

Nelson and Whitman's Cases on Real Estate Transfer, Finance and Development, 2nd Ed., 1114 pages, 1981, with 1983 Supplement (Casebook)

Osborne's Cases and Materials on Secured Transactions, 559 pages, 1967 (Casebook)

Osborne, Nelson and Whitman's Hornbook on Real Estate Finance Law, 2nd Ed., approximately 900 pages, 1985 (Text)

REGULATED INDUSTRIES

Gellhorn and Pierce's Regulated Industries in a Nutshell, 394 pages, 1982 (Text)

Morgan, Harrison and Verkuil's Cases and Materials on Economic Regulation of Business, 2nd Ed., approximately 900 pages, 1985 (Casebook)

Pozen's Financial Institutions: Cases, Materials and Problems on Investment Management, 844 pages, 1978 (Casebook)

See also Mass Communication Law, Banking Law

REMEDIES

Dobbs' Hornbook on Remedies, 1067 pages, 1973 (Text)

Dobbs' Problems in Remedies, 137 pages, 1974 (Problem book)

Dobbyn's Injunctions in a Nutshell, 264 pages, 1974 (Text)

Friedman's Contract Remedies in a Nutshell, 323 pages, 1981 (Text)

Leavell, Love and Nelson's Cases and Materials on Equitable Remedies and Restitution, 3rd Ed., 704 pages, 1980 (Casebook)

McCormick's Hornbook on Damages, 811 pages, 1935 (Text)

O'Connell's Remedies in a Nutshell, 2nd Ed., 325 pages, 1985 (Text)

LAW SCHOOL PUBLICATIONS—Continued

REMEDIES—Continued

York and Bauman's Cases and Materials on Remedies, 4th Ed., approximately 1300 pages, 1985 (Casebook)

REVIEW MATERIALS

Ballantine's Problems
Black Letter Series
Smith's Review Series
West's Review Covering Multistate Subjects

SECURITIES REGULATION

Hazen's Hornbook on The Law of Securities Regulation, Student Ed., approximately 520 pages, 1985 (Text)
Ratner's Securities Regulation: Materials for a Basic Course, 2nd Ed., 1050 pages, 1980 with 1982 Supplement (Casebook)
Ratner's Securities Regulation in a Nutshell, 2nd Ed., 322 pages, 1982 (Text)
Selected Securities and Business Planning Statutes, Rules and Forms, approximately 485 pages, 1985

SOCIAL LEGISLATION

Hood and Hardy's Workers' Compensation and Employee Protection Laws in a Nutshell, 274 pages, 1984 (Text)
LaFrance's Welfare Law: Structure and Entitlement in a Nutshell, 455 pages, 1979 (Text)
Malone, Plant and Little's Cases on Workers' Compensation and Employment Rights, 2nd Ed., 951 pages, 1980 (Casebook)
See also Poverty Law

TAXATION

Dodge's Cases and Materials on Federal Income Taxation, approximately 925 pages, 1985 (Casebook)
Dodge's Federal Taxation of Estates, Trusts and Gifts: Principles and Planning, 771 pages, 1981 with 1982 Supplement (Casebook)
Garbis and Struntz' Cases and Materials on Tax Procedure and Tax Fraud, 829 pages, 1982 with 1984 Supplement (Casebook)
Gunn's Cases and Materials on Federal Income Taxation of Individuals, 785 pages, 1981 with 1985 Supplement (Casebook)
Hellerstein and Hellerstein's Cases on State and Local Taxation, 4th Ed., 1041 pages, 1978 with 1982 Supplement (Casebook)
Kahn's Handbook on Basic Corporate Taxation, 3rd Ed., Student Ed., 614 pages, 1981 with 1983 Supplement (Text)
Kahn and Gann's Corporate Taxation and Taxation of Partnerships and Partners, 2nd Ed., approximately 1300 pages, 1985 (Casebook)

TAXATION—Continued

Kragen and McNulty's Cases and Materials on Federal Income Taxation, 4th Ed., approximately 1200 pages, 1985 (Casebook)
McNulty's Federal Estate and Gift Taxation in a Nutshell, 3rd Ed., 509 pages, 1983 (Text)
McNulty's Federal Income Taxation of Individuals in a Nutshell, 3rd Ed., 487 pages, 1983 (Text)
Posin's Hornbook on Federal Income Taxation of Individuals, Student Ed., 491 pages, 1983 with 1985 pocket part (Text)
Rice and Solomon's Problems and Materials in Federal Income Taxation, 3rd Ed., 670 pages, 1979 (Casebook)
Rose and Raskind's Advanced Federal Income Taxation: Corporate Transactions—Cases, Materials and Problems, 955 pages, 1978 (Casebook)
Selected Federal Taxation Statutes and Regulations, 1255 pages, 1983
Soboloff and Weidenbruch's Federal Income Taxation of Corporations and Stockholders in a Nutshell, 362 pages, 1981 (Text)

TORTS

Christie's Cases and Materials on the Law of Torts, 1264 pages, 1983 (Casebook)
Dobbs' Torts and Compensation—Personal Accountability and Social Responsibility for Injury, approximately 1,050 pages, 1985 (Casebook)
Green, Pedrick, Rahl, Thode, Hawkins, Smith and Treece's Cases and Materials on Torts, 2nd Ed., 1360 pages, 1977 (Casebook)
Green, Pedrick, Rahl, Thode, Hawkins, Smith, and Treece's Advanced Torts: Injuries to Business, Political and Family Interests, 2nd Ed., 544 pages, 1977 (Casebook)—reprint from Green, et al. Cases and Materials on Torts, 2nd Ed., 1977
Keeton, Keeton, Sargentich and Steiner's Cases and Materials on Torts, and Accident Law, 1360 pages, 1983 (Casebook)
Kionka's Torts in a Nutshell: Injuries to Persons and Property, 434 pages, 1977 (Text)
Malone's Torts in a Nutshell: Injuries to Family, Social and Trade Relations, 358 pages, 1979 (Text)
Prosser and Keeton's Hornbook on Torts, 5th Ed., Student Ed., 1286 pages, 1984 (Text)
Shapo's Cases on Tort and Compensation Law, 1244 pages, 1976 (Casebook)
See also Products Liability

TRADE REGULATION

McManis' Unfair Trade Practices in a Nutshell, 444 pages, 1982 (Text)

LAW SCHOOL PUBLICATIONS—Continued

TRADE REGULATION—Continued

Oppenheim, Weston, Maggs and Schechter's Cases and Materials on Unfair Trade Practices and Consumer Protection, 4th Ed., 1038 pages, 1983 (Casebook)

See also Antitrust, Regulated Industries

TRIAL AND APPELLATE ADVOCACY

Appellate Advocacy, Handbook of, 249 pages, 1980 (Text)

Bergman's Trial Advocacy in a Nutshell, 402 pages, 1979 (Text)

Binder and Bergman's Fact Investigation: From Hypothesis to Proof, 354 pages, 1984 (Coursebook)

Goldberg's The First Trial (Where Do I Sit?, What Do I Say?) in a Nutshell, 396 pages, 1982 (Text)

Hegland's Trial and Practice Skills in a Nutshell, 346 pages, 1978 (Text)

Herr, Stempel and Haydock's Fundamentals of Pre-Trial Litigation, approximately 700 pages, 1985 (Casebook)

Hornstein's Appellate Advocacy in a Nutshell, 325 pages, 1984 (Text)

Jeans' Handbook on Trial Advocacy, Student Ed., 473 pages, 1975 (Text)

McElhaney's Effective Litigation, 457 pages, 1974 (Casebook)

Nolan's Cases and Materials on Trial Practice, 518 pages, 1981 (Casebook)

Parnell and Shellhaas' Cases, Exercises and Problems for Trial Advocacy, 171 pages, 1982 (Coursebook)

Sonsteng, Haydock and Boyd's The Trialbook: A Total System for Preparation and Presentation of a Case, Student Ed., 404 pages, 1984 (Coursebook)

TRUSTS AND ESTATES

Atkinson's Hornbook on Wills, 2nd Ed., 975 pages, 1953 (Text)

Averill's Uniform Probate Code in a Nutshell, 425 pages, 1978 (Text)

Bogert's Hornbook on Trusts, 5th Ed., 726 pages, 1973 (Text)

Clark, Lusky and Murphy's Cases and Materials on Gratuitous Transfers, 3rd Ed., approximately 1200 pages, 1985 (Casebook)

TRUSTS AND ESTATES—Continued

Gulliver's Cases and Materials on Future Interests, 624 pages, 1959 (Casebook)

Gulliver's Introduction to the Law of Future Interests, 87 pages, 1959 (Casebook)—reprint from Gulliver's Cases and Materials on Future Interests, 1959

McGovern's Cases and Materials on Wills, Trusts and Future Interests: An Introduction to Estate Planning, 750 pages, 1983 (Casebook)

Mennell's Cases and Materials on California Decedent's Estates, 566 pages, 1973 (Casebook)

Mennell's Wills and Trusts in a Nutshell, 392 pages, 1979 (Text)

Powell's The Law of Future Interests in California, 91 pages, 1980 (Text)

Simes' Hornbook on Future Interests, 2nd Ed., 355 pages, 1966 (Text)

Turrentine's Cases and Text on Wills and Administration, 2nd Ed., 483 pages, 1962 (Casebook)

Uniform Probate Code, 5th Ed., Official Text With Comments, 384 pages, 1977

Waggoner's Future Interests in a Nutshell, 361 pages, 1981 (Text)

WATER LAW

Getches' Water Law in a Nutshell, 439 pages, 1984 (Text)

Trelease's Cases and Materials on Water Law, 3rd Ed., 833 pages, 1979, with 1984 Supplement (Casebook)

See also Energy Law, Natural Resources Law, Environmental Law

WILLS

See Trusts and Estates

WOMEN AND THE LAW

Kay's Text, Cases and Materials on Sex-Based Discrimination, 2nd Ed., 1045 pages, 1981, with 1983 Supplement (Casebook)

Thomas' Sex Discrimination in a Nutshell, 399 pages, 1982 (Text)

See also Employment Discrimination

WORKERS' COMPENSATION

See Social Legislation

LAW AND THE MENTAL HEALTH SYSTEM

CIVIL AND CRIMINAL ASPECTS

By

Ralph Reisner

Professor of Law
University of Illinois-Champaign

AMERICAN CASEBOOK SERIES

WEST PUBLISHING CO.
ST. PAUL, MINN., 1985

COPYRIGHT © 1985 By WEST PUBLISHING CO.
50 West Kellogg Boulevard
P.O. Box 64526
St. Paul, Minnesota 55164–0526

Printed in the United States of America

Library of Congress Cataloging in Publication Data

Reisner, Ralph, 1931–
   Law and the mental health system, civil and criminal
aspects.

   (American casebook series)
   Includes index.
   1. Mental health laws—United States—Cases. 2. Mental
health personnel—Legal status, laws, etc.—United States
—Cases. 3. Insanity—Jurisprudence—United States—
Cases. 4. Insane—Commitment and detention—United States
—Cases. I. Title. II. Series.
KF3828.A7R44 1985   344.73'044   84–25764
ISBN 0–314–85286–7   347.30444

To

Danute and Carol

*

Preface

My initial intention was to develop teaching materials for use solely in law school instruction. However, my later involvement in interdisciplinary teaching prompted me to pursue a broader objective. In 1976 I was invited to teach a course on mental health law for students in the department of psychology. Later I was asked to teach a similar course for psychiatric residents in the department of psychiatry. My development of teaching materials for these courses caused me to conclude that materials could be developed which might be employed for teaching not only in a law school setting but also in courses enrolling students in the mental health field. As a side benefit, it seemed to me that materials suitable for interdisciplinary use might also serve to close some of the conceptual gaps between the legal and mental health professions that have persisted for too long.

Those familiar with the techniques used in law school teaching will find these materials similar to those generally used in law school courses. The emphasis is on the use of reported cases as a basis both to evaluate existing law and to address issues which changes in biotechnology or practice might bring to the forefront. The standard case approach which this book adopts is, however, tempered by the inclusion of extensive amounts of explanatory materials designed to provide the reader with the overall context in which the individual cases must be considered. Materials drawn from both legal and non-legal sources have been included in the questions and comments sections which follow the primary cases. The inclusion of these materials is designed both to emphasize the diversity of the approaches that have been adopted by various jurisdictions and also to facilitate student discussion of the issues raised by the cases themselves.

Any number of logical and sensible schemes for organizing and presenting the materials contained in this book were available. The approach adopted, however, was to group and relate problems, subjects and issues together as they commonly seem to arise in the adjudicative, regulatory and administrative contexts. This structure had the advantage of simplicity and clarity. Whatever may have been lost by adopting this approach in intellectual elegance or sophistication will, I hope, be more than offset by gains in the ease with which the book may be used for reference and for teaching.

A book dealing with mental health law must have several objectives. First, it should give the student an insight into the fundamental questions of how and to what degree the legal system can be used to implement desired social objectives. Second, it should provide the student with information concerning the current status of legal doctrine in the field and the dominant issues which surround particular doctrinal resolutions. Third, the book should provide an awareness of the value choices which are implicit in any such resolution of particular issues. Finally, it should sensitize both lawyers and other professionals active in the field to the delicate interrelationships among the various legal and social structures involved.

To further these varied ends, the book is divided into two principal parts. The first, "The Mental Health Professions and the Law" deals with the structure of the mental health profession (chapter 1) and the duties owed by practitioners and researchers to patients or clients; i.e., the duties of reasonable care (chapter 2), of rendering treatment within the boundaries agreed upon with the patient or as defined by law, (chapter 3), and of preserving the confidences of the client (chapter 4). The second, "The Mental Health Systems" shifts the focus to the issues and rules at the interface between the mentally ill or incapacitated individual and the institutional systems and processes designed to deal with such persons. Here we look at the legal parameters of voluntary (chapter 5) and involuntary (chapter 6) psychiatric hospitalization, the special issues governing the protection of the mentally incompetent (chapter 7), and finally, the mental health issues which relate to the criminal process.

Teachers using this book for classes not principally composed of law students may want to use certain supplementary materials. Most important, in my view, would be materials designed to give students an overview of the basic structures of the American legal system including sources of law, the authority and jurisdiction of various courts and tribunals, and the relationship of state and federal law. Similarly, law teachers may wish to eliminate certain materials in the book, such as some of the introductory materials on malpractice and informed consent, which may be adequately covered in more basic courses.

The subject of this book is a field which has undergone rapid and substantial change during the past two decades. As both law and the behavioral sciences have taken a more sophisticated stance towards the mentally disabled, the interaction of the two fields has become greater and more complex. This book is the culmination of an effort to bring clarity to this interaction in the hope that, through greater interest in the problems discussed herein, policies may be developed that are more sensitive to the varied interests of both the mentally disabled and of society at large.

Some comments concerning the citation form and editing of the cases may be in order. Citations conform to the Uniform System of Citation (13th edition, 1981). Most cases have been edited substantially. The deletion of *textual* portions is indicated by three asterisks. The deletion of *citations* or *footnotes* is not indicated by an asterisk or other signal. When case footnotes have been included they are *numbered* as in the original text; my footnotes are *lettered.*

I am indebted to many people whose encouragement, counsel, and assistance furthered this endeavor. In particular I am indebted to Ms. Sherry Cibelli who has worked beside me these past six years and whose extraordinary skill and patience made the book possible. It has also been my good fortune for over twenty years to have as a colleague, Wayne R. LaFave. His advice and encouragement has been signally important to me. Whatever understanding I may have gained of the criminal law process is largely the result of his mentorship.

I have also benefited greatly from my collaboration with colleagues in the mental health field. Dr. John Loesch, who in past years commuted from Chicago to Champaign to work with me in the teaching of seminars and courses here at the law school, taught me much. Similarly, I am indebted to Drs. Harry Little and Lawrence Jeckel who have generously given of their time in co-teaching the mental health law courses at this law school. Also, I have benefited greatly from my longstanding association with Jack Heller, Esq., Naomi Heller, M.D. of Washington, D.C. and Herbert Semmel, Esq. of New York. My thanks as well to Roger Adelman, Esq., of the U.S. Attorney's Office in Washington, D.C. for the help he has given me and his many helpful suggestions.

A number of former students, who are now in the practice of law, contributed more than one could reasonably expect from research assistants. In particular, I would like to acknowledge the contributions of Philip McConnaughay and Judy Poltz who worked with me in the initial drafts of this text. More recently, I have benefited from the talented help of Kevin Howley, Dean Gramlich, James Marvin, and Richard Yant. I also would like to acknowledge the editorial help of Susan Patterson whose review of the manuscript has made it more readable than it otherwise might have been.

The congenial and supportive environment here at the University of Illinois deserves mention. In particular, I would like to thank Dean Peter Hay for the encouragement and support he has given me over the years. I also owe a debt of gratitude to my colleagues, too numerous to mention, for their advice and counsel.

Finally, what has encouraged and sustained me throughout the project has been the understanding, support, and unselfish patience of my wife, Danute, and my children.

RALPH REISNER

Champaign, Illinois
December, 1984

Acknowledgments

The author wishes to acknowledge, with gratitude, permission to reprint the following copyrighted materials.

Freud's Fragmented Legacy, by Dava Sobel, from THE NEW YORK TIMES MAGAZINE, October 26, 1980, p. 28. Copyright © by The New York Times Company. Reprinted by permission.

Sex Therapy: As Popularity Grows, Critics Question Whether It Works, by Dava Sobel, from THE NEW YORK TIMES, November 14, 1980, p. 17. Copyright © by The New York Times Company. Reprinted by permission.

From THE PSYCHIATRISTS, by Arnold A. Rogow. Copyright © 1970 by Arnold A. Rogow. Reprinted by permission of G.P. Putnam's Sons.

From THE PROFESSION OF PSYCHOLOGY, by Wilse B. Webb. Copyright © 1962 by Holt, Rinehart and Winston, Inc. Reprinted by permission of Holt, Rinehart and Winston, CBS College Publishing.

From THE PROFESSIONAL PSYCHOLOGIST TODAY, by Herbert Dorken and Associates. Copyright © 1976 by Jossey-Bass, Inc., Publishers. Reprinted by permission of Jossey-Bass, Inc., Publishers.

Licensing Mental Therapists, by Daniel B. Hogan, from THE NEW YORK TIMES, July 18, 1979, p. A–23. Copyright © by The New York Times Company. Reprinted by permission.

Doctors, Damages and Deterrence, by Schwartz and Komesar, New England Journal of Medicine 298 (1978). Copyright © 1978 by the New England Journal of Medicine. Reprinted by permission of The New England Journal of Medicine, (Vol. 298, pp. 1284, 1978).

From PSYCHIATRY AND THE LAW, by Manfred S. Guttmacher and Henry Weihofen. Copyright © 1952 by W.W. Norton & Company, Inc. Reprinted by permission of W.W. Norton & Company, Inc.

From LAW, LIBERTY AND PSYCHIATRY by Thomas S. Szasz, M.D. Copyright © 1963 by Thomas S. Szasz, M.D. Reprinted by permission of Macmillan Publishing Co., Inc.

"Voluntary" Hospitalization of the Mentally Ill, by Janet A. Gilboy and John R. Schmidt, 66 Northwestern Law Review 429 (1971).

printed by permission of the California Law Review, Inc. and Fred Rothman & Co.

Psychiatry on the Presumption of Expertise: Flipping Coins in the Courtroom, by Bruce J. Ennis and Thomas R. Litwach, 62 California Law Review 693 (1974). Copyright © 1974 by the California Law Review, Inc. Reprinted by permission of the Califoria Law Review, Inc. and Fred Rothman & Co.

Involuntary Psychiatric Commitments to Prevent Suicide, by David F. Greenberg, 49 New York University Law Review 227 (1974). Copyright © 1974 by the New York University Law Review. Reprinted by permission of the New York University Law Review.

The New Snake Pits, from *Newsweek* (May 15, 1978), p. 93. Copyright © 1978 by Newsweek, Inc. Reprinted by permission of Newsweek, Inc.

A New Trade in Lunacy: The Recommodification of the Mental Patient, by Andrew Scull, 24 American Behavioral Scientist 724 (1981). Copyright © 1981 by the American Behavioral Scientist. Reprinted by permission of Sage Publications, Inc.

The Judicial Power of the Purse, by Gerald E. Frug, 126 University of Pennsylvania Law Review 715 (1978). Copyright © 1978 by Gerald E. Frug. Reprinted by permission of the University of Pennsylvania Law Review.

The Privilege Against Self-Incrimination in Civil Commitment Proceedings, by Marianne Wesson, 1980 Wisconsin Law Review 697 (1980). Copyright © 1980 by Marianne Wesson. Reprinted by permission of the Wisconsin Law Review.

From MENTAL HEALTH LAW, by David B. Wexler. Copyright © 1981 by David B. Wexler. Reprinted by permission of Plenum Publishing Corporation.

The Waivability of Recommitment Hearings, by David B. Wexler, 20 Arizona Law Review 175 (1978). Copyright © 1978 by Arizona Board of Regents. Reprinted by permission of the Arizona Board of Regents.

From DECARCERATION, by Andrew T. Scull. Copyright ©. 1977 by Prentice-Hall, Inc. Reprinted by permission of Prentice-Hall, Inc.

Limiting the Therapeutic Orgy: Mental Patient's Right to Refuse Treatment, by Robert Plotkin, 72 Northwestern Law Review 461 (1978). Copyright © 1978 by Northwestern Law Review. Reprinted by permission of the Northwestern Law Review.

Our Exploitation of Mental Patients, by F. Lewis Bartlett, M.D., The Atlantic Monthly (July 1964). Copyright © 1964 by F. Lewis

Bartlett, M.D., as first published in THE ATLANTIC MONTHLY. Reprinted with permission of Atlantic Monthly.

From THE MENTALLY DISABLED AND THE LAW, by Samuel Jan Brakel and Ronald S. Rock. Copyright © 1971 by the American Bar Foundation. Reprinted by permission of the American Bar Foundation.

The Insanity Defense: Historical Development and Contemporary Relevance, by Sheila Hafter Gray, M.D., 10 American Criminal Law Review 555 (1972). Copyright © 1072 by Sheila Hafter Gray, M.D. Reprinted by permission of the American Bar Association Criminal Justice Section.

From THE INSANITY DEFENSE, by Abraham S. Goldstein. Copyright © 1967 by Yale University Press. Reprinted by permission of Yale University Press.

From MADNESS AND THE CRIMINAL LAW, by Norval Morris. Copyright © 1982 by The University of Chicago Press. Reprinted by permission of The University of Chicago Press.

Review of Madness and the Criminal Law, by Paul Johnson, 50 University of Chicago Law Review 1534 (1983). Copyright © 1983 by University of Chicago Law Review. Reprinted by permission of University of Chicago Law Review.

Hinckley Tells Court "I am Ready Now" to Press for Release, from THE NEW YORK TIMES, July 28, 1984, p. 2, col. 1. Copyright © 1984 by The New York Times Company. Reprinted by permission.

Summary of Contents

Table of Contents

*

Table of Cases

The principal cases are in italic type. Cases cited or discussed are in roman type.
References are to Pages.

*

LAW AND THE MENTAL HEALTH SYSTEM

CIVIL AND CRIMINAL ASPECTS

*

Part One

THE MENTAL HEALTH PROFESSIONS AND THE LAW

Chapter One

REGULATION OF THE MENTAL HEALTH PROFESSIONS

Table of Sections

I. INTRODUCTION

A. THE PURPOSES OF REGULATION

Societal recognition of the value of professional counseling for those suffering from emotional maladjustment or mental illness has increased in recent years. Nevertheless, obtaining safe and effective psychiatric or psychological therapy still presents significant difficulties for the average layman. From the standpoint of the patient, a meaningful opportunity for treatment presupposes the ability to identify a suitable therapist. The prospective patient must first determine which profession can best treat his or her particular malady and then choose an individual practitioner from among the myriad varieties of "experts" in the selected mental health field. Consider for a moment the choice confronting a married couple that seeks professional advice to deal with a problem of sexual maladjustment. Initially, they must elect a particular mental health professional from a wide range of professional categories, including psychiatrists, psychologists, marriage and family counselors, and psychiatric social workers. Even within the various professional categories, they may have to choose one of a number of treatment modalities such as sex therapy, transactional analysis, relationship counseling, group therapy, or any one of countless other treatment "specialities."

Selecting the appropriate professional category or specialist is only the first step in obtaining counseling or psychotherapy. Our hypothetical couple will also want to be sure that the practitioner is competent and adequately trained to treat their particular problem. How many psychology or psychiatry courses are necessary to prepare a competent counselor-therapist? How much supervised experience is necessary? Is a degree from a prestigious medical school adequate certification of psychiatric competence? How valid is professional training completed twenty or thirty years ago? Obviously, few patients are sufficiently knowledgeable to reach an informed conclusion on these matters.

Even when the therapist has the appropriate paper qualifications, the patient always runs the risk that the particular professional may not, in fact, be able to provide adequate professional services. In such a situation, the patient is much more vulnerable than he would be if he had contracted for other types of services. In contrast to other commercial situations, the patient-consumer is more likely to rely upon the therapist's judgment. There is likely to be reliance even when the recommended treatment would appear, to most people, either unwise or utterly bizarre. In one case, for example, a young woman was treated by a psychiatrist for schizophrenia. As part of her treatment, the patient was subjected to severe beatings and electroshock. After seven years of treatment, the patient's condition remained unimproved. In another case, a young woman sought treatment for sexual maladjustment. The psychologist's treatment consisted of sexual intimacies and the prescription of various drugs. By prescribing drugs, the psychologist violated a state law prohibiting the practice of medicine by non-physicians; moreover, the treatment he provided aggravated the patient's condition. Patients such as these, injured as a result of professional malpractice, may face the expense and anguish of additional treatment to correct the injury. In some cases, the harm may not be capable of correction. In other cases, treatment by an incompetent practitioner may not aggravate the condition, but cause the patient unnecessary expense of time, effort, and money.

Growing public awareness of the need to protect the consumer of mental health services has triggered a marked increase in the regulation of the mental health profession. This expansion has been of a twofold nature. On the one hand, those professions that traditionally have been subject to some form of regulation have come under more comprehensive state supervision. At the same time, professional groups previously free from formal regulation have increasingly been brought within the ambit of state regulatory systems. Two basic methods of professional regulation have emerged. Under one system, certain types of therapy, such as psychotherapy, can only be performed by those holding a state license. A license, in turn, is only granted upon compliance with established educational and training requirements. The other system consists of a certification procedure, under which the state does not seek to limit the performance of designated functions to license holders. Instead, those meeting state prescribed requirements are authorized to designate themselves as being "certified" in a particular field. Regardless of the regulatory system employed, the state's primary objective is to ensure that those providing professional services to the public are, in fact, minimally qualified.

Governmental regulation of the profession also serves other purposes, including the control of competition. By monitoring entry into a particular profession, the state is able to protect mental health practitioners from excessive and potentially destructive competition. State regulation also serves to allocate power and authority among various competing professions by granting a monopoly over certain functions to a particular profession. For example, only psychiatrists or other licensed physicians are legally empowered to write prescriptions for medical or anti-psychotic drugs. In addition to these direct types of regulation, the allocation of responsibility among professions can be accomplished indirectly through the allocation of public funds. Under the Medicare system, for instance, reimbursement for mental health treatment is provided only when a licensed physician performs the services. In effect, this regulatory provision channels the performance of mental health treatment services to psychiatrists.

B. PERSPECTIVES ON THE MENTAL HEALTH PROFESSIONS

1. The Mental Health Professions: A Developmental Perspective

As psychotherapy has evolved from a service available only to the very wealthy to a profession generating $13 billion in annual revenues and currently treating an estimated 34 million Americans, the number of psychotherapists in the U.S. has experienced similarly dramatic growth. Today the mental health field comprises approximately 29,000 psychiatrists (medical doctors), 26,000 clinical psychologists, 31,000 mental health social workers, 10,000 psychiatric nurses, 10,000 counselors, and numerous unlicensed and untrained persons who provide "counseling" in various crisis and problem situations. In conjunction with the proliferation of mental health professionals, the range of services and types of therapies available have likewise multiplied. Thus, as noted by one commentator:

> [t]he field of psychotherapy is a complicated maze with alleys branching out in hundreds of biomedical, behavioral and psychoanalytic directions, running from shock treatments and psychotropic drugs, introduced over the last 25 years, to behavior modification, hypnotism and talking cures that focus on the individual, the family or some other group. "The Psychotherapy Handbook," edited by Richie Herink, captures this state of profusion in its claim to be "The A to Z Guide to More than 250 Different Therapies in Use Today"

Dava Sobel, "Freud's Fragmented Legacy," *New York Times Magazine*, October 26, 1980, p. 28. In recent years, myriad legal questions have arisen in connection with the provision of mental health services. A full understanding of these legal issues, however, presupposes a familiarity with the various mental health professions and therapies as they have developed since the time of Sigmund Freud. The following introductory materials trace the development of current psychotherapeutic techniques and explain the differences between the various mental health professions. Consider first the excerpts from Dava Sobel's "Freud's Fragmented Legacy," *New York Times Magazine*, October 26, 1980, which provides an overview of the therapeutic approaches being espoused by the different schools and disciplines.

> Sigmund Freud opened his practice for the treatment of "nervous" patients in the late 1880's. To penetrate the all-important unconscious, he and his followers developed the technique of psychoanalysis, which united doctor and patient in a therapeutic alliance to work through internal conflicts, using free association in the interpretation of fantasies, dreams and such everday "accidents" as slips of the tongue.

*   *   *

> Since Freud was a medical doctor and the care of patients his goal, psychoanalysis was immediately established as a part of medicine. Freud himself, however, was the first to admit that medical knowledge "does nothing, literally nothing" toward the understanding and treatment of neurotic personalities. He argued this point eloquently in his 1926 book "The Question of Lay Analysis," where he also predicted the biochemical emphasis that characterizes psychiatry today: "In view of the intimate connection between the things that we distinguish as physical and mental," he wrote, "we may look forward to a day when paths of knowledge *   *   * will be opened up, leading from organic biology and chemistry to the field of neurotic phenomena."

In the United States today, a bitter struggle still rages between psychoanalysts who are medically trained and those who come from psychology, social work or other fields of human relations.

* * *

In traditional psychoanalysis, tools are limited to talk (with or without a couch) and transference—the patient's projection of intense, early feelings and conflicts on the therapist. Since the aim of psychoanalysis is total personality reorganization, the patient can expect symptoms such as anxiety to persist long after treatment begins. Indeed, anxiety is thought by many analysts to be desirable, since the pain of it keeps the patient motivated through the arduous work of reliving the past. Those who derive the most benefit from psychoanalysis have frequently been dubbed "YAVIS," an acronym for the young, attractive, verbal, intelligent and successful individuals analysis seems to favor.

The term psychoanalysis, as it is used popularly today, refers to the original method as practiced by Freud, then modified by Jung and others, as well as to a host of psychoanalytically oriented therapies that are significant departures from those techniques. According to Dr. Judd Marmor of Los Angeles, past president of the American Psychiatric Association, the traditional method is going out of fashion:

> "It has proved—and I speak as an analyst, although not all my psychoanalytic colleagues will agree with me," Dr. Marmor said, "it's proved to be too costly to the patient, both in time and in dollars. What we are developing are new techniques of therapy that are shorter in duration, less costly, that are often still based on psychoanalytic principles, but that involve a much more active part for the therapist—a face-to-face role instead of putting the patient on the couch; seeing the patient once or twice a week instead of four or five times. We are finding that we are getting comparable results."

* * *

The psychoanalytic emphasis on emotions, mental states and internal conflicts rang false to the behavioral psychologists—people like John B. Watson and B.F. Skinner who preferred to concentrate on the observable phenomenon of human or animal behavior. Experiments conducted by Ivan Pavlov, the great Russian physiologist, and others showed that certain environmental factors produced abnormal behavior in rats and dogs.

> "I once saw laboratory rats huddling in the fetal position," Dr. Skinner said recently, "and doing all the right things necessary to be called psychotic." These experiments convinced some scientists that human mental disorders could also be explained by learned experiences and the reinforcement of certain behavior patterns. A self-destructive or discomfiting pattern could be changed, they reasoned, by teaching the person new habits.

Dr. Joseph Wolpe of Temple University in Philadelphia, for example, devised systematic desensitization, a popular form of behavior therapy dating from the 1960's. With this therapy, the patient learns to relax in tense situations, such as going to the dentist, by repetitive practice in the therapist's office (looking at pictures, for example), as well as in the real-life situation. Since no attempt is made to determine the origin of the fear, therapy can often be completed in as few as three sessions. Other behavioral techniques include reinforcement of certain patient behaviors by the therapist, modeling by the therapist of desirable behavior patterns for the patient to emulate, and biofeedback—training the patient to control his heart rate, blood pressure, skin temperature and brain waves.

Psychoanalysts fault behavioral therapies for being superficial, for providing stopgap relief while ignoring underlying problems that are bound to produce other symptoms later on.

* * *

Set apart from psychoanalysis and psychoanalytically oriented psychotherapy, but distinct from behavioral psychology, are the treatment techniques that focus on experiencing feelings, such as Gestalt therapy of Dr. Frederick S. Perls and Arthur Janov's primal therapy. The basic goal in these techniques is to explore and establish the self, body and mind in the face of the modern world's alienation and despair.

Experiential therapies, which consider the individual's capacity for growth to be almost limitless, focus on encouraging patients to live up to their fullest potential. The experiential therapist tries to provide patients with a supportive milieu that allows them to realize their latent abilities, as in the client-centered therapy of Carl R. Rogers. Instead of probing for hidden conflicts or teaching new behaviors, the experiential therapist tries to engage patients, if not with talk, then with bodily sensations, role-playing, screaming, meditation or any other ploy that gets them to focus on their emotions. He rejects the role of doctor or teacher.

Dr. Janov claims that all neurotic behavior arises from early Pain (always capitalized in his writings to distinguish it from the transitory pain of headache or the like) caused, for example, by lack of parental caring that wounds the child and forces him to deny his feelings. Eventually, this repression surfaces as neurosis, excessive smoking and drinking, drug addiction, sexual dysfunction, psychosomatic illness, asthma, hypertension or psychosis. Dr. Janov's therapeutic technique, which has never been published, involves bringing the client to the stage where he can re-experience the Pain. Since this is a volcanic event for the individual, Dr. Janov warns that "the only person qualified to practice primal therapy is someone with a certificate and approval as a primal therapist from the Primal Institute in Los Angeles." Breakdowns and even suicide are said to be the dangers of mishandling at mock-primal clinics.

Beyond these disparate, even warring philosophies is a rapidly growing area of psychiatry devoted to biochemical causes and medical treatments of mental ills, including electroconvulsive (shock) therapy and psychotropic drugs.

Electricity sufficient to cause a general seizure was first applied to a human brain in 1938 by two Italian scientists, Lucio Bini and Ugo Cerletti. The therapy consists of inducing a general seizure by passing an electric current through the brain, which produces a change in mood. Although no one has yet demonstrated why or how it works, electroshock is used predominantly today to treat depression. Elderly patients who may be refusing to eat or drink and who cannot tolerate the side effects of medication are considered prime candidates for this technique. Years ago, the violent thrashing caused by the seizure often resulted in broken bones, but today's patients are anesthetized and given a drug that paralyzes their muscles. The duration of the electrical impulse is only a fraction of a second, but preparation and recovery time can take about an hour. Electroconvulsive therapy (ECT) for elderly depressed patients is usually given over a period of days or weeks as a course of three or four sessions costing between $50 and $250 each, depending upon where it is administered. Forgetfulness and disorientation follow each treatment, but many people recover their full faculties within two weeks and show marked improvement.

Critics of ECT, notably Dr. Peter Breggin of Bethesda, Md., author of "Electroshock: Its Brain-Disabling Effects," say that shock patients sustain structural brain changes and learning difficulties that last the rest of their lives. But a task force of the American Psychiatric Association investigated the treatment and found it safe and effective.

Shock is administered to about 100,000 Americans a year, but there are tens of millions of individuals receiving psychoactive drugs—compounds such as tricyclic antidepressants and monoamine oxidase inhibitors for various depressed states, lithium for the major mood cataclysms of manic depression, neuroleptic drugs for the hallucinations of schizophrenia, and tranquilizers like Valium and Librium for anxiety.

Biochemical psychiatry has generated tremendous research excitement in recent years and has won adherents among psychoanalytically and behaviorally oriented practitioners. The excitement stems partly from the concept of physiological bases for mental illness, which is a comforting thought for many therapists and patients alike.

*   *   *

Many psychiatrists now employ drugs as "adjunctive therapy" along with regular sessions devoted to talk. This way, the patient can shed his anxiety or depression by chemical means and go on to try to understand its source through more traditional psychotherapy. Dr. Karasu, for one, denounced the belief that a therapist must keep a patient's symptoms alive to keep the patient as "an unethical, sadistic or, at best, a misinformed posture."

Psychologists and social workers, lacking medical degrees, cannot administer drugs, but they can collaborate with physicians who write prescriptions for them or recommend medications to be prescribed by the patient's own doctor. And an estimated 54 percent of Americans suffering episodes of mental disorder, or more than 17 million people annually, are treated pharmacologically by general practitioners with no formal training in psychology or psychiatry.

* * *

Questions and Comments

1. The development of specialized techniques for the treatment of sexual dysfunction represents the most important movement in the field over the past twenty years. Current development in this field of specialization and some of the issues which have come to the forefront as a result of its growing popularity are described in a recent *New York Times* article:

Sex Therapy: As Popularity Grows, Critics Question Whether It Works

"Sex," they said, and the world responded with anger, titillation, relief and respect.

That was 15 years ago. Today again, Dr. William H. Masters and Virginia E. Johnson are under attack for the rapid form of psychotherapy they devised to treat marriages burdened by sexual dysfunction. The widely asked question is: Does this treatment, or others like it, really work?

The complaints come from detractors who reject the concept of sexual dysfunction as a "disorder" and sex therapy as a treatment, and from psychiatrists and psychologists who believe they have improved on the original approach, or who question how many people are actually helped by such treatment.

They also come from moralists opposed to the role of prostitutes and surrogate wives in the technique's development and practice, as well as from consumers who have been the victims of unscrupulous practitioners.

For better or worse, the Masters and Johnson therapeutic technique came to be known as sex therapy.

* * *

Statistics on the efficacy of sex therapy are open to debate because they can so easily be distorted by selecting the patient population. The figures vary wildly, from 25 to 98 percent effective, depending on the therapist and the type of problem under treatment.

In August, Bernie Zilbergeld and Michael Evans, both Berkeley psychologists, attacked Masters and Johnson's outcome studies in the magazine Psychology Today. They said that "Masters and Johnson's sex-therapy research is so flawed by methodological errors and slip-shod reporting that it fails to meet customary standards—and their own—for evaluation.

* * *

In an interview, Dr. Zilbergeld, who devotes about 75 percent of his practice to sex therapy, said that although sex therapy is getting quite sophisticated, it would benefit from more realistic assessments of treatment techniques.

* * *

Other therapists agree that not even all sexual problems are amenable to sex therapy.

But the therapy is now well established. Riding a swell of social change atop advances in birth control, women's liberation and the 1960's thirst for freedom and spontaneity, sex therapy quickly took hold as a specialty field with thousands of licensed and unlicensed practitioners and hundreds of thousands of patients worldwide clamoring after the cure.

The Masters and Johnson treatment, widely discussed but often distorted, is a two-week assault on the couple's complaint, requiring daily meetings between them and a male-and-female team of co-therapists. Since all but 10 percent of the 175 to 200 couples seen annually at the Masters & Johnson Institute in St. Louis come from out of town or even out of the country, patients find their own local hotel accommodations where they carry out the prescribed "sensate exercises" in private.

* * *

The cost of the treatment is $3,000 per couple, and only couples need apply.

"The relationship is the medium within which we work," Mrs. Johnson said, "even if it is a relationship of the moment."

Sexual Relations With Therapist

Dr. Robert C. Kolodny, director of training at the institute, said, "We have run into cases among our patients of people who were enticed into sexual relations with a therapist as necessary to their therapy, and *that* in and of itself created major problems. We get letters from such people and requests from their lawyers to serve as expert witnesses or consultants in suits of this type—and we're not talking about one case a year that comes to our attention."

Dr. Kolodny also pointed out that there are no current regulations governing who may call themselves sex therapists.

"An eighth grader who hung out a shingle and printed up some office stationery claiming he was a sex therapist," Dr. Kolodny said, "might, in fact, attract some phone calls." Many people advertise their sex therapy services in newspapers and magazines, frequently claiming "Masters & Johnson techniques." And while such promotion is not proof of unethical behavior, the public has no way of knowing.

Approximately 30,000 physicians, therapists and other professionals have taken courses in treating sexual problems from Masters and Johnson, but only a handful of practitioners apply the teachings in the two-week, co-therapist, couples-only model.

* * *

Dr. Helen Singer Kaplan of the New York Hospital-Cornell Medical Center . . . routinely accepts single patients, out of her observation that many people have sexual disorders before they ever meet their partner.

Dr. Kaplan usually sees patients once a week, instead of every day, over a period of 12 to 25 weeks, depending on the nature of the problem: Her rates are within the $65-to-$150-per-hour range typical of privately practicing sex therapists, although patients at hospital clinics may be seen without charge.

* * *

Dr. Kaplan insists on a thorough physical examination of her patients, as do Masters and Johnson, before accepting anyone for treatment, since impotence, for example, can be caused by hidden medical problems ranging from a subtle circulatory disorder of the penis to hormonal imbalances, severe diabetes, the use of anti-hypertensive medications or the abuse of alcohol, heroin or other drugs.

USE OF DRUGS WITH THERAPY

As a psychiatrist, Dr. Kaplan also uses medicine as part of sex therapy, where indicated. (Masters and Johnson do not.) With sexual phobias and sexual problems secondary to depression, she said, treatment is often ineffective without appropriate psychotropic drugs, notably tricyclic antidepressants.

Another innovative form of sex therapy, used by numerous practitioners today, is group treatment, particularly for anorgasmic—often optimistically called pre-orgasmic—women.

And for the case where a partner is needed and none exists, there is what Dr. Kaplan calls "the surrogate solution."

Sex surrogates may work freelance or in collaboration with a therapist. They are paid for their services, in the range of $40 to $50 per two-hour session, and are thus technically prostitutes. However, their medical affiliation evidently protects them from prosecution in most states.

New York Times, November 14, 1980, p. 17.

2. The Mental Health Professions: Education and Training

The purveyors of mental health treatment can be classified into three major groups—psychiatrists (including psychoanalysts), psychologists, and psychiatric social workers. The educational training and types of services provided by each group vary significantly. Consider first the following descriptions of the educational requirements for practice in each of the three professions.

Psychiatrists

It is important to note at the outset that the definition of who is a psychiatrist or, more important, who is qualified to practice psychiatry is determined at least on a formal level by state law. Under the law of most states *any licensed physician* can practice and render psychiatric services. As a practical matter, however, norms imposed by the medical profession itself serve to ensure that the practice of psychiatry is restricted to those physicians who have completed a psychiatric residency program which is a requirement for membership in the American Psychiatric Association. These informal methods of control are normally exercised at the local level. Thus, only physicians who have completed the residency program and are members of the American Psychiatric Association will receive referrals from other physicians in the community. Similarly, only physicians who are members of the American Psychiatric Association will be accorded hospital privileges which enable them to function as psychiatrists in a hospital setting.

As noted earlier, only licensed physicians are qualified to become psychiatrists. Thus, the training of a psychiatrist necessarily begins with medical school. The psychiatric residency which follows the completion of medical school is normally of three years duration. Residency programs may be either of a generalized nature or specialized in such fields as child or juvenile psychiatry. Whatever the specialty, the programs vary in their academic orientation; some emphasize psychoanalysis, others behavior therapy while some stress psychopharmacological approaches to the treatment of mental illness. In spite of some differences in the orientation of particular programs all will normally have a curriculum which includes formal courses and seminars combined with clinical training. As noted by one observer:

> The central core of the curriculum, however, usually consists of a didactic program focused on the principles and techniques of psychotherapy and somato-therapy (shock treatment and drug therapy). Residents generally are involved with patients from the start of training and in addition take courses and seminars concerned with the psychopathology of neuroses and psychoses, clinical neurology, personality development, personality assessment, child psychiatry, psychopharmacology, research problems, and other topics. Much attention is given to interviewing techniques and the skills involved in probing a patient's history and accurately diagnosing his problems; teaching methods often include observation of patients and therapists through one-way mirrors (the side facing the patient and therapist is the mirror side), closed-circuit television, and tape recordings. In some psychiatry departments one or two residents interview a patient under supervision and then discuss what occurred with the faculty and other residents. Depending on staff interests, residents may also take work in hypnosis, group psychotherapy, family therapy, law and psychiatry, the psychology of sleeping and dreaming, and community or social psychiatry. Psychoanalytic theories are subsumed under

various labels in the didactic program or taught in special courses and seminars.

Arnold Rogow, *The Psychiatrists* (New York: G.P. Putnam's & Sons, 1980), p. 48.

As in the cases of other medical specialties psychiatry is subject to an accreditation procedure established under the auspices of relevant medical professional groups. In the case of psychiatry it is the American Board of Psychiatry and Neurology, whose membership is drawn from the American Medical Association, which certifies candidates in either general psychiatry, child psychiatry or neurology. Certification in one of these fields is available to any candidate who passes a rather rigorous examination and has completed a psychiatry residency. The number of all practicing psychiatrists in the United States who have been what is known as "board certified" has been variously estimated at between 33 and 48 percent. In fact, certification is only a necessity for those psychiatrists who frequently serve as expert witnesses or act as consultants to agencies which require board certification.

In the common parlance psychiatrists are frequently confused with psychoanalysts. While these two professional groups overlap in many ways, they are distinct professional categories. Part of the confusion about the differences and similarities of these two professional categories can be clarified by considering the educational background and institutional affiliation of those entering these fields. The field of psychoanalysis is for all practical purposes controlled by the American Psychoanalytical Association. The present structure of the American Psychoanalytic Institute was established in 1933 and is at present a federation of 29 societies and 20 training institutions. Each of these institutes operates its own training program, which is of six to ten years duration. Admission into a training program is decided by an institute committee. Admission usually requires a medical background, though decisions as to admissibility also take into account the personality characteristics of the applicant in terms of his or her suitability for analytic training. The following excerpt describes a typical training program.

Once admitted for training, the candidate must undergo the preparatory analysis previously noted "four or more times a week" and also carry through a program of assigned reading, lectures, and supervised clinical experience, all of which is designed to provide him with a thorough knowledge of Freud's theories and other relevant psychoanalytic contributions. He is further required to analyze under supervision at least two adult cases, devoting to each a minimum of 150 hours of analysis and "carrying at least one of them through the terminal phase of analysis." It is expected that material from these analyses will be presented by him "in no less than three extended presentations" at clinical conferences, of which he is required to attend at least fifty during his training. At each stage of training his progress is determined by the institute's educational committee. While some part of this determination is based on oral or written examinations, "of greatest importance is the estimation of the quality of the student's work in his supervised clinical experience and in the presentation of cases in clinical conferences. This constitutes a check upon the preparatory analysis as well, and can be expected to show either its adequacy or the need for further personal analysis." If the candidate successfully completes the training program, he is given a written statement to that effect by the institute, and he may then apply for membership in the American Psychoanalytic Association.

Arnold A. Rogow, *The Psychiatrists* (New York: G.P. Putnam's & Sons, 1980), p. 49.

Psychologists

Any description of the educational background of clinical psychologists is complicated, since there are no uniform nationwide standards as to who in any particular jurisdiction is qualified to practice as a psychologist. On the one hand, there are the standards of the American Psychological Association, which have been adopted by various state licensing and certification agencies. In these states practicing psychologists will generally possess a Ph.D. in clinical psychology. In other states there are either no formal educational requirements or lower educational requirements than those imposed by the American Psychological Association.

Thus, the educational standards or requirements for entry vary from state to state. Nevertheless, some generalizations are possible. A master's or Ph.D. degree in clinical psychology is the general rule in those 26 states which license psychologists. These degrees typically have been earned at one of the 134 universities in the U.S. which offer doctoral programs in clinical psychology. In some cases the degree will have been awarded not by universities but by specialized training centers which have developed in recent years. These non-university programs are by and large comparable to the Ph.D. programs offered by universities, though they differ in emphasis by stressing practical training and field work rather than academic research. Most of the university-centered programs as well as some of the special training programs have been accredited by the American Psychological Association, which serves as the professions educational review and accrediting arm.

As in most fields of study there are significant variations in the length of time that it takes for a student to qualify for a Ph.D. degree. The excerpt below describes some common elements of most Ph.D. programs.

Three years of full-time study beyond the baccalaureate degree is the minimum requirement, with the four-year program much more frequent, and five years not unusual. Most graduate departments prefer to emphasize the qualitative requirements rather than the number of credits, but 90 hours of graduate course work is fairly typical of catalog statements, with one third of these representing research credits. The graduate program sometimes includes a few courses, or even a "minor," in other departments: mathematics and mathematical statistics, philosophy, neurology, physiology, anthropology, chemistry, or others. There is usually some comprehensive examination ("prelims") covering the subject matter of certain fields of psychology, given after two or three years of work. The requirement of language examinations (or completion of language courses) is justified on the grounds that much research requires an acquaintance with some foreign literature in psychology, and, perhaps implicitly, that all doctors of philosophy should share a common mark of cultural distinction. The Ph.D. is traditionally a research degree, and the conclusion of a major piece of original work is almost universally required. (Many departments expect the student to take as an intermediate step a master's degree, frequently including the requirement of a less formidable research project.) There is usually a final oral examination of this dissertation research and relevant areas. Most curricula in clinical psychology involve some practical experience, including a year's closely supervised internship in a mental health installation.

Wilse B. Webb, *The Profession of Psychology* (New York: Holt, Rinehart and Winston, 1962), pp. 40–41.

Questions and Comments

The professions primarily involved in the delivery of mental health services include psychiatrists, psychologists, and psychiatric social workers. The manpower base for each of these categories is summarized below.

a. Psychiatrists

There are approximately 20,000 medical practitioners in the U.S. whose major field of specialization is psychiatry. Nearly one half of all psychiatrists are in private practice. However, multiple appointments are common in psychiatry, so that many of these individuals also function in other capacities and hold public employment or are involved in teaching. The percentage of foreign medical graduates is higher in psychiatry than in general medicine. In the early 1970's approximately one third of all residents in specialty training were foreign medical school graduates. According to one study, the percentage of foreign medical graduates in large state psychiatric hospitals exceeds 75 percent. (The principal source for this data is Herbert Dorken and Associates, *The Professional Psychologist Today* (Washington: Jossey-Bass, 1976) p. 17).

b. Psychologists

Given the considerable differences in the training and certification criteria of the various states it is difficult to describe accurately the manpower base of psychologists working in the mental health field. One estimate is based on the responses to surveys conducted by the American Psychological Association [APA] in 1972. This survey, however, was restricted to the approximately 35,000 members of the APA excluding the thousands of practicing psychologists who do not hold Ph.D.'s. Of the psychologists who were surveyed, the vast majority occupied positions with the educational or governmental institutions. Only 7 percent described themselves as being primarily in independent practice.

More recent surveys, however, suggest that as many as one fourth of all Ph.D. psychologists are now primarily in private practice. Recent surveys also indicate that the manpower of professional psychologists has expanded rapidly in recent years. These surveys suggest that the number of clinical psychologists who possess Ph.D.'s is currently in excess of 50,000. (The principal source for this data is Herbert Dorken and Associates, *The Professional Psychologist Today* (Washington: Jossey-Bass, 1976) pp. 1–16).

c. *Psychiatric Social Workers*

Social work has its own confusion in specialty delineation and requisite levels of training that can mar its acceptance as a health care resource. The U.S. Census definition of social worker includes over 240,000 personnel (Spingarn, 1974). However, only 60,000 belong to the National Association of Social Workers (NASW), which on July 1974 shifted from the M.S.W. [Masters of Social Work] to the B.S.W. [Bachelors of Social Work] as its standard of professional preparation. The National Federation of Societies for Clinical Social Work, however, would continue to limit membership to BSWs with several years of clinical experience.

A recent (1973) National Institute of Mental Health (NIMH) staff study of mental health manpower estimates that 14,500 NASW members are in psychiatric or mental health areas, and that there exist yet another 5,500 psychiatric social workers. Of this 20,000, about 600 are in private practice. Licensing procedures have only been adopted in four states, and certification in only nine more. Thus, this profession is internally divided on a definitional problem.

Herbert Dorken and Associates, *The Professional Psychologist Today* (Washington: Jossey-Bass, 1971), p. 18.

3. *Perspectives on the Function of the Mental Health Professions*

As a corollary to the significant differences in educational training noted above, the therapy or treatment provided by each mental health profession also varies greatly. In this regard, the following materials compare the services rendered by each group and trace their historical development.

Psychiatrists

[The following excerpts from Arnold A. Rogow's *The Psychiatrists* provide a profile of the profession based in part on the results of the author's survey of a random sample of 184 psychiatrists practicing in the U.S.]

Psychiatry, unlike psychoanalysis, did not begin in the twentieth century, but its influence and eminence are of relatively recent origin. If we view 1844, the founding year of what later became the American Psychiatric Association, as the official birthdate of American psychiatry, it is possible to suggest that psychiatry did not come of age until World War II, when, quite apart from its usefulness in the war, psychiatry became an accepted part of the American scene and even achieved a certain fashionableness. Since this development owes so much to the impact upon psychiatry of Freudian psychoanalysis—one is tempted to credit Freud with both the birth of psychoanalysis and the rebirth of psychiatry—it is conceivable that psychiatry without psychoanalysis would have taken quite a different direction, perhaps back toward the mental hospital from which it emerged more than a century ago, or toward an easier synthesis with other behavioral sciences. For it is clear that the broad acceptance of psychiatry relates not only to a rising incidence of mental distress but to the prestige of psychoanalysis, the principles of which transformed the nature of psychiatric training, practice, and research. Whatever the future holds, the growth patterns of psychiatry and psychoanalysis have been remarkably similar, and they face somewhat similar problems with respect to orientation and direction.

* * *

Psychiatrists in private practice usually see patients once or twice a week and are mainly interested in the contemporary day-to-day situation. They endeavor to relieve anxieties, clarify issues, promote insight, and increase confidence; as a rule, they try to be supportive in dealing with their patients' problems. Psychoanalysts, by contrast, may see patients in analysis three, four, or even five times each week, although this aspect is becoming less important as more and more analysts experiment with short-term analyses, fewer and shorter sessions per week, analyses the terminal dates of which are fixed in advance, and other innovations. Analysts also emphasize different material than the psychiatrists—for example, dreams, stream of consciousness and free association, childhood memories, sexual fantasies, and so forth. Usually in psychoanalysis the patient lies on a couch with the analyst seated behind him or to one side.

These distinctions do not mean that psychoanalysts do only psychoanalysis and psychiatrists do only psychotherapy. Many analysts have some patients in therapy, and many psychiatrists do some analysis. Further, there are psychoanalysts and psychotherapists who are not medical doctors but Ph.D.'s in psychology, sociology, or even philosophy and political science. Some psychotherapists have social work degrees—usually they hold a Master's degree—and an undetermined number of therapists have only a Bachelor's degree, or no degree at all.

* * *

In their dealings with patients, the preferred therapeutic technique of both psychiatrists and analysts is a dynamic approach, which may be generally defined as the "study of the active, energy-laden, and changing factors in human behavior," with special reference to their motivation, evolution, and progression or regression. More than 90 percent of the analysts and 67 percent of the psychiatrists employ such an approach, with an even larger percentage of the former (94.3 percent) describing themselves as Freudian with reference to that portion of their practice that is psychoanalytic as distinguished from psychotherapeutic. Twenty-eight percent of the psychiatrists rely extensively on drugs and shock therapy, 20 percent utilize a psychobiological approach to patients, and 14 percent are primarily engaged in family and marital therapy. Only 6 percent of psychiatrists are involved in group therapy, while among analysts more than 11 percent do some family and marital therapy.

* * *

These approaches are brought to bear on a large array of problems, especially with reference to the practices of psychiatrists who deal with a considerable number and variety of ill individuals, but there are distinct preferences among both psychiatrists and analysts in terms of problems and patients. Both psychiatrists and analysts prefer to treat neurosis, followed, in the case of analysts, by characterological problems. Psychiatrists rank schizophrenia as their second preference, followed by other psychoses, and characterological problems.

* * *

Diagnosis of the patient's condition is mainly by interview techniques usually directed to gathering information about the patient's history and that of his family. A trial period of consultation is very much the rule with analysts, but much less so with psychiatrists, and analysts also make more use of projective tests, such as the Rorschach. Psychiatrists, on the other hand, rely more on nonprojective tests and evaluations by psychologists.

Psychologists

[The following discussion of the development of psychology as a mental health profession has been excerpted from Herbert Dorken and Associates, *The Professional Psychologist Today* (Washington: Jossey-Bass, 1971)].

Psychology first emerged as a health profession in the middle 1940s. At that time, mental health workers were urgently needed to help the small corps of psychiatrists meet the needs of tens of thousands of World War II veterans with mental and emotional problems. University departments of psychology rapidly expanded their clinical and later their counseling sections to supply highly trained personnel for Veterans Administration hospitals and clinics throughout the country. It is historically significant that in 1946 the VA decided to require a doctoral degree as a condition of employment for psychologists in the department of medicine and surgery. The

VA also established highly competitive pay scales to attract persons qualified at this level.

* * *

[Thus] the first standard of national significance—requiring the doctoral degree (plus appropriate supervised experience) for psychologists qualified to practice in tax-supported health settings—was established by an employer agency. It would be almost thirty more years before the APA would encourage this level of competence for all persons providing psychological services in municipal, state, and federal health and rehabilitation facilities.

* * *

Between 1945 and 1955, clinical psychology built its foundations as a profession. Its role was (and is) structured by the tenor of the times, the setting for practices, the needs of the major target populations, the extent of its skills and knowledge, and its relationships to other health professions. Each of these dimensions has changed radically over the past twenty-five years. The numbers of clinical, counseling, and rehabilitation psychologists have multiplied many times. A steadily increasing proportion of psychologists have been leaving their traditional institutional settings to enter private practice. However, psychology's status as an independent health profession has not increased proportionately with these professional developments.

This lag does not detract from important advances that were made in self-determination and functional autonomy during the decade 1945 to 1955. Paradoxically, these advances emerged from the private-practice sector, where only a small number of psychologists were engaged, in contrast to the preponderance of those working in nonacademic institutional settings. To understand this distribution among settings, one must recall that, until very recently, the APA was committed almost entirely to advancing psychology as a scholarly and scientific discipline. Only in the past few years has the organization extended itself to professional affairs with anything approaching the investment shown for its historic commitments. Thus, professional psychology grew largely unprotected by its national parent.

* * *

By 1970, compared to other more established health professions, psychology had developed into something like a stork standing on one leg. It was visible and erect but lacked the firm stance expected of a mature professional group fully capable of self-determination, autonomy of functioning, and self-regulation. What psychology lacked most was comprehensive standards of practice—standards that finally would include the overwhelming majority of the country's practicing psychologists, who had been systematically exempted from the state psychology laws passed between 1945 and 1972. These psychologists were employed in tax-supported institutional settings, mainly hospitals, clinics, and correctional and rehabilitation centers. For those settings, the American Psychological Association had offered no consistent model for defining the qualified practitioner, no standards of accessibility to clients, nor the types of services to be offered within stipulated limits of autonomy and accountability.

The latest impetus for creating standards emerged from an APA executive board meeting of Division 22 (Rehabilitation Psychology) in 1966. It was noted that recent landmark federal legislation (the Rehabilitation Act of 1965) had stimulated unprecedented expansion of rehabilitation services. In addition to the influx of money for new buildings and programs, unprecedented standard-setting and accreditation manuals appeared to guide the proper staffing and operations of the new and expanded facilities. Although some manuals referred to the "qualified psychologist" in a facility as one defined as such by the American Psychological Association, the APA had not defined training level and mode of functioning for psychologists in institutional practice. As a result, some governmental and private manuals defined the psychologist in institutional settings as one "with a master's degree from an accredited university" (HEW, SRS, 1967, pp. 12; Commission on Accreditation of Rehabilitation Facilities, 1973, pp. 15).

*   *   *

A few basic principles guided the formulation of the APA Standards for Providers of Psychological Services.

It was very strongly held that a single set of standards should cover all types of psychologists in all manner of human service settings for the guidance of all concerned parties, whether they were providers, consumers, payers, or sanctioners of services. It was further held that there should be a single generic definition of the psychologist qualified to offer independent services in whatever setting—as one holding a doctorate. Academic qualification supplemented by appropriate experience was considered the best available and most generally acceptable index of competence. It was also believed that the same standards should uniformly govern provision of psychological services in both the private and public sectors. It was felt that the double standard sustained by licensure laws since 1945, which had permitted a lesser level of psychological services in tax-supported institutional settings, should be rejected.

*   *   *

It is necessary to point out that standards carry no statutory authority. They cannot supersede state statutes. Unlike the code of ethics, they do not even require immediate conformance by APA members. However, the standards do set forth official APA policy on the directions psychologists shall take in improving their services.

*   *   *

[The materials that follow, reprinted from Wilse B. Webb, *The Profession of Psychology* (New York: Holt, Rinehart and Winston, 1962), describes some of the psychologist's major therapeutic functions.]

Psychodiagnosis

One of the first functions for which the clinical psychologist gained recognition was that of administering "mental tests" as an aid to the diagnosis of persons suffering interferences with their psychological functioning.

* * *

Psychodiagnosis is a term that has come to refer to the total study of an individual with a view to ascertaining his psychological functioning at the time of study, what that functioning may have been prior to any intervention of accident or disorder, and what it may reasonably be expected to be if remedial or therapeutic measures are instituted.

* * *

In many clinics it is particularly in psychodiagnostic work that the clinic team does indeed operate as a team. In such instances the social worker frequently is the one who first sees the patient, determines the reasons for the request for service, and takes a detailed case history. The social worker may further contribute by interviewing the family or others able to provide information about the patient, or by visiting the patient's home to make firsthand observations. Similarly, a psychiatrist may make examinations and conduct interviews designed to elicit additional information necessary to an understanding of the patient. Either a psychiatrist or another physician may make physical examinations and order laboratory studies to contribute further to the same end.

* * *

Psychotherapy

The term *psychotherapy* refers to a broad spectrum of work performed by an equally broad range of workers, so that any precise definition of the field is all but impossible. Psychologists who regard themselves as psychotherapists may use approaches very much akin to those of lawyers, ministers, teachers, and others who counsel people in their life adjustments, or they may concentrate on the unconscious roots of their clients' whole life patterns, as in psychoanalysis, for example.

The role of psychologists in the practice of psychotherapy has been the focus of much discussion and controversy. At one extreme there has been the position that psychotherapy should be practiced by psychologists only under strict medical supervision; at the other extreme has been the claim for complete autonomy by the psychologist in the practice of psychotherapy. At least three points can be noted: (1) it has been increasingly demonstrated that psychologists can make valuable and sometimes unique contributions to psychotherapy; (2) psychologists are actively involved in psychotherapy in a wide variety of hospital, clinic, and independent practice settings; and (3) effective collaborative relationships have been worked out between psychologists and physicians in numerous instances. Effective collaboration requires the psychologist to keep in mind the stated policies of the APA that he is " * * * expected to establish and maintain effective intercommunication with a psychologically oriented physician" but " * * * should not compromise the professional standards of psychology or his freedom to pursue his profession."

As long as concepts of "disease" and "illness" predominate in our thinking about problems of emotional adjustment, medical training or supervision may seem essential in the practice of psychotherapy. Many medical as well as nonmedical therapists, however, have cast doubt on the meaningfulness of concepts such as mental "illness" and on the value of a medical monopoly in the field of psychotherapy. The fact is that psychologists are actively and permanently involved in psychotherapy, and therefore the problem to be dealt with realistically is how to bring their competence to its highest possible level.

The Psychiatric Social Worker

Psychiatric social workers generally treat persons whose personal and social maladjustments stem primarily from mental health problems, emotional behavior, or habit disorders. Leland E. Hinsie & Robert Jean Campbell, *Psychiatric Dictionary* (New York: Oxford University Press, 4th ed. 1970). The following excerpt describes the function of the psychiatric social worker:

> Much of the social worker's help to the psychiatric patient takes place when the patient is well along the road to recovery and is preparing to leave the hospital. The very nature of mental illness leaves its victim shaky and insecure, badly in need of someone to be his "ambassador" to the community, someone who paves the way for his return by serving as liaison with his immediate family, his employer, business associates, relatives, friends and neighbors.

> The patient who has had a long period of hospitalization may also need guidance and reassurance on aspects of life usually taken for granted: how to dress, how to write a letter applying for a job, how to pick up the threads of his former life.

> Even after discharge, the ex-mental patient often continues to need the help of his social worker to fortify him in moments of uncertainty or panic. Members of his family, too, need continued support in their own readjustment. Because in many circles mental illness carries a stigma, the social worker in this field must be particularly skilled in helping patient and family cope not only with their own feelings but with the suspicion and hostility of those they come in contact with.

Frances A. Koestler, *Careers in Social Work* (New York: H.Z. Walck, 1965), pp. 48–49. Thus, the job of a psychiatric social worker includes learning the patient's family and social background and problems and conveying this information to the treating personnel; helping the patient respond to his treatment; helping his family make the needed adjustments; and facilitating access to whatever community services may be required to achieve these adjustments.

Questions and Comments

1. The discussion in the preceding section is based upon the premise that the mental health field is made up of different professional categories and that the consumer need only elect the one that most closely fits his needs. In reality, however, prospective patients may have their choice circumscribed by economic or related factors. For instance, if the patient has medical insurance that covers outpatient mental health treatment, the terms of the insurance policy may dictate the choice. It is not uncommon, for instance, for health care insurance policies to require that outpatient mental health treatment be provided by a psychiatrist or alternatively, that psychologists can only be used if there has been a medical referral and the fees are billed through a physician. While numerous states have enacted freedom of choice laws (*See*, Note 2 at page 48 *infra*) which prevent insurance companies from imposing such limitations on the use of psychologists, in some states these types of restrictions remain in effect and consequently serve to channel patients towards psychiatrists and away from other mental health professionals. Dujovne, *Third Party Recognition of Psychological Services*, "Professional Psychology," 574, 575, 1980.

Similar restrictions as to choice may be imposed on those covered by public insurance plans such as Medicare or Medicaid. For instance, under Medicare the *therapeutic* services of psychologists in private practice are not covered. Programs Operation Manual Systems, § 00610.140, 1981. Moreover, payment for reimbursement of *diagnostic* services performed by psychologists who are in private practice will be reimbursed only when "a physician orders such testing." *Id.* While Medicaid programs for the "medically needy" differ somewhat from state to state, most programs provide only limited reimbursement for outpatient psychiatric services. Mitchell and Cromwell, *Medicaid Participation by Psychiatrists in Private Practice*, 139 Am.J. Psychiatry, 810, 813 (1982). Even when outpatient mental health services are covered, some jurisdictions "will reimburse outpatient mental health services only within a clinic setting: office-based psychologists must obtain prior authorization to treat Medicaid patients." *Id.*

2. Aside from insurance considerations, the choice of a therapist will be influenced by the overall economic circumstances of the patient. Those of limited means are likely to be more sensitive to differences in the fee structure of the respective professions and consequently are more likely to seek the services of auxiliary mental health professionals rather than psychiatrists or certified psychologists. *See, generally,* Mitchell and Cromwell, *Medicaid Participation by Psychiatrists in Private Practice*, 139 Am.J. Psychiatry, 810 (1982). Moreover, those who do not qualify under any insurance program and cannot afford the services of professionals in private practice will generally need to rely on the subsidized services provided by community mental health centers. Here, the patients' opportunity to select a particular professional category to provide treatment may be restricted by staff availability or by the assignment practices of the center.

II. THE REGULATORY FRAMEWORK: AN OVERVIEW

A. INFORMAL REGULATION

For most professions an informal system of regulation operates under the auspices of professional organizations. This system, independent of the government regulation, is essentially one of self-regulation. Most professional organizations, for example, have developed and promulgated their own codes of ethics, which frequently influence, at least indirectly, the development of standards applicable to the whole profession. Professional organizations also perform a policing function in that they may investigate allegations of a member's misconduct or malpractice. The organization's peer group review committees may censure a member or even withdraw membership upon a finding of misconduct.

Professional organizations also play a more formal and authoritative role when they have been delegated power by state regulatory agencies. Some states authorize professional organizations to establish review committees or hearing boards to investigate allegations of professional misconduct. When private organizations are delegated such functions, they assume quasi-governmental powers. Professional organizations also exercise considerable influence on the standards governing entry into a particular profession, typically by establishing minimum standards of training and experience. While technically only binding on the members of the organization, these standards are sometimes adopted by state licensing agencies and thus ultimately have the effect of law. As a result, the influence of the professional organization may reach well beyond its immediate membership.

B. FORMAL REGULATION

Although the type of regulatory model adopted by any given state varies from state to state, the authority for all legislative and administrative action has its source in the state's policing power. In its exercise of this power a state is free to enact legislation that is either remedial or preventive. In actuality, the major thrust of most extant regulation of professional conduct is preventive: It seeks to *prevent* the imposition of injury or exploitation of the public. *Remedial* measures are operative only after an injury has occurred and, by either punishing the wrongdoer or providing financial redress to the injured party, seek to deter future transgressions.

The principal remedial mechanism used to shape professional conduct is the civil suit for malpractice, instituted by the injured party against the practitioner accused of wrongdoing. It seeks payment of damages by the wrongdoer. When a practitioner's conduct violates criminal law, the state may invoke criminal prosecution. These criminal actions are initiated only upon violation of a criminal statute, are prosecuted by the state rather than the injured party, and seek to impose criminal penalties, such as imprisonment or a fine payable to the state. See Chapter II for a more detailed discussion of these remedial mechanisms.

Preventive regulation usually takes one of two basic forms—licensing or certification. A license grants a special privilege, by allowing the holder to engage in activities otherwise proscribed by law. Licensing statutes contain two essential aspects: (1) they limit the performance of certain activities or the rendition of specified services to a designated class of persons; and (2) they restrict the acquisition of a license to those who meet established qualifications and follow certain procedures. It is illegal, for example, to practice medicine without a license. A medical license, in turn, can be obtained only by satisfying statutorily defined educational and experience prerequisites and by complying with additional criteria such as satisfactory performance on an examination and the payment of an application fee.

Unlike licensing statutes, certification statutes do not attempt to restrict unlicensed individuals from engaging in designated activities or practices. Rather, they limit the use of designated titles to those who meet specified criteria of training and experience. A certification statute may provide, for example, that only those who have completed a Ph.D. in psychology may describe themselves as "psychologists" or use any other title incorporating the term "psychology" or similar phraseology. A certification statute does *not* prohibit the uncertified practitioner from rendering psychological services; rather, it regulates the practitioner's representations to the public concerning the nature of his training or qualifications. The informal methods of certification by voluntary professional organizations has already been briefly discussed. It was noted that voluntary certification functions as a stamp of approval, informing the public that an individual's training and experience have been deemed adequate by professional colleagues. Certification statutes serve a similar function, but the force of law is added to punish misrepresentation. Additionally, state certification may inspire greater consumer confidence than certification by professional peer organizations, which are not usually well known by the public.

Technically, licensing and certification statutes operate parallel to and independently of the informal, self-disciplinary policies of professional organizations. In practice, however, governmental regulation is heavily influenced, if not controlled, by members of the regulated professions. The process begins at the state legislature with the drafting of regulatory statutes. State legislators, themselves laymen, are likely to rely on the recommendations of professional organizations concerning the nature and extent of regulation and the type of training and experience prerequisite to professional practice. Often statutes merely establish broadly worded requirements and delegate to an administrative board the duty to develop more specific criteria for licensing or certification. These administrative boards may consist partially or entirely of respected members of the profession in question, and any lay members are likely to defer to the opinions of the professional experts.

Members of the regulated profession are also influential in enforcement. The laws allocate to state administrative agencies the responsibility of reviewing individual applications for licenses or certification, the investigation of charges of professional misconduct, and the conduct of hearings for license revocation or other disciplinary action. These functions are also generally entrusted to special panels or boards operating under the control of the agency. And again, most positions are filled by members of the professions. An agency is likely to judge allegations of professional misconduct in the light of standards of practice and codes of ethics promulgated by professional organizations. Additionally, agencies rely upon the testimony of respected professionals at disciplinary hearings. Because of the active participation and significant influence of the profession's own members, critics contend that government regulation is not an external control, but a form of state-approved self-regulation.

For clarity of presentation, the mechanisms of quality control have been described as either regulatory or remedial. In practice, these mechanisms often overlap. For example, an incompetent practitioner who causes injury to a patient may be censured by his professional colleagues and, simultaneously, face both license revocation proceedings and a malpractice suit. Thus, his conduct has provoked the operation of both informal and formal regulatory measures, as well as the remedial measure of a malpractice suit.

Since regulation of mental health professionals has traditionally been within the exclusive control of the states, there is a notable lack of uniformity in the scope and methods of regulation throughout the U.S. Moreover, even within any given state, different regulatory modalities may be applied to various professional groups. The following materials sketch the prevailing regulatory framework for the three major professional categories in the mental health field.

1. *Formal Regulation of Psychiatry.* Historically, the treatment of mental illness, like treatments for bodily ailments, was regarded as a "healing art," within the province of medicine. Psychiatry, the earliest mental health profession, thus developed as a branch of medicine. As medical licensing became prevalent, treatment of mental illness was subsumed under the umbrella of the statutorily protected "practice of medicine."

Current law reflects this historical origin of psychiatry. The statutory regulation in Illinois is illustrative. The Illinois medical licensing statute, like the law of all states, restricts the practice of all branches of medicine to licensed physicians. Thus psychiatry, a branch of medicine, is restricted to licensed physicians. However, the law does not limit the practice of psychiatry to physicians with psychiatric training. At least theoretically, any licensed physician can provide psychiatric services to his patients. It is also noteworthy that Illinois law does not define the terms "psychiatry" and the "practice of psychiatry." Perhaps this omission reflects the difficulty of defining the practice of psychiatry satisfactorily without restricting unfairly the range of services provided by other mental health professions. As a result, though, non-physicians are able to render such a wide range of mental health services as to suggest that the only treatment modality legally and exclusively reserved to psychiatrists and physicians are those involving the prescription of drugs.

2. *Formal Regulation of Psychologists.* The regulation of psychology is a relatively recent phenomenon. In 1953 only 16 states exercised some manner of regulation over this field; however, by 1967, 41 states had enacted statutes regulating the practice of psychology.

States seeking to regulate the provision of psychological treatment adopt one of three regulatory models. The first involves a certification procedure, which enables those individuals meeting certain educational and experience criteria to apply for a state-issued certificate. The state makes no effort to restrict the rendition of professional service by non-certified persons. However, only those it has formally certified are entitled to designate themselves as *certified* psychologists.

The second regulatory model grants to license holders a monopoly of the exercise of designated professional activities. These laws typically condition licensing on a set of experience or educational requirements. In California, for instance, an applicant must hold a Ph.D. from an approved institution and pass written and oral examinations. Those holding a license are permitted to engage in specified activities or services. Unlicensed persons are barred from either calling themselves psychologists or engaging in certain activities or services in return for compensation.

California employs fairly typical language in its licensing statutes. It stipulates that anyone who is not a licensed psychologist cannot render "psychological services" for a fee. The key phrase, "psychological services," is in turn defined as "the application of psychological principles, methods, and procedures of understanding, predicting, and influencing behavior, such as the principles pertaining to learning, perception, motivation, emotions, and interpersonal relationships; and the methods and procedures of interviewing, counseling, psychotherapy, behavior modification, and hypnosis; and of constructing, administering, and interpreting tests of mental abilities, aptitudes, interests, attitudes, personality characteristics, emotions, and motivations" (California Business and Professional Code § 2903 [1978]). As in the case of most licensing statutes, California law permits other professionals such as "family and child counselors" or "duly ordained religious practitioners" to do work of a "psychological nature" (California Business & Professional Code § 2908 [1978]).

While licensing enables the state to exercise significantly greater control over persons practicing psychology than does certification, substantial legal problems arise in drafting licensing laws. As one commentator has observed: "[T]he basic legislative problem which has arisen in every state which has tried to regulate psychology has been to formulate a satisfactory definition of what constitutes the practice of psychology. A good deal of time and study has gone into this question since regulation is impossible if the class cannot be established with clarity, specificity, and rationality." Sidney H. Asch, *Mental Disability in Civil Practice* (Rochester, N.Y.: The Lawyers Co-Operative Publishing Co., 1973), pp. 128–29.

The third regulatory model is referred to as "title licensing," and it incorporates some of the features of both certification and licensing. Unlike typical licensing statutes, this system does not stipulate that mental health services, such as psychological counseling, can be provided only by those holding a state license. Rather, the scope of these statutes is somewhat narrower, for they only prohibit the rendering of the regulated service by an unlicensed practitioner who uses the title of "psychologist" or a similarly proscribed designation. Thus, under this system anyone can provide treatment services so long as he or she does not use any of the proscribed titles or designations. The Illinois law illustrates a typical statute. That law states that no unlicensed person can render clinical services for a fee if the words "psychological, psychologic, psychologist or psychology" have been used to describe such services by the persons offering them (I.R.S. Ch. 111 § 5303(3)(B) 1981). As in the case of regular licensing statutes, a license is only issued to applicants who fulfill certain educational and experience requirements.

Both regular and title licensing statutes suffer from problems of definition that may hamper their enforcement. Unless the licensing statute defines the regulated activity with sufficient clarity, officials cannot identify offenders, and unlicensed practitioners will not have adequate notice of which activities are proscribed. The Illinois law, for instance, makes the offering or rendering of "psychological services" a critical element of any offense. The practice of psychology is defined as:

> the application of established principles of learning, motivation, perception, thinking, and emotional relationships to problems of behavior adjustment, evaluation of persons, and group relations, by persons trained in psychology. The application of said principles includes, but is not restricted to, counseling and the use of psychological remedial measures with persons or groups having adjustment or emotional problems in the areas of work, family, school and personal relationships; measuring and testing of personality, intelligence, aptitudes, public opinion, attitudes, and skills; and the teaching of such

subject matter, and the conducting of research on problems relating to human behavior. I.R.S. Ch. 111 § 5304(4) 1981.

Thus, as with regular licensing statutes, there is the difficulty of designating with sufficient clarity the meaning of the phrase "psychological services."

Questions and Comments

1. What are the relative advantages and disadvantages of certification and licensing schemes? Which is superior for the regulation of the mental health professions? Why?

2. What problems exist when members of the regulated profession exert influence upon government regulation? Is this the best method to insure protection of the public, or does it tend to pervert a consumer protection scheme into a device to insulate and protect professionals?

3. While licensing seems to be an established part of the regulatory landscape, a vocal minority contends that licensing is contrary to the public interest. In this connection, consider the merits of the arguments against licensing advanced by one commentator:

* * * Invariably, the rationale advanced for restricting the right to practice is protection of the public. But a strong case can be made that the only ones really being protected are the professionals themselves. First, psychotherapy is nearly incapable of definition, and regulations invariably encroach on such related fields as education. Second, academic credentials and written examinations are worthless as measures of therapeutic effectiveness. After reviewing the research in this area, David McClelland, a Harvard professor of psychology, has concluded that neither criteria predicts anything but future grades and test scores, no matter what the profession. (Interestingly, by existing prerequisites, giants in the field such as Erik Erikson would never be licensed.)

So licensing does not insure that those practicing are any more competent than those who are not licensed. Not only that, but once licensed, a practitioner need not worry about being disciplined. In 1969, 33 states did not revoke a single physician's license. Fewer than 0.1 percent of all practicing lawyers were disbarred in 1972. When discipline does take place, a study of the New York City Bar found, publicized offenses tend to be punished much more severely than similar, but unpublicized ones, indicating that the professions are more concerned with public image than public protection. Moreover, there are so many negative side effects to licensing that it is hard to imagine when it would be a useful means of regulation: Evidence is accumulating that licensing significantly increases the cost of professional services, decreases the supply of practitioners, inhibits improvements in the organization and delivery of services, stifles innovative training programs, and is discriminatory.

It should be no surprise, then, that many economists and political scientists see in licensing the return of the medieval guilds. The question is whether alternatives exist. Major improvements could obviously be gained by small changes in existing laws. For instance, statutes might only restrict the right to use certain titles while basing the requirements for licensing on competency, not credentials. Such changes, however, don't go far enough. Since we know so little about therapeutic effectiveness, we need regulations that encourage responsible experimentation and diversity, but also protect the public from incompetence and unethical conduct.

All practitioners should be required to register with the state but not to make academic or other credentials a prerequisite to practice. Laws should, however, require therapists to disclose their training and techniques to all clients. An active, powerful and well-financed disciplinary board, a variety of nongovernment certification organizations, and a comprehensive campaign to educate the public are necessary, if this system is to work properly. There are certainly risks involved in this approach, but I believe they are fewer than if we continue on our current path. The fact is that the only sure losers in today's continuing war among the mental-health professions will ultimately be their patients.

Daniel B. Hogan, "Licensing Mental Therapists" *New York Times*, July 18, 1979, p. A–23.

4. In a state with licensing laws such as those adopted by California could a non-licensed person provide therapy utilizing bio-feedback and other relaxation techniques? Could this same therapist legally insert an advertisement in the local paper with the following text:

Is mental, physical, or emotional STRESS grinding you down? Are you looking for help to relax and reduce tensions? Phone Dr. Dogood, 222–1234.

⑤ In a state with title *licensing* such as Illinois could an unlicensed person advertise as follows:

Need psychological assistance? Psychotherapist will help you deal with your problems in living. Call Melrose 1234.

III. ADMINISTRATIVE REGULATION AND REMEDIATION IN OPERATION

A. REGULATION OF ENTRY

1. Introduction

Government regulation of a profession begins with the enactment of a state statute, which usually provides for certification or licensing, as described previously. In either case the statute sets forth criteria for education and experience that are prerequisite either to professional practice or to the use of a professional title. In addition, the statute establishes penalties for unauthorized practice or use of professional titles. Typically violations of the statute are classified as misdemeanors, punishable by a fine or imprisonment of less than one year's duration, or both.

Regulatory statutes need not adopt precise criteria for professional qualification. Often, they set forth criteria in very broad terms and delegate to a designated administrative agency the task of promulgating more precise prerequisites. This agency, which is often titled the Board of Regents or Board of Examiners, frequently has a permanent staff whose governing board is wholly or partly comprised of prominent members of the regulated profession. Legislatures delegate the task of drafting entry prerequisites to agencies staffed by such experts in the hope that the agency will provide more current and meaningful standards than any the legislature itself could draft.

When the regulatory statute contains only broad standards for professional entry, the administrative agency's task is to "fill in the details" by promulgating rules or regulations. These rules may require, for example, a certain type of degree or number of years of education, training, and experience. Additionally, the rules may condition entry into the field on the submission of affidavits and personal history that demonstrate the applicant's good moral character. The agency may also draw up alternative criteria applicable in special circumstances, allowing, for example, substitution of examination for formal education, recognition of sister-state certification or licenses, or "grandfather clauses" that accord professional status to competent persons who had practiced before the regulatory statute took effect. Further, the rules, if not the regulatory statute itself, may recognize exceptions to the licensing or certification requirements in the cases of professionals employed by state-licensed hospitals or other state institutions.

2. Statutory Criteria for the Practice of Psychology

The power of a state to exercise significant control over the provision of mental health services within its borders is not unlimited. The Supreme Court has construed the due process clause of the Fourteenth Amendment to prohibit legislation that is not rationally related to an appropriate end. The state, therefore, must formulate criteria for professional practice that are rationally related to the purposes of regulation. Needless to say, court decisions holding that legislation fails to conform to the low threshold of the rationality test are rare indeed.

In *Williamson v. Lee Optical Co.*, 348 U.S. 483, 75 S.Ct. 461, 99 L.Ed. 563 (1955), the U.S. Supreme Court considered the constitutionality of an Oklahoma law forbidding opticians from fitting eyeglass lenses without a prescription from a licensed eye doctor or optometrist. The opticians, who could not even replace lost or broken lenses without such a prescription, challenged the law as needless, wasteful, and violative of the due process clause of the Fourteenth Amendment. In a decision broadly applicable to state regulation of all professions, the Court rejected the challenge. Refusing to weigh the merits and drawbacks of particular legislative requirements, the

Court limited the judiciary's power to an assessment of whether the statute reveals a rational basis:

> [T]he law need not be in every respect logically consistent with its aims to be constitutional. It is enough that there is an evil at hand for correction, and that it might be thought that the particular legislative measure was a rational way to correct it.

> The day is gone when this Court uses the Due Process Clause of the Fourteenth Amendment to strike down state laws, regulatory of business and industrial conditions, because they may be unwise, improvident, or out of harmony with a particular school of thought. 348 U.S. at 487–88, 75 S.Ct. at 464–65.

The presumption of validity accorded to legislatively enacted licensing criteria applies with equal force when the licensing requirements are formulated by licensing agencies or boards rather than by the legislature directly. In *Jaffee v. Psychology Examining Committee*, 92 Cal.App.3d 160, 154 Cal.Rptr. 687 (1979), an applicant for a license as a psychologist contended that his educational qualifications and working experience qualified him to practice psychology, even though he had failed examinations formulated and administered by the State Psychology Licensing Committee. Sustaining the actions of the Committee and the examination requirement, the California court explained why judicial review of administrative licensing criteria is necessarily limited:

> [C]ourts do not have the expertise required to assess the qualification of an applicant for licensure in such a field. "In cases involving applications for a license, the courts have largely deferred to the administrative expertise of the agency. Courts are relatively ill-equipped to determine whether an individual would be qualified, for example, to practice a particular profession or trade. In a case involving the agency's initial determination whether an individual qualifies to enter a profession or trade the courts uphold the agency decision unless it lacks substantial evidentiary support or infringes upon the applicant's statutory or constitutional rights."

154 Cal.Rptr. at 691.

As noted, the state is free to impose any marginally rational criterion as a prerequisite to a license or certificate. This is clearly permissible when the state seeks to apply admissions standards to those seeking to enter a particular professional field. But what are the limits of state regulatory power as applied to established practitioners? Can the state, for instance, impose newly formulated educational or examination criteria upon those already in practice in that jurisdiction? Or is the discretion of the state narrower when it imposes new regulations on established practitioners? As a general proposition, decisions of the Supreme Court suggest that the powers of the state are equally broad when applied to those already practicing in a particular field.

In *City of New Orleans v. Dukes*, 427 U.S. 297, 96 S.Ct. 2513, 49 L.Ed.2d 511 (1976), the Supreme Court, for instance, upheld a newly enacted ordinance barring established pushcart vendors from selling their wares in the French Quarter of New Orleans. In reaching this result the Court made it clear that the equal protection and due process clauses of the Constitution do not require the invalidation of legislative policy decisions that do not touch fundamental rights or create a suspect classification.

At the same time, isolated state and federal decisions suggest that if the legislature or administrative agency is dealing with persons already established in a field, the range of regulatory discretion is somewhat narrower. The case which follows illustrates judicial invalidation of a legislatively formulated licensing scheme that sought to apply new licensing requirements to an established practitioner.

BERGER v. BOARD OF PSYCHOLOGIST EXAMINERS

United States Court of Appeals, District of Columbia Circuit, 1975.
521 F.2d 1056.

MacKINNON, Circuit Judge:

Appellant Joseph R. Berger, a practitioner of psychology in the District of Columbia since 1961, challenges the constitutionality of a 1971 law requiring that all psychologists practicing in the District be licensed and specifying that licenses shall be issued only to applicants possessed of certain academic credentials. Berger contends that the Due Process Clause of the Constitution guarantees him some alternative means of demonstrating his professional competence, in the nature of a "grandfather" concession to psychologists practicing at the time the licensure requirement was enacted. We agree, and remand to the licensing board for action consistent with this opinion.

I

In 1971 Congress passed the District of Columbia Practice of Psychology Act, P.L. 91–657, D.C.Code § 2–481 *et seq.*, a licensing statute designed to impose minimum educational requirements upon all psychologists practicing in the District. Section 7 of the Act, § 2–486, directs an appointed Commissioner to grant a license to anyone who (a) submits "satisfactory proof" of good moral character, (b) possesses a doctoral degree in psychology or in some other discipline deemed by the Commissioner to be sufficiently closely related, and (c) passes a written or oral examination. Section 8 of the Act is a limited "grandfather" clause which provides less stringent requirements for licensure for an applicant engaged in the practice of psychology in the District at the time the statute was enacted. The pertinent distinction is that section 8 permits substitution of a master's degree or "twenty-four credit hours taken subsequent to a bachelor's degree in courses related to psychology" and seven years' practice for possession of a doctorate and passage of an examination.

*   *   *

Appellant Berger was awarded a BCS degree in accounting from Southeastern University in 1943. He received training in the field of psychology from several psychiatrists and was given credit for numerous courses in various areas of psychology which he took at American University, the United States Department of Agriculture Graduate School, and the Washington School of Psychiatry. Although he has never been certified or licensed to practice in any other jurisdiction and is not a member of any professional psychological association, he has practiced psychology in the District of Columbia for approximately 14 years, co-authored a book on hypnosis published by Prentice-Hall, and lectured and written on clinical topics. The licensing board established by the Act ignored these facts and letters written by some of Berger's colleagues testifying to his competency, and denied his application because of his failure to make the threshold showing required by the Act. The board concluded:

Inasmuch as it is conceded by the applicant that he possesses neither a doctor's degree nor a master's degree in psychology, it is clear that he is not qualified for a license under Section 8 of the Act.

*   *   *

Berger attacks the Act on four grounds: (1) that it fails to prescribe standards for licensure; (2) that the absence of meaningful grandfather rights or an equivalency provision constitutes invidious discrimination and a denial of due process; (3) that a classification which excludes from the profession a successful practitioner of 14 years is arbitrary and capricious; and (4) that a review board comprised of professional psychologists with apparent or actual qualifications under the Act is not a properly impartial adjudicatory body. Arguing for the licensing board, Corporation Counsel for the District of Columbia defends the statute as a rational exercise of congressional police power over the District and insists that this court cannot pass on constitutional issues in what is in essence an administrative proceeding.

*   *   *

III

Our opportunity and obligation to pass on Berger's claim to meaningful grandfather treatment under the District's licensing scheme is in a sense unique. *   *   * [t]he question we confront is no less important for its rarity: appellant, and perhaps many other psychologists in the District of Columbia who have acquired their skills through apprenticeship, may lose the right to practice their profession because the Congress has suddenly decided the field needs regulating. But the very reason psychology has not been regulated before is that it has been and remains an amorphous, inexact and even mysterious discipline. Possession of a graduate degree in psychology does not signify the absorption of a corpus of knowledge as does a medical, engineering, or law degree; rather it is simply a convenient line for legislatures to draw, on the brave assumption that whatever is taught in the varied graduate curricula of university psychology departments must make one a competent psychologist, or at least competent enough to be allowed to take a licensing examination. While it may not be irrational to assume that this academic background should in the future be a prerequisite to the practice of psychology, it is of questionable rationality to insist that current practitioners, who may have studied and practiced at a time when graduate courses in psychology were even less meaningful, are conclusively incapable of meeting today's new standards because they did not take those courses.

* * *

The limited nature of Berger's challenge to the D.C. statute bears reemphasis. He does not argue that anyone has an absolute right to practice a profession. The logic of his argument allows that a legislature might ban the practice of psychology altogether, on a conclusion that the discipline was not beneficial or that it should be subsumed by traditional medical practice. Appellant maintains only that current practitioners should not be denied the opportunity to continue their chosen profession, without prior notice of the licensing requirement and without some occasion to demonstrate their adequacy to the task. In short, in order to protect his "liberty" and "property" interests in his profession, appellant seeks an opportunity to rebut the statutory presumption of his incompetence.

* * *

The Supreme Court has long held irrebuttable statutory presumptions to be disfavored.

Recently the Court has struck down irrebuttable presumptions that unmarried fathers are unqualified to raise children, *Stanley v. Illinois*, 405 U.S. 645, 92 S.Ct. 1208, 31 L.Ed. 551 (1972); that women more than four months pregnant cannot teach school, *Cleveland Board v. Lafleur*, 414 U.S. 632, 94 S.Ct. 791, 39 L.Ed.2d 52 (1974); and that those who apply to the Connecticut State University system as non-residents can never become residents for the purpose of paying lower in-state tuition, *Vlandis v. Kline*, 412 U.S. 441. In *Vlandis*, in response to the argument that the presumption of non-residency provided "a degree of administrative certainty," Justice Stewart noted that "the Constitution recognizes higher values than speed and efficiency." 412 U.S. at 451, 93 S.Ct. 2236.

The principle of *Vlandis* is applicable to the facts of the instant case. A part, and presumably a significant part, of the D.C. licensing process is the administration pursuant to D.C.Code § 2–481 of an examination devised by the licensing board to applicants holding a doctoral degree. No reason has been suggested why the Board could not fashion a similar examination and substitute passage of that test for the current requirement of passing an examination plus holding a degree. As an administrative body the Board cannot ignore or reinterpret parts of the statute under which it operates. But on remand, following a declaration by this court that the statute's irrebuttable presumption does not accord with principles clearly set forth in the case law, the Board could proceed to determine whether Berger's extensive clinical experience, coupled with his limited academic training and apprenticeship, have afforded him a professional competence equivalent to that of a doctor of psychology who has only two years of acceptable postgraduate experience.

We conclude that the Act's irrefutable presumption arbitrarily and unreasonably deprives Berger of his constitutionally recognized interest in the practice of psychology in violation of the Due Process Clause of the Fifth Amendment. Our decision cannot be wholly founded in any single opinion of the Supreme Court cited above, for those cases have involved statutory presumptions invalid as to all individuals covered by the respective acts. Here the irrebuttable presumption of professional incompetence absent a graduate degree is not invalid with respect to future psychologists, but only with respect to current practitioners who have no meaningful grandfather rights.

* * *

The inequity of the statute is that it fails to account for those competent psychologists who embarked upon their profession when no degree was required and who thus are denied a fair opportunity to come within the statute's licensing requirements at this point.

* * *

Accordingly, we remand the case * * * to the licensing board to administer to appellant Berger an examination designed to determine whether his professional skill is commensurate with that of new psychologists being currently licensed under the Act. In so doing, we do not act as a legislature to add this requirement to the statute, but rather strike down as unconstitutional that part of the statute which requires an applicant to have an academic credential as well as a certain number of years experience in order to qualify to take a license examination. Only by this action can we remedy the constitutional defect of the statute as it is applied to Berger and to other psychologists without the requisite academic credentials but possibly possessed of the necessary skills.

Judgment accordingly.

Questions and Comments

1. Note that the Court of Appeals did not find that Berger had an absolute right to continue to practice; rather, the court merely held that he had a constitutional right to a fair hearing to determine whether his

skill and knowledge were equal to that of a new applicant who meets the act's educational requirements.

What if Berger is now permitted to take but fails an examination required of all applicants? If the examination includes materials not commonly taught when Berger was in training and which only indirectly relate to the *practice* of psychology (e.g., research methods and statistics), does Berger have a basis for challenge? In other words, in determining whether Berger possesses equal qualifications, is the commission free to apply all criteria pertaining to proficiency except formal degree requirements? If so, would this be unfair to someone in Berger's position? Would there be a legal remedy or should this matter be left to legislative correction? *Berger would be obligated to hide or keep up w/ the level of knowledge currently existing*

2. The *Berger* decision was based on the constitutional law doctrine of the irrebuttable presumption. The current viability of this doctrine, however, is uncertain. Some commentators have found it noteworthy that the Supreme Court has neither applied nor alluded to the doctrine since 1974.

Also, the Court of Appeals' decision failed to point out that all Supreme Court cases using the irrebuttable presumption doctrine involved a specially protected right, such as the right to travel as in *Vlandis v. Kline,* 412 U.S. 441, 93 S.Ct. 2230, 37 L.Ed.2d 63 (1973), or adversely affected a class entitled to special constitutional protection, such as illegitimates or women.

3. As previously noted, some states inject certain character requirements into the licensing process. Thus, an applicant may be screened for honesty and integrity. When these character requirements are imposed, an applicant is normally required to provide the examining committee with letters of reference that attest to his or her character qualifications. Given the subjective nature of these assessments, it is not surprising that criteria of this type have been the subject of legal attack when an applicant is rejected on character grounds. No reported decisions involving a psychologist applicant directly addresses the character qualification issue. In *Jaffee v. Psychology Examining Committee,* 92 Cal.App.3d 160, 154 Cal.Rptr. 687 (1979), the issue was raised in a slightly different context. One of the grounds relied upon by the petitioner-applicant to challenge the denial of the license was that the committee that had administered the oral part of the examination was prejudiced against him because of a negative evaluation submitted by one of his references. The appellate court reviewing the case, however, found it unnecessary to deal with the validity of the oral examination or the petitioner's contention of unfair prejudice on the part of the examiner since the petitioner had also failed the written portion of the exam, which had been graded without reference to the identity of the applicant.

B. DISCIPLINE AND SANCTIONS: THE MECHANICS OF REMEDIATION

Although some state legislatures do not delegate the task of defining precise criteria for initial entry into the mental health field, nearly all state laws charge an administrative agency with the task of providing ongoing supervision of members of the regulated profession. For example, a legislature may authorize an agency to investigate complaints of professional misconduct and to impose appropriate sanctions on wrongdoers. Permissible sanctions include license revocation or suspension or the imposition of a fine. In a case of alleged professional misconduct, the accused practitioner is entitled to a hearing on the charges. The primary purpose of that hearing is to provide the accused an opportunity to be heard, to present evidence, and to challenge the testimony of adverse witnesses. The hearing need not be a formal trial before a judge or jury; rather, it is usually relatively informal, conducted by an individual member of a panel or by the full board of the regulatory agency. An accused practitioner has various procedural rights, including the right to prior notice of and to be present at the hearing. While the assistance of legal counsel is usually permitted, it has not been viewed as a constitutional right of an individual facing a disciplinary board. Witnesses may present testimony in an informal narrative fashion, rather than in accordance with rules of evidence at trials.

Despite its informality, a disciplinary hearing must, as a matter of constitutional doctrine, comport with basic notions of fairness. The tribunal must reach a decision of guilt or innocence on the basis of probative evidence, and not on the basis of unsupported allegations or prejudice. Normally, an accused practitioner may obtain judicial review of an adverse agency decision. The scope of review is, however, limited. Typically, a court will confine its inquiry to determining whether the accused received a fair hearing, and whether the tribunal based its decision upon substantial probative evidence and not upon speculation, bias, or other arbitrary factors.

The Kansas Supreme Court's decision in *Morra v. State Board of Examiners* set forth below illustrates both the legal issues that are commonly raised in these types of proceedings and the role of courts in reviewing the administrative decisions. The opinion traces the case from the initial disciplinary hearing before the Board of Examiners to final review by the state's highest court.

MORRA v. STATE BOARD OF EXAMINERS OF PSYCHOLOGISTS

Supreme Court of Kansas, 1973.
212 Kan. 103, 510 P.2d 614.

FONTRON, Justice:

In 1967 the Kansas legislature enacted the certification of psychologists act which now appears on the statute books as K.S.A. 74–5301 et seq. This will be referred to hereafter as the act. This act contained for the first time provisions for the certification and registration of qualified psychologists practicing in this state; for the creation of a state board of examiners of psychologists consisting of seven certified psychologists to be appointed by the governor; for the examination by said board of such applicants as request certification (with certain exceptions); and for the revocation or suspension of certificates by the board of examiners after a hearing held in accordance with procedures set out in the act. The present appeal brings the act before this court for the first time.

The record discloses that on April 21, 1971, the attorney general filed an amended petition against Michael A. Morra, a psychologist who had previously been certified by the state board of examiners. This pleading asked that the board revoke or suspend Dr. Morra's right and authority to practice psychology in the state of Kansas. The petition was predicated on the alleged violation of the provisions of K.S.A.1970 Supp. 74–5324(d) and (e). These subsections provide as follows:

> "The certificate of any psychologist may be suspended or revoked by the board upon proof that the psychologist: * * * (d) has been guilty of unprofessional conduct as defined by rules established by the board; or (e) has been guilty of negligence or wrongful actions in the performance of his duties."

The specific violations charged against the doctor pertained to sexual improprieties said to have been addressed by him to two of his women patients. The misconduct was alleged to have occurred during the last part of 1969 and the early months of 1970.

We shall hereafter refer to the state board of examiners of psychologists as the board and to Dr. Morra either by name or as the respondent.

Following an all-day hearing on July 27, 1971, which continued late into the night, the board found Dr. Morra guilty of negligent and wrongful actions, and guilty of behavior in violation of the code of ethics of the American Psychological Association. Its order of revocation is dated September 17, 1971, on which date the board notified Dr. Morra that his license was revoked. A clarifying order of revocation was sent to Dr. Morra on September 29, and on October 14 the board filed extensive findings of fact and five conclusions of law.

The respondent appealed from the order of the board to the district court of Sedgwick County, Kansas, where the appeal was heard. On March 20, 1972, the district court affirmed the orders of the board

*   *   *

Dr. Morra has appealed from the judgment and findings of the district court.

Before proceeding to discuss the several points raised by the appellant it would seem appropriate to restate quite briefly the limited scope of judicial review with respect to an administrative action. We have consistently said that under the separation of powers principle a district court may not, on appeal, substitute its judgment for that of the administrative tribunal, but the judicial function is strictly limited to the determination of three legal questions: (1) Was there substantial evidence to provide a reasonable basis for the conclusion reached by the administrative body? (2) Was the action taken by the administrative board unreasonable, arbitrary, fraudulent or oppressive? (3) Was the action taken within the authority, or competence, of the administrative agency?

With these observations out of the way, we turn to the issues to be decided. Dr. Morra first contends that the order of the board was not supported by substantial evidence. We believe the record shows otherwise. It discloses that both of the female patients against whom the doctor's improper advances were directed appeared in person and testified at the hearing and that they were cross-examined by respondent's counsel. Their testimony supported the allegations set forth in the amended petition. Each witness went into detail concerning the sexual peccadillos of Dr. Morra.

In its findings, the board set out at some length the testimony given by the two women, who had not previously known each other, and found it to be lucid, clear, unambiguous and containing no contradictions. In its conclusions of law the board characterized Dr. Morra's actions as being negligent and wrongful; that he wrongfully ignored a basic duty of a responsible psychologist, *i.e.*, to avoid sexual intimacies with his patients; and that he neglected to consider the well-being of his patients.

Substantial evidence has been defined as that which possesses relevance and substance and which furnishes a substantial basis of fact from which the issues can reasonably be resolved.

* * * The evidence supporting the board's conclusions in this case may be likewise characterized.

Although Dr. Morra categorically denied the accusations of his former patients, it was the function of the board to judge the credibility of the witnesses, to weigh and evaluate their testimony and to resolve any conflicts. The findings reflect this function was performed.

Not only did the board conclude that respondent was guilty of negligent and wrongful actions in performing his duties but it further determined that his behavior violated the code of ethics of the American Psychological Association. The respondent complains this code of ethics had not been incorporated into the rules of the board until some weeks after the hearing was held and that there could be no substantial evidence to support a violation of a rule yet to be promulgated. K.S.A. 74–5308(a) provides that the board shall adopt the code of ethics of the American Psychological Association. The state asserts in its brief that the board did adopt the A.P.A. code at a regularly scheduled meeting in 1968, but that through some misunderstanding it was not promulgated as one of its rules until shortly after Dr. Morra's hearing. Be that as it may, the rule did not become effective until January 1, 1972.

We need not determine what effect, if any, this hiatus may have had with respect to the validity or legal effectiveness of the board's conclusion that the respondent's conduct violated the code of ethics. The state had charged not only that Dr. Morra had been guilty of unprofessional conduct as defined by rules established by the board (K.S.A. 74–5324 [d]) but alleged also that he had been guilty of negligence and wrongful actions in the performance of his duties. (K.S.A. 74–5324 [e].) The evidence appears amply sufficient to support the latter charge, which alone would justify the board in revoking the respondent's license.

Was the action taken by the board arbitrary, capricious, unlawful or unreasonable? A number of incidents and alleged irregularities are said to require an affirmative response.

Dr. Morra complains of erroneous rulings made during the hearing on the admission and rejection of evidence, the examination of witnesses, etc. K.S.A. 74–5333 specifically provides the board shall not be bound by technical rules of procedure, but shall give all parties reasonable opportunity to be heard and to present evidence. The statute further recites that depositions may be received in the discretion of the board.

*   *   *

It may be conceded that the hearing was not conducted with the finesse and legal expertise which one would hope to find in a judicial proceeding. A good deal of dialogue, some of it argumentative, took place between counsel and members of the board. Not every ruling made by the board would pass muster in a court of law bound by technical rules. We recognize, however, that this was a comparatively new board, that its members were lacking in experience and were, moreover, psychologists—not lawyers. Overall, we cannot say that fraud, bad faith or prejudice tainted the proceedings.

*   *   *

The respondent questions the constitutionality of the certification of psychologists act. *   *   * [T]he respondent argues that the term "wrongful actions" set forth in K.S.A. 74–5324(e) as a ground for revoking or suspending a license is unconstitutionally vague, that is, the term is so vague and uncertain that men of common intelligence and understanding will differ as to its meaning and application. *   *   * [O]ur test for measuring vagueness is "whether the language conveys a sufficient definite warning as to the proscribed conduct when measured by common understanding and practice."

We believe that a member of the profession to which the act applies would have no difficulty in comprehending what the term implies so far as his conduct as a psychologist is concerned. The American Psychological Association has adopted a code of ethics by which practicing psychologists are governed with respect to their professional behavior. Dr. Morra was aware of the association's code and he conceded in his testimony that actions of the nature charged against him would violate its provisions.

* * *

It is our opinion that the findings and judgment of the district court must be sustained, and it is so ordered.

Questions and Comments

1. What type of a hearing is constitutionally required in a disciplinary proceeding? Need it be a *public* hearing? Can a professional, facing charges before a state certification board, subpoena witnesses in his own behalf, hire an attorney, or cross-examine adverse witnesses? To answer these questions, a court will apply the balancing test articulated by the Supreme Court in *Mathews v. Eldridge*, 424 U.S. 319, 96 S.Ct. 893, 47 L.Ed.2d 18 (1976). Under this test, the individual's interest in particular procedural safeguards is balanced against the government's interest in expeditious proceedings. On the individual's side, the court will consider what interest the individual stands to lose and what the likelihood would be that the addition of a new procedural safeguard would avoid an erroneous decision. The government's interest, measured in terms of the added fiscal and administrative burdens, is then balanced against the increased individual benefits. To date, the Supreme Court has not applied its balancing test in a case involving a licensed professional's challenge to the procedures used in a disciplinary hearing. Consequently, it is difficult to state with certainty exactly what procedural protections must be provided.

2. Note that one of the principal issues in the *Morra* case was the adequacy of the statutory standard. Dr. Morra had contended that practitioners did not have adequate notice that having sexual relations with a patient constituted "negligence or wrongful actions in the performance of his duties." The Kansas Supreme Court rejected Dr. Morra's contention of unconstitutional vagueness in the standard as applied, in large part because the American Psychological Association's code of ethics proscribes sexual encounters between a clinician and his patient. Why should the adoption of a particular code of professional ethics by a private voluntary association have a bearing on a definition contained in a state statute?

3. What are the advantages, if any, of administratively conducted disciplinary hearings over other remedial actions such as private suits for malpractice or criminal prosecution? To what extent will the monetary costs and other burdens of litigation discourage an injured or aggrieved patient from pursuing his or her private remedies? Are administrative disciplinary proceedings a good substitute? Does the patient obtain relief in this system, even if the disciplinary proceeding results in a sanction against the practitioner?

Note in this connection that one of the possible advantages of disciplinary proceedings is that the patient or witnesses can frequently avoid the publicity that is invariably connected with a public law suit. Under the law of some states, a disciplinary hearing may be closed to the public and the press. Could this be a significant advantage to a complaining witness? To what extent is the accused practitioner prejudiced by a closed hearing if he is represented by counsel?

4. How effective are disciplinary hearings as a remedial device? Is the public interest likely to be adequately protected by hearings conducted and controlled by members of the profession of the accused? Is there any significant risk that leaving the control of discipline to representatives of the profession will lead to policies that are overly protective of the profession and individual practitioners? Any definite answer to these questions is difficult to come by since there have been no systematic studies gauging the efficiency of state disciplinary boards. However, occasionally reported cases suggest that administrative panels controlled by the professions are sometime unduly lax in carrying out their assigned duties. A series of articles in a Florida newspaper, for instance, reported on two cases that received considerable notoriety in the 1970's. One was the case of Dr. Louis Tsavaris, who was charged with the murder of a female patient. Three years later, with the first degree murder charges still pending, Dr. Tsavaris was free on bond and continuing his practice of psychiatry.

The same series also reported the case of Dr. Eduardo Russario, a Florida psychiatrist, who had reportedly impregnated a patient. He later settled a malpractice suit brought by her for $45,000. Subsequently, charges seeking the revocation of Dr. Russario's license were brought before the Florida Board of Medical Examiners. The only sanction imposed by the board was to place Dr. Russario on probation for three years and require that he undergo therapy. Gene Miller, "Sex and the Psychiatrists," *Miami Herald*, June 4–7, 1978. According to one commentator, "[t]he series documents the ineffectuality of the state licensing board in enforcing professional standards." Jonas B. Robitscher, *The Powers of Psychiatry* (Boston: Houghton Mifflin, 1980), p. 532.

5. It is questionable whether boards controlled by the professions they are mandated to regulate are capable of formulating policies that would be injurious to the economic interests of the profession in question. In this connection, consider the history of state regulation of professional advertising. The codes of ethics of many professions, including lawyers, pharmacists, physicians, and dentists, at one time prohibited advertising. The restrictions began as the policies of private voluntary professional organizations and found their way into state law or administrative agency regulations. In this way, state agencies with the power of law behind them began to enforce the prohibition on advertising which was previously only imbedded in the professions code of ethics. In 1976, however, the Supreme Court held that these broad restrictions on professional advertising violated the First Amendment. See *Virginia Pharmacy Board v. Virginia Consumer Council*, 425 U.S. 748, 96 S.Ct. 1817, 48 L.Ed.2d 346 (1976).

IV. EMERGING ISSUES IN THE ALLOCATION OF FUNCTION AMONG THE MENTAL HEALTH PROFESSIONS

As the Congress moves closer to enacting national health insurance, watch for a conspicuously uncivil war to break out among psychiatrists, psychologists and social workers. At issue is who will be certified and entitled to reimbursement for professional services. Billions of dollars in fees are at stake. So is the quality and range of mental-health care available to the public.

The dispute among the professionals has been warming for more than 25 years, ever since psychologists first began to view themselves as psychotherapists. Sensing a threat, in 1954 the American Psychiatric Association, the American Psychoanalytic Association and the American Medical Association issued a joint resolution opposing any laws that would allow other professional groups to practice psychotherapy independently. They lost. By 1977, having lobbied the state legislatures with remarkable success, psychologists were licensed in all 50 states and the District of Columbia.

Psychiatrists are now attempting to block "freedom-of-choice" laws that allow professionals other than psychiatrists to be reimbursed directly by insurance companies for providing mental-health services. The psychiatrists lost the first few rounds of this skirmish also, but the tide may be turning. In Virginia, for instance, the American Psychiatric Association and two of its district branches successfully defeated a freedom-of-choice bill for social workers.

* * *

Daniel B. Hogan, "Licensing Mental Therapists" *New York Times*, July 18, 1979, p. A–23.

As indicated by the above excerpt, professional groups are actively attempting to shape state and federal health legislation to protect their own interests. The following case illustrates one profession's use of federal antitrust laws to force private insurance carriers to modify their reimbursement policies.

✓ VIRGINIA ACADEMY OF CLINICAL PSYCHOLOGISTS v. BLUE SHIELD OF VIRGINIA

United States Court of Appeals, Fourth Circuit, 1980.
624 F.2d 476.

K.K. HALL, Circuit Judge:

This controversy arises over the refusal by defendants Blue Shield of Virginia and Blue Shield of Southwestern Virginia to pay for services rendered by clinical psychologists unless such services are billed through a physician. Plaintiffs Virginia Academy of Clinical Psychologists and Dr. Robert J. Resnick, a practicing clinical psychologist, claim that this policy violates Section 1 of the Sherman Act. 15 U.S.C. § 1. The district court found no violation.

We affirm in part and reverse in part.

Since 1962, Blue Shield of Virginia [BSV or the Richmond Plan] and Blue Shield of Southwestern Virginia [BSSV or the Roanoke Plan] have included outpatient coverage for mental and nervous disorders and for psychotherapy as a method of treating those disorders. Between 1962 and 1972, Richmond Plan coverage included direct payment to psychologists for psychotherapy rendered to subscribers. In 1972, this policy was revised to allow payment only when the services were billed through a physician.

The revised policy of the Richmond Plan was announced after consultation with various provider groups, including the American Psychological Association and the defendant Neuropsychiatric Society of Virginia [NSV]. Contact between the Richmond Plan and NSV, however, was particularly close.

Beginning in 1971, Dr. Levi Hulley, M.D., the head of the Plan's professional relations committee, met several times with NSV's president, Dr. Terrell Wingfield, M.D., over the question of payment for psychotherapy. Cooperation between the two groups followed: NSV, at the Plan's request, conducted a survey of Virginia psychiatrists on various aspects of psychiatric practice and later passed a resolution recommending, inter alia, that the Richmond Plan terminate direct payment to clinical psychologists. Immediately prior to adopting its policy, Richmond Plan officials met with a special NSV committee to discuss the scope of mental health coverage. The Plan adopted some of NSV's recommendations, including that of refusing to cover services rendered by psychologists unless billed by a physician.

* * *

[The court first reversed the district court's holding that the challenged activity was entitled to First Amendment protection. It then rejected the district court's alternative holding that the defendant's agreement was protected by the McCarran-Ferguson Act, which exempts from antitrust liability all state regulated "business of insurance." 15 U.S.C. § 1913(b) (1976)].

The final, critical issue is whether these combinations were "in restraint of trade." 15 U.S.C. § 1. The district court held that under the rule of reason, no violation was established. We disagree.

The district court began: "[t]he starting point in deciding the proper factual context for this case is deciding what sector of the economy is affected. * * * In other words, the court looks to see who is competing with whom." 469 F.Supp. at 560. The court found that clinical psychologists are not equal providers of therapy with psychiatrists because they do not render medical treatment and are not qualified to diagnose nervous and mental disorders or ascertain their source. The court further found that medical necessity in most, if not all cases requires regular contact between the psychologist's patient and a medical doctor.

The district court concluded that the clinical psychologist is not competitive with the psychiatrist unless the clinical psychologist is working under the "supervision" of a medical doctor. A psychologist working with a physician, the court continued, is paid by the Plans on an equal basis with a psychiatrist, except that the psychologist must bill through a physician.

> The court can well understand that plaintiffs do not like to bill through a physician as a matter of professional pride. The evidence shows that billing through a medical doctor is a requirement of the Blue Shield plan as a means of ascertaining that the treatment given and billed for was medically necessary. This procedure also tends to promote contact between the clinical psychologists and the physicians at all stages of treatment, and thus enhances the supervisory process.

469 F.Supp. at 561.

Appellants assert that the evidence establishes a boycott and therefore their exclusion from direct Blue Shield coverage is illegal *per se.* We agree that the challenged policy closely resembles that alleged in *Ballard v. Blue Shield of Southern West Virginia,* 543 F.2d 1075 (4th Cir.1976), which we found to be a boycott. Nor does the comparison necessarily fail because the concerted refusal to deal is conditional, rather than absolute.

The "boycott" characterization, however, avails us little in determining whether an agreement such as this is *per se* illegal. Because of the special considerations involved in the delivery of health services, we are not prepared to apply a *per se* rule of illegality to medical plans which refuse or condition payments to competing or potentially competing providers.

While we agree with the district court's rejection of a *per se* rule in this case, we think the court's analysis was misdirected. The rule of reason looks to the impact of the challenged practice upon competitive conditions.

The district court's finding that "the clinical psychologist is not competitive with the psychiatrist in treating nervous and mental disorders unless the clinical psychologist is working under the supervision of a medical doctor" reflects a value judgment, rather than an evaluation of anticompetitive effects.

The record demonstrates that psychologists and psychiatrists do compete; indeed it is susceptible to judicial notice. Both provide psychotherapy, 469 F.Supp. at 560, and are licensed to do so by State law. Competition in the health care market between psychologist and M.D. providers of psychotherapy is encouraged by the legislature, and its existence is well documented.

The Blue Shield Plans are a dominant source of health care coverage in Virginia. Their decisions as to who will be paid for psychotherapy necessarily dictate, to some extent, which practitioners will be chosen from among those competent under the law to provide such services.

Whether the "medical necessity" of referral and close contact between the therapist and a physician satisfies the rule of reason, as a cost control measure, is a matter not before us. The Plan's requirement that the psychologists' fee be billed through a physician, however, cannot stand.

The issue is more than one of professional pride. State law recognizes the psychologist as an independent economic entity as it does the physician. The Blue Shield policy forces the two independent economic entities to act as one, with the necessary result of diminished competition in the health care field. The subscriber who has a need for psychotherapy must choose a psychologist who will work as an employee of a physician; a psychologist who maintains his economic independence may well lose his patient. In either case, the psychologist ceases to be a competitor.

* * * [W]e are not inclined to condone anticompetitive conduct upon an incantation of "good medical practice." Moreover, we fail to see how the policy in question fulfills that goal. Any assertion that a physician must actually *supervise* the psychologist to assure the quality of the psychotherapy treatment administered is refuted by the policy itself. The Blue Shield policy provides for payment to psychologists for psychotherapy if billed through *any* physician—not just those who regularly treat mental and nervous disorders. It defies logic to assume that the average family practitioner can supervise a licensed psychologist in psychotherapy, and there is no basis in the record for such an assumption.

There are, of course, procompetitive reasons for requiring examination and consultation by a physician in order to assure that psychotherapy is not needlessly performed to treat a problem with physical etiology, but such safeguards must be accomplished in ways which do not sacrifice the economic independence of the psychologist.

The elimination of the bill-through provision does not preclude a variety of other cost control and quality control measures by Blue Shield. It does, however, expand consumer and provider alternatives. In addition, competition from licensed non-M.D. providers is likely to result in lower costs and the elimination of needless duplication of administrative costs created by the bill-through requirement.

Affirmed in Part, Vacated and Remanded in Part.

Questions and Comments

1. The *Blue Shield of Virginia* case illustrates the use of the federal antitrust laws to prevent insurance companies from limiting coverage and reimbursement for psychotherapy unless the services were rendered under the aegis of a licensed physician. However, because the rule applied in the *Blue Shield of Virginia* case stems from the antitrust

laws, a violation occurs only when the insurance carrier's policy is the product of an agreement by the carrier with another entity. Thus, the decision would not preclude an individual company from unilaterally adopting a policy limiting reimbursement for clinical services performed under the supervision of a psychiatrist unless such restrictions are prohibited by state law (*See*, Note 2 infra.)

2.   A number of states have adopted what are known as freedom of choice laws [FOC]. These laws limit the authority of private insurance companies to condition reimbursement for psychotherapy to services that are prescribed and billed through a physician. As of 1979 twenty-nine states had adopted some form of "freedom of choice" legislation. Dorken, "Laws, Regulations, and Psychological Practice," in Kiesler, Cummings, VandenBos, eds., *Psychology and National Health Insurance: A Sourcebook* (New York: American Psychological Association, Inc., 1979), p. 177.

Chapter Two

MALPRACTICE AND THE MENTAL HEALTH PROFESSIONS

Table of Sections

I. INTRODUCTION

As noted in Chapter I, the public interest in protecting the consumer of mental health services has led to a system of state regulation that seeks to ensure the quality of services by limiting entry into the various mental health fields to those who meet certain minimum qualifications. The emphasis of this approach is prospective in the sense that prevention of injury is the main objective. The legal system, however, has also established a regulatory scheme which is remedial in nature. Its emphasis is on furnishing those who are injured by substandard professional care with an opportunity for obtaining relief in a court of law. All claims of this nature fall within the general rubric of what is known as a malpractice suit. The term malpractice, however, does not adequately describe the legal theory under which these law suits are actually brought. As a catchall term it encompasses all actions of this nature, regardless of the specific doctrinal basis of the claim. In fact, private actions for malpractice may be based on any of several legal grounds. Most commonly, they are grounded on the doctrine of negligence. In some instances, the malpractice claim might rest on one of the intentional torts doctrines such as assault and battery, invasion of privacy, or breach of confidentiality. Occasionally it may be based entirely on principles of contract law rather than tort.

   Contrary to the impression conveyed in occasional newspaper reports of celebrated cases, malpractice suits against mental health professionals are still fairly uncommon. Most malpractice litigation against professionals in the mental health field have involved psychiatrists. As a group, however, psychiatrists are involved in significantly less litigation than other groups of medical specialists. Moreover, cases against psychiatrists have usually sought compensation for physical injury allegedly caused by the treatment; suits alleging less tangible psychic injury are relatively rare. One study reviewed all recorded litigation involving psychiatrists between 1946 and 1972 and concluded that:

> The most common suits against psychiatrists have, in the past, related to injuries from insulin or electroconvulsive therapy. Now that use of muscle relaxants has sharply reduced the risk of fractures during induced convulsions, suits in this class are declining. The rising use of drugs which affect mood or behavior makes increasingly likely suits related to adverse drug reactions.

Beresford, *Professional Liability of Psychiatrists,* 21 *Def.L.J.* 123 (1972).

A number of factors account for the relative infrequency of malpractice actions against mental health professionals. A major reason is the lack of professional consensus as to the limits of proper mental health treatment. Additionally, even when psychotherapy is improperly rendered, it is unlikely to result in visible physical injuries. Thus, the potential claimant will face substantial difficulties in proving that injury did in fact occur. Moreover, many former psychiatric patients undoubtedly choose to avoid litigation rather than face public disclosure of the fact that they have undergone treatment.

While these factors appear to have deterred lawsuits in the past, there are indications that the relative immunity enjoyed by mental health professionals over the years may be ending. For instance, a review of recent case law reveals that psychiatrists are no longer the only mental health professionals being charged with malpractice. With greater frequency, psychologists and social workers are sued by former patients or clients. This increase in litigation is in part the result of doctrinal changes in the law. For instance, courts and juries have become more willing to assign liability when therapists have breached their duty of trust by engaging in sexual intimacies with patients. These cases have significantly broadened the bases of malpractice liability to allow recovery in cases involving only psychological injury. Additionally, changes in legal doctrines in some jurisdictions have expanded the class of persons to whom a therapist owes a duty of care. Recent cases have imposed on the therapist a duty of care to persons other than those with whom he has established a professional relationship. The scope of this doctrine and its impact on the mental health profession will be explored more fully later in this chapter.

The materials which follow explore the various theories available to an injured patient seeking redress in a court of law. Part A focuses on the doctrine of negligence as a basis for recovery by a patient who has received substandard professional care. Recovery of damages based on contractual theories is considered in part B. Malpractice cases alleging invasion of privacy or breach of confidentiality are considered in the chapter dealing with confidentiality and the testimonial privilege. The doctrine of informed consent, which has developed as a separate theory of recovery, is dealt with in Chapter Three.

Questions and Comments

1. It is difficult to determine accurately the incidence of law suits against psychiatrists or other mental health professionals. Generally, only appellate decisions are reported; these cases represent only a small fraction of the total number of claims filed. The records of malpractice insurance companies are a good source of information, but access to

these records is generally difficult to obtain.   One author, however, was able to assess the incidence of suits against psychiatrists in southern California by reviewing the records of the principal malpractice insurer in the state.   Slawson, *Psychiatric Malpractice: A Regional Incidence Study*, 126 Am.J.Psych. 1302 (1968).

2.   The general trend of litigation involving psychiatrists has been summarized in the following terms:

> The rising use of drugs which affect mood or behavior makes increasingly likely suits related to adverse drug reactions.   Suits relating to suicide, wrongful commitment or detention, and injuries occurring during hospitalization will probably continue to arise as they have in the past.   Suits deriving from psychotherapy have been rare and will probably remain so.   Because many psychiatric patients are frustrated and angry, some may seek to sue their physicians, whether or not there is reasonable cause.   In this circumstance, their lawyers may best serve them by discouraging costly and futile litigation.

> There are few published studies of litigation involving psychiatrists.   Bellamy analyzed appellate decisions relating to alleged psychiatric malpractice for the fifteen-year period 1946–1961.   He found that the incidence of claims against psychiatrists during the five-year period ending in 1960 rose more steeply than the number of practicing psychiatrists.   Of the eighteen reported cases, nine involved treatment (seven of these relating to electroconvulsive therapy), six involved allegedly wrongful commitment, and one involved suicide.

Beresford, *Professional Liability of Psychiatrists*, 21 Def.L.J. 123 (1972).

The types of malpractice claims filed against psychiatrists during a four year period (1972–1976) are reviewed in Trent, *Psychiatric Malpractice and Its Problems: An Overview* in Barton and Sanborn, Law and the Mental Health Professions (New York: International Universities Press, 1978).

The serious side effects associated with the prolonged use of antipsychotic medication can be expected to lead to an increasing number of malpractice actions against psychiatrists and psychiatric institutions. This trend may, in fact, have already begun.   For instance, in *Clites v. Iowa*, 322 N.W.2d 917 (Iowa App.1982), the appeals court affirmed an award of $760,000 where a mentally retarded patient had developed tardive dyskinesia following six years of the administration of antipsychotic medication.

3.   The increase in psychiatric malpractice claims in recent years has been accompanied by increased malpractice insurance costs.   In 1972 when the American Psychiatric Association initiated its insurance program, a policy with limits of $1,000,000 cost $744 in California and $64 in New Hampshire.   In 1976 the same coverage had risen to $228 in New Hampshire and an average of $3,000 in California.   Trent, *Psychiatric Malpractice and Its Problems: An Overview* in Barton and Sanborn, Law and the Mental Health Professions (New York: International Uni-

versities Press, 1978), p. 101. Since psychiatrists are generally grouped together with general practitioners as a risk category the increases in premiums over the four year period does not necessarily reflect the actual claims experience of the psychiatric profession. *Id.* at 111.

4. What ends is the legal system attempting to achieve by maintaining a system which permits private actions for malpractice? The basic purpose of the system has been described as follows:

> As with negligence law in general, the malpractice system may be understood as a mechanism for signaling the potentially negligent—in this case, a subpopulation of physicians. The signal, when properly received, informs the doctor how much to invest in avoiding mishaps; ✔ the "correct" response, then, is for him to invest his resources up to the level of expected damages.

> To the extent that the usual fee for a service accurately reflects the training and the investment of time needed to meet customary standards of care, non-negligent physicians are appropriately remunerated. By contrast, the negligent physician, who fails to provide the full service but accepts the full price, is shortchanging his patient. With an effective malpractice signal, the potentially negligent physician would be stimulated to invest more time for no increase in pay because he probably could not set his fees higher than those of his more competent colleagues.

> In practice, the negligent physician may modify his behavior in one of several ways. The doctor who tends to skimp on history or physical examination or to rush through procedures must take the time needed for more careful work. But increasing his investment of time on each case may be insufficient. An inadequately trained physician is notified by the damages award that he should invest in further training. The cost of training must then be amortized over future cases. Alternatively, a physician may abandon procedures that he is not competent to perform, even though these procedures are relatively more remunerative than others in his practice.

> The ideal negligence signal is achieved only when every noteworthy incident of malpractice leads to a claim, and every valid claim to a full award. Then (in an ideal or, so to speak, "frictionless," system), the physician is stimulated to invest appropriately in mishap reduction.

Schwartz and Komesar, *Doctors, Damages and Deterrence*, 298 New Eng.J.Med. 1282, 1284 (1978).

5. It has been suggested that the malpractice system suffers from various imperfections. Among the problems that have been highlighted are the increasing tendency of the legal system to penalize non-negligent behavior and its failure at times to detect real negligence. See Schwartz and Komesar, *Doctors, Damages and Deterrence*, 298 New England Journal of Medicine, 1288 (1978). Moreover, it has been argued that "malpractice insurance, as it is currently administered virtually insulates the negligent physician from the damages award and, thus, from the malpractice signal." *Id.* at 1287. Is it arguable, however, that even if

the loss is covered by insurance that the embarrassment caused by the claim and the time spent by the physician in defending suit serve as deterrents to continued negligent behavior?

Would a no-fault system, which would make a practitioner automatically responsible for at least limited damages regardless of fault or negligence, be preferable to the system of negligence that currently prevails in all jurisdictions?

6. The unique characteristics of a therapist's work pose a particular challenge to legal institutions when the quality of the services rendered must be judged. For one thing, psychiatry has been described as both a science, requiring technical skills, and an art, dependent upon the personal relationship between the psychiatrist and his patient. In addition, even experts frequently have difficulty in assessing whether the therapy has been successful. The changes in the patient may be so subtle as to be imperceptible. Moreover, it is sometimes difficult to attribute a particular outcome, be it negative or positive, to the therapeutic intervention.

II. CLAIMS BASED ON NEGLIGENCE

Any professional who renders services has a legal duty to perform his professional functions in a manner comporting with the skill and technical proficiency normally exercised by other professionals in the same field. This duty of ordinary skill or care does not depend on or arise from any affirmative assumption of responsibility by the professional. It is rather an obligation imposed by the law. A professional's failure to meet this legal standard when rendering services establishes the key element of a claim of negligence. But to be successful in a law suit a patient-plaintiff must be able to prove more than that the services were of substandard quality. In fact, negligence has at least four distinct elements, each of which must be established by the plaintiff. These elements have been described in the following terms by one noted commentator:

1. A duty, or obligation, recognized by the law, requiring the actor to conform to a certain standard of conduct, for the protection of others against unreasonable risks.

2. A failure on his part to conform to the standard required. These two elements go to make up what the courts usually have called negligence; but the term quite frequently is applied to the second alone. Thus it may be said that the defendant was negligent, but is not liable because he was under no duty to the plaintiff not to be.

3. A reasonable close causal connection between the conduct and the resulting injury. This is what is commonly known as "legal cause," or "proximate cause."

4. Actual loss or damage resulting to the interests of another.

W. Prosser, *Handbook on the Law of Torts* § 30 (4th ed. 1971).

Each element raises separate problems of interpretation and application. The following materials discuss each element and explore current issues involving their application to legal disputes over the delivery of mental health services.

A. TO WHOM DOES THE THERAPIST OWE A DUTY OF CARE?

A threshold question in any case alleging professional negligence is whether the injured party is a member of the class of persons legally protected under the law of negligence. Traditionally, the answer to this question was relatively clear cut. No duty of care was owed except to those with whom the professional had established a contractual relationship. Thus, if the plaintiff had not been the professional's client, the case was dismissed, unless the plaintiff alleged more than mere negligence. However, the existence of a professional relationship, establishing what is called privity between the patient-claimant and therapist-defendant, is no longer the dispositive factor in professional negligence cases. An increasing number of jurisdictions have modified or repudiated the privity doctrine. Thus, under some circumstances therapists may today be liable to persons with whom no professional relationship has ever been established. Even under this expansive view, however, the presence of a contractual relationship may make it easier for a plaintiff to prevail in his claim. Thus, privity continues to be a significant factor in any action that alleges professional negligence.

As noted earlier, two distinct classes of claimants may seek to hold a therapist liable for negligent treatment—claimants who have received treatment and non-patient claimants who contend that the therapist's duty should be extended beyond the patient-therapist relationship to include third parties. Only for the former group of claimants will the issue of privity arise; the non-patient claimants, of course, acknowledge the absence of a privity relationship.

The following material explores the nature and significance of the professional relationship as an element in a negligence action brought by a former patient. The developments relating to the expansion of the therapist's liability to non-patients are treated separately later in this chapter.

1. The Professional Relationship and the Duty of Care

In our system of jurisprudence, a professional relationship is established by the voluntary actions of the prospective patient, who chooses an individual or an institution for the purpose of receiving mental health treatment. The contract resulting from this relationship presupposes the assent of both parties. This contract, however, need not be formal. The necessary assent can usually be inferred from the actions of the parties; no specific agreement is necessary.

Thus, a contract for services is presumed when a patient consults a therapist and the therapist undertakes to treat the patient.

While in most cases the circumstances readily reveal whether a therapist-patient relationship has been formed, in a number of situations the nature of the relationship may be contested. What, for instance, is the relationship of a therapist to the members of a patient's family whom the therapist involves in the treatment of the primary patient?

Although the professional relationship that establishes a duty of care is usually formed by the voluntary actions of both the therapist and the patient, under some circumstances the acts of only one of the parties may be sufficient to establish a professional relationship. This is the case, for instance, when a physician renders emergency care to an unconscious person. Here, the patient's incapacity prevents him from assenting to the formation of a contract. The patient's assent is presumed, however, and the physician is seen as entering into a professional relationship of a contractual nature. In other cases, professionals employed by a hospital or other treatment facility are not always free to reject a patient. These professionals may have a legal duty to render at least emergency services. The materials that follow consider the scope of this obligation and the circumstances under which it may arise.

Questions and Comments

1. Under the doctrine of vicarious responsibility a *respondent superior* liability may be imposed on an institution or individual practitioner for the negligent acts of employees or personnel under the defendant's supervision. Mental health therapy often involves treatment by a team of professionals, including perhaps a psychiatrist, psychologist, social worker, psychiatric nurse, occupational therapist, or other personnel. Thus, former patients alleging malpractice by one team member may invoke the doctrine of *respondent superior* to seek to hold one professional liable for the negligent acts of another team member. Similarly, the doctrine may be invoked to impose liability on an institution such as a hospital or mental health center for the negligence of one of its staff.

Professional or institutional liability for a subordinate's negligence can only be imposed, however, if two conditions are satisfied. First, the professional must have the right or ability to control the subordinate in his work. The necessary control is generally based upon an employment relationship between the defendant individual or institution and the subordinate. Even without an employer-employee relationship, a defendant who has exercised extensive control over the employee of another employer may be held liable for the subordinate's negligence under the "borrowed servant" doctrine.

Thus, because the crucial element of control is lacking, a professional will not be liable for the malpractice of another professional whom he recommends to a patient, nor will he be liable for the negligence of a professional called in for consultation or independent assistance in treating the patient. For instance, in *Stovall v. Harms*, 214 Kan. 835, 522 P.2d 353 (1974), a general medical practitioner referred a patient to a psychiatrist for treatment. The patient was later injured in a car accident allegedly caused by an excess of medication prescribed by the psychiatrist. In a malpractice suit naming both doctors as defendants, the general practitioner was not held liable for the psychiatrist's acts. The court reasoned that because the doctor had exercised reasonable care in selecting the psychiatrist and had no control over the psychiatric treatments, the doctrine of *respondent superior* was inapplicable.

The second prerequisite for application of *respondent superior* is that the subordinate must have been engaged in serving the purposes of the defendant. In part, this means that when a subordinate strays too far from the assigned work and becomes engaged in what is known as a "frolic and detour," his employer will no longer be held liable for the subordinate's negligence. For example, suppose a psychiatrist directs his nurse to drive directly to a patient's home to administer medication. Instead of taking the shortest route, the employee nurse takes a slightly longer route and negligently runs over a pedestrian. Because the nurse took only a slight detour from the psychiatrist's instructions, and because the major purpose of her actions was to serve the psychiatrist, she was acting within the scope of her employment at the time of the accident. Thus, her negligence will be imputed to the psychiatrist under the doctrine of *respondent superior*, and the psychiatrist will be liable for the injuries caused by her negligence. Suppose, however, that the nurse, after administering the medication, drove out of town to visit her family and on her return trip was involved in an accident. In this instance, the employee was acting outside of the employment relationship, on a frolic of her own. Thus, the psychiatrist would not be liable for the results of her negligence.

From a policy standpoint, four factors support the doctrine of *respondent superior*. First, because the negligent subordinate is unlikely to be as affluent or as well insured as his employer or supervisor, the imposition of derivative liability allows full compensation to an injured patient. Second, if a defendant is held liable for the negligence of his subordinates, he will be more careful in their selection and supervision. Third, the supervising professional or institution is able to spread the loss among all patients so that no one individual incurs ruinous expenses. And finally, since the defendant reaps the benefits of the business, payment of damages resulting from the business is properly imposed as one of the risks of business.

a. The Duty of Care to the Non-patient: The Traditional View

HAMMER v. POLSKY

Supreme Court, Special Term, New York County, 1962.
36 Misc.2d 482, 233 N.Y.S.2d 110.

[Plaintiff sued the defendant, a psychiatrist, for malpractice and invasion of privacy alleging that the psychiatrist had communicated erroneous diagnostic information to a third party. Because the complaint failed to allege that the relationship of plaintiff to defendant was that of patient-therapist, the defendant moved to dismiss the case.]

TILZER, Justice:

The second cause of action is also rested, as plaintiff asserts, in malpractice. It is therein alleged that the defendant did see the plaintiff on several occasions when plaintiff's wife was usually present, that plaintiff's wife was "the basic patient", that upon that basis defendant willfully and negligently diagnosed plaintiff's condition as "schizophrenia, paranoid in type", that such diagnosis, as defendant well knew, required skill and detailed careful inquiry to make, which careful inquiry the defendant had failed to make, that with gross negligence and contrary to the standards of care and practice obtaining in the area and upon inadequate, improper and insufficient examination, defendant negligently and unskillfully evaluated the data, upon which he claimed to have based his opinion and diagnosis. The sole objection with respect to the second cause of action is that plaintiff has failed to allege that the defendant was his physician. The court reaches the conclusion that such an explicit statement is lacking in the second cause of action as well. It is [therefore] insufficient [to state a cause of action by the plaintiff].

*   *   *

The motion is granted with leave to plaintiff to serve an amended complaint within 20 days from service of a copy of this order with notice of entry.

Questions and Comments

1. *Hammer v. Polsky* adopts the traditional view, which limits the therapist's duty of care to those with whom he has established a therapist-patient relationship. While this approach still has considerable vitality, it has been eroded somewhat in recent years by judicial decisions holding therapists liable to non-patient third parties.

Thus, for an aggrieved party other than the primary patient, for example, a family member involved in therapy sessions, there are two alternative approaches to establish his position as a member of the class to whom the defendant therapist owes a duty of care. First, the claimant family member may assert that, as a participant in the family therapy, he, too, had become one of the therapist's patients. To be successful in this argument, the claimant would have to convince the court to accept a broad definition of "patient" for purposes of establishing the professional relationship, which in turn would trigger a duty of care from therapist to claimant. In the alternative the claimant could argue that, even though he was not a patient of the therapist, the therapist's duty should be expanded to include certain non-patient third parties. Although the legal arguments are somewhat different, a successful claimant in either case would increase the traditional scope of the therapist's duty of care. Which approach do you think a court would be more likely to adopt? Which provides a narrower basis for holding the therapist liable? What factors would be relevant to the patient's choice of theory?

2. Is it possible that the *Hammer* decision is a product of earlier approaches to mental health? Traditionally, therapeutic interventions involved only the patient needing treatment. Joint or family therapy did not come into vogue until relatively recently. Is it, therefore, possible that the plaintiff's attorney was hesitant to assert that the patient's spouse, who was interviewed once or twice was, in fact, also a patient rather than merely a "bystander"?

3. With the increasing tendency of therapists to deal with the family as a unit, at what point and under what circumstances is a therapist-patient relationship established with other members of the family? Would one or two interviews, designed to elucidate the dynamics of family interaction, suffice to convert those family members interviewed into patients for purposes of establishing a duty of care to them? Or would the contact need to be more prolonged, involving some effort by the therapist to change the perceptions or behavior of the family member?

4. The past decade has witnessed a significant expansion of liability of professionals to *non-patients*. This trend has been accompanied by a major doctrinal shift in the law of negligence. This subject will be treated separately in a later part of this chapter.

5. In some situations the legal system may compel a service provider to provide treatment to designated members of the public. For instance, while as a general rule a hospital has no obligation to admit a patient (nor does the patient have an absolute right to be admitted), a number of states have enacted laws requiring hospitals that operate emergency wards to provide emergency care to anyone seeking admission. In other states the same result has been reached by judicial decision. When the duty has been established by court decision rather than by statutory enactment, the courts have reasoned that by operating an emergency ward the hospital has voluntarily undertaken a responsibility to render emergency aid. *Wilmington General Hospital v. Manlove*, 54 Del. 15, 174 A.2d 135 (1961) illustrates this recent trend.

Suppose a private hospital that operates an emergency ward refuses to admit a person who is suffering from an overdose of drugs. If that person is injured by a vehicle shortly after being refused admission, might the hospital be liable? What might be the liability of the psychiatrist who was on call that evening and who, after being telephoned by the nurse in charge of the emergency room, advised her to deny admission?

b. *What Conduct Is Encompassed by the Professional Relationship?*

Once a therapist-patient relationship has been established, are all actions of the therapist to protect the patient subject to the standard of care that is normally applicable to the profession? Are there situations in which a distinction may be made between interactions with a patient that are professional in nature and, therefore, clearly subject to the professional standard, and those undertaken by the therapist in a private or non-treatment capacity? The next two cases examine this question.

HESS v. FRANK

Supreme Court, Appellate Division, 1975.
47 A.D.2d 889, 367 N.Y.S.2d 30.

PER CURIAM.

Order, Supreme Court, New York County, entered May 15, 1974, which granted defendant's motion to the extent of dismissing on the merits the second cause of action, and which denied the motion insofar as it sought summary judgment or dismissal of the first cause of action, so far as appealed from, unanimously reversed on the law and the first cause of action dismissed. Appellant shall recover of respondent $60 costs and disbursements of this appeal.

The complaint sets forth two causes of action. In the first cause of action it is alleged that defendant, a psychiatrist, treated the plaintiff from 1961 to September of 1969. It is further alleged that on September 26, 1969 during a regularly scheduled session, the defendant, without any just cause, became abusive to the plaintiff, uttering various words and phrases which the defendant knew or should have known in his professional capacity would cause grave mental anguish to the plaintiff and would be injurious to his health. The record also indicates that the alleged abusive statements were uttered during the course of the parties' argument over fees as well as the appointment schedule. The first cause of action seeks damages in the sum of $100,000.

*   *   *

We believe that the second cause of action was properly dismissed, but conclude that the first cause of action should also have been dismissed. The Supreme Court upheld the first cause of action as being one sounding in malpractice—which was apparently the theory urged by plaintiff. However, the complaint failed to set forth the traditional elements of a claim for malpractice. As stated in New York Jurisprudence, "Negligence is the basis of a malpractice action which is tortious in nature and predicated upon a failure to exercise requisite skill." (45 N.Y.Jur. Physicians and Surgeons § 159.) The conduct complained of, however, was not part of the course of treatment and there is no claim or indication that defendant failed to provide medical services in accordance with accepted standards or that he did not exercise requisite skills in the treatment of the plaintiff. The argument which ensued between the parties and the abusive language allegedly employed by the defendant, if it may in some manner be considered a tortious act, may not be considered an act of professional misconduct, and, indeed, was unrelated to the medical treatment which was being rendered.

Questions and Comments

1. In *Hess* was there a foreseeable risk of harm to the patient from the therapist's use of abusive language? If so, was it realistic for the court to characterize the discussion over fees as being outside of the professional treatment relationship?

ZIPKIN v. FREEMAN

Supreme Court of Missouri, 1968.
436 S.W.2d 753.

[In a 1963 malpractice suit, Margaret Zipkin obtained a judgment in the amount of $17,000 against a psychiatrist, Dr. Robert Freeman. The original suit had alleged malpractice by Dr. Freeman. In the present suit, the plaintiff is suing Dr. Freeman's malpractice insurance company to collect the judgment obtained against Dr. Freeman. The company has acknowledged that the policy was in effect at the time that Ms. Zipkin was under treatment but had refused to pay the amount awarded to the plaintiff in the original malpractice suit. In its defense, the insurance company contended that it was not liable because the insurance policy only covered "professional services." Thus, the company argued, it was not required to compensate the plaintiff for the injuries she sustained as a result of activities "extraneous to * * * professional treatment." 436 S.W.2d at 756. The trial court rejected this defense, and the defendant insurance company has appealed from a judgment in plaintiff's favor.]

The facts contained in the partial transcript of the original case are these:

Respondent Ada Margaret Zipkin prior to April 1959, lived on a farm west of Columbia, Missouri for twelve years, as the wife of L.D. Baurichter. They had three children. She was active in community affairs such as PTA, the farm club, and in church. She and her husband entertained neighbors and friends, attended sports events, and one year were selected as the outstanding farm couple. About two years prior to April 1959, Mrs. Zipkin developed a chronic diarrhea, and about two months prior to that date she began to have severe headaches. Her regular doctor, Dr. Charles Lampke, treated her for these conditions but was not able to alleviate them, and, after many tests to try to find the causes, suggested she needed a psychiatrist and mentioned Dr. Freeman, of Columbia. She decided to see Dr. Freeman, made an appointment, took preliminary tests and saw him on April 18, 1959. There was a general discussion of what Dr. Lampke had reported to Dr. Freeman and he "asked me questions about my home and my family." She told him she had a good home, a good husband and thought she was very happy. During the first months the treatment "was limited to conversations, general talking. Most of all he asked me about my husband, if I was sure that he really loved me and that we were as happy as we thought we were."

After about two months of treatment the conditions for which Mrs. Zipkin went to Dr. Freeman "were completely gone". She asked him if it was necessary that she stay in treatment, which cost $17.50 per hour, two treatments a week. Dr. Freeman told her she could leave if she wanted to, but that her symptoms would return, she would have diarrhea and headaches again, and that it would probably be better if she stayed until they got to the root of what was really the problem, so she continued treatment.

* * *

In agreeing to continue the treatments after the headaches and diarrhea ceased, Mrs. Zipkin testified she was following Dr. Freeman's advice as to what she needed to correct her condition permanently. By this time "I had begun to feel nothing for my family or my husband * * * [and] thought I was in love with the doctor." He told her " * * * this was what I needed to get completely well, that this is what I would do" and she followed his directions in detail. She told Dr. Freeman she loved him and he told her he loved her too, this being three or four months after she started treatment.

In the summer of 1959, Dr. Freeman invited Mrs. Zipkin into his home, "saying that this was group therapy." She went to parties there, and a swimming party, [which involved nude bathing by Dr. Freeman and a number of his guests] and once a week Dr. Freeman had skating parties attended by eight to ten patients and their spouses. The social activities around Columbia continued through the winter, and she took a trip to New Orleans with Dr. Freeman and Mrs. Freeman and about a dozen other persons, including patients, in the early months of 1960. Dr. Freeman told her the occasion of the trip was a vacation, "and at times he would take some of his patients along for this group therapy, or because, maybe, sometimes the patients felt lost when they were not close to the doctor, and this was one way to treat them."

At a date not shown, she made an overnight trip with Dr. Freeman and a married couple, also his patients, to Lawrence, Kansas to visit a nursing home there, because there had been some talk of the doctor's starting a nursing home in Columbia. Dr. Freeman told her the trip was both social and group therapy, "Because at this time a lot of patients would say things * * * in other words, would lose a few of their inhibitions, maybe, and you could therefore study a patient closer."

About four or five months after she began treatment, Mrs. Zipkin gave up her active part in PTA, church and club activities, community affairs and visits with friends and neighbors because "They no longer had any interest for me * * * they meant nothing to me", the same being true as to her family and husband.

During the above time Dr. Freeman asked about Mrs. Zipkin's inheritance of an estate, and said "he would advise me as to how to handle it and I would thereby be a rich woman." He told her he was making $50,000 a year and a farm would be good for him for tax purposes. He also convinced her that her own home was not good enough for her.

* * *

They discussed buying 190 acres, and Mrs. Zipkin discussed it with her husband and her family attorney, who advised her against going in with the doctor and that perhaps she and her husband should buy the farm. Her husband said that he wanted no part of it. Soon after that she left him, moved at the doctor's suggestion to his apartment over his office with her three children and invested what money she could get from the estate in the farm, $14,000, which was later paid back by the doctor with interest, under threat of foreclosure. After a month in the apartment, she and the children (including the twins) moved to the farm, known as "Roads End", in the first part of June 1960, upon the understanding she would pay $100 per month rent.

As to Mrs. Zipkin's subconscious problems, Dr. Freeman told her she had a character disorder; she had a desire to be a male; that she thought she had to compete with males in order to be anything; that she did not know what it was to be a woman; and that she had a religious problem and a deep-seated rebellion and hostility toward her family. The basic diagnosis was that she was a neurotic, and had "an inferiority complex."

* * *

Dr. Freeman told Mrs. Zipkin to divorce her husband, "that I must do that in order to get completely well." She did file suit in June 1960, but the divorce was denied. She also filed an accounting suit against her husband, which suit was eventually dropped. She filed a suit against her brother for estate money he was supposed to have taken and which rightfully belonged to her, and the suit was dismissed. Dr. Freeman advised her on all these procedures, and explained to her that it was one way to rid herself of the pent-up hostility that was in her toward her family. This was why she filed the lawsuits, not to win them. For that same purpose, as part of his treatment and counselling, Dr. Freeman told her to go back to her former home. She went there alone, broke in, and took a few small things, "just to get some of this hostility out of me." He went with her on a later occasion and they took a desk, and some beds which went into his home for his two boys. She was told by him to take some of the livestock which her husband had, but she was unsuccessful, and he directed her to return with a pistol he gave her and to shoot anyone who got in the way and to take anything she might want. He told her "this was a war of hostility at that time between my family and myself and that I was on the front line and I had to take care of myself."

* * *

She admitted giving conflicting false testimony in her divorce hearing, on deposition, and at a hearing involving Dr. Freeman before the Board of Healing Arts, and testified that she was directed by Dr. Freeman to testify as she did. She also testified she had sexual relationships with him and had been his mistress.

* * *

The social trips and associations stopped in November 1961 and Mrs. Zipkin left Roads End in March 1962.

* * *

Dr. Flynn testified that the type of swimming parties where a number were not dressed is not group therapy, although this is an accepted type of psychiatric treatment where patients come to see the psychiatrist as a group and discuss their problems together; the type of skating parties described in evidence is not group therapy; the taking of trips, some overnight, by another couple, Mrs. Zipkin and Dr. Freeman, where he stated he could perform therapeutic treatments, is not accepted treatment—one would be entering into a social relationship with patients and Dr. Flynn could not see how it would have anything at all to do with therapy. He considered it improper treatment.

It is our opinion and we hold that the defendant insurer was obligated to defend this case and is liable under its policy. It refused to defend on the ground that the acts and omissions of Dr. Freeman were not professional services rendered by him in the practice of his profession. It makes no claim that part of what Dr. Freeman did is covered and part is not. It contends that none of what gave rise to plaintiff's claim were professional services covered by the policy, that these "were things any butcher, baker, beggar man or thief was capable of doing". It quotes the testimony of Dr. Flynn that the swimming parties and skating parties were not therapy and had the effect of distorting "the entire transference situation" and turning the patient-physician relationship into a social relationship. Parenthetically, we observe that the context of Dr. Flynn's testimony is more that these were not proper therapy or properly handled than that they were completely unrelated to therapy.

At any rate, defendant argues that by no stretch of the imagination can any of what the doctor did be considered professional services, that there was no way they could have litigated this aspect of the matter in the Zipkin v. Freeman case and hence it was under no duty to defend and is now under no duty to pay.

However, it is an oversimplification to focus on the more spectacular and extreme acts of the doctor as determinative of the issue. Under the extremely broad terms of the policy before us, defendant agreed to pay damages "based on"—which would also mean resulting from, or caused by, or due to—professional services rendered or which should have been rendered. The word "damages" is not limited to any particular kind of damage or injury and applies to any claim or suit, with certain specific exceptions not here material. Defendant would limit the damages to the very act itself of professional services, but the policy clearly covers the results and liability flowing from professional services rendered or which should have been rendered.

The gravamen of the petition is that defendant did not treat Mrs. Zipkin properly and as a result she was injured. He mishandled the transference phenomenon, which is a reaction the psychiatrists anticipate and which must be handled properly. He mishandled it over a long period of time. As Dr. Flynn explained, to take the relationship outside the office into social relationships, "would allow the patient to develop all sorts of unusual ideas just around the feelings that she has about the doctor", and that a psychiatrist should no more take an overnight trip with a patient than shoot her; that "Patients have enough trouble with their feelings that they develop about the doctor without adding to them by actual events." He said transference should be handled in the office situation.

* * *

Once Dr. Freeman started to mishandle the transference phenomenon, with which he was plainly charged in the petition and which is overwhelmingly shown in the evidence, it was inevitable that trouble was ahead. It is pretty clear from the medical evidence that the damage would have been done to Mrs. Zipkin even if the trips outside the state were carefully chaperoned, the swimming done with suits on, and if there had been ballroom dancing instead of sexual relations. It might not have been exactly clear at the beginning of the failure to treat properly how the trouble would manifest itself, but under the petition and the evidence Dr. Freeman did not give Mrs. Zipkin the professional services he should have. The damages which she sustained resulted from such failure and are within the policy coverage.

* * * [T]he judgment is affirmed.

Questions and Comments

1. The *Zipkin* case is only one of numerous actions that former patients have brought in recent years against psychiatrists who have become sexually involved with their patients. Other reported cases include *Seymour v. Lofgreen,* 209 Kan. 72, 495 P.2d 969 (1972); *Greenberg v. McCabe,* 453 F.Supp. 765 (E.D.Pa.1978) at p. 88 *infra.*

Even social contact of a non-sexual nature has been the basis of malpractice liability in England. *See,* for instance, *Landau v. Werner,* 105 Sol.J. 1008 (1961).

c. Terminating the Professional Relationship

BRANDT v. GRUBIN

Superior Court of New Jersey, Law Division, 1974.
131 N.J.Super. 182, 329 A.2d 82.

DREIER, J.D.C., Temporarily Assigned.

In this medical malpractice action defendant Dr. Charles J. Grubin has moved for summary judgment. This case raises an issue of first impression in New Jersey concerning the alleged abandonment by a physician who had referred a patient for specialized services.

Defendant Dr. Grubin is a licensed and practicing physician of the State of New Jersey engaged in the general practice of medicine. He is alleged to have been the physician of plaintiff, the decedent's mother, but her depositions show his earlier services had been limited to signing one or two death certificates for the family. On October 25, 1971, and for some time prior thereto, decedent, George F. Brandt, Jr., then 21 years of age, was alleged to have experienced periods of anxiety, loneliness and insomnia, as described by Dr. Grubin. On this date (and perhaps one other occasion) decedent consulted Dr. Grubin for examination, care and treatment of these conditions.

At his deposition Dr. Grubin characterized the decedent's mental condition on October 25, 1971 as "an anxiety syndrome." He admitted that he was not a psychiatrist, but nevertheless prescribed thorazine to be taken by decedent "to take the edge off his anxiety." He admitted that the principal contraindication for the use or prescription of thorazine is depression, and the second most important contraindication is liver disease. With respect to depression as a contraindication, he noted that "the literature says in the presence of depression thorazine should be used very cautiously and that's all I have to see and I don't touch it."

After this one visit, and perhaps an additional contact a few days later decedent <u>did not return to Dr. Grubin</u>. A month later, on November 21, 1971, decedent was treated at the Elizabeth General Hospital Emergency Room and was again advised to go to the Union County Psychiatric Clinic for further treatment. Two days later (on November 23, 1971) he was again admitted into the hospital's medical ward, and then placed in the psychiatric ward just prior to his suicide on November 26, 1971.

On the subject of Dr. Grubin's later alleged unavailability, decedent's sister, Mrs. Frances Freda, stated in her depositions that the family attempted repeatedly to contact Dr. Grubin the week prior to decedent's confinement at Elizabeth General Hospital on November

23, 1971. She testified that "for the whole weekend we tried to reach Dr. Grubin and we just got a series of runarounds," and further:

> At one point my mother called him and spoke with the nurse again. We explained to him all these times it was an emergency, that we had to speak to him immediately. We told him who we were, who we were calling for, and this last time when my mother called she asked him has Dr. Grubin returned yet and the nurse said, "Returned? He's always been here. He hasn't gone anyplace."

* * *

In short, the three claims of malpractice are Dr. Grubin's (1) inadequate assessment of the "seriousness of the situation," (2) "inadequate" treatment and (3) abandonment of the patient.

[The court found no basis in fact to support the first two claims advanced by the plaintiff.]

The question of abandonment of a patient was considered in detail in Clark v. Wichman, [where it was argued by plaintiff] * * * that the surgeon abandoned her when she was committed to the mental hospital, but the court held that this argument was without merit, particularly when the transfer had been pursuant to an order of the court.

* * * This is not a case of unwarranted forsaking of a patient without notice or without providing a competent substitute physician [citing authorities]. Where a physician under appropriate circumstances ceases to attend a patient, his responsibility ordinarily ceases without any formality [citing cases]. An abandonment consists of "a failure by the physician to continue to provide service to the patient when it is still needed in a case for which the physician has assumed responsibility and from which he has not been *properly* relieved."

* * *

The general statement of the rule concerning a physician's withdrawal from the case is expressed as follows:

> It is the settled rule that one who engages a physician to treat his case impliedly engages him to attend throughout that illness, or until his services are dispensed with. In other words, the relation of physician and patient, once initiated, continues until it is ended by the consent of the parties or revoked by the dismissal of the physician, or until the latter's services are no longer needed. However, the relationship of physician and patient may also be terminated by the physician's withdrawal from the case. *It is well recognized that the physician has a right to withdraw from the case, but only after giving the patient reasonable notice so as to enable him to secure other medical attendance, and such a withdrawal does not constitute abandonment.*

* * *

This principle is merely an expansion of the brief statement quoted earlier and is supported in the Annotation and Supplements by cases too numerous to cite.

The foregoing statements of the rule pertain to a physician who has undertaken the general treatment of a patient without an agreement limiting his services. A modified rule pertains, however, to a physician who has been employed only for a specific occasion or service, and such physician "is under no duty to continue his visits or treatment thereafter, and is consequently not liable for abandonment if he ceases treatment of his patient after performance of the specific service."

This court is of the opinion that the same rule must apply if a patient is examined by a physician who by reason of his general practice determines that he is unable to provide needed specialized treatment and that the patient must therefore be referred to a specialist. In this case the reference was made to specific clinics where specialized help would be available, and the patient actually underwent care at one of these clinics. The fact that the decedent's mother had briefly utilized defendant's services on an earlier occasion did not render him decedent's physician under any general contract to provide care. The only proofs before the court by way of expert reports, depositions and interrogatory answers show that decedent visited Dr. Grubin for a specific purpose, and after this one visit Dr. Grubin found that he was incapable of providing the requested services. This was explained to decedent, and the subsequent events cannot be legally ascribed to any abandonment by Dr. Grubin. Whatever efforts were made by decedent's family to contact Dr. Grubin are of no legal import since no duty then flowed from Dr. Grubin to decedent.

* * *

Defendant Grubin's motion for summary judgment is therefore granted.

Questions and Comments

1. One of the arguments advanced by the *Brandt* plaintiffs was abandonment. In effect, the plaintiffs were alleging that if the physician had continued to treat the decedent, the suicide could have been prevented. This type of claim raises problems of proving proximate cause, another element of a negligence claim; this issue is discussed in subsection II.C., *infra*.

2. A therapist has no legal duty to continue treatment indefinitely. If he wishes to terminate his relationship with the patient, he is merely obligated to give the patient sufficient time to arrange other treatment before withdrawing from the case. The amount of time that constitutes "reasonable notice" varies from case to case and ultimately will be submitted as a question of fact if the matter is adjudicated.

3. To date, the requirement that a therapist give his patient reasonable notice before terminating treatment has only been applied to physicians. However, the considerations underlying the rule would seem to apply with equal force to treatment by other mental health professionals.

4. The doctrine of abandonment poses particular problems to those in the mental health field. When a disturbed patient comes to a therapist's office, the therapist will frequently want to conduct at least a preliminary interview to determine the nature of the problem and the amenability of the individual to treatment. ✗ To what extent does a preliminary diagnostic interview subject a therapist to potential liability for abandonment in the event that he decides at the conclusion of the initial interview not to accept the person as a patient? If the therapist decides not to continue with the case, must he continue to see the patient for a period of time sufficient to permit the patient to establish contact with another therapist? Or may the therapist terminate treatment immediately? *AS LONG AS NO EMERGENCY - YES*

INTERVIEW CAN BE CONTRUED AS INITIATING TX

5. The standard of reasonable notice embodies no clear rules as to when a therapist may terminate treatment. Suppose, for example, a patient does not improve and the therapist determines that the patient should see another professional. Does the therapist have a duty to see that his patient successfully makes the transition, or can he simply send him on his way? What about the patient who does not pay his bill? Does the duty of care continue? Suppose a patient simply stops coming to regularly scheduled appointments. Should the therapist have a duty to attempt to contact the patient? To what extent would your answer depend on the severity of the disorder being treated?

MAY BE CONSIDERED AS PT. HAS TERMINATED TX - WOULD BE A CONSTRUCTIVE DISMISSAL - NO OBLIGATION

B. "DUE CARE" AS AN ELEMENT OF NEGLIGENCE
1. Introduction

The occurrence of a mishap or injury is not sufficient to impose liability on mental health professionals providing treatment. Liability for negligence can only attach if those rendering the treatment did not exercise the knowledge and skill attributable to the reasonably well-qualified practitioner in the same field or specialty. Application of this standard, which is commonly known as the requirement of "ordinary" or "due" care, requires the trier of fact to focus on several points. First, the fact finder must take into account the defendant's particular profession. Whether a psychiatrist exercised due care is judged, not by the training and knowledge of mental health professionals in general, but by the particular knowledge and expertise ordinarily possessed by medically trained persons. Similarly, the actions of a Ph.D. clinical psychologist are judged by a different standard than those of a psychologist holding only a master's degree. In each case the knowledge and expertise of the professional being charged with negligence is evaluated according to the standards of his professional specialty.

A second issue pertains to the actual level of skill which the due care standard incorporates. What is the specific standard by which due care is to be judged? The test in the medical context has been analyzed in the following terms:

> How can the ability of other physicians of a community or an area be measured so that it can be used as a comparative guide for the law's purposes? Is the doctor who is charged with negligence measured against the skill and ability of the best, the worst, or the average among his colleagues? All three bases of comparison specifically have been repudiated by the courts. It is unfair to a defendant doctor to require that he be as good as the best. Likewise, it is unfair to the plaintiff patient to allow the doctor to be compared to none other than the worst. Depending upon conditions in the comparative area, it may be unfair to one party or the other to require the defendant to possess the skill of the average among other physicians if indeed such an "average" exists except as a verbal term. It is often stated that the physician must possess the skill and exercise the care which an ordinarily prudent physician would possess and exercise under the same or similar circumstances. It is apparent, therefore, that the physician is supposed to be judged according to something like a median skill and carefulness presently existing among practitioners of the same type in the same or a similar community. It is further apparent that the verbalization of the standard means little until it is applied to a particular set of facts.

David W. Lowisell and Harold Williams, *The Parenchyma of Law* (Rochester, N.Y.: Professional Medical Publications, 1960), pp. 179–180.

Finally, the test of due care sometimes incorporates a geographic limitation. In some jurisdictions the standard of due care is judged in terms of the knowledge, expertise, and practice of the particular community where the services were rendered. The use of this criterion, known as the locality rule, was at one time essential in medical malpractice cases, because the quality of services, medical facilities, and level of professional expertise varied considerably from one locality to another. This rule reflected the courts' belief that because a doctor from a small town or rural area would not have access to the resources available to physicians living in cities or near large medical centers, the quality of each doctor's services should be gauged not against an absolute standard, but rather against the standard of care expected from a doctor practicing in similar conditions.

2. *What Is Meant by the Concept of "Ordinary Care?"*

PETTIS v. STATE DEPARTMENT OF HOSPITALS

Court of Appeals of Louisiana, 1976.
336 So.2d 521.

[The plaintiff, Cecil Pettis, sustained multiple fractures as a result of the administration of shock treatments at a state mental hospital.]

The above shock treatments were administered to Pettis without the use of any premedication, except atropine. The medical evidence is uniform to the effect that fractures frequently are sustained by patients where shock treatments are performed without first administering a tranquilizer or paralyzing drug, such as "Anectine." The experts estimated that from two to 30 percent of the patients who are given shock treatments without the use of a paralyzing drug sustain fractures. Usually the fractures relate to the vertebrae, but occasionally other bones of the body are fractured, such as the shoulders, arms and hips. It is very rare for fractures of the femur to result from those treatments.

* * *

Plaintiff contends, first, that the defendant doctors were negligent in not administering a muscle relaxant or a muscle paralyzing drug, such as Anectine, to Pettis before performing each shock treatment. He argues that these treating physicians thus failed to exercise the degree of skill ordinarily employed by members of their profession in the same community or locality, and that they failed to use reasonable care and diligence, along with their best judgment, in the application of their skills to the case.

The applicable law was stated by our Supreme Court as follows:

"A physician, surgeon or dentist, according to the jurisprudence of this court and of the Louisiana Courts of Appeal, is not required to exercise the highest degree of skill and care possible. As a general rule it is his duty to exercise the degree of skill ordinarily employed, under similar circumstances, by the members of his profession in good standing in the same community or locality, and to use reasonable care and diligence, along with his best judgment, in the application of his skill to the case."

The burden of proof rests on the plaintiff in a malpractice suit to establish that the defendant physician deviated from the required standard of skill and care.

Eight doctors testified in this case, including the three doctors who are defendants. Seven of them expressed opinions as to whether it is good or accepted medical practice for a physician to administer a shock treatment without the use of a muscle relaxant or muscle paralyzing drug, such as Anectine. Some of them preferred to use that type drug in administering shock treatments, while others preferred not to use it. All recognized the fact that there is a greater danger of the patient sustaining fractures if the drug is not used but that there is a slightly greater danger of loss of the patient's life, due to respiratory failure or cardiac arrest, if the drug is used. All of the medical experts seem to agree, however, that either procedure is acceptable to members of the medical profession in good standing in that community, and that the doctor who administers that treatment may, consistent with good medical practice, use his best judgment as to whether to use the tranquilizer or muscle paralyzing drug, or not to use it, in any case.

We find no negligence on the part of Dr. Kirkpatrick or Dr. Kent in failing to use Anectine, or a similar drug, in performing shock treatments on plaintiff.

[The Court, however, found that defendant was negligent in administering electric shock to the plaintiff on several occasions *after* he had already suffered a fracture of the vertebrae at the initial session.]

Questions and Comments

1. A departure from the standard of due care may result from either the election of an inappropriate therapy or improper *implementation* of the therapy. The improper use of a treatment modality might involve either its use when no beneficial result could reasonably be expected or its use when one could reasonably anticipate exacerbation of the condition or some other side effect. Because, for example, the administration of thorazine is contradicted in the case of an individual suffering from depression, its administration to a depressed patient who subsequently commits suicide might result in liability. *See, e.g., Brandt v. Grubin*, 131 N.J.Super. 182, 329 A.2d 82 (1974). An example of improper implementation of customary therapeutic modality would be the administration of ECT without the administration of the muscle relaxant. It might also include the uninterrupted and prolonged administration of psychotropic medication coupled with a failure to terminate treatment upon the appearance of symptoms of tardive dyskinesia. *See, e.g. Clites v. State*, 322 N.W.2d 917 (Iowa App.1982).

2. Adherence to the locality rule, as articulated by the court in *Pettis*, created a number of problems for the plaintiff, who was required to establish the community's medical standards of care and to prove that the defendant had deviated from that standard. In many jurisdictions the plaintiff was traditionally required to obtain expert testimony on the standard of care in the relevant community or locality. Because of the natural reluctance on the part of doctors to testify against one another, the plaintiff was frequently unable to obtain the expert testimony of a physician who actually lived in the community.

Gradually, the locality rule was broadened to include the standard of care applicable in similar localities; thus, the plaintiff could present the testimony of doctors practicing in other towns or cities. This relaxation of the standard lightened the plaintiff's burden because doctors were more likely to agree to testify against practitioners in communities other than their own. With improved means of communication, transportation, access to medical literature, and consultation, the locality rule has been broadened even further, so that the community standard is now merely one factor to be considered in establishing a general professional standard.

Locality Rule Has Been Gradually Abandoned

3. The court in *Pettis* found that the doctor's failure to use a muscle relaxant in the administration of ECT did not constitute negligence as measured against the standards of that particular community. Had the standard been national rather than local, the result may have been different. In that connection, it is perhaps significant to note that only in the last ten years has the use of muscle relaxant drugs become a recognized medical procedure in the administration of shock therapy. Thus, courts in future cases are much more likely to impose liability on physicians who fail to use a muscle relaxant, even if the court applies the restrictive locality rule.

3. Innovative Therapy and the Standard of Due Care

As with every aspect of a therapist's performance of his duties, the selection of one therapy over another is measured by the standard of due care, i.e., what members of the profession would customarily do under the circumstances. The legal yardstick for measuring liability thus focuses on what is customary. While a finding that the therapeutic approach used was not "customary" does not necessarily lead to liability, proof of conformity to custom generally precludes a finding of liability. Thus, whether a particular treatment is "customary" or "accepted" by the profession may well be dispositive of the issue of liability. However, "customary" does not mean that the therapeutic approach in question is used by the majority of practitioners. In some jurisdictions it is enough that use of the therapy is supported by a "respectable minority" of those in the field. *See Leech v. Bralliar*, 275 F.Supp. 897 (D.Ariz.1967). Other jurisdictions have articulated the test in terms of whether the mode of treatment has the approval of a "considerable number" of professionals in good standing. *See McHugh v. Audet*, 72 F.Supp. 394 (M.D.Pa.1947).

Satisfying the standard of due care is made more difficult where the physician departs entirely from established modes of treatment and adopts a unique or novel procedure. Because no meaningful measure of approval by the medical/professional community is available for dramatically innovative techniques, the reasonableness of the selected treatment must be determined by other criteria. Whether the use of a particular therapeutic mode is found reasonable generally turns on a combination of factors including (1) the present and predicted conditions of the patient; (2) the probability of success of a given therapy; and (3) the probability, type and severity of risks collateral to the therapy. Jon R. Waltz and Fred E. Inbau, *Medical Jurisprudence* (New York: Macmillan, 1971), pp. 190–191. In cases of extreme departures from customary practice a court may hold that the physician's treatment constituted a lack of due care as a matter of law and the issue is not to be put to the jury. The case of *Kershaw v. Tilbury*, 214 Cal. 679, 8 P.2d 109 (1932) illustrates this situation. There, a licensed osteopathic physician undertook to treat the plaintiff's inflamed leg with a black box that purportedly emitted diagnostic and therapeutic radio waves. The defendant physician incorrectly diagnosed the patient's affliction and permanent disability resulted before proper treatment could be obtained elsewhere. The trial court kept the question of the reasonableness of defendant's approach from the jury, allowing liability to attach after a finding that the defendant's unorthodox method caused the plaintiff's injuries.

On the other hand, where the circumstances clearly warrant the use of experimental methods, the issue of experimentation may also be decided as a matter of law. For instance, in one of the early heart transplant cases it was shown that the patient's condition was not amenable to any known treatment and that death was imminent. Given those circumstances, the court of appeals affirmed the trial court's directed verdict on the issue of experimentation. *See Karp v. Cooley*, 493 F.2d 408 (5th Cir.1974).

Questions and Comments

1. Was the case of *Hammer v. Rosen* which appears at p. 78 more like *Kershaw v. Tilbury* or *Karp v. Cooley?* Was it sufficiently clear that there was a departure from the ordinary standard of due care that the issue should not have been submitted to the jury?

2. The only reported similar case imposing liability on a psychologist using innovative therapy is *Abraham v. Zaslow* (San Francisco, Cy.Sup. Ct.1972) reported in *New York Times*, July 5, 1972, p. 27 and APA *Monitor*, Mar. 1973. The therapy in question was called "Rage Reduction Therapy or Z-Process." This involved breaking down the patient's resistance, by applying extensive physical stimulation to an immobilized patient in order to reduce the repressed compulsion to escape. The process was originally developed for use on autistic children, but Dr. Zaslow expanded it for use with disturbed adults. At trial the plaintiff testified, "I was tortured, including choking, beating, holding and tying me down and sticking fingers in my mouth." Ralph Slovenko, *Psychiatry and Law* (Boston: Little, Brown, 1973), p. 428, n. 39.

3. The standards governing the liability of physicians undertaking experimental or innovative therapy have undergone a marked change in recent years. As one commentator notes, "The rule to be extracted from the early cases involving human experimentation is that physicians vary from established treatment at their own peril." Michael H. Shapiro and Roy G. Spence, *Bioethics and Law* (St. Paul, Minn.: West Pub. Co., 1981), p. 871. "The more modern courts take a less restrictive view of untried medical treatment and surgical procedures; and several decisions establish the right of the general field of medicine and surgery to progress and advance to some experimentation." *Id.*

4. The development of the present legal standards of assessing liability for experimentation results from an attempt to promote the

advancement of medical science while protecting society from reckless innovation. *See Carpenter v. Blake*, 60 Barb. 488 (S.Ct.N.Y.1871). Has the proper balance been struck? How confident must a physician, breaking new ground, be that his techniques are "reasonable" before he exposes his patients and himself to the attendant risks? Will the patient about to undergo experimental treatment have more or less reason to trust his doctor's judgment if he knows the standard to which he will be held?

5. The present controversy concerning the use of hemodialysis to treat schizophrenia raises interesting issues concerning the liability of physicians who administer such experimental treatment. Some reseachers have suggested the "possibility that schizophrenia may be caused by a mysterious substance in the blood and cured by removing it with hemodialysis techniques used for kidney disease." "Dialysis for Schizophrenia? Doctors Debate Effects," *New York Times*, March 7, 1981, pg. 1, col. 1. Dialysis, however, may be "so stressful that it often produces unpleasant psychological effects," including a high incidence of depression and suicide among renal dialysis recipients. *Id.*

"Dialysis is presently considered by most psychiatric researchers to represent only an experimental approach and treatment modality. *Id.* Some studies have cast substantial doubt on the efficacy of dialysis as an acceptable treatment for schizophrenia. For instance, researchers at the National Institute of Mental Health recently issued a report finding hemodialysis to be totally ineffective in relieving schizophrenic patients of their hallucinations or other psychiatric symptoms. Nevertheless, some families of schizophrenic patients "desperately seeking a new promise of help are pursuing dialysis despite its great expense and grave dangers." *Id.* While actual statistics are not known, some researchers have estimated the number of schizophrenics receiving hemodialysis in the hundreds. *Id.*

Given the present state of knowledge, what should be the liability of a psychiatrist who prescribes dialysis treatment for a schizophrenic patient who subsequently manifests depression which results in suicide? Should the fact that a small minority of professionals believe that hemodialysis can effectively treat schizophrenia be relevant in determining whether the use of this procedure establishes a *prima facie* case of negligence? Would a holding that the use of the procedure constitutes a lack of due care as a matter of law stifle legitimate medical experimentation? Should the result perhaps rest on whether the treatment was offered as customary therapy as distinct from closely controlled experimentation?

6. It is important to note that the liability of therapists who use innovative or experimental methods may rest on either the doctrine of negligence or on the separate doctrine of informed consent. The latter is a distinct form of action involving elements of proof substantially different from those required by the law of negligence. The doctrine of informed consent is considered in greater detail in Chapter Three. Thus,

the earlier comments which suggest a relaxation of the standards applicable to experimental therapy only apply to the law of negligence. In fact, as suggested by the chapter dealing with informed consent, the legal standards governing that doctrine have, if anything, become more stringent in recent years.

7. Generally, proof that a practitioner adhered to custom in providing treatment precludes the imposition of liability. In rare cases courts have departed from this position, however. Thus, the courts of at least two jurisdictions have held a particular therapeutic procedure to be negligent in spite of uncontradicted expert evidence stating that the procedures used conformed to the customary practices of the profession. *See Helling v. Carey*, 83 Wn.2d 514, 519 P.2d 981 (1974) *and Barton v. Owen*, 71 Cal.App.3d 484, 139 Cal.Rptr. 494 (1977).

4. *Allocation of Evidentiary Burdens and the Issue of Due Care*

As a practical matter, the result in a negligence case is often more the function of the evidentiary rules applied than of the substantive doctrine itself. For instance, in the typical malpractice case the patient has suffered an injury while undergoing medical treatment. In substantive law the central issue is whether the therapist exercised due care while treating the patient. Ordinarily, however, before a plaintiff can present the merits of the case to the trier of fact, he must introduce the testimony of an expert witness to establish the applicable standard of care. In other words, unless the plaintiff can find medical experts who will describe how a reasonably qualified practitioner would have treated the plaintiff, the plaintiff is unable to present evidence of the defendant's alleged negligence. Thus, in the absence of expert testimony, the defendant generally prevails, regardless of the facts of the particular case. This burden of adducing sufficient proof by the use of expert testimony is part of what is called the plaintiff's burden of production. In two situations, however, the plaintiff is relieved of his burden of establishing the applicable standard of care through expert testimony. In the first, if the facts are such that even a layman could reasonably conclude that the conduct failed to conform to the applicable standard of care, the absence of expert testimony is not fatal to the plaintiff's case. This "common knowledge" exception allows a court to find the defendant's conduct patently unreasonable and to compensate a plaintiff who has been unable to find a medical expert to testify against the defendant. The other situation involves the application of what is called the *res ipsa loquitur* rule. This doctrine allows the plaintiff to introduce circumstantial evidence of the defendant's negligence in instances in which direct proof is unavailable to him. In both of these situations a plaintiff need only adduce evidence of the fact of injury and the general circumstances under which the injury occurred. These evidentiary rules and the circumstances in which they are invoked are examined in the following materials. At the same time, this section illustrates the application of the due care concept in various treatment contexts.

a. The Expert Witness Requirement

DILLMANN v. HELLMAN

District Court of Appeals of Florida, 1973.
283 So.2d 388.

COWART, JOE A., Jr., Associate Judge. *[handwritten: Did Hosp. fall below standard of care?]*

Nine days after the appellant had been admitted and confined in the hospital, her psychiatrist, the appellee, thought she had progressed sufficiently to be transferred from the west wing to the more rehabilitative but less secure east wing of the same ward. Within twenty-four hours she jumped from an open window and injured herself.

When sued for negligence, the appellee moved for summary judgment, filing his own deposition and that of the appellant's present physician. Both depositions affirm that appellee's treatment conformed to the medical standards of the community. The appellant filed no opposition affidavits or evidence and appeals the summary judgment entered against her.

The cases cited by the appellant are distinguishable from the facts in this case. This is not a case where lay persons can observe physical facts which may themselves be evidence of medical negligence * * *.

All that is left is the hindsight argument that the psychiatrist was negligent because if it were his judgment that the appellant could be safely transferred to an area of less security the result proves he erred. This argument is no substitute for admissible evidence and disregards the fact that physicians and other professionals practice the arts and must be allowed a wide range in the exercise of judgment and discretion. They cannot insure results and cannot be held liable under law for honest errors of judgment made while pursuing methods, courses, procedures and practices recognized as acceptable by their profession. *[handwritten in margin: The fact that something bad happened doesn't nec. mean you breached duty of care if signif. # believe you did what is generally acceptable then no case]*

The order granting summary judgment in favor of appellee is affirmed.

Questions and Comments

1. Note that the *Dillmann* court entered judgment for the defendant at the close of the plaintiff's case. Note also that the plaintiff did *not* introduce expert testimony to support his allegation that the doctor's decision to transfer the decedent to a relatively unsupervised ward constituted negligence. Had the plaintiff introduced expert testimony on this point, the result may have been different.

2. A different result was reached by the court in *Wright v. State*, 31 A.D.2d 421, 300 N.Y.S.2d 153 (1969). There the court held that in view of the known suicidal tendencies of the plaintiff, no expert testimony was required to show negligent supervision by the hospital staff. This "common knowledge" exception is discussed in the following case.

3. The court in *Dillmann* did not discuss causation. Is it necessarily true that the death was the result of the doctor's decision to transfer the patient to a less restrictive ward? In this connection consider the materials on proximate cause, in subsection A3, *infra*.

b. The "Common Knowledge" Exception to the Expert Witness Requirement

HAMMER v. ROSEN
New York Court of Appeals, 1960.
7 N.Y.2d 376, 198 N.Y.S.2d 65, 165 N.E.2d 756.

[Dr. John Nathaniel Rosen, a psychiatrist, "had developed immediately after World War II a reputation for dramatic success in treatment and cure of schizophrenic patients (those suffering from a serious mental disorder marked by a loss of contact with reality)."

* * *

Dr. Rosen treated schizophrenics rather than neurotics. To bridge the communication gap which treating persons of this much lower mental level posed, Dr. Rosen, after ascertaining his patient's mental level and before attempting to raise the mental level of his patient, attempted to project himself on the communicable mental plateau of his patient in order to establish mental contact and eventually rapport and trust. In executing this technique, which of course was highly personalized, but which was consented to by the spouse, next of kin, or legal guardian of each patient, it would certainly be presumed that Dr. Rosen might touch certain patients from time to time with differing degrees of force, depending upon the mental condition and needs of the patient, in order to effectively and fully explore and utilize the possibilities and potentialities which his method offered." Morse, *The Tort Liability of the Psychiatrist*, 18 Syracuse L.R. 691, 704–707 (1967).]

FULD, Judge.

Alice Hammer, suffering from schizophrenia, was treated for some seven years by Dr. Rosen, a psychiatrist. In 1955 she and her father instituted this action, the patient seeking damages for malpractice, * * * and for fraud. Their efforts have been signally unsuccessful. The trial court dismissed the malpractice and fraud causes of action at the close of the plaintiff's case, * * * and the Appellate Division, by a divided court, affirmed the resulting judgment. Although we agree with the disposition made of the other counts, we believe, as did the dissenting justice in the Appellate

Division, that the count charging malpractice should have been submitted to the jury.

With respect to the evidence, it is necessary merely to point out that the testimony given by three of the plaintiff's witnesses, indicating that the defendant had beaten Alice on a number of occasions, made out a prima facie case of malpractice which, if uncontradicted and unexplained and credited by the jury, would require a verdict for the plaintiff.

NEED XPERT WITNESS TO TESTIFY TO THOSE THINGS ONLY XPERTS WOULD KNOW — DON'T NEED XPERT TO TESTIFY TO THOSE THINGS THAT EVERYONE KNOWS

As to the second of the defendant's arguments—that there was no expert testimony to support the plaintiff's charge of malpractice—the *"COMMON knowledge"* simple answer is that the very nature of the acts complained of bespeaks improper treatment and malpractice and that, if the defendant chooses to justify those acts as proper treatment, he is under the necessity of offering evidence to that effect. In point of fact, the defendant can hardly urge that the plaintiff must call an expert to demonstrate the impropriety of the assaultive acts charged against him in view of the acknowledgment, contained in his brief in this court, that any mode of treatment which involves assaults upon the patient is "fantastic".

* * *

The judgment appealed from should be modified by reversing so much thereof as dismissed the malpractice cause of action, [and] a new trial [is] granted as to such cause.

Questions and Comments

1. Generally "the burden is on the plaintiff to establish a standard of care and to prove a deviation from that standard by *expert* medical testimony unless the deviation is so grossly apparent that a layman would have no difficulty in recognizing it." *Doctors Hospital, Inc. v. Kovats*, 16 Ariz.App. 489, 494 P.2d 389 (1972). However, in the Doctors Hospital case, the court, just as in *Hammer v. Rosen*, held that expert testimony was not necessary to establish the liability of a hospital for permitting a psychiatric patient who assaulted another patient to slip out of his restraints.

2. Dr. Rosen's techniques were the subject of favorable comment by a number of prominent psychiatrists of that period. One psychiatrist found Dr. Rosen's method to be "a promising and important original contribution." Morse, *The Tort Liability of Psychiatrists*, 18 Syracuse L.Rev. 691, 706 (1971). Dr. Rosen's techniques also drew the following comments:

> [Psychiatrist Jule Eisenbud noted] Dr. Rosen has absolutely no hostility toward the patient, toward the psychotic patient. This, I think is a very important factor * * * [H]e has no hostility toward the patient whatsoever. * * * I don't believe that there are many people who could approach the psychotic with * * * the complete absence of hostility * * * that characterizes Dr. Ro-

sen's approach." Mellitta Schmideberg, M.D., said: "Dr. Rosen is to be admired for achieving results in 37 out of 38 cases. * * * " And Hyman Spotnitz, M.D., said: "I want to compliment Dr. Rosen on his coverage and on his deep insight in this field. I feel it requires a great deal of courage, devotion and sincerity to do this type of work." *Id.*

However, at the trial neither the plaintiff nor the defense introduced any evidence either as to the reasonableness or acceptability to the psychiatric profession of the experimental therapy developed by Dr. Rosen. Thus, the case was decided in the absence of an expert testimony. Might the result have been different if Dr. Rosen had introduced expert testimony attesting to the efficacy of his therapeutic approach or evidence that the therapy was viewed as promising by some accepted segment of the psychiatric profession? Yes

3. Was the decision in *Hammer v. Rosen* correct? What is the purpose of the expert testimony requirement? Can a judge or a jury properly assess whether a given treatment meets the requisite standard of care? Does the fact that the doctor's method was extraordinarily and perhaps shocking necessarily mean that he was negligent from a medical standpoint? Suppose the treatment in question had been generally successful in the past. Should the success rate be the determining factor?

c. The Res Ipsa Loquitur Exception

The doctrine of *res ipsa loquitur,* like the "common knowledge" exception, serves to ease the evidentiary burden of the plaintiff. In some circumstances a plaintiff who has suffered an injury will find it difficult to produce direct evidence that the injury was the result of someone's negligence. For example, a patient who undergoes surgery may have difficulty establishing the exact circumstances under which the surgery was performed and, consequently, whether there was negligence on the part of the physician. The only evidence available may be the injury itself and circumstantial proof that the type of injury suffered does not readily occur in the absence of negligence. (For instance, a surgical sponge has been left in a body cavity.) Direct evidence of negligence need not be produced if it can be shown that (1) the injury probably would not have occurred without negligence on someone's part; (2) the instrumentality that caused the injury was under the defendant's control; and (3) the plaintiff himself had no responsibility for the injury.

Even when applicable, a doctrine of *res ipsa loquitur* does not automatically result in a judgment for the plaintiff. It only serves to allow submission of a case to the jury in the absence of direct proof that the defendant departed from the ordinary standard of care. Nevertheless, this evidentiary doctrine can be of substantial benefit to a plaintiff who might otherwise be precluded from having his claim submitted to a jury.

Unhappily, it is often difficult to predict whether the doctrine will be applied in a particular situation. In part this uncertainty stems from the nature of the test itself, which requires courts to make individual judgments of probabilities. As noted by one court, "The doctrine of *res ipsa loquitur* is predicated on inferences deductible from circumstantial evidence and the weight to be given them." *Clark v. Gibbons*, 66 Cal.2d 399, 58 Cal.Rptr. 125, 426 P.2d 525, 532 (1967). It is also not entirely clear when a plaintiff will be required to introduce expert testimony for the purpose of establishing the *probabilities* which exist in regard to a particular occurrence. At times courts have relied on "common knowledge" to make these assessments while at other times they have required expert testimony. *Id.* Application of the *res ipsa loquitur* doctrine in the mental health cases has been particularly unpredictable. In the only two reported cases dealing with the administration of ECT, both courts refused to apply the doctrine of *res ipsa* where the patient suffered fractures in the course of the administration of ECT. *Johnston v. Rodis*, 251 F.2d 917 (D.C.Cir.1958) and *Farber v. Olkon*, 40 Cal.2d 503, 254 P.2d 520 (1953). Similarly, in *Wees v. Creighton Memorial Hospital*, 194 Neb. 295, 231 N.W.2d 570 (1975), where the plaintiff, a severely regressed psychiatric patient, suffered a broken arm, the doctrine of *res ipsa loquitur* was held inapplicable. In *Meier v. Ross General Hospital*, 69 Cal.2d 420, 71 Cal.Rptr. 903, 445 P.2d 519 (1968), however, the court held the doctrine of *res ipsa loquitur* to be applicable where the decedent, a psychiatric patient, committed suicide by jumping through an open window of the hospital room.

Questions and Comments

1. In appropriate circumstances both the *res ipsa loquitur* doctrine and the common knowledge doctrine permit the plaintiff to get to the jury without an expert witness. What then is the distinction between the two doctrines? *Res ipsa* applies in the context of a particular fact situation of an injury which does not ordinarily result in the absence of negligence. Having proven an injury and the overall factual context from which it resulted, the plaintiff is released from having to establish proximate cause and also to prove by expert testimony that the defendant's actions constituted a departure from the ordinary standard of care.

The common knowledge exception, on the other hand, does not release the plaintiff from having to prove proximate cause. It only applies where a specific proven act led to an established injury; the only issue left to be resolved is whether the defendant's act was consistent with the exercise of due care.

2. Where the act in question is clearly outside the bounds of acceptable professional behavior, the court will apply the common knowledge exception to release the plaintiff of having to establish by expert testimony a deviation from the ordinary standard of care. For instance, the common knowledge exception would undoubtedly be applied where a

physician was shown to have performed minor surgery in his office with an unsterilized pocket knife.

3. One of the requirements for the application of *res ipsa* is that the "accident was not due to any voluntary action or contribution" on the part of the plaintiff. *Meier v. Ross General Hospital*, 69 Cal.2d 420, 71 Cal.Rptr. 903, 445 P.2d 519, 524 (1968). In spite of this requirement at least one state supreme court has held that *res ipsa loquitur* instructions must be given even where the cause of injury or death resulted from the suicide of the plaintiff. *Id.* In that case, however, the decedent had been a hospitalized psychiatric patient with known suicidal tendencies.

C. PROXIMATE CAUSE AS AN ELEMENT OF NEGLIGENCE

The element of proximate cause in a medical malpractice case raises issues similar to those surrounding the existence and scope of a duty of care. Though identical questions are often involved in the applications of the two concepts, they are two different elements of the plaintiff's case. Typically, the determination of whether the defendant owed the plaintiff a duty of care depends on the nature of the relationship between the plaintiff and defendant. A threshold question is whether the relation between the two parties was sufficient to impose an obligation of due care on the defendant. Once the duty is established, the issue of proximate cause becomes relevant, and the plaintiff must establish a sufficient causal connection between the breach of the defendant's obligation and the injuries suffered by the plaintiff.

CASTILLO v. UNITED STATES OF AMERICA

United States Court of Appeals, Tenth Circuit, 1977.
552 F.2d 1385.

BARRETT, Circuit Judge.

Corrine Castillo, (Castillo), as Administratrix of the Estate of Richard Montoya, Deceased, appeals from a judgment in favor of the United States Government following trial to the court on a suit filed by Castillo * * *

The action was filed following the death of Richard Montoya after his "elopement" from the Veterans Administration hospital psychiatric ward facilities located in Albuquerque, New Mexico.

Castillo alleges in her complaint that Montoya, who had voluntarily entered the hospital for psychiatric care and treatment, was permitted to depart from the facility undetected for a period in excess of three (3) hours, during which time he traveled to Belen, New Mexico, some 25 miles away, where he was run over by a train in the Belen train yard; that his death would not have occurred except for the negligence of the hospital staff in failing to "closely observe"

Montoya's activities and promptly notifying his relatives of his departure as required by Veterans Administration's hospital regulations.

Richard Montoya was a voluntary patient hospitalized in the psychiatric ward of the Veterans Administration hospital located in Albuquerque, on some nine separate occasions between 1970 and the date of his death in October, 1972. In 1972 the hospital staff had diagnosed his condition as "chronic undifferentiated schizophrenia." During this two-year period of voluntary hospitalization, Montoya had exhibited episodes of bizarre behavior, *i.e.*, physical aggression toward others, acute psychotic periods, and visual and auditory delusions. Even so, the hospital staff did not believe that he was dangerous to himself or others.

On each of his four admissions prior to his final admission on October 16, 1972, Montoya remained at the hospital for a short time and he departed without notifying the staff in advance despite the staff recommendation that he should continue treatment. The hospital refers to departure under these conditions as "elopement." When he "eloped" from the hospital, Montoya would either walk or take a cab to the home of one of his relatives in Belen, New Mexico, some 25 miles away.

On October 18, 1972, Montoya was last seen by the hospital staff at approximately 5:00 P.M., after which he eloped from the hospital. At about 7:30 P.M. that day he was seen approaching the engine of a train in the Santa Fe railroad yards near Belen. The brakeman on the train yelled at him, and Montoya then turned and started towards the rear of the train which was moving at about six to eight miles per hour. Shortly afterwards, he was run over by the train and killed.
* * *

II.

Quite possibly in anticipation of rejection of her negligence per se contention, Castillo further urges that the trial court's findings of fact require, as a matter of law, a judgment finding the United States guilty of common law negligence. In New Mexico, as is universally the case, liability in the area of negligence requires not only that the defendant be negligent, but that the negligence be a proximate cause of the injury complained of and, "[p]roximate cause is that which, in a natural or continuous sequence, produces the injury and without which the injury would not have occurred. It need not be the last act nor the sole cause, but it must be a concurring cause. And the injury resulting from the alleged negligent act must be such that a reasonably prudent person would have anticipated it.

Assuming *arguendo* that the United States, through some purported negligence on the part of its employees at the Veterans Hospital in Albuquerque, breached a duty to "closely observe" the deceased, liability for his untimely death does not necessarily follow. Montoya had been diagnosed as late as October, 1972, as neither dangerous to himself nor to others, a finding of the trial court which Castillo does not challenge. Under the totality of these circumstances, Montoya's death cannot have been the "natural consequence" of the negligence alleged here. Following each of Montoya's four voluntary admissions prior to that of October 16, 1972, Montoya "eloped" by either walking or taking a cab safely to his residence in Belen. The hospital staff had no cause to believe that Montoya's "elopement" on October 18, 1972, would result in his death when he was struck and killed by a train in Belen. We observe that even had the staff "closely observed" Montoya, such would not very likely have altered the sequence of events in view of the trial court finding that the hospital staff was without authority to restrain Montoya from leaving. His admission was voluntary and not by commitment. Under all of these circumstances, any failure of the staff to "closely observe" the deceased, even if considered negligence, could hardly be the "proximate cause" of his death.

Castillo has further relied heavily on a Texas decision which although similar in many respects to the case at bar, is not controlling. In that case the deceased, who was killed by a train, was found by the court to be incapable of caring for or protecting himself; furthermore, he had been committed to the hospital on a nonvoluntary basis.

We Affirm.

Questions and Comments

1. The problem of civil liability for the suicide of another has not been easy for the courts to resolve. On the one hand, that the attending psychiatrist could have taken action or refrained from a particular action argues in favor of holding the psychiatrist liable. The plaintiff may argue, for example, that the defendant could have prevented the suicide by hospitalizing the patient or by refusing to prescribe the drugs that ultimately caused the patient's death. On the other hand, a contrary argument views suicide as an independent intervention on the part of the patient that breaks the chain of causation, thus releasing the psychiatrist from liability.

2. In *Lando v. State*, 47 A.D.2d 972, 366 N.Y.S.2d 679 (1975), modified 39 N.Y.2d 803, 385 N.Y.S.2d 759, 351 N.E.2d 426 (1976) the administrator of the estate of a deceased mental patient sued the state hospital for negligence in failing to promptly conduct a search for the patient after she disappeared from the hospital grounds. The body was not found until eleven days after her disappearance. At the trial the extent and thoroughness of the search were seriously questioned, and the testimony as to the measures taken by the hospital was sharply disputed. Reversing an award for the plaintiff's administrator, the court concluded that the element of proximate cause had not been adequately proved:

> To demonstrate entitlement to an award in this situation, the claimant must establish the existence of a duty; that the duty was

breached and that the breach was the proximate cause of death. Even if we assume the existence of a duty and assume but do not concede its breach, the claim here must *fail because of a lack of proof that the breach was the proximate cause of the result.* Without this connection between the duty and the result, there can be no recovery * * * The deceased may have been the victim of foul play or she may have died from natural causes and the time of death is uncertain. There is no proof as to when Miss Lando's body fell or was placed or thrown into the obscuring foliage. Hence, several possibilities as to what occurred exist and, since the State would not be responsible for one or more of these possibilities, the claimant cannot recover without proving that the death was sustained wholly or in part by a cause for which the State was responsible * * * To conclude here that the failure to make an adequate search was the proximate cause requires speculation of the rankest sort.

Id. at 973, 366 N.Y.S.2d at 680. [On review by New York's highest court the decision of the appellate division denying the claim for decedent's wrongful death was affirmed. However, the father's claim for damages for mental anguish resulting from his being "denied access and control over the body of his deceased daughter for a period of 11 days" was reinstated. 39 N.Y.2d 803, 385 N.Y.S.2d 759, 351 N.E.2d 426 (1976).]

3. One major problem in establishing proximate cause is the question of whether a new act intervened to break the chain of causation between the breach of the standard of care and the injury. Sometimes this act is referred to as a "new and independent" cause and at other times as an "intervening" cause; in both cases it is an additional obstacle the plaintiff must overcome. The basic facts of the *Lando* case provide a useful model for analysis. Assume that the *Lando* plaintiff had been able to make a *prima facie* case of negligence, *i.e.*, the hospital had been negligent in not conducting a timely search. The hospital would be able, nevertheless, to interject the issue of intervening cause as a defense. This might involve proof that the patient died immediately from a fall immediately after her departure. The thrust of the defendant's argument would be that the patient's death would have occurred even if hospital personnel had conducted a diligent search. This would allow the court to find that a new and independent cause of the patient's death was of sufficient causal importance to release the hospital from liability.

D. DAMAGES

In addition to showing that the defendant (the mental health practitioner) deviated from the applicable standard of reasonable care, a plaintiff must show that he has suffered "actual loss or damage." Even an admittedly negligent defendant will not be liable to a plaintiff who received negligent care yet suffered no injury as a result. On that basis the court in *Di Giovanni v. Pessel*, 104 N.J. Super. 550, 250 A.2d 756 (1969), while recognizing the defendant's negligence, refused to award damages to the unharmed plaintiff. Not all injuries, however, give rise to compensation. Traditionally, only those injuries accompanied by a physical impact or injury are compensable. In the mental health field, where aggrieved plaintiffs frequently seek compensation for non-physical injuries allegedly caused by negligent treatment, the "physical impact rule" effectively insulates many mental health practitioners from liability for their negligence. As the following section illustrates recent court decisions have modified this rule.

Once the plaintiff has established that he has suffered an injury entitled to legal redress, the method and scope of compensation must be determined. Generally, the law of damages seeks to restore the plaintiff to the position he would have been in if the injury had not occurred. In certain situations, however, an injured plaintiff may also be entitled to recover punitive damages, awarded not as compensation for the plaintiff but rather to punish the defendant. This additional aspect of the element of damages is discussed below.

1. *What injuries Are Compensable Under the Law of Negligence?*

The traditional judicial definition of compensable injury is relatively straightforward: a plaintiff injured by the defendant's negligent conduct could recover damages for all physical injuries suffered and for mental injuries suffered in connection with a physical injury or impact. In the absence of physical impact, however, the plaintiff's non-physical injuries could not be compensated. For example, a mother who suffered a serious nervous shock and required hospitalization upon seeing her child severely injured by a negligent third person would be without legal remedy because her damages were limited to mental illness or anguish. Had the woman suffered the same shock before she herself was hit by an oncoming car, however, her mental as well as physical injuries would be compensable.

Presumably, this physical impact rule is the result of the courts' reluctance to engage in speculation about a plaintiff's mental state when there is no tangible evidence of injury and their concern that a plaintiff could easily fabricate a claim for damages for which the sole, almost unrebuttable, proof would be the plaintiff's own description of his mental injuries. Moreover, the courts frequently found that the plaintiff's proof of causation was tenuous in the absence of proof of physical impact (see subsection II.C. *supra* on proximate cause). One well-established exception to this traditional rule, however, granted compensation to a plaintiff whose exclusively mental injuries had been caused by the defendant's intentional acts. Thus, a plaintiff who suffered severe embarrassment and humiliation when wrongly accused of shoplifting and then was detained illegally could recover damages.

Though the physical impact rule is still the law in nearly all jurisdictions, recent developments indicate that courts are likely to reexamine, modify, or abrogate the rule in order to provide compensation for a plaintiff who has sustained serious mental injuries. The Hawaii Supreme Court was the first to make a definitive break from the physical impact rule. In *Rodrigues v. State*, 52 Hawaii 156, 472 P.2d 509 (1970), the court held that the plaintiff is entitled to compensation for the defendant's negligent infliction of serious mental distress.

Questions and Comments

1. Other courts, more cautious than the Hawaii Supreme Court (which decided the case of *Rodrigues v. State*), have chosen a less radical departure to compensate plaintiffs who have suffered severe mental injury. For instance, in *Vanoni v. Western Airlines*, 247 Cal. App.2d 793, 56 Cal.Rptr. 115 (1967), the court held that severe shock constituted "physical" injury.

2. An individual suffering from a mild neurosis known as the "harried housewife syndrome" visits a psychotherapist for treatment. As part of the therapy, the defendant therapist convinced the patient to engage in sexual relations with him. The plaintiff's mental condition deteriorates severely. She sues the defendant and at trial presents proof that she has suffered permanent psychosis as a result of the defendant's negligence. Suppose you are in a jurisdiction that has explicitly rejected *Rodrigues v. State*. What legal arguments could you, as attorney for the plaintiff, offer to persuade the court to award damages to your client? Would your client have any hope of recovering against the therapist? See *Greenberg v. McCabe*, 453 F.Supp. 765 (E.D.Pa.1978), *infra*.

2. Assessment of Damages

Once the court has ruled that the plaintiff is entitled to receive compensation, the specific rules governing damages in the particular jurisdiction become relevant. Depending on the factual situation, both compensatory and punitive damages may be available to the plaintiff.

As the term indicates, compensatory damages are intended to place the plaintiff in the position he would have been in if the injury had not occurred. Thus, the plaintiff will be entitled to a monetary award calculated to compensate him for his past and future loss of earnings, his medical and caretaking expenses, as well as for such intangible damages as loss of normal life, pain, suffering, inconvenience, and humiliation.

In awarding compensatory damages, a court may make a distinction between "general damages" and "special damages." General damages are those that commonly occur with the type of negligence the defendant has committed; special damages consist of any unique injury the plaintiff has suffered. Each kind of legal injury has its own rules of general and special damages. The distinction is important, not because the rules of compensation are different for each category, but rather because in many categories the plaintiff must specially plead special damages in his complaint, while general damages are presumed. This requirement evolved at common law because of the court's concern that the defendant be given actual notice of what the plaintiff is seeking to recover. While a defendant can be presumed to be aware of the general damages that typically follow from a particular injury, the plaintiff's special damages will probably not be known to him. Thus, the plaintiff may be required to list those damages in the initial complaint.

In addition, the distinction between special and general damages may be relevant to the plaintiff's proof of causation. While a negligent defendant will be liable for those items of general damages that were even remotely caused by his negligence, the courts apply a much stricter causation limitation on the plaintiff's claims for special damages. In that way only those special damages with a strong causal connection to the defendant's negligence will be recoverable. The following case illustrates the approach of courts to the assessment of special damages.

GREENBERG v. McCABE

United States District Court, Eastern District of Pennsylvania, 1978.
453 F.Supp. 765.

OPINION

JOSEPH S. LORD, III, Chief Judge.

Plaintiff in this psychiatric malpractice case alleges that defendant negligently treated her, principally by engaging in a sexual relationship with her in the course of therapy and by improperly administering drugs, from June 1968 through February 1974 and that she sustained permanent psychiatric damages as a result of this negligence. The jury returned a verdict for the plaintiff in the amount of $665,000: $275,000 for compensatory damages exclusive of costs for future psychiatric care, $90,000 for future psychiatric care and $300,000 for punitive damages. We will address at some length two of the points raised by defendant in his motion for judgment notwithstanding the verdict or for a new trial: that plaintiff's claim is barred as a matter of law by the Pennsylvania statute of limitations and that the record does not support the award for future psychiatric treatment. [The court found that plaintiff's action was not barred by the Statute of Limitations.]

II. DAMAGES FOR FUTURE PSYCHIATRIC TREATMENT:

Plaintiff sought compensatory damages for future psychiatric treatment, and the jury awarded her $90,000 for such expenses. The defendant argues that that award was not supported by the evidence, and we agree that it was improper to submit this claim of damages to the jury.

Under the law of Pennsylvania, a plaintiff bears the burden of proof by the preponderance of evidence with regard to damages to be incurred in the future.

It follows that the mere possibility of future damages is insufficient proof and that such damages cannot be presumed on the basis of injury itself.

The plaintiff must demonstrate, accordingly, the probability of all the elements which are necessary for the future expenses to be incurred—including the fact that the treatment will be performed as well as the fact of the injury itself. We conclude as a matter of law that the plaintiff did not demonstrate that it was probable she would undergo future psychiatric care, based on her own testimony that she would not undergo therapy and could not trust another doctor (apparently meaning therapist).

The testimony of plaintiff's expert supported the unlikelihood that she would undergo therapy in the future by describing the difficulties that would have to be overcome in order for her to submit to such treatment. There was no evidence concerning the likelihood of plaintiff submitting to another kind of psychiatric care.

The only evidence from which an inference that the plaintiff is likely to undergo therapy in the future conceivably could be drawn is two-fold: her testimony that she has been able to trust and talk freely to doctors, and her expert's statement that "I hope that I could prevail upon her to accept treatment eventually." We find these evidentiary scraps insufficient to support a finding that the plaintiff was likely, by a preponderance of the evidence, to undergo future psychiatric care. Plaintiff's other contentions concerning the jury's award for future medical expenses, e.g., that the award was reasonably calculated and that the parameters of future treatment necessary to arrive at the award were testified to sufficiently, are not relevant to our finding that the jury could not reasonably have concluded such future treatment was probable.

Because this element of damages should not have been submitted to the jury, we will reduce the plaintiff's verdict by the $90,000 that was awarded her for future treatment.

Questions and Comments

1. *Stowers v. Wolodzko*, 386 Mich. 119, 191 N.W.2d 355 (1971), raises interesting questions about the proper measure of damages. The psychiatrist in *Stowers* was held liable for false imprisonment and assault and battery for actions taken pursuant to a court order that had authorized the temporary commitment of the plaintiff pending a sanity hearing. The plaintiff, a homemaker without outside employment, had been forcibly dragged from her home and taken to a private hospital where she had been denied the right to receive or write letters, make phone calls, or consult an attorney. She was also forced to submit to

treatment that she had attempted to refuse. The jury awarded her $40,000 for her detention, which lasted approximately eleven days. The Supreme Court of Michigan affirmed. How would you determine the proper measure of damages in this type of case? What factors would you consider? Should punitive damages be awarded? Generally, punitive damages are awarded only if the defendant knowingly and intentionally caused the plaintiff's injury. As the name implies, their purpose is to punish the defendant for his intentional conduct. Therefore, the wealth of the defendant rather than the damage inflicted should provide the basis for calculating the award. Should courts permit insurance companies to pay the punitive damages awarded against an insured? *See* D. Dobbs, *Remedies* § 3.9 (1973).

2. In *Di Giovanni v. Pessel*, 104 N.J.Super. 550, 250 A.2d 756 (1969), the defendant doctor who certified that the plaintiff was insane for purposes of commitment disregarded his statutory duty to examine the plaintiff within ten days of the commitment. The court found that this deviation from the statutory prescribed standard of conduct constituted proof of his negligence. Nevertheless, the court held that the dismissal of the malpractice claim against the doctor was proper. The court concluded that the plaintiff had failed to prove injury and also found uncontradicted evidence that she was in need of the hospitalization and treatment she received.

3. *Punitive Damages*

If the defendant's negligent conduct was intentional, willful, wanton, malicious, or extremely reckless, the court may enter an award of punitive damages. As they are intended to punish the defendant and to deter other prospective defendants, the nature and extent of the plaintiff's injury are but two factors considered in the calculation of a punitive damages award. Other relevant aspects include the defendant's state of mind at the time of the injury. The following two cases illustrate the application of the rules pertaining to punitive damages.

McDONALD v. MOORE

District Court of Appeals of Florida, 1976.
323 So.2d 635.

PER CURIAM.

This is an appeal by Gary P. McDonald, plaintiff in the trial court, from a judgment on a jury verdict for compensatory damages in the amount of $5,000 in the plaintiff's favor, in an action for malpractice against Dr. Thomas Earl Moore. McDonald contends that the amount of the verdict is inadequate due to the trial court's striking his claim for punitive damages.

The plaintiff, a narcotics addict, underwent treatment by Dr. Moore, a psychiatrist. The treatment included daily prescriptions for methadone. McDonald agreed to permit Dr. Moore to perform a series of six electric shock treatments in order to cure his addiction to methadone without the pain of withdrawal. During the fifth treatment, McDonald complained of extreme pain in his left shoulder. The doctor minimized the importance of his complaint and convinced McDonald to proceed with the sixth treatment on the next day. After the sixth treatment, McDonald discovered that his shoulder had been dislocated and fractured by the shock treatments. The evidence showed that Dr. Moore failed to warn McDonald of the danger of a shoulder fracture and that he did not administer a muscle relaxant before the electric shock. One of the plaintiff's medical experts testified that it was not the usual practice to give shock treatments without utilizing the muscle relaxant; the other testified that such omission fell below the standard of care. They both testified that failure to advise the patient of the risk of fractures encountered with shock treatments was conduct below the standard of care.

During the trial, after the plaintiff had presented all of his evidence relating to the issue of punitive damages, the trial court struck his claim for punitive damages.

* * *

The record presented in the instant case fails to demonstrate wanton disregard for the plaintiff's rights or an entire want of care raising a presumption of conscious indifference to the consequences. Thus, we cannot say that the trial judge committed reversible error in striking the claim for, and refusing to charge the jury on, punitive damages.

McDonald's other two points, as well as the points raised on appeal by Dr. Moore, are not well taken and will not be discussed.

Affirmed.

ROY v. HARTOGS

Supreme Court, Appellate Term, 1976.
85 Misc.2d 891, 381 N.Y.S.2d 587.

MEMORANDUM DECISION

* * *

Counsel asserted in the opening statement that the defendant, a psychiatrist, had treated the plaintiff, as his patient, during the period March, 1969 through September, 1970. It was further averred that, during the last thirteen months of her treatment, plaintiff was induced to have sexual intercourse with the defendant as part of her prescribed therapy. As a result of this improper treatment, counsel alleged that the plaintiff was so emotionally and mentally injured that she was required to seek hospitalization on two occasions during 1971.

* * *

In this proceeding, the injury to the plaintiff was not merely caused by the consummation of acts of sexual intercourse with the defendant. Harm was also caused by the defendant's failure to treat the plaintiff with professionally acceptable procedures. By alleging that his client's mental and emotional status was adversely affected by this deceptive and damaging treatment, plaintiff's counsel asserted a viable cause of action for malpractice in his opening statement.

The award of $50,000 in compensatory damages for defendant's aggravation of plaintiff's pre-existing mental disorders, is, however, in our opinion excessive. Plaintiff's condition was of long standing, and began years before she became defendant's patient. There is no evidence to support a permanent worsening of the condition by defendant's acts; nor is there proof demonstrating a permanent impairment of her ability to work in a position comparable to that she had before or during the period she was defendant's patient. Given the fact that she may recover only for the aggravation of her condition by defendant we conclude that an award of more than $25,000 would be excessive.

The jury's finding, implicit in its award of punitive damages, that the defendant was actuated by evil or malicious intentions when the parties had sexual intercourse was against the predominating weight of the credible evidence. Viewing all the facts and circumstances incident to the occurrences most favorably to the plaintiff as disclosed in this record the weight of the evidence did not justify the jury's finding that defendant's conduct, while inexcusable, was so wanton or reckless as to permit an award for punitive damages.

The other points of error raised in defendant's brief are clearly without merit and need not be explored in this decision.

Judgment, entered July 29, 1975 (Myers, J. and jury), reversed and new trial ordered limited to the issue of compensatory damages, with $30 costs to appellant to abide the event that plaintiff recovers less than $25,000 in compensatory damages, unless respondent within ten days after service of a copy of the order entered hereon with notice of entry, stipulates to reduce the recovery to $25,000, in which event judgment modified accordingly and as modified, affirmed without costs.

Questions and Comments

1. The preceeding two cases illustrate the courts' careful scrutiny of claims for punitive damages and suggest a judicial reluctance to enter a punitive damages award without evidence of extremely egregious misconduct by the defendant.

2. A fuller account of the facts in *Roy v. Hartogs* is reported in the book *Betrayal* by Lucy Freeman & Julie Roy (New York: Stein and Day, 1976). According to the authors, evidence presented in the proceedings established that Dr. Hartogs had induced the complaining witness into engaging in sexual intercourse for ostensibly therapeutic purposes.

There was also evidence that Dr. Hartogs had engaged in sexual relations with other patients.

The jury awarded Julie Roy, the plaintiff, $250,000 compensatory damages and $100,000 punitive damages. Subsequently, the trial court judge reduced the compensatory damages by $200,000, leaving only $50,000 in that category, on the basis that the plaintiff had failed to prove that permanent emotional damages had ensued. The trial judge allowed the punitive damages to remain at $100,000 concluding that "a patient must not be fair game for a lecherous doctor." However, as indicated in the opinion contained herein the Court of Appeals surprisingly eliminated punitive damages altogether on the basis that actions contributing malpractice were not "wanton or reckless."

All but a few courts permit the jury to award punitive damages in a tort action when there are "circumstances of aggravation or outrage, such as spite or 'malice,' or a fraudulent or evil motive on the part of the defendant, or such a conscious and deliberate disregard of the interests of others that his conduct may be called willful or wanton." W. Prosser, *Handbook of the Law of Torts*, § 2, pp. 9–10 (4th ed. 1971). Given this standard for awarding punitive damages, why did the appellate court in *Hartogs* conclude that the evidence did not justify imposing punitive damages? What type of misconduct would the court in the *Hartogs* case require before allowing punitive damages?

E. NEW DIRECTIONS IN THE DUTY OF CARE: LIABILITY TO THIRD PARTIES

A previous section of this chapter explained that the traditional limit on professional liability was the contractual relationship, usually called privity of contract, between the professional and his client. Thus, the threshold question in a negligence suit was always whether the plaintiff had been the defendant's client. Unless a professional relationship had existed between the two parties, the court would usually dismiss the plaintiff's negligence suit. The privity doctrine, however, is no longer the dispositive factor in professional negligence cases. An increasing number of jurisdictions have modified or repudiated this doctrine, concluding that while the privity limit on liability provides certainty in the law, it may not promote justice or deter negligent conduct. A move away from traditional limitations on a professional's liability to third parties (those with whom no contractual relationship exists) is traceable to a 1928 decision rendered by one of the most influential state courts of the time.

In the landmark case of *Palsgraf v. Long Island Railroad*, 248 N.Y. 339, 162 N.E. 99 (1928), the New York Court of Appeals established a test of foreseeability to determine whether the actor had a duty of care to the injured party. Under this test, the court asked whether the defendant actor should have reasonably foreseen that his actions would injure the plaintiff. If that question was answered affirmatively, the defendant would be found liable.

In *Palsgraf* a passenger was attempting to board one of the defendant's trains while carrying a bulky and apparently fragile package. The defendant railroad's employees while attempting to help the passenger board the train, jostled him, and the package fell to the ground. The unmarked package contained fireworks, which exploded upon impact. The force of the explosion knocked over a platform scale thirty feet away, which in turn fell upon and injured another passenger, the plaintiff in the case. At trial the jury found the defendant's employees negligent and entered an award for the plaintiff. New York's highest court, however, reversed that decision, concluding that although the trainmen might have been negligent toward the passenger boarding the train, those trainmen could not have foreseen that their negligent actions would injure the plaintiff, who had been standing thirty feet away. The relationship between the parties, Chief Justice Cardozo said, would determine whether the defendant's actions constituted negligence toward the plaintiff: To be found liable to the plaintiff, the defendant must have been able to reasonably foresee that his actions would result in injury to the plaintiff. The court characterized this limitation on the extent of liability for negligence as follows:

> [T]he risk reasonably to be perceived defines the duty to be obeyed, and risk imports relation; it is risk to another or to others within the range of apprehension.

248 N.Y. at 344, 162 N.E. at 100.

Foreseeability of injury to a third person, therefore, may constitute an alternative basis of professional malpractice liability, imposing liability on a defendant-therapist who had no contractual relationship with the injured party. This foreseeability criterion, though a convenient benchmark of liability, is decidedly imprecise of measurement and extends professional liability beyond the limits set by the privity doctrine.

The following materials trace the development of the third-person liability doctrine in the context of mental health treatment.

TARASOFF v. REGENTS OF UNIVERSITY OF CALIFORNIA

Supreme Court of California, 1976.
17 Cal.3d 425, 131 Cal.Rptr. 14, 551 P.2d 334.

TOBRINER, Justice.

On October 27, 1969, Prosenjit Poddar killed Tatiana Tarasoff. Plaintiffs, Tatiana's parents, allege that two months earlier Poddar confided his intention to kill Tatiana to Dr. Lawrence Moore, a psychologist employed by the Cowell Memorial Hospital at the University of California at Berkeley. They allege that on Moore's request, the campus police briefly detained Poddar, but released him when he appeared rational. They further claim that Dr. Harvey

Powelson, Moore's superior, then directed that no further action be taken to detain Poddar. No one warned plaintiffs of Tatiana's peril.

Concluding that these facts set forth causes of action against neither therapists and policemen involved, nor against the Regents of the University of California as their employer, the superior court sustained defendants' demurrers to plaintiffs' second amended complaints without leave to amend.[2] This appeal ensued.

Plaintiffs' complaints predicate liability on two grounds: defendants' failure to warn plaintiffs of the impending danger and their failure to bring about Poddar's confinement pursuant to the Lanterman-Petris-Short Act.

Defendants, in turn, assert that they owed no duty of reasonable care to Tatiana * * *

We shall explain that defendant therapists cannot escape liability merely because Tatiana herself was not their patient. When a therapist determines, or pursuant to the standards of his profession should determine, that his patient presents a serious danger of violence to another, he incurs an obligation to use reasonable care to protect the intended victim against such danger. The discharge of this duty may require the therapist to take one or more of various steps, depending upon the nature of the case. Thus it may call for him to warn the intended victim or others likely to apprise the victim of the danger, to notify the police, or to take whatever other steps are reasonably necessary under the circumstances.

In the case at bar, plaintiffs admit that defendant therapists notified the police, but argue on appeal that the therapists failed to exercise reasonable care to protect Tatiana in that they did not confine Poddar and did not warn Tatiana or others likely to apprise her of the danger.

* * *

1. PLAINTIFFS' COMPLAINTS

Plaintiffs, Tatiana's mother and father, filed separate but virtually identical second amended complaints. The issue before us on this appeal is whether those complaints now state, or can be amended to state, causes of action against defendants. We therefore begin by setting forth the pertinent allegations of the complaints.

Plaintiffs' first cause of action, entitled "Failure to Detain a Dangerous Patient," alleges that on August 20, 1969, Poddar was a voluntary outpatient receiving therapy at Cowell Memorial Hospital.

---

2. The therapist defendants include Dr. Moore, the psychologist who examined Poddar and decided that Poddar should be committed; Dr. Gold and Dr. Yandell, psychiatrists at Cowell Memorial Hospital who concurred in Moore's decision; and Dr. Powelson, chief of the department of psychiatry, who countermanded Moore's decision and directed that the staff take no action to confine Poddar.

* * *

Poddar informed Moore, his therapist, that he was going to kill an unnamed girl, readily identifiable as Tatiana, when she returned home from spending the summer in Brazil. Moore, with the concurrence of Dr. Gold, who had initially examined Poddar, and Dr. Yandell, assistant to the director of the department of psychiatry, decided that Poddar should be committed for observation in a mental hospital. Moore orally notified Officers Atkinson and Teel of the campus police that he would request commitment. He then sent a letter to Police Chief William Beall requesting the assistance of the police department in securing Poddar's confinement.

Officers Atkinson, Brownrigg, and Halleran took Poddar into custody, but, satisfied that Poddar was rational, released him on his promise to stay away from Tatiana. Powelson, director of the department of psychiatry at Cowell Memorial Hospital, then asked the police to return Moore's letter, directed that all copies of the letter and notes that Moore had taken as therapist be destroyed, and "ordered no action to place Prosenjit Poddar in 72-hour treatment and evaluation facility."

Plaintiffs' second cause of action, entitled "Failure to Warn On a Dangerous Patient," incorporates the allegations of the first cause of action, but adds the assertion that defendants negligently permitted Poddar to be released from police custody without "notifying the parents of Tatiana Tarasoff that their daughter was in grave danger from Posenjit Poddar." Poddar persuaded Tatiana's brother to share an apartment with him near Tatiana's residence; shortly after her return from Brazil, Poddar went to her residence and killed her.

* * *

2. Plaintiffs Can State a Cause of Action Against Defendant Therapists for Negligent Failure to Protect Tatiana

The second cause of action can be amended to allege that Tatiana's death proximately resulted from defendants' negligent failure to warn Tatiana or others likely to apprise her of her danger. Plaintiffs contend that as amended, such allegations of negligence and proximate causation, with resulting damages, establish a cause of action. Defendants, however, contend that in the circumstances of the present case they owed no duty of care to Tatiana or her parents and that, in the absence of such duty, they were free to act in careless disregard of Tatiana's life and safety.

In analyzing this issue, we bear in mind that legal duties are not discoverable facts of nature, but merely conclusory expressions that, in cases of a particular type, liability should be imposed for damage done.

* * *

* * * [Duty] is not sacrosanct in itself, but only an expression of the sum total of those considerations of policy which lead the law to say that the particular plaintiff is entitled to protection.

* * *

We depart from "this fundamental principle" only upon the "balancing of a number of considerations"; major ones "are the foreseeability of harm to the plaintiff, the degree of certainty that the plaintiff suffered injury, the closeness of the connection between the defendant's conduct and the injury suffered, the moral blame attached to the defendant's conduct, the policy of preventing future harm, the extent of the burden to the defendant and consequences to the community of imposing a duty to exercise care with resulting liability for breach, and the availability, cost and prevalence of insurance for the risk involved."

The most important of these considerations in establishing duty is foreseeability. As a general principle, a "defendant owes a duty of care to all persons who are foreseeably endangered by his conduct, with respect to all risks which make the conduct unreasonably dangerous." As we shall explain, however, when the avoidance of foreseeable harm requires a defendant to control the conduct of another person, or to warn of such conduct, the common law has traditionally imposed liability only if the defendant bears some special relationship to the dangerous person or to the potential victim. Since the relationship between a therapist and his patient satisfies this requirement, we need not here decide whether foreseeability alone is sufficient to create a duty to exercise reasonably care to protect a potential victim of another's conduct.

Although, as we have stated above, under the common law, as a general rule, one person owed no duty to control the conduct of another nor to warn those endangered by such conduct the courts have carved out an exception to this rule in cases in which the defendant stands in some special relationship to either the person whose conduct needs to be controlled or in a relationship to the foreseeable victim of that conduct (see Rest.2d Torts, supra, §§ 315–320). Applying this exception to the present case, we note that a relationship of defendant therapists to either Tatiana or Poddar will suffice to establish a duty of care; as explained in section 315 of the Restatement Second of Torts, a duty of care may arise from either "(a) a special relation * * * between the actor and the third person which imposes a duty upon the actor to control the third person's conduct, or (b) a special relation * * * between the actor and the other which gives to the other a right of protection."

Although plaintiffs' pleadings assert no special relation between Tatiana and defendant therapists, they establish as between Poddar and defendant therapists the special relation that arises between a patient and his doctor or psychotherapist. Such a relationship may support affirmative duties for the benefit of third persons. Thus, for example, a hospital must exercise reasonable care to control the behavior of a patient which may endanger other persons. A doctor must also warn a patient if the patient's condition or medication renders certain conduct, such as driving a car, dangerous to others.

Although the California decisions that recognize this duty have involved cases in which the defendant stood in a special relationship *both* to the victim and to the person whose conduct created the danger, we do not think that the duty should logically be constricted to such situations. Decisions of other jurisdictions hold that the single relationship of a doctor to his patient is sufficient to support the duty to exercise reasonable care to protect others against dangers emanating from the patient's illness. The courts hold that a doctor is liable to persons infected by his patient if he negligently fails to diagnose a contagious disease or, having diagnosed the illness, fails to warn members of the patient's family.

Since it involved a dangerous mental patient, the decision in *Merchants Nat. Bank & Trust Co. of Fargo v. United States* comes closer to the issue. The Veterans Administration arranged for the patient to work on a local farm, but did not inform the farmer of the man's background. The farmer consequently permitted the patient to come and go freely during nonworking hours; the patient borrowed a car, drove to his wife's residence and killed her. Notwithstanding the lack of any "special relationship" between the Veterans Administration and the wife, the court found the Veterans Administration liable for the wrongful death of the wife.

* * *

Defendants contend, however, that imposition of a duty to exercise reasonable care to protect third persons is unworkable because therapists cannot accurately predict whether or not a patient will resort to violence. In support of this argument amicus representing the American Psychiatric Association and other professional societies cites numerous articles which indicate that therapists, in the present state of the art, are unable reliably to predict violent acts; their forecasts, amicus claims, tend consistently to overpredict violence, and indeed are more often wrong than right. Since predictions of violence are often erroneous, amicus concludes, the courts should not render rulings that predicate the liability of therapists upon the validity of such predictions.

The role of the psychiatrist, who is indeed a practitioner of medicine, and that of the psychologist who performs an allied function, are like that of the physician who must conform to the standards of the profession and who must often make diagnoses and predictions based upon such evaluations. Thus the judgment of the therapist in diagnosing emotional disorders and in predicting whether a patient presents a serious danger of violence is comparable to the judgment which doctors and professionals must regularly render under accepted rules of responsibility.

We recognize the difficulty that a therapist encounters in attempting to forecast whether a patient presents a serious danger of violence. Obviously we do not require that the therapist, in making that determination, render a perfect performance; the therapist need only exercise "that reasonable degree of skill, knowledge, and care ordinarily possessed and exercised by members of [that professional specialty] under similar circumstances."

Within the broad range of reasonable practice and treatment in which professional opinion and judgment may differ the therapist is free to exercise his or her own best judgment without liability; proof, aided by hindsight, that he or she judged wrongly is insufficient to establish negligence.

In the instant case, however, the pleadings do not raise any question as to failure of defendant therapists to predict that Poddar presented a serious danger of violence. On the contrary, the present complaints allege that defendant therapists did in fact predict that Poddar would kill, but were negligent in failing to warn.

Amicus contends, however, that even when a therapist does in fact predict that a patient poses a serious danger of violence to others, the therapist should be absolved of any responsibility for failing to act to protect the potential victim. In our view, however, once a therapist does in fact determine, or under applicable professional standards reasonably should have determined that a patient poses a serious danger of violence to others, he bears a duty to exercise reasonable care to protect the foreseeable victim of that danger. While the discharge of this duty of due care will necessarily vary with the facts of each case, in each instance the adequacy of the therapist's conduct must be measured against the traditional negligence standard of the rendition of reasonable care under the circumstances.

* * *

* * * In sum, the therapist owes a legal duty not only to his patient, but also to his patient's would-be victim and is subject in both respects to scrutiny by judge and jury."

The risk that unnecessary warnings may be given is a reasonable price to pay for the lives of possible victims that may be saved. We would hesitate to hold that the therapist who is aware that his patient expects to attempt to assassinate the President of the United States would not be obligated to warn the authorities because the therapist cannot predict with accuracy that his patient will commit the crime.

Defendants further argue that free and open communication is essential to psychotherapy that "Unless a patient * * * is assured that * * * information [revealed by him] can and will be held in utmost confidence, he will be reluctant to make the full disclosure upon which diagnosis and treatment * * * depends."

The giving of a warning, defendants contend, constitutes a breach of trust which entails the revelation of confidential communications.

We recognize the public interest in supporting effective treatment of mental illness and in protecting the rights of patients to privacy and the consequent public importance of safeguarding the confidential character of psychotherapeutic communication. Against this interest, however, we must weigh the public interest in safety from violent assault. The Legislature has undertaken the difficult task of balancing the countervailing concerns. In Evidence Code section 1014, it established a broad rule of privilege to protect confidential communications between patient and psychotherapist. In Evidence Code section 1024, the Legislature created a specific and limited exception to the psychotherapist-patient privilege: "There is no privilege * * * if the psychotherapist has reasonable cause to believe that the patient is in such mental or emotional condition as to be dangerous to himself or to the person or property of another and that disclosure of the communication is necessary to prevent the threatened danger."

We realize that the open and confidential character of psychotherapeutic dialogue encourages patients to express threats of violence, few of which are ever executed. Certainly a therapist should not be encouraged routinely to reveal such threats; such disclosures could seriously disrupt the patient's relationship with his therapist and with the persons threatened. To the contrary, the therapist's obligations to his patient require that he not disclose a confidence unless such disclosure is necessary to avert danger to others, and even then that he do so discreetly, and in a fashion that would preserve the privacy of his patient to the fullest extent compatible with the prevention of the threatened danger.

The revelation of a communication under the above circumstances is not a breach of trust or a violation of professional ethics; as stated in the Principles of Medical Ethics of the American Medical Association (1957), section 9: "A physician may not reveal the confidence entrusted to him in the course of medical attendance * * * *unless he is required to do so by law or unless it becomes necessary in order to protect the welfare of the individual or of the community.*" (Emphasis added.) We conclude that the public policy favoring protection of the confidential character of patient-psychotherapist communications must yield to the extent to which disclosure is essential to avert danger to others. The protective privilege ends where the public peril begins.

Our current crowded and computerized society compels the interdependence of its members. In this risk-infested society we can hardly tolerate the further exposure to danger that would result from a concealed knowledge of the therapist that his patient was lethal. If the exercise of reasonable care to protect the threatened victim requires the therapist to warn the endangered party or those who can reasonably be expected to notify him, we see no sufficient societal interest that would protect and justify concealment. The containment of such risks lies in the public interest. For the foregoing reasons, we find that plaintiffs' complaints can be amended to state a cause of action against defendants Moore, Powelson, Gold, and Yandell, and against the Regents as their employer, for breach of a duty to exercise reasonable care to protect Tatiana.

[The court went on to reject a claim by the defendants that release of information obtained from Poddar would violate a state statute governing the disclosure of confidential information in the possession of state officials. The court also held that the plaintiffs' claim was not barred by the state's governmental immunity statute in so far as it related to the psychiatrist's failure to warn third persons.]

WRIGHT, C.J., and SULLIVAN and RICHARDSON, JJ., concur.

MOSK, Justice (concurring and dissenting).

I concur in the result in this instance only because the complaints allege that defendant therapists did in fact predict that Poddar would kill and were therefore negligent in failing to warn of that danger. Thus the issue here is very narrow: we are not concerned with whether the therapists, pursuant to the standards of their profession, "should have" predicted potential violence; they allegedly did so in actuality. Under these limited circumstances I agree that a cause of action can be stated.

* * *

I would restructure the rule designed by the majority to eliminate all reference to conformity to standards of the profession in predicting violence. If a psychiatrist does in fact predict violence, then a duty to warn arises. The majority's expansion of that rule will take us from the world of reality into the wonderland of clairvoyance.

CLARK, Justice (dissenting).

Until today's majority opinion, both legal and medical authorities have agreed that confidentiality is essential to effectively treat the mentally ill, and that imposing a duty on doctors to disclose patient threats to potential victims would greatly impair treatment. Further, recognizing that effective treatment and society's safety are necessarily intertwined, the Legislature has already decided effective and confidential treatment is preferred over imposition of a duty to warn.

The issue whether effective treatment for the mentally ill should be sacrificed to a system of warnings is, in my opinion, properly one for the Legislature, and we are bound by its judgment. Moreover, even in the absence of clear legislative direction, we must reach the same conclusion because imposing the majority's new duty is certain to result in a net increase in violence.

The majority rejects the balance achieved by the Legislature's Lanterman-Petris-Short Act. (Welf. & Inst. Code, § 5000 et seq., hereafter the act.) In addition, the majority fails to recognize that, even absent the act, overwhelming policy considerations mandate against sacrificing fundamental patient interests without gaining a corresponding increase in public benefit.

*   *   *

COMMON LAW ANALYSIS

Entirely apart from the statutory provisions, the same result must be reached upon considering both general tort principles and the public policies favoring effective treatment, reduction of violence, and justified commitment.

Generally, a person owes no duty to control the conduct of another. Exceptions are recognized only in limited situations where (1) a special relationship exists between the defendant and injured party, or (2) a special relationship exists between defendant and the active wrongdoer, imposing a duty on defendant to control the wrongdoer's conduct. The majority does not contend the first exception is appropriate to this case.

*   *   *

Overwhelming policy considerations weigh against imposing a duty on psychotherapists to warn a potential victim against harm. While offering virtually no benefit to society, such a duty will frustrate psychiatric treatment, invade fundamental patient rights and increase violence.

The importance of psychiatric treatment and its need for confidentiality have been recognized by this court.

"It is clearly recognized that the very practice of psychiatry vitally depends upon the reputation in the community that the psychiatrist will not tell." (Slovenko, *Psychiatry and a Second Look at the Medical Privilege* (1960) 6 Wayne L.Rev. 175, 188.)

Assurance of confidentiality is important for three reasons.

DETERRENCE FROM TREATMENT

First, without substantial assurance of confidentiality, those requiring treatment will be deterred from seeking assistance. It remains an unfortunate fact in our society that people seeking psychiatric guidance tend to become stigmatized. Apprehension of such stigma—apparently increased by the propensity of people considering treatment to see themselves in the worst possible light—creates a well-recognized reluctance to seek aid. This reluctance is alleviated by the psychiatrist's assurance of confidentiality.

FULL DISCLOSURE

Second, the guarantee of confidentiality is essential in eliciting the full disclosure necessary for effective treatment. The psychiatric patient approaches treatment with conscious and unconscious inhibitions against revealing his innermost thoughts. "Every person, however well-motivated, has to overcome resistances to therapeutic exploration. These resistances seek support from every possible source and the possibility of disclosure would easily be employed in the service of resistance."

Until a patient can trust his psychiatrist not to violate their confidential relationship, "the unconscious psychological control mechanism of repression will prevent the recall of past experiences."

Successful Treatment

Third, even if the patient fully discloses his thoughts, assurance that the confidential relationship will not be breached is necessary to maintain his trust in his psychiatrist—the very means by which treatment is effected.

* * * All authorities appear to agree that if the trust relationship cannot be developed because of collusive communication between the psychiatrist and others, treatment will be frustrated.

Given the importance of confidentiality to the practice of psychiatry, it becomes clear the duty to warn imposed by the majority will cripple the use and effectiveness of psychiatry. Many people, potentially violent—yet susceptible to treatment—will be deterred from seeking it; those seeking it will be inhibited from making revelations necessary to effective treatment; and, forcing the psychiatrist to violate the patient's trust will destroy the interpersonal relationship by which treatment is effected.

Violence and Civil Commitment

By imposing a duty to warn the majority contributes to the danger to society of violence by the mentally ill and greatly increases the risk of civil commitment—the total deprivation of liberty—of those who should not be confined. The impairment of treatment and risk of improper commitment resulting from the new duty to warn will not be limited to a few patients but will extend to a large number of the mentally ill. Although under existing psychiatric procedures only a relatively few receiving treatment will ever present a risk of violence, the number making threats is huge, and it is the latter group—not just the former—whose treatment will be impaired and whose risk of commitment will be increased.

Both the legal and psychiatric communities recognize that the process of determining potential violence in a patient is far from exact, being fraught with complexity and uncertainty. In fact precision has not even been attained in predicting who of those having already committed violent acts will again become violent, a task recognized to be of much simpler proportions.

This predictive uncertainty means that the number of disclosures will necessarily be large. As noted above, psychiatric patients are encouraged to discuss all thoughts of violence, and they often express such thoughts. However, unlike this court, the psychiatrist does not enjoy the benefit of overwhelming hindsight in seeing which few, if any, of his patients will ultimately become violent. Now, confronted by the majority's new duty, the psychiatrist must instantaneously calculate potential violence from each patient on each visit. The difficulties researchers have encountered in accurately predicting violence will be heightened for the practicing psychiatrist dealing for brief periods in his office with heretofore nonviolent patients. And, given the decision not to warn or commit must always be made at the psychiatrist's civil peril, one can expect most doubts will be resolved in favor of the psychiatrist protecting himself.

Neither alternative open to the psychiatrist seeking to protect himself is in the public interest. The warning itself is an impairment of the psychiatrist's ability to treat, depriving many patients of adequate treatment. It is to be expected that after disclosing their threats, a significant number of patients, who would not become violent if treated according to existing practices, will engage in violent conduct as a result of unsuccessful treatment. In short, the majority's duty to warn will not only impair treatment of many who would never become violent but worse, will result in a net increase in violence.

The second alternative open to the psychiatrist is to commit his patient rather than to warn. Even in the absence of threat of civil liability, the doubts of psychiatrists as to the seriousness of patient threats have led psychiatrists to overcommit to mental institutions. This overcommitment has been authoritatively documented in both legal and psychiatric studies.

Given the incentive to commit created by the majority's duty, this already serious situation will be worsened, contrary to Chief Justice Wright's admonition "that liberty is no less precious because forfeited in a civil proceeding than when taken as a consequence of a criminal conviction."

CONCLUSION

*   *   *

The tragedy of Tatiana Tarasoff has led the majority to disregard the clear legislative mandate of the Lanterman-Petris-Short Act. Worse, the majority impedes medical treatment, resulting in increased violence from—and deprivation of liberty to—the mentally ill.

We should accept legislative and medical judgment, relying upon effective treatment rather than on indiscriminate warning.

The judgment should be affirmed.

McCOMB, J., concurs.

Questions and Comments

1. The decision of the California Supreme Court in *Tarasoff* has been surprisingly influential. By mid-1984, state and federal courts in at

least three jurisdictions, Michigan, Nebraska, and New Jersey, had applied the *Tarasoff* doctrine to hold a psychiatrist or psychologist liable for having failed to warn a potential victim. *McIntosh v. Milano*, 168 N.J.Super. 466, 403 A.2d 500 (1979), *Lipari v. Sears, Roebuck & Co.*, 497 F.Supp. 185 (D.Neb.1980), *Davis v. Lhim*, 124 Mich.App. 291, 335 N.W.2d 481 (1983). At least one state (Maryland) has rejected the *Tarasoff* theory of liability, finding that the statutorily enacted law of privileged communications (see Privileged Communications in Chapter IV) bars any disclosure to third persons by a psychotherapist. *Shaw v. Glickman*, 45 Md.App. 718, 415 A.2d 625 (1980). A majority of states have privilege laws substantially similar to Maryland's. Up to now too few cases have been decided to indicate whether the Tarasoff theory of liability will be generally accepted by other jurisdictions and particularly those that have laws similar to Maryland's.

2. Note that the *Tarasoff* opinion does not decide whether Dr. Moore or the University of California outpatient clinic was negligent. The case merely holds that the plaintiff has stated a cause of action that, if proved at trial, would entitle the plaintiff to relief. On remand to the lower court, the trier of fact would have had to decide whether Dr. Moore's failure to notify the victim or her family did in fact constitute a breach of his duty to the third-party victim. A jury might also have found that by notifying the police Dr. Moore had exercised due care and thus was not negligent. (The *Tarasoff* case was settled by the parties out of court prior to retrial.)

3. The majority decision in *Tarasoff* strives to make the formulation of new doctrine appear as a natural and logical extension of existing doctrine. In reaching its conclusion that the therapist has a duty to third parties, the majority pursues three lines of analysis. First, it cites earlier medical cases from other jurisdictions that imposed a duty on physicians to notify third parties who are likely to come into contact with a patient suffering from a contagious disease. The majority opinion, however, fails to distinguish imposing a duty when there is a clearly diagnosable and invariably contagious disease from the facts of *Tarasoff*, where the duty was triggered not by a clearly diagnosible condition, but by a clinical prediction of probable future conduct on the part of the patient.

Second, the majority opinion looks to Section 315 of the Restatement of Torts Second, which provides:

There is no duty so to control the conduct of a third person as to prevent him from causing physical harm to another unless

(a) a special relation exists between the actor and the third person which imposes a duty upon the actor to control the third person's conduct, or

(b) a special relation exists between the actor and the other which gives to the other a right to protection.

Although the wording of Section 315 seems compatible with the majority's holding in *Tarasoff*, the commentaries to this section should not be overlooked. They emphasize that the duty attaches only in certain enumerated "special relations," when, for example, the defendant is an innkeeper, common carrier, or landowner. Presumably, therefore, the drafters of the Restatement Second did not intend to include the psychiatrist-patient relationship in Section 315.

The third part of the court's opinion was a policy analysis. Here the court addressed the competing interests of affording protection to persons who may be endangered by a patient against the interest of protecting the integrity of the therapist-patient relationship. The court concluded as a matter of policy that the need to protect persons from serious harm outweighed the possibly destructive effects on the patient-therapist relationship that might be caused from a rule requiring disclosure to third parties.

4. Quite aside from the merits of the court's reasoning, is it desirable that broad policy questions with no implications for constitutional law be resolved by courts rather than legislatures? To what extent are courts equipped to resolve issues of the type posed by the *Tarasoff* case? Would a legislature acting through its committees be better able to address and resolve the question? Should it make any difference to the court whether the legislature has already entered the field by enacting the rules governing the confidentiality of patient-therapist communications? In this connection consider the case of *Shaw v. Glickman*, 45 Md. App. 718, 415 A.2d 625 (1980), which appears on page 232.

5. The factual situation of *Tarasoff* is clearly distinguishable from those cases that have imposed liability on a psychiatric facility that had custody of a patient who injured someone outside the institution following his release or escape. Section 319 of the Restatement of Torts Second provides a basis for imposing liability on the institution in this situation:

> One who takes charge of a third person whom he knows or should know to be likely to cause bodily harm to others if not controlled is under a duty to exercise reasonable care to control the third person to prevent him from doing such harm.

The commentaries to this section of the Restatement make clear that the institution may be liable to a third party who is injured by a patient if:

1. A patient is released when the facility knew or had reason to know of the patient's dangerous proclivities;

2. The institution fails to conduct an adequate predischarge examination of a patient with a history of violent behavior; or

3. The institution's failure to take adequate precautions allows a patient to escape.

Recent cases have generally imposed liability on a psychiatric facility for releasing a patient that the institution knew or should have known to be dangerous. *Estate of Mathes v. Ireland*, ___ Ind.App. ___, 419 N.E.2d 782 (1981); *Semler v. Psychiatric Institute of Washington, D.C.*, 538 F.2d 121 (4th Cir.1976). In *Semler* the psychiatric facility had custody of a convicted felon, who was placed on outpatient status. Without proper court authorization the patient killed an individual, and in a subsequent wrongful death suit the institution was found liable to the victim's parents.

However, some states have enacted laws that specifically grant immunity to institutions that improvidently release a patient or prisoner who subsequently injures a third party. In *Beauchene v. Synanon Foundation, Inc.*, 88 Cal.App.3d 342, 151 Cal.Rptr. 796 (1979), the court construed a state immunity statute, which on its face applied only to state correctional facilities, to protect private institutions that provide inpatient treatment to convicted criminals placed on probation. In denying relief to the plaintiff, who had been shot by a former patient of the institution, the court observed:

> [O]f paramount concern is the detrimental effect a finding of liability would have on prisoner release and rehabilitation programs. Were we to find a cause of action stated we would in effect be encouraging the detention of prisoners in disregard of their rights and society's needs.

At 348.

6. To what extent are the divergent conclusions of the majority as expressed by Justice Tobriner's opinion and the dissenting opinion of Justice Clark founded on different perceptions as to the ability of clinicians to predict dangerous or abnormal behavior? Do any policy considerations support the imposition of a duty to warn if, in fact, the ability of the therapist to predict dangerous behavior correctly is very limited? In this context, see the discussion in Chapter VI, subsection II.C. on the problem of predicting dangerous behavior.

7. In his concurring opinion Justice Mosk would limit the duty to warn to those cases in which the "psychiatrist does in fact predict violence." Presumably this means that liability cannot be imposed unless the psychiatrist has actually concluded that the patient is likely to be violent. One commentator has praised this approach:

> Making the legal duty dependent on the therapist's subjective determination of the patient's dangerousness would of course extremely limit the number of instances in which suit could successfully be brought. In the usual case, once the therapist has convinced himself that a patient is certainly dangerous, he will take some action. Only where he has reached this conclusion—and made it clear in records or consultation—and then failed to act would liability be imposed. Unlike the *Tarasoff* standard, then, this formulation would provide no incentive to the therapist to overpredict dangerousness early in the treatment process and to act to warn potential victims who might or might not be in serious danger. It seems to me quite clear that both the public interest and the patient's needs are better served by a legal standard which does not serve to discourage or undermine the effective treatment of potentially dangerous individuals. Moreover, the safety of the potential victims may well be more successfully promoted by such a standard, since premature action by the therapist is likely to terminate the therapeutic relationship, with the result that patients whose illnesses might have been successfully

treated would remain a source of danger to those they originally threatened.

Stone, *The Tarasoff Decisions: Suing Psychotherapists to Safeguard Society*, 90 Harv.L.Rev. 358, 375–376 (1976).

How practical is Justice Mosk's standard? Are the arguments in favor of it convincing? What evidence would a plaintiff have to introduce to establish the existence of a duty? Would this approach in effect permit the psychiatrist to insulate himself from liability? In other words, would not any psychiatrist be able to avoid liability for failure to warn by merely refusing to formulate predictions?

8. If Dr. Moore had initiated commitment proceedings rather than merely notifying the university police, would his potential liability have been any different? In connection with that question, consider the following hypothetical situation. Assume that the dangerous patient was admitted as an involuntary emergency admission (the nature of emergency admissions are considered in Chapter Six). The psychiatric facility released him after several days, and shortly thereafter the patient murdered an acquaintance. Assume further that the therapist who had originally initiated the commitment proceedings had not warned either the victim or the victim's family; the therapist, however, knew of the patient's violent intentions. Could the therapist still be held liable under these circumstances? In answering this question consider the section on *proximate cause* in section 3 of this chapter.

9. The expanding concept of the duty of care to third persons has not been confined to the psychiatric setting. The *Tarasoff* court cited three California decisions that had imposed third-party liability for the actions of another. In *Ellis v. D'Angelo*, 116 Cal.App.2d 310, 253 P.2d 675 (1953), the court recognized a cause of action against the parents of a child who failed to warn a babysitter of the violent proclivities of their child. *Johnson v. State of California*, 69 Cal.2d 782, 73 Cal.Rptr. 240, 447 P.2d 352 (1968), sustained a cause of action against the state for its failure to warn foster parents of the dangerous personality traits of their ward. And in *Morgan v. Yuba County*, 230 Cal.App.2d 938, 41 Cal.Rptr. 508 (1964), a cause of action was similarly upheld when the sheriff failed to carry out his promise to warn the decedent before releasing a dangerous prisoner. Implicit in these cases is judicial recognition that victims of violent crimes should have a remedy for their injuries. Of course, victims can sue the person who committed the offense, but in most cases the offender is penniless. As a result, victims must search for a "deep pocket" and seek compensation from someone who stands in a special relationship to the person who caused the injury. It is in determining both whether this special relationship exists, and, if so, what actions should be taken to avoid similar future injuries that have caused the greatest difficulty.

In *Grimm v. Arizona Board of Pardons and Paroles*, 115 Ariz. 260, 564 P.2d 1227 (1977), the Arizona Supreme Court held that the state parole board had a duty to individual members of the general public to avoid the grossly negligent or reckless release of a highly dangerous prisoner. The court also concluded that the parole board members could claim only qualified immunity for their administrative acts. The doctrine of immunity of the state and officials and employees of the state is governed largely by statute. Thus, the liability of state-run hospitals and the therapists working there depends upon the scope of the immunity which may have been granted by the legislature.

1. Defining the Boundaries of the Tarasoff Doctrine

LEEDY v. HARTNETT
United States District Court, Middle District of Pennsylvania, 1981.
510 F.Supp. 1125.

MUIR, District Judge.

This case arose out of an assault upon the Plaintiffs allegedly by one John J. Hartnett, now deceased. * * * The Plaintiffs allege that the Veterans Hospital was negligent in failing to warn the Leedys of Hartnett's alleged violent tendencies. * * *

The facts insofar as they are relevant to the hospital's motion for summary judgment are not substantially disputed. To the extent that there are disputes as to material facts, the Court will for the purposes of this motion assume as true the Plaintiffs' factual contentions.

John Hartnett was a disabled veteran of the Korean War. From 1956 through March 1978 he had been a patient at the Lebanon Veterans Administration Hospital on more than 20 occasions. During most of those hospitalizations, he was treated for paranoid schizophrenia and chronic alcoholism. Although at one time Hartnett may have been involuntarily committed, during the times relevant to this action he was a voluntary patient at the hospital. It is the Plaintiffs' contention that Harrison Leedy met Hartnett in Leedy's capacity as a service officer of the Lebanon Veterans of Foreign Wars in 1974. Leedy performed various services for Hartnett such as offering him rides, companionship, and the like. This relationship between Hartnett and Leedy was known to personnel of the hospital.

Throughout his course of treatment at the hospital, its personnel were aware of a history of violent outbursts by Hartnett with incidents spanning at least 10 years. Medical personnel at the hospital had since at least 1977 diagnosed Hartnett as being aggressive, impulsive, and exhibiting unstable behavior caused in large part by his alcoholism and his continued drinking in spite of that condition.

On September 26, 1977, Hartnett discharged himself from the hospital and informed hospital personnel that he would be staying with the Plaintiffs and that his funds could be forwarded to that address. At that time, Hartnett told hospital personnel that he had a standing offer to move in with Mr. Leedy. On March 21, 1978, Hartnett left the hospital and for a few days resided at a hotel in the

City of Lebanon. On approximately March 29, 1978, he moved into the Leedy residence at Mr. Leedy's invitation. It was the intention of the Leedys that Hartnett would remain there for a few days until other living arrangements could be made for Hartnett. The Plaintiffs claim that Hartnett was a social guest at their home.

On March 31, 1978, the Plaintiffs and Hartnett went to the Myerstown Veterans of Foreign Wars Club to celebrate Hartnett's birthday. During the course of the evening, Mrs. Leedy had two or three mixed drinks, Mr. Leedy had six or seven small bottles of beer and Hartnett drank approximately 24 12-oz. bottles of beer. At approximately 2:00 A.M. the next morning, they left the club and went to the Leedys' residence. After their return, Hartnett drank several more bottles of beer and took 400 milligrams of Thorazine. At some time during that night the Leedys were beaten.

* * *

It is the position of the Leedys that Hartnett assaulted them and that the hospital owed to them a duty to warn them of Hartnett's alleged assaultive tendencies and that the breach of that duty was a substantial cause of the assault inflicted on them by Hartnett.

* * *

The Court concludes that * * * as a matter of law the hospital owed no duty to warn the Leedys of any danger posed by Hartnett.

* * * The question presented by the Plaintiffs as to the hospital's duty to them appears to be one of first impression in Pennsylvania. Plaintiffs' theory of liability is that because of the hospital's relationship to Hartnett, which was essentially that of psychiatrist to patient, the hospital owed to the Leedys a duty to warn them of Hartnett's alleged violent tendencies. This theory of liability has been adopted to a certain extent by the states of California, New Jersey, and Florida. The United States District Courts for the Districts of North Dakota and Nebraska have held that such would be the law in those states. The most complete statement of the rationale behind this legal theory is that given by the California Supreme Court in *Tarasoff.*

In *Tarasoff,* * * * the Court, far from imposing a broad duty on therapists, held that plaintiffs could state a cause of action by "asserting that the therapists in fact determined that [the patient] presented a serious danger of violence to [the victim] or pursuant to the standards of their profession should have so determined, but nevertheless failed to exercise reasonable care to protect her from that danger." *Tarasoff v. Regents of University of California,* 17 Cal.3d 425, 450, 551 P.2d 334 (1976).

The California Supreme Court has refused to extend the rationale of *Tarasoff.* In *Thompson v. County of Alameda,* 167 Cal.Rptr. 70, 27 Cal.3d 741, 614 P.2d 728 (1980), the Court was confronted with a claim against a county alleging negligence in releasing from custody a juvenile delinquent who was known to have dangerous and violent propensities toward young children and who within 24 hours after being released sexually assaulted and murdered plaintiffs' son who resided in the community into which the juvenile was released. In rejecting the plaintiffs' contention that their complaint stated a cause of action, the Supreme Court of California emphasized that in *Tarasoff* there was a specifically foreseeable and identifiable victim. While the Court stated that the intended victim need not be specifically named, he must be "readily identifiable."

The Court rejected the contention that as a neighborhood child the plaintiffs' decedent was a foreseeable victim of the released juvenile. In circumstances in which an individual poses a risk of danger to a significant portion of the community the Court declined to impose any duty to give warnings primarily because it determined that the value of such warnings was not great. In *Tarasoff* the warnings were directed at making the victim aware of the danger to which she was "uniquely exposed." The threatened target was "precise." * * * In contrast to that situation, the case presented in *Thompson* was one in which there was a need to give warnings to a broad segment of the population and the warnings could be only general in nature because no specific threat had been made. Under those circumstances, the Court found that such warnings because of their necessary generality could not be expected to "stimulate increased safety measures."

The New Jersey case of *McIntosh v. Milano*, 168 N.J.Super. 466, 403 A.2d 500 (1979), which relied heavily on the California Supreme Court's decision in *Tarasoff*, also involved a situation where it was clear to the psychiatrist that his patient posed a particular threat to the decedent. In *McIntosh* the patient had reported numerous fantasies about the decedent and the psychiatrist knew that he had shot a B.B. gun at a car in which the decedent was riding sometime prior to having killed her.

* * *

Plaintiffs, recognizing that their case does not fall squarely within the confines of *Tarasoff*, seek to convince the Court that there exists a material issue of fact as to whether they were part of a readily identifiable group of people to whom Hartnett posed a special risk of danger. They seek to define this group as those who had frequent social contact with Hartnett. The Plaintiffs do not contend that Hartnett ever made any threats against them or that he was more likely to become violent toward people in whose presence he was comfortable. Indeed, the past acts of violence relied on by the Plaintiffs to show that Hartnett was dangerous do not fall into any pattern. At most, they demonstrate that Hartnett was prone to violent behavior and that that tendency was aggravated when he drank. There is no evidence from which it can be concluded that even when he drank Hartnett was more likely to become violent toward the people with whom he was drinking rather than others in the area. Plaintiffs appear to be arguing that since Hartnett had a tendency to commit violent acts, people with whom he had frequent contact would be more likely to be victims of such acts and for that reason a special duty was owed to any such people known to the hospital's personnel.

* . * *

In order for the rule of liability announced in *Tarasoff* to be kept within workable limits, those charged with the care of potentially dangerous people must be able to know to whom to give warnings. When, as in *Tarasoff* and *McIntosh*, a particular victim can be identified, there is good reason to impose upon psychiatrists or custodians a duty to warn the intended victim of the danger posed by the person under their care. On the facts of this case, however, Hartnett did not pose any danger to the Leedys different from the danger he posed to anyone with whom he might be in contact when he became violent. This is not a case in which it is alleged that the propensity to violence is increased by frequent contacts with the same people; rather, Plaintiffs' claim that they represent a readily identifiable group rests solely on a statistical probability that the more one saw Hartnett the more likely it is that one would be a victim of any violent outbreak by him. This is not the type of readily identifiable victim or group of victims to which the California Supreme Court made reference in *Tarasoff* or *Thompson*.

* * *

Questions and Comments

1. *Leedy v. Hartnett* follows *Thompson v. County of Alameda*, 167 Cal.Rptr. 70, 614 P.2d 728 (1980), which establishes the rule that a therapist will not be liable unless there is a *readily identifiable* potential victim. The manner in which the "identifiable victim" standard is applied will materially influence the ultimate scope of the *Tarasoff* doctrine. Strict construction will limit the circumstances under which liability may be found; an expansive interpretation will enlarge them.

Several recent decisions indicate that the identifiable victim requirement is likely to be broadly construed. For instance, in *Jablonski v. United States*, 712 F.2d 391 (9th Cir.1983), the patient who had served a five year prison term for raping his wife subsequently killed his girlfriend after attempting to rape her mother. In holding the psychiatrist liable, the court ruled that although the patient had not made a *specific* threat "[h]is psychological profile indicated that his violence was likely to be directed against women very close to him." Id. at 398. Similarly, in *Davis v. Lhim*, 124 Mich.App. 291, 335 N.W.2d 481 (1983), where the patient shot and killed his mother during a scuffle the psychiatrist was found liable. The mother was found to be a foreseeable victim on the basis of evidence that two years before the homicide the patient had acted "strangely" and had threatened her for money. This together with the fact that the therapist had knowledge that the patient was a drug addict and would need money to obtain drugs was "sufficient to support a jury finding that defendant [the psychiatrist] should have known * * * that [the patient] posed a serious threat to his mother." Id. at 490. *See also, Hedlund v. Superior Court of Orange County*, 34 Cal.3d 695, 194 Cal.Rptr. 805, 669 P.2d 41 (1983).

The requirement of a clearly foreseeable victim does not apply in an action against an institution for negligently releasing an individual where the facility's staff knew or should have known that the patient was likely to impose harm on others. Where the patient is improperly released, the institution may be held liable even where the specific victim was not foreseeable. *See, Lipari v. Sears, Roebuck & Co.*, 497 F.Supp. 185 (D.Neb.1980).

2. May liability be imposed on a psychotherapist if he fails to warn a potential victim when the victim had actual knowledge of the patient's intentions? In *Hedlund v. Superior Court of Orange County*, 34 Cal. 3d 695, 194 Cal.Rptr. 805, 669 P.2d 41 (1983), a psychologist was held liable for having failed to warn the victim in spite of evidence that the victim had actual knowledge that the patient intended to inflict serious bodily harm on her. The *Hedland* case also represents an extension of the foreseeable victim requirement in its finding of liability for the serious emotional injuries suffered by the three-year-old son who was seated next to his mother when she was shot by the patient.

3. *McIntosh v. Milano*, 168 N.J.Super. 466, 403 A.2d 500 (1979), cited in *Leedy*, involved a fact situation very similar to *Tarasoff*. In that case, a 20-year old male patient had undergone two years of treatment for drug abuse and what was described as "an adjustment reaction of adolescence." During therapy the psychiatrist learned that the patient was infatuated with a female neighbor. The patient also revealed to the psychiatrist his feelings of intense jealousy and possessiveness. Moreover, the psychiatrist learned that the patient had purchased a knife and had on one occasion fired a BB gun at a car in which the neighbor girl was riding while on a date. The patient later shot and killed the girl.

The patient was charged with first-degree murder. At the criminal trial the treating psychiatrist in testifying for the defense revealed that he had been aware of the patient's aggressive and hostile intentions toward the victim. Some months after criminal trial, which resulted in a guilty verdict, the parents of the victim filed a wrongful death action against the psychiatrist, charging him with negligence for his failure to warn the victim or her family of the danger imposed by the patient. On appeal, the court adopted the *Tarasoff* doctrine and held that the failure to warn the victim constituted actionable negligence from which liability may arise.

BELLAH v. GREENSON

California Court of Appeals, 1978.
81 Cal.App.3d 614, 146 Cal.Rptr. 535.

ROUSE, Associate Justice.

Plaintiffs, Melanie and Robert Bellah, are the heirs of Thomasin (Tammy) Bellah, their daughter, who succumbed to a self-inflicted overdose of pills on April 12, 1973. Tammy had been under the care of defendant, Daniel Greenson, a psychiatrist in Berkeley, for an unspecified period of time prior to her death. It appears that, during that time, defendant concluded that Tammy was disposed to suicide, and that he recorded his conclusion in his written notes. At the time of Tammy's death, plaintiffs were temporarily living in Princeton, New Jersey, where they were spending the 1972–73 academic year.

On April 11, 1975, some two years after Tammy's death, plaintiffs instituted the present action for wrongful death, alleging that defendant had failed to personally take measures to prevent Tammy's suicide; that he failed to warn plaintiffs of the seriousness of Tammy's condition and of circumstances which might cause her to commit suicide; and that he had failed to inform plaintiffs that Tammy was consorting with heroin addicts in plaintiffs' home. Plaintiffs' complaint purported to state two causes of action, one based upon simple negligence, and one based upon defendant's negligent performance of his contract with plaintiffs to care for their daughter, which contract allegedly contained the implied term that defendant would use reasonable care to prevent Tammy from harming herself or the property of another. Plaintiffs sought to recover damages which would compensate them for Tammy's wrongful death and for certain thefts from their home which were apparently committed by the heroin addicts with whom Tammy was consorting.

* * *

The primary issue to be decided on appeal from a judgment rendered following the sustaining of a demurrer is whether, considering all allegations in the complaint to be true, plaintiffs have stated facts sufficient to entitle them to some relief.

* * *

In the present case, a second issue is whether the action is barred by the statute of limitations, as alleged in the demurrer below.

In order to state a cause of action for negligence, the complaint must allege facts sufficient to show a legal duty on the part of the defendant to use due care, a breach of such legal duty, and the breach as the proximate or legal cause of the resulting injury. The duty of care is always related to some circumstance of time, place and person. The determination of whether a duty exists is primarily a question of law. Thus, in the present case, we must determine whether plaintiffs have alleged facts sufficient to give rise to a duty on the part of defendant to take steps to prevent Tammy from committing suicide or to advise plaintiffs about the existence of conditions which might cause Tammy to take her own life, so that they could take such steps.

It has been held that the requisite special relationship does exist in the case of a patient under the care of a psychiatrist and that a psychiatrist who knows that his patient is likely to attempt suicide has a duty to take preventive measures. Thus, in *Vistica v. Presby-*

terian Hospital (1967) 67 Cal.2d 465, 62 Cal.Rptr. 577, 432 P.2d 193, and *Meier v. Ross General Hospital* (1968) 69 Cal.2d 420, 71 Cal. Rptr. 903, 445 P.2d 519, it was held that a wrongful death action would lie where the plaintiffs' decedent committed suicide while undergoing psychiatric treatment in a hospital. In *Vistica*, the cause of action was held to exist against the hospital, which was the only named defendant, and in *Meier*, it was found to exist against both the hospital and the decedent's treating physician.

Vistica was cited in *Tarasoff v. Regents of University of California* (1976) 17 Cal.3d 425, 436, 131 Cal.Rptr. 14, 551 P.2d 334, for the proposition that a *hospital* must exercise reasonable care to control the behavior of a patient which may endanger other persons.

However, on their facts, *Vistica* and *Meier* are readily distinguishable from the case at hand. Each involved situations where the patient was confined in a hospital at the time of the event which constituted the basis for subsequent litigation. Obviously, the duty imposed upon those responsible for the care of a patient in an institutional setting differs from that which may be involved in the case of a psychiatrist treating patients on an out-patient basis.

Here, the complaint alleged the existence of a psychiatrist-patient relationship between defendant and Tammy, knowledge on the part of the defendant that Tammy was likely to attempt suicide, and a failure by defendant to take appropriate preventive measures. We are satisfied that these allegations are sufficient to state a cause of action for the breach of a psychiatrist's duty of care towards his patient. The nature of the precautionary steps which could or should have been taken by defendant presents a purely factual question to be resolved at a trial on the merits, at which time both sides would be afforded an opportunity to produce expert medical testimony on the subject. From the face of plaintiffs' complaint, we are unable to determine whether defendant did or did not take preventive steps which were consonant with good medical practice in the community. However, that question is not before us in the demurrer stage of these proceedings.

We disagree with plaintiffs in their contention that *Tarasoff v. Regents of University of California*, created a duty on the part of the defendant in this instance to breach the confidence of a doctor-patient relationship by revealing to them disclosures made by their daughter about conditions which might cause her to commit suicide. In *Tarasoff*, the California Supreme Court held that, under certain circumstances, a therapist had a duty to warn others that a patient under the therapist's care was likely to cause personal injury to a third party. There the court said, "Although * * * under the common law, as a general rule, one person owed no duty to control the conduct of another [citations], nor to warn those endangered by such conduct [citations], the courts have carved out an exception to this rule in cases in which the defendant stands in some special relationship to either the person whose conduct needs to be controlled or in a relationship to the foreseeable victim of that conduct [citation]."

Applying that exception to the facts of *Tarasoff*, the court held that where a therapist knows that his patient is likely to injure another and where the identity of the likely victim is known or readily discoverable by the therapist, he must use reasonable care to prevent his patient from causing the intended injury. Such care includes, at the least, informing the proper authorities and warning the likely victim. However, the court did not hold that such disclosure was required where the danger presented was that of self-inflicted harm or suicide or where the danger consisted of a likelihood of property damage. Instead, the court recognized the importance of the confidential relationship which ordinarily obtains between a therapist and his patient, holding that "the therapist's obligations to his patient require that he *not disclose a confidence unless such disclosure is necessary to avert danger to others * * *.*"

Far from imposing a duty to warn others of the likelihood of any and all harm which might be inflicted by a patient, *Tarasoff* requires that a therapist *not* disclose information *unless* the strong interest in confidentiality is counterbalanced by an even stronger public interest, namely, safety from violent assault.

The imposition of a duty upon a psychiatrist to disclose to others vague or even specific manifestations of suicidal tendencies on the part of the patient who is being treated in an out-patient setting could well inhibit psychiatric treatment. In his amicus brief, counsel points out that the dynamics of interaction between the psychotherapist and the patient seen in office visits are highly complex and subtle. Intimate privacy is a virtual necessity for successful treatment. Were it not for the assurance of confidentiality in the psychotherapist-patient relationship, many in need of treatment would be reluctant to seek help. Even those who do seek help under such circumstances may be deterred from fully disclosing their problems. An element usually assumed essential is the patient's trust that matters disclosed in therapy will be held in strict confidence.

We conclude that *Tarasoff v. Regents of University of California*, requires only that a therapist disclose the contents of a confidential communication where the risk to be prevented thereby is the danger of violent assault, and not where the risk of harm is self-inflicted harm or mere property damage. We decline to further extend the holding of *Tarasoff*.

* * *

The order sustaining the demurrer without leave to amend is modified by adding thereto a paragraph dismissing the action. The judgment of dismissal is affirmed.

F. THE DOCTRINE OF SOVEREIGN IMMUNITY AS A LIMITATION ON THE LIABILITY OF PUBLIC EMPLOYEES AND GOVERNMENTAL AGENCIES

As the preceding section makes clear, a mental health professional who provides substandard care or fails to conform to legal requirements such as informed consent may be liable for damages. The employing agency also may be liable for damages caused by the mental health professional. However, when the employing agency is a governmental one, such as a Veterans Administration hospital, or the professional is a public employee, special rules often apply to limit liability. These rules stem from the doctrines of sovereign immunity and official immunity.

The doctrine of sovereign immunity is largely historical in nature. When the United States was created from the former colonies of Great Britain, the new government inherited the sovereign immunity that had been enjoyed by the king. The doctrine was based on a monarchical semi-religious tenet that "the king can do no wrong," and its effect was to prevent the government from being sued without its consent. Justice Holmes stated the proposition in a more pragmatic way when he wrote in *Kawanankoa v. Polyblank*, 205 U.S. 349, 353, 27 S.Ct. 526, 527, 51 L.Ed. 834 (1907):

> A sovereign is exempt from suit, not because of any formal conception or obsolete theory, but on the logical and practical ground that there can be no legal right as against the authority that makes the law on which the right depends.

Sovereign immunity is rooted in social policy as well as in history. It is seen as preserving government's control over its funds, property, and instrumentalities. Without immunity, it is argued, the government would be hampered in its essential functions. In addition, some argue that a democratic society needs sovereign immunity to prevent individuals from depleting the treasury at the expense of the majority of the population.

The immunity doctrine has come under increasing criticism, however, as government has become larger and more pervasive. It is argued that injuries caused by the government should be born by the entire society as a cost of government rather than by the particular individual injured.

Originally the federal government alleviated this burden upon individuals on a case by case basis, with Congress adopting private acts allowing certain individuals to sue the government. In 1946, however, Congress passed the Federal Tort Claims Act [FTCA], which waived the federal government's immunity from suit in a broad range of circumstances. Through the FTCA, Congress intended to compensate victims of the negligent conduct of government activities in circumstances in which a victim could collect damages from a private tort feasor.

The FTCA, however, excludes some torts from coverage, and thus the immunity doctrine remains in effect for those causes of action. For example, the federal government remains immune from suit for damages resulting from combat activities in time of war. A section of the FTCA provides that the United States will not be liable for "any claim arising out of arrest, battery, false imprisonment, false arrest, malicious prosecution, abuse of process, libel, slander, misrepresentation, deceit, or interference with contract rights" except in law enforcement cases. 28 U.S.C. § 2680(b). This provision has sometimes been broadly construed to preclude recovery from the government for medical malpractice. Thus, a claim of battery for an operation performed in a Veterans Administration hospital on the wrong leg of the plaintiff was denied in *Moos v. United States*, 118 F.Supp. 275 (D.Minn.1954), *affirmed* 225 F.2d 705 (8th Cir.1955).

The FTCA also excludes the federal government from liability for acts or omissions that are within the "discretionary function or duty" of any federal agency or employee. 28 U.S.C. § 2680(a). The distinction between discretionary and non-discretionary duties is often difficult. Almost every act performed by a government official includes some discretion in the manner in which it is performed. Therefore, the discretionary function exclusion has been construed by courts to involve a planning/operational distinction. *Dalehite v. United States*, 346 U.S. 15, 73 S.Ct. 956, 97 L.Ed. 1427 (1953). Under this test, the federal government has been held to be immune from suit based on negligence in making top-level planning decisions such as whether to export fertilizer. *Dalehite, id.* In contrast, the federal government may be held liable for the negligence of federal employees in the "operational" level of government in carrying out the plans even though such actions may involve a certain amount of discretion. For example, the Supreme Court in *Indian Towing Co. v. United States*, 350 U.S. 61, 76 S.Ct. 122, 100 L.Ed. 48 (1955), found that checking the electrical system of a lighthouse was at the "operational level" and did not involve discretion within the meaning of the FTCA. The government was therefore not immune from suit to recover damages suffered by a barge that ran aground while a Coast Guard lighthouse was not operating.

The FTCA additionally places various procedural requirements on persons with claims against the government. The most important is the requirement of exhaustion of administrative remedies. The injured party must have been denied relief from the agency from which recovery is sought before suit may be brought in court. In this way Congress sought to encourage compromise and to minimize the burden added to the courts when immunity was waived.

The principle that the sovereign cannot be sued without its consent applies with full force to the various states of the United States. Absent waiver, states, state agencies, and state officers in their official capacities are generally immune from suit. The doctrine has been criticized by some state courts, however, and appears to be in disfavor. See e.g., *Crowder v. Department of State Parks*, 228 Ga. 436, 185 S.E.2d 908 (1971), *cert. denied*, 406 U.S. 914, 92 S.Ct. 1768, 32 L.Ed.2d 113 (1972); *Muskopf v. Corning Hospital District*, 55 Cal.2d 211, 11 Cal.Rptr. 89, 359 P.2d 457 (1961). The Supreme Court of Colorado totally abandoned the doctrine in *Evans v. Board of County Commissioners*, 174 Colo. 97, 482 P.2d 968 (1971). Every state has, to at least some extent, consented to be sued by adopting legislation waiving sovereign immunity in some circumstances. These statutes, although generally not as comprehensive as the FTCA, serve much the same purpose. Immunity is waived only for those circumstances explicitly set forth in the statute and only if the prescribed procedures are followed. There are some circumstances, however, in which a state or state agency may be sued even though it has not waived its immunity. Such a circumstance arises when the state is acting not in its governmental capacity, but in a "proprietary" capacity, as when the state creates an agency to engage in a primarily commercial venture.

There is no uniform rule declaring whether state and municipal hospitals exist under the proprietary or governmental function of the state. The maintenance of a hospital for the service of the public health and to treat indigent patients is generally held to be a governmental function, and thus the hospital is immune from suit absent waiver of immunity. In contrast, the operation of a hospital for the purpose of obtaining a pecuniary profit is generally considered to be a proprietary function not immune from suit. Unfortunately, the majority of state hospitals fall within a middle category for which generalizations are impossible. *See* generally Annot. 25 A.L.R.2d 203, 228 (1952) and Supp. (1981).

Some cases arise in which the governmental agency is immune from suit, but the employee who actually committed the wrong is amenable to suit in his individual capacity. Such an action may be possible when its result will not affect the state's actions. Additionally, a plaintiff may wish to seek recovery from both the government agency and the individual employee. However, in any suit against a government employee one must consider the doctrine of official immunity.

Government employees are, of course, not absolved from their private and personal tort liabilities merely because of their employment. When, however, a person is injured as a result of government (federal, state, or local) action, the employee causing the injury may be immune from liability under the doctrine of official immunity.

Official immunity has been recognized by the courts as a means of relieving the burden that would otherwise fall upon government officials if they were held accountable in private tort suits for every action taken or decision made. The immunity allows government employees to execute their duties without unreasonable fear of liability and prevents qualified persons from being discouraged from entering government employment out of such fear. Courts have, however, recognized that not every government employee requires the same type of protection. The scope of the immunity therefore varies among government employees.

In essence there are two types of immunity: absolute and qualified. Judges have long been granted absolute immunity for their judicial acts, even when their conduct is corrupt or malicious. Such an immunity was recognized in order to preserve an independent judiciary by eliminating the possibility of vexatious suits. Because the immunity extends to all members of the judicial branch, such mental health professionals as hearing officers in commitment proceedings and psychiatrists appointed by the court benefit from the doctrine. A doctor who signs papers in a commitment process or who testifies at a commitment hearing has "absolute immunity" from liability for actions taken in his capacity as an officer of the court. *Duzynski v. Nosal*, 324 F.2d 924 (7th Cir.1963); *Williams v. Westbrook Psychiatric Hospital*, 420 F.Supp. 322 (E.D.Va.1976).

Additionally, federal courts have tended to extend absolute immunity to executive branch officers of a lower degree. Courts have recognized that many officers in federal administrative agencies (*e.g.*, administrative law judges) perform functions similar to those traditionally performed by the judiciary. Thus those officers performing a "quasi-judicial" function have been granted absolute immunity in some situations.

In general, however, lower administrative officers are afforded only a qualified immunity, and this qualified immunity is only applied to those officers whose duties are regarded as "discretionary" as opposed to "ministerial." The distinction between discretionary and ministerial employees is largely one of degree. Certainly every act requires some degree of discretion. But qualified immunity is limited to those officers who are involved in the decision-making phase of government and denied those who merely follow orders or whose duties require few choices. Government employees are held to the normal negligence standard when performing ministerial duties.

If qualified immunity does apply, the officer cannot be held liable for any act within his governmental duties that was performed in good faith. Thus, for example, a psychiatrist employed by a state mental hospital who negligently determines that a civilly committed patient remains mentally ill and denies the patient release would be immune from liability for false imprisonment. If, however, the psychiatrist makes his report knowing that the patient is qualified for release, his report is probably in bad faith, and qualified immunity will not protect him from liability. *See e.g., Hoffman v. Halden*, 268 F.2d 280 (9th Cir.1959); *Mierop v. State*, 22 Misc.2d 216, 201 N.Y.S.2d 2 (1960).

Actions that are wholly outside of the authority of the official, however, are not protected by the doctrine of official immunity. This limitation of the doctrine applies whether the immunity is absolute or qualified and may even allow plaintiffs to recover for discretionary acts of the official. However, courts will often extend the immunity to the officer if determination of the scope of his authority would have required a determination of legal questions that could perplex a court. Thus, if an officer acted under authority of a statute later determined to be unconstitutional, he is protected by the same immunity he would have if the statute had been valid.

This rule is modified slightly in a federal civil rights action. *O'Connor v. Donaldson*, 422 U.S. 563, 95 S.Ct. 2486, 45 L.Ed.2d 396 (1975), involved a state hospital superintendent who held a patient under authority of a state statute that was later declared to be unconstitutional. In an action for damages brought by the patient, the Supreme Court held that the superintendent's immunity depended on whether he "knew or reasonably should have known that the action he took within his sphere of responsibility would violate the constitutional rights of [the patient], or if he took the action with the malicious intention to cause a deprivation of constitutional rights or injury to [the patient]." 422 U.S. at 577, 95 S.Ct. at 2494, citing, *Wood v. Strickland*, 420 U.S. 308, 322, 95 S.Ct. 992, 1000, 43 L.Ed.2d 214 (1975). The test thus stated is in effect only a special application of the qualified immunity good faith requirement to a constitutional violation.

The various types of immunity recognized for governments and government employees have come under increasing attack as the role of government has increased in this country. Many have argued that liability should be borne by all as a cost of government and that government employees should not enjoy more privileges than they would have if employed in a similar function in the private sector. Certainly many of the original justifications for the immunities have changed. Courts and legislatures have therefore adjusted the immunity doctrines to try to deal with these changes by waiving or eroding immunity in some areas and extending it into others. That process continues today. Whatever the ultimate outcome, government and official immunity will undoubtedly continue to have an important place in litigation involving the mental health professions.

III. RECOVERY AND DAMAGES UNDER ALTERNATIVE THEORIES

A. CLAIMS BASED ON CONTRACT

Even though the professional services rendered fall well below the ordinary standard of care, the patient-plaintiff can have difficulty in establishing all the elements of an action for negligence. In those situations, it is possible for a plaintiff to base his claim on another legal theory. One alternative involves basing a claim on deprivation of federal civil rights and is discussed in the following section. A second alternative is discussed here: basing a claim for relief on a breach of contract.

JOHNSTON v. RODIS

United States Court of Appeals, District of Columbia Circuit, 1958.
251 F.2d 917.

EDGERTON, Chief Judge.

The complaint makes the following allegations. The plaintiff Kathryn Johnston consulted the defendant Dr. Rodis for the purpose of obtaining certain treatments and "questioned" him concerning the treatments. He advised her "that the treatments as given by him were perfectly safe". "Relying upon the statements" he made, she submitted herself to him for the treatments. On May 10, 1952, he commenced a treatment "and upon her regaining consciousness she learned that while under the direction, care and supervision of the defendant she sustained a fracture of her left arm." Serious, permanent and painful injuries resulted.

The defendant's answer says that because of the plaintiff's condition he gave her electric shock therapy in accordance with the approved method and practice of physicians specializing in psychiatry.

*   *   *

The District Court gave summary judgment for the defendant and the plaintiffs appeal. * * * Doubtless a physician's statement that he would cure a disease could seldom if ever be regarded as a warranty. But that is not this case. The statement attributed to the defendant, that shock treatments are "perfectly safe", contains less of prediction and more of present fact. We think this statement, if the defendant made it and did not qualify it in any way, might properly be found to be a warranty. It follows that summary judgment should not have been granted.

Reversed.

Questions and Comments

1. In the therapist-patient relationship a claim of breach of contract can arise two ways. The therapist can, as was described in the preceding case of *Johnston v. Rodis*, make an express promise of a particular outcome. If the therapy does not produce the promised result, the practitioner will be liable for breaching the express terms of his contract. This liability will attach even if the quality of the services rendered conforms to the highest standards of the profession.

A contract claim, however, need not necessarily arise from any *express* promise made by the practitioner. An *implied* warranty of the contract for services may also form the basis for a malpractice suit alleging breach of contract. The contract between the patient and therapist will generally be interpreted to include an implied warranty that the services to be rendered will be of reasonable quality and conform to prevailing standards of the therapist's profession. When a therapist's performance fails to meet this standard, he has breached his contract. *See, e.g., Anclote Manor Foundation v. Wilkinson,* 263 So.2d 256 (Fla.App.1972).

2. Even where the treatment provided was substandard, the plaintiff can find it difficult to establish one or more of the elements required by the doctrine of negligence. For instance, a plaintiff may suffer an injury but may encounter difficulty in establishing whether the cause of the injury was the consequence of the improper treatment or another factor. This was the situation in *Anclote Manor Foundation v. Wilkinson,* 263 So.2d 256 (Fla.App.1972). The plaintiff in that case was a former husband of a patient who had committed suicide several months after being released from the defendant-hospital. Evidence presented at the trial showed that the wife had been seduced by the supervising psychiatrist. Upon being released from the hospital, the patient divorced her husband. In the next several months both the patient's grandmother and only brother died, the latter as a result of suicide. Rather than suing for negligence which would have required a showing that the improper treatment resulted in or contributed to the suicide, the plaintiff chose to base his claim on breach of contract. He recovered $28,628 as restitution of the fees and charges paid to the hospital for the care of the deceased wife.

3. Although a patient seeking redress for inadequate or substandard professional care may be able to assert a legal claim based on either a contract or negligence theory, he will usually find it advantageous to use the negligence theory of tort. Undoubtedly, the factor that ordinarily leads a plaintiff to choose negligence is the nature of damages that may be recovered. In a suit based on a theory of contract the patient will be awarded damages only if the court concludes that the injuries he suffered were or could have been reasonably foreseen by the parties at the time the contract for treatment was formed. To recover in an action based on negligence, however, the injury need not have been foreseeable at any time prior to the injury; if the injury was a natural and probable consequence of the defendant's negligent act, liability will attach. In most situations either test will work.

Nothing is ever totally clear cut, and there are cases in which an injury will not have been reasonably foreseeable but will, nevertheless, be deemed to have been the natural and probable consequence of the defendant's negligent action. Thus, the doctrine of negligence ordinarily provides somewhat greater latitude to a plaintiff in establishing legally compensable damages.

An action in negligence also provides other advantages for the plaintiff seeking to recover the maximum amount of damages. The plaintiff in a tort suit may recover damages for pain and suffering and may, at least in the case of intentional torts, recover punitive damages from the defendant. These "general damages" are usually not available to the plaintiff in a contract action. Where such damages have been awarded in a suit alleging breach of contract, it has generally been because the contract breach was also found to constitute a tort.

There are, however, a limited number of circumstances in which a plaintiff will find it advantageous to bring suit against a practitioner under a contract theory. Once a court has determined that a practitioner has breached a contractual duty, whether express or implied, the plaintiff's cause of action will not be defeated by his contributory negligence. If the claim rests on negligence, however, the law of some states will prevent recovery if the plaintiff is found to have contributed to his injury by his own negligence.

A contract or quasi-contract theory may be attractive to the plaintiff if it is clear that the practitioner has not met his duty of care, but the plaintiff can show no specific demonstrable injury. This might be the case, for instance, when the patient's only injury from the substandard services he received was that his condition remained unchanged. In a suit alleging breach of contract, the plaintiff would then be able to recover the fees he had paid to the defendant.

Perhaps the most frequent reason why a plaintiff chooses to base his suit on contract theory is the differences in the applicable statutes of limitations. Most jurisdictions allow plaintiffs more time in which to bring a suit based on a contract than on negligence. Typically, the statute of limitations for a contract action will be five years, whereas the limitations period for a negligence action will be two years. Some states, however, have adopted statutes providing a uniform limitations period for all suits brought against physicians, whether based on negligence or contract. Finally, a contract action may be necessary when a plaintiff sues some hospitals. In many states, charitable institutions are immune from liability arising out of negligence. That immunity does not, however, protect the institution from liability under contract.

B. CLAIMS BASED ON FEDERAL CIVIL RIGHTS LAWS

Certain federal statutes, collectively known as the Civil Rights Statutes, allow patients to sue mental health professionals for deprivations of their civil rights. The most widely used of these statutes provides that:

> Every person who, under color of any statute, ordinance, regulation, custom, or usage, of any State or Territory, subjects, or causes to be subjected, any citizen of the United States or other person within the jurisdiction thereof to the deprivation of any rights, privileges, or immunities secured by the Constitution and laws, shall be liable to the party injured in an action at law, suit in equity, or other proper proceeding for redress.

42 U.S.C. § 1983 (1970).

Although these statutes were originally passed after the Civil War to assure the rights of the newly emancipated slaves, since the civil rights movements of the 1960's and 70's the scope of their application has continuously expanded beyond racial discrimination. Accordingly, the number of civil rights actions filed each year has increased from 296 in 1960 to 3,985 in 1970, and to 16,332 in 1981 (Director, Administrative Office of the United States Courts, Annual Report [1982]). Today a mental health patient can bring a civil rights action against a mental health professional if he can show that: (1) the conduct complained of was committed by a person acting under color of state law; (2) this conduct deprived the patient of rights, privileges, or immunities secured by the Constitution or laws of the United States; and (3) the conduct complained of was not protected by the professional's "good faith" immunity.

While meeting these three requirements will often be somewhat burdensome, the advantages of the civil rights action over the traditional state tort action will often justify this effort. The most obvious advantage in seeking a federal forum is that the plaintiff-patient will be able to remove his case from the state court, which may have subtle political ties to the state agency involved. This neutrality in the federal court may be somewhat undercut by the presence of a local jury even in the district court, but it may still be to the patient's advantage to be in federal court. The federal forum may also be necessary to avoid state created limitations on liability, whether it be the creation of a fixed ceiling of liability or the non-recognition of punitive damages for particular actions. However, as noted below, certain immunities may still operate to limit recovery of damages. Where the patient seeks only relief that is equally available under state tort law, the advantages of a federal action may be outweighed by the additional elements of proof which confront a plaintiff in a federal civil rights action. A choice between a state or federal cause of action must be made on the basis of the facts of the case, the party taking into account the obstacles to relief under state law and the difficulties of meeting the evidentiary requirements of the federal civil rights laws.

The most commonly used statute to redress non-criminal deprivations of civil rights, the Civil Rights Act of 1871, entails proof of the three elements listed above. The following discussion describes these elements and considers their application in the context of the delivery of mental health services.

1. Persons Acting Under Color of Law

The threshold requirement for a civil rights action is that the conduct complained of be that of one acting under color of state law, i.e., that the state was somehow involved in the deprivation of the plaintiff's federal rights. The statute does not sanction actions against *private* citizens; rather the "color of law" requirement is coextensive with the "state action" requirement for violations of due process under the Fourteenth Amendment. One of the most common ways of establishing the color of law requirement is to show that the defendant is an employee of the state. Any mental health professional who works at a state institution is acting under color of law. *Hoffman v. Halden,* 268 F.2d 280 (9th Cir.1959).

Even though a mental health professional does not work directly for the state, he may still be acting under color of law. For example, the mental health professional may be paid from funds provided by the state for a special program. Or the professional might work under the control of a state agency, such as the welfare commission. In either of these cases the professional may be found to have been acting under the color of law. *Campbell v. Glenwood Hills Hospital, Inc.,* 224 F.Supp. 27 (D.Minn.1963).

A professional employed by a private hospital may also be found to be acting under color of law. For instance, the state's mental health laws could effect the commitment of an individual to a private hospital. This rationale was used by the court in *Holmes v. Silver Cross Hospital,* 340 F.Supp. 125, 134 (N.D.Ill.1972), to find that the admission of a patient into a private hospital met the color of law requirement. A later case, however, rejected the rationale of *Holmes,* saying that the emerging decisions were contra to *Holmes. Gerrard v. Blackman,* 401 F.Supp. 1189 (N.D.Ill.1975). The court in *Gerrard* suggested that to meet the color of law requirement, the state's involvement had to have a more direct causal connection to a participation in the activity that resulted in the civil rights injury.

Another way of proving that the mental health professional is acting under color of law is to show that the hospital is acting under color of law. If the hospital itself is under color of law, then of all its agents and employees also act under color of law. A hospital may be acting under color of law if it receives substantial federal, state, or city funds; *Pollock v. Methodist Hospital,* 392 F.Supp. 393 (E.D.La. 1975); *Suckle v. Madison General Hospital,* 362 F.Supp. 1196 (W.D. Wis.1973), affirmed 499 F.2d 1364 (W.D.Wis.1974); or if there is other substantial state involvement; *Greco v. Orange Memorial Hospital Corp.,* 513 F.2d 873 (5th Cir.1975), *rehearing denied* 515 F.2d 1183 (5th Cir.1975), *cert. denied,* 423 U.S. 1000, 96 S.Ct. 433, 46 L.Ed.2d 376 (1975) (suggesting that a state or county representative on the hospital's board of directors might constitute sufficient involvement).

The law is very unclear as to what constitutes sufficient state involvement to bring a private hospital under color of law. One frequently asserted ground is receipt by the hospital of Hill-Burton funds for the initial construction of the hospital. The Hill-Burton Act, 42 U.S.C. § 291 et seq. (1970), passed in 1944, was designed to survey the need for new hospitals and to funnel federal funds through state agencies for the construction of non-profit hospitals. The federal courts, however, are split as to whether receipt of such funds is sufficient to satisfy the color of law requirement. Compare *Pollock v. Methodist Hospital,* 392 F.Supp. 393 (E.D.La.1975) (receipt of 36% of total construction costs from Hill-Burton funds constitutes color of law) and *Simkins v. Moses H. Cone Memorial Hospital*, 323 F.2d 959 (4th Cir.1963) (receipt of 15% of total construction costs through Hill-Burton constitutes color of law) with *Watkins v. Mercy Medical Center*, 520 F.2d 894 (9th Cir.1975) (receipt of Hill-Burton funds combined with tax exemptions not sufficient to meet color of law requirement) and *Barrett v. United Hospital*, 376 F.Supp. 791 (S.D.N.Y.1974). Predicting whether a particular hospital falls within the color of law requirement is difficult; but at least three factors should be considered: (1) Is the government funding a significant amount of either construction or operation of the hospital? (2) Is there a nexus between the complained of conduct and the government funds; and (3) Are the government funds used to further the unconstitutional activity? While a positive answer to any of these questions may not be dispositive, an affirmative finding as to any one would make it more likely that the color of law requirement would be declared satisfied.

2. Deprivation of Federal Rights

Section 1983 is intended to protect the patient from "the deprivation of any rights, privileges, or immunities secured by the Constitution and laws" 42 U.S.C. § 1983 (1970). The statute covers only violations of rights guaranteed by the federal Constitution and federal laws and not those guaranteed by state law. However, there is no creation of a federal substantive law, the statute merely creates federal jurisdiction and a remedy where jurisdiction might otherwise be unavailable.

Two kinds of rights are protected by the Civil Rights Statutes: substantive rights and procedural rights. Substantive rights include those guaranteed by the Bill of Rights. Due process procedural rights are created by the Fourteenth Amendment. These rights protect against deprivations of life, liberty, or property without due process of law, the inference being that such deprivations are not necessarily a violation of rights if there is proper procedural due process.

The hospital's virtual control over a patient's life provides abundant opportunities for violations of a patient's civil rights. If a patient were denied the right to practice his religion or to vote in a federal election during his hospitalization, for example, he would be able to bring a civil rights action against the person responsible. The same holds true if the patient is denied other substantive rights created by federal law.

Frequently, mental health professionals find themselves defendants in civil rights cases based on the treatment, or lack thereof, received by a patient. In *Knecht v. Gillman*, 488 F.2d 1136 (8th Cir. 1973), the plaintiff had been an inmate in a mental institution where the patients were given apomorphine, a drug that induces vomiting, when they violated certain hospital rules such as swearing or lying.

The court found that this use of apomorphine was not an accepted nor recognized form of treatment and that the use of this drug on an involuntary basis was cruel and inhuman punishment. The physician responsible for its administration was held liable in a civil rights action brought by the patient. In *Philipp v. Carey*, 517 F.Supp. 513 (N.D.N.Y.1981), the plaintiffs were mentally retarded voluntary residents of a state mental health facility, who complained that they were being given debilitating psychotropic drugs as a substitute for treatment and rehabilitation. The court found that they had a 1983 cause of action for violation of Section 504 of the Rehabilitation Act, a federal law prohibiting the denial of benefits to handicapped persons by a facility receiving federal funding. 29 U.S.C. § 794.

A mentally ill patient may also attack the conditions of his confinement through a civil rights action. In *Jobson v. Henne*, 355 F.2d 129 (2d Cir.1966), the patient was assigned uncompensated work for up to sixteen hours a day. The work was not part of a therapy program, nor was it related to the patient's housekeeping needs. The court held that this stated a possible cause of action as a violation of the patient's Thirteenth Amendment right (freedom from involuntary servitude).

Other conditions of a patient's confinement may give rise to a civil rights action against a mental health professional. In *Gerrard v. Blackman*, 401 F.Supp. 1189 (N.D.Ill.1975), the court held that a psychiatrist who monitored an involuntary patient's calls to her attorney could be subject to a possible civil rights action. In *Jones v. Superintendent*, 370 F.Supp. 488 (W.D.Va.1974), the court refused to find a civil rights violation where the patient who was a vegetarian for religious reasons had been denied a special diet. The plaintiff was unable to show any physical injury, however, and the case suggests that an action might lie where there is such harm.

Whether deprivations which are the result of mere negligence are covered under section 1983 has not been entirely resolved by the U.S. Supreme Court. The loss of *property* due to the negligence of public officials was held to not be actionable when there was no indication that the negligence was the direct result of state authorized procedures or policy. *Parratt v. Taylor*, 451 U.S. 527, 101 S.Ct. 1908, 68 L.Ed.2d 420 (1981). Subsequent lower court cases have, however, refused to extend this exemption to deprivations of substantive constitutional rights in contrast to procedural due process, *see, e.g., Wolf-Lillie v. Sonquist*, 699 F.2d 864 (7th Cir.1983); see generally, Sheldon Nahmod, Civil Rights & Civil Liberties Litigation, (Colorado Springs, Co.: Shepard's/McGraw-Hill, 1979).

3. "Good Faith" Immunity

A mental health professional acting under color of law is a state executive official and is entitled to qualified immunity similar to that described in the section on sovereign immunity. Although the U.S.

Supreme Court has rejected the notion that executive officers are entitled to absolute immunity from civil rights actions, a balancing of the individuals rights and the need for decision-makers to be free to exercise discretionary judgments has resulted in a "good faith" immunity for defendants. *Wood v. Strickland,* 420 U.S. 308, 319–20, 95 S.Ct. 992, 999–1000, 43 L.Ed.2d 214 (1974). The test arrived at by the court involves both an objective and a subjective analysis. Under the objective aspect of the test, a civil rights plaintiff must show that the mental health professional "knew or reasonably should have known that the action he took within his sphere of official responsibility would violate the constitutional rights of [the patient]." *O'Connor v. Donaldson,* 422 U.S. 563, 577, 95 S.Ct. 2486, 2494, 45 L.Ed.2d 396 (1975), quoting *Wood v. Strickland,* 420 U.S. 308, 322, 95 S.Ct. 992, 1000, 43 L.Ed.2d 214 (1975). Thus, the test is satisfied by proof that the defendant knew or should reasonably have known that the plaintiff's rights were being violated. This standard obviously imposes some burden on the professional to become aware of the law governing patients' rights.

Liability may also be imposed if the defendant "took the action with the malicious intention to cause a deprivation of constitutional rights or other injury." *Wood v. Strickland,* 420 U.S. 308, 322, 95 S.Ct. 992, 1000, 43 L.Ed.2d 214 (1975). Thus, the mere fact of injury having been inflicted with malice, even if unaccompanied by knowledge that the action constituted a legal wrong, would be sufficient to result in liability.

Even if liability does attach where a professional acting under color of law "should have known that the actions he took * * * would violate the constitutional rights" of the patient, the liability may only be extended to those situations in which the violated legal right was "settled and indisputable." *Wood v. Strickland,* 420 U.S. 308, 321, 95 S.Ct. 992, 1000, 43 L.Ed.2d 214 (1975). It is impossible to state with certainty the degree of resolution that this qualification contemplates. One court has said that the professional should not be "charged with predicting the future course of constitutional law." *Pierson v. Ray,* 386 U.S. 547, 557, 87 S.Ct. 1213, 1219, 18 L.Ed.2d 288 (1967). Another court has dealt with this problem in the context of an emergency commitment statute. In *Reese v. Nelson,* 598 F.2d 822 (3d Cir.1979) the plaintiff was temporarily institutionalized after he sent a series of threatening letters to various county officials, who became concerned for their safety. Pursuant to emergency commitment procedures, the plaintiff was picked up and kept under observation for a week before he was released as unsuitable for treatment. He subsequently brought suit against, among others, the examining physician who suggested that the observation period take place, alleging violation of due process in the failure to provide a hearing before this deprivation of liberty. The court, contemplating the unconstitutionality of the statute involved, found that the objective test of the good faith defense was met since at the time of the commitment the statute was not clearly perceived to be constitutionally deficient. The court relied on *Procunier v. Navarette*, 434 U.S. 555, 98 S.Ct. 855, 55 L.Ed.2d 24 (1978), in refusing to use hindsight and limited the defendant's objective responsibility to the protection of constitutional rights that were clearly established at the time the act was committed. The question still remains as to how extensive a court will expect the legal knowledge of mental health officials to be. If the standard seems at first glance overly burdensome, mental health professionals can expect to find little sympathy from the U.S. Supreme Court: "Such a standard imposes neither an unfair burden upon a person assuming a responsible public office requiring a high degree of intelligence and judgment for the proper fulfillment of its duties, nor an unwarranted burden in light of the value which civil rights have in our legal system." *Wood v. Strickland*, 420 U.S. at 322, 95 S.Ct. at 1000.

In *Tenney v. Brandhowe*, 341 U.S. 367, 71 S.Ct. 783, 95 L.Ed. 1019 (1951) and *Pierson v. Ray*, 386 U.S. 547, 87 S.Ct. 1213, 18 L.Ed. 2d 288 (1967), the U.S. Supreme Court extended absolute immunity to state legislators and judges acting within their official jurisdictions. Judicial immunity is available not only to judges but also to all officers of the court. If a mental health professional can come within the definition of an officer of the court, he may enjoy a greater measure of immunity in a civil rights action. A court-appointed psychiatrist may be an example of a mental health professional acting as an officer of the court. If, as part of the commitment process, a doctor must sign certain papers or testify at a commitment hearing, he may be immune from actions taken in this capacity. *Duzynski v. Nosal*, 324 F.2d 924 (7th Cir.1963); *Williams v. Westbrook Psychiatric Hospital*, 420 F.Supp. 322 (E.D.Va.1976).

It is not uncommon for a patient to attack the validity of his commitment order in the context of a civil rights action. If the commitment proceedings do not comply with the applicable statutory provisions, they are void, and the patient may not be legally detained. However, if the commitment order is valid on its face, the hospital staff is immune from civil rights liability based on defects in the confinement order. *Hoffman v. Halden*, 268 F.2d 280 (9th Cir.1959); *Bartlett v. Duty*, 174 F.Supp. 94 (N.D.Ohio 1959); *Kenney v. Fox*, 232 F.2d 288 (6th Cir.1956). In *Kenney* the court was emphatic that not only should doctors not be required to go behind a commitment order valid on its face, but also they should not even be permitted to do so. 232 F.2d at 290. The *Hoffman* court declared that the physician who confines a patient on the basis of an invalid commitment order is like the jailer who confines a prisoner whose conviction is later reversed. Neither is liable, regardless of any malicious motive or intent. 268 F.2d at 300.

Although most psychiatric civil rights actions are brought under § 1983, two other sections should be noted. The first is 42 U.S.C. § 1985 (1970). This section is very similar to § 1983, but provides a remedy for a conspiracy to violate civil rights. The second is 18 U.S.C. § 242 (1970), which provides for criminal sanctions for a violation of civil rights. The major difference between the civil and criminal statutes is intent. Criminal law generally is based on the assumption that the wrongdoer understands that he is doing something wrong and that he should be punished. Civil law, on the other hand, is simply a method of allocating losses. The intent requirement, therefore, in a criminal civil rights action is more stringent, and, indeed, the statute itself declares that the deprivation must be "willful." The U.S. Supreme Court has interpreted this to mean that the act must be done intentionally and with the specific intent to deprive the victim of a constitutional right. *Screws v. United States*, 325 U.S. 91, 65 S.Ct. 1031, 89 L.Ed. 1495 (1945). If, for example, the supervising psychiatrist of a mental hospital knew that a patient was sane and not dangerous, yet refused to authorize the patient's discharge, the psychiatrist could be held guilty of a criminal violation of the patient's rights.

Chapter Three

INFORMED CONSENT

I. INTRODUCTION

The fundamental principle that every person should have the right to determine what should be done with his body has deep-seated roots in our jurisprudence. In 1914 Justice Cardozo affirmed this basic right in *Schloendorff v. Society of New York Hospital*, 211 N.Y. 125, 129–130, 105 N.E. 92, 93 (1914), in the following terms:

> Every human being of adult years and sound mind has a right to determine what shall be done with his own body; and a surgeon who performs an operation without his patient's consent commits an assault, for which he is liable in damages.

For many years, however, the right of self-determination was honored more in the abstract than in reality. It is only relatively recently that the right has been given meaningful expression by courts and legislatures. The Supreme Court's 1976 disposition of the abortion cases provides the most dramatic evidence of this shift. Acknowledging the primacy of a woman's right to terminate an unwanted pregnancy, the Court rested its holding on the basic principle that every person has the right to determine what happens to his or her body.

This growing recognition of the individual's right to bodily self-determination can also be seen in another line of cases, those dealing with the prerogative of self-decision as to medical treatment. A limited right to self-determination had been a traditional part of our jurisprudence for many years. Courts were quite prepared, even before the turn of the century, to classify as a battery the rendering of medical treatment that involved a touching performed without the patient's approval or consent. The consent necessary to immunize the physician from liability was, however, very limited and required nothing more than the patient's general agreement to the proposed treatment. The patient had no recognized right to receive comprehensible information about the treatment's risks. Thus, a physician would escape liability if the patient agreed to treatment, even if the patient was totally unaware of the risks it involved.

Only since 1960 has the doctrine of consent emerged as something more than a mere technicality. In a series of cases decided in the early 1960's various state courts ruled that the patient could not give meaningful consent unless he had received adequate information about the risks of the therapy and any available alternative treatments. The courts found that consent based on inaccurate or incomplete information deprived the patient of the right to charter his own course as to treatment and use of his body.

The doctrine of informed consent in its present form comprises two separate elements. One involves the duty of *disclosure* of relevant information to the patient; the other pertains to the patient's *consent* to the proposed therapy. The courts, however, disagree on both the precise doctrinal source of this right as well as its actual scope and dimension. As the materials in this chapter make clear, in some jurisdictions informed consent is subsumed under the doctrine of assault and battery. In others, violations of this right is treated as a form of professional negligence. The implications of these different approaches are explored in the materials that follow.

It is important to note that the doctrine of informed consent has to date only been applied in medical cases. Even in the area of psychiatric malpractice, its application has been limited to physically intrusive treatment methods such as electro-convulsive or insulin shock therapy or the administration of psychotropic drugs. No reported cases have applied the doctrine to any psychotherapy, whether performed by a psychiatrist or a psychologist.

Two reasons may explain why the doctrine has been limited to the bio-medical field. One reason relates to the peculiarities of the law of damages. In general, recovery of monetary damages under most tort theories requires that the injured party has suffered some physical injury. Physical injury is, of course, a much more frequent result of surgery or drug therapy than of conventional psychotherapy. Thus, under current law, a patient who has been deprived of the right to give informed consent to psychiatric or psychological treatment is unlikely to qualify for more than nominal damages. This alone reduces a patient's incentive to bring suit against a therapist and may explain, in part, the absence of cases applying the doctrine to the psychotherapy counseling field. In recent years, however, courts have demonstrated a marked tendency in other areas of law to compensate for non-physical injuries. A continuation of this trend may well result in exposing psychotherapists to increased risks of liability under the informed consent doctrine.

There is, however, an additional but related problem in extending the doctrine beyond the medical field. A cause of action predicated on the lack of informed consent requires that the patient's injury be the direct and proximate cause of the treatment. This element of proof becomes increasingly difficult if an injury is not immediately identifiable as the direct consequence of the treatment. This point is illustrated by the following hypothetical fact situation. A patient feels that she is not advancing in her job as her intellectual potentials might dictate due to excessive passivity and an inability to direct subordinates. On the therapist's recommendation, the patient undergoes assertiveness training. The training is successful to the extent that the patient has become much more assertive; however, her assertiveness and change of personality cause marital difficulties. Since her husband is unable to adjust to her new and more assertive personality, the patient now contends that she would not have consented to the therapy if she had been informed of its risks. In this situation the patient faces the significant difficulty of proving both that the psychotherapy in fact led to the personality change and that this fact was the proximate cause of the destruction of the marriage. While this burden of proof might not be altogether impossible to meet, it presents problems far more formidable than demonstrating that a particular physical injury was the direct and proximate cause of a surgical procedure. In spite of the various doctrinal and practical difficulties, it is likely that the concept of informed consent will eventually be applied to non-medical treatment situations. The field of psychological research, which has in the past been all too often characterized by a widespread disregard of any notion of informed consent, would seem particularly vulnerable to this form of legal regulation.

For those professionals whose activities are covered by the doctrine of informed consent, the impact can be formidable. Under this doctrine the possibility of civil liability no longer hinges on a departure from the exercise of reasonable skill in providing treatment. Rather, professionals can face liability even when the treatment was flawless. Recovery for the patient or research subject is predicated solely on the lack of appropriate consent to treatment. The following materials provide an overview of the doctrine's current development. Keep in mind, however, that the doctrine is still in its embryonic stage, and that major issues remain to be resolved.

II. ORIGINS OF THE DOCTRINE OF INFORMED CONSENT

A. AN EARLY CASE ESTABLISHING THE DUTY TO INFORM

MITCHELL v. ROBINSON

Supreme Court of Missouri, 1960.
334 S.W.2d 11.

BARRETT, Commissioner.

William Mitchell has been awarded $15,000 damages against the Doctors Robinson and their associates, particularly Dr. Jack DeMott, for malpractice, and the essentially meritorious problem is whether upon the record there is any evidence to support the jury's finding of negligence.

Mitchell and Dr. DeMott were boyhood schoolmates in Independence, Kansas, attended Kansas University at the same time, and were both living in Independence when Dr. DeMott began the practice of medicine there. So when in 1951, at age 35, Mitchell was beset with serious emotional problems he sought out Dr. DeMott who was then a specialist in neurology and psychiatry and was then associated with Doctor Robinson and the Neurological Hospital in Kansas City, Missouri. Mitchell had "a rather severe emotional illness," process schizophrenia, but he was not mentally incompetent; his illness was characterized by serious depression and rather severe anxiety, complicated by alcoholism. It is not necessary at this point to detail his case history and symptoms; it was the opinion of the doctors that he should have "combined electro-shock and insulin subcoma therapy." The general purpose of electroshock treatment is to build up the patient's "defenses and controls and self-confidence" while insulin relieves "basic anxiety" and "disturbance of the mood." The desired physical reaction and intended purpose of electroshock is to induce convulsive seizures of forty to fifty seconds duration. The desired physical reaction of insulin shock is the induction of unconsciousness, a "subcoma" state, but it is neither intended nor desired, as it is with electroshock, that the patient suffer a convulsion. One of the unpredictable results of insulin shock, however, is an unpreventable convulsion and one of the hazards of convulsions, whether from insulin or electroshock, is fractured vertebrae, fractured legs and various other injuries.

On October 25, 1951, Mitchell had his first electroshock treatment, the next day another, and, after two days' rest, his first insulin shock October 28 and the next day another, and on the 30th his third electroshock and on the 31st another insulin treatment. There were convulsions with the electroshock treatments but no untoward results; the insulin treatments came off with normal results and reactions except that on the 31st Mitchell suffered a convulsion and that particular treatment was successfully terminated by an intravenous injection of glucose. Insulin treatment, reduced to 25 units, was resumed November 2, but Mitchell went out for a walk and came in drunk and the treatments were "started over" again on November 4 with 25 units, increased to 40 units November 5 and on November 7, with his seventh insulin treatment of 40 units, he had "a hard generalized convulsion," a grand mal seizure, which resulted in a compression fracture of the fifth, sixth and seventh dorsal vertebrae. It is to recover damages for these specific injuries that Mitchell instituted this action.

These briefly noted facts are excerpted as background for certain basic distinctions in this and other malpractice cases and eventually to point up the problem precisely involved upon this appeal. The appellant doctors, relying on the general rules contend that their motions for a directed verdict should have been sustained because "There was no expert testimony to show that the insulin therapy administered to Mitchell failed to conform to the required standards of an ordinarily careful and prudent neurologist or psychiatrist in the community," indeed, the greater part of their brief is devoted to this subject. This phase of the appellants' argument has but little, if any, bearing upon the basic problem involved here; it may be that they could not anticipate just what position the plaintiff would take. But the plaintiff has made it perfectly clear that there is no claim of negligence in any of these general respects * * * [P]laintiff does not question the technique of administering the insulin, nor does he deny that it should have been administered. * * *

* * *

The defendants produced as a witness Dr. Pool, a radiologist connected with a veterans' hospital, Fort Roots Hospital, North Little Rock, Arkansas. While he was neither a neurologist nor a psychiatrist and disclaimed any special qualification in these fields he had made two case studies of the incidence of fractures from shock therapy as they occurred in his hospital. In one study of 46 insulin shock patients he testified that eighteen per cent of them sustained fractures, that in the course of combined electro and insulin shock treatment of 53 patients nineteen per cent sustained fractures, and in another group of 32 patients twenty-five per cent sustained fractures.

* * *

This finally brings us to the really meritorious question of whether in the circumstances of this case, the illness and treatment involved, the doctors were under a duty to inform the plaintiff that one of the hazards of insulin treatment is the fracture of bones not involved in either the illness or the treatment. That the hazard exists is beyond question; Dr. G. Wilse Robinson, Jr., said that fractured bones, serious paralysis of limbs, irreversible coma and even death were hazards incident to shock therapy and further that there are no completely reliable or successful precautions. In their amended answer the defendants "state that the fracture of bones is a danger and risk that is inherent in insulin shock therapy, and that compression fractures of the spine, and fractures of the limbs can and frequently do occur when said insulin shock therapy is properly administered." The plaintiff's principal claim here is that "There was evidence of a negligent failure to disclose to plaintiff the hazards of insulin treatment," and, of course, evidence that plaintiff would not have consented to the treatment had he known of the dangers. In his argument plaintiff states his position in this language: "He relies on defendants' negligent failure to warn him of the danger of injury from this therapy and on defendants' negligent assurance that there was no danger, and failure to use due care as submitted to the jury." The appellants, on the other hand, do not attempt to demonstrate or elaborate, they simply say that "Failure to inform Mitchell of the risks of the treatment, if there was such a failure, is not negligence." Thus, the serious hazards being admitted, the problem is whether in the circumstances of this record the doctors were under a duty to inform their patient of the hazards of the treatment, leaving to the patient the option of living with his illness or of taking the treatment and accepting its hazards.

*   *   *

*   *   * Mitchell testified that *   *   * Drs. Robinson and DeMott recommended the electroshock and insulin therapies, that he personally had no knowledge of the possibilities of fractures from insulin, that they explained the "process" to him "but there was nothing in his conversation to me that indicated any risk or disability as a result of the insulin treatment or any risk of disability at all." He categorically denied that either of the doctors advised him of the possibility of bone injuries or death from the treatments. He said that he asked Dr. DeMott if there was any danger and "His answer was that the treatments had only a temporary effect, a confusion that would last only a matter of an hour or so. He didn't say there would be any lasting effect at all"—in fact the doctor replied, "no danger."

*   *   *

Mitchell did not sign a written consent to the treatment; however, in his brief he repeatedly states that he needed the treatment and "Indeed, he consented to that," but, he says, he would not have consented had he been informed of the hazards. His then wife (they were divorced in 1952 and both have remarried) did sign a consent which contained this sentence: "This is to certify that I have been informed of the possible dangers of the shock treatment with curare and electro-shock, or with insulin in the case of William Mitchell and that I hereby give permission to the Neurological Hospital and staff to administer this treatment and request that this be done. We assume responsibility for any complications or accident resulting from the administration of these treatments." Mitchell testified that he did not authorize his wife to sign the consent and that he never heard of it until long after he had been discharged from the hospital and therefore had no notice from the consent of the hazards of the treatment. It is not necessary to say whether the consent Mitchell's wife signed was a valid assumption of the hazards of the treatment, the problem is whether it warned of the dangers *   *   *

*   *   *

While the fairly relevant cases may be indicative but inconclusive the authoritative literature is more specific and helpful to a positive and rather confident conclusion.

*   *   *

*   *   * The proper solution is to recognize that *the doctor owes a duty to his patient to make reasonable disclosure of all significant facts,* i.e., the nature of the infirmity (so far as reasonably possible), the nature of the operation *and some of the more probable consequences and difficulties inherent in the proposed operation. It may be said that a doctor who fails to perform this duty is guilty of malpractice."* (Italics supplied.)

*   *   * There was no emergency here, it was not even claimed that Mitchell was critically or dangerously ill and that immediate spectacular treatment was imperative. He was "emotionally" ill and the treatment was "recommended," but it was not immediately necessary to save his life or even his sanity. The doctors said that he had "a rather severe emotional illness," he was "upset, agitated, anxious, depressed, crying." He had been drinking excessively, he was having marital difficulties, was not sleeping well, could not think things through, had unsuccessfully attempted to work for his father and later unsuccessfully attempted to work for his then father-in-law. As indicated, when Mitchell came to the doctors he was not mentally incompetent or in delirium, he had some understanding of his problems and the need for treatment.

In the particular circumstances of this record, considering the nature of Mitchell's illness and this rather new and radical procedure with its rather high incidence of serious and permanent injuries not connected with the illness, the doctors owed their patient in possession of his faculties the duty to inform him generally of the possible serious collateral hazards; and in the detailed circumstances there was a submissible fact issue of whether the doctors were negligent in failing to inform him of the dangers of shock therapy.

[The Court concluded that various errors in the instructions given the jury required reversal in spite of the fact that the plaintiff's pleadings and proof were sufficient to sustain a judgment.]

Questions and Comments

1. *Mitchell v. Robinson* is one of the earliest cases recognizing the therapist's duty to disclose collateral risk information. Shortly before the *Mitchell* decision was handed down, the Supreme Court of Kansas, in *Natanson v. Kline*, 186 Kan. 393, 350 P.2d 1093 (1960), *clarified* 187 Kan. 186, 354 P.2d 670 (1960), expressly held that failure to disclose collateral risk data could constitute negligence. Though *Mitchell* and *Natanson* were decided within weeks of each other, most commentators agree that *Natanson* has been far more influential in shaping legal developments. Undoubtedly, one reason for this is that the *Natanson* opinion was better drafted, while the Mitchell court was somewhat "unclear about what it was up to." Capron, "Informed Consent In Catastrophic Disease Research and Treatment," 123 U.Pa.L.Rev. 340, 347 n. 20 (1974).

2. *Mitchell v. Robinson* and *Natanson v. Kline* are generally viewed as having ushered in the modern doctrine of informed consent. Prior to these cases, courts typically treated problems of consent as interlocked with the law of assault and battery, which insulated the physician from liability if the patient merely assented to the medical procedure. Adequate information was not a necessary component of a binding consent. The particular significance of the *Mitchell* and *Natanson* cases, and to some extent such earlier cases as *Salgo v. Leland Stanford Jr. University Board of Trustees*, 154 Cal.App.2d 560, 317

P.2d 170 (1957), is the court's recognition that a patient's consent cannot be meaningful or binding unless it is based upon sufficient information concerning the risks of the treatment. It is important to note that while a clear majority of states have accepted the *Mitchell-Natanson* approach, it has not been universally adopted. The trend, however, is clearly toward a wider recognition of the therapist's duty to provide adequate information.

3. Numerous cases, some decided as early as the beginning of the century, used a theory of battery to impose liability on physicians who performed medical procedures without the patient's authorization. Typically, these cases involved one of two basic fact situations. In one the physician performed a medical or surgical procedure different than the one authorized by the patient. For instance, in *Hively v. Higgs*, 120 Or. 588, 253 P. 363 (1927), a surgeon who during an operation on a patient's nose also removed the patient's tonsils was held liable for battery. Similarly, a dentist who had been authorized to extract two teeth, but removed eight while the patient was under sodium pentathol, was held liable in battery. *Moore v. Webb*, 345 S.W.2d 239 (Mo.App.1961).

The second situation leading to liability has involved the performance of a procedure consented to by the patient, but on a different part of the body than the patient had authorized. For instance, in *Mohr v. Williams*, 95 Minn. 261, 104 N.W. 12 (1905), the physician initially diagnosed the patient's right ear as requiring surgery (an ossiculectomy). The patient consented to undergo the recommended procedure, but during the operation the surgeon discovered a more serious defect in the left ear and performed an ossiculectomy on that instead. The court found that these facts established a basis for liability under a theory of battery. It is important to note, however, that in none of these early cases was liability predicated on the physician's failure to disclose information about collateral risks inherent in the treatment. Moreover, the physician could establish a complete defense with evidence that he had informed the patient of the planned procedure and that the patient had authorized the proposed treatment.

4. The modern doctrine of informed consent has been applied under different doctrinal headings. Some courts have chosen to view the failure to inform as vitiating any technical consent which might have been given, thus rendering the physician liable for assault and battery. More commonly, however, courts have characterized violations of the duty to inform as giving rise to an action based on negligence. A few jurisdictions have permitted the plaintiff-patient to proceed on both a negligence and an assault and battery rationale. *See, e.g., Belcher v. Carter*, 13 Ohio App.2d 113, 234 N.E.2d 311 (1967).

5. Whether a jurisdiction appends informed consent to the doctrine of assault and battery rather than negligence is of more than theoretical interest and can have important practical implications for the litigants. At least four major consequences can follow the choice of one doctrine over the other. First, negligence actions generally are subject to a longer statute of limitations than those based on a theory of battery. A

court's decision to subsume informed consent under battery may preclude a lawsuit that was still viable under the state's statute of limitations for negligence.

Second, the burden of proof imposed on the respective parties may vary with the theory chosen. For instance, when the action is based on battery, it is easier for the plaintiff to recover without introducing expert testimony to establish the prevailing medical practice as to the scope of disclosure. A full explanation of this point is provided in the notes following *Canterbury v. Spence,* 464 F.2d 772 (D.C.Cir.1972), which appears in the next section.

Third, the measure of damages may depend on which theory is utilized. Since battery is an intentional tort, the plaintiff may be able to recover punitive damages, particularly if he can show an element of malice. Also, under the battery theory the plaintiff may receive nominal damages even without a showing of actual injury. In negligence actions, on the other hand, damages are ordinarily awarded only in relation to the injuries actually suffered.

Fourth, under the terms of malpractice insurance policies, the defendant physician or therapist might not be covered if the action alleges battery, since intentional torts are specifically excluded in some policies.

6.   What type of information must be disclosed to the patient?   Can disclosure be limited to the collateral risks of the proposed therapy or must the therapist also describe any alternative forms of therapy that may be available, as well as the collateral risks of each alternative? Consider these questions in the context of the cases which follow.

III. ELEMENTS OF THE DOCTRINE OF INFORMED CONSENT

A. THE DISCLOSURE REQUIREMENT

1. *Standards Governing the Scope of Disclosure*

As indicated in the preceding section, the doctrine of informed consent requires that the therapist disclose the collateral risks of the proposed treatment. However, a rule framed in these general terms does not provide standards by which to evaluate the scope of disclosure given by the doctor. For instance, must there be disclosure of every minimal risk, or is it sufficient if the doctor informs the patient of only the more severe and more probable adverse consequences? Or does the doctrine establish a variable standard of disclosure, by requiring that the doctor provide only a level of disclosure that is consistent with reasonable and proper medical procedures? The cases which follow represent two divergent approaches to these fundamental questions.

AIKEN v. CLARY

Supreme Court of Missouri, 1965.
396 S.W.2d 668.

FINCH, Judge.

Plaintiff went to trial on Count III of a malpractice action wherein he alleged negligence of defendant in failing sufficiently to advise plaintiff of the hazards and risks involved in insulin shock therapy to enable plaintiff to give an informed consent for the treatment. Plaintiff alleged that as a result of such therapy administered by defendant he was caused to lapse into a coma and to suffer organic brain damage, resulting in total disability. He sought recovery of $150,000. The jury returned a verdict for defendant. After an unavailing motion for new trial, plaintiff appealed to this court.

* * * We proceed * * * to examine the evidence, which, insofar as pertinent to this assignment and viewed most favorably to plaintiff, was as follows:

After military service from 1941 to 1945 plaintiff entered employment of the Frisco Railroad, ultimately serving as an electrician in the diesel engine department. Early in 1961 plaintiff became irritable and "changed almost his entire personality." He was cross with the children, particularly a teen-age daughter, spent money on things for which he had never spent money before, and had trouble sleeping so that he lost a great amount of sleep and rest. His wife discussed with him the matter of seeing a doctor, but he maintained that his wife needed a doctor as much as he did, and that it was she who was "way out in left field." He agreed to see a doctor if she would, and they then consulted Dr. Lewis E. Jorel of Springfield, who previously had treated their daughter.

Following conferences by the doctor with both plaintiff and his wife, plaintiff entered St. John's Hospital at Springfield, Missouri, on June 3, 1961, for a complete physical examination. Numerous tests and procedures were utilized, as a result of which Dr. Jorel found no physical ailments. Dr. Jorel then discussed with plaintiff a need for psychiatric examination and arranged for defendant, Dr. William F. Clary, to examine and talk to plaintiff and evaluate him for psychiatric help. Dr. Clary testified that this examination was made and, among other things, related that plaintiff charged his wife with infidelity but in their conversation had no evidence or basis for such charge, and the doctor was convinced that this was a figment of his imagination. Dr. Clary's diagnosis was that plaintiff was a paranoid schizophrenic, and he recommended to plaintiff that he have both electric and insulin shock therapy. Plaintiff at that time said that he would think about the matter of such treatment, and Dr. Clary said he would talk further to Dr. Jorel. Thereafter, Dr. Clary talked to Dr. Jorel of his diagnosis and recommendation, and also talked to plaintiff's wife. She testified that Dr. Clary told her that plaintiff was a very sick man, that he needed treatment, but Dr. Clary didn't think plaintiff would submit thereto himself. She said that Dr. Clary suggested that they see if they could talk plaintiff into taking the treatment and if not that proceedings be started to force the treatment since he thought plaintiff was that sick. Meanwhile, plaintiff talked to his wife and to Dr. Jorel and plaintiff told him that he wanted to take the treatment and would take it willingly. Subsequently, Dr. Clary had a second conversation with plaintiff about coming down to the psychiatry section and having a course of electric shock and insulin therapy.

With respect to the information given by Dr. Clary to plaintiff in these conversations as to the nature of the treatment and the risks involved, plaintiff offered in evidence certain statements of the defendant given in an earlier deposition. That testimony was as follows:

"Q. When you talked to him previous to the moving down to psychiatry and signing the release, did you tell him what the possible effects of insulin shock therapy might be?

"A. I told him it would put him to sleep, I told him there was risks involved, I told him the same thing about electric shock therapy. I didn't belabor the point, I told him it was risky because this guy was real shook, but I told him it was risky, and he had no questions.

"Q. Did you tell him it might possibly result in his death?

"A. I implied it. In talking about the anesthetic, I said people take anesthetic, and there are hazards. Some people over-react to anesthetics, and insulin, I told him, it is like being put to sleep, there are risks involved. In terms of specifically telling him, 'This can kill you,' no, sir, I didn't.

"Q. Did you tell him it might possibly result in a delayed awakening, possible brain damage?

"A. No, I didn't tell him that."

Dr. Clary testified that he thought the plaintiff had the mental capacity at least to understand the ordinary affairs of life, understand what the treatment really was and what it might do to him. He again related what he had told plaintiff and stated that he tried to explain it to him on a level he would understand, and he thought plaintiff knew exactly what he was getting into. At the second conference between Dr. Clary and plaintiff, the latter agreed to take whatever treatment Dr. Clary recommended.

Accordingly, on June 9, 1961, a nurse in the psychiatric ward presented to plaintiff a form of "Consent to Shock Therapy." It read as follows: "I (We) hereby request and authorize Dr. Clary and whomever he may designate to assist him, to administer insulin and/ or electroshock therapy to Mr. Aiken; and to continue to administer such therapy and such other supplemental treatment as he may deem advisable from time to time. The effect and nature of shock and/or insulin treatment have been fully explained to me (us), as well as the hazards involved. Notwithstanding the fact that there are risks to the patient inherent in this treatment, I (we) voluntarily accept the risks involved. No assurance has been made by anyone with respect to the results that may be obtained. I have been given a copy of the pamphlet 'Information to Relatives.' " The nurse testified that she did not explain anything about the dangers involved in the therapy when she presented the consent for signature. The plaintiff read the consent in her presence and she asked him if he had any questions, but he had none and he signed the consent.

Beginning on June 12, 1961, and continuing through June 22, 1961, plaintiff was given a series of shock treatments which involved insulin in increasing amounts of from 40 to 260 units. On June 22, 1961, plaintiff went into a deep coma. He suffered a delayed awakening from the insulin and did not respond to the procedures used for the purpose of bringing the patient out of the coma. A specialist in internal medicine was called in and plaintiff was transferred to the intensive care unit but the coma was prolonged and as a result plaintiff suffered brain damage.

Dr. Robert L. Lam, M.D., a specialist in neurology and psychiatry, testified for plaintiff that from an examination made by him at the Veterans Hospital in Little Rock, Arkansas, on January 16, 1964, his opinion was that plaintiff had severe organic brain damage, that he was totally incapacitated in terms of employment and that his condition was permanent as a result of the prolonged insulin coma. Plaintiff was still in the Veterans Hospital at the time of trial.

Dr. Lam was interrogated as to dangers in insulin shock therapy and he testified that the possible dangers or complications thereof are coma and death or prolonged coma resulting in various degrees of brain damage, or that there might be the production of epilepsy or localized paralysis, or there might be a vascular disturbance. In addition, he said that with convulsions that may occur one could have fractures of certain types, either of the vertebrae or the extremities. The doctor was not asked and did not undertake to testify as to the frequency of occurrence of such events, or any of them, and said that no doctor could predict which patient would be the one to have trouble, saying, "So that the only thing one can say is that, when one has a patient getting deep coma insulin, that there is a possibility that this could occur." Dr. Lam also testified that there was nothing improper in the administration of the insulin shock therapy and that the administration thereof was according to good medical practice. Dr. Lam was not asked about the adequacy of defendant's disclosures to plaintiff.

* * *

Defendant first asserts that plaintiff failed to make a submissible case because he failed to offer any expert medical evidence as to what a reasonably careful and prudent physician engaged in similar practice would do under the same or similar circumstances with respect to disclosure of risks involved in the proposed therapy. There is no dispute but that plaintiff did not offer any expert testimony on this matter of what a reasonably prudent practitioner would disclose. We must determine, therefore, whether plaintiff is required to offer such proof in order to make a submissible case.

The basic philosophy in malpractice cases is that the doctor is negligent by reason of the fact that he has failed to adhere to a standard of reasonable medical care, and that consequently the service rendered was substandard and negligent. In our judgment, this is true whether the alleged malpractice consists of improper care and treatment (the usual malpractice case) or whether it is based, as here, on an alleged failure to inform the patient sufficiently to enable him to make a judgment and give an informed consent if he concludes to accept the recommended treatment.

How, then, is a jury to determine whether a physician has been negligent in failing to inform his patient adequately to enable him to make an informed decision whether to consent to recommended treatment? What proof must a plaintiff offer? Obviously, in addition to evidence as to plaintiff's condition and the treatment proposed and administered, there must be testimony as to what risks are involved and what disclosures were made by the doctor. These necessarily are a part of plaintiff's case. Such evidence was offered by plaintiff in this case. The real issue here is whether plaintiff is required to go further and as a part of his case offer evidence as to a standard of medical conduct with reference to disclosures by the physician to his patient or whether this is a matter which the jury may decide without such expert testimony. There are cases from some states which hold that such expert testimony is necessary as a part of plaintiff's case and cases from other states holding that such evidence is not required.

*   *   *

We have reexamined this question and have concluded that the question of what disclosure of risks incident to proposed treatment should be made in a particular situation involves medical judgment and that expert testimony thereon should be required in malpractice cases involving that issue. The question to be determined by the jury is whether defendant doctor in that particular situation failed to adhere to a standard of reasonable care. These are not matters of common knowledge or within the experience of laymen. Expert medical evidence thereon is just as necessary as is such testimony on the correctness of the handling in cases involving surgery or treatment.

[Expert testimony as to the correctiveness of the level of disclosure required in a particular case would need to take into account such factors as] the state of the patient's health, the condition of his heart and nervous system, his mental state, and * * * among other things, whether the risks involved were mere remote possibilities or something which occurred with some sort of frequency or regularity. This determination involves medical judgment as to whether disclosure of possible risks may have such an adverse effect on the patient as to jeopardize success of the proposed therapy, no matter how expertly performed. (Defendant in this case testified that plaintiff was "real shook.") After a consideration of these and other proper factors, a reasonable medical practitioner, under some circumstances, would make full disclosure of all risks which had any reasonable likelihood of occurring, but in others the facts and circumstances would dictate a guarded or limited disclosure. In some cases the judgment would be less difficult than in others, but, in any event, it would be a medical judgment.

* * *

Accordingly, we hold that plaintiff, in order to sustain his burden of proof, is required to offer expert testimony to show what disclosures a reasonable medical practitioner, under the same or similar circumstances, would have made, or, stated another way, that the disclosures as made by the defendant do not meet the standard of what a reasonable medical practitioner would have disclosed under the same or similar circumstances. To whatever extent Mitchell v. Robinson is inconsistent with the views herein expressed, it is disapproved.

Once plaintiff has offered sufficient proof to make a submissible case, including the required expert testimony which we have discussed, then the ultimate determination of whether defendant did or did not fail to disclose to plaintiff in accordance with the standard of what a reasonable medical practitioner would have done is a jury question under proper instructions from the court.

* * *

In view of the fact that plaintiff made no offering of any expert testimony relative to the extent of disclosure a reasonable medical practitioner would have made under the same or similar circumstances, he failed to make a submissible case for the jury. However, we will not affirm this case on that basis for the reason that counsel for plaintiff asserted in the presentation of the case that in the case of Mitchell v. Robinson, supra, this court had stated that expert testimony is not necessary in cases involving extent of duty to warn, and that he relied thereon in offering no proof of that character. In the light of language used in the opinion of Mitchell v. Robinson, supra, it was reasonable for counsel to assume the lack of a requirement of such testimony in this case. Under those circumstances, we feel compelled to reverse and remand for a new trial in order to afford plaintiff an opportunity to offer expert testimony on the standard of disclosure required.

* * *

The judgment is reversed and the cause remanded for a new trial. All of the Judges concur.

Questions and Comments

1. Note that although the *Aiken* court sustained the defendant's legal argument, it reversed the judgment in defendant's favor and remanded the case for retrial. The court reached this unusual outcome on the basis that the plaintiff's lawyer had erroneously relied on a previous case involving a different but related factual situation. Normally when an attorney errs in this way, appellate courts are less forgiving than the *Aiken* court, and the client is precluded from a second opportunity to litigate the case.

2. Under *Aiken v. Clary* the scope of required disclosure is established by a determination of what a reasonable medical practitioner would disclose under the same or similar circumstances. This reasonableness standard is very flexible, for it allows the practitioner to take into account not only the remoteness of the possibility of adverse consequences but also whether "disclosure of possible risks may have such an adverse affect on the patient as to jeopardize success of the proposed therapy no matter how expertly performed." 396 S.W.2d 668, 674 (Mo.1965).

What specifically are the adverse effects that disclosure might engender? Does the *Aiken* court assume that psychological stress might result from knowledge of the risk and thereby impede recovery? Is there any evidence to support this assumption in the case of conventional medical treatment, including surgery? Is the risk of psychiatric complication more likely if the patient is also suffering from a psychiatric disorder? The scope of what is known as the "privilege of non-disclosure" is covered in greater detail in subsection A.2 at p. 59.

3. Does *Aiken* in effect hold that if a particular risk is not normally disclosed by medical practitioners, the patient cannot therefore recover under an informed consent theory? If so, does this allow the medical profession to determine the actual scope of the doctrine of informed consent? Does this standard reflect an appropriate compromise between the patient's interests in receiving sufficient information upon which to base the decision to accept or reject treatment and the interest of the medical profession in being able to carry out its professional function without undue risk of liability?

4. In the situation presented by the *Aiken* case (insulin coma therapy), would reasonable medical practice require the doctor to inform the patient of the risks of brain damage? What if the risk of brain damage is estimated to be only 0.1%?

Would the *Aiken* standard require disclosure of the risk of bone fracture, which is fairly rare when a muscle relaxant is administered?

What if a bone fracture occurs only once in every 8,000 cases in which a relaxant is used? *See generally* Krouner, *Shock Therapy and Psychiatric Malpractice: The Legal Accommodation to a Controversial Treatment,* 2 Forensic Sci. 397 (1973); see also Note, *Regulation of Electro-convulsive Therapy,* 75 Mich.L.Rev. 363, 367 (1976).

CANTERBURY v. SPENCE

United States Court of Appeals, District of Columbia Circuit, 1972.
464 F.2d 772.

SPOTTSWOOD W. ROBINSON, III, Circuit Judge:

This appeal is from a judgment entered in the District Court on verdicts directed for the two appellees at the conclusion of plaintiff-appellant Canterbury's case in chief. His action sought damages for personal injuries allegedly sustained as a result of an operation negligently performed by appellee Spence, a negligent failure by Dr. Spence to disclose a risk of serious disability inherent in the operation, and negligent post-operative care by appellee Washington Hospital Center. On close examination of the record, we find evidence which required submission of these issues to the jury. We accordingly reverse the judgment as to each appellee and remand the case to the District Court for a new trial.

At the time of the events which gave rise to this litigation, appellant was nineteen years of age, a clerk-typist employed by the Federal Bureau of Investigation. In December, 1958, he began to experience severe pain between his shoulder blades. He consulted two general practitioners, but the medications they prescribed failed to eliminate the pain. Thereafter, appellant secured an appointment with Dr. Spence, who is a neurosurgeon.

Dr. Spence examined appellant in his office at some length but found nothing amiss. On Dr. Spence's advice appellant was x-rayed, but the films did not identify any abnormality. Dr. Spence then recommended that appellant undergo a myelogram—a procedure in which dye is injected into the spinal column and traced to find evidence of disease or other disorder—at the Washington Hospital Center.

Appellant entered the hospital on February 4, 1959. The myelogram revealed a "filling defect" in the region of the fourth thoracic vertebra. Since a myelogram often does no more than pinpoint the location of an aberration, surgery may be necessary to discover the cause. Dr. Spence told appellant that he would have to undergo a laminectomy—the excision of the posterior arch of the vertebra—to correct what he suspected was a ruptured disc. Appellant did not raise any objection to the proposed operation nor did he probe into its exact nature.

* * *

Dr. Spence performed the laminectomy on February 11 at the Washington Hospital Center.

* * * The laminectomy revealed several anomalies: a spinal cord that was swollen and unable to pulsate, an accumulation of large tortuous and dilated veins, and a complete absence of epidural fat which normally surrounds the spine. A thin hypodermic needle was inserted into the spinal cord to aspirate any cysts which might have been present, but no fluid emerged. In suturing the wound, Dr. Spence attempted to relieve the pressure on the spinal cord by enlarging the dura—the outer protective wall of the spinal cord—at the area of swelling.

For approximately the first day after the operation appellant recuperated normally, but then suffered a fall and an almost immediate setback. Since there is some conflict as to precisely when or why appellant fell, we reconstruct the events from the evidence most favorable to him. Dr. Spence left orders that appellant was to remain in bed during the process of voiding. These orders were changed to direct that voiding be done out of bed, and the jury could find that the change was made by hospital personnel. Just prior to the fall, appellant summoned a nurse and was given a receptacle for use in voiding, but was then left unattended. Appellant testified that during the course of the endeavor he slipped off the side of the bed, and that there was no one to assist him, or side rail to prevent the fall.

Several hours later, appellant began to complain that he could not move his legs and that he was having trouble breathing; paralysis seems to have been virtually total from the waist down. Dr. Spence was notified on the night of February 12, and he rushed to the hospital. * * * The surgical wound was reopened and Dr. Spence created a gusset to allow the spinal cord greater room in which to pulsate.

Appellant's control over his muscles improved somewhat after the second operation but he was unable to void properly. As a result of this condition, he came under the care of a urologist while still in the hospital. In April, following a cystoscopic examination, appellant was operated on for removal of bladder stones, and in May was released from the hospital. He reentered the hospital the following August for a 10-day period, apparently because of his urologic problems. For several years after his discharge he was under the care of several specialists, and at all times was under the care of a urologist. At the time of the trial in April, 1968, appellant required crutches to walk, still suffered from urinal incontinence and paralysis of the bowels, and wore a penile clamp.

* * *

* * * The damages appellant claims include extensive pain and suffering, medical expenses, and loss of earnings.

II

Appellant filed suit in the District Court on March 7, 1963, four years after the laminectomy and approximately two years after he attained his majority. The complaint stated several causes of action against each defendant. Against Dr. Spence it alleged, among other things, negligence in the performance of the laminectomy and failure to inform him beforehand of the risk involved. Against the hospital the complaint charged negligent post-operative care in permitting appellant to remain unattended after the laminectomy, in failing to provide a nurse or orderly to assist him at the time of his fall, and in failing to maintain a side rail on his bed. The answers denied the allegations of negligence.

*   *   *

Appellant introduced no evidence to show medical and hospital practices, if any, customarily pursued in regard to the critical aspects of the case, and only Dr. Spence, called as an adverse witness, testified on the issue of causality. Dr. Spence described the surgical procedures he utilized in the two operations and expressed his opinion that appellant's disabilities stemmed from his pre-operative condition as symptomized by the swollen, non-pulsating spinal cord. *   *   * Dr. Spence further testified that even without trauma paralysis can be anticipated "somewhere in the nature of one percent" of the laminectomies performed, a risk he termed "a very slight possibility." He felt that communication of that risk to the patient is not good medical practice because it might deter patients from undergoing needed surgery and might produce adverse psychological reactions which could preclude the success of the operation.

At the close of appellant's case in chief, each defendant moved for a directed verdict and the trial judge granted both motions. The basis of the ruling, he explained, was that appellant had failed to produce any medical evidence indicating negligence on Dr. Spence's part in diagnosing appellant's malady or in performing the laminectomy; that there was no proof that Dr. Spence's treatment was responsible for appellant's disabilities; and that notwithstanding some evidence to show negligent post-operative care, an absence of medical testimony to show causality precluded submission of the case against the hospital to the jury. The judge did not allude specifically to the alleged breach of duty by Dr. Spence to divulge the possible consequences of the laminectomy.

We reverse. The testimony of appellant and his mother that Dr. Spence did not reveal the risk of paralysis from the laminectomy made out a prima facie case of violation of the physician's duty to disclose which Dr. Spence's explanation did not negate as a matter of law. There was also testimony from which the jury could have found that the laminectomy was negligently performed by Dr. Spence, and that appellant's fall was the consequence of negligence on the part of the hospital. * * * These considerations entitled appellant to a new trial.

* * *

III

Suits charging failure by a physician adequately to disclose the risks and alternatives of proposed treatment are not innovations in American law. They date back a good half-century, and in the last decade they have multiplied rapidly. There is, nonetheless, disagreement among the courts and the commentators on many major questions, and there is no precedent of our own directly in point. For the tools enabling resolution of the issues on this appeal, we are forced to begin at first principles.

The root premise is the concept, fundamental in American jurisprudence, that "[e]very human being of adult years and sound mind has a right to determine what shall be done with his own body. * * *" True consent to what happens to one's self is the informed exercise of a choice, and that entails an opportunity to evaluate knowledgeably the options available and the risks attendant upon each. The average patient has little or no understanding of the medical arts, and ordinarily has only his physician to whom he can look for enlightenment with which to reach an intelligent decision. From these almost axiomatic considerations springs the need, and in turn the requirement, of a reasonable divulgence by physician to patient to make such a decision possible.

A physician is under a duty to treat his patient skillfully but proficiency in diagnosis and therapy is not the full measure of his responsibility. The cases demonstrate that the physician is under an obligation to communicate specific information to the patient when the exigencies of reasonable care call for it.

* * *

The context in which the duty of risk-disclosure arises is invariably the occasion for decision as to whether a particular treatment procedure is to be undertaken. To the physician, whose training enables a self-satisfying evaluation, the answer may seem clear, but it is the prerogative of the patient, not the physician, to determine for himself the direction in which his interests seem to lie. To enable the patient to chart his course understandably, some familiarity with the therapeutic alternatives and their hazards becomes essential.

* * *

We now find, as a part of the physician's overall obligation to the patient, a similar duty of reasonable disclosure of the choices with respect to proposed therapy and the dangers inherently and potentially involved.[31]

31. Some doubt has been expressed as to ability of physicians to suitably communicate their evaluations of risks and the advantages of optional treatment, and as to the lay patient's ability to understand what the physician tells him.

This disclosure requirement, on analysis, reflects much more of a change in doctrinal emphasis than a substantive addition to malpractice law. It is well established that the physician must seek and secure his patient's consent before commencing an operation or other course of treatment. It is also clear that the consent, to be efficacious, must be free from imposition upon the patient. It is the settled rule that therapy not authorized by the patient may amount to a tort—a common law battery—by the physician. And it is evident that it is normally impossible to obtain a consent worthy of the name unless the physician first elucidates the options and the perils for the patient's edification. Thus the physician has long borne a duty, on pain of liability for unauthorized treatment, to make adequate disclosure to the patient. The evolution of the obligation to communicate for the patient's benefit as well as the physician's protection has hardly involved an extraordinary restructuring of the law.

IV

Duty to disclose has gained recognition in a large number of American jurisdictions, but more largely on a different rationale. The majority of courts dealing with the problem have made the duty depend on whether it was the custom of physicians practicing in the community to make the particular disclosure to the patient. If so, the physician may be held liable for an unreasonable and injurious failure to divulge, but there can be no recovery unless the omission forsakes a practice prevalent in the profession. We agree that the physician's noncompliance with a professional custom to reveal, like any other departure from prevailing medical practice, may give rise to liability to the patient. We do not agree that the patient's cause of action is dependent upon the existence and nonperformance of a relevant professional tradition.

There are, in our view, formidable obstacles to acceptance of the notion that the physician's obligation to disclose is either germinated or limited by medical practice. To begin with, the reality of any discernible custom reflecting a professional concensus on communication of option and risk information to patients is open to serious doubt. We sense the danger that what in fact is no custom at all may be taken as an affirmative custom to maintain silence, and that physician-witnesses to the so-called custom may state merely their personal opinions as to what they or others would do under given conditions. We cannot gloss over the inconsistency between reliance

We do not share these apprehensions. The discussion need not be a disquisition, and surely the physician is not compelled to give his patient a short medical education; the disclosure rule summons the physician only to a reasonable explanation. That means generally informing the patient in nontechnical terms as to what is at stake: the therapy alternatives open to him, the goals expectably to be achieved, and the risks that may ensue from particular treatment and no treatment. So informing the patient hardly taxes the physician, and it must be the exceptional patient who cannot comprehend such an explanation at least in a rough way.

on a general practice respecting divulgence and, on the other hand, realization that the myriad of variables among patients makes each case so different that its omission can rationally be justified only by the effect of its individual circumstances. Nor can we ignore the fact that to bind the disclosure obligation to medical usage is to arrogate the decision on revelation to the physician alone. Respect for the patient's right of self-determination on particular therapy demands a standard set by law for physicians rather than one which physicians may or may not impose upon themselves.

* * *

V

Once the circumstances give rise to a duty on the physician's part to inform his patient, the next inquiry is the scope of the disclosure the physician is legally obliged to make. The courts have frequently confronted this problem but no uniform standard defining the adequacy of the divulgence emerges from the decisions. Some have said "full" disclosure, a norm we are unwilling to adopt literally. It seems obviously prohibitive and unrealistic to expect physicians to discuss with their patients every risk of proposed treatment—no matter how small or remote—and generally unnecessary from the patient's viewpoint as well. Indeed, the cases speaking in terms of "full" disclosure appear to envision something less than total disclosure, leaving unanswered the question of just how much.

The larger number of courts, as might be expected, have applied tests framed with reference to prevailing fashion within the medical profession. Some have measured the disclosure by "good medical practice," others by what a reasonable practitioner would have bared under the circumstances, and still others by what medical custom in the community would demand. We have explored this rather considerable body of law but are unprepared to follow it. The duty to disclose, we have reasoned, arises from phenomena apart from medical custom and practice. The latter, we think, should no more establish the scope of the duty than its existence. Any definition of scope in terms purely of a professional standard is at odds with the patient's prerogative to decide on projected therapy himself. That prerogative, we have said, is at the very foundation of the duty to disclose, and both the patient's right to know and the physician's correlative obligation to tell him are diluted to the extent that its compass is dictated by the medical profession.

In our view, the patient's right of self-decision shapes the boundaries of the duty to reveal. That right can be effectively exercised only if the patient possesses enough information to enable an intelligent choice. The scope of the physician's communications to the patient, then, must be measured by the patient's need, and that need is the information material to the decision. Thus the test for determining whether a particular peril must be divulged is its materiality to the patient's decision: all risks potentially affecting the decision must be unmasked. And to safeguard the patient's interest in achieving his own determination on treatment, the law must itself set the standard for adequate disclosure.

* * *

From these considerations we derive the breadth of the disclosure of risks legally to be required. The scope of the standard is not subjective as to either the physician or the patient; it remains objective with due regard for the patient's informational needs and with suitable leeway for the physician's situation. In broad outline, we agree that "[a] risk is thus material when a reasonable person, in what the physician knows or should know to be the patient's position, would be likely to attach significance to the risk or cluster of risks in deciding whether or not to forego the proposed therapy."

The topics importantly demanding a communication of information are the inherent and potential hazards of the proposed treatment, the alternatives to that treatment, if any, and the results likely if the patient remains untreated. The factors contributing significance to the dangerousness of a medical technique are, of course, the incidence of injury and the degree of the harm threatened. A very small chance of death or serious disablement may well be significant; a potential disability which dramatically outweighs the potential benefit of the therapy or the detriments of the existing malady may summons discussion with the patient.

There is no bright line separating the significant from the insignificant; the answer in any case must abide a rule of reason. Some dangers—infection, for example—are inherent in any operation; there is no obligation to communicate those of which persons of average sophistication are aware. Even more clearly, the physician bears no responsibility for discussion of hazards the patient has already discovered, or those having no apparent materiality to patients' decision on therapy. The disclosure doctrine, like others marking lines between permissible and impermissible behavior in medical practice, is in essence a requirement of conduct prudent under the circumstances. Whenever nondisclosure of particular risk information is open to debate by reasonable-minded men, the issue is for the finder of the facts.

* * *

As in much malpractice litigation, recovery in nondisclosure lawsuits has hinged upon the patient's ability to prove through expert testimony that the physician's performance departed from medical custom. This is not surprising since, as we have pointed out, the majority of American jurisdictions have limited the patient's right to know to whatever boon can be found in medical practice. We have already discussed our disagreement with the majority rationale. We now delineate our view on the need for expert testimony in nondisclosure cases.

There are obviously important roles for medical testimony in such cases, and some roles which only medical evidence can fill. Experts are ordinarily indispensible to identify and elucidate for the factfinder the risks of therapy and the consequences of leaving existing maladies untreated. They are normally needed on issues as to the cause of any injury or disability suffered by the patient and, where privileges are asserted, as to the existence of any emergency claimed and the nature and seriousness of any impact upon the patient from risk-disclosure. Save for relative infrequent instances where questions of this type are resolvable wholly within the realm of ordinary human knowledge and experience, the need for the expert is clear.

The guiding consideration our decisions distill, however, is that medical facts are for medical experts and other facts are for any witnesses—expert or not—having sufficient knowledge and capacity to testify to them. It is evident that many of the issues typically involved in nondisclosure cases do not reside peculiarly within the medical domain. Lay witness testimony can competently establish a physician's failure to disclose particular risk information, the patient's lack of knowledge of the risk, and the adverse consequences following the treatment. Experts are unnecessary to a showing of the materiality of a risk to a patient's decision on treatment, or to the reasonably, expectable effect of risk disclosure on the decision. These conspicuous examples of permissible uses of nonexpert testimony illustrate the relative freedom of broad areas of the legal problem of risk nondisclosure from the demands for expert testimony that shackle plaintiffs' other types of medical malpractice litigation.

[The court next determined that the issues of whether the defendant Dr. Spence had performed the laminectomy negligently and whether the hospital was negligent in the aftercare should have been submitted to the jury.]

X

This brings us to the remaining question, common to all three causes of action: whether appellant's evidence was of such caliber as to require a submission to the jury. On the first, the evidence was clearly sufficient to raise an issue as to whether Dr. Spence's obligation to disclose information on risks was reasonably met or was excused by the surrounding circumstances. Appellant testified that Dr. Spence revealed to him nothing suggesting a hazard associated with the laminectomy. His mother testified that, in response to her specific inquiry, Dr. Spence informed her that the laminectomy was no more serious than any other operation. When, at trial, it developed from Dr. Spence's testimony that paralysis can be expected in one percent of laminectomies, it became the jury's responsibility to decide whether that peril was of sufficient magnitude to bring the disclosure duty into play.

[Reversed and remanded for new trial.]

Questions and Comments

1. Note that although the courts in *Aiken v. Clary* and *Canterbury v. Spence* anchored the duty of disclosure to the doctrine of negligence, the operational standard by which liability was to be determined was very different in each case.

2. Most jurisdictions which have recognized the doctrine of informed consent (numbering twenty-two states as of 1967) adhere to the *Aiken v. Clary* formulation of the appropriate standard. As of 1977, only two jurisdictions, California and Rhode Island, had adopted the *Canterbury v. Spence* rule.

3. Note that the court in *Canterbury v. Spence* did recognize a medical privilege to withhold collateral risk data. The court's discussion of this point is reprinted in the following subsection entitled "Exceptions to the duty to disclose."

4. What reasons led the *Canterbury* court to reject the majority rule, which measures the duty to disclose by prevailing medical practice? Was it concern that there is no professional consensus on the customary scope of disclosure in particular classes of cases? Is it reasonable to expect that professional standards would be developed in the course of litigation? Was the court more concerned that the majority rule requiring expert medical testimony to establish prevailing medical practices indirectly allows the medical profession to shape and limit the scope of disclosure?

5. *Canterbury* defines the breadth of required disclosure to include any risk which either singly or in combination with other risks would be deemed significant by the average patient in deciding whether to accept or forego the therapy. "Materiality" is the shorthand expression of this principle. Whether a particular risk or combination of risks was material in a given situation can be established by lay witnesses exclusively and, in all likelihood, will rest largely if not exclusively on the plaintiff's testimony that a particular risk would have been material to his decision. To what extent does this approach invite intentional or unintentional fabrication by the plaintiff? Does the *Canterbury* approach leave the possibility of therapist liability wide open and expose a professional to incalculable and unknown risks of liability? Does a standard that adopts a layman's definition of materiality give professionals adequate notice of what disclosure the law demands.

6. Courts choosing among the various standards seek to find an appropriate balance between competing interests. There is, on the one hand, the interest of the patient to obtain all information necessary for a meaningful decision on the proposed therapy. In addition, the medical and other treating professions have an interest in carrying out their professional functions efficiently and with a minimum of open-ended risk of liability. The looser or more uncertain the legal standard, the more difficult it becomes for professionals to adhere to a standard of conduct that will eliminate the risk of liability. And, finally, there is also a broader societal interest in maximizing access to needed professional

services, which means, of course, that the cost of these services must be reasonable. As experience with malpractice shows, the greater the liability exposure of a profession, the higher the cost of malpractice insurance; higher premiums are in turn reflected in the fee structure and the costs of medical services. Does the majority rule outlined in *Aiken* or the minority rule of *Canterbury* better reconcile these competing interests?

7. To what extent does either the majority or minority view require disclosure of additional alternative therapies? Could a therapist be held liable if he has disclosed all collateral risks of the proposed therapy but has failed to point out alternatives? Does either case speak to this point?

8. What is the therapist's liability for non-disclosure of risk data not known by him? In the instance of established therapies, as distinguished from experimental therapies (which are considered separately in a following section), the therapist has a duty to disclose only those risks known to him or that are generally known by a reasonably proficient practitioner. The *Canterbury* court defined this rule in the following terms:

> The category of risks which the physician should communicate is, of course, no broader than the complement [*sic*] he could communicate. The duty to divulge may extend to any risk he actually knows, but he obviously cannot divulge any of which he may be unaware.

464 F.2d 772, 787 n. 84 (D.C.Cir.1972).

However, if the therapist is unaware of risks that are generally known by practitioners in the field, non-disclosure could give rise to a claim based on negligence. As noted by the court in *Canterbury:*

> Nondisclosure of an unknown risk does not, strictly speaking, present a problem in terms of the duty to disclose although it very well might pose problems in terms of the physician's duties to have known of it and to have acted accordingly.

Id.

9. Is it possible that the materiality of the risk might change over period of time? For instance, the side effects of a particular medical drug may not be discovered until the drug has been in use for several years. When initially prescribed, the actual risks may have been unknown or perceived as less severe. To what extent does the *Canterbury* approach invite a court to gauge materiality by the state of knowledge prevailing at the time of trial rather than at the time of treatment? Would the *Aiken* requirement of expert testimony lessen this risk?

10. The doctrine of informed consent under either the majority or minority approach poses particular problems for the adjudicatory process. In medical malpractice, resolution of the case requires the trier of fact to assess the *conduct* or actions of the therapist. Liability will attach when the actions fall below normal professional standards. In an informed consent case, however, the therapist's performance is not an issue. In fact, liability can attach even if the defendant acted with

optimum skill and proficiency. Resolution of the case depends entirely on whether disclosure of information was sufficient.

When the parties agree on what was communicated, all that must be adjudicated is whether this quantum of information was sufficient. Not infrequently, however, the extent of disclosure will be disputed by the parties. In this situation, the trier of fact must decide what the therapist in fact disclosed by weighing the credibility of the respective parties. Once the factual questions have been resolved, application of the governing legal standard will produce the verdict. This initial stage of fact determination imposes particular stresses on the adjudicatory system. Unless the disclosure has been reduced to writing, the only evidence available is the parties' conflicting testimony. Quite apart from the risk of intentional distortion, there is the possibility of inadvertent distortion, since a witness may be required to recollect the substance of verbal communication that took place several years earlier. In other areas of the law, where the communications between the parties form the cornerstone of the claim, the legal system has adopted special rules to guard against inaccurate recollection of facts. For instance, most contracts involving substantial claims cannot be enforced unless the terms have been reduced to writing.

Can therapists protect themselves against claims based on faulty patient recollection of what was disclosed? Is it feasible to make audio recordings of risk disclosure sessions? How long should the recordings be kept? Alternatively, is it feasible to reduce to writing a description of the risks of therapy and require the patient to read and sign such document? What problems is this procedure likely to produce? These issues are considered in greater detail in subsection *C.2. infra.*

11. To date, the only forms of psychiatric treatment that have engendered litigation based on the patient's lack of informed consent have involved insulin-coma and electro-convulsive therapy. (*See, e.g., Woods v. Brumlop,* 71 N.M. 221, 377 P.2d 520 (1962): *Mitchell v. Robinson,* 334 S.W.2d 11 (Mo.1960)). Why have there not been more reported cases involving the nonintrusive forms of psychotherapy? Is it because psychotherapy does not involve collateral risks of *physical* injury proximately related to the treatment? Or is it because the risks of treatment are generally unknown even to the therapist, and it would be unreasonable to impose a duty of disclosure under these circumstances?

12. As noted previously, to date there have been no reported cases imposing liability on a psychotherapist on grounds of informed consent where conventional verbal psychotherapy techniques were used. This result is undoubtedly explained in large part by the evidentiary problems which would confront any patient-plaintiff. Putting aside these practical difficulties are there not numerous situations in everyday practice which at least technically violate the rights of the patient to informed consent? To what extent would the doctrine of informed consent require disclosure in the following situations?

(a) There is a substantial body of expert opinion that long-term outpatient psychotherapy involves a significant risk of "negative effects." *See* Hadley and Strupp, *Contemporary Views of Negative*

Effects in Psychotherapy, 33 Archives of General Psychiatry 1291 (1976). Is there any obligation on the part of the therapist to disclose the risks of the potentially negative effects prior to the commencement of a prolonged course of treatment?

(b) In some instances a patient who is close to decomposition may not tolerate intense psychoanalysis. In these cases the risk is that the analysis will, in fact, trigger decomposition. Must this risk be communicated when, in the analyst's view, there is any reasonable possibility that the analysis will result in decomposition?

(c) An established novelist has for some time suffered from intermittent bouts of anxiety and occasional episodes of depression. The novelist consults an analyst to explore the possibilities of treatment. At the initial interview the patient expresses some fear that successful treatment might detract from or at least reduce his creative abilities. In response to a direct question as to the risks of therapy the therapist answers: "To the extent that your creativity is the result of neurosis, there may be some loss, but your true creativity will be enhanced by the removal of neurotic blocks, inhibitions, and distortions." Would this reply constitute a sufficient disclosure of the risks inherent in therapy? *See* Jonus B. Robitscher, *The Powers of Psychiatry* (Boston: Houghton Mifflin, 1980).

2. *Exceptions to the Duty to Disclose*

CANTERBURY v. SPENCE

United States Court of Appeals, District of Columbia Circuit, 1972.
464 F.2d 772.

(The main body of the opinion is set out in the preceding Section.)

VI

Two exceptions to the general rule of disclosure have been noted by the courts. Each is in the nature of a physician's privilege not to disclose, and the reasoning underlying them is appealing. Each, indeed, is but a recognition that, as important as is the patient's right to know, it is greatly outweighed by the magnitudinous circumstances giving rise to the privilege. The first comes into play when the patient is unconscious or otherwise incapable of consenting, and harm from a failure to treat is imminent and outweighs any harm threatened by the proposed treatment. When a genuine emergency of that sort arises, it is settled that the impracticality of conferring with the patient dispenses with need for it. Even in situations of that character the physician should, as current law requires, attempt to secure a relative's consent if possible. But if time is too short to accommodate discussion, obviously the physician should proceed with the treatment.

The second exception obtains when risk-disclosure poses such a threat of detriment to the patient as to become unfeasible or contraindicated from a medical point of view. It is recognized that patients occasionally become so ill or emotionally distraught on disclosure as to foreclose a rational decision, or complicate or hinder the treatment, or perhaps even pose psychological damage to the patient. Where that is so, the cases have generally held that the physician is armed with a privilege to keep the information from the patient, and we think it clear that portents of that type may justify the physician in action he deems medically warranted. The critical inquiry is whether the physician responded to a sound medical judgment that communication of the risk information would present a threat to the patient's well-being.

The physician's privilege to withhold information for therapeutic reasons must be carefully circumscribed, however, for otherwise it might devour the disclosure rule itself. The privilege does not accept the paternalistic notion that the physician may remain silent simply because divulgence might prompt the patient to forego therapy the physician feels the patient really needs. That attitude presumes instability or perversity for even the normal patient, and runs counter to the foundation principle that the patient should and ordinarily can make the choice for himself. Nor does the privilege contemplate operation save where the patient's reaction to risk information, as reasonably foreseen by the physician, is menacing. And even in a situation of that kind, disclosure to a close relative with a view to securing consent to the proposed treatment may be the only alternative open to the physician.

Questions and Comments

1. In its recognition of the limitation exception to a therapist's duty to disclose, the court in *Canterbury v. Spence* adhered to the rule applicable in virtually all jurisdictions that have adopted the doctrine of informed consent. As the opinion clarifies, however, the exception is limited; it does not permit the therapist to remain silent "simply because the divulgence might prompt the patient to forego therapy the physician feels the patient really needs."

Presumably, non-disclosure is justified in three instances: first, where disclosure is likely to cause the patient to become so "ill or emotionally distraught" as to "foreclose a rational decision"; second, where the disclosure will "complicate or hinder the treatment"; and third, where the disclosure will result in "psychological damage to the patient." Unhappily, the *Canterbury* court, like other courts that have dealt with the exception, failed to provide much guidance as to the scope of the exception.

2. A minority of courts have also allowed the privilege of non-disclosure "where an explanation of every risk attendant upon a treatment procedure may well result in alarming a patient who is already apprehensive and who may, as a result, refuse to undertake surgery or treatment in which there is minimal risk * * *" *Woods v. Brumlop,* 71 N.M. 221, 228, 377 P.2d 520, 525 (1962). Can an exception explained in these terms be applied without devouring the disclosure rule itself?

3. Does the privilege to withhold information also allow a therapist to misrepresent the nature of the treatment or diagnosis to an emotional-

ly disturbed patient in order to induce the patient to undergo needed therapy? In a somewhat unusual case of *Kraus v. Spielberg*, 37 Misc.2d 519, 236 N.Y.S.2d 143 (1962), the plaintiff, who had a tuberculosis phobia, consulted a physician because of acute stomach pains. To induce the patient to agree to chemotherapy treatment, the therapist led the plaintiff to believe that the tuberculous germs had spread to her stomach. In fact, however, the doctor had not verified the exact location of the tubercular condition. The plaintiff consented to the therapy and later suffered unpleasant side effects. Finding that the misrepresentation was necessary to induce the plaintiff to undergo needed treatment, the court held for the defendant-therapist. Is it likely that the case would be decided the same way today in jurisdictions recognizing the doctrine of informed consent?

4. The rule permitting non-disclosure of risks appears to have particular relevance when the patient is mentally ill. Assume the following situation: A psychiatrically hospitalized patient, suffering from a number of phobias and delusions, believes that death will inevitably follow any prolonged period of impotency. In addition to the psychiatric disorder, the patient also suffers from high blood pressure. A commonly used drug for the treatment of high blood pressure is inderal. One of the possible but unlikely side effects of this drug is impotency. Would the treating physician be justified in prescribing inderal without disclosing to the patient the risk of impotency?

5. Clearly the rule set forth in *Canterbury*, which permits non-disclosure where the disclosure may cause the patient to become "so ill or emotionally distraught on disclosure as to foreclose a rational decision or complicate or hinder treatment or even pose psychological damage to the patient", poses problems of interpretation. For instance, what degree of psychological damage justifies non-disclosure? Would the risk of moderate to severe depression be a sufficient justification? Alternatively, would anticipation of a severe but transient anxiety reaction justify nondisclosure?

The *Canterbury* exception also includes those situations in which disclosure would cause the patient to become so ill or emotionally distraught as to foreclose a rational decision. Again, what degree of irrationality will justify non-disclosure? Keep in mind that if the matter were litigated, the defendant-therapist would have the burden of establishing that the patient's condition justified the non-disclosure. How difficult would this be if the matter is litigated two or even three years later and the patient no longer exhibits the mental disabilities he did at the time of treatment?

The California Supreme Court has articulated the medical disclosure exception in somewhat different terms. In *Cobbs v. Grant*, 8 Cal.3d 229, 104 Cal.Rptr. 505, 502 P.2d 1 (1972) the court observed that

> A disclosure need not be made beyond that required within the medical community when a doctor can prove by a preponderance of the evidence he relied upon facts which would demonstrate to a reasonable man the disclosure would have so seriously upset the

patient that the patient would not have been able to dispassionately weigh the risks of refusing to undergo the recommended treatment. *Id.* at 516.

6. Can a patient waive his right to be informed, and can the therapist rely on such waiver? This issue has not been conclusively resolved; however, the California Supreme Court has stated in *dictum:*

> "[A] medical doctor need not make disclosure of risks when the patient requests that he not be informed."

Cobbs v. Grant, 8 Cal.3d 229, 104 Cal.Rptr. 505, 516, 502 P.2d 1, 12 (1972).

B. OTHER ELEMENTS NECESSARY TO ESTABLISH A CLAIM

1. *Causation*

Mere non-disclosure of a risk is not sufficient to impose liability on the therapist. Liability results only if an *injury* occurs that would not have occurred *but for* the non-disclosure. Thus, a patient must prove that if the risk of injury been disclosed, he would not have consented to the therapy that resulted in the injury. "Causation" is the shorthand legal term used to describe the relationship that must exist between the breach of duty (non-disclosure of a material fact) and the resulting injury. The following materials describe more fully the concept of causation as it applies to informed consent.

AIKEN v. CLARY
Supreme Court of Missouri, 1965.
396 S.W.2d 668.

(The main body of the opinion is set forth in the preceding Section.)

Finally, defendant contends that plaintiff did not make a submissible case in the absence of proof that plaintiff would not have consented to the insulin shock therapy if he had been informed adequately of the risks involved. Such testimony is not required, and this contention is overruled. Such a requirement would make recovery impossible in the case of a patient who died or, as here, was unable to testify. This does not mean, however, that plaintiff is not required to establish a causal connection between the doctor's failure sufficiently to inform and the injury for which recovery is sought. The matter of causation still must be submitted to the jury. Obviously, if the jury was convinced from all the evidence that a more complete disclosure would have made no difference to plaintiff, and that he still would have consented to the therapy or procedure, then plaintiff has not established a right of recovery. For example, if the evidence was that the plaintiff was about to die and chances for survival were one out of ten, a jury might well conclude that a more complete disclosure of hazards involved in an operation would have made no difference to plaintiff in deciding whether to consent to an operation which, if successful, would make his survival reasonably likely. On the other hand, a jury could find from all the facts and circumstances in a particular case that had plaintiff been properly informed he would not have consented to the treatment, and this is so even though plaintiff does not specifically so testify.

Questions and Comments

1. Causation must be distinguished from the element of materiality. Material risks, as noted previously, are those to which the patient is "likely to attach significance * * * in deciding whether or not to forego the proposed therapy." *Canterbury v. Spence*, 464 F.2d 772, 787 (D.C.Cir.1972). Not all material risks, of course, would prompt a patient to refuse therapy. In such a case, disclosure would be irrelevant to the patient's final decision. Waltz and Schoneman provide an example of this distinction: "(I)t would be reasonable to conclude that a patient who required brain surgery to survive would not have refused it even had he known of an undisclosed risk of speech impediment. At the same time the risk of a speech impediment could well be deemed to constitute nondisclosure of a material fact". Waltz and Schoneman, *Informed Consent to Therapy*, 64 Nw.U.L.Rev. 628, 648 (1970).

2. As discussed above, the element of causation requires the fact-finder to determine whether the plaintiff would have foregone the therapy if he had been informed of the risk that actually materialized. In resolving his question, the fact-finder must decide how an individual would have acted under a hypothetical set of circumstances. Obviously, any decision of this type is at best an educated guess.

Basically two approaches can be used to determine causation. In one, the fact-finder focuses on the particular plaintiff and determines whether that individual would have foregone the therapy if the risk had been disclosed. This "subjective" approach focuses on the plaintiff's testimony. Thus, the plaintiff generally would prove causation by testifying that he would have foregone a particular therapy if he had been aware of the risk that eventually materialized. Of key importance here is the plaintiff's credibility as judged by the fact-finder.

Alternatively, under the "objective" approach, the causation issue is posed not in terms of the particular plaintiff, but in terms of the effect that nondisclosure of a material risk would have on a reasonable person in plaintiff's position. While the plaintiff's testimony is still relevant, it is less influential; the issue is how a reasonable person in plaintiff's position—rather than the plaintiff himself—would have acted when faced with the disclosure risk. Undoubtedly, the outcome of informed consent cases is very much influenced by the court's choice of approach. Under the subjective approach causation is much less likely to be a barrier to recovery; consequently, the plaintiff has a greater chance of recovery than under the objective approach. The cases that follow explore in greater detail the respective merits of these two approaches to proof of causation.

CANTERBURY v. SPENCE

United States Court of Appeals, District of Columbia Circuit, 1972.
464 F.2d 772.

[The main body of the opinion is set forth at p. 148 *supra*].

A causal connection exists when, but only when, disclosure of significant risks incidental to treatment would have resulted in a decision against it. The patient obviously has no complaint if he would have submitted to the therapy notwithstanding awareness that the risk was one of its perils. On the other hand, the very purpose of the disclosure rule is to protect the patient against consequences which, if known, he would have avoided by foregoing the treatment. The more difficult question is whether the factual issue on causality calls for an objective or a subjective determination.

It has been assumed that the issue is to be resolved according to whether the factfinder believes the patient's testimony that he would not have agreed to the treatment if he had known of the danger which later ripened into injury. We think a technique which ties the factual conclusion on causation simply to the assessment of the patient's credibility is unsatisfactory.

*   *   *

[W]hen causality is explored at a post-injury trial with a professedly uninformed patient, the question whether he actually would have turned the treatment down if he had known the risks is purely hypothetical: "Viewed from the point at which he had to decide, would the patient have decided differently had he known something he did not know?" And the answer which the patient supplies hardly represents more than a guess, perhaps tinged by the circumstance that the uncommunicated hazard has in fact materialized.

In our view, this method of dealing with the issue on causation comes in second-best. It places the physician in jeopardy of the patient's hindsight and bitterness. It places the factfinder in the position of deciding whether a speculative answer to a hypothetical question is to be credited. It calls for a subjective determination solely on testimony of a patient-witness shadowed by the occurrence of the undisclosed risk.

Better it is, we believe, to resolve the causality issue on an objective basis: in terms of what a prudent person in the patient's position would have decided if suitably informed of all perils bearing significance. If adequate disclosure could reasonably be expected to have caused that person to decline the treatment because of the revelation of the kind of risk or danger that resulted in harm, causation is shown, but otherwise not. The patient's testimony is relevant on that score of course but it would not threaten to dominate the findings.

*   *   *

SCOTT v. BRADFORD

Supreme Court of Oklahoma, 1979
606 P.2d 554

DOOLIN, Justice:

This appeal is taken by plaintiffs in trial below, from a judgment in favor of defendant rendered on a jury verdict in a medical malpractice action.

Mrs. Scott's physician advised her she had several fibroid tumors on her uterus. He referred her to defendant surgeon. Defendant admitted her to the hospital where she signed a routine consent form prior to defendant's performing a hysterectomy. After surgery, Mrs. Scott experienced problems with incontinence. She visited another physician who discovered she had a vesico-vaginal fistula which permitted urine to leak from her bladder into the vagina. This physician referred her to an urologist who, after three surgeries, succeeded in correcting her problems.

Mrs. Scott, joined by her husband, filed the present action alleging medical malpractice, claiming defendant failed to advise her of the risks involved or of available alternatives to surgery. She further maintained had she been properly informed she would have refused the surgery.

The case was submitted to the jury with instructions to which plaintiffs objected. The jury found for defendant and plaintiffs appeal.

*   *   *

The cause of action, based on lack of informed consent, is divided into three elements: the duty to inform being the first, the second is causation, and the third is injury. The second element, that of causation, requires that plaintiff patient would have chosen no treatment or a different course of treatment had the alternatives and material risks of each been made known to him. If the patient would have elected to proceed with treatment had he been duly informed of its risks, then the element of causation is missing. In other words, a causal connection exists between physician's breach of the duty to disclose and patient's injury when and only when disclosure of material risks incidental to treatment would have resulted in a decision against it. A patient obviously has no complaint if he would have submitted to the treatment if the physician had complied with his duty and informed him of the risks. This fact decision raises the difficult question of the correct standard on which to instruct the jury.

The court in *Canterbury v. Spence,* although emphasizing principles of self-determination permits liability only if non-disclosure would have affected the decision of a fictitious "reasonable patient," even though actual patient testifies he would have elected to forego therapy had he been fully informed.

Decisions discussing informed consent have emphasized the *disclosure* element but paid scant attention to the consent element of the concept, although this is the root of causation. Language in some decisions suggest the standard to be applied is a subjective one, i.e., whether that particular patient would still have consented to the treatment, reasonable choice or otherwise.

Although the *Canterbury* rule is probably that of the majority, its "reasonable man" approach has been criticized by some commentators as backtracking on its own theory of self-determination. The *Canterbury* view certainly severely limits the protection granted an injured patient. To the extent the plaintiff, given an adequate disclosure, would have declined the proposed treatment, and a reasonable person in similar circumstances would have consented, a patient's right of self-determination is *irrevocably lost*. This basic right to know and decide is the reason for the full-disclosure rule. Accordingly, we decline to jeopardize this right by the imposition of the "reasonable man" standard.

If a plaintiff testifies he would have continued with the proposed treatment had he been adequately informed, the trial is over under either the subjective or objective approach. If he testifies he would not, then the causation problem must be resolved by examining the credibility of plaintiff's testimony. The jury must be instructed that it must find plaintiff would have refused the treatment if he is to prevail.

Although it might be said this approach places a physician at the mercy of a patient's hindsight, a careful practitioner can always protect himself by insuring that he has adequately informed each patient he treats. If he does not breach this duty, a causation problem will not arise.

* * *

Because we are imposing a new duty on physicians, we hereby make this opinion prospective only, affecting those causes of action arising after the date this opinion is promulgated.

* * *

We find no basis for reversal.

Affirmed.

2. *Damages*

The previous section pointed out that a successful plaintiff must prove that a material risk of the therapy was not disclosed and that a reasonable person in the plaintiff's position would not have consented to the therapy had the risk been disclosed. What remains to be considered is the measure of damages applicable to this type of case. While few cases have addressed this question, it has generally been assumed that a successful plaintiff is entitled to damages to compensate for the loss or injury resulting from the risk that materialized. Thus, the measure of damages is generally the same as in a malpractice case. It has been argued that this rule is unduly harsh from the therapist's perspective and that the recovery should be reduced by an amount attributable to whatever injury or loss would have occurred if no therapy had been undertaken or if an alternative therapy had been adopted. Thus, under this view, if the plaintiff inevitably would have suffered physical deterioration if he had received no therapy whatsoever, that factor would reduce the amount of damages he can recover.

These general rules of damages may vary somewhat in the few jurisdictions that treat the doctrine of informed consent as a variant of an action in assault and battery. In those jurisdictions, because the basis of the claim is an "unauthorized touching," the therapist can be liable for monetary damages even if the plaintiff suffered no actual injury. Also, since battery is viewed as an intentional tort, the defendant can be assessed punitive or exemplary damages. However, most courts would not impose exemplary damages unless the physician was guilty of actual malice.

It is important to note that prevailing rules on damages significantly limit the impact of the doctrine of informed consent. Unless some *physical injury* results from the treatment, it is unlikely that a patient can recover anything more than nominal damages. Under the present state of the law, mental distress, fright, shock, humiliation, or similar violations of psychological integrity do not ordinarily constitute compensable injuries unless accompanied by physical impact. Thus, at least for the present, the doctrine of informed consent is limited to those professions that use treatment methods capable of inflicting physical harm. As a result, conventional psychotherapists, unless they also use treatment modalities such as drugs, which have the potential of inflicting physical harm, are relatively immune from liability. Undoubtedly, this explains in large part the total absence of reported cases against psychotherapists for failure to secure the patient's informed consent. It also explains why behavioral science researchers, in spite of numerous reported violations of the requirements of informed consent, have escaped liability. However, the trend is clearly toward recognition of psychological harm as a sufficient basis for the recovery of monetary damages even when not associated with any physical injury. With these considerations in mind consider the following hypothetical fact situation:

> A patient consults a psychotherapist to overcome his flying phobia, which in view of his occupational need to travel is proving to be an increasing handicap to his professional advancement. The therapist agrees to treat the patient, and over a period of the next three months gives him a series of desensitization procedures coupled with hypnotherapy.

The patient is informed that he has made material progress and the next step is to take a short flight. The patient is not alerted to the possibility that he will feel great anxiety during the flight. In fact, the therapist assures him that he is entirely ready to take the next step. Pursuant to the therapist's recommendations, the patient secures a ticket and boards an airline flight to the next city. Shortly after takeoff, in spite of the patient's use of a tape-recorder designed to facilitate self-hypnosis, the patient experiences a severe anxiety attack. By the time the airplane lands 30 minutes later, the patient is in a state of total collapse. He is taken by ambulance to the nearest hospital and is placed under sedation. Upon release a week later, the patient remains in a highly agitated and anxious state, which is accompanied by insomnia. As a result of this condition he is absent from work for the next three weeks. Upon his return to work, he learns that during his absence he was considered but rejected for a promotion, on the grounds that his records indicated that he had health problems. Badly shaken by the experience and somewhat angry at the therapist for having encouraged him to take the flight, he consults an attorney to inquire whether he has any basis to sue the therapist.

Encouragement rather than assurances [handwritten marginalia]

What is the attorney likely to advise? Would the result be different in a jurisdiction which requires physical injury?

C. ISSUES PERTAINING TO PATIENT ACKNOWLEDGMENT AND UNDERSTANDING

1. Introduction

In its original form, legally sufficient consent required nothing more than patient assent to the proposed treatment. Failure to obtain consent subjected the therapist to liability for assault and battery. The modern doctrine, on the other hand, requires that the consent be an *informed* one.

The elements of informed consent are twofold. First, the therapist must disclose information pertaining to the risks of the proposed therapy. Second, as under the original doctrine, the patient must agree to undergo the therapy. In law the agreement that the patient must give to authorize the therapist to start the therapy is known as consent.

Two types of problems arise in connection with the element of consent or agreement. One pertains to the evidentiary requirements imposed by the legal system. In other words, what actions or expressions on the part of the patient will suffice to establish consent? A second and more complex problem relates to the level of patient understanding that must accompany the consent or agreement. More specifically, does the legal system require that the patient understand the nature and degree of risk that was disclosed? If so, can the requisite level of understanding be presumed, or must the therapist establish its existence? These interrelated issues are explained in the materials that follow.

Both legal opinions and the writings of legal commentators have advanced the view that "[t]o establish consent to a risk it must be shown that the patient was aware of the risk and assented to the encountering of it". Jon R. Waltz and Fred E. Inbau, *Medical Jurisprudence* (New York: Macmillan, 1971), p. 164. What these assertions leave unanswered, however, is whether the patient must have actual rather than imputed knowledge. Consider for a moment the legal efficacy of a consent given by a patient who has been fully informed of all risks and alternatives but who, unknown to the physician, fails to adequately understand the information he has received. Two different approaches can be followed in dealing with this problem.

One alternative focuses on the therapist's disclosure. If that disclosure is deemed adequate, in the sense that an ordinary patient would comprehend the information transmitted, awareness will be imputed without regard to the patient-plaintiff's *actual level of comprehension*. It is this approach that the *Canterbury v. Spence* court advocated. In a footnote, the court observed that "the physician discharges the duty when he makes a reasonable effort to convey sufficient information *although the patient, without fault of the physician, may not fully grasp it*". 464 F.2d 772, 780 n. 15 (D.C.Cir.1972) [Emphasis added]. Thus, under this approach, the therapist has discharged his duty when he has made full disclosure in terms that would be comprehensible to the average patient.

Under the other approach, a patient's consent would not be effective unless he had *actual* knowledge and understanding of the therapist's disclosure. In the event of litigation, then, the fact-finder would be required to determine whether the *particular* patient-plaintiff had understood what the therapist had told him. One commentator has explained the rationale for this approach:

> Even when the information presented is adequate, therefore, the consenting process may be nothing more than a "ritual" if the patient-subject remains "uneducated and uncomprehending." To avoid this result, the physician could be held responsible for taking reasonable steps to ascertain whether the information presented has been understood, so that if it has not he may supplement it as needed or may convey the same information in a manner more comprehensible to the particular patient.

Capron, *Informed Consent in Catastrophic Disease Research and Treatment* 123 U.Pa.L.Rev. 340, 414 (1974).

The weight of legal opinion has, however, rejected the "subjective" approach on a variety of grounds. As Waltz and Inbau have observed:

> One difficulty with this view is that the patient's testimony, undeniably admissible at trial, in fact controls the issue of consent. And the

trial lawyer's healthy cynicism tells him that a claimant's testimony is sometimes susceptible to modification based upon hindsight. Another difficulty is that it leaves no room for reasonable communication or interpretation mistakes by the physician; he assumes the risk of incorrectly concluding that the patient in fact understood and assented to the risks communicated. As the entire history of contract law attests, legal relationships based on communication cannot practicably be made to depend on the vagaries of the parties' subjective intent.

John Waltz and Fred Inbau, *Medical Jurisprudence* (New York: Macmillan Co., 1971), p. 165.

Question and Comment

As a practical matter, the question whether the patient's awareness should be measured objectively or subjectively has only rarely arisen in modern informed consent cases. The reasons for this are twofold. First, modern cases have emphasized the element of disclosure. To the extent that the physician fails to inform the patient adequately, the question of awareness is typically never reached, since the case can be disposed of on that ground. Thus, the scope of patient awareness would only be an issue if the fact-finder determined that the therapist had given adequate disclosure, and the patient contended that he did not understand its content. Cases based on this type of contention are, however, very hard to win, which at least in part explains their absence. Moreover, a patient's case would be weakened by the dual contentions that there was insufficient disclosure and that he lacked awareness because he did not understand what was disclosed. While these are not necessarily inconsistent positions, the plaintiff's lawyer would be concerned that emphasis on the patient's lack of comprehension might buttress the defendant's contentions that there was full disclosure and that the patient, through no fault of the therapist, failed to understand what was said.

2.　The Determination of Patient Assent: Evidentiary Problems

As has been noted, consent consists of the dual ingredients of awareness and assent. To establish consent to a risk it must be shown that the patient is made aware of the risk and knowingly assented to the treatment. Thus, in the event of litigation, the fact-finder must determine whether the patient's expressions in their totality (both verbal and nonverbal) support the conclusion that he assented to the treatment. The test is an objective one; intent is gauged by what is known as the reasonable person standard. Under this test the question is whether a reasonable therapist would have concluded from the patient's statements and behavior that the patient was aware of the risks that had been communicated and that he had manifested a willingness to undergo the therapy or procedure. Any other approach would, of course, subject the therapist to the unreasonable risk that a patient who manifests assent could subsequently deny it on the basis of unexpressed mental reservations.

When divorced from the question of knowledge, however, the element of assent is not likely to be an issue. The mere fact that the patient had some interaction with the therapist generally establishes assent to at least some form of treatment. But the issue is likely to be much broader. The crucial question for the fact-finder is usually not whether there was assent in the narrow sense, but whether the assent was coupled with sufficient knowledge and awareness. As might be expected, this factual determination poses problems of an evidentiary nature. Most commonly, an informed consent case will, if litigated, turn at least in part on the credibility of the parties to the action. The patient will contend that because of inadequate disclosure, he was not made aware of the risks of the treatment. The therapist, on the other hand, may have a substantially different recollection of what was disclosed. To lower the risk of erroneous recollection, a therapist would be wise to keep a written summary of the information communicated to the patient and a written record of a patient's consent.

Questions and Comments

1. What are the implications of various studies showing that within a relatively short period of time patients frequently lose recall of much of the medical data disclosed during the consent obtaining process. In one study which involved 200 cancer patients, it was found, for instance, that one day after receiving relevant information on the risks of chemotherapy, "[O]nly 60 per cent understood the purpose and the nature of the procedure, and only 55 per cent correctly listed even one major risk or complication." Cassileth, Zupkis, Sutton-Smith, and March, "Informed Consent—Why Are Its Goals Imperfectly Realized?" 302 New. Eng.J.Med. 896 (1980). *See also* Epstein and Lasagna, "Obtaining Informed Consent: Form or Substance?," 123 Arch Inter.Med. 682 (1969); Schultz, Pardee, Ensinck, "Are Research Subjects Really Informed?," 123 West.J.Med. 76 (1975).

Do studies such as the one described above call into question the overall utility of the informed consent doctrine? Do they at least point to the need for those providing treatment to maintain adequate records evidencing the disclosures made to the patient?

2. A number of states have enacted statutes that spell out the evidentiary requirement for informed consent to medical or surgical procedures. Typically, these statutes require that the attending physician provide the patient with a document that sets forth the procedures of treatment to be undertaken and the major risks. At the same time, they require that the patient sign a document acknowledging that the disclosure of information has been made and that all of his questions pertaining to the treatment have been answered. In turn, the fulfillment of these documentary requirements constitutes either *prima facia* or

conclusive evidence that informed consent to treatment has been given. The Iowa statute illustrates this approach to proof of informed consent:

> A consent in writing to any medical or surgical procedure or course of procedures in patient care which meets the requirements of this section shall create a presumption that informed consent was given. A consent in writing meets the requirements of this section if it:
>
> 1. Sets forth in general terms the nature and purpose of the procedure or procedures, together with the known risks, if any, of death, brain damage, quadriplegia, paraplegia, the loss or loss of function of any organ or limb, or disfiguring scars associated with such procedure or procedures, with the probability of each such risk if reasonably determinable.
>
> 2. Acknowledges that the disclosure of that information has been made and that all questions asked about the procedure or procedures have been answered in a satisfactory manner.
>
> 3. Is signed by the patient for whom the procedure is to be performed, or if the patient for any reason lacks legal capacity to consent, is signed by a person who has legal authority to consent on behalf of that patient in those circumstances.

Iowa Code Ann. § 147.137 (Supp.1977).

Note that the Iowa Statute only requires disclosure of certain major risks that are itemized in Section 1 of the Statute. Also, note that the statute does not require any information on alternative treatment.

In those states with statutes regulating informed consent, the question of legislative preemption arises. A court in one of those states may have to determine whether the legislature has preempted the entire area or whether there is room for judicially developed remedies to supplement the statutory provisions.

3. Is it possible for a patient who has signed a form that exhaustively lists the risks and hazards of the therapy to contend that although he signed the form he did not, in fact, understand its content? The answer to this question would presumably turn on whether under the law of the state controlling the disposition of the case, the signing of a statement is *conclusive* evidence of informed consent on the part of the patient. If it is only *prima facie* evidence, the patient's signature on a consent form would not preclude the contention that he was not, in fact, adequately informed. This suggests that for maximum protection the therapist should do more than obtain the patient's written consent on a form that recites the significant risks. In addition, the therapist should verbally explain the risks and alternatives and then enter a notation in the patient's file recounting the general nature of the conversation.

4. Note that standardized consent forms that merely recite that the patient has been informed of "all risks" are likely to be of little legal protection. Valid consent requires disclosure of the specific risks and available alternative therapy.

Therefore, a summary consent form merely attesting that "all risks" have been communicated will not foreclose the admission of evidence that there was not, in fact, a sufficient disclosure. Not surprisingly, fairly detailed standardized consent forms are becoming more frequent. Illustrative of the standardized forms that have been developed is the one set out below for obtaining consent to electroshock therapy (ECT).

CONSENT TO ELECTRIC SHOCK THERAPY

A.M.
Date _____ Time _____ P.M.

1. I authorize Dr. _____, and assistants of his choice, to administer electric shock treatment, and relaxant drugs and other medication, to _____ and to continue
(name of patient)
such treatment at such intervals as he and his assistants may deem advisable.

2. I understand that this treatment consists of passing a controlled electric current between two electrodes applied to the patient's temples. In some instances, the patient may be given medication prior to treatment to reduce tension and produce muscular relaxation. I understand that the patient will not feel the electric current and will feel no pain. When the electric current is administered, the patient becomes unconscious and has strong convulsive muscular contractions which may last from 35 to 50 seconds. The patient gradually regains consciousness and his confusion clears within 15 to 60 minutes. The patient may experience headache and nausea.

3. I understand that the treatments may cause temporary confusion and memory impairment. I also understand that certain risks and complications are involved in the treatment. The most common risk is fracture and dislocation of the limbs and vertebrae. I acknowledge that these and other risks and complications of this procedure have been explained to me.

4. In addition to the foregoing, the strict care which will be required immediately following treatment and during convalescence has been fully explained to me.

5. The alternative methods of treatment have been explained and no guarantee or assurance has been given by anyone as to the results that may be obtained.

Signed _____

Witness_____

5. The right to consent implies the right to revoke any consent that has been given. Thus, a patient may withdraw his consent at any time before the treatment has been concluded. However, under the law of most states this principle does not apply to the consent given by a patient entering an institution through a voluntary admission procedure. Typically, laws governing admission to psychiatric facilities stipulate that a voluntary patient may be forcibly detained for a designated period even after he has withdrawn his voluntary admission consent. This problem is considered in greater detail in Chapter Five.

3. Impediments to Valid Consent: Coercion and Duress

Because the consent that the patient gives the therapist to authorize the treatment is an act having legal significance, it has attendant legal rights. There are, of course, numerous other instances in law where an individual's act establishes the responsibilities and rights of those who are a party to the transaction. Such is the case, for instance, in the law of contracts; an individual's acceptance of an offer creates a contract. In each instance some specific and intentional act has legal significance.

Because of the potentially far-reaching and important consequences that can attach, these legally significant acts will not be
given effect unless they are voluntary. In fact, the law has traditionally refused to recognize or enforce any legally significant act that is
the product of force or coercion. The reasons behind this principle
are grounded in basic notions of fairness. Enforcement of involuntary acts would both recognize the legitimacy of force and violence and
at the same time make the state a partner to the coercion.

While all are probably willing to accept a rule requiring consent to
be voluntary, there may be less agreement as to exactly what
conditions should render it involuntary. Unfortunately, the legal
literature is not very informative on this question, at least in the
context of consent to medical treatment. By what criteria then is the
voluntariness of consent to be judged? To some extent the answer
will depend on the particular model of behavior that one subscribes
to. One can, for instance, adopt a free-will model, which perceives
human behavior as the product of a free and autonomous will.
Involuntary actions result when the free will is overwhelmed by some
external force or pressure. An inquiry using this model will focus on
an abstraction known as the "ordinary or reasonable man" and
determine whether the pressures or forces exerted were of such
magnitude as to override the free will of the model person. While
this approach with its emphasis on free will may not accord with
modern behavioral science doctrines on the nature of man and the
psychic apparatus, it is a workable one. Unlike other models presently available, it provides a frame of reference that judges and juries
can use to decide specific cases in a manner generally acceptable to
the public.

The issue, then, for the trier of fact is whether a particular set of
circumstances was sufficiently coercive as to lead to the conclusion
that, but for such pressure, consent would have been withheld. In
making this decision, a judge or jury is likely to apply certain
commonly held presumptions. We are all prepared, for instance, to
assume that a decision reached at the point of a gun is likely to be
involuntary. But other forms of duress or coercion aside from the
threat of physical force may render the consent invalid. Even the
promise of a benefit or the threat to withhold some privilege may
constitute coercion under some circumstances. Certainly this would
be the case if consent to participation in a biomedical research project
were obtained from a prisoner serving an indeterminate sentence in
exchange for a promise of early release. Consent here is likely to be
viewed as coerced, not because the individual did not have an effective choice (as is the case when physical force is used or threatened),
but rather because the "bargain" was basically unfair. The finding
of unfairness here, of course, takes into account the particular
vulnerability of the consenting individual. The perceived unfairness
derives not so much from the inequality of the detriment in relation

to the benefit, but rather from the particular vulnerability of the person giving the consent. What is called for in every case of this type is basically a moral judgment that takes into account the benefit in relation to the detriment and more important, the overall vulnerability of the consenting individual. This, of course, suggests that not every beneficial promise made to a prisoner that induces consent is necessarily coercive, thus rendering the consent invalid. An agreement by prisoners to donate blood in exchange for reasonable remuneration would not necessarily be viewed as unfair and therefore coercive. But even this conclusion is being challenged; some critics contend that the overall control that the institution or staff is likely to exercise over a prisoner or patient is sufficient to call into question the voluntary nature of consent to any medical procedure that is not of direct therapeutic benefit to the consenting person. However, this absolutist position has not found general acceptance; these cases are still decided on their own particular facts.

Whatever the actual dynamics of patient decision-making in an institution, the legal system assumes that treatment decisions made by a competent patient are voluntary unless shown, upon adequate proof, to be otherwise. As is further developed in Chapter Six ("Involuntary Psychiatric Hospitalization"), *some* treatment decisions, particularly those pertaining to the treatment of psychiatric disorders, are not always subject to the informed consent requirement. The institution, either by statute or judicial interpretation, is permitted to administer certain treatments, such as psychotropic medication, to involuntarily hospitalized patients without the patient's consent. In the treatment of nonpsychiatric disorders of institutionalized patients, the requirement of informed consent prevails, at least when the patient is legally competent and his consent is presumed voluntary unless shown to be otherwise.

This general presumption, however, does not necessarily apply when the treatment is administered in the experimental or research context. As we will see, the use of experimental treatment procedures on institutionalized patient-subjects, particularly if the procedures are physically intrusive, raise unique problems in determining the voluntariness of the patients' informed consent. Nor is this problem an insignificant one. While it is difficult to arrive at a numerical estimate, it is undoubtedly true that institutionalized persons have for many years been one of the prime sources of experimental subjects. In fact, the bulk of biomedical psychiatric research has by and large been carried out on institutionalized patients. It is, therefore, somewhat surprising that these practices have engendered relatively little litigation to date. In fact, only one decision, *Kaimowitz v. Department of Mental Health,* has directly dealt with the issue of whether institutionalized persons have the capacity to give voluntary informed consent to intrusive experimental therapies. That decision, moreover, was only a trial court opinion; no appellate court has passed on the issues it sought to resolve. Nevertheless, the opinion is worth considering because it is the only decision that has come to grips with the extremely difficult questions underlying the application of any experimental procedures to institutionalized populations.

KAIMOWITZ v. DEPARTMENT OF MENTAL HEALTH FOR THE STATE OF MICHIGAN

Circuit Court for Wayne County, 1973.
Civil Action No. 73–19434–AW.

OPINION

This case came to this Court originally on a complaint for a Writ of Habeas Corpus brought by Plaintiff Kaimowitz on behalf of John Doe and the Medical Committee for Human Rights, alleging that John Doe was being illegally detained in the Lafayette Clinic for the purpose of experimental psychosurgery.

John Doe had been committed by the Kalamazoo County Circuit Court on January 11, 1955, to the Ionia State Hospital as a Criminal Sexual Psychopath, without a trial of criminal charges, under the terms of the then existing Criminal Sexual Psychopathic law. He had been charged with the murder and subsequent rape of a student nurse at the Kalamazoo State Hospital while he was confined there as a mental patient.

In 1972, Drs. Ernst Rodin and Jacques Gottlieb of the Lafayette Clinic, a facility of the Michigan Department of Mental Health, had filed a proposal "For the Study of Treatment of Uncontrollable Aggression.

This was funded by the Legislature of the State of Michigan for the fiscal year 1972. After more than 17 years at the Ionia State Hospital, John Doe was transferred to the Lafayette Clinic in November of 1972 as a suitable research subject for the Clinic's study of uncontrollable aggression.

Under the terms of the study, 24 criminal sexual psychopaths in the State's mental health system were to be subjects of experiment. The experiment was to compare the effects of surgery on the amygdaloid portion of the limbic system of the brain with the effect of the drug cyproterone acetate on the male hormone flow. The comparison was intended to show which, if either, could be used in controlling aggression of males in an institutional setting, and to afford lasting permanent relief from such aggression to the patient.

Substantial difficulties were encountered in locating a suitable patient population for the surgical procedures and a matched controlled group for the treatment by the anti-androgen drug. As a matter of fact, it was concluded that John Doe was the only known appropriate candidate available within the state mental health system for the surgical experiment.

The complete "Informed Consent" form signed by John Doe is as follows:

"Since conventional treatment efforts over a period of several years have not enabled me to control my outbursts of rage and anti-social behavior, I submit an application to be a subject in a research project which may offer me a form of effective therapy. This therapy is based upon the idea that episodes of anti-social rage and sexuality might be triggered by a disturbance in certain portions of my brain. I understand that in order to be certain that a significant brain disturbance exists, which might relate to my anti-social behavior, an initial operation will have to be performed. This procedure consists of placing fine wires into my brain, which will record the electrical activity from those structures which play a part in anger and sexuality. These electrical waves can then be studied to determine the presence of an abnormality.

"In addition electrical stimulation with weak currents passed through these wires will be done in order to find out if one or several points in the brain can trigger my episodes of violence or unlawful sexuality. In other words, this stimulation may cause me to want to commit an aggressive or sexual act, but every effort will be made to have a sufficient number of people present to control me. If the brain disturbance is limited to a small area, I understand that the investigators will destroy this part of my brain with an electrical current. If the abnormality comes from a larger part of my brain, I agree that it should be surgically removed, if the doctors determine that it can be done so, without risk of side effects. Should the electrical activity from the parts of my brain into which the wires have been placed reveal that there is no significant abnormality, the wires will simply be withdrawn.

"I realize that any operation on the brain carries a number of risks which may be slight but could be potentially serious. These risks include infection, bleeding, temporary or permanent weakness or paralysis of one or more of my legs or arms, difficulties with speech and thinking, as well as the ability to feel, touch, pain and temperature. Under extraordinary circumstances, it is also possible that I might not survive the operation.

"Fully aware of the risks detailed in the paragraphs above, I authorize the physicians of Lafayette Clinic and Providence Hospital to perform the procedures as outlined above.

October 27, 1972	/S/ Louis M. Smith
Date	Signature
Calvin Vanee	/S/ Emily T. Smith/Harry
	L. Smith
	Signature of responsible relative or guardian

John Doe signed an "informed consent" form to become an experimental subject prior to his transfer from the Ionia State Hospital. He had obtained signatures from his parents giving consent for the experimental and innovative surgical procedures to be performed on his brain, and two separate three-man review committees were established by Dr. Rodin to review the scientific worthiness of the study and the validity of the consent obtained from Doe.

[Following a review of the research protocol both committees approved the proposal.]

Even though no experimental subjects were found to be available in the state mental health system other than John Doe, Dr. Rodin prepared to proceed with the experiment on Doe, and depth electrodes were to be inserted into his brain on or about January 15, 1973.

Early in January, 1973, Plaintiff Kaimowitz, a legal services attorney, became aware of the work being contemplated on John Doe and made his concern known to the Detroit Free Press. Considerable newspaper publicity ensued and this action was filed shortly thereafter.

Upon the request of counsel, a Three-Judge Court was empanelled, * * * [and Counsel was appointed to represent John Doe].

With the rush of publicity on the filing of the original suit, funds for the research project were stopped by * * * the Department of Mental Health, and the investigators, Drs. Gottlieb and Rodin, dropped their plans to pursue the research set out in the proposal. They reaffirmed at trial, however, their belief in the scientific, medical and ethical soundness of the proposal.

Three ultimate issues were framed for consideration by the Court. The first related to the constitutionality of the detention of Doe. The full statement of the second and third questions, to which this Opinion is addressed, are set forth in the text below.

[At an initial hearing on March 23, 1973 the Court determined that the detention of John Doe was unconstitutional and ordered his release. Following this development the state contended that consideration of the other issue—whether the proposed surgical procedures could be carried out on a subject [sic] in Doe's former status was now moot. In holding that the case had not been mooted and was appropriate for a declaratory judgment the court advanced the view that "even though the original experimental program was terminated, there was nothing that would prevent it from being instituted again in the near future" * * *]

The two issues framed for decision in this declaratory judgment action are as follows:

1. After failure of established therapies, may an adult or a legally appointed guardian, if the adult is involuntarily detained, at a facility within the jurisdiction of the State Department of Mental

Health give legally adequate consent to an innovative or experimental surgical procedure on the brain, if there is demonstrable physical abnormality of the brain, and the procedure is designed to ameliorate behavior, which is either personally tormenting to the patient, or so profoundly disruptive that the patient cannot safely live, or live with others?

2.   If the answer to the above is yes, then is it legal in this State to undertake an innovative or experimental surgical procedure on the brain of an adult who is involuntarily detained at a facility within the jurisdiction of the State Department of Mental Health, if there is demonstrable physical abnormality of the brain, and the procedure is designed to ameliorate behavior, which is either personally tormenting to the patient, or so profoundly disruptive that the patient cannot safely live, or live with others?

Throughout this Opinion, the Court will use the term psychosurgery to describe the proposed innovative or experimental surgical procedure defined in the questions for consideration by the Court.

At least two definitions of psychosurgery have been furnished the Court. Dr. Bertram S. Brown, Director of the National Institute of Mental Health, defined the term as follows in his prepared statement before the United States Senate Subcommittee on Health of the Committee on Labor and Public Welfare on February 23, 1973:

> "Psychosurgery can best be defined as a surgical removal or destruction of brain tissue or the cutting of brain tissue to disconnect one part of the brain from another, with the intent of altering the behavior, even though there may be no direct evidence of structural disease or damage to the brain."

Dr. Peter Breggin, a witness at the trial, defined psychosurgery as the destruction of normal brain tissue for the control of emotions or behavior or the destruction of abnormal brain tissue for the control of emotions or behavior, where the abnormal tissue has not been shown to be the cause of the emotions or behavior in question.

The psychosurgery involved in this litigation is a sub-class, narrower than that defined by Dr. Brown. The proposed psychosurgery we are concerned with encompasses only experimental psychosurgery where there are [no] demonstrable physical abnormalities in the brain. Therefore, temporal lobectomy, an established therapy for relief of clearly diagnosed epilepsy is not involved, nor are accepted neurological surgical procedures, for example, operations for Parkinsonism, or operations for the removal of tumors or the relief of stroke.

It is clear from the record in this case that the understanding of the limbic system of the brain and its function is very limited. Practically every witness and exhibit established how little is known of the relationship of the limbic system to human behavior, in the absence of some clearly defined clinical disease such as epilepsy.

The record in this case demonstrates that animal experimentation and non-intrusive human experimentation have not been exhausted in determining and studying brain function. Any experimentation on the human brain, especially when it involves an intrusive, irreversible procedure in a non life-threatening situation, should be undertaken with extreme caution, and then only when answers cannot be obtained from animal experimentation and from non-intrusive human experimentation.

Psychosurgery should never be undertaken upon involuntarily committed populations, when there is a high-risk low-benefits ratio as demonstrated in this case. This is because of the impossibility of obtaining truly informed consent from such populations. The reasons such informed consent cannot be obtained are set forth in detail subsequently in this Opinion.

* * *

The Court does not in any way desire to impede medical progress. We are much concerned with violence and the possible effect of brain disease on violence. Much research on the brain is necessary and must be carried on, but when it takes the form of psychosurgery, it cannot be undertaken on involuntarily detained populations. Other avenues of research must be utilized and developed.

As pointed out above, psychosurgery is clearly experimental, poses substantial danger to research subjects, and carries substantial unknown risks. There is no persuasive showing on this record that the type of psychosurgery we are concerned with would necessarily confer any substantial benefit on research subjects or significantly increase the body of scientific knowledge by providing answers to problems of deviant behavior.

The dangers of such surgery are undisputed. Though it may be urged, as did some of the witnesses in this case, that the incidents of morbidity and mortality are low from the procedures, all agree dangers are involved, and the benefits to the patients are uncertain.

Absent a clearly defined medical syndrome, nothing pinpoints the exact location in the brain of the cause of undesirable behavior so as to enable a surgeon to make a lesion, remove that portion of the brain, and thus affect undesirable behavior.

Psychosurgery flattens emotional responses, leads to lack of abstract reasoning ability, leads to a loss of capacity for new learning and causes general sedation and apathy. It can lead to impairment of memory, and in some instances unexpected responses to psychosurgery are observed. It has been found, for example, that heightened rage reaction can follow surgical intervention on the amygdala, just as placidity can.

It was unanimously agreed by all witnesses that psychosurgery does not, given the present state of the art, provide any assurance that a dangerously violent person can be restored to the community.

Simply stated, on this record there is no scientific basis for establishing that the removal or destruction of an area of the limbic brain would have any direct therapeutic effect in controlling aggressivity or improving tormenting personal behavior absent the showing of a well defined clinical syndrome such as epilepsy.

To advance scientific knowledge, it is true that doctors may desire to experiment on human beings, but the need for scientific inquiry must be reconciled with the inviolability which our society provides for a person's mind and body. Under a free government, one of a person's greatest rights is the right to inviolability of his person, and it is axiomatic that this right necessarily forbids the physician or surgeon from violating, without permission, the bodily integrity of his patient.

Generally, individuals are allowed free choice about whether to undergo experimental medical procedures. But the State has the power to modify this free choice concerning experimental medical procedures when it cannot be freely given, or when the result would be contrary to public policy. For example, it is obvious that a person may not consent to acts that will constitute murder, manslaughter, or mayhem upon himself. In short, there are times when the State for good reason should withhold a person's ability to consent to certain medical procedures.

It is elementary tort law that consent is the mechanism by which the patient grants the physician the power to act, and which protects the patient against unauthorized invasions of his person. This requirement protects one of society's most fundamental values, the inviolability of the individual. An operation performed upon a patient without his informed consent is the tort of battery, and a doctor and a hospital have no right to impose compulsory medical treatment against the patient's will. These elementary statements of tort law need no citation.

It is obvious that there must be close scrutiny of the adequacy of the consent when an experiment, as in this case, is dangerous, intrusive, irreversible, and of uncertain benefit to the patient and society.

Counsel for Drs. Rodin and Gottliev argues that anyone who has ever been treated by a doctor for any relatively serious illness is likely to acknowledge that a competent doctor can get almost any patient to consent to almost anything. Counsel claims this is true because patients do not want to make decisions about complex medical matters and because there is the general problem of avoiding decision making in stress situations, characteristic of all human beings.

He further argues that a patient is always under duress when hospitalized and that in a hospital or institutional setting there is no such thing as a volunteer. Dr. Ingelfinger in Volume 287, page 466, of the New England Journal of Medicine (August 31, 1972) states:

> " * * * The process of obtaining 'informed consent' with all its regulations and conditions, is no more than an elaborate ritual, a device that when the subject is uneducated and uncomprehending, confers no more than the semblance of propriety on human experimentation. The subject's only real protection, the public as well as the medical profession must recognize, depends on the conscience and compassion of the investigator and his peers."

Everything defendants' counsel argues militates against the obtaining of informed consent from involuntarily detained mental patients. If, as he agrees, truly informed consent cannot be given for regular surgical procedures by non-institutionalized persons, then certainly an adequate informed consent cannot be given by the involuntarily detained mental patient.

We do not agree that a truly informed consent cannot be given for a regular surgical procedure by a patient, institutionalized or not. The law has long recognized that such valid consent can be given. But we do hold that informed consent cannot be given by an involuntarily detained mental patient for experimental psychosurgery for the reasons set forth below.

Informed consent is a requirement of variable demands. Being certain that a patient has consented adequately to an operation, for example, is much more important when doctors are going to undertake an experimental, dangerous, and intrusive procedure than, for example, when they are going to remove an appendix. When a procedure is experimental, dangerous, and intrusive, special safeguards are necessary. The risk-benefit ratio must be carefully considered, and the question of consent thoroughly explored.

To be legally adequate, a subject's informed consent must be competent, knowing and voluntary.

In considering consent for experimentation, the ten principles known as the Nuremberg Code give guidance. They are found in the Judgment of the Court in *United States v. Karl Brandt*. There the Court said:

> " * * * Certain basic principles must be observed in order to satisfy moral, ethical and legal concepts:
>
> 1. The Voluntary consent of the human subject is absolutely essential.
>
> This means that the person involved should have legal capacity to give consent; should be so situated as to be able to exercise free power of choice, without the intervention of any element of force, fraud, deceit, duress, overreaching, or other ulterior form of constraint or coercion; and should have sufficient knowledge and comprehension to enable him to make an understanding and enlightened decision. This latter element requires that before the acceptance of an affirmative decision by the experimental subject there should be

made known to him the nature, duration and purpose of the experiment; the methods and means by which it is to be conducted; all inconveniences and hazards reasonably to be expected; and the effects upon his health or person which may possibly come from his participation in the experiment.

The duty and responsibility for ascertaining the quality of the consent rests upon each individual who initiates, directs, or engages in the experiment. It is a personal duty and responsibility which may not be delegated to another with impunity.*

We must first look to the competency of the involuntarily detained mental patient to consent. Competency requires the ability of the subject to understand rationally the nature of the procedure, its risks, and other relevant information. The standard governing required disclosures by a doctor is what a reasonable patient needs to know in order to make an intelligent decision.

Although an involuntarily detained mental patient may have a sufficient I.Q. to intellectually comprehend his circumstances (in Dr. Rodin's experiment, a person was required to have at least an I.Q. of 80), the very nature of his incarceration diminishes the capacity to consent to psychosurgery. He is particularly vulnerable as a result of his mental condition, the deprivation stemming from involuntary confinement, and the effects of the phenomenon of "institutionalization."

The very moving testimony of John Doe in the instant case establishes this beyond any doubt. The fact of institutional confinement has special force in undermining the capacity of the mental patient to make a competent decision on this issue, even though he be intellectually competent to do so. In the routine of institutional life, most decisions are made for patients. For example, John Doe testified how extraordinary it was for him to be approached by Dr. Yudashkin about the possible submission to psychosurgery, and how unusual it was to be consulted by a physician about his preference.

Institutionalization tends to strip the individual of the support which permits him to maintain his sense of self-worth and the value of his own physical and mental integrity. An involuntarily confined mental patient clearly has diminished capacity for making a decision about irreversible experimental psychosurgery.

The second element of an informed consent is knowledge of the risk involved and the procedures to be undertaken. It was obvious from the record made in this case that the facts surrounding experimental brain surgery are profoundly uncertain, and the lack of knowledge on the subject makes a knowledgeable consent to psychosurgery literally impossible.

---

* Trial of War Criminals before the Nuremberg Military Tribunals. Volume 1 and 2, "The Medical Case," Washington, D.C.; U.S. Government Printing Office (1948) reprinted in 'Experimentation with Human Beings,' by Katz (Russel Sage Foundation (1972) page 305.

We turn now to the third element of an informed consent, that of voluntariness. It is obvious that the most important thing to a large number of involuntarily detained mental patients incarcerated for an unknown length of time, is freedom.

The Nuremberg standards require that the experimental subjects be so situated as to exercise free power of choice without the intervention of any element of force, fraud, deceit, duress, overreaching, or other *ulterior form of constraint or coercion*. It is impossible for an involuntarily detained mental patient to be free of ulterior forms of restraint or coercion when his very release from the institution may depend upon his cooperating with the institutional authorities and giving consent to experimental surgery.

The privileges of an involuntarily detained patient and the rights he exercises in the institution are within the control of the institutional authorities. As was pointed out in the testimony of John Doe, such minor things as the right to have a lamp in his room, or the right to have ground privileges to go for a picnic with his family assumed major proportions. For 17 years he lived completely under the control of the hospital. Nearly every important aspect of his life was decided without any opportunity on his part to participate in the decision-making process.

* * *

Involuntarily confined mental patients live in an inherently coercive institutional environment. Indirect and subtle psychological coercion has profound effect upon the patient population. Involuntarily confined patients cannot reason as equals with the doctors and administrators over whether they should undergo psychosurgery. They are not able to voluntarily give informed consent because of the inherent inequality in their position.

It has been argued by defendants that because 13 criminal sexual psychopaths in the Ionia State Hospital wrote a letter indicating they did not want to be subjects of psychosurgery, that consent can be obtained and that the arguments about coercive pressure are not valid.

The Court does not feel that this necessarily follows. There is no showing of the circumstances under which the refusal of these thirteen patients was obtained, and there is no showing whatever that any effort was made to obtain the consent of these patients for such experimentation.

The fact that thirteen patients unilaterally wrote a letter saying they did not want to be subjects of psychosurgery is irrelevant to the question of whether they can consent to that which they are legally precluded from doing.

The law has always been meticulous in scrutinizing inequality in bargaining power and the possibility of undue influence in commercial fields and in the law of wills. It also has been most careful in excluding from criminal cases confessions where there was no clear showing of their completely voluntary nature after full understanding of the consequences. No lesser standard can apply to involuntarily detained mental patients.

The keystone to any intrusion upon the body of a person must be full, adequate and informed consent. The integrity of the individual must be protected from invasion into his body and personality not voluntarily agreed to. Consent is not an idle or symbolic act; it is a fundamental requirement for the protection of the individual's integrity.

We therefore conclude that involuntarily detained mental patients cannot give informed and adequate consent to experimental psychosurgical procedures on the brain.

[The petitioners challenged the proposed psychosurgery on the alternate ground that the procedure if carried out would violate his first amendment rights. The Court held that in the absence of a compelling state interest which the state had failed to demonstrate, an involuntarily detained mental patient may not be subjected to experimental psychosurgery without violating his first amendment rights.]

For the reasons given, we conclude that the answer to question number one posed for decision is no.

In reaching this conclusion, we emphasize two things.

First, the conclusion is based upon the state of the knowledge as of the time of the writing of this Opinion. When the state of medical knowledge develops to the extent that the type of psychosurgical intervention proposed here becomes an accepted neurosurgical procedure and is no longer experimental, it is possible, with appropriate review mechanisms, that involuntarily detained mental patients could consent to such an operation.

Second, we specifically hold that an involuntarily detained mental patient today can give adequate consent to accepted neurosurgical procedures.

In view of the fact we have answered the first question in the negative, it is not necessary to proceed to a consideration of the second question, although we cannot refrain from noting that had the answer to the first question been yes, serious constitutional problems would have arisen with reference to the second question.

Questions and Comments

1. If followed, does the *Kaimowitz* decision preclude any use of innovative psychosurgical procedures involving involuntary patients? Consider the three elements of effective consent focused on by the court: competency, voluntariness, and knowledge. The *Kaimowitz* court first declared that institutionalization vitiates the patient's *competence* to make important decisions by fostering dependence and eliminating the need to make autonomous choices. The court reasoned further that the

inherent coercive atmosphere of the institution, in which the patient is dependent on the staff's goodwill for all privileges, renders *voluntary* decision-making impossible. Wouldn't the reasoning of the court effectively preclude an institutionalized patient from giving informed consent in *any* treatment context? Does the court properly balance the interests of a patient who may perceive the treatment as a means of possible recovery and release from the institution? How would this reasoning apply to a patient in need of a heart transplant?

The court also found that knowledge, the third element could never be sufficient to support informed consent when experimental methods are involved. Wouldn't this conclusion also preclude *competent* persons from giving informed consent to experimental procedures?

A final, and even more incongruous, element of the court's reasoning is its suggestion that if greater knowledge of the dangers and risks involved in psychosurgery was available, then informed consent might be possible after all. Can this suggestion be reconciled with the court's findings that institutionalization eliminates both competence and voluntariness in patient decision-making?

2.   Similar concerns were expressed in Note, Kaimowitz, v. Department of Mental Health: *A Right to be Free from Experimental Psychosurgery?*, 54 B.U.L.Rev. 301 (1974) at 326:

> If *Kaimowitz* is followed, its determination of "public policy" would preclude a court from approving the consent of an involuntarily committed person to experimental psychosurgery even if consent had been found competent and voluntary by an acceptable review committee. Therefore, it is possible that experimental psychosurgery might someday be unavailable only to the small class of institutionalized persons who truly desire the operation. Ironically, then, the *Kaimowitz* per se rule may be creating a situation in which a "right" to be free from treatment could be used to deny the privilege to make personal medical decisions which the court was at pains to secure in John Doe's particular case.

See also, Annas, Glantz, Katz, *Informed Consent to Human Experimentation* (Cambridge, Mass., Ballinger Publishing Co., 1977) 147–151.

3.   It has been suggested that the reasoning of *Kaimowitz* would effectively preclude the use of any volunteer drawn from among longtime institutionalized prisoners or patients. *See*, Annas, Glantz, Katz, *Informed Consent to Human Experimentation*, Ballinger Publishing Co. 1977, 147–151. If read this way, the *Kaimowitz* opinion cannot be reconciled with later cases such as *Bailey v. Lally*, 481 F.Supp. 203 (D.Md.1979), which have rejected claims that institutionalization rendered invalid the consent given by prisoners to participate in a medical research program.

4.   The result reached by the court in *Kaimowitz* has also been criticized on policy grounds. In this connection, consider the merits of the following commentary:

> The final point worth making about *Kaimowitz*, and the most important one from a practical standpoint, is that the main reasoning

of the court quite ironically *goes against* a major thrust of liberal reform in the mental health-prison area in recent years. In trying to win for patients and/or prisoners the rights to do such things as vote, get married, manage their own money, consent (or refuse to consent) to *normal* medical procedures, etc., it has been necessary to insist again and again that one may not infer incompetence from the mere fact of institutionalization. A person might justifiably be committed to an institution and yet remain perfectly competent to manage—if not all—at least a very wide and complex range of his affairs; the mere fact of institutionalization, in other words, must not be allowed to demote an inmate from the status of an autonomous person and a bearer of rights. But now, in *Kaimowitz*, the court seems to be saying (by implication) that the above reform was all a mistake, that the mere fact of institutionalization *does* establish incompetence. The *Kaimowitz* decision was enthusiastically welcomed by liberals who seek to reduce the coercion experienced by inmates in total institutions. Ironically, the decision provides the basis for making the very coercion feared by liberals *easier* to justify!

Murphy, *Total Institutions and the Possibility of Consent to Organic Therapies*, 5 Human Rights 25, 37–38 (1975).

4. Special Problems: Minors and the Mentally Disabled

a. Minors

The previously discussed rule that medical treatment may be administered only with the patient's consent is generally deemed inapplicable in the case of minors. In order to protect children from their own inexperience, and to protect the interests of the parents who bear the financial responsibility for their children's support, the basic consent model for minors requires the substituted consent of the child's parents. Thus, children are for the most part legally incapable of consenting to their own medical treatment.

Although the substituted consent model is at least partially predicated on the interests of the parents, that interest must give way to the interests of the child in some cases. One purely practical exception to the parental consent rule permits treatment in cases of emergency when the parents are unavailable to consent to treatment necessary to save the child from death or irreparable injury. Because of the child's own legal incapacity to give consent, this exception is analogous to the emergency treatment of unconscious adults.

Two further exceptions to the rule requiring parental consent to treatment are premised on the realization that in certain situations the interests of parents and their children may not coincide. The first instills in the courts the power to order necessary medical treatment for a minor whose parents refuse to authorize needed treatment. These cases normally arise when the parents have religious convictions which forbid them to consent to certain types of medical treatment, such as surgery or blood transfusions. Where the child is in a life threatening situation or at risk of irreparable damage in the absence of treatment, courts will often override the wishes of the parent's and provide the necessary substituted consent.

In addition to the "religious objection" cases, some state statutes provide for treatment in the absence of parental consent when the treatment is both necessary and relatively risk-free, and the parental consent requirement would have a "chilling effect" on the child's propensity to obtain treatment on his own. Such statutes allow the minor to provide the necessary consent to treatment involving venereal disease, pregnancy testing, contraception and drug dependency. A number of state statutes also authorize minors to receive mental health treatment without parental consent. An Illinois statute provides, for example, that: "Any minor fourteen years of age or older may request and receive counseling services or psychotherapy on an outpatient basis. The consent of the parent, guardian, or person in loco parentis shall not be necessary to authorize outpatient counseling or psychotherapy." Ill.Rev.Stat. Ch. 91½, ¶ 3–501(a) (1983).

Two other closely related exceptions to the parental consent requirement also permit minors to make their own treatment decisions. Under the emancipation doctrine, children who are in fact no longer subject to parental control, guidance, or financial support can give independent consent to treatment. Children can achieve emancipated status through acts of independence such as marriage or enlistment in the armed forces, through failure of the parents to meet their legal responsibilities, or through judicial decree. Similarly, a number of jurisdictions have adopted "mature minor" rules which give legal validity to consent to treatment given by older minors who demonstrate the intelligence and maturity of judgment necessary to satisfy the adult informed consent model. Prospective reliance on these exceptions by treating professionals is often discouraged, however, by the need to determine their applicability through a partially subjective case by case determination.

Though the substituted consent model, with its exceptions applicable to minors, does afford some degree of guidance in the area of conventional therapeutic treatment, the application of these principles to research and experimentation remains clouded. Generally, both parents and the emancipated or mature minor may consent to experimentation when the objective is therapeutic. No legal guidelines have emerged, however, to deal with non-therapeutic research and experimentation.

Commentators have suggested that a workable rule must take into account both the risks involved and the potential benefit to be enjoyed by the child. Accordingly, experimentation and research that poses no significant risk should be able to proceed upon the consent of either parents or emancipated or mature minors. As the degree of risk increases, some question the utility of the parental consent model as an adequate safeguard of the interest of the child. *See*, Ellis, *The*

Rights of Children in Research and Treatment: A Conceptual Framework for Consent, Proceedings, The Rights of Children as Research Subjects, University of Illinois at Urbana-Champaign, pp. 22–23, October 14–16, 1976. Because it is unlikely that potential risks to individual children will be tolerated on the basis of their interest in benefiting children as a class, it may be impossible, absent direct benefit to the subject, to involve children in experimentation when they are unable to consent for themselves.

Questions and Comments

1. The United States Supreme Court relied on constitutional grounds to avoid the "chilling effect" of parental consent requirements in abortion cases. In holding that privacy rights were violated by a requirement that all minor women obtain parental consent before having an abortion, the Court in *Planned Parenthood of Central Missouri v. Danforth,* 428 U.S. 52, 74, 96 S.Ct. 2831, 2843, 49 L.Ed.2d 788 (1976) stated: "Constitutional rights do not mature and come into being magically only when one attains the state defined age of majority. Minors, as well as adults, are protected by the Constitution and have constitutional rights."

2. Although a rule requiring a direct benefit to any minor involved in experimentation may inhibit the study of many disorders unique to children, it is unlikely that the law will retreat from this position for some time. One of the leading advocates of this position has stated the case in no uncertain terms:

> No *adult* has the legal power to consent to experiments on an infant unless the treatment is for the benefit of the *infant.* * * * It is the lamentable use in experiments of such subjects as infant children, incompetents in mental institutions, unconsenting soldiers subject to military discipline—as has been done—that is indefensible; and no rational social order will or should tolerate it.

Burger, *"Reflections on Law and Experimental Medicine,"* 15 U.C. L.A.L.Rev. 436, 438 (1968).

b. Mentally Disabled

Recall that the doctrine of informed consent incorporates two elements: the communication of relevant information and assent predicated upon an adequate understanding of the communicated information. The application of this model in the mental health treatment context, however, raises particular problems. Psychiatric patients and those who are developmentally disabled are by definition more likely than the average population to suffer from impairments which may diminish or interfere with the requisite comprehension. In the instance of retardation, the barrier to understanding manifests itself at the cognitive level. In the case of mental illness, the impediment to informed consent is more likely to involve a distortion of the information provided or an impairment in the patient's ability to communicate his intentions. One commentator has provided the following description of the way that mental illness can interfere with the giving of informed consent:

> * * * how does one obtain consent from a severely ill catatonic schizophrenic who sits and stares at a blank wall all day, refusing to speak to anyone? Certainly if a patient is psychotic or hallucinating and cannot assimilate information about a proposed procedure, he does not have the capacity to reach a decision about the matter in question. Some mental patients are incapable of evaluating information in what most people would call a rational manner. A treatment decision might ordinarily be based on considerations of perceived personal objectives, or long-term versus short-term risks and benefits. But there are patients whose acceptance or rejection of a treatment is not made in relation to any "factual" information. To add to this dilemma, while a mental patient may refuse to give his consent to a procedure, his refusal may only be a manifestation of his illness, having little resemblance to his actual desires.

G. Annas, L. Glantz, and B. Katz, *Informed Consent to Human Experimentation: The Subject's Dilemma* (Cambridge, Mass.: Ballinger Publishing Co., 1977) at 152.

When it is clear that the patient's psychiatric condition precludes the giving of informed consent, non-emergency treatment cannot be administered without a judicial determination that the patient is legally incompetent and consent is provided by an appointed guardian. (The competency adjudication process and the mechanism for the giving of substituted consent are discussed in Chapter Seven.) Thus, unless the patient has already been adjudicated to be incompetent, any substantial doubt as to the patient's capacity to give consent would call for the initiation of competency proceedings by the physician or mental facility.

In some instances, however, the capacity of a particular patient to give informed consent will not be altogether clear. Assessments are frequently complicated by the fact that "competency is not necessarily a fixed state that can be assessed with equivalent results at any one of a number of times. Like the patient's mental status as a whole, a patient's competency may fluctuate as a function of the natural course of his or her illness, response to treatment, psychodynamic factors * * * metabolic status, intercurrent illnesses, or the effects of medication." Appelbaum and Roth, *Clinical Issues on the Assessment of Competency*, 138 Am.J. of Psychiatry, 1462–1465 (1981). The physician's assessment may be further clouded by the lack of clear legal guidelines as to what constitutes capacity to consent (*See infra*, Chapter Seven Section IIA).

At the same time it would be impractical for those involved in treatment to seek an adjudication of incompetency whenever there is some element of doubt. Psychiatric commentators have noted that "[A]n immediate resort to the courts whenever the question of

incompetency arises [would be] too time consuming and expensive."
Appelbaum and Roth, at 1462. Furthermore, even an adjudication
followed by a finding of competency would not necessarily establish
the ability of the patient to give informed consent at some *later
point in time*. Thus, those providing treatment theoretically may
run some risk that a patient previously deemed legally competent
would in subsequent litigation be found to have lacked capacity to
give informed consent to treatment administered after the initial
determination.

Exposure to liability is minimized, however, by the judicially
announced rule that a "physician discharges the duty when he makes
a reasonable effort to convey sufficient information although the
patient, without fault of the physician, may not fully grasp it."
Canterbury v. Spence, 464 F.2d 772, 780 n. 15 (D.C.Cir.1972). Thus
if the clinical determination of capacity at the time of the giving of
consent involves the exercised due care, those providing treatment
would be insulated from liability even if the assessment were subsequently deemed to have been erroneous.

Questions and Comments

1. The capacity of psychiatric patients to understand and correctly
interpret medical information has been the subject of numerous empirical
studies. *See* Roth, *Competency to Consent to or Refuse Treatment*, in
Psychiatry 1982: The American Psychiatric Annual Review, 350, L.
Grinspoon, ed. (Washington, D.C., American Psychiatric Press, 1982).
By and large, these studies indicate that psychotic patients frequently
suffer severe impairment of competency to consent to medical treatment.
For instance a 1978 study of hospitalized schizophrenic patients receiving
antipsychotic medication included the following findings:

"while the schizophrenic patients, as compared with medical patients,
did not have defective understanding of the side effects and risks of
medication, the schizophrenic patients were less knowledgeable about
how their medication related to the nature of their problem. To the
extent that schizophrenic patients fail to understand the nature of
their problem, it may be anticipated that they will also fail to
understand the risks and benefits of treatment or to weigh risks and
benefits in deciding whether to accept treatment." *Id.* at 357.

Similarly, another study of the understanding of schizophrenic patients
of the risks and benefits of medication indicated "poor patient understanding." Also as reported by Roth, a study conducted in 1981 found
"that even after having been carefully informed, most of the schizophrenic outpatients treated in a cognitive disorder clinic did not absorb or
understand information about tardive dyskinesia." Id. On the other
hand, a study of persons suffering from psychotic depression found that
most patients in this category (more than 75 percent) "were able to
understand the information the consent form gave about electro-convulsive treatment. Roth, 357–358. *See also*, Roth, Meisel, Lidz, *"Tests of
Competency to Consent to Treatment"*, 134 Am.J. Psychiatry 279, 283

(1977); Roth and Appelbaum, *"Obtaining Informed Consent for Research With Psychiatric Patients,"* 6 Psychiatric Clinics of North America 551, 556–558 (1983).

IV. RESEARCH AND INFORMED CONSENT

A. INTRODUCTION

An earlier section considered the doctrine of informed consent in the context of treatment, including treatment modalities which are innovative or experimental. However, experimentation is not always limited to treatment intended to enhance the well-being of the subject. Specifically, in research situations, the activities in which the experimental subject is involved are primarily or wholly designed to develop or contribute to scientific or medical knowledge. Because the interests of the researcher and the subject are thus potentially in conflict, special regulations have been developed to protect the rights of experimental subjects.

The materials in this section will examine the legal regulation of both biomedical and behavioral research on human subjects. Since the risk to subjects is ordinarily greater in biomedical research, most current regulations were promulgated with that type of research in mind. Biomedical research may be defined as a scientific inquiry having a direct or immediate physical effect on the subject, which in turn produces some biological change. Biomedical research includes almost all medical research and psychiatric research aimed at the physiological origins of psychopathology.

Behavioral research is defined as a scientific inquiry into the factors determinative of human attitudes and behavior. In contrast to biomedical research, behavioral research generally involves no physical intrusion of the subject. Behavioral research may be divided into three categories, each distinguished by its effects on the subject's perception. One form consists of passive observation of the subject, with or without the subject's awareness. A second involves manipulation of the subject's environment without significant deception of the subject. A third also involves manipulation of the subject's environment, but coupled with overt deception of the subject.

B. PROFESSIONAL AND LEGAL REGULATION

The evolution of professional and legal standards to control research involving human subjects largely parallels the development of the doctrine of informed consent in the therapeutic treatment context. Thus, it was not until the early 1960's that courts, legislatures and professional organizations began to seriously search for methods to protect research subjects. Much of the impetus for this activity came from the disclosure of abuses in various research programs. For example, during the 1960's researchers at the Tuskegee Institute began a study of black males suffering from syphilis. The Tuskegee researchers intentionally deprived the subjects of treatment in order to study the degenerative effects of syphilis, a fact that, when revealed later, led to much criticism of the study and its researchers. In the social sciences, Stanley Milgram's obedience experiments, in which subjects were given the illusion that they were administering painful electric shocks to other persons, drew considerable criticism. Although these experiments are not typical of biomedical and behavioral research, fear of such overzealousness in the cause of science has been a primary motive for the regulation of human-subject research.

1. Self-Regulation

To a certain degree, researchers police their own activities through a process of self-questioning normally a part of any legitimate scientific inquiry. That scientists are encouraged to publish the results of their studies also affects the procedures utilized in research. Individual journals, for instance, can refuse to publish results of experiments that were not conducted in conformance with guidelines established by agencies such as the Department of Health and Human Services. Also, publication itself means both the results and research methods become available to the research community at large, which can then offer its own critique. The ethical codes and policy statements of professional organizations have also played a part in the process of self-regulation, particularly in the area of biomedical research. Internationally, the World Medical Association issued the Declaration of Helsinki in 1967 and a second document in 1975, known as Helsinki II. These policy statements espoused general principles, such as the necessity of fully informed consent, which have become the touchstone of both professional and legal regulation. In the United States, the American Medical Association's "Ethical Guidelines for Clinical Investigation" (1966) has had considerable influence on biomedical research methods, particularly in restricting the use of children and incompetent persons as subjects. Most of these guidelines, however, have only limited application to behavioral research. This gap has been partially filled by the Belmont Report, which was developed by the National Commission for the Protection of Human Subjects (an advisory group created by Congress to propose guidelines for federal regulations), and which presents the ethical principles applicable to all human-subject research. National Commission for the Protection of Human Subjects of Biomedical and Behavioral Research. *The Belmont Report: Ethical Principles and Guidelines for the Protection of Human Subjects of Research,* DHEW Pub. No. (OS) 78–0012 (1978).

2. Legal Regulation

Although a professional organization may impose sanctions on those members who violate organization guidelines, only the state can provide a remedy for subjects harmed by research or directly punish researchers and their sponsors. Legal regulation of human-subject research resulting from legislative and administrative agency action has had a significant impact on the conduct of human-subject research. However, these regulations have been designed as a means of preventing future injury to human subjects, not as means of remedying past injuries. Research subjects seeking compensation for injuries resulting from researcher misconduct must look to the law of torts, or the Federal Civil Rights statutes for redress.

a. Statutory and Administrative Regulation

Congress and several state legislatures have shown their awareness of the public concern over the propriety of human-subject experimentation by enacting legislation. Congress created two regulatory mechanisms, both under the aegis of the Department of Health and Human Services (HHS) to insure the proper conduct of human-subject research. Both the Food and Drug Act of 1938 (21 U.S.C. § 355) and the National Research Act of 1974 (42 U.S.C. 2891–2) empower the Secretary of HHS to promulgate regulations affecting human-subject research. Several states, including New York and California, have also enacted legislation which in some respects parallels the federal regulation.

Two principal checks on biomedical and behavioral research are created by the HHS regulations. First, researchers must submit detailed protocols describing their proposed research to an Institutional Review Board (IRB) made up of representatives drawn from different academic disciplines. These IRBs must be established in each HHS-funded institution and oversee the conduct of all human-subject research; they are empowered to either prohibit or modify the research being proposed. 45 C.F.R. § 46.113. In reviewing proposals, the IRBs are under a mandate to insure that risks to human subjects are minimized. Moreover, each proposal must reasonably balance the risk to human subjects against the anticipated benefit of the research. 45 C.F.R. § 46.111(1), (2). Where the proposed research involves pregnant women, fetuses, children, or prisoners, additional criteria must be met. The National Commission for the Protection of Human Subjects has proposed special regulations pertaining to the mentally infirm, but HHS has not adopted these proposed regulations. See 43 Fed.Reg. 11,328 (1978).

A second feature of the regulations is the requirement of informed consent of all subjects. Thus, as in the therapy situation, researchers must disclose all appropriate alternative procedures and all foreseeable risks. The HHS regulations also impose requirements in addition to those necessary where the intrusion is solely for therapeutic purposes. For instance, the researcher must also inform the subject that he or she may withdraw at any time. Additionally, the researcher must inform the subject of any compensation available should the subject suffer injury as a result of participation.

The Food and Drug Act of 1938 creates a second area of federal regulation of human-subject research. The act empowers the Secretary of HHS to approve the use of investigational drugs and medical devices. All researchers administering investigational drugs and devices must certify that the informed consent of either the subject or their proxies will be obtained. The FDA informed consent standard is substantially identical to the traditional therapeutic standard. The regulations require consent "except where [it] is not feasible, or, in the investigator's professional judgment, is contrary to the best interests of the subject." 21 C.F.R. § 312.1(12).

A number of states, such as California and New York, have enacted legislation similar to the HHS regulations. *See* Cal.Penal Code §§ 2670–2678 (West 1983); N.Y.Pub.Health Law §§ 2440–2446 (McKinney 1977). Like the HHS regulations, both New York and California require the subject's informed consent. Unlike HHS regulations, both the California and New York statutes cover all medical research conducted within the state, not just research in institutions receiving state funding. Neither the California nor the New York statutes explicitly cover behavioral research, unlike the HHS regulations, which cover all human-subject research, but do explicitly exempt several categories of behavioral research including surveys, educational testing, and observation of public behavior. 45 C.F.R. § 46.101(b).

As previously noted, neither federal or most state regulations provide specific remedies for human subjects injured while participating in research. HHS merely denies funding to institutions with whom an offending researcher is affiliated, while California imposes criminal penalties on medical researchers who fail to obtain their subject's informed consent. Cal.Health & Safety Code § 21476 (West Supp.1982). Some private remedy may nevertheless be available to an injured patient under state tort law or conceivably under one of the Federal Civil Rights statutes. The scope of the Federal Civil Rights laws and their impact on the mental health treatment field is discussed in Chapter Two.

b. *Private Remedies*

Claims related to nontherapeutic research have rarely been the subject of litigation. Consequently, there is only a very limited body of case law defining the rights of research subjects under either the common law or the Constitution. Some attention, however, has been given to the validity of the informed consent of institutionalized persons. In *Kaimowitz v. Department of Mental Health for the State of Michigan*, Wayne County Cir.Ct.C.A. No. 73–19434–AW (Mich.1973), which is set out in an earlier part of this chapter, a Michigan trial court held that institutionalized patients could not give informed consent to highly intrusive experimental surgery. A similar issue was the subject of litigation in *Bailey v. Lally*, 481 F.Supp. 203

(D.Md.1979), which challenged the validity of the consent provided by persons participating in high-risk medical research involving exposure to infectious diseases. Documented informed consent was obtained, but the plaintiff prisoners claimed that subtle coercive factors in the prisoner's environment (*i.e.*, higher level of pay, better living conditions for subjects) vitiated their consent, thereby giving them a cause of action under federal civil right statutes. The district court held that the inducements offered to the prisoners did not amount to coercion negating their fully informed consent. In any event, the defendant researchers were found to have qualified immunity to suit under 42 U.S.C.A. § 1983.

Questions and Comments

1. An important contributing factor in the movement for reform not only in the U.S. but also in other countries was the disclosure of human rights abuses carried out under the guise of scientific experimentation by Nazi scientists during World War II. *See*, Ratnoff & Smith, *Human Laboratory Animals: Martyrs for Medicine*, 36 Ford.L.Rev. 673, 679 (1968). The World Medical Association has been at the forefront of efforts to develop international standards for the control of human experimentation. One result of these efforts is the first and second Helsinki Declaration. *See, generally*, Jon R. Waltz and Fred E. Inbau, *Medical Jurisprudence*, pg. 381–383 (Macmillan Press, 1971).

The Tuskegee study and other abuses which stimulated the movement towards greater regulation are discussed in Nathan Hershey and Robert D. Miller, *Human Experimentation and the Law* (Aspen System Corp., Germantown, Md., 1976) pg. 153–156.

2. The ethical and legal issues which may be raised by experimentation with human subjects has been the subject of increasing attention by medical and legal scholars. *See, generally*, Paul A. Freund, ed., *Experimentations With Human Subjects*, (George Braziller, New York, 1970); Katz, Jay (with the assistance of Alexander Capron and Elenor Swift Glass), *Experimentation With Human Beings* (Russell Sage Foundation, New York, 1972); Symposium: *Medical Experimentation on Human Subjects*, 25 Case Wester.L.Rev. 431 (1975); National Academy of Sciences, *Experiments and Research With Humans: Values in Conflict* (Wash., D.C.1975); George Annas, Leonard H. Glantz and Barbara F. Katz, *Informed Consent to Human Experimentation: The Subject's Dilemma* (Ballinger Press, Cambridge, Mass.1977).

3. The HHS regulations under the National Research Act delegate to each institution's IRB the power to review all consent forms and procedures. But the regulations do not indicate to what degree IRB representatives should intervene in the consent process to insure that subjects are truly informed. Some commentators have argued that IRBs have concentrated too heavily on the review and revision of consent forms, suggesting that subjects might receive better protection if IRB representatives more frequently intervened in the consent process itself. *See* Robertson, "Taking Consent Seriously: IRB Intervention in the

Consent Process," 4 *IRB: A Review of Human Subject Research* 10 (1982) (citing study by Gray (1975) in which 40% of subjects signing consent form did not know they were involved in research).

4.   Under the HHS regulations, determinations of a subject's risks in proposed research have significant impact on whether the IRB will approve the proposed research.   Accordingly, the definition of risk of harm will be pertinent to a court's determination of whether a researcher acted negligently.   Neither state nor federal regulations, however, adequately define risk of harm.   The HHS regulations define "minimal risk" as that risk of harm "not greater, considering probability and magnitude, than those ordinarily encountered in daily life * * * "   45 C.F.R. § 46.102.   But such definitions say nothing about what kind of harm must be considered by IRBs.   Risk of harm would certainly include physical harm, but what kinds of psychological harm could be included?

Some individual IRBs have sought to eliminate this uncertainty by providing a definition of "risk of harm."   For example, the University of Illinois's IRB provides researchers with lists of research examples.   One list covers research involving minimal risk.   A second list covers research involving greater than minimal risk (*e.g.*, studies of the effects of prescribed tranquilizers on driving skills).

5.   In *Bailey v. Lally*, cited in the text above, the court did find that researchers had not always informed prisoners that participation would not affect consideration for parole.   However, the court concluded that this omission did not affect the validity of consent because researchers did not expressly promise parole board consideration of the subjects' participation.

Current regulations promulgated by the HHS would clearly prohibit the consent procedures followed in *Lally*.   Under special HHS regulations concerning prisoners, the researcher must inform each prisoner-subject that participation in research will have no effect on consideration of the prisoner-subject's parole.   45 C.F.R. § 46.305(a)(6).   The *Lally* case does illustrate the restrictive approach to the rights of human subjects that could be applied to research not covered by HHS regulations.

C. SPECIAL PROBLEMS ASSOCIATED WITH BEHAVIORAL RESEARCH

In biomedical research the subject's knowledge about the research usually has little or no effect on research outcomes.   In contrast, behavioral research frequently requires some deception of the subject as to the nature and purpose of the experiment.   Consequently, strict imposition of the informed consent requirement would severely limit the behavioral research that could be conducted.

It has therefore been argued that some adjustment in the informed consent doctrine developed for biomedical research is called for in behavioral research.   Moreover, it has been suggested that the need for strict informed consent standards is somewhat reduced by the nature of the risks posed by behavioral research, which rarely poses risk of physical harm. Some types of behavioral research, however, may expose the subject to risk of legally compensable psychological harm. Because the magnitude of these risks depends on the type of behavioral research conducted, it may be useful in evaluating current and proposed standards of informed consent to consider the legal implications associated with different types of behavioral research.

1. Passive Observation Studies

Passive observation of subjects in public places, without any modification of their environment, normally poses no risk of psychological harm. For example, in an experiment conducted by Bryan and Test (1967), the researchers measured the effect that the employment of black or white Santas as Salvation Army bell ringers had on frequency of donation. The mere act of giving or not giving constituted an experience of ordinary life which the researchers did not alter. Participants were completely unaware of ever having participated in the experiment.

In some instances, however, passive observation studies could subject the researcher to legal liability. For instance, in one controversial experiment by Humphreys (1970), the researcher stationed himself in public restrooms and posed as "lookout" for male homosexuals engaging in sex acts. By pretending to stand watch for intruders, the researcher was able to witness hundreds of sexual acts and sometimes follow up on these observations with interviews in which the purpose of the experiment was disclosed.

In this instance, even though the acts were committed in a public place, the nature of the activities plus the reasonable expectations of the parties would presumably give rise to protected privacy interests. Thus, by failing to inform the subjects of the true purpose of his presence, the researcher would in some jurisdictions become liable for invasion of privacy. *See supra* Chapter Four. *See also Katz v. United States*, 389 U.S. 347, 88 S.Ct. 507, 19 L.Ed.2d 576 (1967); Fried, Problems of Consent in Sex Research: Legal and Ethical Considerations in Ethical Issues in Sex Therapy and Research, 31 (Masters, Johnson, Koldney, and Weems, ed. 1980).

An action for invasion of privacy occurs when the defendant publishes a matter concerning the private life of a person which is highly offensive and is not of legitimate concern to the public. Rest. (Second) of Torts § 652D (1965). Thus, if an acquaintance of one of the subjects in the Humphreys's experiment had been able to identify the subject from the information presented in the published findings, the research might have constituted a form of invasion of privacy.

The HHS regulations promulgated under the National Research Act take into account the subject's right to privacy in research involving passive observation. The regulations generally exempt passive observation from coverage. Researchers lose the exemption, however, if (1) the researchers keep records which identify the subject, (2) publication of the records would expose the subject to legal liability or financial loss, and (3) the research concerns sensitive aspects of the subject's behavior. 45 C.F.R. § 46.101(4).

2. *Surveys and Manipulation Studies Without Overt Deception*

A second type of behavorial research involves some manipulation of the subject's environment, but without any significant deception of the subject. One famous experiment by Meritz and Fowler (1944) involved the use of a "lost letter" technique to test the honesty of persons in various cities. Two different kinds of addressed envelopes were distributed, one containing a letter and the other containing a coin-shaped slug. The difference in the percentage of returns between the two kinds of letters was expected to indicate the honesty of the general population. The experiment would have been impossible to perform if informed consent had been required. The researchers, however, had no duty to inform because participation posed no risk to the subjects greater than that encountered in ordinary life.

Similarly, survey interviews normally create little risk of harm to the subject. But if the subject's responses concern sensitive or personal matters, the researcher has a legal duty to insure the anonymity of the subject. If the subject must be identified in the researcher's records, the researcher may need to take special precaution to insure that the subject's responses remain confidential. Again, HHS regulations exempt interviews and surveys, provided that the researcher maintain the subject's anonymity, the subject's responses do not place the subject at risk of legal liability, and the responses do not pertain to sensitive aspects of the subject's behavior. 45 C.F.R. § 46.101.

3. *Studies Involving Deception*

A third type of behavorial research combines manipulation of the subject's environment with some form of deception. One study found that as much as 44% of recent research in social psychology involved deception of the subjects. Diener & Crandall, *Ethics in Social and Behavioral Research*, 74 (1978). Some social scientists have expressed concern that the use of deceit lessens public respect for the social sciences and may, because of participants' suspicions that researchers employ deception, become valueless as a research tool. *Id.* at 80.

Nevertheless, deceit is a necessity in some types of behavioral research. Knowledge of the manipulation by the research subject would in many situations compromise the validity of the research outcome. Imposing traditional standards of informed consent on researchers would obviously preclude the conduct of research involving deception. Behavioral studies frequently entail manipulation of some external variables under controlled conditions. The HHS regulations recognize this problem by allowing an IRB to completely waive the informed consent requirement where the research poses no more than minimal risk to the subject.   45 C.F.R. § 46.117(c), (z).

The nature and degree of risk of psychological harm varies with the type of deception employed by the researcher.   Psychological harm might arise from the subject's planned misapprehension of what appears to be an emergency situation.   For example, in an experiment conducted by the United States Army, military recruits were placed in an aircraft and flown to an altitude of 5,000 feet.   The researcher then instructed the pilot to turn off the plane's propellers. The subjects were allowed to overhear communications designed to convince them that the pilot would be forced to crash land the plane. The behavior of the subjects under these artificial stress conditions was monitored by researchers who were also aboard the aircraft.

The threat of psychological harm also might arise from a deception that causes subjects to misapprehend the nature of their own personalities.   In a study by Bergin (1965) on dissonance theory, researchers falsely told male subjects that personality tests had revealed that the subjects had latent homosexual tendencies.   Eventually researchers "dehoaxed" the subjects, but not before many of the subjects suffered a blow to their self-esteem.

Either of these experiments could have exposed the researchers to liability for failure to obtain informed consent or for the tort of intentional infliction of emotional distress.   To demonstrate intentional infliction of emotional distress, the plaintiff subject would have to show that the plaintiff's action amounted to conduct "so outrageous in character, and so extreme in degree, as to go beyond all possible bounds of public decency."   Rest. (Second) of Torts, § 46 commented (1965).   Some states have the added requirement that the emotional distress cause some physical manifestation of illness or injury.   Thus, under the standards which prevail today the subjects in both the Army and Bergen Studies could, at least in those states which do not require a physical manifestation of the injury, conceivably prevail in an action for intentional infliction of mental distress.

Questions and Comments

1.   It has been contended by some commentators that the low risk of injury from participation in behavioral research brings into question the necessity of applying the HHS regulations to behavioral research situations.   *See* Pattullo, "Who Risks What in Social Research," 2 *IRB: A Review of Human Subject Research* 1, 3 (1980).   Cumbersome IRB procedures have undoubtedly discouraged some researchers from engaging in valuable scientific inquiry.   *See* Hunt, *Research Through Deception*, N.Y. Times, Sept. 12, 1982, § 6 (Magazine) at 143.   At the same time, the overwhelming consensus both within and outside the social sciences profession is that some regulation and institutional control of the actions of individual researchers is necessary.

2. Researchers employing deception have developed several safeguards to decrease the risks that subjects will become emotionally upset as a result of the deception. Most researchers as a matter of course debrief their subjects at the experiment's conclusion. In debriefing sessions, researchers meet with subjects and fully disclose the hoax. Disturbed subjects are comforted and reassured. To what extent does such debriefing protect against any psychological trauma which may have accompanied the experiment?

3. Behavioral and biomedical researchers have also developed several forms of "consent" that fall short of giving the subject all the information required to satisfy legal standards of informed consent. Some researchers have asked their subjects to consent to not being informed of the real purposes of the experiment. Levine, "Consent to Incomplete Disclosure as an Alternative to Deception," 4 *IRB: A Review of Human Subject Research* 10 (1982). Another technique consists of asking subjects to waive their right to disclosure without any forewarning to the subject that the research involves deception. Still another technique, heretofore used primarily in biomedical research, is to inform an incompetent subject's proxy of the experiment, but withhold the option of denying consent from the proxy. Within a specific period after the beginning of the experiment, however, the researcher must obtain the proxy's consent. The theory behind this technique, called "deferred consent," is that by delaying the consent decision, the subject's proxy will have more time to consider the matter and come to a "correct" decision. The HHS regulations under the National Research Act appear to authorize such techniques, but only if the research poses no more than minimal risk to the subject. 45 CFR § 46.116(d). *See* Fost & Robertson, "Deferring Consent with Incompetent Patients in an Intensive Care Unit," 2 *IRB: A Review of Human Subject Research* 5 (1980). *Cf.* Beauchamp, The Ambiguities of "Deferred Consent," 2 *IRB: A Review of Human Subject Research* 6 (1980) (article critical of deferred consent technique).

Would any of these techniques provide a defendant researcher with a defense to an informed consent action filed on behalf of the incompetent subject?

Chapter Four

CONFIDENTIALITY, PRIVACY, AND PATIENT ACCESS TO RECORDS

I. PROTECTION OF PRIVACY AND CONFIDENTIALITY

A. INTRODUCTION

1. *The Importance of Confidentiality in Psychotherapy*

Confidentiality is especially important in the unique setting of psychotherapy. The patient must reveal "his private personality, that which he keeps secret from the world," and "communicate all his thoughts, real and fantasy, to the therapist." Note, Psychiatrists' Duty To The Public: Protection From Dangerous Patients, 1976 U.Ill. L.F. 1103, 1112–1113. Typically, the attitudes expressed in therapy are grossly at variance with those of the patient's daily life. A minister, for example, may reveal hostile or aggressive impulses. Public disclosure of these communications could destroy the patient's reputation. Thus, the psychotherapeutic relationship originates in the patient's trust that the psychiatrist will not divulge his communications.

Confidentiality in psychotherapy is necessary not only to protect the patient from embarrassment and disgrace, but also to accomplish treatment, which is the purpose of the relationship. A patient will not speak freely with a psychotherapist if public disclosure is likely, but effective treatment calls for true and complete communication by the patient of all his ideas and associations. To accomplish these complete revelations a patient must overcome inhibitions which "seek support from every possible source * * * including the possibility of disclosure." Goldstein & Katz, *Psychiatrist-Patient Privilege: The GAP Proposal and the Connecticut Statute,* 36 Conn.B.J. 175, 179 (1962). Thus, with remarkable uniformity, authoritative commentators assert that treatment through psychotherapy requires confidentiality to be successful.

Confidentiality fosters a related public interest: it induces the hesitant person, in need of treatment, to seek it. Receiving psychotherapy occasions social stigma; even in enlightened communities patients in psychotherapy may be viewed with curiosity or suspicion. Furthermore, the stigma may exert an exaggerated effect upon persons who would benefit from therapy because they tend "to see themselves in the worst possible light." Confidentiality both as to the *fact* that a person is the patient of a psychiatrist, as well as to the *contents* of his disclosures, is thus important. By fostering treatment for those in need, confidentiality serves both the patient and society at large.

While the statement above relates particularly to psychotherapy, confidentiality is clearly important in the context of all psychiatric or psychological services. The results of personality and intelligence tests, for example, are no less sensitive than a patient's verbal confidences to a therapist. Of like sensitivity are the statements of a youth who confides to a social worker or counsellor that he fears that he has contacted a venereal disease or that he has been struggling with a drug or alcohol problem. This chapter begins a study of therapists' and counsellors' obligations to maintain the confidentiality of patient and client information.

We say "begin" because the obligation of confidentiality raises a host of problems as it conflicts with such equally important societal values such as protecting the safety of the client as well as that of the community, meeting the obligations of fact finding in criminal and civil trials, and advancing scientific knowledge through research, debate, and teaching. It is these conflicts which must be balanced by courts and legislatures as they struggle to develop appropriate standards.

2. *Professional/Ethical Foundations*

The obligation of confidentiality is well recognized by the psychiatric profession. Psychiatrists, like physicians, are ethically bound by the Hippocratic oath, which states in part, "Whatever, in connection with my professional practice, or not in connection with it, I see or hear, in the life of men, which ought not to be spoken of abroad, I will not divulge, as reckoning that all such should be kept secret."

The modern code of ethics promulgated by the American Medical Association reiterates this ancient injunction to maintain confidentiality. According to the code, breaches of confidentiality are permissible only when compelled by law or necessary to protect the welfare of the patient or community. In annotations to this code of ethics, the American Psychiatric Association has explained that confidentiality is essential to psychiatric treatment, not only because of the traditional ethical relationship between physician and patient, but also because of the special nature of psychiatric treatment.

Psychologists are similarly impressed with the practical and ethical importance of confidentiality in therapy. "Ethical Standards for Psychologists," the code of ethics of the American Psychological Association, provides that "safeguarding information about an individual that has been obtained by the psychologist in the course of his teaching, practice or investigation is a primary obligation of the psychologist". (Ethical Standards for Psychologists, Principle 6). Conditions which a psychologist must consider before divulging information in order to protect the client or society, to further the interests of the client, or to advance scientific knowledge are set forth in the code. The conditions relate to such factors as the immediacy of danger, if any, the scope and purpose of the disclosure, the client's awareness of the limits of confidentiality, and the client's consent to allow disclosure.

3. *Legal Regulation*

Various legal mechanisms exist to enforce the ethical obligation of confidentiality in psychiatric or psychological treatment. Perhaps the

most obvious is enforcement of professional obligations set forth in
licensing and certification statutes. Such statutes may include an
express provision concerning the confidentiality of patient or client
information. Statutory provisions mandating confidentiality frequently provide a corresponding testimonial "privilege," that is, a
right on the part of the therapist to refuse to testify in court
concerning his patients (*see* the later section on testimonial privilege).
Violation of the statutory obligations of confidentiality may give rise
to disciplinary proceedings and imposition of penalties as set forth in
the statute. Penalties may range from a fine to license suspension or
revocation.

In addition to, or in place of, explicit statutory provisions concerning confidentiality, a licensing or certification statute may incorporate
a general obligation to adhere to the code of ethics promulgated by
designated professional organizations. In the case of psychiatrists
and psychologists, these codes include obligations to insure confidentiality of patient or client information.

Even if the licensing statute does not expressly refer to the
professional code of ethics, however, the mere fact that the profession is state-licensed or state-certified may *imply* an obligation on the
part of practitioners to comply with professional ethical standards.
Such an implied obligation was found, for example, in the license
revocation case, *Morra v. State Board of Examiners*, set forth in the
earlier chapter on Regulation of the Mental Health Professions. In
that case, the court found an obligation to comply with professional
ethical standards was implied by the state licensing statute.

Of course, the obligation of confidentiality would be meaningless
if it did not extend to safeguarding patient and client records maintained by the therapist or by his employer. In some cases, the
confidential patient records may be protected independently of the
therapist's obligations, by a statute protecting institutional records
generally. This is often the case in state hospitals for the mentally ill
or retarded. In some states, similar statutes protect educational
records maintained in public and private schools. Statutes of this
sort usually provide that information contained in client records may
not be disclosed, except for certain authorized purposes, without the
client's knowledge or consent, or the knowledge and consent of his
parent or guardian if the client is a minor or incompetent.

Perhaps the most effective and certainly the most common
method to enforce a therapist's duty of confidentiality is the civil
damage suit. A patient aggrieved by a therapist's wrongful disclosure of confidential information may sue the therapist under a
number of legal theories.

A successful suit will result in an award of monetary damages for
the disclosure itself, for any real injuries, such as damage to the
patient's business or employment due to the disclosure, for non-

economic losses, such as damage to the patient's reputation in the community or for mental anguish caused by the disclosure. While monetary damages may not correct the injury, such awards, it is hoped, will assuage the patient's injured feelings, assure a legally sanctioned vent for righteous anger, and incidentally punish the malfeasant therapist and thereby deter abuse.

Although the nature of a patient's grievance may be readily understandable, the patient-plaintiff in a lawsuit must frame his complaint as an allegation of a wrong which is legally recognized. The torts which most commonly apply to improper disclosures of confidential information are defamation, invasion of privacy, and breach of duty arising from a confidential professional relationship. While these are distinct theories of wrong, very often a single act of wrongful disclosure will satisfy the elements of all three theories. In such cases the plaintiff will frequently elect to frame his complaint in terms of any one or all of these individual theories of liability.

The following materials examine briefly each of these separate doctrines. The first two—defamation and invasion of privacy—are not specific to the psychotherapist/patient relationship but apply to anyone who improperly communicates information concerning another. On the other hand, the tort of breach of the patient/therapist relationship is applicable only to those involved in rendering of psychotherapeutic treatment.

B. LEGAL REMEDIES FOR WRONGFUL DISCLOSURE

1. *General Remedies*

a. *Actions Based on Breach of Privacy*

A private remedy based on an infringement of privacy is today recognized in almost every jurisdiction *in either limited or a more comprehensive form.* See Jon R. Waltz and Fred E. Inbau, *Medical Jurisprudence* (New York: Macmillan, 1971), Ch. 18. There are essentially four distinct types of privacy actions.

In one the privacy refers to a physical intrusion into a person's private affairs, such as wiretapping his telephone. In the second aspect of the doctrine the phrase refers to appropriation, *i.e.,* the use of another person's photograph or likeness for advertising without permission. A third form entails publication of incomplete or misleading information which places another person in a "false light" in the public eye. For instance, use of a person's photograph to illustrate a story about drug addicts, when that person is neither a drug addict nor has any relationship to the story, may violate his privacy rights. A fourth and final aspect of the right to privacy and the one that most concerns the therapist is the revelation of confidential information about the plaintiff. The action is founded on the premise that if information that the patient could reasonably expect to remain private is disclosed, a cause of action may arise based on that disclosure. This branch of privacy is most often referred to as the public disclosure of private facts and covers the disclosure of those matters that would be embarrassing to the average individual. The following case illustrates the application of this doctrine.

COMMONWEALTH v. WISEMAN

Supreme Judicial Court of Massachusetts, 1969.
356 Mass. 251, 249 N.E.2d 610.

CUTTER, Justice.

This bill seeks, among other relief, to enjoin all showings of a film entitled "Titicut Follies," containing scenes at Massachusetts Correctional Institution at Bridgewater (Bridgewater), to which insane persons charged with crime and defective delinquents may be committed. The film was made between April 22, and June 29, 1966. Mr. Wiseman and Bridgewater Film Company, Inc. (BFC) appeal from an interlocutory decree, an order for a decree, and the final decree which enjoins showing the film "to any audience" and requires Mr. Wiseman and BFC to deliver up to the Attorney General for destruction specified films, negatives, and sound tapes. The plaintiffs appeal from the final decree because it did not order sums realized by various defendants from showing the film to be held for distribution as the court might direct.

The trial judge made a report of material facts. The evidence (2,556 pages of proceedings on eighteen trial days and sixty-four exhibits) is reported. The facts, except as otherwise indicated, are stated on the basis of the trial judge's findings and certain exhibits. The film has been shown to the Justices participating in this decision.

In 1965, Mr. Wiseman first requested permission from the Superintendent and from the Commissioner to make an educational documentary film concerning Bridgewater. His first request was denied. On January 28, 1966, permission was granted, subject to the receipt of a favorable opinion from the Attorney General (that the officials could grant permission) and to the conditions (a) that "the rights of the inmates and patients * * * [would be] fully protected," (b) that there would be used only "photographs of inmates and patients * * * legally competent to sign releases," (c) that a written release would be obtained "from each patient whose photograph is used in the film," and (d) that the film would not be released "without first having been * * * approved by the Commissioner and Superintendent." The existence of the final condition was the subject of conflicting evidence but there was oral testimony upon which the trial judge could reasonably conclude that it had been imposed.

* * *

In April, 1966, Mr. Wiseman and his film crew started work at Bridgewater. They were given free access to all departments except the treatment center for the sexually dangerous, whose director made "strong objections" in writing to any photography there without compliance with explicit written conditions. In three months, 80,000 feet of film were exposed. Pictures were made "of mentally incompetent patients * * * in the nude * * * [and] in the most personal and private situations."

In approaching the Commissioner and the Superintendent, Mr. Wiseman had indicated that he planned a documentary film about three people: an adult inmate, a youthful offender, and a correctional officer. It was to be an effort "to illustrate the various service performed—custodial, punitive, rehabilitative, and medical." The judge concluded (a) that the "plain import of [Mr.] Wiseman's representations was that his film was to be * * * non-commercial and non-sensational," whereas, in the judge's opinion, it was "crass * * * commercialism"; (b) that, in fact, the film "constitutes a most flagrant abuse a of the privilege * * * [Mr. Wiseman] was given"; and (c) that, instead of "a public service project," the film, as made, is "to be shown to the general public in movie houses."

* * *

In September, 1967, Mr. Wiseman made an agreement with Grove for distribution of the film for "showing to the general public * * * throughout the United States and Canada," with Mr. Wiseman to receive "50% of the theatrical gross receipts, and 75% from any television sale." Grove, for promotion of the film, was to have "complete control of the manner and means of distribution." The film was shown privately, and to the public for profit, in New York City in the autumn of 1967.

The trial judge ruled, inter alia, (a) that such "releases as may have been obtained [from inmates] are a nullity"; (b) "that the film is an unwarranted * * * intrusion * * * into the * * * right to privacy of each inmate" pictured, degrading "these persons in a manner clearly not warranted by any legitimate public concern"; (c) that the "right of the public to know" does not justify the unauthorized use of pictures showing identifiable persons "in such a manner as to * * * cause * * * humiliation"; (d) that "it is the responsibility of the State to protect" the inmates "against any such * * * exploitation"; and (e) that the Commonwealth is under "obligation * * * to protect the right of privacy of those * * * committed to its * * * custody."

Reactions to the film set out in the record vary from the adversely critical conclusions of the trial judge to those expressed by witnesses

a. Among the findings are the following: The film "is a hodge-podge of sequences * * * depicting mentally ill patients engaged in repetitive, incoherent, and obscene rantings * * *. The film is excessively preoccupied with nudity. * * * [N]aked inmates are shown desparately attempting to hide * * * their privates with their hands. * * * There is a scene of * * * [a priest] administering the last rites of the church to a dying patient [and] the preparation of corpse for burial. * * * A * * * patient, grossly deformed by * * * congenital brain damage, is paraded before the camera."

who regarded it as fine journalistic reporting, as education, and as art.[b] The Attorney General (Mr. Richardson) testified that the film "was impressive in many ways * * * powerful in impact." He, however, expressed concern about the problem of obtaining valid releases, even from those "conceivably competent," since the releases would have been given before the inmates "could have any idea how they would be depicted." There was testimony from experts about the value of the film for instruction of medical and law students, and "exposure of conditions in a public institution."

*   *   *

1. [As an initial matter, the Court held that since the film constituted documentary evidence the appellate court could undertake its appraisal without regard to the findings of the trial court.]

2. The Commissioner and the Superintendent would have acted wisely if they had reduced any agreement to writing rather than to have risked the misunderstandings possible in oral discussions. They also might have avoided dispute if they had supervised the filming itself much more closely.

*   *   *

Early in the negotiations, Mr. Wiseman represented in writing that only pictures of inmates "legally competent to sign releases" would be used and that the "question of competency would * * * be determined by the Superintendent and his staff." In the 1966 request for the Attorney General's opinion, Mr. Wiseman was quoted as giving assurance that a written release would be obtained "from each * * * patient whose photograph is used." The latter assurance was quoted in the opinion (March 21, 1966) stating that the Superintendent had power to permit the film to be made. In the circumstances, the judge reasonably could conclude that these representations were a part of the arrangement.

The judge was also clearly justified in deciding on the basis of expert testimony, that some of sixty-two inmates identified as shown in the film were incompetent to understand a release and, on the basis of a stipulation, that releases were obtained only from eleven or twelve of the numerous inmates depicted. There was ample basis for concluding that Mr. Wiseman had not fulfilled important undertakings clearly designed to assure that the film would show only those

b. For example the Life review said, in part, "The Bridgewater atmosphere is one of aimless hopelessness. * * * A psychiatrist turns an interview with an inmate into a sadistic baiting, or, with malicious cheerfulness, forcefeeds a dying old man, while we wonder whether the ash from the doctor's carelessly dangling cigarette is really going to fall into the glop being funneled into the convulsively shuddering throat. A society's treatment of the least of its citizens * * * is perhaps the best measure of its civilization. The repulsive reality * * * forces us to contemplate our capacity for callousness. No one seeing this film can but believe that reform of the conditions it reports is urgent business. * * *

consenting in writing to their appearance in the film and competent to understand and to give such consent.

3. The film shows many inmates in situations which would be degrading to a person of normal mentality and sensitivity. Although to a casual observer most of the inmates portrayed make little or no specific individual impression, others are shown in close-up pictures. These inmates are sufficiently clearly exhibited (in some instances naked) to enable acquaintances to identify them. Many display distressing mental symptoms. There is a collective, indecent intrusion into the most private aspects of the lives of these unfortunate persons in the Commonwealth's custody.

We need not discuss to what extent in Massachusetts violation of privacy will give rise to tort liability *to individuals*. [Emphasis added]

We think, in any event, that Mr. Wiseman's massive, unrestrained invasion of the intimate lives of these State patients may be prevented by properly framed injunctive relief. The Commonwealth has standing and a duty to protect reasonably, and in a manner consistent with other public interests, the inmates from any invasions of their privacy substantially greater than those inevitably arising from the very fact of confinement.

There is a "general power of the Legislature, in its capacity as parens patriae, to make suitable provision for incompetent persons." A "comprehensive system for their care and custody" is contained in [Massachusetts Statutory Provisions]. The Legislature has exercised that power with specific reference to Bridgewater, among other institutions. These general provisions import all reasonable power, and the duty, to exercise proper controls over the persons confined and the conditions of their custody and to afford the inmates protection and kindness consistent with the terms and rehabilitative purposes of their commitments.

The Commissioner and Superintendent, under reasonable standards of custodial conduct, could hardly permit merely curious members of the public access to Bridgewater to view directly many activities of the type shown in the film. We think it equally inconsistent with their custodial duties to permit the general public (as opposed to members of groups with a legitimate, significant, interest) to view films showing inmates naked or exhibiting painful aspects of mental disease.

These considerations, taken with the failure of Mr. Wiseman to comply with the contractual condition that he obtain valid releases from all persons portrayed in the film, amply justify granting injunctive relief to the Commonwealth. The impracticability of affording relief to the inmates individually also supports granting this collective relief to the Commonwealth as parens patriae, in the interest of all the affected inmates. We give no weight to any direct interest of the Commonwealth itself in suppressing the film.

4. The defendants contend that no asserted interest of privacy may be protected from the publication of this film because the conditions at Bridgewater are matters of continuing public concern, as this court has recognized.

Indeed, it was concern over conditions at Bridgewater which led various public officials in 1965 and 1966 to consider a documentary film, in the hope that, if suitable, it might arouse public interest and lead to improvement.

Even an adequate presentation to the public of conditions at Bridgewater, however, would not necessitate the inclusion of some episodes shown in the film, nor would it justify the depiction of identifiable inmates, who had not given valid written consents and releases, naked or in other embarrassing situations. We agree with the trial judge that Mr. Wiseman's wide ranging photography amounted to "abuse of the privilege he was given to make a film" and a serious failure to comply with conditions reasonably imposed upon him. Mr. Wiseman could hardly have fairly believed that officials, solicitous about obtaining consent and releases from all inmates portrayed, could have been expected to approve this type of film for general distribution.

The record does not indicate to us that any inmate shown in the film, by reason of past conduct, had any special news interest as an individual. Each inmate's importance to the film was that he was an inmate of Bridgewater, that he suffered from some form of mental disease, and that he was undergoing in the Bridgewater facilities particular types of custody and treatment. Recognizable pictures of individuals, although perhaps resulting in more effective photography, were not essential. In the circumstances, there will be no unreasonable interference with any publication of matters of public concern if showing the film to the general public is prevented (a) to protect interests of the inmates in privacy, and (b) because Mr. Wiseman went unreasonably beyond the scope of the conditional permission to enter, and take pictures upon, State owned premises properly not generally open for public inspection and photography.

The case is distinguishable from decisions which have permitted publication of newsworthy events where the public interest in reasonable dissemination of news has been treated as more significant than the private interests in privacy. We need not now consider to what extent Mr. Wiseman could have been wholly excluded from making a film at Bridgewater. In this aspect of the case, we hold merely that he violated the permission given to him, reasonably interpreted, and did not comply with valid conditions that he obtain written releases.

* * *

5. That injunctive relief may be granted against showing the film to the general public on a commercial basis does not mean that all showings of the film must be prevented. As already indicated the film gives a striking picture of life at Bridgewater and of the problems affecting treatment at that or any similar institution. It is a film which would be instructive to legislators, judges, lawyers, sociologists, social workers, doctors, psychiatrists, students in these or related fields, and organizations dealing with the social problems of custodial care and mental infirmity. The public interest in having such persons informed about Bridgewater, in our opinion, outweighs any countervailing interests of the inmates and of the Commonwealth (as parens patriae) in anonymity and privacy.

The effect upon inmates of showing the film to persons with a serious interest in rehabilitation, and with potential capacity to be helpful, is likely to be very different from the effect of its exhibition merely to satisfy general public curiosity. There is possibility that showings to specialized audiences may be of benefit to the public interest, to the inmates themselves, and to the conduct of an important State institution. Because of the character of such audiences, the likelihood of humiliation, even of identifiable inmates, is greatly reduced. In any event the likelihood of harm seems to us less than the probability of benefits.

* * * The decree is to be modified to permit (according to standards to be defined in the decree) the showing of the film to audiences of the specialized or professional character already mentioned.

* * *

[The Court held that individual inmates who had been filmed were not entitled to damages.]

Questions and Comments

1. This action, which was brought by the state of Massachusetts, relied on the *parens patriae* power of the state to protect persons unable to care for themselves. The dimensions of this power will be explored in greater detail in Chapter Six.

2. Note that in *Wiseman* the defendant did not concede that the permission given by the authorities was predicated on the obtaining of the consent of any inmates who would be included in the film. The trial court, however, accepted the state's version that the patients' consent was an express condition. Suppose the evidence had clearly indicated that no condition of consent had been imposed. Would the state have been able to enjoin the showing of the film under these facts? If so, on what theory?

3. Some inmates were so afflicted with mental illness as to lack capacity to consent to the filming. Could state authorities acting under the *parens patriae* power consent on behalf of these patients? If not,

under what circumstances, if any, could they be filmed? Issues relating to this question are taken up in Chapter Seven.

4. The *Wiseman* case is illustrative of the application of privacy as the basis for a right of action which may be asserted against private individuals. There is also a constitutionally based right to privacy, however, which can be invoked to limit only *governmental* intrusions. *Hawaii Psychiatric Society v. Ariyoshi*, 481 F.Supp. 1028 (D.Hawaii 1979) illustrates the application of this doctrine in the psychiatric sphere. In 1978, in an effort to curb Medicaid fraud, the legislature of the State of Hawaii adopted an administrative inspection scheme which required each health provider to maintain records fully describing the care being provided to Medicaid recipients and to make such records available to authorized state officials. A key provision in the statute authorized the issuance of administrative inspection warrants upon a showing of "probable cause." This provision in turn provided the statutory basis for the subsequent issuance by an administrative search warrant which authorized the inspection of a clinical psychologist's Medicaid records, including "therapeutic notes, patient history forms, medical records and reports, and diagnoses." *Id.* at 1034.

In *Ariyoshi* a psychologist, together with the Hawaii Psychiatric Society, challenged the constitutionality of the search warrant portion of the statute, both on its face and as applied to the plaintiff. The district court, in granting a preliminary injunction, concluded that it was highly probable that the statute violated constitutional prohibitions against invasion of privacy and unreasonable searches without the requisite compelling justification. *Id.*

5. The existing rules designed to protect the privacy and confidentiality of patient's medical records were developed in an era when these records were maintained in the physician's office itself. Since that time, there have been significant changes in the way that medical data is recorded and stored. Several factors are responsible. The development of computerized data storage systems and data transmission networks that connect these systems make it possible to establish centralized medical record filing systems with virtually unlimited capacities. In addition, changes in the structure of the medical profession itself and in the way that medical care is financed have effected the locations and methods of the storage of patient's medical data.

The movement toward medical health care organizations and away from individual practice has been accompanied by increasing reliance on centralized computerized files. At the same time, health care is increasingly being financed through public and private insurance programs. In fact, it has been estimated that approximately 75% of all medical services are either totally or in part paid for by public or private insurance programs. *Note,* Computers, *The Disclosure of Medical Information, and the Fair Credit Reporting Act,* III Computer/Law Journal, 619 (1982); Dubro, *Your Medical Records. How Private Are They?* 3 Cal. Lawyer 33, 34 (1983). As a consequence of these changes, those involved in providing health care must share medical treatment information with those agencies which finance health care costs. The consent of the patient, which is usually required by insurance companies as a condition of reimbursement, authorizes this exchange of personal medical information.

Centralization of medical records has also been furthered by the formation of pooled record systems. By far the largest of these systems is that developed under the auspices of the Medical Information Board (MIB), which has collected data on over 11 million persons and is tied to a group of insurance companies that together write nearly 95% of the medical insurance policies issued in the United States. Note, *Computers, The Disclosure of Medical Information, and the Fair Credit Reporting Act*, III Computer/Law Journal 619 (1982). These files consist mainly of medical records supplied by the insurers themselves who obtain them directly from reporting physicians. *Id.* at 626. In the past such files even included data on sexual deviancy and social maladjustment, though this type of information was subsequently deleted by the MIB. *Id.*

Similar centralized data systems have been developed in the mental health field. The most comprehensive of these systems is the Multi-State Information System for Psychiatric Patient Records (MSIS), which collects data supplied by the institutions of at least seven states. Lawrence Tancredi, *Legal Issues in Psychiatric Care* (New York: Harper and Row, 1975), p. 55. It has been estimated that over 30% of the patients in state-operated mental hospitals in the U.S. are in facilities that in some way participate in this system. Jonas Robitscher, *The Power of Psychiatry* (Boston: Houghton Mifflin, 1980), p. 225. When insurance is provided by an employer, disclosure may also result from specific requests from the employer for information held by the insurance company. Note, *Computers, The Disclosure of Medical Information, and the Fair Credit Reporting Act*, III Computer/Law Journal 619, 626 (1982).

These changes, brought about by advanced data systems and a restructured medical profession, have led many to question the adequacy of traditional doctrines such as the law of privacy and defamation to provide sufficient safeguards to prevent abuses of these systems. A 1980 Senate bill recently attempted to address the problem of misuse of medical information at the federal level. The proposed Privacy of Medical Information Act would have required a record to be made of any agency or individual that gains access to a medical record bank. Strong lobbying by law enforcement and intelligence authorities, as well as by the medical profession itself, led to the defeat of the bill.

Limited efforts at controlling the release of medical information have also been undertaken on the state level. A number of states have enacted legislation promoting the confidentiality of psychiatric treatment records. Generally, these purport to prevent the disclosure of treatment information of those undergoing psychiatric therapy, excepting information sought for the purposes of research. Lawrence Tancredi, *Legal Issues in Psychiatric Care* (New York:

Harper and Row, 1975), p. 56. At least one state, New York, has passed special legislation seeking to limit access to psychiatric records available for entry into computerized MSIS systems. *Id.* California has enacted legislation based on the National Association of Insurance Commissioner's Model Bill. This act regulates some of the circumstances under which insurance companies disclose information to other agencies. The act also authorizes individual patients to inspect their insurance records and correct errors. Dubro, *Your Medical Records: How Private Are They?* 3 Cal.Lawyer, 33, 36 (1983).

b. Defamation

Defamation is the tort of making a statement to a third person which tends to injure the reputation of another, that is, which tends to diminish the person's esteem and respect in the eyes of the community or to excite adverse or unpleasant opinions about him. When the statement is oral, the tort is called slander; when it is written, the tort is called libel. Sometimes courts require that the statement be made with malice or ill will toward the plaintiff. Even when the speaker made the statement without actual malice, however, he may be held liable for the injury to the plaintiff. In such cases the malice is said to be implied.

There are two defenses to any defamation action. One is truth; the second is privilege. The privilege in the law of defamation is not coextensive with the testimonial privilege to be discussed later. Privilege here means that certain statements which might otherwise be considered defamatory are immune from attack given the context in which they were spoken. For example, statements made by a therapist during the course of judicial or quasi-judicial proceedings are absolutely immune from legal challenge. This would apply to a therapist's testimony in commitment or malpractice trials.

It is also a general rule that defamatory statements, if made in good faith to discharge a legitimate duty with which the speaker is charged or to advance a valid, and important, interest of the speaker, are privileged if the statements are made to another person having a corresponding interest or responsibility. This interest need not necessarily be of a legal nature, but may arise from a moral or social imperative.

While a detailed analysis of the law of defamation is beyond the scope of these materials, it may be useful to consider a case which illustrates its application in the context of treatment.

HOESL v. UNITED STATES OF AMERICA AND DR. DAVID ALLEN KASUBOSKI

United States Court of Appeals, Ninth Circuit, 1980.
629 F.2d 586.

* * *

I. FACTUAL BACKGROUND

This statement of facts is based on the complaint, whose allegations the Court assumes to be true for the purposes of the pending motions.

In May 1975, plaintiff was employed by the United States Department of the Navy as a civilian electrical engineer at the Naval Air Rework Facility ("NARF") in Alameda, California. On May 9, 1975, plaintiff's supervisors at NARF directed him to report on the same day to the Navy Regional Medical Center at Oakland, California, for a medical examination, and plaintiff complied. The examination was conducted by Dr. Kasuboski, a psychiatrist employed by the Navy, and its purpose was to determine whether plaintiff suffered from any mental disability which made him unable to carry out his responsibilities. Based on this examination, Dr. Kasuboski concluded that plaintiff did suffer from such a disability. Plaintiff alleges that Dr. Kasuboski was negligent in making this diagnosis and that the diagnosis was incorrect.

After the examination Dr. Kasuboski prepared a written report setting forth his findings. He sent this report to the NARF Industrial Medical Department, which forwarded it to plaintiff's supervisors. Relying on the conclusions reached by Dr. Kasuboski in his report, the supervisors placed plaintiff on an emergency suspension for medical reasons. Plaintiff was subsequently terminated as medically disabled.

Plaintiff appealed these actions through administrative channels, and the Civil Service Commission eventually reinstated him to his original position and awarded him at least partial back pay for the period of his suspension and separation.

* * *

Plaintiff claims that as a result of Dr. Kasuboski's negligence in preparing his report, "he has suffered permanent and irreparable harm to his professional reputation * * *" and impairment of his earning capacity. Other claimed elements of damage include severe mental anguish, the expenses which plaintiff incurred in his efforts to obtain relief in administrative and judicial proceedings, and the rest of his back pay. The general damages sought are seven million dollars and as yet unascertained special damages.

* * *

Plaintiff states a cause of action for defamation under California law. The substantive tort law of California governs plaintiff's claim under the FTCA because the allegedly tortious conduct was committed in California and because the alleged injury to plaintiff caused by that conduct was suffered by him in this state.

California Civil Code § 45 defines libel as

"Libel is a false and unprivileged publication by writing, printing, picture, effigy, or other fixed representation to the eye, which exposes any person to hatred, contempt, ridicule, or obloquy, or which causes him to be shunned or avoided, or which has a tendency to injure him in his occupation."

Plaintiff's complaint contains allegations which state a claim under this section.

First, the complaint alleges that Dr. Kasuboski's diagnosis of plaintiff was false.

Second, plaintiff alleges that the defamatory matter applies to and concerns him, as California Code of Civil Procedure § 460 requires.

Third, plaintiff has alleged the publication of this allegedly false diagnosis. Publication consists of the communication of the defendant's characterization of the plaintiff to a person other than the plaintiff.[a]

* * * Plaintiff alleges that Dr. Kasuboski sent a copy of his diagnostic report to his superiors, who then forwarded it to plaintiff's supervisors.

Fourth, Dr. Kasuboski communicated his diagnosis to plaintiff's superiors by means of a written report, so the publication was in writing.

Finally, plaintiff alleges that the publication of this diagnosis tended "to injure him in his occupation." Cal.Civ.Code § 45. California applies a broad definition to injuries to reputation, *Moore v. Greene*, 431 F.2d 584, 592 (9 Cir.1970), and language alleged to be libelous need only be fairly included within the statutory definition of libel. *Schomberg v. Walker*, 132 Cal. 224, 227, 64 P. 290, 291 (1901). The imputation of severe psychological problems to an individual is generally held defamatory on its face.

Like other courts, California courts have refused to hold defamatory on its face or defamatory at all an imputation of mental disorder which is made in an oblique or hyperbolic manner (statement made "not to describe the plaintiff as a person who was mentally ill but as one who was unreasonable in his actions and his demands"); (letter implying that mental patient released by hospital should still be institutionalized is not libelous per se); (characterization of plaintiff as "paranoid" and "schizophrenic" constitutes nondefamatory hyperbole). However, in a case involving the unambiguous and considered publication to an employer that an employee has a specified mental disorder serious enough to make him unfit for his job, California courts would unquestionably follow other courts and hold the publication defamatory on its face.

Dr. Kasuboski's report is such a publication. It did more than impute or imply plaintiff's unfitness for his position; it explicitly

a. Throughout this opinion, the Court uses the term publication in this specialized sense which has no necessary connotation of communication to the public generally or to large numbers of people.

stated that he was unfit because of a psychiatric disorder. Even if this defamatory publication was not libelous on its face, it is still actionable provided that plaintiff "alleges and proves that he has suffered special damage as a proximate result thereof." Plaintiff has satisfied that requirement because he alleges that the publication of the report led directly to his suspension and termination.

If one of plaintiff's coworkers had accused him of the kind of psychiatric disorder that Dr. Kasuboski diagnosed, plaintiff could sue only for defamation, and the mere fact that defendant in this case is a physician and that he obtained the allegedly defamatory information about plaintiff during the course of a professional consultation does not mean that he committed some tort other than defamation. Under the law of California and other jurisdictions, a doctor who communicates untrue medical information about his patient to a third party commits defamation, unless of course the publication is privileged.

* * *

The disclosure by a doctor to third persons of medical information about a patient may in some circumstances give rise to a statutory cause of action or to a cause of action for invasion of privacy or for a breach of contract. But those circumstances are not present in this case. Disclosure is actionable only when it is improper because, for example, the patient has not authorized the doctor to disclose the information. Plaintiff does not allege that it was improper for Dr. Kasuboski to communicate his diagnosis to plaintiff's supervisors. He claims only that Dr. Kasuboski should not have communicated the wrong diagnosis.

The tortious conduct that plaintiff alleges, the communication to his employer of a report falsely calling him unfit, is the kind of conduct that gives rise to defamation actions. All the injuries which plaintiff alleges were caused by an injury to his reputation. Dr. Kasuboski's report about his unfitness resulted in his suspension and termination, and his claimed emotional injuries are the kind recoverable in defamation actions. In light of these factors, it is clear that under California law, the tort which Dr. Kasuboski allegedly committed was defamation.

* * *

III. LIABILITY OF DR. KASUBOSKI

Plaintiff is not entitled to any relief from Dr. Kasuboski because Dr. Kasuboski's report was privileged.

The scope of personal immunity of federal employees like Dr. Kasuboski is a matter of federal common law. The state of this federal law, especially in connection with absolute immunity, is somewhat uncertain. In 1959, the Supreme Court held that high-level executive officers have absolute immunity in defamation actions for statements made "within the outer perimeter of [their] line of duty * * *." *Barr v. Matteo*, 360 U.S. 564, 575, 79 S.Ct. 1335, 1341, 3 L.Ed.2d 1434 (1959).

*   *   *

Recent Supreme Court cases involving the scope of executive immunity under the civil rights laws have suggested that executive employees may be entitled only to a qualified immunity in common-law actions. It is unnecessary for this Court to enter that debate. For it is clear that Dr. Kasuboski's report is protected by a qualified privilege even if it is not absolutely privileged.

The law of defamation has long recognized a qualified or conditional privilege for publications made in a reasonable manner and for a proper purpose. Prosser, *supra* § 115, at 785–786; Restatement of Torts, *supra*, §§ 593–612, at 285–305; *see* Cal.Civ.Code § 47(3). This qualified privilege may be invoked when publication is necessary to protect the interests of persons other than the publisher. Prosser, *supra*, at 787–789; Restatement of Torts, *supra*, § 595, at 268. It is, for example, permissible to inform an employer of the unfitness of one of his employees, Restatement of Torts, *supra*, § 595 Comment (i), at 273, and this category of privileged publications includes warnings by a physician to the employer of a patient. *See* cases cited in Prosser, *supra*, at 788 n. 2.

A qualified privilege is lost if the publisher acts with malice or if the publisher abuses the occasion of publication. Malice exists when the publisher knows the published matter to be false or acts in reckless disregard as to its truth or falsity, Restatement of Torts, *supra*, § 600, at 288, or perhaps if the publisher is motivated by spite or ill will toward the subject of the communication. Negligence in ascertaining the facts in the allegedly defamatory publication does not meet this scienter requirement.

*   *   *

The factual allegations of plaintiff's complaint demonstrate that Dr. Kasuboski's report was privileged under the qualified immunity for reports about an employee's fitness to his employer. Dr. Kasuboski's job was to evaluate the fitness of government employees when instructed to do so, and when plaintiff's supervisors made the entirely legitimate request that Dr. Kasuboski examine him, Dr. Kasuboski complied, as he should have done. The doctor sent his report only to those people who needed access to it, and there is no allegation that he included extraneous or scurrilous matter irrelevant to his diagnosis. Plaintiff alleges only that Dr. Kasuboski acted negligently in gathering the facts which he stated in his report, and mere negligence does not satisfy the scienter requirement of the qualified privilege.

Because Dr. Kasuboski's report was privileged and because the facts underlying the privilege appear on the face of the complaint, plaintiff's claim against Dr. Kasuboski must be dismissed for failure to state a claim upon which relief for defamation may be granted.

*   *   *

2. Remedies Arising From the Patient/Therapist Relationship

In addition to defamation and invasion of privacy, wrongful disclosure of patient or client information may be actionable as a breach of duty that arises from the confidential nature of the professional relationship between therapist and patient. This tort was first recognized in suits against physicians for unauthorized disclosure of patient information. More recently, various states have enacted laws giving a patient a cause of action against a psychotherapist who wrongfully disclosed confidential information. In other states a cause of action has been found to arise not from any express statutory enactment but rather from related laws, such as state-licensing statutes governing the testimonial privilege or those providing for the confidentiality of patient records. The case of *Doe v. Roe*, which follows, illustrates the role of courts in filling in gaps created by legislative inaction.

DOE v. ROE

Supreme Court, New York County, 1977.
93 Misc.2d 201, 400 N.Y.S.2d 668.

MARTIN B. STECHER, Justice:

This action for an injunction and for damages for breach of privacy is a matter of first impression in this State, and so far as I am able to ascertain, a matter of first impression in the United States. It arises out of the publication, verbatim, by a psychiatrist of a patient's disclosures during the course of a lengthy psychoanalysis. I have made and filed detailed findings of fact which are briefly summarized here.

Dr. Joan Roe is a physician who has practiced psychiatry for more than fifty years. Her husband, Peter Poe, has been a psychologist for some 25 years. The plaintiff and her late, former husband were each patients of Dr. Roe for many years. The defendants, eight years after the termination of treatment, published a book which reported verbatim and extensively the patients' thoughts, feelings, and emotions, their sexual and other fantasies and biographies, their most intimate personal relationships and the disintegration of their marriage. Interspersed among the footnotes are Roe's diagnoses of what purport to be the illnesses suffered by the patients and one of their children.

The defendants allege that the plaintiff consented to this publication. This defense is without substance. Consent was sought while the plaintiff was in therapy. It was never obtained in writing. In Dr. Roe's own words consent "was there one day and not there another day. That was the nature of the illness I was treating, unreliable." I need not deal with the value of an oral waiver of confidentiality given by a patient to a psychiatrist during the course of treatment. It is sufficient to conclude that not only did the defendants fail to obtain the plaintiff's consent to publication, they were well aware that they had none. [The plaintiff contended that in the absence of a statutory provision expressly recognizing a cause of action against a therapist who wrongfully discloses confidential information, an action is impliedly authorized by various state laws including sections of the New York Civil Practice Law and Rules (Sec. 4504(a)) and provisions of the New York Licensing and Disciplinary Statutes (Ed.L. 6509 et seq.). Following a review of the text and history of these statutory provisions the court concluded that these sections standing by themselves did not authorize a private cause of action. The court next addressed the plaintiff's intention that other theories including the right to privacy and rights flowing from the contract between the therapist and patient grant a cause of action for wrongful disclosure.]

* * *

As hereafter indicated there are theories on which liability may be predicated other than violation of the CPLR [4504(a)], the licensing and disciplinary statutes [Ed.L. 6509 et seq.] and what I perceive as this State's public policy. In two of the very few cases which have come to grips with the issue of wrongful disclosure by physicians of patients' secrets [*Hammonds v. Aetna Casualty & Surety Company*, 243 F.Supp. 793 [N.D.Ohio, 1965]; and *Horne v. Patton*, 291 Ala. 701, 287 So.2d 824 [1973] the courts predicated their holdings on the numerous sources of obligation which arise out of the physician-patient relationship.

* * *

I too find that a physician, who enters into an agreement with a patient to provide medical attention, impliedly covenants to keep in confidence all disclosures made by the patient concerning the patient's physical or mental condition as well as all matters discovered by the physician in the course of examination or treatment. This is particularly and necessarily true of the psychiatric relationship, for in the dynamics of psychotherapy "(t)he patient is called upon to discuss in a candid and frank manner personal material of the most intimate and disturbing nature * * * He is expected to bring up all manner of socially unacceptable instincts and urges, immature wishes, perverse sexual thoughts—in short the unspeakable, the unthinkable, the repressed. To speak of such things to another human being requires an atmosphere of unusual trust, confidence and tolerance.

* * *

There can be little doubt that under the law of the State of New York and in a proper case, the contract of private parties to retain in confidence matter which should be kept in confidence will be enforced by injunction and compensated in damages

The contract between the plaintiff and Dr. Roe is such a contract.

* * *

Every patient, and particularly every patient undergoing psychoanalysis, has such a right of privacy. [Eminating from the plaintiff's contract right to confidentiality and other state laws including the licensing and disciplinary statute and the New York civil practice law.] Under what circumstances can a person be expected to reveal sexual fantasies, infantile memories, passions of hate and love, one's most intimate relationship with one's spouse and others except upon the inferential agreement that such confessions will be forever entombed in the psychiatrist's memory, never to be revealed during the psychiatrist's lifetime or thereafter? The very needs of the profession itself require that confidentiality exist *and be enforced*. As pointed out in *Matter of Lifschutz*, 2 Cal.3d 415, 85 Cal.Rptr. 829, 467 P.2d 557 [1970] "a large segment of the psychiatric profession concurs in Dr. Lifschutz's strongly held belief that an absolute privilege of confidentiality is essential to the effective practice of psychotherapy" [*cf.* Annotation, 20 A.L.R.3d, 1109, 1112]. Despite the fact that in no New York case has such a wrong been remedied due, most likely, to the fact that so few physicians violate this fundamental obligation, it is time that the obligation not only be recognized but that the right of redress be recognized as well.

What label we affix to this wrong is unimportant [although the category of wrong could, under certain circumstances—such as determining the applicable statute of limitations—be significant]. It is generally accepted that "There is no necessity whatever that a tort must have a name. New and nameless torts are being recognized constantly". [Prosser, Torts (2d ed.), p. 3]. What is important is that there must be the infliction of intentional harm, resulting in damage, without legal excuses or justification.

* * *

The defendants contend that the physician's obligation of confidentiality is not absolute and must give way to the general public interest. The interest, as they see it in this case, is the scientific value of the publication.

It is not disputed that under our public policy the right of confidentiality is less than absolute. * * *

Despite the duty of confidentiality courts have recognized the duty of a psychiatrist to give warning where a patient clearly presents a danger to others to disclose the existence of a contagious disease, to report the use of "controlled substances" in certain situations and to report gunshot and other wounds.

In no case, however, has the curiosity or education of the medical profession superseded the duty of confidentiality. I do not reach the question of a psychiatrist's right to publish case histories where the identities are fully concealed for that is not our problem here, nor do I find it necessary to reach the issue of whether or not an important scientific discovery would take precedence over a patient's privilege of non-disclosure. I do not consider myself qualified to determine the contribution which this book may have made to the science or art of psychiatry. I do conclude, however, that if such contribution was the defendants' defense they have utterly failed in their proof that this volume represented a major contribution to scientific knowledge. The evidence is to the contrary and this defense must necessarily fail.

Nor is the argument available that by enjoining the further distribution of this book the court will be engaging in a "prior restraint" on publication.

*   *   *

There is no prior restraint in the case at bar. The book has been published and it does offend against the plaintiff's right of privacy, contractual and otherwise, not to have her innermost thoughts offered to all for the price of this book. There is no prior restraint and, therefore, no censorship within constitutional meaning.

*   *   *

The liability of Dr. Roe to respond in damages is clear; and Mr. Poe's liability is equally clear. True, he and the plaintiff were not involved in a physician-patient relationship and he certainly had no contractual relationship to her. But, the conclusion is unassailable that Poe, like anyone else with access to the book, knew that its source was the patient's production in psychoanalysis. He knew as well as, and perhaps better than Roe, of the absence of consent, of the failure to disguise. If anyone was the actor in seeing to it that the work was written, that it was manufactured, advertised and circulated, it was Poe. He is a co-author and a willing, indeed avid, co-violator of the patient's rights and is therefore equally liable.

The plaintiff seeks punitive damages and suggests that a proper measure of those damages, in addition to compensatory damage, is approximately $50,000, the sum plaintiff has thus far expended on and incurred for attorneys' fees.

*   *   *

In order to warrant an award of punitive damages, it must have been affirmatively demonstrated that the wrong committed was willful and malicious, that the act complained of was "morally culpable or *   *   * actuated by evil and reprehensible motives, not only to punish the defendant but to deter him, as well as others *   *   *"

Where the act complained of is willful, malicious and wanton, punitive damages are sometimes available to "express indignation at the defendants' wrong rather than a value set on plaintiff's loss." Certainly, the acts of the defendants here are such as to warrant an expression of indignation and punishment for the purpose of deterring similar acts by these defendants or others. The difficulty, however, is that the defendants' acts were not willful, malicious or wanton—they were merely stupid. I have no doubt that the defendants were of the opinion that they had sufficiently concealed the identity of the plaintiff and her family. I have no doubt that in addition to the commercial success they hoped to have, they believed that they were rendering a public service in publishing what they considered an in-depth description of the plaintiff's family. But there was no motive to harm. Under these circumstances, punitive damages are not available.

*   *   *

The plaintiff has suffered damage as a consequence of this publication. She suffered acute embarrassment on learning the extent to which friends, colleagues, employer, students and others, had read or read of the book. Her livelihood, as indicated in the findings, was threatened; but fortunately, the actual cash loss was only some $1,500. Medical attention, principally treatment with Dr. Lowenfeld, cost an additional $1,400. But beyond these sums the plaintiff suffered in health. She had insomnia and nightmares. She became reclusive as a consequence of the shame and humiliation induced by the book's publication and her well-being and emotional health were significantly impaired for three years. In my opinion the fair and reasonable value of the injury she sustained—to the extent it can be compensated in damages—is $20,000.

Damages, of course, do not provide an adequate remedy; for should the book circulate further, beyond the 220 copies already sold, the damage must accrue anew. The plaintiff is entitled to a judgment permanently enjoining the defendants, their heirs, successors and assigns from further violating the plaintiff's right to privacy whether by circulating this book or by otherwise disclosing any of the matters revealed by the plaintiff to Dr. Roe in the course of psychotherapy.

*   *   *

Questions and Comments

1. A duty of confidentiality does not arise unless a treatment relationship has been established between the patient and therapist. When it is clear from the outset that the physician or psychotherapist is examining or diagnosing a person at the request of a third party, no duty of confidentiality arises. Under these circumstances otherwise confidential matters may be included in the report that the therapist communicates to the third party.

2. A patient may voluntarily waive the right of confidentiality. For instance, insurance companies frequently require an applicant to supply his medical background and, in that connection, request that the applicant authorize the insurance company to obtain information from any physician or other persons who may have provided health care in the past. Also, insurance carriers which provide coverage for psychological counseling often require reports of the services performed by the therapist as a condition for payment. In this situation, the patient may be asked to authorize certain disclosures to the insurance carrier. Disclosures even when authorized by the patient present some problems for

the therapist. It is not always clear what information may be disclosed. Is it the fact of treatment or the diagnosis or may it include other information, such as the disability of the patient?

3. One of the defenses in *Doe v. Roe* was that the plaintiff had consented to the publication. The Court rejected the defense because "[i]t was sought while the patient was in therapy." Does this suggest that any consent to publication obtained in a course of treatment is not binding and cannot be relied on by the therapist? What considerations support this rule?

4. To what extent may a therapist disclose confidential information to other professionals without the patient's expressed consent? Similarly, what are the limits of disclosure for the purpose of research or the training of professionals? There is little developed case law on these points. However, as suggested by the court in *Wiseman* a professional appears to have somewhat greater latitude in being able to communicate information where the purpose involves the training of other professionals. The exact scope of this latitude has not been authoritatively resolved by decided cases. In any event, a treating professional can always obtain protection against subsequent claims by obtaining the patient's informed consent to having the information disclosed in the context of the publication of research findings or for training.

MacDONALD v. CLINGER

Supreme Court, Appellate Division, Fourth Department, 1982.
84 App.Div.2d 482, 446 N.Y.S.2d 801.

DENMAN, Justice.

We here consider whether a psychiatrist must respond in damages to his former patient for disclosure of personal information learned during the course of treatment and, if he must, on what theory of recovery the action may be maintained. We hold that such wrongful disclosure is a breach of the fiduciary duty of confidentiality and gives rise to a cause of action sounding in tort.

The complaint alleges that during two extended courses of treatment with defendant, a psychiatrist, plaintiff revealed intimate details about himself which defendant later divulged to plaintiff's wife without justification and without consent. As a consequence of such disclosure, plaintiff alleges that his marriage deteriorated, that he lost his job, that he suffered financial difficulty and that he was caused such severe emotional distress that he required further psychiatric treatment. The complaint set forth three causes of action: breach of an implied contract; breach of confidence in violation of public policy; and breach of the right of privacy guaranteed by article 5 of the Civil Rights Law. Defendant moved to dismiss for failure to state a cause of action, asserting that there was in reality only one theory of recovery, that of breach of confidence, and that such action could not be maintained against him because his disclosure to plaintiff's wife was justified. The court dismissed the third cause of action but denied the motion with respect to the first two causes of action and this appeal ensued.

Research reveals few cases in American jurisprudence which treat the doctor-patient privilege in this context. That is undoubtedly due to the fact that the confidentiality of the relationship is a cardinal rule of the medical profession, faithfully adhered to in most instances, and thus has come to be justifiably relied upon by patients seeking advice and treatment. This physician-patient relationship is contractual in nature, whereby the physician, in agreeing to administer to the patient, impliedly covenants that the disclosures necessary to diagnosis and treatment of the patient's mental or physical condition will be kept in confidence.

Examination of cases which have addressed this problem makes it apparent that courts have immediately recognized a legally compensable injury in such wrongful disclosure based on a variety of grounds for recovery: public policy; right to privacy; breach of contract; breach of fiduciary duty. As the Supreme Court of Washington stated in *Smith v. Driscoll*, 94 Wash. 441, 442, 162 P. 572:

> Neither is it necessary to pursue at length the inquiry of whether a cause of action lies in favor of a patient against a physician for wrongfully divulging confidential communications. For the purposes of what we shall say it will be assumed that, for so palpable a wrong, the law provides a remedy.

An excellent and carefully researched opinion exploring the legal ramifications of this confidentiality is *Doe v. Roe*, 93 Misc.2d 201, 400 N.Y.S.2d 668, a decision after a non-jury trial in which plaintiff sought injunctive relief and damages because of the verbatim publication by her former psychiatrist of extremely personal details of her life revealed during years of psychoanalysis. The court considered several proposed theories of recovery, including violation of public policy and breach of privacy rights. We agree with the court's observation that the several statutes and regulations requiring physicians to protect the confidentiality of information gained during treatment are clear evidence of the public policy of New York but that there is a more appropriate theory of recovery than one rooted in public policy.

Neither do we believe that an action for breach of the right of privacy may be maintained despite some current predictions to the contrary.

*   *   *

* * * I * * * find that a physician, who enters into an agreement with a patient to provide medical attention, impliedly covenants to keep in confidence all disclosures made by the patient concerning the patient's physical or mental condition as well as all matters discovered by the physician in the course of examination or treatment. This is particularly and necessarily true of the psychiatric relationship, for in the dynamics of psychotherapy "[t]he patient is

called upon to discuss in a candid and frank manner personal material of the most intimate and disturbing nature * * * He is expected to bring up all manner of socially unacceptable instincts and urges, immature wishes, perverse sexual thoughts—in short, the unspeakable, the unthinkable, the repressed. To speak of such things to another human requires an atmosphere of unusual trust, confidence and tolerance.

* * *

It is obvious then that this relationship gives rise to an implied covenant which, when breached, is actionable. If plaintiff's recovery were limited to an action for breach of contract, however, he would generally be limited to economic loss flowing directly from the breach and would thus be precluded from recovering for mental distress, loss of his employment and the deterioration of his marriage. We believe that the relationship contemplates an additional duty springing from but extraneous to the contract and that the breach of such duty is actionable as a tort. Indeed, an action in tort for a breach of a duty of confidentiality and trust has long been acknowledged in the courts of this state.

* * * When such duty grows out of relations of trust and confidence, as that of the agent to his principal or the lawyer to his client, the ground of the duty is apparent, and the tort is, in general, easily separable from the mere breach of contract. * * *

* * *

Such duty, however, is not absolute, and its breach is actionable only if it is wrongful, that is to say, without justification or excuse. Although public policy favors the confidentiality described herein, there is a countervailing public interest to which it must yield in appropriate circumstances. Thus where a patient may be a danger to himself or others a physician is required to disclose to the extent necessary to protect a threatened interest.

* * *

Although the disclosure of medical information to a spouse may be justified under some circumstances, a more stringent standard should apply with respect to psychiatric information. One spouse often seeks counselling concerning personal problems that may affect the marital relationship. To permit disclosure to the other spouse in the absence of an overriding concern would deter the one in need from obtaining the help required. Disclosure of confidential information by a psychiatrist to a spouse will be justified whenever there is a danger to the patient, the spouse or another person; otherwise information should not be disclosed without authorization. Justification or excuse will depend upon a showing of circumstances and competing interests which support the need to disclose (cf. *Berry v. Moench*, 8 Utah 2d 191, 331 P.2d 814, *supra*). Because such showing is a matter of affirmative defense, defendant is not entitled to dismissal of the action.

The order should be modified to dismiss the cause of action for breach of contract and as modified should be affirmed.

Order modified on the law and as modified affirmed with costs to defendant.

SIMONS, J.P., concurs in a separate opinion.

SIMONS, Justice Presiding (concurring).

Plaintiff seeks in this action to recover from defendant, his psychiatrist, for defendant's allegedly unjustified and damaging disclosure of confidential information about plaintiff's condition to plaintiff's wife. The members of the court are agreed that he may do so and that the action sounds in tort. We are divided about the nature of the cause of action, however, the majority believing it to be a "breach of fiduciary duty to confidentiality," while I believe the cause of action to be for malpractice. The difference is one of substance, for the majority hold plaintiff may recover if he submits evidence of the professional relationship, the disclosure of confidential information and damages. Once plaintiff does so, it is for the doctor to offer evidence of justification and for the jury to weigh it. Plaintiff's right to recover, as they see it, rests on proof of an unauthorized disclosure, the breach of an implied promise to hold confidential information received during treatment. In my view, plaintiff's right to recover must rest upon his proof that the disclosure was wrongful or unjustified.

When a physician undertakes treatment of a patient, he impliedly represents that he possesses, and the law places upon him the duty of possessing, the reasonable degree of learning and skill possessed by physicians in the community generally. Culpable fault exists if the physician fails to live up to this standard.

* * * Confidentiality, particularly in the case of a psychiatrist, is a significant and important aspect of medical treatment and a promise of non-disclosure may readily be implied from the physician-patient relationship. Thus, the relationship has elements of a contract, as plaintiff's first cause of action suggests, but commonly malpractice is a tort action predicated upon the physician's violation of his duty to supply the quality of care promised when he undertook to treat the patient. The physician's duty to honor this implied promise of confidentiality is merely another aspect of the treatment rendered and should be judged similarly.

The majority, by taking the cause of action out of the malpractice area, hold that all unauthorized disclosures, *prima facie*, violate reasonable medical care. The disclosure may be excused only if defendant proves that it was precipitated by danger to the patient, spouse or another. No other disclosure is permissible, apparently, even if mandated by statute. But further than that, the established rules of professional malpractice base liability upon an objective standard measured by the general quality of care of the professional community. The rule advanced by the majority permits the standard of care in unauthorized disclosure cases to be set by the jury. Thus, in every case of disclosure, the physician is exposed to the danger of a damage verdict resting upon the jury's subjective view of his explanation of his conduct even if it was in accordance with accepted medical practice. Thus, a jury disbelieving a physician's evaluation that a patient is assaultive or suicidal may hold the physician liable for the most limited but necessary disclosure relating to such commonplace matters as advice to ensure that the patient takes prescribed medication or avoids stressful situations.

In short, to avoid a non-suit, a plaintiff should submit evidence of more than an unauthorized disclosure by the physician. There should be evidence that the physician has engaged in the unskilled practice of medicine. The relationship between the parties, after all, is medical, not fiduciary. The doctor is hired to treat the patient and his liability, if any, should be predicated upon his failure to do so properly.

*   *   *

Questions and Comments

1. Regardless of the plaintiff-patient's choice of legal theory, the defendant-therapist may raise certain defenses whose merits will usually determine the outcome of the case. All of these defenses may best be understood as falling within four possible categories: absolute privilege, qualified privilege, patient consent, or absence of malice.

"Privilege" is a term frequently used in discussions about confidential information. Perhaps the best way to understand the term is to think of privilege as an exemption from liability which would otherwise attach to the actor's disclosure or withholding of information. A privilege may be either "absolute" or "qualified." An absolute privilege attaches whenever disclosure is compelled by law. Examples of compelled disclosure, which are treated in greater detail in another section of this chapter, includes reports of child abuse, drug dependency, or illnesses which pose a threat to the public safety, such as persons with venereal disease or other serious contagious diseases. Disclosure may also be compelled by courts or legislative and administrative agencies.

When disclosure of confidential information is not unequivocally mandated by law, a therapist's disclosures may nevertheless be immune under the doctrine of "qualified privilege," which allows disclosure only if certain conditions are met. The first condition is that the therapist's purpose in disclosing the confidential information must be to achieve some societal purpose of importance comparable to the patient's interest in preserving confidentiality. Such interests may include, for example, protection of the safety of another endangered by a violent patient or disclosures made in good faith in proceedings for the civil commitment of a patient. A second condition is that the disclosure be no greater than reasonably necessary to achieve the purpose sought. Third, the disclosure must be by a method which is appropriate under the circumstances to achieve the purpose sought. A therapist will usually not be liable, for example, for entrusting a confidential report to an office secretary for typing. He may incur liability, on the other hand, for submitting the report to the patient's employer, when such action is neither authorized nor necessary to achieve any legitimate purpose outweighing the patient's interest in confidentiality.

2. If the patient or client has authorized disclosure, the therapist cannot be held liable for disclosures in compliance with the patient's authorization. The patient's consent thus constitutes a third possible defense in an action for wrongful disclosure. The issue of consent is not as simple as it may appear at first. First it is not always clear whether a patient has consented to disclosure. If disclosure of psychological reports to teachers and school officials is a routine practice at a psychological clinic, for example, can it be said that a patient who seeks counselling there has implicitly consented to such disclosures? *See Iverson v. Frandsen*, 237 F.2d 898 (10th Cir.1956).

Second, even if the patient's express consent is obtained, however, the scope of consent is not always clear. A patient may consent to allow a therapist to disclose to the patient's prospective employer that he has received therapy. Does this consent authorize disclosure of the nature of the patient's problem, or of the nature or length of treatment, or specific facts about the patient relating to his suitability for employment?

II. LIMITATIONS ON THE DUTY OF CONFIDENTIALITY

A. INTRODUCTION

The preceding materials have explored doctrines which protect patients from unauthorized disclosures by professionals with whom they have entered into a patient/therapist relationship. The patient's rights of privacy, however, are not absolute, and in some circumstances a therapist may be under a legal duty to make disclosure to either agencies of the state or private citizens.

There are three situations where *disclosure of information* by the therapist may be required. One exception is created by compulsory reporting statutes which cover such matters as child abuse or narcotics addiction. The second category, which so far has been adopted by only a minority of states, is the obligation of a therapist to communicate to third parties the known dangerous propensities of the patient.

A third category of compelled disclosure is the duty to give testimony in a judicial proceeding. However, this duty is not applied universally, and in fact the legal system has carved out special exceptions for professionals including physicians and psychotherapists. These exceptions fall within the ambient of what is known as the testimonial privilege, are fairly technical in nature, and do not apply with equal force in all jurisdictions. While any comprehensive treatment of the testimonial privilege is beyond the purview of these materials, section D below seeks to set forth the general legal framework governing the application of the privilege.

B. MANDATORY REPORTING REQUIREMENTS

Nearly all states have enacted laws which require physicians to disclose to designated authorities certain types of patient information, even if the information would otherwise be confidential. Most states, for instance, require the reporting to health authorities the fact that a patient is suffering from certain communicable diseases. *Hammonds v. Aetna Casualty & Surety Co.*, 243 F.Supp. 793 (N.D. Ohio 1965). Nearly all states also impose a duty on physicians or hospital administrators to report to police authorities any case where a patient appears for treatment of gunshot injuries. Jon R. Waltz and Fred E. Inbau, *Medical Jurisprudence* (New York: Macmillan, 1971), p. 364. Some states also require attending or consulting physicians to report the name of any person known to be "a habitual user of a narcotic drug." *Id.* at 365. Finally, most states require any physician who has reasonable cause to suspect an incidence of child abuse to report such fact to a designated agency. *Id.* at 320–322. None of these statutes expressly cover non-physician psychotherapists who may obtain information of child abuse as a result of treating the parent. Thus, it is possible that in some jurisdictions psychiatrists are covered by these provisions whereas other mental health professionals are not. In any event, legal reporting requirements override the usual rules governing the confidentiality of patient/therapist relationships.

Questions and Comments

Recent cases suggest that there are constitutional limits on the power of legislatures to impose medical reporting requirements. For instance, a majority of the justices of the Supreme Court have found broad state law requirements for notification of the parents of minors seeking an abortion to be constitutionally defective. *Bellotti v. Baird*, 443 U.S. 622, 99 S.Ct. 3035, 61 L.Ed.2d 797 (1979). But see, *H.L. v. Matheson*, 450 U.S. 398, 101 S.Ct. 1164, 67 L.Ed.2d 388 (1981).

In the psychiatric context a California Appeal Court has held that a state law provision that required institutions to notify a "responsible relative" of the patient prior to the administration of ECT or psychosurgery violated the patient's right to privacy. *Aden v. Younger*, 57 Cal. App.3d 662, 129 Cal.Rptr. 535 (1976).

C. DISCLOSURES OF THE DANGEROUS PROPENSITIES OF THE PATIENT

TARASOFF v. REGENTS OF THE UNIVERSITY OF CALIFORNIA

Supreme Court of California, 1976.
17 Cal.3d 425, 131 Cal.Rptr. 14, 551 P.2d 334.

(The opinion is set out at page 94).

SHAW v. GLICKMAN

Court of Special Appeals of Maryland, 1980.
45 Md.App. 718, 415 A.2d 625.

[Plaintiff, Daniel Shaw, a dentist, had been undergoing group therapy treatment conducted by the defendant psychiatrist and his wife, a psychiatric nurse. Among the other patients in the group were Mr. and Mrs. Billian. Unknown to Mr. Billian, an amorous relationship developed between Mrs. Billian and Dr. Shaw. Upon learning of the extramarital affair, one of the therapists disclosed the information to Mr. Billian at a private therapy session. Some days later, Mr. Billian broke into Dr. Shaw's home. Finding his wife in bed with Dr. Shaw, Mr. Billian fired five shots at the doctor. Dr. Shaw filed an action to recover for his injuries, naming as defendants both Mr. Billian and the psychiatric team that had been conducting the group therapy sessions. The complaint charged that the defendant therapists had failed to warn him of Mr. Billian's "unstable and violent condition and the foreseeable and immediate danger that it presented to the plaintiff."]

GILBERT, Chief Judge:

Shaw points to *Tarasoff v. Regents of the University of California*, 17 Cal.3d 425, 131 Cal.Rptr. 14, 551 P.2d 334 (1976), as authority for the proposition that the psychotherapist-patient relationship imposes on the therapists a duty to control his patient and the concomitant duty to protect the patient's would-be victim.

*   *   *

The Court, in *Tarasoff*, noted that there was no question of a missed diagnosis or failure to predict the future conduct of the patient. What was involved was the fact that the patient did tell the therapist of the plan to kill Tatiana, and the therapist, while correctly predicting the event, negligently failed to warn the victim.

The court turned away the contention that "the therapist should be absolved of any responsibility for failing to act to protect the potential victim." Rather the court opined that "once a therapist . . . determine[s], or under applicable professional standards reasonably should have determined, that a patient poses a serious danger of violence to others, he bears a duty to exercise reasonable care to protect the foreseeable victim of that danger." The court concluded that each case must stand on its own facts, as measured against traditional negligence standards of reasonable care under the circumstances.

We neither accept nor reject the rationale of *Tarasoff* because, in our view, it is inapposite to the instant case.

Here there was no threat revealed to the "team" by Billian to kill or injure Dr. Shaw; there was apparently no confiding by Billian in the doctor or his staff, concerning any animosity or hatred toward Dr. Shaw. The record, at least, is devoid of the existence of any such feeling. Although Billian was known by Dr. Gallant to tote a gun, that fact does not give rise to the inference that Billian did so for the purpose of harming Dr. Shaw. The matter *sub judice* is unlike *Tarasoff* in that the intent to kill or injure was not disclosed.

Underlying Dr. Gallant's obligation to his patients was the Hippocratic oath. That oath, in pertinent part, states: "All that may come to my knowledge in the exercise of my profession or outside of my profession or in daily commerce with men, which ought not to be spread abroad, I will keep secret and will never reveal."

Of course, it may be argued that when as in *Tarasoff*, a patient informs a doctor of the patient's plan to kill another person, such information is not within the proscription of the Hippocratic oath, but rather "ought to be spread abroad" in order to prevent injury or loss of life. Clearly, had Billian confided in Dr. Gallant, or any of the team, that he, Billian, planned to shoot Dr. Shaw, Dr. Gallant would have faced a dilemma, *i.e.*, to breach Billian's confidence and tip off Shaw, or keep Billian's confidence and, figuratively speaking, throw Shaw to the wolves.

Even that dilemma is not without some legislative guidance. Md. Courts and Judicial Proceedings Code Ann. (1974) § 9–109(b) provides:

> "Unless otherwise provided, in all judicial, legislative, or administrative proceedings, a patient or his authorized representative has a privilege to refuse to disclose, and to prevent a witness from disclosing, communications relating to diagnosis or treatment of the patient's mental or emotional disorder."

* * *

The statute provides also for the exceptions to its tenets. None of the exceptions are germane to the issue before us, however. It seems to us that inasmuch as the statute confers a privilege of confidentiality on the communication between patient and psychiatrist-psychologist in judicial, legislative, or administrative proceedings, which privilege is that of the patient, no lesser privilege is existent when the matter is not judicial, legislative, or administrative. With the exception of those instances where the privilege of confidentiality is expressly prohibited, the lips of the psychiatrist or psychologist have been statutorily sealed shut subject solely to being unsealed by the patient or the patient's authorized representative.

We hold that under current Maryland law, it would have been a violation of the statute for Dr. Gallant or any member of his psychiatric team to disclose to Dr. Shaw any propensity on the part of Billian to invoke the old Solon law and shoot his wife's lover.

* * *

Because we believe no cause of action exists on the part of Dr. Shaw against the psychiatric team, under the circumstances of this case, we affirm the judgment of the Superior Court of Baltimore.

Judgment Affirmed.

Questions and Comments

1. What rationale led the *Shaw v. Glickman* court to reject the adoption of the *Tarasoff* doctrine?   Could the court's decision be reversed by the legislature?

2. Since many states have enacted statutes protecting the confidentiality of psychotherapist-patient communications, other courts could similarly reject the *Tarasoff* doctrine in favor of the rationale of the *Shaw v. Glickman* court.   Too few cases have been decided in other jurisdictions to indicate the direction in which the law is likely to develop.

3. Numerous states also authorize a physician or mental health professional to disclose any confidential information when the patient's condition makes it necessary to set in motion commitment proceedings. For instance, in Illinois records and communications may be disclosed where it is "necessary to the provision of emergency medical care to a recipient" or in "commitment proceedings." Ill.Rev.Stat. Ch. 91½ § 8–11 (Supp.1979) (Mental Health and Development Disability Confidentiality Act, 1979).   In fact, failure of a therapist to initiate commitment where warranted could lead to civil liability for negligence.   Thus, liability might attach where a therapist has failed to initiate civil commitment of a clearly suicidal patient.

D. JUDICIAL PROCEEDINGS AND THE TESTIMONIAL PRIV-ILEGE

1. Introduction

In many situations society, through an arm of government, needs information known only to a few.   In these situations, according to an old maxim, the public has a right to every man's evidence.   That is, each person has a duty to disclose information of vital importance to society.   The duty to disclose arises when society's need to ascertain the truth outweighs the individual's interest in concealing the information.   The public, through the coercive forces of government, may then compel disclosure.   The usual contexts in which the need for information arises include civil and criminal trials and hearings and investigations by legislatures and administrative agencies. In each of these contexts, the ascertainment of truth is essential to an important societal interest.

In a civil trial the dispute before the court may concern the interpretation of a contract, a disputed claim to property, or a claim for damages for an injury allegedly caused by another person's negligent conduct. The parties stand as adversaries competing to produce evidence helpful to their respective causes. The court, on behalf of society, seeks to achieve substantial justice between the parties. Ascertainment of the facts is essential in this task, but the basis of the court's decision must be limited to the evidence adduced at trial. Thus, not only do the individual parties have an interest in obtaining information, but the court, on behalf of society and in the interests of justice, seeks to assure each litigant's ability to obtain information necessary to his case.

The need for information is perhaps more dramatic in a criminal trial, where the guilt or innocence of an accused person is at stake. Society has a dual interest in ascertaining the facts in criminal cases. First, society seeks to assure that offenders are apprehended and punished. The state's task at a trial is to prove beyond a reasonable doubt that the accused person is guilty as charged. Ascertainment of facts surrounding the crime is essential in this task. Second, and equally important, is the guarantee of a fair trial and a just verdict. In the interest of fairness, society must guarantee an accused person the availability of information necessary to his defense. Indeed, the federal Bill of Rights guarantees criminal defendants' right to compel witnesses' testimony, as do most state constitutions. The cause of justice is served by assuring the availability of information to both sides, so that the truth may emerge.

In addition to the familiar settings of trials, public need for information and an individual's corresponding duty to disclose may arise in the context of legislative hearings and investigations. Whether the area is securities regulation or care of the mentally ill, legislative decisions must rest in part on balancing diverse political interests. Equally important, however, the legislature needs access to factual information. Legislative fact-finding is accomplished through hearings and investigations at which the legislature may compel testimony. In investigating charges of widespread abuse in the care of the mentally ill, for example, the legislature may compel testimony by institution administrators, behavioral scientists, and professional organizations concerned with formulating standards of treatment.

The final setting in which a duty to disclose information is likely to arise is before an administrative agency. Administrative agencies may perform functions of each of the three branches of government. Pursuant to legislatively delegated authority, an agency may draft rules regulating an industry. The agency may be authorized to perform such executive functions as granting licenses and conducting investigations of alleged violations. Finally, an agency may serve as the primary tribunal for prosecuting alleged violations. See, Chapter One, Section III.B. In each capacity fact-finding is essential. Like courts and legislatures, administrative agencies may have authority to compel testimony. More commonly, however, agencies must rely upon court orders to compel testimony from reluctant witnesses.

Whether the context is a trial, a hearing, or an investigation, the ascertainment of truth is paramount. The presiding governmental unit facilitates the endeavor by issuing subpoenae or by invoking a court's authority to issue subpoenae. A subpoena is a writ commanding a named person to appear and testify before the issuing tribunal. The first part of the witness's duty is to appear and to answer questions. Unexcused failure to comply constitutes contempt, for which the penalty may be a fine, imprisonment, or both. Additionally, the witness must testify truthfully. Lying under oath constitutes perjury.

Aside from imposing a duty to disclose information, a subpoena affords a witness protection from certain adverse consequences which might otherwise flow from his appearance or disclosures. For example, a subpoenaed witness is immune from arrest when traveling to and from the proceeding and during his stay at the place of the proceeding. Additionally, witnesses are immune from civil liability for any statement made under oath. That is, a witness may not be sued for defamation, regardless of whether his testimony damages another person's reputation. This immunity extends even to perjured testimony.

In some circumstances required information may be in written form. For example, in a suit for personal injuries, the records of a physician who treated the injured party may contain relevant information. Similarly, an accountant's records may contain information relevant to an investigation of a business merger which is suspected of violating antitrust laws. In such a case, the court or other tribunal may compel production of the documents in question by issuing a subpoena *duces tecum*, that is, a writ commanding production of the documents before the court.

Limitation of Witness's Duty: Testimonial Privilege

Governmental authority to compel disclosure is not unlimited. It extends only as far as necessary to achieve the governmental purpose at hand. Thus, no witness may be compelled to testify concerning matters irrelevant to the case before the court or other tribunal.

Governmental authority is also limited when mandatory disclosure conflicts with rights or interests which are highly valued in a free society. To preserve important rights and interests, courts and other tribunals may recognize a "privilege" on the part of a witness to decline to answer certain questions. For example, no person may be compelled to make statements which might incriminate him. The privilege against self-incrimination is inherent in the American concept of liberty. Long recognized under the English common law, the privilege was incorporated in the Fifth Amendment to the federal Constitution and is made applicable to the states through the Fourteenth Amendment. Similarly, under the First Amendment guarantees of free speech and religion, no person may be compelled to state his political or religious beliefs under oath. Of course, a witness may waive the privilege and volunteer this information. The privilege merely protects against compulsory disclosure.

In addition to privileges which arise under the Constitution, legislatures may create testimonial privileges by statutes. In the absence of a statute or constitutional mandate, courts may recognize a privilege because of the importance of the interests thereby protected.

A testimonial privilege may protect certain *topics*, such as the witness's political or religious beliefs or information tending to incriminate the witness. Another form of privilege protects confidential communications in the context of certain relationships which society seeks to foster. When such a privilege is asserted, *neither* party to such a relationship may be compelled to disclose information exchanged in confidence. Relationships which traditionally have given rise to privilege of this sort include those between attorney and client, physician and patient, husband and wife, and priest and penitent. In recent years privilege for confidential communications has been extended by statute or by courts in various states to such diverse professional groups as journalists, accountants, and psychotherapists.*

Traditionally, privilege for confidential communications is justified when four conditions are met. First, the relationship must be one which society seeks to foster. Second, the communications must originate in a confidence that they will not be disclosed. Third, the element of confidentiality must be essential to achieve the purpose of the relationship. Finally, injury to the relationship resulting from compelled disclosure must be greater than the benefit gained in correct disposal of litigation. Many courts, legislatures, and scholars have recognized that these conditions are clearly met in the psychotherapeutic relationship. Whether between a psychiatrist and a patient, or between a psychologist or other mental health professional and a client, the psychotherapeutic relationship is clearly one which

---

* The reader may recall that the term "privilege" arises in many contexts. Generally, the term privilege refers to an exemption from liability for an action which would ordinarily give rise to liability. See, for example, the discussion of privilege as a defense to defamation in the earlier chapter on therapists' duty of confidentiality. In the present context, the action which would ordinarily give rise to liability is the withholding of subpoenaed testimony or information. Although the ordinary penalty for withholding subpoenaed information may be fine or imprisonment, the valid assertion of a recognized testimonial privilege exempts a witness from liability.

society seeks to foster. Moreover, effective therapy is generally thought to require a patient's complete disclosure of his innermost thoughts and feelings. Fear of compulsory disclosure may inhibit a patient's ability to confide, and it may deter some persons from seeking psychotherapy. The assurance of confidentiality thus facilitates disclosures which are essential to effective treatment and induces hesitant persons to seek needed treatment.

The availability and scope of testimonial privilege depends upon the profession of the psychotherapist and upon the law of the particular jurisdiction. Confidential communications between psychiatrist and patient are protected by physician-patient privilege statutes, which have been passed in about two-thirds of the states. In addition, statutes in a few states provide a comprehensive psychiatrist-patient privilege. In most states statutes licensing psychologists provide a privilege for communications between psychologist and client. Finally, in a small number of states, statutes provide a privilege for other mental health professionals who provide psychotherapy, such as marriage counselors and social workers. Privilege statutes, however, are frequently ambiguous, and the availability and scope of the privilege in various context may be difficult to ascertain. The following materials illustrate some of the issues courts confront in applying the statutory provisions governing the privilege.

2. Conditions Giving Rise to the Privilege

a. Communications Made in the Course of Treatment

STATE v. COLE

Supreme Court of Iowa, 1980
295 N.W.2d 29

*   *   *

LARSON, Justice.

This defendant appeals her conviction, in a jury-waived trial, of first-degree murder in violation of section 690.2, The Code 1977. She challenges the trial court's rulings in regard to psychiatric evidence secured by depositions and in-trial testimony * * * We affirm the trial court.

It is undisputed that on September 15, 1977, the defendant shot and killed Dr. Alan Tyler, her ex-husband, in his office at Wilden Clinic. Immediately after the shooting, she proceeded to the reception area and announced that she had "shot her husband." She then called the police and waited for them at the clinic. She was brought before a magistrate for an initial appearance where she was represented by Lawrence Scalise and Thomas Levis. At that time an order was signed by the magistrate to take the defendant to Iowa Lutheran Hospital "to undergo psychiatric and physical examination and evaluation." It is this order and the related evidence concerning the mental condition of the defendant which give rise to the most troublesome issues.

I. THE PSYCHIATRIC EVIDENCE

A. *Effect of the commitment order.* Pursuant to the court's order, the defendant was first examined by Dr. Michael Taylor, a psychiatrist who had been treating her on a private basis since before the shooting. He ceased his examination of her on September 30, 1977, at which time he was replaced by Dr. Vernon Varner. The defendant filed notice, * * * that she intended to rely upon the defense of diminished capacity. The State then sought to obtain psychiatric evidence through these doctors' depositions and in-trial testimony.

Upon application of the State, and over defendant's objections, pretrial depositions of Doctors Taylor and Varner were ordered by the court. Dr. Varner complied, and his deposition was taken. * * * Again over objection, the trial court permitted Dr. Taylor to testify at trial in the State's case in chief.

Defendant argues the trial court's rulings on the admissibility of the psychiatric evidence was erroneous because they violated her doctor-patient privilege, set out in section 622.10, The Code, as follows:

> No practicing attorney, counselor, physician, surgeon, or the stenographer or confidential clerk of any such person, who obtains such information by reason of his employment, minister of the gospel or priest of any denomination shall be allowed, in giving testimony, to disclose any confidential communication properly entrusted to him in his professional capacity, and necessary and proper to enable him to discharge the functions of his office according to the usual course of practice or discipline. Such prohibition shall not apply to cases where the person in whose favor the same is made waives the rights conferred. * * *

As the following authorities established, not every doctor-patient relationship provides a basis for exclusion of the doctor's testimony. In some cases the privilege never arises; in others it exists but is held to be waived by the patient. The privilege did not exist at common law, and its embodiment by statute has been criticized by at least one writer.

While our cases have evidenced no hostility to the rule itself, they have uniformly required three elements to be established: (1) the relationship of doctor-patient; (2) acquisition of the information or knowledge during this relationship; and (3) the necessity of the information to enable the doctor to treat the patient skillfully.

The order signed by the magistrate was as follows:

ORDER FOR PSYCHIATRIC EVALUATION AND REPORT

Now, on this 15th day of September, 1977, this matter having been brought to the attention of the court, and the court being fully advised of the charges against the defendant in the above captioned cause, and the present condition of the defendant; it is the considered opinion of this court that before further proceedings may be had an evaluation of the above-named defendant's physical and psychological state should be made by competent professionals in the fields of medicine and psychology in order that the court may be more fully advised and that the best interests of the parties and of justice may be realized.

*   *   *

The effect of [the Court's] order, and of the medical relationship which followed it, are determinative on the issue of whether or not the defendant could assert the doctor-patient privilege. In court-ordered evaluations, the third requirement of the privilege is lacking; the communication is not for the purpose of treatment but to determine the existence of a fact or condition for the benefit of the court. Therefore, "[t]he physician-patient privilege does not arise where on order of the court a defendant is examined to determine his mental or physical condition."

*   *   * The order clearly provided for evaluation and report to the court and made no provision for diagnosis or treatment.

The defendant, while acknowledging that the order appears to be for evaluation and report, argues it was really only intended to provide for her safekeeping in order to avoid a possible suicide. We do not believe the intentions of the parties can be properly used to countermand the unambiguous provisions of a court order.

*   *   *

Even if we were to consider the intentions of the parties, as appellant suggests, we do not believe the record supports her contention that "[t]he record unquestionably shows that Kathleen Cole was sent to Lutheran Hospital for the primary, if not the sole purpose, of obtaining diagnosis and treatment." Even under her own evidence, the commitment was for her protection; no one testified she was committed for treatment.

*   *   *

We find no reversible error; we therefore affirm the trial court.

Affirmed.

All Justices concur except HARRIS, J., who dissents, joined by REES and ALLBEE, JJ.

*   *   *

Questions and Comments

1. The *Cole* case affirms the basic rule that the privilege only attaches where the client's relationship to the psychologist or psychiatrist was in the course of treatment. Problems may arise in the application of this rule when the professional relationship involves both diagnosis undertaken as a result of a court order and treatment which is carried out at the initiative of the examining faculty.

2. Where the psychiatrist or psychologist examines a person on behalf of the court or an adverse party, is there any obligation on the part of the examiner to inform the person being examined as to the nature of the relationship and that any disclosures that are made will not be privileged? This question has only been addressed in the context of criminal cases where it has generally been held that, unless the person being examined is specifically informed that the purpose of the examination is not for treatment, any disclosures that may be made are not admissible in a subsequent criminal trial. *See, State v. Shaw*, 106 Ariz. 103, 471 P.2d 715 (1970) and *State v. Cole*, 295 N.W.2d 29, 34 (Iowa 1980).

KOERNER v. WESTLAND

Appellate Court of Illinois, 4th District, 1977.
48 Ill.App.3d 172, 6 Ill.Dec. 331, 362 N.E.2d 1153.

* * *

MILLS, Justice.

We must reverse, remand.

* * *

The facts are neither complicated nor lengthy. Petitions were filed alleging that Mary Westland's five minor children were neglected and dependent. At the hearing on the petitions, testimony was given by Mary, her psychiatrist, a psychiatric nurse and the natural father of one of the children. Dr. Robert Talbert, Mary's treating psychiatrist, testified that he had treated her while she was hospitalized in the psychiatric ward of St. Elizabeth's Hospital in 1972 and 1973, and again in September and October, 1975. He diagnosed her as an "undifferentiated schizophrenic" who, as of November 1975, was unable to care for herself and was prescribed large daily doses of Thorazine. In fact, he did not expect Mary ever to completely recover. All of Dr. Talbert's testimony was given over the objection that it was subject to the patient-psychiatrist privilege.

Myrna Barney, who had been a nurse on the psychiatric ward, testified to Mary's conduct during several of the hospitalizations. The trial court prohibited testimony concerning contact with Mrs. Westland while Mrs. Barney was a sustaining care worker with the

Mental Health Department upon the ground that such testimony was protected by the statutory social worker's privilege. (Ill.Rev.Stat. 1975, ch. 23, par. 5320.) For the same reason the court prohibited testimony by Mary Pope, a home care worker employed by the Department of Children and Family Services.

Mrs. Westland testified that, at the time of the hearing, she had been released from the hospital and was residing in a shelter care home. It is apparent from the record that she had some difficulty in recalling the names of the fathers of the children, and the birthdates of some of the children. She testified to her desire to provide a home for all her children and her concern for them.

Because of our resolution of the issues we need not present the testimony in any further detail.

I

The first issue is whether the trial court erroneously permitted the psychiatrist, Dr. Talbert, to testify. This contention is based on the statutory psychiatrist-patient privilege which states:

"In civil and criminal cases, in proceedings preliminary thereto, and in legislative and administrative proceedings, a patient or his authorized representative and a psychiatrist or his authorized representative have the privilege to refuse to disclose, and to prevent a witness from disclosing, communications relating to diagnosis or treatment of the patient's mental condition between patient and psychiatrist * * *."

(Ill.Rev.Stat.1975, ch. 51, par. 5.2)

The statute proceeds to then list four exceptions to the privilege, which, it is conceded, are not involved here. Mrs. Westland argues that the statute clearly covers the situation at bar and therefore it was error to have admitted the psychiatrist's testimony. But the respondent argues that, for policy reasons, the statute should not be so read.

Our first task appears to be to zero in on the meaning of the critical words, "communication relating to diagnosis or treatment." If the words cover only verbal statements made by Mrs. Westland, then the majority of Dr. Talbert's testimony was not covered by the privilege. It is both informative and helpful to compare other privilege statutes to this one.

The *marital privilege* statute also speaks of "communication":

"* * * [N]either may testify as to any communication or admission made by either of them to the other or as to any conversation between them during coverture * * *." (Ill.Rev.Stat.1975, ch. 51, par. 5) *EVERYTHING IS SACROSANCT*

In this State, and in most states, such privilege is limited to verbal exchanges between the marital couple. The words "admission" and "conversation" reinforce that interpretation. That "communications" may have a broader meaning in the patient-psychiatrist privilege statute is possible because the psychiatrist's trained observation is an important factor in diagnosis and treatment.

The *physician-patient privilege* is phrased differently:

"No physician or surgeon shall be permitted to disclose any *information* he may have acquired in attending any patient * * *." (Emphasis supplied.) (Ill.Rev.Stat.1975, ch. 51, par. 5.1)

[handwritten margin note: can disclose observations & inferences]

At least one writer has stated that "information" and "communication" are treated as synonymous terms by the courts in the context of this privilege. However, the legislature has used two different words and the implication, at least, is that different meanings are to be attached.

Dr. Talbert, in his testimony, only once directly attributed a statement to Mrs. Westland. However, other information to which he testified is obviously the result of his conversations with his patient, as he testified that he had little, if any, contact with her outside the hospital. Information concerning her dependency on her mother, and the causes of her mental breakdowns could only be obtained from "communications" with her. To our view, that information could not properly be directly testified to, nor, we think, would it be proper to introduce it indirectly by proceeding straight to Dr. Talbert's diagnosis. While it might have been proper for Dr. Talbert to testify to any of his observations, the testimony was not so limited.

* * *

* * * [T]he judgment and orders of the Circuit Court of Vermilion County are reversed and the cause remanded for further proceedings.

Reversed and Remanded.

Questions and Comments

1. It is sometimes difficult to determine whether a specific professional group, particularly in the mental health field, is covered by a particular privilege statute and, if so, the extent of the exemption. States have commonly enacted separate privilege statutes for various professional groups such as physicians, psychologists, marriage counselors, and social workers. Various problems are raised by the existence of multiple privilege statutes. For instance, in the absence of explicit legislative direction should psychiatrists be entitled to the special privilege for psychologists which is normally broader and more comprehensive than the physician's privilege? In one jurisdiction the court held that the psychologist privilege did *not* cover psychiatrists. *See Ritt v. Ritt*, 98 N.J.Super. 590, 238 A.2d 196 (1967). In another state it was held

that the psychologist privilege did cover psychiatrists, since the psychiatrist in question "worked with" the psychologist to whom the privilege applied. *See Day v. State*, 378 So.2d 1156 (Ala.Cr.App.1979), reversed sub nom. *Ex parte Day*, 378 So.2d 1159 (Ala.1979).

Similar problems are encountered where the coverage of the privilege for psychologists and marriage counsellors differ. For instance, in New Jersey the privilege for marriage counsellors is virtually absolute, and confidential communications are not admissible in a divorce proceeding. However, under the practicing Psychology Licensing Act the privilege would not necessarily bar the admission of confidential information in a divorce proceeding. In *Wichansky v. Wichansky*, 126 N.J.Super. 156, 313 A.2d 222 (1973), the court held that a psychologist who engages in marriage counseling is covered by the broader marriage counsellor's privilege, even though he is not a licensed marriage counsellor.

2. When privilege protects confidential communications with a psychotherapist, the privilege extends as well to the patient records the psychotherapist maintains. Generally, such records are protected to the same extent as the communications they describe. When patient records are maintained at a hospital, school, or other public agency, however, the status of privilege is unclear. Similarly, when a patient is committed for treatment at a mental hospital, a variety of personnel may have access to his records. Courts, therefore, may regard the records as non-confidential and hence not privileged. On the other hand, other courts view nurses and ward staff as agents of the patient's psychiatrist and, accordingly, extend any applicable psychiatrist-patient or physician-patient privilege to hospital records.

Records at publicly funded hospitals pose additional problems. A few courts have found no confidential relationship between a resident-patient and psychiatrists employed at a state hospital, and hence no privilege for psychiatric records of state hospital patients. Additionally, courts sometimes treat state hospital records as public documents and therefore not privileged, or privileged under privilege statutes for government documents generally, and hence subject to waiver by the government, without consent of the patient. (*See*, for example, dissent in *Taylor v. United States*, 222 F.2d 398, 404 (D.C.Cir.1954) and New York cases cited therein.)

3. A number of states have enacted privilege statutes for social workers. For instance, in Illinois the statute provides:

> No social worker may disclose any information he may have acquired from persons consulting him in his professional capacity which was necessary to enable him to render services in his professional capacity. * * * (Ill.Rev.Stat.1975, ch. 23, par. 5320).

In the *Westland* case set out above, the court held that the privilege is only available to social workers who are registered under the Social Workers Registration Act. *In re Westland*, 48 Ill.App.3d 172, 6 Ill.Dec. 331, 362 N.E.2d 1153, 1157 (1977).

b. Scope of the Privilege: Communications Made in the Presence of Other Persons

GILHAM v. GILHAM

Supreme Court of Pennsylvania, 1955.
177 Pa.Super. 328, 110 A.2d 915.

HIRT, Judge.

Although the master recommended a divorce on the ground of adultery in this case, the court sustained exceptions to his report and dismissed the complaint. A consideration of the entire record convinces us that the case was properly decided. The order will be affirmed.

The parties were married in August 1941 and they lived together until November 26, 1942 in the Borough of Lehighton, when libellant was inducted into the armed forces.

*   *   *

During the period respondent lived with her parents in East Stroudsburg. After his discharge from the service libellant returned to Lehighton on November 30, 1945. Because of a housing shortage he was unable to set up a separate home and respondent remained in the home of her parents. The parties did resume marital relations however during weekends and respondent lived with her husband continuously, at the home of his parents for several weeks early in 1946. Libellant testified that on June 6, 1946 while taking his wife to her parents' home in an automobile he became suspicious because of her attitude toward him and he then insisted that she tell him the reason for what he interpreted as a disturbed conscience. In response, according to his testimony, she said that she had been out with one Carl Hamill at least once a month from July 1944 until just before libellant's return in November 1945. According to his testimony when she stated further that she was afraid that she had contracted a venereal disease, libellant drove back to Lehighton with his wife in the car and reported her confession to his parents, whereupon they all went to the office of Dr. Roger R. Rupp in Lehighton for the purpose of an examination of the defendant for venereal infection. Dr. Rupp testified that in his office he asked her: "Is there any reason for you to be examined *   *   * Were you out with anybody? And she said 'Yes.' " That was the extent of the questioning. A nurse in attendance testified that the above admission was made to Dr. Rupp in her presence and in the presence of libellant's parents. The result of the examination was negative.

Under the circumstances, the admission made to Dr. Rupp was confidential and privileged by the Act of June 7, 1907, P.L. 462, 28 P.S. § 328, and since the nurse was in attendance in her professional capacity, the same principle closed her mouth. Accordingly we are bound to disregard their testimony as to the above admission. However the conversation was overheard by libellant's parents and their testimony was competent and credible evidence of the admission which the defendant then made. Third persons may testify to communications, overheard by them, however privileged as to the parties to the conversation.

[The court, however, held that the action was properly dismissed since in Pennsylvania a divorce based on adultery could not be based on only a confession unsupported by additional collaborating evidence which the plaintiff here failed to provide.]

Questions and Comments

1. It is unclear to what extent multiple-person interactions are protected by the rules of privileged communication. If a "casual third party" is present during communications between patient and therapist, then such communications usually are not privileged. There is a presumption that the patient did not intend that the information remain confidential. Thus, persons in group therapy appear to be unprotected from other group members who may, without malice, reveal problems discussed during therapy to outsiders. (However, "the therapist may have aides present without destroying the confidential nature of the communication"). Schwitzgebel & Schwitzgebel, Law and Psychological Practice, 1980

2. Marriage counsellors as well as psychotherapists in general are increasingly resorting to co-joint therapy of both the husband and wife. As a result, in some therapy sessions both spouses may be present. This practice presents a particular problem in terms of confidentiality, particularly where the parties may later be involved in litigation against each other such as in a divorce proceeding. To what extent, for instance, are decisions made during a therapy session in the presence of a spouse privileged? Under the traditional test no privilege would attach to prevent a spouse from testifying as to the communications made during a therapy session. At least one state (Colorado) has enacted legislation which

> prohibits the questioning of any persons who have participated in group therapy sessions "concerning any knowledge gained during the course of such therapy without the consent of the person or persons to whom the testimony sought relates.

Schwitzgebel at 209.

3. It has been suggested that disclosures by patient members of joint therapy groups could be controlled by having the member of the group enter into a contract prior to the commencement of the sessions binding each signatory to preserve the confidentiality of the sessions. See, Schwitzgebel at 209. It is not certain, however, that such contract could be enforced to prevent disclosure in a court proceeding. Also see,

Note, *Group Therapy at Privileged Communications*, 45 Ind.L.Rev. 93 (1967).

3.　Waiver of the Privilege

A common element of psychotherapist-patient privilege is that its purpose is to protect the *patient's* interest in confidentiality. It is the patient, not the therapist, who is injured by compulsory public disclosure, for the patient is thereby deterred from seeking needed treatment or from confiding fully during therapy. Privilege, therefore, belongs to the patient, not to the therapist, and a patient's assertion or waiver of privilege is binding upon the therapist. That is, if a patient asserts privilege, the therapist may not be compelled to testify, nor may he voluntarily testify concerning confidential communications. Similarly, if a patient waives privilege, the therapist may not invoke the privilege to refuse to testify.

A patient must assert or waive privilege when a party to litigation seeks to compel disclosure of confidential information. A litigant may compel testimony from the patient or from the psychotherapist by obtaining a subpoena issued by the court, and he may compel production of a psychotherapist's records by obtaining a subpoena *duces tecum*. The patient need not be a party to the litigation to assert the privilege.

A patient may waive privilege in two ways. First, he may simply fail to assert privilege when confidential information is sought by a party in litigation. That is, the patient may provide the information himself, or he may consent to its acquisition from the therapist. The therapist, however, is under an affirmative duty to assert the privilege for the patient, if the patient is not present or is incapable of asserting privilege. Second, a patient may waive privilege by making his mental or emotional condition an element of a claim or defense. This form of waiver is often called the patient-litigant exception to privilege. In some jurisdictions a criminal defendant who raises an insanity defense, for example, may not invoke privilege to bar testimony concerning the results of a psychiatric interview to evaluate his sanity. See, e.g., *People v. Edney* at p. 255 *infra*. Similarly, a patient who initiates a malpractice suit against his therapist may not invoke the privilege to preclude testimony concerning the conduct of therapy. Finally, a patient makes his mental condition an element of a claim, and thereby waives privilege, when he seeks to recover damages for mental or emotional distress allegedly caused by another person's actions.

Generally, courts attempt to limit compulsory disclosures to those elements of the communications which are essential to the issues of a case. The practice reflects recognition of the sensitive nature of the information and accords with a general policy to protect witnesses and litigants from unnecessary harassments.

Privilege persists despite the termination of therapy, even after the patient's death. Although usually only a patient may waive privilege, in some circumstances a patient's personal representative, acting on behalf of the patient, may waive the privilege. Persons who may be granted this authority include the guardian of a mentally incompetent patient and the heirs or persons appointed to manage the estates of a deceased patient. Waiver of privilege after the death of a patient occurs most often in disputes concerning the patient's mental capacity at the time of making a will.

a. Circumstances Leading to Express or Implied Waiver of the Privilege

i. Civil Proceedings

IN RE LIFSCHUTZ

Supreme Court of California, 1970.
2 Cal.3d 415, 85 Cal.Rptr. 829, 467 P.2d 557.

TOBRINER, Justice.

Dr. Joseph E. Lifschutz, a psychiatrist practicing in California, seeks a writ of habeas corpus to secure his release from the custody of the Sheriff of the County of San Mateo. Dr. Lifschutz was imprisoned after he was adjudged in contempt of court for refusing to obey an order of the San Mateo County Superior Court instructing him to answer questions and produce records relating to communications with a former patient. Dr. Lifschutz contends that this underlying court order was invalid as unconstitutionally infringing his personal constitutional right of privacy, his right effectively to practice his profession, and the constitutional privacy rights of his patients. He also attacks the order, or more specifically, the statutory provisions which authorize the compulsion of his testimony in these circumstances, as unconstitutionally denying him the equal protection of the laws since, under California law, clergymen could not be compelled to reveal certain confidential communications under these circumstances.

The instant proceeding arose out of a suit instituted by Joseph F. Housek against John Arabian on June 3, 1968, for damages resulting from an alleged assault. Housek's complaint alleged that the assault caused him "physical injuries, pain, suffering and severe mental and emotional distress." Defendant Abrabian deposed the plaintiff and during the course of that deposition Housek stated that he had received psychiatric treatment from Dr. Lifschutz over a six-month period approximately 10 years earlier. Nothing in the record indicates that the plaintiff revealed the nature or contents of any conversation with or treatment by Dr. Lifschutz.

Arabian then subpoenaed for deposition Dr. Lifschutz and all of his medical records relating to the treatment of Housek. Although Dr. Lifschutz appeared for the deposition, he refused to produce any of his medical records and refused to answer any questions relating to his treatment of patients; the psychiatrist declined even to disclose whether or not Housek had consulted him or had been his patient.

*   *   *

[Plaintiff] Housek has neither expressly claimed a psychotherapist-patient privilege, statutory or constitutional, nor expressly waived such a privilege.

In response to the psychiatrist's refusal to cooperate, defendant Arabian moved for an order of the superior court compelling the production of the subpenaed records and the answers to questions on deposition.

Relying on the patient-litigant exception of section 1016 of the Evidence Code, the superior court determined that because the plaintiff, in instituting the pending litigation, had tendered as an issue his mental and emotional condition, the statutory psychotherapist-patient (Evid. Code, § 1014) privilege did not apply. On December 20, 1968, the court therefore ordered Dr. Lifschutz to comply with the subpena and to answer questions posed during deposition. On January 15, 1969, defendant attempted to continue with the deposition of Dr. Lifschutz as ordered by the superior court, but petitioner remained resolute in his refusal to respond or produce records.

*   *   *

*   *   * Evidence Code, section 912, subdivision (a), provides that: "*   *   * the right of any person to claim a privilege provided by Section *   *   * 1014 (psychotherapist-patient privilege) *   *   * is waived with respect to a communication protected by such privilege if any holder of the privilege, without coercion, has disclosed a significant part of the communication or has consented to such disclosure made by anyone. Consent to disclosure is manifested by any statement or other conduct of the holder of the privilege indicating his consent to the disclosure, including his failure to claim the privilege in any proceeding in which he has the legal standing and opportunity to claim the privilege."

Since Housek, the holder of the privilege disclosed at a prior deposition that he has consulted Dr. Lifschutz for psychiatric treatment, he has waived whatever privilege he might have had to keep such information confidential.*   *   *

Defendant contended in the superior court, however, that *any* communication between the plaintiff and Dr. Lifschutz has lost its privileged status because the plaintiff has filed a personal injury action in which he claims recovery for "mental and emotional distress." Defendant relies on section 1016 of the Evidence Code, the patient-litigant exception to the psychotherapist-patient privilege, which provides that: "[t]here is no privilege under this article as to a communication relevant to an issue concerning the mental or emotional condition of the patient if such issue has been tendered by: (a) the patient * * *." To avoid the necessity for further contempt proceedings or delaying appellate review in the instant case, we have considered whether defendant has accurately identified the proper reach of the patient-litigant exception.

As we explain more fully below, the patient-litigant exception allows only a limited inquiry into the confidences of the psychotherapist-patient relationship, compelling disclosure of only those matters directly relevant to the nature of the specific "emotional or mental" condition which the patient has voluntarily disclosed and tendered in his pleadings or in answer to discovery inquiries. Furthermore, even when confidential information falls within this exception, trial courts, because of the intimate and potentially embarrassing nature of such communications, may utilize the protective measures at their disposal to avoid unwarranted intrusions into the confidences of the relationship.

In interpreting this exception we are necessarily mindful of the justifiable expectations of confidentiality that most individuals seeking psychotherapeutic treatment harbor. As has been aptly pointed out by Judge Edgerton in *Taylor v. United States* (1955) 95 U.S.App. D.C. 373, 222 F.2d 398, 401 (quoting from Guttmacher, M., et al., Psychiatry and the Law (1952) p. 272), " 'The psychiatric patient confides more utterly than anyone else in the world. He exposes to the therapist not only what his words directly express; he lays bare his entire self, his dreams, his fantasies, his sins, and his shame. Most patients who undergo psychotherapy know that this is what will be expected of them, and that they cannot get help except on that condition. * * * It would be too much to expect them to do so if they knew that all they say—and all that the psychiatrist learns from what they say—may be revealed to the whole world from a witness stand.' "

We believe that a patient's interest in keeping such confidential revelations from public purview, in retaining this substantial privacy, has deeper roots than the California statute and draws sustenance from our constitutional heritage.

* * *

Dr. Lifschutz presents a novel challenge, attempting to raise far-reaching questions of constitutional law. From the affidavits and correspondence included in the record we note that a large segment of the psychiatric profession concurs in Dr. Lifschutz's strongly held belief that an absolute privilege of confidentiality is essential to the effective practice of psychotherapy.

We recognize the growing importance of the psychiatric profession in our modern, ultracomplex society. The swiftness of change—economic, cultural, and moral—produces accelerated tensions in our society, and the potential for relief of such emotional disturbances offered by psychotherapy undoubtedly establishes it as a profession essential to the preservation of societal health and well-being. Furthermore, a growing consensus throughout the country, reflected in a trend of legislative enactments, acknowledges that an environment of confidentiality of treatment is vitally important to the successful operation of psychotherapy. California has embraced this view through the enactment of a broad, protective psychotherapist-patient privilege.

The nature of the actual interests involved in this case can only be properly evaluated against the California statutory background. Although petitioner, in pressing for judicial acceptance of a genuine and deeply held principle, seeks to cast the issue involved in this case in the broadest terms, we must properly address, in reality, a question of more modest dimensions. We do not face the alternatives of enshrouding the patient's communication to the psychotherapist in the black veil of absolute privilege or of exposing it to the white glare of absolute publicity. Our choice lies, rather, in the grey area.

Properly viewed, the broadest issue before our court is whether the Legislature, in attempting to accommodate the conceded need of confidentiality in the psychotherapeutic process with general societal needs of access to information for the ascertainment of truth in litigation, has unconstitutionally weighted its resolution in favor of disclosure by providing that a psychotherapist may be compelled to reveal relevant confidences of treatment when the patient tenders his mental or emotional condition in issue in litigation. For the reasons discussed below, we conclude that, under a properly limited interpretation, the litigant-patient exception to the psychotherapist-patient privilege, at issue in this case, does not unconstitutionally infringe the constitutional rights of privacy of either psychotherapists or psychotherapeutic patients. As we point out, however, because of the potential of invasion of patients' constitutional interests, trial courts should properly and carefully control compelled disclosures in this area in the light of accepted principles.

*   *   *

The primary contention of Dr. Lifschutz's attack on the judgment of contempt consists of the assertion of a constitutional right of a psychotherapist to absolute confidentiality in his communications with, and treatment of, patients. Although, as we understand it, the alleged right draws its substance primarily from the psychological needs and expectations of patients, Dr. Lifschutz claims that the Constitution grants him an absolute right to refuse to disclose such confidential communications, regardless of the wishes of a patient in a particular case.

[The court held that the privilege is that of the patient and that a psychotherapist has no constitutional right to assert the privilege in his own behalf.]

* * *

The second basis of petitioner's contention raises a more serious problem. Petitioner claims that if the state is authorized to compel disclosure of some psychotherapeutic communications, psychotherapy can no longer be practiced successfully. He asserts that the unique nature of psychotherapeutic treatment, involving a probing of the patient's subconscious thoughts and emotions, requires an environment of total confidentiality and absolute trust. Petitioner claims that unless a psychotherapist can truthfully assure his patient that all revelations will be held in strictest confidence and never disclosed, patients will be inhibited from participating fully in the psychotherapeutic process and proper treatment will be impossible. Petitioner concludes that the patient-litigation exception involved here conflicts with the preservation of an environment of absolute confidentiality and unconstitutionally constricts the field of medical practice.

Petitioner's argument, resting as it does on assertions of medical necessity, exemplifies the type of question to which the judiciary brings little expertise. Although petitioner has submitted affidavits of psychotherapists who concur in his assertion that total confidentiality is essential to the practice of their profession, we cannot blind ourselves to the fact that the practice of psychotherapy has grown, indeed flourished, in an environment of a non-absolute privilege. No state in the country recognizes as broad a privilege as petitioner claims is constitutionally compelled. Whether psychotherapy's development has progressed only because patients are ignorant of the existing legal environment can only be a matter for speculation; psychotherapists certainly have been aware of the limitations of their recognized privilege for some time.

Petitioner's broad assertion, moreover, overlooks the limited nature of the intrusion into psychotherapeutic privacy actually at issue in this case. As we explain more fully in part III infra, the patient-litigant exception of section 1016 of the Evidence Code compels disclosure of only those matters which the patient himself has chosen to reveal by tendering them in litigation. We do not know, of course, to what extent patients are deterred from seeking psychotherapeutic treatment by the knowledge that if, at some future date, they choose to place some aspect of their mental condition in issue in litigation, communications relevant to that issue may be revealed. We can only surmise that an understanding of the limits of section 1016, and the realization that the patient retains control over subsequent disclosure, may provide a measure of reassurance to the prospective patient.

* * *

In previous physician-patient privilege cases the exception [to the privilege of confidentiality] has been generally applied only to compel disclosure of medical treatment and communication concerning the very injury or impairment that was the subject matter of the litigation. There is certainly nothing to suggest that in the context of the more liberal psychotherapist-patient privilege this exception should be given a broader reading.

If the provision had as broad an effect as is suggested by petitioner, it might effectively deter many psychotherapeutic patients from instituting any general claim for mental suffering and damage out of fear of opening up all past communications to discovery. This result would clearly be an intolerable and overbroad intrusion into the patient's privacy, not sufficiently limited to the legitimate state interest embodied in the provision and would create opportunities for harassment and blackmail.

In light of these considerations, the "automatic" waiver of privilege contemplated by section 1016 must be construed not as a complete waiver of the privilege but only as a limited waiver concomitant with the purposes of the exception. Under section 1016 disclosure can be compelled only with respect to *those mental conditions* the patient-litigant has "disclose[d] * * * by bringing an action in which *they* are in issue" communications which are not directly relevant to those specific conditions do not fall within the terms of section 1016's exception and therefore remain privileged. Disclosure cannot be compelled with respect to other aspects of the patient-litigant's personality even though they may, in some sense, be "relevant" to the substantive issues of litigation. The patient thus is not obligated to sacrifice all privacy to seek redress for a specific mental or emotional injury; the scope of the inquiry permitted depends upon the nature of the injuries which the patient-litigant himself has brought before the court.

In some situations, the patient's pleadings may clearly demonstrate that his entire mental condition is being placed in issue and that records of past psychotherapy will clearly be relevant.

*   *   *

In other cases, however, the determination of the specific "mental condition" in issue may present more complex problems. The difficulties involved in analyzing the applicability of the exception in the instant case may be illustrative. The plaintiff's complaint, containing the typical allegations of "mental and emotional distress" arising out of a physical assault, does not specifically identify the nature of the "mental or emotional condition" at issue. In incorporating this allegation in his complaint, plaintiff obviously neither disclosed his entire medical history if treatment for mental or emotional conditions nor realistically waived his interest in maintaining the confidentiality of that treatment. The generality of the claim, however, does create the possibility that some feature of plaintiff's psychological history will be directly relevant to the determination of whether his emotional or mental distress can be properly attributed to the alleged assault. Although we doubt that the 10-year-old therapeutic treatment sought to be discovered from Dr. Lifschutz would be sufficiently relevant to a typical claim of "mental distress" to bring it within the exception of section 1016, we cannot determine from the present state of the record whether plaintiff's "mental and emotional" distress is merely the "normal" distress experienced as a result of physical assault or whether it includes unusual or particularly serious elements upon which prior history may be directly relevant.

Because only the patient, and not the party seeking disclosure, knows both the nature of the ailments for which recovery is sought and the general content of the psychotherapeutic communications, the burden rests upon the patient initially to submit some showing that a given confidential communication is not directly related to the issue he has tendered to the court. A patient may have to delimit his claimed "mental or emotional distress" or explain, in general terms, the object of the psychotherapy in order to illustrate that it is not reasonably probable that the psychotherapeutic communications sought are directly relevant to the mental condition that he has placed in issue. In determining whether communications sufficiently relate to the mental condition at issue to require disclosure, the court should heed the basic privacy interests involved in the privilege.

* * *

Inasmuch as plaintiff had already disclosed that he had consulted Dr. Lifschutz for psychotherapeutic treatment, petitioner could not properly have refused to answer at least that question concerning the communications; since neither plaintiff nor the psychotherapist has as yet made any claim that the subpenaed records are not directly relevant to the specific "mental and emotional" injuries for which plaintiff is claiming relief, Dr. Lifschutz had no right to refuse to produce the records. Thus the trial court's order requiring the production of records and the answering of questions was valid; the trial court properly adjudged Dr. Lifschutz in contempt of court for intentionally violating that valid court order.

The order to show cause is discharged and the petition for writ of habeas corpus is denied.

MOSK, Acting C.J., McCOMB, PETERS, BURKE, and SULLI-VAN, JJ., and MOLINARI, J. pro tem., concur.

Questions and Comments

1. *Lifschutz* in effect requires the plaintiff-patient to "disclose at least part of the contents of protected communications to his lawyer and the trial judge as a condition to retaining its confidentiality of the communication." *Caesar v. Mountanos*, 542 F.2d 1064, 1075 (9th Cir. 1976). This result has been criticized because it forces a plaintiff who wants to preserve confidentiality to elect either to make partial disclosure or possibly forego recovery for mental distress. Some, like Judge Hufstedler of the Ninth Circuit Court of Appeals, would avoid this problem by restricting compelled disclosures in a personal injury action to "the fact of treatment, the time and length of treatment, the cost of

treatment, and the ultimate diagnosis unless the party seeking disclosure establishes in the trial court a compelling need for its production." *Caesar v. Mountanos*, 542 F.2d 1064, 1075 (9th Cir.1976), (Hufstedler, J., concurring and dissenting).

ii. Criminal Proceedings

PEOPLE v. EDNEY

Court of Appeals of New York, 1976.
39 N.Y.2d 620, 385 N.Y.S.2d 23, 350 N.E.2d 400.

GABRIELLI, Judge.

Defendant was charged with kidnapping and the brutal killing of the eight-year-old daughter of his former girlfriend. He interposed the defense of insanity.

The jury found defendant guilty, as charged, of manslaughter, first degree and kidnapping in the first and second degrees. He was sentenced to a term of 25 years to life on the first degree kidnapping charge and to concurrent terms of up to 25 years on the other charges. The Appellate Division unanimously affirmed.

The critical and principal issue is whether the testimony of a psychiatrist, who had examined defendant prior to trial at the request of his attorney, was admissible over objections that the physician-patient and attorney-client privilege acted to bar its admission.

At trial, the prosecution showed that late in the afternoon on July 24, 1968, defendant grabbed Lisa Washington, the victim, off the street where she was playing with friends, and forcibly pushed her into a taxicab. At approximately 8:30 p.m., Lisa's aunt, with whom she was residing, received a call from defendant who stated that "If you don't get 'C' [the nickname of Lisa's mother] on the phone in the next couple of hours, I am going to rape and kill Lisa". A barmaid testified that defendant and a young girl were in the Nu-Way Lounge at about 9:30 p.m. and that she observed defendant leave the tavern with the girl, walk around a corner toward the back of the building, and return a short while later without her. Less than an hour later, police officers, responding to a call by a woman who had reported a disturbance in her backyard which adjoined the rear of the Nu-Way Lounge, found Lisa's lifeless body. She had been stabbed 11 times. The police questioned persons in the bar and learned of defendant's presence in the bar earlier in the evening with a little girl.

Defendant was located at his father's home early the next morning and taken into custody. As he was leaving with the officers, he was asked by his father whether he had "hurt that little child", to which he replied "I'm sorry, I'm sorry". Granules of dirt taken from defendant's trousers confirmed that defendant had been in the area behind the Nu-Way Lounge.

Following his arrest, and after receiving the standard preinterrogation admonitions defendant volunteered to a detective that he had been in the Nu-Way Lounge that evening, that he had been hearing voices which told him that God wanted Lisa, and that he might have killed Lisa but he was not sure. Taking the witness stand in his own defense, defendant testified that on the day in question, he had drunk large quantities of alcohol, had been smoking marijuana cigarettes, and that sometime after 9:00 p.m., he and Lisa had left the Nu-Way Lounge to go to his father's place; that he might have killed Lisa but he was not sure he had done so. He recalled walking to a cab across the street from the bar but could remember no more. He explained that he regained consciousness under a tree near his father's home and that he walked inside and blacked out; the next thing he was able to remember was someone pounding on him to wake up because the police were there.

A psychiatrist called by the defense testified that defendant suffered from paranoid schizophrenia of mild severity and that the condition was of long standing. It was his opinion that defendant was mentally ill to such an extent that he was unaware of the nature and quality of his act and did not know that his act was wrong.

In rebuttal, the prosecution called Dr. Daniel Schwartz, a psychiatrist, who originally examined defendant at the behest of defendant's attorney, who was not present during the examination. The defense unsuccessfully objected to his testifying on the ground that the attorney-client and physician-patient privileges barred his testimony. Dr. Schwartz described defendant as having an alcoholic psychosis which occasionally manifested itself through hallucinations and delusions; however, he found no evidence of an underlying disease or defect. It was his opinion that at the time of the murder defendant knew and appreciated the nature of his conduct and knew that such conduct was wrong.

Another rebuttal psychiatrist, who had independently examined the defendant for the prosecution, supported the conclusions of Dr. Schwartz that defendant knew and appreciated the nature of his conduct and that such conduct was wrong.

Two other psychiatrists, produced by the defense as surrebuttal witnesses, each testified that he was unable to form an opinion as to whether defendant knew or appreciated the nature of his acts, or whether such acts were wrong, although they did agree that defendant had some form of mental disease.

People v. Al-Kanani, 33 N.Y.2d 260, 351 N.Y.S.2d 969, 307 N.E.2d 43, is dispositive of the physician-patient privilege claim. There we held

> "that where insanity is asserted as a defense and ＊ ＊ ＊ the defendant offers evidence tending to show his insanity in support of this plea, a complete waiver is effected, and the prosecution is then permitted to call psychiatric experts to testify regarding his sanity

even though they may have treated the defendant. When the patient first fully discloses the evidence of his affliction, it is he who has given the public the full details of his case, thereby disclosing the secrets which the statute was designed to protect, thus creating a waiver removing it from the operation of the statute and once the privilege is thus waived, there is nothing left to protect against for once the revelation is made by the patient there is nothing further to disclose 'for when a secret is out it is out for all time and cannot be caught again like a bird, and put back in its cage. * * * The legislature did not intend to continue the privilege when there was no reason for its continuance and it would simply be an obstruction to public justice.' * * *.''

Our holding in the case now before us comports with this rationale and is but a logical extension of our determination in *Al-Kanani*.

Equally unavailing to defendant is the claim that the attorney-client privilege bars admission of Dr. Schwartz' testimony. Essentially, defendant relies on decisions in other jurisdictions which have excluded such testimony apparently because a psychiatrist would inevitably be required to reveal a defendant's statements to him to justify his opinion and because a contrary rule would deter attorneys from freely seeking sound professional advice as to the soundness of an insanity plea. We do not find the reasoning of these cases compelling and, accordingly, do not follow them. Rather, we think the better rationale underlies the *Al-Kanani* rule that a plea of innocence by reason of insanity constitutes a complete and effective waiver by the defendant of any claim of privilege.

A defendant who seeks to introduce psychiatric testimony in support of his insanity plea may be required to disclose prior to trial the underlying basis of his alleged affliction to a prosecution psychiatrist. Hence, where, as here, a defendant reveals to the prosecution the very facts which would be secreted by the exercise of the privilege, reason does not compel the exclusion of expert testimony based on such facts, or cross-examination concerning the grounds for opinions based thereon. It follows that no harm accrues to the defense from seeking pretrial psychiatric advice where an insanity plea is actually entered, for in such circumstances, the underlying factual basis will be revealed to the prosecution psychiatrist. Conversely, were the defendant not to enter an insanity plea, no physician-patient waiver would occur and any information divulged to the psychiatrist would remain privileged. There is, therefore, no deterrent to seeking expert psychiatric advice for, in one instance, there will be disclosure to the prosecution in any event and, in the other, disclosure will never occur. In short, no reason appears why a criminal defendant who puts his sanity in issue should be permitted to thwart the introduction of testimony from a material witness who may be called at trial by invoking the attorney-client privilege anymore than he should be able to do so by invoking the physician-patient privilege.

This is not to say, however, that an attorney cannot consult a psychiatrist in order to obtain advice concerning the efficacy of an insanity plea or, for that matter, any trial strategy, without fear of later courtroom disclosure. The product of such a consultation is protected, of course, by the work product doctrine (see CPLR 3101). However, that doctrine affords protection only to facts and observations disclosed *by the attorney*. Thus, it is the information and observations of the attorney that are conveyed to the expert which may thus be subject to trial exclusion. The work product doctrine does not operate to insulate other disclosed information from public exposure.

It is significant that the underlying purpose of the attorney-client privilege would not be diminished by the admission of the testimony of Dr. Schwartz. The privilege is grounded in the salutary policy of encouraging "persons needing professional advice to disclose freely the facts in reference to which they seek advice, without fear that such facts will be made public to their disgrace or detriment by their attorney" * * * That policy is not harmed, however, by the admission of evidence which, in any event, in these circumstances would be available to the prosecution. Indeed, with respect to the testimony of Dr. Schwartz, it is readily apparent that the traditional and statutory requirements of an attorney-client relationship were simply not established (CPLR 4503, subd. [a]). We hold, therefore, that the privilege was inapplicable.

We find no merit in defendant's other contentions.

Accordingly, the order of the Appellate Division should be affirmed.

[The dissenting opinion of Fuchsberg is omitted.]

STATE v. PRATT

Court of Appeals of Maryland, 1979.
284 Md. 516, 398 A.2d 421.

DIGGES, Judge.

The question presented by this criminal cause is one of first impression in this State, and yet, it involves "the oldest of the privileges for confidential communications"—that which exists between an attorney and his client. Stated succinctly, we are asked to decide whether this privilege was violated when, over objection, a psychiatrist, who was retained by defense counsel to examine his client in preparing an insanity defense, was permitted to testify at the instance of the prosecution. Because we conclude that this fundamental privilege was invaded, we will direct a new trial.

The factual background here is uncomplicated and may be briefly related. On the morning of October 23, 1976, respondent Margaret

Melton Pratt, after a sleepless night during which she contemplated the taking of her own life, shot and killed her still-slumbering husband, William S. Pratt, in their Montgomery County apartment. After the shooting, the wife packed an overnight bag and drove to a friend's farm near Front Royal, Virginia, to visit the gravesite of her dog; she stayed several hours and then proceeded to a nearby motel to spend the night. The next morning Mrs. Pratt returned to her home and, after a short stay there, began driving aimlessly around the Bethesda-Rockville area. Realizing she would eventually be apprehended, the respondent went to the Montgomery County police and informed them of her husband's death. The officers, after verifying Mrs. Pratt's story concerning what had taken place, arrested her for murder.

Upon being indicted by the grand jury for murder and related offenses, the respondent entered pleas of not guilty and interposed a defense of insanity at the time of the commission of the alleged crimes. Thereafter, the Circuit Court for Montgomery County, ordered that the Department of Health and Mental Hygiene conduct a mental examination of Mrs. Pratt to determine her "sanity or insanity at the present time and at the time of the commission of the crime, and * * * her competenc[y] to stand trial at the present time * * *." After an examination, the department, by its report dated December 30, 1976, informed the court that Mrs. Pratt was presently competent to stand trial and was sane at the time of the commission of the alleged offenses. Trial on the indictment began on April 18, 1977, and three days later the jury found Mrs. Pratt was sane at the time of the commission of the alleged crimes and guilty of both murder in the second degree and the use of a handgun in the commission of a felony.

Throughout the trial, Mrs. Pratt did not dispute that she had killed her husband but, instead, strenuously urged that she was insane at the time she fired the fatal shots. In support of her insanity plea, respondent presented two psychiatrists, Dr. Gerald Polin and Dr. Leon Yochelson, who testified that at the time of the act Mrs. Pratt was, in their opinion, suffering from a mental illness of such severity that she lacked substantial capacity to conform her conduct to the requirements of the law. In rebuttal, the State produced three psychiatrists, all of whom agreed that the respondent was suffering from some degree of mental disorder when the shooting took place. Nonetheless, two of these medical experts testified that, under Maryland law, Mrs. Pratt was legally responsible for her act. Of these two, one, Dr. Brian Crowley, had examined the accused at the request of her attorney after being retained by him to aid in preparing support for Mrs. Pratt's insanity plea. It is the evidence given by Dr. Crowley, who testified during the trial at the request of the State and over the objection of the defense, that precipitated the controversy now before us. On appeal to the Court of Special

Appeals, that court concluded that the permitting of Dr. Crowley's testimony violated the attorney-client privilege and ordered a new trial. We agree.

In this State the attorney-client privilege, * * * is a rule of evidence that forever bars disclosure, without the consent of the client, of all communications that pass in confidence between the client and his attorney during the course of professional employment or as an incident of professional intercourse between them.

* * * While never given an explicit constitutional underpinning, the privilege is, nevertheless, closely tied to the federal, as well as this State's, constitutional guarantees of effective assistance of counsel and could, if limited too severely, make these basic guarantees virtually meaningless.

Initially we observe that, given the complexities of modern existence, few if any lawyers could, as a practical matter, represent the interest of their clients without a variety of nonlegal assistance. Recognizing this limitation, it is now almost universally accepted in this country that the scope of the attorney-client privilege, at least in criminal causes, embraces those agents whose services are required by the attorney in order that he may properly prepare his client's case. Consequently, in line with the views of the vast majority of the courts in our sister jurisdictions, we have no hesitancy in concluding that in criminal causes communications made by a defendant to an expert in order to equip that expert with the necessary information to provide the defendant's attorney with the tools to aid him in giving his client proper legal advice are within the scope of the attorney-client privilege.

This is uniquely so in cases concerning the question of a criminal defendant's sanity, because the need of an attorney to consult with a qualified medical expert is paramount. Such a medical expert not only provides testimony that usually is necessary at trial to support an insanity defense, but also "attunes the lay attorney to unfamiliar but central medical concepts and enables him, as an initial matter, to assess the soundness and advisability of offering the defense * * * and perhaps most importantly, * * * permits a lawyer inexpert in the science of psychiatry to probe intelligently the foundations of adverse testimony."

The State here does not dispute the inclusion of psychiatric communications within the scope of the attorney-client privilege; instead, it contends that when Mrs. Pratt interposed a defense of insanity, she waived the privilege with respect to all statements she may have made to any medical expert, whether in her employ or in that of the State. While there is little doubt that a client may waive this right to confidentiality, which may be done either expressly or impliedly, we have been made aware of only one decision in which a court, the New York Court of Appeals, has held that raising the defense of insanity, without more, is a relinquishment of the attorney-client privilege as to communications between the client and his alienist. In its opinion the court justified its conclusion that a defendant's insanity plea waived the attorney-client privilege on the following basis:

> A defendant who seeks to introduce psychiatric testimony in support of his insanity plea may be required to disclose prior to trial the underlying basis of his alleged affliction to a prosecution psychiatrist. Hence, where, as here, a defendant reveals to the prosecution the very facts which would be secreted by the exercise of the privilege, reason does not compel the exclusion of expert testimony based on such facts, or cross-examination concerning the grounds for opinions based thereon. It follows that no harm accrues to the defense from seeking pretrial psychiatric advice where an insanity plea is actually entered, for in such circumstances, the underlying factual basis will be revealed to the prosecution psychiatrist. [*People v. Edney*, 385 N.E.2d 400, 403 (1976).]

While there appears to be some logic, at least in a technical sense, to New York's highest court's reasoning, nonetheless we find that the chilling effect such a result would have upon a client's willingness to confide in his attorney or any defense-employed consultants requires that we align ourselves with the overwhelming body of authority and reject that court's conclusion.

Moreover, a further drawback to the New York rule is the prejudice inherent in disclosing to the trier of fact that the source of this adverse testimony is an expert originally employed by the defendant. This factor will almost certainly carry added weight with the jury, which usually is the prosecution's principal purpose for producing the defense-employed psychiatrist as a witness. Note, *Protecting the Confidentiality of Pretrial Psychiatric Disclosures: A Survey of Standards*, 51 N.Y.U.L.Rev. 409, 411 (1976).

* * *

An additional consequence of the State's suggested waiver rule, if adopted by us, is that the defense, in essence, would be required to assist the prosecution in discharging its burden of proof. In Maryland, as in most other jurisdictions, the government not only bears the burden of showing that the defendant perpetrated the alleged criminal act, but, once the sanity of the accused has been placed in doubt by the defense, it is also saddled with the ultimate burden of proving, beyond a reasonable doubt, that the defendant was sane at the time he committed the act.

* * *

If, in its efforts to establish the mental responsibility of the accused following a plea of insanity, the State is permitted to utilize a psychiatrist hired by the defendant, both the defense attorney and his client will be inhibited from "consulting one or more experts, with possibly conflicting views, by the fear that in doing so [they] may be assisting the government in meeting its burden of proof on the [sanity] issue." Breaching the attorney-client privilege in this situation also would have the effect of inhibiting the free exercise of a defense attorney's informed judgment by confronting him with the likelihood that, in taking a step obviously crucial to his client's defense, he is creating a potential government witness who theretofore did not exist. The possible impact upon the federal and State constitutional rights of the defendant of a rule permitting such testimony further persuades us that we should be reluctant to hold there is a waiver, under the circumstances here, of the attorney-client privilege.

Accordingly, we affirm the judgment of the Court of Special Appeals, which comports with the ruling we make here.

III. PATIENT ACCESS TO RECORDS

GOTKIN v. MILLER

United States Court of Appeals, Second Circuit, 1975.
514 F.2d 125.

HAYS, Circuit Judge:

Janet Gotkin, a former mental patient, and her husband Paul brought an action in the United States District Court for the Eastern District of New York under 42 U.S.C. § 1983 and 28 U.S.C. § 1343 (1970) seeking to have Mrs. Gotkin's records at Brooklyn State Hospital, Long Island Jewish-Hillside Medical Center, and Gracie Square Hospital made available to her. Judge Travia granted summary judgment in favor of the defendants. He held that the plaintiffs had failed to demonstrate that they had a constitutional right to inspect and copy Mrs. Gotkin's records. Gotkin v. Miller, 379 F.Supp. 859 (E.D.N.Y.1974). We affirm.

I.

The facts are essentially undisputed. Between 1962 and 1970 Janet Gotkin was voluntarily hospitalized on several occasions mainly because of a series of suicide attempts. She has not received treatment since September, 1970. In April, 1973, the Gotkins contracted to write a book about Janet's experiences. In order to verify her recollections of various incidents, she wrote to three hospitals at which she had been a patient asking them to send her copies of her records. Brooklyn State Hospital and Long Island Jewish-Hillside Medical Center refused her request, and Gracie Square Hospital did not respond.

The Gotkins then filed suit against the directors of the three hospitals and the New York State Commissioner of Mental Hygiene, alleging that the policies of the hospitals against granting requests such as Mrs. Gotkin's violated the rights of former mental patients under the First, Fourth, Ninth, and Fourteenth Amendments of the United States Constitution. The complaint demanded declaratory and injunctive relief in favor of the Gotkins and all others similarly situated. The court granted the defendants' motion for summary judgment. It held that Paul Gotkin was not a proper plaintiff because he was not a former mental patient and had not requested access to his or his wife's records. 379 F.Supp. at 862. As to Janet Gotkin and other members of her purported class, the court held that former mental patients have no First Amendment right to receive information contained in their hospital records, 379 F.Supp. at 862–63; that the Fourth Amendment prohibition of unreasonable searches and seizures is inapplicable, id. 379 F.Supp. at 863; that plaintiffs enjoy no right of privacy entitling them to their records for purposes of publishing a book, id.; and that plaintiffs had not been deprived of "liberty" or "property" protected by the due process clause of the Fourteenth Amendment, id. 379 F.Supp. at 864–68.

II.

Appellants' main argument on this appeal is that the refusal by the hospitals to allow former mental patients to inspect their records deprives the patients of property without due process of law. We can find no basis for the proposition that mental patients have a constitutionally protected property interest in the direct and unrestricted access to their records which the appellants demand.

In Board of Regents of State Colleges v. Roth, 408 U.S. 564, (1972), the Supreme Court held that the Fourteenth Amendment is not an independent source of property rights. The due process clause protects only those property interests already acquired as a result of "existing rules or understandings that stem from an independent source such as state law—rules or understandings that secure certain benefits and that support claims of entitlement to those benefits." Id.

In an attempt to satisfy the *Roth* criteria, appellants argue that under New York case law, patients have a property interest in their hospital records. However, none of the cases cited by appellants indicates that patients have a right to unrestricted access to their records. The majority of the cited cases hold simply that under the discovery provisions of New York law, patients are entitled to a court order granting them access to their records for purposes of litigation.

* * *

New York statutory law also establishes that while patients may exercise a considerable degree of control over their records, they do not have the right to demand direct access to them. Under the Mental Hygiene Law records may not be released to third parties without the consent of the patient, except in certain enumerated situations. Section 17 of the Public Health Law provides for the release of medical records to a hospital or physician designated by the patient. These sections indicate the existence of substantial limitations on the right of access claimed by appellants. We therefore hold that the Fourteenth Amendment does not support appellants' claim that former mental patients have a constitutionally protected, unrestricted property right directly to inspect and copy their hospital records.

III.

Appellants also argue that the hospitals' policy violates the Fourteenth Amendment because it deprives former mental patients of liberty without due process of law. They claim that since the policy against unrestricted disclosure is in part based on the fear that such disclosure could have an adverse effect on the patient, the refusal by the hospitals to grant Mrs. Gotkin access to her records stigmatizes her as mentally ill, although she is now sane and competent.

We agree that the due process clause applies not only when one's physical liberty is threatened but also "[w]here a person's good name, reputation, honor, or integrity is at stake." Wisconsin v. Constantineau, 400 U.S. 433. However, the contention that Mrs. Gotkin is being stigmatized by the hospitals is without merit. No one has branded her as mentally ill or otherwise incompetent. Mrs. Gotkin has no valid claim of deprivation of liberty under the Fourteenth Amendment.

*   *   *

We agree with the district court that the defendants were entitled to summary judgment regardless of the outcome of these factual disputes. Plaintiffs in this action sought nothing short of unrestricted, direct access to Mrs. Gotkin's records. They failed to establish a constitutional basis for this claim, and it was therefore unnecessary for the district court to judge the wisdom of the hospitals' screening procedures or to decide if those procedures were properly administered.

Affirmed.

PALMER v. DURSO

Supreme Court, Special Term, Kings County, 1977.
90 Misc.2d 110, 393 N.Y.S.2d 898.

ARTHUR S. HIRSCH, Justice.

On August 11, 1953 petitioner was certified by the Department of Mental Hygiene of the State of New York as a mentally incompetent person under Section 74 of the former Mental Hygiene Law and was confined in Brooklyn State Hospital for a period of six months. More than twenty-three years later, petitioner moved in this court last year to have the certification vacated and all records thereto expunged. His motion was denied and petitioner is proceeding *pro se* in appealing said motion to the Appellate Division.

The instant motion is for an order directing the release to petitioner of all sealed records relating to a Department of Mental Hygiene certification of petitioner on August 11, 1953 filed in the Office of the County Clerk of the County of Kings, which petitioner claims is necessary for the preparation of the appeal.

The relevant statute, Mental Hygiene Law 31.31 concerning sealed records of a hearing on an involuntary admission of a patient pursuant to medical certification provides:

> (f) The papers in any proceeding under this article which are filed with the county clerk shall be sealed and shall be exhibited only to the parties to the proceeding or someone properly interested, upon order of the court.

As a party to the proceeding which resulted in the commitment, the petitioner is one of the designated persons listed in the statute who may have access to sealed records filed in the Office of the County Clerk, should the court decide petitioner's request for said records is legitimate and appropriate.

Respondent, County Clerk, in objecting to the release of the records argues that petitioner is merely seeking relief denied in his motion now being appealed. He contends that records of a patient in a mental hospital are of such confidential nature that public policy requires they not be revealed except on a strong showing of legitimate and proper call therefor. To buttress this contention, respondent cites a 1953 case (*Application of Hild*, Sup., 124 N.Y.S.2d 271.) The *Hild* court acknowledged that the purpose of the prevailing 1927 Mental Hygiene statute (comparable to the present statute) was to make records to a patient of a mental facility accessible, provided a commissioner or a judge of a court of record, after considering the facts of a given case, passed upon the propriety of the requested action. (Id. at 273) The court, therefore, under appropriate circumstances could unseal records and make them available to former patients. The court in *Hild* denied the application only because petitioner had not shown that the records were germane to issues raised in a pending divorce action in a foreign state for which purpose they were to be used.

There is no question that the records in the instant case are competent, material and relevant to petitioner's appeal from an order denying his request to have those same records vacated and expunged. He is seeking in this motion to have access to the records unlike his initial motion in which he asked that they be destroyed. His ability to competently argue his appeal which he intends to do *pro se* may well hinge on his study of the very records that are the focal point of the proceeding.

In regard to respondent's reference to public policy, it is to be noted the Mental Hygiene Law which allows for concealment of mental institution records was enacted primarily to save patients from humiliation, embarrassment and disgrace (*Munzer v. Blaisdell*, 183 Misc. 773, 49 N.Y.S.2d 915). This rationale for keeping records sealed cannot seriously be applied to the instant situation as it is the petitioner who waived the privilege in order to prepare himself for the appeal. Public policy, especially in light of today's positive attitude towards openness and against bureaucratic concealment would demand that a litigant be facilitated in obtaining his records.

A second case is offered by respondent to support his objections (*Gotkin v. Miller* (D.C.1974) 379 F.Supp. 859, affd. 2 Cir., 514 F.2d 125). The United States District Court ruled that the withholding from plaintiff of records of certain mental hospitals was not a violation of plaintiff's constitutional rights. In *Gotkin,* the plaintiff had been a voluntary mental patient at mental hospitals for a series of threatened suicides. She wanted the record of her stay at these institutions to help her verify some data which she had included in a soon to be published book about her psychiatric experiences.

The court succinctly differentiated between plaintiff's need for the records as opposed to the needs of a litigant in a pending legal action (379 F.Supp. at 868). The petitioner in the instant action is of the latter group, having filed his notice of appeal in the Appellate Division of this state.

The use to which records will be put is a determinant factor in unsealing records of mental institutions. If an applicant needs to obtain information necessary to proceed with litigation, it is reasonable that he should be afforded the opportunity to review and to receive a copy of those records he needs including the order for his commitment, the papers upon which it was granted, as well as all records pertaining thereto. (*Lee v. State,* 183 Misc. 615, 49 N.Y.S.2d 836).

The court concludes petitioner has shown sufficient and legitimate need for records to be used in a pending litigation and further, that respondent has shown no public policy requiring a denial of petitioner's access to said records.

Accordingly, upon the foregoing papers, the petitioner's motion is granted. Petitioner may examine the sealed records of his commitment on file in the County Clerk's Office under such supervision as the County Clerk may deem proper.

Questions and Comments

1. As the two preceeding cases indicated, there was no common law right by a patient to information in his medical records. The patient was not perceived as having a property interest in the records nor as having an implied contractual right. In recent times various jurisdictions have passed specific legislation for providing patients and particularly those patients who have undergone psychotherapy with a right of access to their records. A typical statute is that enacted by the State of Illinois in 1979, the Illinois Mental Health and Developmental Disability Confidentiality Act. This law provides that any recipient of mental health and development disabilities services "shall be entitled upon request, to

inspect a copy of [his/her] record or any partial thereof." Ill.Rev.Stats. ch. 91½, § 802 (1983). Moreover, the Illinois statute gives this right to any recipient who is 12 years of age or older.

It is, however, noteworthy that the Illinois statute like that of other states with similar legislation distinguishes between the "patients record" and the therapist's "personal notes." The latter term is defined to include:

> (i) information disclosed to the therapist in confidence by other persons on condition that such information would never be disclosed to the recipient or other persons;

> (ii) information disclosed to the therapist by the recipient which would be injurious to the recipient's relationships to other persons; and

> (iii) the therapist's speculations, impressions, hunches, and reminders.

Thus, by restricting access to the patient's *official record*, these statutes make it possible for therapists to closely regulate and limit the amount of information that is actually available to the patient. Cf. California, which grants a patient access to his records unless in the view of the physician or administrative officer in question, release of such records to the patient would not "serve his best interests." Ann.Cal. Code § 5328.9 (1983).

2. What policy reasons support the recipient's access to the records of his mental health services? Are statutes which provide access merely protecting an abstract interest in the patient's right to know, or are there more practical reasons why the patient should have access to his records? Does the answer to this question depend in any sense on the scope of the therapist's authority to disclose information to third parties? In other words, to the extent that even the common law or statutory law of the state permits or at least does not prevent disclosure to third parties, the patient arguably may have a very substantial interest in screening his record so as to ensure that misinformation is not transmitted. However, if under the prevailing state law the therapist's powers to transmit to third parties are closely controlled, what is the patient's interest in gaining access to his records?

3. Are there any possible negative consequences in a psychiatric patient gaining access to their records? Would a diagnosis which is merely tentative have a potential of becoming self-fulfilling if the patient learns of the tentative diagnosis? Is this problem more or less in the case of children who are under treatment? Note, in this connection, that in some jurisdictions such as Illinois, any recipient of services over the age of 12 has the right to inspect records maintained by a provider of services.

*

Part Two

THE MENTAL HEALTH SYSTEMS

Chapter Five

VOLUNTARY PSYCHIATRIC HOSPITALIZATION

Table of Sections

I. INTRODUCTION

In terms of the legal process there are basically two ways that a person can enter a residential psychiatric facility. An individual may enter voluntarily in which case his status is similar to that of a patient entering any medical facility. In other words, entry is effected through what is presumed to be the free and voluntary action of the patient. Alternatively, an individual may be admitted by way of a coercive process authorized by law. In the latter case, where the admission is "involuntary," the normal prerogatives of the individual to elect or reject treatment and hospitalization are overridden and the final decision is made by an administrative or judicial officer.

Thus, on a formal level there are two separate and distinct methods of admission. In reality, however, the distinction between voluntary and involuntary methods of admission are less clear than the governing statutory laws suggest. In some cases an individual may be admitted as a voluntary patient not because he, in fact, desires to be hospitalized but rather because he has been induced or pressured into executing the necessary voluntary admission application. As the materials which follow will make clear, many incentives or pressures are available to persuade an individual to execute or apply for voluntary admission.

While the distinction between voluntary and involuntary admissions may not be as clear as the statutes which govern admissions procedures suggest, there are nonetheless many individuals who, in fact, freely and voluntarily chose to avail themselves of the opportunity for voluntary admission to a psychiatric facility. And there are significant differences in the legal issues which courts may be called upon to address when an individual enters on a voluntary basis. This chapter focuses on the voluntary form of admission; the issues raised by admissions that are explicitly involuntary are treated in the following chapter.

II. OVERVIEW OF THE VOLUNTARY ADMISSIONS PROCESS

A. INTRODUCTION

Voluntary hospitalization of the mentally ill has been widely acclaimed in recent years as a welcome alternative to involuntary commitment. Voluntary or consensual hospitalization is intended to remove the coercion, trauma, and stigma normally associated with involuntary hospitalization and to provide the same opportunity for treatment for mentally ill persons as is available to those suffering from physical illness.

Most state statutes provide for two different types of consensual admission—informal voluntary admission and formal voluntary admission. The basic difference between the two types lies in the statutory provisions regulating release. Under the informal type of admission, the patient generally must be released immediately upon request, while under the more formal admission, the patient may be detained for a specified period of days following his request. In Michigan, for example, an "informal voluntary patient may terminate his hospitalization and leave the hospital, at any time during the normal day shift hours of the hospital", Mich.Stat.Ann. § 330.1412 (1976). On the other hand, a "formal voluntary patient * * * may be hospitalized for up to 3 days, excluding Sundays and holidays, after he gives written notice of his intention to terminate his hospitalization." *Id.*, § 333.1419.

Whether a patient is informally or formally admitted to the hospital depends primarily on the method of application. Thus, continuing with Michigan as the example, an individual may be hospitalized as an informal voluntary patient if he merely "requests" hospitalization as an informal patient and if the hospital director deems him clinically suitable for that form of hospitalization. *Id.*, § 330.1411. As a practical matter the informal method of admission is rarely utilized largely because of the unwillingness of administrators of psychiatric facilities to admit patients on this basis. Consequently, nearly all persons who enter a facility on a consensual basis are subject to the mandatory detention periods associated with the formal type of voluntary admission.

The materials that follow examine the various issues related to the voluntary mode of hospitalization. The theoretical objective of voluntary hospitalization as well as some of the criticisms of this form are reviewed in the section, General Perspectives, immediately following. Issues specifically related to the application and interpretation of statutory provisions governing the voluntary admission process are considered in section III. Section IV considers those issues which may arise after an individual has been admitted as a voluntary patient. Section V considers the special problems raised by the admission of minors and incompetent persons.

B. GENERAL PERSPECTIVES

COMMENT, "HOSPITALIZATION OF THE MENTALLY DISABLED IN PENNSYLVANIA: THE MENTAL HEALTH–MENTAL RETARDATION ACT OF 1966"
71 Dick.L.Rev. 307, 308–309 (1967).

The term "voluntary admission" refers to procedures for admission to a mental facility which are commenced originally by the affirmative action of the patient himself or of someone empowered by law to act in the patient's behalf. With the modern advance of psychiatry, the availability of effective treatment through the use of tranquilizers, and a more enlightened understanding of the problems of mental health by the public, there has been an increasing emphasis on voluntary admission as the most desirable method of hospitalization of the mentally disabled. This method enjoys the unique position of being favored by all of the groups concerned with influencing legislation in this field. The medical profession endorses this procedure because of its simplicity and the complete lack of any court action. The patient who can recognize his illness and seek hospitalization on his own volition is the one who will actively participate in his treatment, cooperate with his doctor, and benefit the most from the treatment. As a result the voluntary patient will be discharged more rapidly, thereby alleviating the generally crowded conditions that exist in most mental facilities. Those who are concerned with civil liberties of mental patients are reassured, since the dangers of wrongful detention exist only in involuntary hospitalization procedures.

MANFRED S. GUTTMACHER AND HENRY WEIHOFEN, *PSYCHIATRY AND THE LAW*

(New York: Norton, 1952), pp. 305–308.

Whereas commitment connotes a legal command by which a person is placed in an institution, voluntary admission signalizes recognition of the new conception of "insanity" as a form of illness calling for medical care. Such a conception was, of course, impossible so long as commitment was resorted to only as a means of confining the dangerous insane. But after the view became accepted, legally as well as medically, that commitment might be proper, not only where it was necessary for the safety of the public or of the patient, but also where it might be conducive to his restoration to health, it was inevitable that we should come to regard mental illness as not essentially different from physical illness, and to believe that a person able to realize that he is mentally ill should be able to obtain hospital treatment as easily and as informally as he can for physical illness.

THOMAS S. SZASZ, *LAW, LIBERTY, AND PSYCHIATRY*

(New York: Macmillan, 1963), pp. 81–83.

Until recently, all mental hospital admissions were involuntary. This was consistent with the view, once widely held, that mental patients were "demented." Hence, one did not seek their cooperation. Since the end of the Second World War, there has been a growing interest in voluntary admission to public mental hospitals. Voluntary—or, more precisely, ostensibly voluntary—admission policies have been adopted in a number of places, partly in an effort to sustain the myth that mental illness is just like any other illness. Indeed, the fact that voluntary mental hospitalization is available is now being interpreted as evidence of the similarity between bodily and psychiatric illness. It is in this spirit that Guttmacher and Weihofen (1952) have advocated voluntary admission laws. They wrote:

Whereas commitment connotes a legal command by which a person is placed in an institution, *voluntary admission signalizes recognition of the new conception of "insanity" as a form of illness calling for medical care.* Such a conception was, of course, impossible so long as commitment was resorted to only as a means of confining the dangerous insane. But after the view became accepted, legally as well as medically, that *commitment might be proper, not only where it was necessary for the safety of the public or of the patient, but also where it might be conducive to his restoration of health,* it was inevitable that we should come to regard mental illness as not essentially different from physical illness, and to believe that a person able to realize that he is mentally ill should be able to obtain hospital treatment as easily and as informally as he can for physical illness [italics added; pages 305–306].

The logic of this argument is astonishing. Guttmacher and Weihofen assert that by the mere act of treating A and B in the same way, we shall uncover and establish similarities between them. This is nonsense. Whether mental disease is comparable to physical disease, and if so, in what ways, must be investigated by empirical research and epistemological analysis. Instead of undertaking either of these tasks, the authors, and many others, advocate social action to establish empirical facts and logical constructs.

*   *   *

III. SOME PROBLEMS IN THE APPLICATION OF STATUTORY STANDARDS

The reality of voluntary admission (as distinguished from the theoretical legal model) raises two types of problems: First, to what extent should the informed consent model described in the previous chapter apply to the admission process? As was noted in the context of outpatient treatment, consent obtained through duress or coercion has no legal validity. What is the legal status of an application for voluntary admission where the applicant is threatened with either criminal prosecution or civil commitment if he does not agree to enter as a voluntary patient? Would or should either of these "inducements" serve to invalidate the voluntary admission?

The resolution of this problem must take into account a number of factors. First and foremost, if the law were to move toward true voluntary admission, it would undoubtedly serve to increase the number of involuntary commitments. Clearly, some individuals who now enter psychiatric hospitals as voluntary patients would, if all coercion were to be eliminated, enter by way of the involuntary process with its attendant "hearing." This would undoubtedly serve to increase the number of "commitments" and place additional strain on the court system and legal resources in general, *i.e.*, prosecutors and defendants' lawyers. The problem is analogous to what would occur if plea bargaining in the criminal process were to be reduced or eliminated. Any change would, therefore, have to take into account the capacity of the legal system to handle a significantly increased case load.

Application of the informed consent standard to the voluntary admission process raises a second problem. The informed consent model previously considered in the context of consent to outpatient treatment presumes that the patient *understands* both the nature of the proposed treatment and the alternatives open to him. However, some psychiatric patients may temporarily lack the capacity for full understanding and awareness. Thus, to the extent that the full requirements of informed consent were to be imposed, it is thus doubtful whether some who currently enter as voluntary patients would meet the requisite legal standard. The problem is more complicated where the prospective admittee is not legally incompetent but rather is only partially disabled in his understanding or cognition. When the incapacity is substantial, it may lead to the institution of incompetency proceedings and the appointment of a guardian. The special problems related to the institutionalization of incompetent persons are treated in Chapter Seven. More commonly, however, the person is only partially incapacitated. It is in such cases that there is some tension between the legal model and empirical reality. Thus, if true voluntariness and understanding were to be required, present procedures may have to be modified. For one thing, it may be necessary to have some independent decision-maker interposed in the process to determine whether the requisite of level of understanding or awareness exists. This would still leave open the question of how to deal with individuals who are found not to have sufficient aware- ness to give meaningful informed consent but who are not legally incompetent. Thus, there are obvious problems in the use of an admissions procedure which at least in theory contemplates free and informed individual choice on the part of the prospective admittee. The material which follows seeks to explore some of these questions.

A. WHAT IS A "VOLUNTARY" APPLICATION?

GILBOY AND SCHMIDT, "VOLUNTARY HOSPITALIZA- TION OF THE MENTALLY ILL"
66 Nw.L.Rev. 429 (1971).

The use of voluntary rather than involuntary procedures for the hospitalization of the mentally ill has been widely acclaimed in recent years by both medical and legal scholars. One legal study states that "the availability of voluntary hospitalization procedures has been favored by practically every group concerned with drafting effective legislation in this field." Psychiatrists and hospital officials advocate voluntary admission as "extremely desirable from the viewpoint of effective medical treatment." Making the patient responsible for his own treatment, rather than committing him forcibly to an institution, is said to increase his feelings of self worth and his receptivity to psychiatric treatment. Voluntary admission also avoids a formal judicial involuntary commitment hearing, "an experience which itself often increases mental instability."

* * *

Both the medical and legal proponents of voluntary care share a conception of voluntary admission as an individual decision to accept mental treatment, made entirely apart from involuntary commitment procedures, thereby avoiding the therapeutic and legal problems of coercion. We have recently studied the use of voluntary admission procedures in Illinois, a state in which a substantial majority of persons hospitalized in mental institutions are now admitted under voluntary procedures. The results of our study indicate that the foregoing conception is wrong.

In a majority of cases voluntary admission is utilized to hospitalize persons who are already in some form of official custody. Voluntary admission avoids procedural complexity and the need for officials to assume responsibility, both inherent drawbacks to compulsory commitment from the officials' point of view. Individuals are therefore induced to voluntarily commit themselves with the threat of involuntary commitment as the principal means of persuasion, and with little concern for the adequacy of the information on which the individual's decision is based or whether it is "voluntary" at all. * * *

DEFINITION OF VOLUNTARY ADMISSION

Under Illinois law there are two different procedures for voluntary admission to mental hospitals. Under the first procedure, known as "informal admission," an individual is admitted to a mental hospital without formal application and is free to leave at any time during normal day-shift hours. Under the second procedure, known as "voluntary admission," an individual is admitted to a mental hospital upon formal application and is free to leave "within 5 days, excluding Saturdays, Sundays and holidays, after he gives any professional staff person notice of his desire to leave * * *". However, during that 5-day notice period, the hospital officials may ask a court to hold an involuntary commitment hearing, which must be set within 5 days after such petition. The patient continues to be hospitalized pending a final order of the court at the hearing. Thus, informal admission may be described as an entirely voluntary process. Voluntary admission, in contrast, requires an initial voluntary decision on the part of the patient, but, once that decision is made, the patient is subject to restraint on his right to leave the hospital, and may be required to remain a week or more after he expresses a desire to leave.

A striking preliminary fact which our study disclosed is that informal admission is almost never utilized. In fact, in only about one percent of the cases admitted to mental institutions in Illinois is "informal admission" utilized. In contrast, voluntary admission is used in about 68% of all cases. The reason for the greater use of voluntary admission appears to be the additional restraining power the procedure gives the hospital over the patient. "With 'informal admission' the units just do not feel enough control over the patient," one hospital admissions officer remarked. Another hospital official described informal admission as an "inconvenience" to hospital staff personnel and an unnecessary "allowance" to patients. In one case described to us by an admissions officer, informal admission was used to house overnight an individual admittedly not in need of hospitalization, but for whom no other immediate shelter could be found.

The almost total refusal to use the entirely voluntary informal admission procedure is suggestive at the outset of the general attitude of officials toward voluntary admission procedures. The value of such procedures to officials, as will be more evident below, is not primarily in allowing individuals to remain in control of their own circumstances, but rather in hospitalizing individuals with a minimum of official responsibility and difficulty.

POLICE CUSTODY CASES

The case which proponents of voluntary admission almost always have in mind is that of an individual who arrives at a mental institution by himself, or accompanied by a physician, family, relatives or friends, and asks to be admitted for treatment. We call these "non-custody cases" to denote the absence of any official custody prior to the individual's decision to commit himself.

* * *

Our study disclosed that about 40% of all voluntarily admitted patients are brought to the mental hospital by the police * * * While some studies of civil commitment have recognized that a significant number of persons are brought to mental institutions by the police, there has been little recognition that such cases often result in voluntary rather than involuntary commitment. * * *

* * *

COURT CASES

Our study disclosed that approximately 10–11% of voluntary admissions to mental hospitals result from decisions made, or announced, in court at the time of an involuntary commitment hearing. Voluntary admission occurs in approximately 35% of the cases which come to court for involuntary commitment hearings. * * *

A decision to accept voluntary admission by a defendant at a court hearing raises the same issue of adequate disclosure discussed earlier in connection with voluntary admission of persons brought by the police to the hospital admissions office. It might be expected that the involvement of the public defender and the judge at the time of a court hearing would insure that any decision on admission would be fully informed. However, the judges involved appear to give no consideration to the defendant's awareness of his situation. Any indication that the public defender and state's attorney are agreeable to voluntary admission and that the patient will agree is sufficient to dispose of the case.

* * *

Where persons come to civil commitment hearings after having initially been arrested on criminal charges (a majority of the cases in Chicago), a further legal issue is raised. In these cases the individuals are under an added pressure: the threat of criminal prosecution if they should successfully resist civil commitment. If the individual is committed, voluntarily or involuntarily, the criminal charge against him is usually dropped. * * *

CONCLUSION

Our study disclosed that in a majority of the cases in which voluntary admission procedures were used, the individuals were already under some form of official custody and were faced with the threat of involuntary commitment proceedings as the principal alternative to voluntary admission. * * *

Questions and Comments

1. The authors of the preceding article seemed particularly concerned with the voluntariness of an individual's consent to hospitalization when the alternative is threatened criminal or involuntary hospitalization proceedings. Could it be argued that a decision to voluntarily admit oneself under such circumstances represents a rational decision by the patient that such admission is in his or her best interest? This assessment might include the judgment that there is less social approbrium associated with a "voluntary" admission.

2. How could the problems addressed in the preceding article be avoided? Is there any alternative except to require judicial review of every "voluntary" admission to ensure that the individual's consent to admission was truly voluntary? If judicial review were required, what standard of voluntariness might emerge?

3. Should voluntary hospitalization require that every prospective patient be appraised of the possible alternative to hospitalization, much as would be required by the doctrine of informed consent?

4. The issue of voluntariness has arisen in various other contexts. For instance, it is a rule of constitutional dimension that confessions of criminal conduct are only admissible in a criminal proceeding if they were made "voluntarily." In fact, in *Malloy v. Hogan*, 378 U.S. 1, 84 S.Ct. 1489, 12 L.Ed.2d 653 (1964), the Supreme Court held that a waiver of the defendant's right to remain silent must be the "unfettered exercise of his [the defendant's] will." The application of this standard by courts has, however, proved troublesome and has required *ad hoc* case by case determinations. The difficulties inherent in the evaluation of voluntariness in criminal proceedings have been described in the following terms:

> [I]n the sense that the situation always presents a "choice" between two alternatives, either one disagreeable, to be sure, *all* confessions are "voluntary."

* * *

As police interrogators made greater use of "psychological" techniques over the years, the always difficult problems of proof confronting the alleged victims of improper interrogation practices became increasingly arduous. Disputes over whether physical violence occurred are not always easy to resolve, but evidence of "mental" or "psychological" coercion is especially elusive. Frequently, the defendant was inarticulate, which aggravated the difficulties of recreating the tenor and atmosphere of the police questioning or the *manner* in which the appropriate advice about the suspect's rights might have been given or, if properly given, subsequently undermined.

Y. Kamisar, W. LaFave, J. Israel, *Modern Criminal Procedure* (St. Paul, Minn.: West, 1980), p. 557.

Would these same problems arise if genuine voluntariness were required for voluntary admissions into psychiatric facilities? What types of pressures or inducements should serve to invalidate such admission?

B. IS INFORMED CONSENT A REQUIREMENT?

The only reported case where the issue of informed consent in the context of voluntary admission has been addressed is *Application for Certification of William R*, 9 Misc.2d 1084, 172 N.Y.S.2d 869 (1958). Even in that case the issue was not really one requiring judicial resolution, since the judicial proceedings had, in effect, been terminated by the patient's subsequent placement in a private home, thereby rendering the issue of admission into a psychiatric facility moot. Nevertheless, the court made the following observation with respect to use of the "voluntary" admissions procedures for the institutionalization of senile persons into state psychiatric facilities:

I have previously called to the attention of the organized Bar that the pink form is being increasingly used by the Department of Mental Hygiene for the transfer and admission to state mental institutions, without judicial consideration, of most of the senile aged who do not make *positive objection*, and that it accounted for more than 1,000 such transfers within a period of nine months in 1957 from Kings County Hospital alone. ＊ ＊ ＊ This newly used technique effectively shunts seniles into involuntary confinement without awareness by them of their plight and without their actual approval or judicial surveillance. These unwanted seniles may not even hope to escape factually involuntary confinement because the possibility of private care, often provided at a judicial hearing, is denied to them and, of course, they cannot thereafter effect their own release.

Moreover, the denial of judicial hearing or sanction is based on a statute of questionable constitutionality because it is grounded on a fictitious consent given by one who concededly is confused and disoriented. Even if *positive objection* is not required by the Mental Hygiene Department, the consent thus extracted is dubious because the senile is not likely to understand that the admitting institution is a mental institution, even if he be told that it is. Often he is chagrined and humiliated following family rejection and has neither the will nor the capacity to object even if he be carefully advised. That he is aware of his right to object or of the significance of his failure to object is doubtful. In short, the pink sheet procedure, in my view, is little less than a ruse designed to circumvent the need for judicial consideration or review of the transfer of the senile to a mental institution.

Questions and Comments

1. Justice Brenner registers staunch disapproval of the procedure whereby an individual may be admitted to a mental institution if he or she makes no "positive objection," arguing that "[t]his newly used technique effectively shunts seniles into involuntary confinement without awareness by them of their plight and without their actual approval or judicial surveillance." Is there any validity to the view as expressed by one commentator who argued that "non-protesting persons" statutes can be justified by the "need for a simple, non-traumatic admission process for those individuals who either do not recognize their need for hospitalization or are unwilling to seek admission, but nevertheless do not object when others initiate the admission process." Note, "District of Columbia Hospitalization of the Mentally Ill Act," 65 Colum.L.Rev. 1062, 1065 (1965). Does Justice Brenner's opinion adequately address (or weigh) these considerations?

Is increased judicial involvement in voluntary or non-protesting hospitalization procedures necessary to safeguard the interests of the prospective patient? Are these interests likely to be adequately protected by the supervising mental health professional?

2. Implicit throughout Justice Brenner's opinion is that many voluntary or non-protesting patients may be incapable of giving informed consent to their hospitalization because of their mental illness or disability. Is such an individual ever a proper candidate for "voluntary" hospitalization?

3. In addition to "voluntary admissions" procedures, a number of states allow for the non-judicial hospitalization of "non-protesting" persons. The District of Columbia's statute, for example, provides that:

A friend or relative of a person believed to be suffering from a mental illness may apply on behalf of that person to the admitting psychiatrist of a hospital by presenting the person, together with a referral from a practicing physician. For the purpose of examination and treatment, a private hospital may accept a person so presented and referred, and a public hospital shall accept a person so presented and referred, if, in the judgment of the admitting psychiatrist, the need for examination and treatment is indicated on the basis of the person's mental condition and the person signs a statement at the time of the admission stating that he does not object to hospitalization. The statement shall contain in simple, non-technical language the fact that the person is to be hospitalized and a description of the right to release [immediately on request]. The admitting psychiatrist may admit a person so presented, without referral from a practicing physician, if the need for an immediate admission is apparent to the admitting psychiatrist upon preliminary examination.

D.C.Code, § 21–513 (1973). The drafters of the District of Columbia statute apparently felt "there is a need for a simple, non-traumatic admission process for those individuals who either do not recognize their need for hospitalization or are unwilling to seek admission, but nevertheless do not object when others initiate the admission process." 65 Colum.L.Rev. 1062 at 1065 (1965).

4. As noted, the question of whether a *voluntary* admission must accord with the requirements of informed consent has to date not been authoritatively resolved by any court. In fact, few courts have even had occasion to consider the issue for largely procedural reasons. For one thing a person who has been either pressured into signing an application for voluntary admission or who has signed such application without fully understanding the consequences of the application for admission is unlikely to have standing to raise the issue since he can, at any time, request to be released. Such an individual will then either be released pursuant to his request or be *committed* pursuant to the legal provisions for involuntary admission. In either event, the issue of wrongful or improper voluntary admission will have been mooted, thereby depriving a court of jurisdiction to pass on the underlying issues pertaining to the voluntary admission.

IV. STATUS AND RIGHTS OF THE VOLUNTARY PATIENT

A. IS THERE A RIGHT TO ADMISSION?

The issues pertaining to psychiatric hospitalization that have received the most attention by the press and commentators in general have, by and large, focused on the abuses of the involuntary civil commitment power and the legal rights of psychiatric patients. Of equal importance, though far less often the subject of attention and debate, are questions going to access to services, including in-patient treatment. In fact, for some individuals obtaining access to in-patient services may be of crucial importance.

The issue of access, particularly where the individual is competent and has reached majority, most often arises in the voluntary admissions process when an individual makes application to a state-operated facility but is denied admission as a voluntary patient. The same basic issue arises when the individual has been admitted as a voluntary patient and is then discharged against his will, either because he is deemed to no longer require in-patient treatment or because of budgetary limitations that require the discharge of some of the patients in the facility.

In addressing these issues one may start by noting that if a *right* to state services exists, its source will be in either a state or federal statute or in the Constitution. Whether a right exists under a particular statute depends on the wording of the statute and the meaning ascribed to the statute by the administration or any courts that may be called upon to interpret it. Ordinarily most statutes governing voluntary admission invest the administrator of the particular facility with considerable discretion in admitting or retaining voluntary patients. A typical provision is found in the Illinois Mental Health and Disability Code which provides:

> Any person 16 or older may be admitted to a mental health facility as a voluntary patient for treatment of a mental illness upon the filing of an application with the facility director of the facility if the facility director deems such person clinically suitable for admission as a voluntary patient.

Ill.Rev.Stats. ch. 91½, 83–400 (1983).

Illinois law also gives a person who is rejected for in-patient treatment as a voluntary patient a right to a hearing before a Utilization Review Committee of the facility to which the individual is seeking admission. However, since the governing statutory standard is very general and gives wide discretion to the facility in accepting or rejecting patients, the same measure of discretion is applicable to the actions of the review committee. Thus, it is highly doubtful whether a person who is rejected in Illinois after a hearing before the review committee would have any further legal recourse, even if admission were medically indicated.

In some limited situations a *federal* statute may provide the basis for a statutory right to admission into a state operated psychiatric facility. For instance, the Education For All Handicapped Children Act of 1975, 20 U.S.C. 1401–1420 (1976), which entitles handicapped children between the ages of three and 21 to "appropriate public education" has been construed to require those states covered by the act to provide residential placement for "seriously emotionally disturbed children" if such placement is necessary to provide "special education" and "related services." *Papacoda v. State of Connecticut*, 528 F.Supp. 68 (D.Conn.1981). However, aside from this one exception, no federal statute has to date been construed as giving persons suffering from a mental disorder the right to in-patient treatment.

The Constitution has been posited as a possible source of a right to in-patient treatment. However, little support for this view can be found in current case law. As noted by one commentator:

> Seemingly, the only doctrinal ground that could be invoked to challenge the exclusion of voluntary patients is the equal protection clause. The core of the argument would be that there is no meaningful difference between the voluntary and involuntary patient except the label attached to them by the state. Individuals in both classes require hospitalization either because they are in need of treatment or they are dangerous to themselves or others. To the extent that those seeking equal "treatment" could show that they are clinically the equivalent of those involuntarily committed, their argument would

have considerable force. A more difficult question is posed when the equal protection argument is raised by persons who are not "equivalent" either because their mental disorder is less profound or because they fail to meet some other criterion such as the requisite degree of dangerousness. Here the result would undoubtedly turn on the standard of review that would be applied. The Supreme Court has recently emphasized that in the area of social welfare, statutes need only pass the traditional or rational basis equal protection test. If tested by this standard it is doubtful that any exclusion or difference in treatment could be successfully challenged at least to the extent that there are clinical differences between the two classes of patients in question.

Reisner, *"Psychiatric Hospitalization and the Constitution: Some Observations on Emerging Trends,"* 1973 U.Ill.Law F. 9, 19–20.

Questions and Comments

1.   There is no reported case to date which has addressed the issue of whether there is a right to in-patient treatment under state law. Whether a patient who has been admitted on a voluntary basis has a legal right under either federal law or the federal Constitution to challenge his discharge has been the subject of comment in only one reported case. See *Goodman v. Parwatikar,* 570 F.2d 801 (8th Cir.1978). The patient contended that she was threatened with discharge and sought to obtain a declaration that a discharge under prevailing circumstances would be unconstitutional. While declining to reach the issue, the court made the following observations:

> In Count II plaintiff claims that the part of the Missouri voluntary discharge statute, which reads, "He [the head of the hospital] may discharge any voluntary patient if to do so would, in the judgment of the head of the hospital, contribute to the most effective use of the hospital in the care and treatment of the mentally ill," is unconstitutional. Plaintiff claims it is unconstitutional because it confers such arbitrary and uncontrolled discretion upon the head of the hospital that it enables him to deny a patient his constitutional right to treatment and because it discriminates between patients at the mental institution on the irrational basis of whether they are voluntary or involuntary.

> However, we do not reach this constitutional issue because it is not necessary for the resolution of the conflict before us. It does not appear from the record that Rachel has ever been discharged or denied admission on the basis of this statute.

> *   *   * [D]efendant Parwatikar filed an affidavit with the district court in which he stated that Rachel is currently in need of treatment and there is no intention to discharge her pursuant to section 202.787 "unless and until it is determined that she is no longer in need of treatment from this facility or her discharge is requested by her court-appointed guardian." Thus, we are not presented with a

factual situation in which the validity of the statute is actually involved in an adversarial context.

at 806.

2.   Much of the debate concerning the possible right of individuals to voluntary in-patient status is undoubtedly tied up with the broader question of whether individuals who cannot afford a particular social service, such as in-patient psychiatric treatment, may be denied access to such services merely because of their economic status.   This issue is not dissimilar from the debate concerning the obligation of the states to provide general medical treatment to indigents or low-income families. For a further discussion of this point see, Brakel and Rock, *The Mentally Disabled and the Law* (1971) at 20.

B.   IS THERE A RIGHT TO IMMEDIATE RELEASE?

As noted in the introduction to this chapter, states typically have two types of non-compulsory admissions procedures, "voluntary" and "informal."   The principal distinction is that persons admitted as "voluntary" may be detained for a set time after their request for release; "informal" patients just leave.   During this period of mandatory detention the state may initiate involuntary commitment procedures which, if successful, result in the individual being detained as an *involuntary* patient.   Significantly, various studies disclose that state-operated facilities generally refuse to admit persons "informally," thereby forcing individuals to seek admission as formal "voluntary" patients.   This results in making the overwhelming majority of individuals who are admitted on a non-compulsory basis subject to the mandatory detention provisions.   Such mandatory detention provisions have been the subject of particular controversy.   The nature of this debate is considered by the following materials.

1.   *General Perspectives*

COMMENT, "HOSPITALIZATION OF THE MENTALLY
DISABLED IN PENNSYLVANIA: THE MENTAL
HEALTH–MENTAL RETARDATION ACT OF 1966"

71 Dick.L.Rev. 307, 315 (1967).

When a statutory scheme for truly voluntary admission is analyzed, it quickly becomes apparent that the free release procedures that accompany this method can become disconcerting and frustrating to the staff of the facility.   They are constantly faced with the dilemma of having to discharge a patient before his treatment has been completed or even begun.   The problem is especially acute in those cases in which a person applies for admission during a lucid interval, and then expresses the desire to leave after he passes into another stage of his illness, usually when his condition becomes severe.

MANFRED S. GUTTMACHER AND HENRY WEIHOFEN, *PSYCHIATRY AND THE LAW*

(New York: Norton, 1952), p. 306.

With regard to provisions for release, two opposing considerations must be weighed. On the one hand, complete freedom to leave the hospital at any time will almost certainly lead a number of patients to leave a few days after being admitted, for restlessness and dissatisfaction with the restraints of hospitalization are common and natural, especially during the first period of adjustment. This makes the admission a complete waste of time and money. On the other hand, refusal to release a voluntary patient on demand would not only be difficult to justify legally but would be highly undesirable, because resort to voluntary admission will be discouraged unless it is made quite clear that a patient may change his mind and leave. Most voluntary admission statutes meet the problem by providing that a voluntary patient shall be released within a specified number of days after he gives written notice of his desire to leave, unless in the meanwhile the hospital authorities start proceedings to have his status changed to that of involuntary patient. It has been held that detention for a reasonable number of days after written demand for release is proper, although a refusal to release, without legal proceedings being taken, is illegal and may be ground for claiming damages for false imprisonment.

THOMAS S. SZASZ, *LAW, LIBERTY, AND PSYCHIATRY*

(New York: Macmillan, 1963), p. 83.

In my opinion, this [voluntary hospitalization procedures] amounts to luring the patient into the hospital with false promises. If voluntary hospitalization were really voluntary, the mental patient would be free to enter and leave the mental hospital in the same manner as he enters and leaves a medical hospital. But this is not the case. Voluntary admission is in fact voluntary commitment. Or, to put it another way, the voluntary mental patient's role is a cross between the roles of medical patient and prisoner.

2. *Legal Perspectives*

EX PARTE LLOYD

United States District Court, Eastern District of Kentucky, 1936.
13 F.Supp. 1005.

FORD, District Judge.

This is a petition for a writ of habeas corpus filed by Emery Lloyd, an inmate of the United States Narcotic Farm at Lexington, Ky.

The petitioner charges that he has never been tried or convicted of any crime, yet he is imprisoned and restrained of his liberty by the superintendent of the United States Narcotic Farm at Lexington, Fayette County, Ky., and that such detention is in violation of his rights under the Constitution of the United States.

In response to a rule to show cause why the writ of habeas corpus should not be granted, the respondent, Dr. Lawrence Kolb, medical officer in charge of the narcotic farm, while in effect admitting the compulsory detention of the petitioner, asserts the right to so detain him under the provisions of the Act of Congress of January 19, 1929, c. 82, 45 Stat. 1085–1089 (title 21, §§ 221–237, U.S.C.A.).

The response alleges, in substance, that on December 10, 1935, the petitioner Emery Lloyd made application to the Secretary of the Treasury for admission to the narcotic farm for the purpose of receiving treatment for his addiction to the use of narcotic drugs; that, upon medical examination, it was ascertained that the petitioner was an addict to the use of such drugs and in need of such treatment; that, thereafter, upon the petitioner's application and the disclosure of said facts to the Secretary of the Treasury, authority was given for his admission upon the condition, however, that he agree and obligate himself to submit to confinement at the farm for such period as was estimated by the Surgeon General to be necessary to effect a cure of his addiction or until he ceased to be an addict within the meaning of the law; that upon these conditions being made known to the petitioner, he signed a writing by which he agreed to comply with said conditions in consideration of admission to the farm, and thereby granted to those lawfully in charge of the farm authority to use any reasonable method of restraint to prevent the petitioner's departure until eligible for release, under the terms and conditions of his contract. It is further alleged that, upon the execution of said agreement, the petitioner was admitted to the institution as a voluntary patient and is now so held and detained under medical treatment for his particular type of addiction; that the period estimated by the Surgeon General for his cure has not expired; that at the present time he is still an "addict" with an extremely unstable personality, with inebriate impulses and emotional instability; that he has not received the maximum benefit of the prescribed treatment and in the opinion of the medical board should not be dismissed or released from the institution.

* * *

It appears that the narcotic farm at Lexington, wherein the petitioner is detained, was constructed by the federal government primarily for the confinement and treatment of prisoners convicted of offenses against the United States who are addicted to the use of habit-forming narcotic drugs. The confinement and treatment of addicts who voluntarily submit themselves to the institution is expressly authorized but is clearly a secondary consideration. * * *

The provisions regulating the admission of addicts who are not prisoners and who have not been convicted of any offense against the United States are contained in section 12 of the act (title 21 U.S.C.A. § 232). This section authorizes such persons to apply to the Secretary of the Treasury or his authorized representative for admission. It provides for an examination by the Surgeon General or his authorized agent to determine whether the applicant is an addict within the meaning of the law and whether his addiction is susceptible of a cure by treatment at the institution, together with the estimated length of time necessary to effect such a cure. Upon receiving such application and report, the Secretary of the Treasury is authorized, in his discretion, if room is available, to admit the applicant to the institution. Then follows this provision: "No such addict shall be admitted unless he voluntarily submits to treatment for the maximum amount of time estimated by the Surgeon General of the Bureau of the Public Health Service as necessary to effect a cure. * * * Provided, That if any addict voluntarily submits himself to treatment he may be confined in a United States narcotic farm for a period not exceeding the maximum amount of time estimated by the Surgeon General of the Bureau of the Public Health Service as necessary to effect a cure of the addiction or until he ceases to be an addict within the meaning of this chapter: And provided further, That any person who voluntarily submits himself for treatment at a United States narcotic farm shall not forfeit or abridge thereby any of his rights as a citizen of the United States; nor shall such submission be used against him in any proceeding in any court, and that the record of his voluntary commitment shall be confidential and not divulged."

It is apparently the contention of the respondent that the purpose of the act, properly interpreted, is to authorize specific enforcement of the terms and conditions of the contract entered into by a voluntary inmate by subjecting him to compulsory confinement at the institution for the time specified in the contract. Such interpretation, if adopted, would necessarily carry with it the implication of power to enforce upon such voluntary inmate all prescribed rules and regulations * * *.

That such a construction of the act would encounter serious, if not fatal, constitutional barriers to its validity, is scarcely open to doubt. To give rise to such doubts, it is only necessary to refer to the Fifth Amendment providing that no person shall be deprived of liberty without due process of law, and to the Thirteenth Amendment providing that involuntary servitude, except as a punishment for crime, whereof the party shall have been duly convicted, shall not exist within the United States or any place subject to their jurisdiction.

The fact that the petitioner at some previous time consented to submit himself to confinement does not withdraw the present imprisonment, which is now enforced against his will, from the condemnation of these provisions of the Constitution. The full intent of the constitutional provisions could be defeated with obvious facility if citizens could be held to involuntary servitude or enforced imprisonment, through the guise of such contracts. The contract exposes the petitioner to liability for any damages suffered as the result of the breach but not to involuntary servitude in any form nor to the loss of his liberty or any of its essential attributes without due process of law. *Bailey v. Alabama*, 219 U.S. 219.

In the case of *Ex parte McClusky* (C.C.) 40 F. 71, 74, the court said:

> "Has any person the right to surrender his liberty * * * secured to him * * * by the fifth amendment to the constitution of the United States? No man or no power has the right to take away another's liberty, even though with consent, except by due process of law. Due process of law, in a case like the one charged against petitioners, means compliance by the government with a fundamental requisite, such as that the party shall be charged with the crime in the way provided by the constitution and laws of the United States. Liberty, under such constitution and laws, is an inalienable prerogative, of which no man by mere agreement can divest himself. Any divestiture not occurring by due process of law is null. 1 Whart.Crim.Law (9th Ed.) § 145. * * *

*   *   *

From the fact that an act of Congress has authorized the making of a certain character of contract, it does not follow, by mere implication, that Congress intended to grant to one contracting party the power or authority to use force or coercion upon the other party to prevent his breach of the contract. Nothing less than compelling language would justify the conclusion that Congress intended or contemplated the grant of a power so inconsistent with the universally recognized rights and relations of contracting parties.

That guaranteed constitutional rights embrace the right not only to make contracts but also to terminate or renounce them, leaving the remedy for the breach to civil damages, subject only to the jurisdiction of equity to decree specific performance in proper cases, has been so often recognized and acted upon as to admit of no further doubt. * * *

*   *   *

Although the privilege of abiding at the farm may be denied or withdrawn, I am of the opinion that the law does not authorize coercion of continued acceptance of the government's charity and benevolence by subjecting voluntary patients to compulsory confinement or detention at the institution, even though such enforced confinement may be for their personal welfare and in specific performance of the patient's agreement to submit thereto. * * *

It follows that the demurrer to the response should be sustained and the petition for the writ of habeas corpus should be granted. If, upon its return, no additional facts are shown to justify the detention of the petitioner, an order will be entered directing his forthwith release.

ORTEGA v. RASOR

United States District Court, Southern District of Florida, 1968.
291 F.Supp. 748.

ATKINS, District Judge.

This cause is before the Court pursuant to the petition for writ of habeas corpus filed by Raul Herberto Ortega.

The petitioner filed a petition in this Court on March 25, 1968 pursuant to Title III of the Narcotic Rehabilitation Act of 1966, 42 United States Code, § 3411 et seq. He voluntarily requested the Court to order him civilly committed for treatment of a narcotic addiction. After a hearing, held on March 26, 1968, Raul Herberto Ortega was ordered committed to the custody of the Surgeon General for confinement in a hospital for examination for a period not to exceed 30 days. The Surgeon General was directed to report his findings to the Court in accordance with Section 3413 of the Act. The petitioner at the hearing signed a Waiver of Further Court Appearances wherein he waived his right to return to this Court for a hearing in the event the Surgeon General, after examination, finds that the petitioner is eligible for further hospitalization because he is an addict who is likely to be rehabilitated through treatment. The petitioner further agreed that in such event the Court could enter its order committing him, in absentia and without further hearing, to the care and custody of the Surgeon General for treatment for a period not to exceed six months and such posthospitalization treatment as may be provided for in Title III of the Act. Upon receipt of the report of the examining psychiatrist wherein he recommended treatment, the Court entered its order of confinement. The petitioner now seeks to voluntarily withdraw from his treatment.

The power of the Congress of the United States to promulgate laws for the betterment of the public health, morals, safety, and welfare is beyond question. Whether or not Congress has acted within its powers depends upon whether or not there is a reasonable nexus between the subject matter of the suspect legislation and the results sought to be achieved. If the answer to this question is "fairly debatable," the legislation must be upheld.

* * * In the case at bar, the Court is not concerned with a situation of compulsory treatment as such. The petitioner, Raul Herberto Ortega, initially instituted the proceeding for his civil commitment with the filing of a petition on his own behalf. The statute involved in this case, because of this difference, finds more support from the above quotation from Robinson v. State of California, supra, than was even involved in the facts of *Robinson*. * * * The

Court, having independently recollected the hearing held pursuant to Mr. Ortega's petition for civil commitment, which hearing was brought before the Court by the government, and having reviewed the transcript of that hearing, is convinced that the petitioner acted of his own volition in requesting civil commitment and not because he was under the influence of narcotics and did not know what he was doing. The transcript of the hearing as well as the petition for voluntary civil commitment and Waiver of Further Court Appearance, both signed by Mr. Ortega established without a doubt that Mr. Ortega was fully apprised of his responsibilities under the Act and in fact understood those responsibilities. The Court will not permit the petitioner to terminate his treatment simply because the road to recovery is bumpy.

The court, for the above reasons, hereby

Orders and adjudges that the petition for writ of habeas corpus filed by Raul Herberto Ortega be and the same is hereby denied and the petition be and the same is hereby dismissed.

Questions and Comments

1. In *Ortega*, the court refused to release the petitioner from a narcotic rehabilitation program. Is that case distinguishable from *Ex Parte Lloyd?* Note that in *Ortega*, the petitioner had "voluntarily requested *the Court to order him civilly committed* for treatment of narcotic addiction" (emphasis added). Does this element of judicial involvement make Ortega's situation more analogous to lawful involuntary hospitalization after trial than to unlawful confinement after withdrawal of consent?

Are the different outcomes of the *Ortega* and *Lloyd* cases, therefore, distinguishable by the fact that the paper signed by Ortega was an official court document, while the paper signed by Lloyd was a mere contractual agreement?

Was the difference in outcome in Lloyd and Ortega perhaps the result of different release standards? What was the standard for release in *Ex Parte Lloyd?* Was the standard different than in *Ortega*, and if so, what was it?

2. Are the delayed release provisions of voluntary admissions procedures which typically allow detention for 2 to 5 days more like those in *Ortega* or *Lloyd?* Why should the length of the delayed detention period make a difference in terms of constitutional law requirements? If short delayed detention provisions are constitutionally allowable, is it because an individual may contractually waive his constitutional right to liberty for short but not long periods? Are there any parallels to this view of waiver of constitutional rights? In this connection, consider the following excerpt, commenting on the waiver of constitutional rights:

Whatever the rationale for permitting waiver, courts have applied two principles limiting its application. First, * * * [the waiver] to be effective, must be an "intentional relinquishment or abandonment of a known right." This standard stresses the consensual, "free choice" character of waiver and its ultimate reliance upon the individual's freedom to forgo benefits or safeguards through the uncoerced exercise of his rational faculties. * * *

Second, there may be some procedural incidents of the criminal process which the accused cannot waive. The Supreme Court has said that the right to jury trial, for example, is a right not only of the accused, but of the government, and that it would not be unconstitutional to require the government's and the court's concurrence in a waiver.

Tiger, *Foreword: Waiver of Constitutional Rights: Disquiet in the Citadel*, 84 Harv.L.Rev. 1, 8 (1970).

As previously noted, most states have two types of consensual admissions. In a few states, such as Washington, no distinction is made in terms of release time between "informal" and other voluntary admissions, and all voluntarily admitted patients must be released immediately upon request. West's R.C.W.A. 71.05.050 (1976).

What, if any, policy considerations support the enactment by the state of two separate voluntary admissions procedures, one of which permits delayed release? To what extent do delayed release provisions in formal voluntary admission statutes discourage prospective patients from seeking treatment for mental illness and thereby negate any beneficial aspects delayed release accomplishes in ensuring completion of a treatment program?

3. While the delayed release provisions associated with the voluntary admission process may be questioned on the grounds that they serve to discourage voluntary admissions, there seems to be no constitutional impediment to the enforcement of such provisions. No reported case has to date, in any event, found the enforcement of a delayed release policy to be constitutionally invalid. At the same time, the court of at least one jurisdiction has indirectly expressed its disapproval of such provisions. In *In re Robinson*, Superior Court for the District of Columbia, Family Division, Mental Health Number 578–72, May 30, 1973 (unreported), the District of Columbia trial court found that the overall legislative scheme governing psychiatric hospitalization reflected a "legislative policy which favors voluntary admission." This finding caused the court to disallow civil commitment proceedings to be initiated against a patient who was in the facility as a voluntary patient.

C. RIGHTS OF THE VOLUNTARY PATIENT

GOODMAN v. PARWATIKAR

United States Court of Appeals, Eighth Circuit, 1978.
570 F.2d 801.

STEPHENSON, Circuit Judge.

This suit was brought by Mortimer Goodman, as guardian of the person and estate of Rachel Goodman, individually and as a class representative of all mental patients in the St. Louis State Hospital. Plaintiff is seeking injunctive and monetary relief. In Count I of this section 1983 action plaintiff contends that Rachel Goodman received constitutionally inadequate medical treatment.

*   *   *

St. Louis State Hospital is a facility operated under the aegis of the Missouri Department of Mental Health to provide care and treatment for the mentally ill. Plaintiff is the father and legal guardian of Rachel Goodman. He was appointed legal guardian of her person and estate by the probate court of St. Louis County on November 24, 1976, at which time Rachel was adjudicated incompetent.

Since 1965 Rachel has been discharged and readmitted as a patient in the hospital at least eight times. On numerous other occasions she has eloped from the hospital and has been released to half-way houses, usually with allegedly disastrous results.

The district court specifically found: "From the briefs and documents [affidavits] submitted in support of, and in opposition to, the various motions filed by defendants, it appears that Rachel Goodman was at all times a voluntary patient at the St. Louis State Hospital, although she has since been adjudged incompetent."

*   *   * [I]n plaintiff's affidavit it is alleged that on September 12, 1976, Rachel, while an in-patient at the hospital, was beaten by another patient and taken to City Hospital. Although there is nothing in the Constitution which requires the state of Missouri to admit all patients seeking treatment, once Rachel was admitted as a patient, voluntary or involuntary, she had a constitutional right to a basically safe and humane living environment.

The state has a duty to provide a humane living environment which includes a duty to protect inmates from assault by fellow inmates and staff, which if callously disregarded may constitute a violation of civil rights.

If plaintiff can establish at trial a sufficient helplessness on the part of Rachel and a deliberate indifference toward Rachel's serious medical needs, including protection from assault, on the part of those caring for her, then plaintiff will have proved that she was denied her constitutional right to a humane and safe living environment while confined under state authority.

*   *   *

Jurisdiction of the district court in this case is based upon the claim of a violation of civil rights. *   *   * For plaintiff to establish a claim cognizable under section 1983, he must show that defendants, under color of state law, deprived Rachel Goodman of a right secured by the United States Constitution; and to recover damages he must also establish the requisite knowledge or malice of the defendants.

We conclude that while section 1983 does not create a general federal law of torts, the complaint and affidavits could conceivably encompass a federal cause of action for damages should plaintiff be able to establish a malicious or wanton disregard of duty by defendants as opposed to a mere negligent failure to afford proper care and treatment. Therefore, the district court should not have granted defendants' motion for summary judgment.

On remand, the district court may eventually conclude, after more complete development of the facts, that plaintiff's claim is only one of negligence or malpractice at most. In such event, section 1983 would not afford relief. However, on the record before us, we are unable to say that if plaintiff is able to prove the allegations in his complaint that this case fails to cross the line between tort and civil rights action.

* * *

The judgment of the district court is vacated, and the case is remanded for further proceedings consistent with this opinion.

Questions and Comments

1. The *Parwatikar* case establishes the basic principle that a voluntary patient retains the right to seek legal repress for injuries suffered in the institution as a voluntary patient. This may include recovery of damages in an action for negligence or, if the institution in question was state operated, the patient may also maintain an action under Section 1983 of the Civil Rights Act of 1871. The requirements for an action under Section 1983 are discussed in greater detail at pp. 124–131 *supra*.

2. In order to prevail in an action under Section 1983, the *Parwatikar* court made clear that it is not enough for the plaintiff to establish improper treatment and an injury. The plaintiff must also establish knowledge or malice on the part of the defendant(s).

If Section 1983 claims to impose greater evidentiary burdens, in that the plaintiff must also prove malice or knowledge, what factors might cause a plaintiff to utilize this ground rather than basing the claim on the doctrine of negligence? Several factors may explain the choice of one rather than the other theory. First, an action under Section 1983 would avoid state sovereign immunity limitations, which might serve to limit the amount of damages a plaintiff might otherwise recover. Second, by seeking a remedy under Section 1983, the plaintiff is assured that the case will be tried in a federal rather than a state court. Finally, a successful action under Section 1983 may make it easier for the plaintiff to obtain punitive or exemplary damages.

3. May a voluntary patient be required to accept psychotropic medication as a condition to be treated in a psychiatric facility? At least one appellate court has rejected the argument that a voluntary patient has a right to refuse psychotropic medication and continue as a patient. In *Rogers v. Okin*, 634 F.2d 650 (1st Cir.1980), *vacated* 457 U.S. 291, 102

S.Ct. 2442, 73 L.Ed.2d 16 (1982), the court addressed the issue in the following terms:

> One point that our analysis leaves unaddressed is whether patients who voluntarily enter a state mental health facility have a right to refuse antipsychotic medication. The district court held that "the voluntary patient has the same right to refuse treatment in a non-emergency as does the involuntary patient." 478 F.Supp. at 1368. The court apparently rejected defendants' argument that voluntary patients can be forced to choose between leaving the hospital and accepting prescribed treatment.
>
> In so holding, the district court in effect found that Massachusetts citizens have a constitutional right upon voluntary admittance to state facilities to dictate to the hospital staff the treatment that they are given. The district court cited no authority for this finding, and we know of none. Massachusetts law provides for the voluntary admission of mental health patients who are "in need of care and treatment * * * providing the admitting facility is suitable for such care and treatment." Mass.Gen.Laws Ann. ch. 123 § 10(a). The statute does not guarantee voluntary patients the treatment of their choice. Instead, it offers a treatment regimen that state doctors and staff determine is best, and if the patient thinks otherwise, he can leave. We can find nothing even arguably unconstitutional in such a statutory scheme.

V. SPECIAL PROBLEMS

A. ADMISSION OF MINORS BY PARENTAL ACTION

SILVERSTEIN, CIVIL COMMITMENT OF MINORS: DUE AND UNDUE PROCESS
58 N.C.L.Rev. 1133 (1980).

Since changes in mental health laws for juveniles have been patterned after changes in criminal procedure in juvenile cases, it is helpful to examine those changes first. The basic philosophy of the legal system in dealing with juveniles has been very different from that in dealing with adults. Beginning in 1899 with the first juvenile court in Cook County, Illinois, the goal of the juvenile justice system was to offer the adolescent "individualized justice and treatment rather than impartial justice and punishment." Therefore, instead of being dealt with as a criminal, the minor was committed for treatment in a civil proceeding. In addition, hearings were often conducted informally and secretly in an effort to spare the juvenile embarrassing publicity. Since the goal was to insure help for the child, the standard of proof of guilt was not the same as with adults, and offenses such as truancy, talking back to one's parents, or incorrigibility could draw potentially lengthy sentences.

As a result of their supposed *parens patriae* function juvenile courts were accorded substantial latitude and authority. Juveniles coming before a juvenile court judge were to be helped instead of punished. On this theory, juveniles who were institutionalized for what would be criminal offenses if committed by adults were sent not to prison, but to so-called "reform" or "training" schools. The goal of such special treatment was to temper the severity of the traditional criminal justice system. There has been a growing suspicion, however, that this *parens patriae* function, instead of providing wayward youth with rehabilitation, has unfortunately "served society only as an old-fashioned jailor." As a result, the juveniles received the worst of both worlds: they were stripped of many of the due process safeguards accorded adults, and were often thrust into brutal and punitive state institutions.

Another problem endemic to the juvenile justice system was the lack of real dispositional alternatives. For example, in many states, juvenile statutes did not differentiate between neglected and delinquent children in describing the judge's dispositional alternatives. As a result, youths with very different needs and very different backgrounds would end up in the same facilities.

[In 1967 "this disparity between the theory and practice of the juvenile justice system" led to the Supreme Court's decision of *In re Gault*, which "became a milestone in the establishment of legal rights for minors."]

While the opinion was limited to the adjudicatory stage of the juvenile court process and thus did not consider questions raised by arrest, detention, or disposition, it did provide for rights in the areas of notice, counsel, privilege against self-incrimination, and confrontation of witnesses available for cross-examination.

Accompanying the significant changes in juvenile court procedures in the past decade have been efforts to similarly revise mental health laws for minors. These efforts, however, have been complicated by the traditional role of parents in our society. For example, parents are often allowed to force or "volunteer" their children for services that the children might not choose for themselves. In addition, it is permissible in most states for parents or legal guardians to "voluntarily" admit their children into a hospital. This type of parental prerogative has recently come under vigorous attack. The criticism has been focused on the loss of liberty involved in such "voluntary" hospitalizations and the need for the same type of due process safeguards accorded those subject to the juvenile justice system. Nevertheless, as one commentator has pointed out,

> [t]here are three justifications that could be used for forcing hospitalization on young patients who would not be subject to such commitment if they were adults. (1) Children are not old enough to make a mature judgment about whether they need treatment or not, and therefore someone else must make it for them. (2) Children are subject to the decisions made for them by their parents, and a commitment decision is within the scope of parental authority. (3)

Mental disorders are much more tractable when the patient is young, and therefore there is a greater state interest in forcing treatment on mildly ill young persons than on mildly ill adults.

Furthermore, "[t]he autonomy of the natural family unit from external control by the state and others, and the concomitant authority over the conduct of a child, are deeply imbedded values in our society," and have long been "central to the American concept of freedom and individuality." Interference, then, with a joint decision by a mental health facility and parents to commit a child runs contrary to some basic American values and departs from the privileges and responsibilities than parents customarily exercise in raising their children.

PARHAM v. J.R. et al.

Supreme Court of the United States, 1979.
442 U.S. 584, 99 S.Ct. 2493, 61 L.Ed.2d 101.

[The plaintiffs in this class action were two minors who had been institutionalized in a psychiatric facility operated by the state of Georgia at the initiation of their guardians. One of the plaintiffs, J.L., was initially admitted into Central State Hospital at the age of six. At the time of his admission he had been expelled from school for "uncontrollable behavior" and had manifested "extremely aggressive" behavior at home. For a period of time J.L. was permitted to go home, but his behavior during these visits was "erratic," and the parents asked for discontinuance of the home visits. Two years later a new program was implemented that permitted J.L. to live at home and attend school in the hospital. However, when the parents found they were unable to control J.L.'s behavior, they requested his readmission into Central State Hospital.

The second plaintiff, J.R., was declared a neglected child and removed from his natural parents when he was three months old. He lived in a succession of foster homes until he reached the age of seven, when his disruptive and "incorrigible" behavior both at home and school led his seventh set of foster parents to request his removal. J.R. was thereafter institutionalized in Central State Hospital at the initiative of the Georgia Department of Family and Student Services. At the time of his admission, he was diagnosed as "borderline retarded" and suffering from "unsocialized aggressive reaction."]

Mr. Chief Justice BURGER delivered the opinion of the Court.

The question presented in this appeal is what process is constitutionally due a minor child whose parents or guardian seek state administered institutional mental health care for the child and specifically whether an adversary proceeding is required prior to or after the commitment.

*   *   *

A three-judge District Court was convened pursuant to 28 U.S.C. §§ 2281 and 2284. After considering expert and lay testimony and extensive exhibits and after visiting two of the State's regional mental health hospitals, the District Court held that Georgia's statutory scheme was unconstitutional because it failed to protect adequately the appellees' due process rights.

To remedy this violation the court enjoined future commitments based on the procedures in the Georgia statute. It also commanded Georgia to appropriate and expend whatever amount was "reasonably necessary" to provide nonhospital facilities deemed by the appellant state officials to be the most appropriate for the treatment of those members of plaintiffs' class, who could be treated in a less drastic, nonhospital environment.

Appellants challenged all aspects of the District Court's judgment.

*   *   *

Georgia Code, § 88–503.1 provides for the voluntary admission to a state regional hospital of children such as J.L. and J.R. Under that provision admission begins with an application for hospitalization signed by a "parent or guardian." Upon application the superintendent of each hospital is given the power to admit temporarily any child for "observation and diagnosis." If, after observation, the superintendent finds "evidence of mental illness" and that the child is "suitable for treatment" in the hospital, then the child may be admitted "for such period and under such conditions as may be authorized by law."

Georgia's mental health statute also provides for the discharge of voluntary patients. Any child who has been hospitalized for more than five days may be discharged at the request of a parent or guardian. Even without a request for discharge, however, the superintendent of each regional hospital has an affirmative duty to release any child "who has recovered from his mental illness or who has sufficiently improved that the superintendent determines that hospitalization of the patient is no longer desirable."

Georgia's Mental Health Director has not published any statewide regulations defining what specific procedures each superintendent must employ when admitting a child under 18. Instead, each regional hospital's superintendent is responsible for the procedures in his or her facility. There is substantial variation among the institutions with regard to their admission procedures and their procedures for review of patients after they have been admitted.

*   *   *

After admission the staff reviews the condition of each child every week. In addition, there are monthly utilization reviews by nonstaff mental health professionals; this review considers a random sample of children's cases. The average length of each child's stay in 1975 was 161 days.

II

In holding unconstitutional Georgia's statutory procedure for voluntary commitment of juveniles, the District Court first determined that commitment to any of the eight regional hospitals constitutes a severe deprivation of a child's liberty. The court defined this liberty interest both in terms of a freedom from bodily restraint and freedom from the "emotional and psychic harm" caused by the institutionalization. Having determined that a liberty interest is implicated by a child's admission to a mental hospital, the court considered what process is required to protect that interest. It held that the process due "includes at least the right after notice to be heard before an impartial tribunal." 412 F.Supp., at 137.

In requiring the prescribed hearing, the court rejected Georgia's argument that no adversary-type hearing was required since the State was merely assisting parents who could not afford private care by making available treatment similar to that offered in private hospitals and by private physicians. The court acknowledged that most parents who seek to have their children admitted to a state mental hospital do so in good faith. It, however, relied on one of appellees' witnesses who expressed an opinion that "some still look upon mental hospitals as a 'dumping ground.'" *Id.*, at 138. No specific evidence of such "dumping," however, can be found in the record.

The District Court also rejected the argument that review by the superintendents of the hospitals and their staffs was sufficient to protect the child's liberty interest. The court held that the inexactness of psychiatry, coupled with the possibility that the sources of information used to make the commitment decision may not always be reliable, made the superintendent's decision too arbitrary to satisfy due process.

* * *

III

In an earlier day, the problems inherent in coping with children afflicted with mental or emotional abnormalities were dealt with largely within the family. Sometimes parents were aided by teachers or a family doctor. While some parents no doubt were able to deal with their disturbed children without specialized assistance, others especially those of limited means and education, were not. Increasingly, they turned for assistance to local, public sources or private charities. Until recently most of the states did little more than provide custodial institutions for the confinement of persons who were considered dangerous.

As medical knowledge about the mentally ill and public concern for their condition expanded, the states, aided substantially by federal grants, have sought to ameliorate the human tragedies of seriously disturbed children. Ironically, as most states have expanded their efforts to assist the mentally ill, their actions have been subjected to increasing litigation and heightened constitutional scrutiny. Courts have been required to resolve the thorny constitutional attacks on state programs and procedures with limited precedential guidance.

* * *

The parties agree that our prior holdings have set out a general approach for testing challenged state procedures under a due process claim. Assuming the existence of a protectible property or liberty interest, the Court has required a balancing of a number of factors:

> "First, the private interest that will be affected by the official action; second, the risk of an erroneous deprivation of such interest through the procedures used, and the probable value, if any, of additional or substitute procedural safeguards; and finally, the Government's interest, including the function involved and the fiscal and administrative burdens that the additional or substitute procedural requirement would entail."

Matthews v. Eldridge, 424 U.S. 319, 335, 96 S.Ct. 893, 903, 47 L.Ed.2d 18 (1976), quoted in *Smith v. Organization of Foster Families*, 431 U.S. 816, 848–849, 97 S.Ct. 2094, 2111–2112, 53 L.Ed.2d 14 (1977).

In applying these criteria, we must consider first the child's interest in not being committed. Normally, however, since this interest is inextricably linked with the parents' interest in and obligation for the welfare and health of the child, the private interest at stake is a combination of the child's and parents' concerns. Next we must examine the State's interest in the procedures it has adopted for commitment and treatment of children. Finally, we must consider how well Georgia's procedures protect against arbitrariness in the decision to commit a child to a state mental hospital.

(a) It is not disputed that a child, in common with adults, has a substantial liberty interest in not being confined unnecessarily for medical treatment and that the State's involvement in the commitment decision constitutes state action under the Fourteenth Amendment.

We also recognize that commitment sometimes produces adverse social consequences for the child because of the reaction of some to the discovery that the child has received psychiatric care.

This reaction, however, need not be equated with the community response resulting from being labeled by the state as delinquent, criminal, or mentally ill and possibly dangerous. The state through its voluntary commitment procedures does not "label" the child; it provides a diagnosis and treatment that medical specialists conclude the child requires. In terms of public reaction, the child who exhibits abnormal behavior may be seriously injured by an erroneous decision not to commit. Appellees overlook a significant source of the public reaction to the mentally ill, for what is truly "stigmatizing" is the symptomatology of a mental or emotional illness. The pattern of untreated, abnormal behavior—even if nondangerous—arouses at least as much negative reaction as treatment that becomes public knowledge. A person needing, but not receiving, appropriate medical care may well face even greater social ostracism resulting from the observable symptoms of an untreated disorder.

However, we need not decide what effect these factors might have in a different case. For purposes of this decision, we assume that a child has a protectible interest not only in being free of unnecessary bodily restraints but also in not being labeled erroneously by some because of an improper decision by the state hospital superintendent.

(b) We next deal with the interests of the parents who have decided, on the basis of their observations and independent professional recommendations, that their child needs institutional care. Appellees argue that the constitutional rights of the child are of such magnitude and the likelihood of parental abuse is so great that the parents' traditional interests in and responsibility for the upbringing of their child must be subordinated at least to the extent of providing a formal adversary hearing prior to a voluntary commitment.

Our jurisprudence historically has reflected Western Civilization concepts of the family as a unit with broad parental authority over minor children. Our cases have consistently followed that course; our constitutional system long ago rejected any notion that a child is "the mere creature of the State" and, on the contrary, asserted that parents generally "have the right, coupled with the high duty, to recognize and prepare [their children] for additional obligations."

Surely, this includes a "high duty" to recognize symptoms of illness and to seek and follow medical advice. The law's concept of the family rests on a presumption that parents possess what a child lacks in maturity, experience, and capacity for judgment required for making life's difficult decisions. More important, historically it has recognized that natural bonds of affection lead parents to act in the best interests of their children.

As with so many other legal presumptions, experience and reality may rebut what the law accepts as a starting point; the incidence of child neglect and abuse cases attests to this. That some parents "may at times be acting against the interests of their child" creates a basis for caution, but is hardly a reason to discard wholesale those pages of human experience that teach that parents generally do act in the child's best interests. The statist notion that governmental power should supersede parental authority in *all* cases because *some* parents abuse and neglect children is repugnant to American tradition.

Nonetheless, we have recognized that a state is not without constitutional control over parental discretion in dealing with children when their physical or mental health is jeopardized. Moreover, the Court recently declared unconstitutional a state statute that granted parents an absolute veto over a minor child's decision to have an abortion. Appellees urge that these precedents limiting the traditional rights of parents, if viewed in the context of the liberty interest of the child and the likelihood of parental abuse, require us to hold that the parents' decision to have a child admitted to a mental hospital must be subjected to an exacting constitutional scrutiny, including a formal, adversary, preadmission hearing.

Appellees' argument, however, sweeps too broadly. Simply because the decision of a parent is not agreeable to a child or because it involves risks does not automatically transfer the power to make that decision from the parents to some agency or officer of the state. The same characterizations can be made for a tonsillectomy, appendectomy or other medical procedure. Most children, even in adolescence, simply are not able to make sound judgments concerning many decisions, including their need for medical care or treatment. Parents can and must make those judgments. * * * The fact that a child may balk at hospitalization or complain about a parental refusal to provide cosmetic surgery does not diminish the parents' authority to decide what is best for the child.

*   *   *

In defining the respective rights and prerogatives of the child and parent in the voluntary commitment setting, we conclude that our precedents permit the parents to retain a substantial, if not the dominant, role in the decision, absent a finding of neglect or abuse, and that the traditional presumption that the parents act in the best interests of their child should apply. We also conclude, however, that the child's rights and the nature of the commitment decision are such that parents cannot always have absolute and unreviewable discretion to decide whether to have a child institutionalized. They, of course, retain plenary authority to seek such care for their children, subject to a physician's independent examination and medical judgment.

(c) The State obviously has a significant interest in confining the use of its costly mental health facilities to cases of genuine need. The Georgia program seeks first to determine whether the patient seeking admission has an illness that calls for in-patient treatment. To accomplish this purpose, the State has charged the superintendents of each regional hospital with the responsibility for determining, before authorizing an admission, whether a prospective patient is mentally ill and whether the patient will likely benefit from hospital care. In addition, the State has imposed a continuing duty on hospital superintendents to release any patient who has recovered to the point where hospitalization is no longer needed.

*   *   *

The State also has a genuine interest in allocating priority to the diagnosis and treatment of patients as soon as they are admitted to a hospital rather than to time-consuming procedural minutes before the admission. One factor that must be considered is the utilization of the time of psychiatrists, psychologists and other behavioral specialists in preparing for and participating in hearings rather than performing the task for which their special training has fitted them. Behavioral experts in courtrooms and hearings are of little help to patients.

The *amicus* brief of the American Psychiatric Association points out at page 20 that the average staff psychiatrist in a hospital presently is able to devote only 47% of his time to direct patient care. One consequence of increasing the procedures the state must provide prior to a child's voluntary admission will be that mental health professionals will be diverted even more from the treatment of patients in order to travel to and participate in—and wait for—what could be hundreds—or even thousands—of hearings each year. Obviously the cost of these procedures would come from the public monies the legislature intended for mental health care.

(d) We now turn to consideration of what process protects adequately the child's constitutional rights by reducing risks of error without unduly trenching on traditional parental authority and without undercutting "efforts to further the legitimate interests of both the state and the patient that are served by" voluntary commitments. We conclude that the risk of error inherent in the parental decision to have a child institutionalized for mental health care is sufficiently great that some kind of inquiry should be made by a "neutral factfinder" to determine whether the statutory requirements for admission are satisfied. That inquiry must carefully probe the child's background using all available sources, including, but not limited to, parents, schools and other social agencies. Of course, the review must also include an interview with the child. It is necessary that the decisionmaker have the authority to refuse to admit any child who does not satisfy the medical standards for admission. Finally, it is necessary that the child's continuing need for commitment be reviewed periodically by a similarly independent procedure.

We are satisfied that such procedures will protect the child from an erroneous admission decision in a way that neither unduly burdens the states nor inhibits parental decisions to seek state help.

Due process has never been thought to require that the neutral and detached trier of fact be law-trained or a judicial or administrative officer. Surely, this is the case as to medical decisions for "neither judges nor administrative hearing officers are better qualified than psychiatrists to render psychiatric judgments." Thus, a staff physician will suffice, so long as he or she is free to evaluate independently the child's mental and emotional condition and need for treatment.

It is not necessary that the deciding physician conduct a formal or quasi-formal hearing. A state is free to require such a hearing, but due process is not violated by use of informal traditional medical investigative techniques. Since well-established medical procedures already exist, we do not undertake to outline with specificity precisely what this investigation must involve. The mode and procedure of medical diagnostic procedures is not the business of judges. What is best for a child is an individual medical decision that must be left to the judgment of physicians in each case. We do no more than emphasize that the decision should represent an independent judgment of what the child requires and that all sources of information that are traditionally relied on by physicians and behavioral specialists should be consulted. * * * [One of the] problem(s) with requiring a formalized, factfinding hearing lies in the danger it poses for significant intrusion into the parent-child relationship. Pitting the parents and child as adversaries often will be at odds with the presumption that parents act in the best interests of their child. It is one thing to require a neutral physician to make a careful review of the parents' decision in order to make sure it is proper from a medical standpoint; it is a wholly different matter to employ an adversary contest to ascertain whether the parents' motivation is consistent with the child's interests.

Moreover, it is appropriate to inquire into how such a hearing would contribute to the long range successful treatment of the patient. Surely, there is a risk that it would exacerbate whatever tensions already existed between the child and the parents. Since the parents can and usually do play a significant role in the treatment while the child is hospitalized and even more so after release, there is a serious risk that an adversary confrontation will adversely affect the ability of the parents to assist the child while in the hospital. Moreover, it will make his subsequent return home more difficult. These unfortunate results are especially critical with an emotionally disturbed child; they seem likely to occur in the context of an adversary hearing in which the parents testify. A confrontation over such intimate family relationships would distress the normal adult parents and the impact on a disturbed child almost certainly would be significantly greater.

* * *

By expressing some confidence in the medical decisionmaking process, we are by no means suggesting it is error free. On occasion parents may initially mislead an admitting physician or a physician may erroneously diagnose the child as needing institutional care either because of negligence or an overabundance of caution. That there may be risks of error in the process affords no rational predicate for holding unconstitutional an entire statutory and administrative scheme that is generally followed in more than 30 states. "[P]rocedural due process rules are shaped by the risk of error inherent in the truthfinding process as applied to the generality of cases, not the rare exceptions." In general, we are satisfied that an independent medical decisionmaking process, which includes the thorough psychiatric investigation described earlier followed by additional periodic review of a child's condition, will protect children who should not be admitted; we do not believe the risks of error in that process would be significantly reduced by a more formal, judicial-type hearing.

*   *   *

IV

(a) Our discussion in Part III was directed at the situation where a child's natural parents request his admission to a state mental hospital. Some members of appellees' class, including J.R., were wards of the State of Georgia at the time of their admission. Obviously their situation differs from those members of the class who have natural parents. While the determination of what process is due varies somewhat when the state, rather than a natural parent, makes the request for commitment, we conclude that the differences in the two situations do not justify requiring different procedures at the time of the child's initial admission to the hospital.

For a ward of the State, there may well be no adult who knows him thoroughly and who cares for him deeply. *   *   * Contrary to the suggestion of the dissent, however, we cannot assume that when the State of Georgia has custody of a child it acts so differently from a natural parent in seeking medical assistance for the child.

*   *   *

Once we accept that the State's application of a child for admission to a hospital is made in good faith, then the question is whether the medical decisionmaking approach of the admitting physician is adequate to satisfy due process. We have already recognized that an independent medical judgment made from the perspective of the best interests of the child after a careful investigation is an acceptable means of justifying a voluntary commitment. We do not believe that the soundness of this decisionmaking is any the less reasonable in this setting.

Indeed, if anything, the decision with regard to wards of the State may well be even more reasonable in light of the extensive written records that are compiled about each child while in the State's custody.

*   *   *

Since the state agency having custody and control of the child *in loco parentis* has a duty to consider the best interests of the child with respect to a decision on commitment to a mental hospital, the State may constitutionally allow that custodial agency to speak for the child, subject, of course, to the restrictions governing natural parents.

*   *   *

(b) It is possible that the procedures required in reviewing a ward's need for continuing care should be different from those used to review a child with natural parents. As we have suggested earlier, the issue of what process is due to justify continuing a voluntary commitment must be considered by the District Court on remand. In making that inquiry the District Court might well consider whether wards of the State should be treated with respect to continuing therapy differently from children with natural parents.

The absence of an adult who cares deeply for a child has little effect on the reliability of the initial admission decision, but it may have some effect on how long a child will remain in the hospital. We noted in *Addington v. Texas, supra,* —— U.S., at ——, 99 S.Ct., at 1811, "the concern of family and friends generally will provide continuous opportunities for an erroneous commitment to be corrected." For a child without natural parents, we must acknowledge the risk of being "lost in the shuffle."

*   *   *

Whether wards of the State generally have received less protection than children with natural parents, and, if so, what should be done about it, however, are matters that must be decided in the first instance by the District Court on remand, if the Court concludes the issue is still alive. *   *   * [W]e are satisfied that Georgia's medical factfinding processes are reasonable and consistent with constitutional guarantees. Accordingly, it was error to hold unconstitutional the State's procedures for admitting a child for treatment to a state mental hospital. The judgment is therefore reversed and the case is remanded to the District Court for further proceedings consistent with this opinion.

Reversed and remanded.

Mr. Justice STEWART, concurring in the judgment.

*   *   * [T]he basic question in this case is whether the Constitution requires Georgia to ignore basic principles so long accepted by our society. For only if the State in this setting is constitutionally compelled always to intervene between parent and child can there be any question as to the constitutionally required extent of that intervention. I believe this basic question must be answered in the negative.

Under our law parents constantly make decisions for their minor children that deprive the children of liberty, and sometimes even of life itself. Yet surely the Fourteenth Amendment is not invoked when an informed parent decides upon major surgery for his child, even in a state hospital. I can perceive no basic constitutional differences between commitment to a mental hospital and other parental decisions that result in a child's loss of liberty.

For these reasons I concur in the judgment.

Mr. Justice BRENNAN, with whom Mr. Justice MARSHALL and Mr. Justice STEVENS join, concurring in part and dissenting in part.

I agree with the Court that the commitment of juveniles to state mental hospitals by their parents or by state officials acting *in loco parentis* involves state action that impacts upon constitutionally protected interests and therefore must be accomplished through procedures consistent with the constitutional mandate of due process of law. I agree also that the District Court erred in interpreting the Due Process clause to require preconfinement commitment hearings in all cases in which parents wish to hospitalize their children. I disagree, however, with the Court's decision to pretermit questions concerning the post-admission procedures due Georgia's institutionalized juveniles. While the question of the frequency of post-admission review hearings may properly be deferred, the right to at least one post-admission hearing, can and should be affirmed now. I also disagree with the Court's conclusion concerning the procedures due juvenile wards of the State of Georgia. I believe that the Georgia statute is unconstitutional in that it fails to accord pre-confinement hearings to juvenile wards of the State committed by the State acting *in loco parentis*.

I

RIGHTS OF CHILDREN COMMITTED TO MENTAL INSTITUTIONS

Commitment to a mental institution necessarily entails a "massive curtailment of liberty," and inevitably effects "fundamental rights."

* * * [O]ur cases have made clear that commitment to a mental hospital "is a deprivation of liberty which the State cannot accomplish without due process of law." In the absence of a voluntary, knowing and intelligent waiver, adults facing commitment to mental institutions are entitled to full and fair adversarial hearings in which the necessity for their commitment is established to the satisfaction of a neutral tribunal. At such hearings they must be accorded the right to "be present with counsel, have an opportunity to be heard, be confronted with witnesses against [them], have the right to cross-examine, and to offer evidence of [their] own."

These principles also govern the commitment of children. "Constitutional rights do not mature and come into being magically only when one attains the state-defined age of majority. Minors as well as adults are protected by the Constitution and possess constitutional rights."

Indeed, it may well be argued that children are entitled to more protection than are adults. The consequences of an erroneous commitment decision are more tragic where children are involved. Children, on the average, are confined for longer periods than are adults. Moreover, childhood is a particularly vulnerable time of life and children erroneously institutionalized during their formative years may bear the scars for the rest of their lives. Furthermore, the provision of satisfactory institutionalized mental care for children generally requires a substantial financial commitment that too often has not been forthcoming.

* * *

In addition, the chances of an erroneous commitment decision are particularly great where children are involved. Even under the best of circumstances psychiatric diagnosis and therapy decisions are fraught with uncertainties.

* * *

II

RIGHTS OF CHILDREN COMMITTED BY THEIR PARENTS

Notwithstanding all this Georgia denies hearings to juveniles institutionalized at the behest of their parents. Georgia rationalizes this practice on the theory that parents act in their children's best interests and therefore may waive their children's due process rights. Children incarcerated because their parents wish them confined, Georgia contends, are really voluntary patients. I cannot accept this argument.

* * *

This does not mean States are obliged to treat children who are committed at the behest of their parents in precisely the same manner as other persons who are involuntarily committed. The demands of due process are flexible and the parental commitment decision carries with it practical implications that States may legitimately take into account. While as a general rule due process requires that commitment hearings precede involuntary hospitalization, when parents seek to hospitalize their children special considerations militate in favor of postponement of formal commitment proceedings and against mandatory adversarial preconfinement commitment hearings.

First, the prospect of an adversarial hearing prior to admission might deter parents from seeking needed medical attention for their children. Second, the hearings themselves might delay treatment of children whose home life has become impossible and who require some form of immediate state care. Furthermore, because adversarial hearings at this juncture would necessarily involve direct challenges to parental authority, judgment or veracity, preadmission hearings may well result in pitting the child and his advocate against the parents. This, in turn, might traumatize both parent and child and make the child's eventual return to his family more difficult.

Because of these special considerations I believe that States may legitimately postpone formal commitment proceedings when parents seek in-patient psychiatric treatment for their children. Such children may be admitted, for a limited period, without prior hearing, so long as the admitting psychiatrist first interviews parent and child and concludes that short term in-patient treatment would be appropriate.

Georgia's present admission procedures are reasonably consistent with these principles. To the extent the District Court invalidated this aspect of the Georgia juvenile commitment scheme and mandated preconfinement hearings in all cases, I agree with the Court that the District Court was in error.

I do not believe, however, that the present Georgia juvenile commitment scheme is constitutional in its entirety. Although Georgia may postpone formal commitment hearings, when parents seek to commit their children, the State cannot dispense with such hearings altogether.

* * *

The informal postadmission procedures that Georgia now follows are simply not enough to qualify as hearings—let alone reasonably prompt hearings. The procedures lack all the traditional due process safeguards. Commitment decisions are made *ex parte*. Georgia's institutionalized juveniles are not informed of the reasons for their commitment; nor do they enjoy the right to be present at the commitment determination, nor the right to representation, the right to be heard, the right to be confronted with adverse witnesses, the right to cross-examine, or the right to offer evidence of their own. By any standard of due process, these procedures are deficient.

The special considerations that militate against preadmission commitment hearings when parents seek to hospitalize their children do not militate against reasonably prompt postadmission commitment hearings. In the first place, postadmission hearings would not delay the commencement of needed treatment. Children could be cared for by the State pending the disposition decision.

Second, the interest in avoiding family discord would be less significant at this stage since the family autonomy already will have been fractured by the institutionalization of the child. In any event, postadmission hearings are unlikely to disrupt family relationships. At later hearings the case for and against commitment would be based upon the observations of the hospital staff and the judgments of the staff psychiatrists, rather than upon parental observations and recommendations. The doctors urging commitment, and not the parents, would stand as the child's adversaries. As a consequence, postadmission commitment hearings are unlikely to involve direct challenges to parental authority, judgment or veracity. To defend the child, the child's advocate need not dispute the parents' original decision to seek medical treatment for their child, or even, for that matter, their observations concerning the child's behavior. The advocate need only argue, for example, that the child had sufficiently improved during his hospital stay to warrant out-patient treatment or outright discharge. Conflict between doctor and advocate on this question is unlikely to lead to family discord.

As a consequence, the prospect of a postadmission hearing is unlikely to deter parents from seeking medical attention for their children and the hearing itself is unlikely to so traumatize parent and child as to make the child's eventual return to the family impracticable.

* * *

III

Rights of Children Committed by Their State Guardians

Georgia does not accord prior hearings to juvenile wards of the State of Georgia committed by state social workers acting *in loco parentis*. The Court dismisses a challenge to this practice on the grounds that state social workers are obliged by statute to act in the children's best interest.

* * *

To my mind, there is no justification for denying children committed by their social workers the prior hearings that the Constitution typically requires. * * * The rule that parents speak for their children, even if it were applicable in the commitment context, cannot be transmuted into a rule that state social workers speak for their minor clients. The rule in favor of deference to parental authority is designed to shield parental control of childrearing from state interference.

* * * The social worker-child relationship is not deserving of the special protection and deference accorded to the parent-child relationship and state officials acting *in loco parentis* cannot be equated with parents.

Second, the special considerations that justify postponement of formal commitment proceedings whenever parents seek to hospitalize their children are absent when the children are wards of the State and are being committed upon the recommendations of their social workers. The prospect of preadmission hearings is not likely to deter state social workers from discharging their duties and securing psychiatric attention for their disturbed clients. Moreover, since the children will already be in some form of state custody as wards of the State, prehospitalization hearings will not prevent needy children from receiving state care during the pendency of the commitment proceedings. Finally, hearings in which the decisions of state social workers are reviewed by other state officials are not likely to traumatize the children or to hinder their eventual recovery.

For these reasons I believe that, in the absence of exigent circumstances, juveniles committed upon the recommendation of their social workers are entitled to preadmission commitment hearings. As a consequence, I would hold Georgia's present practice of denying these juveniles prior hearings unconstitutional.

Questions and Comments

1. Numerous state statutes, including Georgia's, authorize the admission of a minor with parental or guardian's consent where the disorder or condition would not enable the state to civilly commit the individual through civil action. In other words, a minor may be admitted into a psychiatric facility when his condition is not of the severity required by the involuntary commitment law. What policy considerations, if any, justify the admission of a minor by parental action when the minor would not be committable if he were an adult?

2. Note that the majority's opinion in *Parham* imposes the requirement of an inquiry by a "neutral fact finder to determine whether the state requirements for admission are satisfied." Moreover, such inquiry must include a careful "probe of the child's background" and "an interview with the child." Is it clear from the opinion whether such inquiry must precede the actual admission of the child? Would it be permissible to conduct such inquiry shortly after admission?

Note also that the majority characterizes the inquiry as a "medical-psychiatric" decision. Is there anything in the opinion to suggest that the neutral fact finder must be a medically trained person? Would this foreclose as a matter of constitutional law the utilization of psychologists or other professionals as actual fact finders?

Note also that a state is not precluded from establishing procedural requirements which are more rigorous than those called for by *Parham*. In fact, a number of states require a full adversary hearing when a minor is institutionalized.

3. Does the majority opinion in *Parham* decide the procedures and nature of the hearing that must be utilized when the hospitalized child is a ward of the state?

B. INCOMPETENT PERSONS

[The issues pertaining to the admission of persons judicially determined to be incompetent are treated in Chapter Seven.]

Chapter Six

INVOLUNTARY PSYCHIATRIC HOSPITALIZATION

Table of Sections

III. Commitment Procedures.
    A. Overview of the Commitment Process.
        1. Emergency Commitment Procedures.
        2. Commitment by Court Order.
    B. Issues Pertaining to Emergency Commitment.
        1. Introduction.
        2. Probable Cause Hearings.
            a. The Purpose of the Probable Cause Hearing.
            b. Timing of the Hearing.
            c. Elements of the Probable Cause Hearing.
    C. Procedural Requirements for the Full Hearing.
        1. Introductory Comments: Right to a Fair Hearing.
        2. Right to Notice.
        3. The Nature of the Hearing—Must It Be Before a *Judicial* Officer?
        4. Confrontation of Witnesses and the Right to Be Present.
        5. Is There a Right to a Trial by Jury?
        6. Right to Legal and Psychiatric Assistance.
            a. Legal Assistance.
            b. Psychiatric Assistance.
        7. Standard of Proof in Commitment Proceedings.
        8. Privilege Against Self-Incrimination.
    D. Revocation of Conditional Release: Procedural Requirements.

IV. Rights of Involuntarily Committed Persons.
    A. The Right to Treatment.
    B. The Right to Decline Treatment.
        1. Introduction.
        2. Psychotropic Medication.
            a. Clinical Application.
            b. Legal Perspectives.
        3. Electroconvulsive Therapy.
            a. Clinical Application.
            b. Legal Perspectives.
        4. Psychosurgery.
            a. Clinical Application.
            b. Legal Perspectives.
        5. Behavior Modification Therapy.
            a. Clinical Application.
            b. Legal Perspectives.
    C. Miscellaneous Rights of the Institutionalized Patient.
        1. Freedom From Physical Restraints.
        2. Mandatory Work Assignments.
        3. Communication With Persons Outside the Institution.
    D. The Right to Periodic Redetermination of Commitability.

I. THE COMMITMENT PROCESS: PRELIMINARY OVERVIEW

A. INTRODUCTION

In dealing with the many issues posed by involuntary commitment, it is appropriate to establish the principal characteristics of the commitment process and how this process relates to other forms of governmental intervention directed toward social control and the protection of the public. The major method of controlling deviant behavior has traditionally been criminal law, in which an essential prerequisite for governmental action and the denial of an individual's liberty is the commission of an overt act by the offender. Incarceration or the imposition of punishment can generally follow only once the commission of an overt act is proven beyond a reasonable doubt.

In contrast to criminal law, civil commitment, which also may lead to a deprivation of liberty, does not necessarily require that any particular proscribed act has been committed by the individual. Rather, the process is prospective in that civil commitment may be used in anticipation of the commission of an act. Thus, the initiation of civil commitment may involve merely the prediction of some act or conduct. It is precisely this aspect of the civil commitment process that has generated the most controversy and that presents some of the most challenging issues in the realm of constitutional litigation.

Civil commitment also differs from incarceration following conviction in terms of the societal purpose behind the exercise of the state's power. A strong, if not dominant, ingredient of the criminal process is the imposition of punishment designed to deter. The principal purpose of civil commitment, on the other hand, is treatment and protective isolation of the individual. It is this difference in basic purpose that presumably justifies the differences in the procedures which are utilized to effect incarceration in the civil context.

Few areas pertaining to the exercise of governmental authority have in recent years been the subject of as much intense attention by court and legislature as those pertaining to civil commitment. Some of these changes have been the result of constitutional litigation. Other changes reflect shifts in legislative policy. In both cases the modifications in legal doctrine reflect changing notions of individual rights, individual responsibility, and the role of the mental health profession. This chapter examines the nature of the issues which have arisen and evaluates the capacity of the legal system to develop workable solutions.

B. HISTORICAL BACKGROUND AND LEGAL FOUNDATIONS

1. Historical Background

WILLIAM J. CURRAN, *HOSPITALIZATION OF THE MENTALLY ILL*

31 N.C.L.Rev. 274, 274 (1953).

The ignorance and apathy of the general public concerning mental illness and the mentally ill were a part of our social structure until only about one hundred years ago. It was naturally reflected in the law.

In colonial times an "insane person" (only the acutely disturbed, violent and dangerous, were recognized as such) could be confined in any available place. There were no hospitals where the mentally ill were accepted. They were disposed of as criminals or paupers, confined in jails, poorhouses, in private cages, or strong-rooms.

During the early years of the Republic, when special legislation began to appear in which these "furiously mad" creatures were mentioned, such laws were statutes relating to the "suppression of Rogues, Vagabonds, Common Beggars and other idle, disorderly, and lewd persons."

When the early asylums were established, commitment could be achieved with greater ease. Institutionalization was confined to the indigent insane, however. If private funds could provide a sturdy cage for the unfortunate creature, the state would concern itself no further. Even as the state mental hospitals for universal care were established and psychiatry became a part of the science of medicine, these easy practices of admission and discharge continued. There was little concern for the personal rights of the individuals committed. It is notable, however, that the legal order had long had elaborate provisions for the disposition of the *property* of the insane.

As the humanitarian movement for the decent care and treatment of the mentally ill began to achieve some success in the middle of the nineteenth century, the amazing void in the law concerning commitment came to public attention.

PAUL S. APPELBAUM, *CIVIL COMMITMENT*

TO APPEAR IN KLERMAN G. (Ed.), *PSYCHIATRY, VOL. 5, EPIDEMIOLOGY, LEGAL AND SOCIAL PSYCHIATRY.* (Philadelphia: J.B. LIPPINCOTT AND NEW YORK, BASIC BOOKS).

Prior to the establishment of hospitals for the treatment of mental illness, which began to appear in large numbers with the development of state hospital systems in the second quarter of the nineteenth century, there was little formal legal regulation of the care of the mentally ill. Some states, such as New York, had enacted statutes permitting the detention of the "furiously mad," while others responded to individual cases of particular need with appropriations to permit families to care for ill relatives at home. It is clear, however, that these represented the exceptional cases. For the most part, the mentally ill were either ignored or dealt with by the two major systems of social control, the criminal laws and the poor laws.

The detailed memoranda of Dorothea Dix, who combed much of the nation in the 1840s and 1850s to document the need for hospitals in which to treat the "insane," reveal that nearly every county jail had its share of deranged inmates, confined there in abominable conditions for want of more suitable alternatives. When the mentally ill could not be charged with a crime, they were likely to end up in the public almshouse, an important institution in almost every county in nineteenth-century America, confined on the order of the overseers of the poor. There they received basic sustenance, but often in circumstances of filth and disorder. In either case, their liberty was constrained, without therapeutic pretext, and often with frankly punitive intent.

At the same time as jails and almshouses were filling up with mentally ill inmates, a number of experiments were being launched in hospital care of the mentally ill. The first psychiatric admission in the American colonies occurred at the Pennsylvania Hospital in Philadelphia in 1752. By the third decade of the nineteenth century, a handful of similar charitable institutions, under private auspices but often supported by public funds, had developed in such major cities as New York and Boston. In addition, a few states, such as Virginia and Kentucky, had opened small public facilities for the care of the mentally ill.

Before the 1830s, admission to the institutions that existed was almost entirely free of legal regulation. The private institutions established their own rules, which often required that the potential patient's admission be accompanied by a guarantee of payment by a family member or friend, and certified by an attending physician. It was assumed that admissions would be involuntary, in that insane persons were thought as a matter of course to be unable to recognize their own interests. Family members and friends were assumed to have the right to act for the patient's interests, a right that was supported by a number of early court decisions.

The beginning of legal regulation of the commitment process came with the great wave of establishing state-run hospitals for the insane in the second quarter of the century. State involvement brought a need for enabling legislation, and some modicum of outside control. In many states commitment could still be effected by concerned family members who were willing to pay the costs of care, but if the state were to assume the costs, some judicial certification of the need for commitment, along with medical approval, was generally required. In the early days of the formal commitment system, judicial involvement sometimes appeared to be more a form of cost control than a mechanism for the protection of individual rights. In some states, for example, those paupers already supported in almshouses could be committed by overseers of the poor with no further legal intervention.

* * *

Questions and Comments

1. Writing over a quarter of a century ago, Professor Curran declared, "the striking of a balance between the requirements for legal safeguards and medical discretion in medical matters is the great dilemma in the commitment laws today." Curran, *Hospitalization of the Mentally Ill*, 31 N.C.L.Rev. 274, 277 (1953). This observation is no less

true today. Throughout this chapter, we will encounter numerous areas where effective medical treatment seems obstructed by legal safeguards, and where legal safeguards seem obliterated by overzealous providers of treatment for mental illness. The basic problem will be to reconcile an individual's desire to avoid unnecessary intrusions on his freedom of choice with the state's interest to provide protection for the community and care and treatment for the mentally ill.

2. The next two cases provide some historical insight into the legal power of the state to force preventive treatment on an individual and to incarcerate an individual against his will for medical purposes.

2. *Legal Foundations*

JACOBSON v. MASSACHUSETTS
Supreme Court of the United States, 1905.
197 U.S. 11, 25 S.Ct. 358, 49 L.Ed. 643.

This case involves the validity, under the Constitution of the United States, of certain provisions in the statutes of Massachusetts relating to vaccination.

The Revised Laws of that Commonwealth, c. 75, § 137, provide that "the board of health of a city or town if, in its opinion, it is necessary for the public health or safety shall require and enforce the vaccination and revaccination of all the inhabitants thereof and shall provide them with the means of free vaccination. Whoever, being over twenty-one years of age and not under guardianship, refuses or neglects to comply with such requirement shall forfeit five dollars."

Mr. Justice HARLAN, after making the foregoing statement, delivered the opinion of the court. * * * The defendant insists that his liberty is invaded when the State subjects him to fine or imprisonment for neglecting or refusing to submit to vaccination; that a compulsory vaccination law is unreasonable, arbitrary and oppressive, and, therefore, hostile to the inherent right of every freeman to care for his own body and health in such way as to him seems best; and that the execution of such a law against one who objects to vaccination, no matter for what reason, is nothing short of an assault upon his person. But the liberty secured by the Constitution of the United States to every person within its jurisdiction does not import an absolute right in each person to be, at all times and in all circumstances, wholly freed from restraint. There are manifold restraints to which every person is necessarily subject for the common good. On any other basis organized society could not exist with safety to its members. Society based on the rule that each one is a law unto himself would soon be confronted with disorder and anarchy. Real liberty for all could not exist under the operation of a principle which recognizes the right of each individual person to use his own, whether in respect of his person or his property, regardless of the injury that may be done to others. This court has more than once recognized it as a fundamental principle that "persons and property are subjected to all kinds of restraints and burdens, in order to secure the general comfort, health, and prosperity of the State; of the perfect right of the legislature to do which no question ever was, or upon acknowledged general principles ever can be made, so far as natural persons are concerned." In *Crowley v. Christensen*, 137 U.S. 86, 89, 34 L.Ed. 620, 621, 11 Sup.Ct.Rep. 13, we said: "The possession and enjoyment of all rights are subject to such reasonable conditions as may be deemed by the governing authority of the country essential to the safety, health, peace, good order and morals of the community. Even liberty itself, the greatest of all rights, is not unrestricted license to act according to one's own will. * * * "

* * *

We are not prepared to hold that a minority, residing or remaining in any city or town where smallpox is prevalent, and enjoying the general protection afforded by an organized local government, may thus defy the will of its constituted authorities, acting in good faith for all, under the legislative sanction of the State. If such be the privilege of a minority then a like privilege would belong to each individual of the community, and the spectacle would be presented of the welfare and safety of an entire population being subordinated to the notions of a single individual who chooses to remain a part of that population. We are unwilling to hold it to be an element in the liberty secured by the Constitution of the United States that one person, or a minority of persons, residing in any community and enjoying the benefits of its local government, should have the power thus to dominate the majority when supported in their action by the authority of the State. * * *

MOORE v. DRAPER

Supreme Court of Florida, 1952.
57 So.2d 648.

MATHEWS, Justice.

This is a case of original jurisdiction.

The petitioner was confined in the Southwest Florida State Sanitarium at Tampa pursuant to a commitment issued by the County Judge of Dade County, under the provisions of [a state statute.]

The petitioner claims that the statute in question is unconstitutional and that his confinement thereunder is unlawful, a denial of due process of law, and further alleges as follows:

"1. The statute abridges the constitutional guaranteed right to freedom and violates the due process clause of the 14th Amendment to the United States Constitution.

"2. The statute imposes indefinite loss of liberty for reasons other than conviction of crime.

"3. The statute fails to provide any definite or mandatory form of release.

"4. The statute discriminates against all persons other than those of a certain religious faith and belief.

Recent history of public health matters shows that tuberculosis was recognized as one of the most dreadful diseases and one of the greatest killers. The State has spent millions of dollars prior to 1949 in an attempt to minimize as far as possible the spread of this terrible disease. It had established a few hospitals and clinics and had carried on a program of detection, education and advice. It was recognized that those afflicted with this disease were a menace to society. They walked the streets; went to public places such as theatres, hotels and restaurants; they rode in common carriers; in their homes and other places they came in close contact with relatives and friends and the general public. They not only suffered themselves, but left disease, misery, sorrow and death in their wake.

*   *   *

Vital statistics showed that tuberculosis was taking an awful toll. The death rate was startling. In 1949 it was recognized that the Legislature would probably levy sufficient taxes and appropriate sufficient money to erect suitable sanitaria where people suffering with tuberculosis could be confined and treated. This law was enacted by the Legislature in anticipation that sufficient facilities would be provided. The Cigarette Tax Law, provided sufficient funds to carry on this work and some of the sanitaria have already been completed and others are nearing completion.

In the case of People v. Robertson, the court said:

*   *   *

"That the preservation of the public health is one of the duties devolving upon the state as a sovereign power will not be questioned. Among all the objects sought to be secured by governmental laws none is more important than the preservation of public health. The duty to preserve the public health finds ample support in the police power, which is inherent in the state, and which the state cannot surrender. Every state has acknowledged power to pass and enforce quarantine, health, and inspection laws to prevent the introduction of disease, pestilence, and unwholesome food, and such laws must be submitted to by individuals for the good of the public. The constitutional guaranties that no person shall be deprived of life, liberty, or property without due process of law, and that no state shall deny to any person within its jurisdiction the equal protection of the laws, were not intended to limit the subjects upon which the police power of a state may lawfully be asserted in this any more than in any other connection."

*   *   *

All questions raised in this petition have been carefully considered and we do find the Act to be a proper exercise of the police power, and not violative of Petitioner's constitutional rights.

When the Petitioner feels that he has been cured or that his disease has been so arrested that he is not and will not be dangerous to others, the Courts of the State will be open to him and he should be afforded ample opportunity to obtain his release, if an examination, scientific tests and other evidence justifies it.

The petition for writ of habeas corpus is denied, but without prejudice to the right of the petitioner to take appropriate action in seeking his release in any of the courts of this state having jurisdiction over him and the subject matter, when he conceives that he is able to come under the terms of the preceding paragraph of this opinion.

SEBRING, C.J., and CHAPMAN and ROBERTS, JJ., concur.

Questions and Comments

1. The opinions in *Jacobson* and *Moore* reflect the basic proposition that individual rights must at some point give way for the good of society. As the *Jacobson* court put it, "[r]eal liberty for all could not exist under the operation of a principle which recognizes the right of each individual person to use his own, whether in respect of his person or his property, regardless of the injury that may be done to others." Implicit in this proposition is the recognition of a *societal* power to preserve itself. All exercises of state authority derive from his power.

The *Moore* opinion identifies this power as the *police power*. Generally speaking, the state under its police power may enact any law reasonably necessary to the promotion of the public welfare—"public welfare" being an exceptionally broad and inclusive term. Thus, in upholding the petitioner's confinement for treatment of tuberculosis, the *Moore* court noted that "the duty to preserve the public health finds ample support in the police power."

Traditionally the police power has been used to support those exercises of state authority which prevent harm *to others*. Thus, courts often cite the state's police power as the basis for upholding criminal laws, traffic laws, zoning and building regulations, and most other protective laws enacted by a state legislature. The police power generally is *not* cited as authority for those laws which seek to protect an individual only from himself—such as laws requiring motorcyclists to wear helmets or laws concerning suicide. Rather, when the state acts to protect an individual from his or her own acts, it is acting under its power as *parens patriae*, which means it acts as guardian to those members of society unable to care for their *own* interests. As the U.S. Supreme Court has explained,

> The concept of *parens patriae* is derived from the English constitutional system. As the system developed from its feudal beginnings, the King retained certain duties and powers, which were referred to as the "royal prerogative." * * * These powers and duties were said to be exercised by the King in his capacity as guardian of persons under legal disabilities to act for themselves. For example,

Blackstone refers to the sovereign or his representative as "the general guardian of all infants, idiots and lunatics," and as the superintendent of all "charitable uses in the kingdom." In the United States, the "royal prerogative" and the "parens patriae" function of the King passed to the States. *Hawaii v. Standard Oil*, 405 U.S. 251, 92 S.Ct. 885, 31 L.Ed.2d 184 (1971).

Neither the police power nor the *parens patriae* power, however, represents an unlimited authority in government to enact laws for the general welfare or for the protection of individuals. Both powers are subject to the overriding constraint of the U.S. Constitution. Thus, for example, although a state law regulating commercial advertising might be a legitimate exercise of the state's police power, such a law would, nonetheless, be invalid if it unreasonably interfered with the exercise of First Amendment rights protected by the U.S. Constitution. Similarly, although most laws regulating the use of controlled substances are valid exercises of the state's police power, if the enforcement of such laws were to rely on extensive governmental intrusion into the privacy rights of the individual they might violate either the first or fifth amendments to the Constitution. Thus, although the police and *parens patriae* powers give the states broad authority to regulate on behalf of societal or individual interests, each exercise of those powers must also be consistent with the specific civil right protections of the Constitution.

By and large, the specific source of governmental action, whether derived from the police or the *parens patriae* power, does not have any practical consequence in terms of the *scope* of governmental power. In each case the governmental action is subject to the same constitutional constraints.

Together, the police power and the *parens patriae* power provide the legal foundation for state laws regarding civil commitment of the mentally disabled. When the state seeks to hospitalize a mentally disabled individual because he or she is dangerous *to others*, it is acting under its police power. When the state seeks to hospitalize a mentally disabled individual who is unable to care for himself or herself or is dangerous to himself or herself, it is acting under its power as *parens patriae*.

2. Are the opinions in *Jacobson* and *Moore* good authority for the proposition that the state has power to force medical treatment on individuals as long as the treatment is reasonably related to the good of society or the good of the individual? Note that the courts in both *Jacobson* and *Moore* were addressing the validity of forced vaccinations or treatment for *contagious* diseases. Note also that the vaccination and treatment laws addressed in those cases were founded on reasonably accurate predictions of the dire *consequences* attending a failure to abide by the laws—in other words, it was predictable with a reasonable degree of medical certainty that persons failing to receive vaccinations were likely to contract and spread smallpox and that persons failing to consent to hospitalization and treatment for tuberculosis were likely to spread that disease. Moreover, the persons subject to vaccination or treatment also were identifiable with reasonable certainty—*all* persons were sub-

ject to vaccination and only those persons diagnosed as tubercular were subject to forced treatment.

Given these factual bases of the *Jacobson* and *Moore* opinions, might not those opinions be read as allowing forced treatment *only* when the individuals subject to treatment are identifiable with reasonable medical certainty, and only when a failure to treat would almost certainly result in a significant harm to society? If this is the reading to be given those cases, how would civil commitment laws fare under such an analysis? In answering this question, is it relevant to ask whether mental illness can be diagnosed with as much certainty as a physical disorder such as tuberculosis? Is it relevant to ask whether the dangerousness of individuals can be predicted as accurately as the likelihood of contagion in the instance of smallpox? Much of the current debate on civil commitment concerns the extent to which civil commitment may or should be grounded on diagnoses and predictions arguably less certain than those involved in *Jacobson* and *Moore*. It is this basic question that is explored in greater depth later in this chapter.

C. CONTEMPORARY PERSPECTIVES

Three issues underlie most of the current debate concerning civil commitment. The most basic of these is whether the commitment process is or should be within the powers that may be exercised by government. For those who deny the legitimacy of civil commitment based on the libertarian notation that the state may not deprive an individual of liberty outside of the criminal law system, no further questions need be addressed.

For those who accept the legitimacy of civil commitment under at least some circumstances, there are two other issues which, depending on how they are answered, will shape the resolution of subsidiary questions. One of these concerns the limits, if any, of governmental authority to define the grounds for civil commitment. Thus, civil commitment might be permissible to achieve some ends but not others.

The other basic issue concerns the procedures which must be employed to effect civil commitment. For some, commitment is only tolerable when accompanied by all the procedural safeguards of a criminal prosecution. For others, civil commitment is deemed as essentially benign and, therefore, requires a lesser degree of procedural due process protection. It may be useful as a starting point to consider the most fundamental of these questions—whether civil commitment should be among the powers available to government. The material that follows considers this question from the perspective of several leading commentators. The other basic, though subsidiary, questions which ultimately need to be resolved in terms of constitutional doctrine are considered in the parts of this chapter dealing with standards and procedures.

MORSE, *A PREFERENCE FOR LIBERTY: THE CASE AGAINST INVOLUNTARY COMMITMENT OF THE MENTALLY DISORDERED*

70 Cal.L.R. 54, 59–65 (1982).

The primary theoretical reason for allowing involuntary commitment of only the mentally disordered is the belief that their legally relevant behavior is the inexorable product of uncontrollable disorder, whereas the legally relevant behavior of normal persons is the product of free choice. It is believed, for example, that a normal person who experiences an impulse to commit a crime is capable of repenting or being deterred by the sanctions of the criminal law, and hence may choose not to commit the crime. Thus, to preserve the person's autonomy and dignity, a normal person cannot be incarcerated until he or she actually offends the criminal law, even if the person's future dangerousness is highly predictable. On the other hand, the disordered person is thought to lack understanding or behavioral control, and therefore cannot change his or her mind or be deterred. Because the individual will ultimately have little or no choice in deciding whether to act violently, it does not violate the disordered person's dignity or autonomy to hospitalize him or her preventively, even in the absence of strong predictive evidence of future dangerousness.

The belief that disordered persons particularly lack competence or behavioral control is a strongly ingrained social dogma that underlies the special legal treatment accorded mentally disordered persons.

* * *

But the assertion that the crazy behavior of mentally disordered persons is compelled, in contrast to the freely chosen behavior of normal persons, is a belief that rests on commonsense intuitions and not on scientific evidence. Indeed, the degree of lack of behavioral control necessary to justify involuntary commitment is fundamentally a moral, social, and legal question—not a scientific one. Social and behavioral scientists can only provide information about the pressures affecting an actor's freedom of choice. The law must determine for itself when the actor is no longer to be treated as autonomous.

In fact, empirical evidence bearing on the question of the control capacity of mentally disordered persons would seem to indicate that mentally disordered persons have a great deal of control over their crazy behavior and legally relevant behavior related to it, indeed, often they may have as much control over their behavior as normal persons do.

* * *

For comparison, imagine the case of a habitually hot-tempered person who takes offense at something his doctor says and threatens to harm the doctor. Is this person more in control or rational than the delusional person? Or, consider the case of a severely ill cardiac patient who refuses to modify dietary, exercise, or smoking habits because the person prefers his or her habitually unhealthy lifestyle. The person's behavior can disrupt the well-being of the family, help drive up health care and insurance costs, and, if the result is an untimely death, impoverish the family. Is this person more in control or rational than the delusional person, and if so, in what sense? Of course, we all "understand" the behavior of the hot-tempered person and the cardiac patient, while the behavior of the delusional person makes no sense whatsoever. Still, there is no conclusive means to prove that any of these persons has greater or lesser control than any of the others.

*   *   *

A second possible reason that only crazy persons may be committed is the belief that they are especially dangerous. If so, society might be justified in instituting special measures that would make it particularly easy to intervene in the lives of crazy persons for either their own good or the good of society. This argument, however, may be disposed of with relative ease. Mental disorder is both an over and underinclusive predictor of dangerousness; most crazy persons are not dangerous and many normal persons are.

Indeed, although it is hard to obtain firm data on this question, mentally disordered persons are probably no more dangerous than normal persons.

*   *   *

A third reason given for allowing commitment of only the mentally disordered is that such persons are especially incompetent, that is, incapable of rationally deciding what is in their own best interests. The concept of incompetence is difficult to analyze, but it is clear that it refers to an *inability* to decide rationally or to manage one's life, rather than to the fact that the individual in question makes decisions that might be considered irrational or based upon seemingly irrational reasons. In order to protect liberty and autonomy, the legal system focuses on the decisionmaking process rather than decisional outcomes: so long as a person is capable of rational decisionmaking and managing, the person will be left free to make irrational decisions or to mismanage his or her life and to suffer the consequences; only if the person is not so capable does overriding the actor's judgment and substituting the judgment of the state appear justified.

Are the mentally disordered particularly incompetent? The question is crucial because involuntary commitment substitutes the state's judgment about the necessity for hospitalization (and often for treatment as well) for the judgment of the individual. Although commitment rarely includes a formal finding of legal incompetence at present, it at least implies the judgment that in some cases the person

cannot cope or make decisions in his or her own best interest.
*   *   *

There is, however, little empirical or theoretical justification for the belief that the mentally disordered as a class are especially incapable of managing their lives or deciding for themselves what is in their own best interests. Available empirical evidence demonstrates that the mentally disordered as a class are probably not more incompetent than normal persons as a class. Indeed, there is no necessary relationship between mental disorder and legal incompetence.

*   *   * While some disordered persons are clearly incompetent according to any reasonable criteria, the social goal of reducing the consequences of incompetence is not well served by allowing involuntary hospitalization, guardianship, or treatment of only the mentally disordered.

A final reason for allowing commitment of only mentally disordered persons is the belief that they are especially treatable. The mental disorders themselves and the dangerous and incompetent behaviors that allegedly ensue from mental disorder supposedly are particularly ameliorable by mental health treatment methods. Although this assertion seems reasonable, once again there is little evidence to support it. There is every reason to believe that normal persons who are dangerous or incompetent are equally treatable. Indeed, there is good reason to believe that normality is positively correlated with likelihood of treatment success. Moreover, the consequent social disabilities, which are in many cases more worrisome than mental health symptoms, are far harder to treat than the symptoms themselves. Differential treatability is thus not a supportable rationale for allowing involuntary commitment of the mentally disordered.

*   *   *

BRUCE J. ENNIS, *PRISONERS OF PSYCHIATRY*
(New York: Harcourt Brace Jovanovich, Inc., 1972), pp. 227–228.

Consider the paradox. Whatever his past, we never put a man in jail because of something he *might* do in the future. If he has not actually committed a dangerous or criminal act, we let him alone, no matter how "sure" we may be that he will do something wrong in the future. Yet we are not at all reluctant to put the same man in a mental hospital. The added ingredient "mental illness" somehow justifies incarceration. We condemn preventive detention of the sane but welcome preventive detention of the insane. But is the victim any happier for learning that his assailant, though dangerous, was sane and thus left at liberty? If we really wanted to prevent future dangerous behavior, we would incarcerate everyone considered dangerous, sane or not.

Why, then, do we single out the mentally ill for preventive detention? The answer is complex. We do so, in part, for historical reasons—it has always been done that way—and in part for sociological reasons—mental patients are considered second-class citizens whose rights need not be respected as strenuously as the rights of the sane. * * *

There are also philosophical and practical objections to the "need-for-treatment" justification, which authorizes the involuntary hospitalization of nondangerous persons on the ground that it will be good for them.

The essential premise of liberty is that people can do whatever they want—including things that are bad for them—so long as they do not injure others. We permit people to smoke, though we know smoking shortens lives. We permitted Justice Robert Jackson to resume his seat on the United States Supreme Court after a heart attack, though his doctors had told him, correctly, that the work load would cause a fatal attack within a year. We allow persons to give away their fortunes, destituting themselves for a cause. Every day, each of us does something that another would criticize, or fails to do something that another would urge. That is what liberty means.

Consider the patient in a general hospital with a physical, rather than a mental, disease. He has the legal right to refuse surgery, though it may save his life. We might think he has made a wrong or irrational decision, but he is permitted to make it. Transfer the same patient down the corridor to the psychiatric wing of the hospital, and he will no longer be permitted to make the decisions that affect his life.

Why is this so? Why is it that persons can do whatever they want with their lives until the moment someone else says they are mentally ill? Why is it that mental patients are stripped of rights that the general patient, and everyone else, can take for granted? It is because we accept without question the assumption that the mental patient, if sane, would choose for himself exactly what the doctors say he should choose.

There are many problems with that assumption. The first is that it is self-fulfilling. It can never be proved wrong because disagreement with the doctor is itself considered evidence of insanity.

THOMAS S. SZASZ, *LAW, LIBERTY AND PSYCHIATRY*
(New York: Macmillan, 1963), pp. 41–47, 247–248.

Because of the large number of persons affected by commitment procedures, and because of the extensive deprivations of civil rights which commitment entails, the compulsory hospitalization of mentally ill persons is a matter of considerable legal, moral, and social—as well as psychiatric—significance.

* * *

As a rule, no single reason can account for the commitment of a particular person at a given time. * * *

The so-called psychotic state of an individual is neither a necessary nor a sufficient cause for his commitment. Impecunious elderly persons, addicts, and offenders are committed; yet, they are not usually considered to be psychotic. Conversely, many persons whom psychiatrists regard as psychotic remain at liberty.

A person's dangerousness, to himself or others, is a more relevant consideration. However, dangerousness is undefined. Hence, this criterion also fails to offer a reliable guide for explaining the commitment of one person and the noncommitment of another equally as dangerous.

* * *

In my opinion, whether or not a person is dangerous is not the real issue. It is rather *who* he is, and *in what way* he is dangerous. Some persons are allowed to be dangerous to others with impunity. Also, most of us are allowed to be dangerous in some ways, but not in others.

Drunken drivers are dangerous both to themselves and to others. They injure and kill many more people than, for example, persons with paranoid delusions of persecution. Yet, people labeled paranoid are readily committable, while drunken drivers are not.

Some types of dangerous behavior are even rewarded. Race-car drivers, trapeze artists, and astronauts receive admiration and applause. In contrast, the polysurgical addict and the would-be suicide receive nothing but contempt and aggression. Indeed, the latter type of dangerousness is considered good cause for commitment. Thus, it is not dangerousness in general that is at issue here, but rather the manner or style in which one is dangerous.

* * *

Because the concept of mental illness is infinitely elastic, almost any moral, political, or social problem can be cast into a psychiatric mold. Thus, despite the fact that in a free society public policy should be determined by democratic political methods within a framework of constitutional guarantees, this process may easily become transformed into a bureaucratic administration of public health measures.

* * *

It seems to me that the increasing intrusion of psychiatry into public policy is both the cause and the result of a similar situation. People seem tired of their moral responsibilities. They try to escape from their moral freedom by delegating their responsibility for moral decisions to the experts in human relations, especially the psychiatrists. Of course, this is self-deception. But just as counterfeit money, if accepted as real, can buy many things, so this type of moral counterfeiting may work, and may be a powerful social force, until it is unmasked.

Where is this moral counterfeiting leading us? In controversies over public policy, we substitute judgments of mental health for judgments of moral value. I believe we are thus heading toward moral Fascism. Unlike political Fascism, which sought its justification in the value of the "good of the state," and subordinated everything else to it, the moral Fascism we have been cultivating subordinates all to the value of the "welfare of the people." The expression "welfare state" is an understatement. For the state is fast becoming not merely an adminsitrator of the general welfare, but a veritable therapist. Recently, a psychiatrist proudly extolled the promise of "community psychiatry," the ultimate purpose of which is to "transform a state into a great therapeutic community."

*   *   *

BERNARD L. DIAMOND, *BOOK REVIEW, LAW, LIBERTY AND PSYCHIATRY*

52 Cal.L.Rev. 899–907 (1964).

Law, Liberty and Psychiatry is an irresponsible, reprehensible, and dangerous book. It is irresponsible and reprehensible because the author must surely know better. It is dangerous because its author is clever, brilliant, and articulate—the book reads well and could be most convincing to the intelligent, but uncritical reader. Dr. Szasz has had the best of training in medicine, psychiatry, and psychoanalysis. His teaching and clinical experience have been most extensive, and he well-earned his post as professor of psychiatry at the State University of New York Upstate Medical Center in Syracuse. Many outstanding psychiatrists, and particularly psychoanalysts, are abysmally ignorant about the complex and conflictive relationship between psychiatry and the law. Every so often one will write an article on a medico-legal issue in which the author's naiveté is betrayed. Such articles are harmless—at worst they provide useful citations for legal authors who wish to demonstrate that psychiatry is not an "exact science."

*   *   *

Nor is *Law, Liberty and Psychiatry* concerned with the unimportant, the irrelevant or the technical. Rather, it is concerned with the basic social functions of psychiatry. Szasz believes that psychiatry is a "form of social engineering" and that "psychiatric activity is medical in name only." He believes that the mental health concept contains within itself social values of deposition which masquerade under the guise of "false psychiatric liberalism." And most certainly, Szasz does not evade. He meets the issues bluntly and head-on. As a proclaimed libertarian, he devotes the major portion of his book to an attempted demonstration that psychiatry—especially legal psychiatry—is an insidious brain-washing process which is used to undermine our traditional moral values and to impose authoritarian restrictions upon individual liberties.

Szasz is not only convinced that psychiatrists are not true members of the healing profession, but that there is nothing analogous between illness of the body or brain and illness of the mind.

* * *

The problem of the psychologic versus the organic is disposed of neatly and simply: since there is no such thing as mental illness, there is no need to explain deviant behavior in other than social, ethical, and legal terms. The deviant is not sick or helpless. Rather, he is deficient in moral, ethical, and social responsibility. If psychiatrists claim to heal these deviants, in reality they are only imposing their own brand of "moral Fascism." "And upon those unwilling to heed peaceful persuasion, the values of the state will be imposed by force: in political Fascism by the military and the police; in moral Fascism by therapists, especially psychiatrists. I think that we are rapidly heading toward the Therapeutic State."

* * *

The struggle for the humane care of the mentally ill and the elimination of the snake-pits of the old custodial institution has been long and difficult. And no one knows better than the psychiatric profession how much is yet to be accomplished. Most certainly the dangers of forensic psychiatry are recognized by almost all psychiatrists. The dangers, however, are not of "economic enrichment" and "professional aggrandizement" as claimed by Szasz. The dangers are hopelessly antiquated legal rules of criminal responsibility, miserably inadequate financial appropriations for the care of the mentally ill, and primitive, superstitious public fears of the mentally disordered. These are the forces which create the hospital which is worse than the jail, the institution of barren custody and social ostracism, and the deprivation of even the minimal human rights—yet alone, civil rights—of the mentally ill. Here I would go further than Szasz. I would insist that the mentally ill comprise the most discriminated against and persecuted class of individuals in the United States today.

In urging upon us his own political ideology, an ideology of extreme libertarianism, and individual responsibility, which equates any type of government intervention for welfare or security purposes as Fascism, Szasz appears to abandon his sense of professional integrity and to leave behind his clinical skills and experience. He discusses clinical cases and quotes extensively from the professional literature to support his conclusions. I am familiar with the details of certain of these cases, and I know very well the professional articles from which he draws material. I am indignant and outraged by the apparent distortion and falsity of this material. He constantly makes inferences and draws the reader towards conclusions which seem quite logical as Szasz presents the material, but which simply are untruthful in the context of the originals.

*   *   *

PAUL CHODOFF, THE CASE FOR INVOLUNTARY HOSPITALIZATION OF THE MENTALLY ILL

Am. Journal of Psychiatry, pp. 497–98 (May 1976).

THE ABOLITIONISTS

Those holding this position would assert that in none of the cases I have described should involuntary hospitalization be a viable option because, quite simply, it should never be resorted to under any circumstances. As Szasz has put it, "we should value liberty more highly than mental health no matter how defined" and "no one should be deprived of his freedom for the sake of his mental health." Ennis has said that the goal "is nothing less than the abolition of involuntary hospitalization."

Prominent among the abolitionists are the "anti-psychiatrists," who, somewhat surprisingly, count in their ranks a number of well-known psychiatrists. For them mental illness simply does not exist in the field of psychiatry. They reject entirely the medical model of mental illness and insist that acceptance of it relies on a fiction accepted jointly by the state and by psychiatrists as a device for exerting social control over annoying or unconventional people. The anti-psychiatrists hold that these people ought to be afforded the dignity of being held responsible for their behavior and required to accept its consequences. In addition, some members of this group believe that the phenomena of "mental illness" often represent essentially a tortured protest against the insanities of an irrational society. They maintain that society should not be encouraged in its oppressive course by affixing a pejorative label to its victims.

Among the abolitionists are some civil liberties lawyers who both assert their passionate support of the magisterial importance of individual liberty and react with repugnance and impatience to what they see as the abuses of psychiatric practice in this field—the commitment of some individuals for flimsy and possibly self-serving reasons and their inhuman warehousing in penal institutions wrongly called "hospitals."

The abolitionists do not oppose psychiatric treatment when it is conducted with the agreement of those being treated. I have no doubt that they would try to gain the consent of the individuals described earlier to undergo treatment, including hospitalization.

*   *   *

If efforts to enlist voluntary compliance with treatment failed, the abolitionists would not employ any means of coercion. Instead, they would step aside and allow social, legal, and community sanctions to take their course. If a human being should be jailed or a human life lost as a result of this attitude, they would accept it as a necessary evil to be tolerated in order to avoid the greater evil of unjustified loss of liberty for others.

THE MEDICAL MODEL PSYCHIATRISTS

I use this admittedly awkward and not entirely accurate label to designate the position of a substantial number of psychiatrists. They believe that mental illness is a meaningful concept and that under certain conditions its existence justifies the state's exercise, under the doctrine of parens patriae, of its right and obligation to arrange for the hospitalization of the sick individual even though coercion is involved and he is deprived of his liberty.

*   *   *

Despite the revisionist efforts of the anti-psychiatrists, mental illness *does* exist. It does not by any means include all of the people being treated by psychiatrists (or by nonpsychiatrist physicians), but it does encompass those few desperately sick people for whom involuntary commitment must be considered. In the words of a recent article, "The problem is that mental illness is not a myth. It is not some palpable falsehood propagated among the populace by power-mad psychiatrists, but a cruel and bitter reality that has been with the human race since antiquity."

II. COMMITMENT STANDARDS

A. INTRODUCTION

The process leading to the involuntarily institutionalization of an individual can be conceptualized in terms of the application of two interrelated elements: (1) the substantive standard establishing the characteristics of those subject to commitment, and (2) the procedural rules governing the conduct of the commitment process. This section focuses on the first of these elements. It bears noting that in nearly all jurisdictions the basic substantive standard governing commitment is embodied in a statute enacted by the legislature. Frequently, however, the language used by these statutes is sufficiently general as to invite judicial interpretation or refinement. Thus, the governing standard is generally the product of an interplay between the legislative and judicial branches of government.

While there are considerable variations among the states in the wording of their civil commitment laws, a basic pattern is neverthe-less discernible. Generally, all jurisdictions require the presence of two separate and distinct elements. One pertains to the *mental condition* of the individual facing commitment. Thus, nearly every statute requires a threshold finding that the individual is "mentally ill" or, as stated in some statutes, suffers from a "mental disorder."

A second element calls for a finding that *some specified adverse consequence* will follow if the individual is not committed. Thus, a statute will typically provide that a person who is mentally ill is committable if he or she is reasonably expected at the time that the determination is made to "injure other persons." Nearly all statutes also authorize commitment to prevent harm or injury to the afflicted person, but statutes vary considerably in terms of the kinds of anticipated injury.

We will use the current District of Columbia statute to illustrate a typical commitment statute, although we will explore in this section statutes of other states. The District of Columbia statute subjects to involuntary hospitalization any person who is "mentally ill, and because of the illness is likely to injure himself or other persons if allowed to remain at liberty." D.C.Code § 21–541 (1981).

The first step in interpreting any statute is to isolate those elements that must be proved. What elements must be proved in order to commit an individual through civil procedure in the District of Columbia? There are three. First, the individual must be mentally ill. Second, the individual must be dangerous to himself or others if allowed to remain at liberty. Third, the dangerousness must result from the mental illness. The failure to prove *any one* of these elements will result in a dismissal of the commitment proceedings. Thus, a dangerous person may not be committed unless he also is mentally ill, and a mentally ill person may not be committed unless he also is dangerous. Similarly, an individual may be both mentally ill and dangerous but not committable because the dangerousness does not result from the mental illness.

The second step in statutory interpretation is to decide whether the facts of a particular case fall within the meaning of the terminology used in the statute. For example, does "mentally ill" in the District of Columbia statute include sociopathic personalities? Does "danger to self" include only the infliction of physical harm or also consequences resulting from self-neglect? Does "dangerous to other persons" include dangerousness to another person's property? These questions are merely illustrative of the innumerable problems of statutory interpretation courts confront daily.

The substantive standards governing commitment—as distinct from the procedures—were until recently rarely challenged on constitutional grounds. As a consequence, legislatures were deemed to have unfettered discretion in establishing such standards. Lately, however, the grounds for commitment, as every other aspect of the commitment process, have increasingly been the subject of litigation and challenge on constitutional grounds. As a consequence, there is rapidly developing a constitutional jurisprudence by which all statutory standards must be measured. The materials which follow seek to isolate the legal issues that most commonly confront legislatures, courts and mental health agencies in the formulation and application of the standards governing commitment.

Questions and Comments

1. The standards governing civil commitment have been far from static, as dramatic changes have occurred in the past twenty years. Standards governing involuntary civil commitment prior to 1960 were extremely general and as a result broad discretion was vested in courts and mental health professionals to give content to these laws. By the mid-1960s, however, vast changes were beginning to occur. As noted by one commentator:

> [L]awyers interested in civil rights turned their attention to involuntary hospitalization at the same time that various conceptual and political critiques of psychiatry, especially institutional psychiatry, gathered momentum. In addition, the theory of community mental health and the wide usage of psychotropic drugs appeared to render long term involuntary hospitalization less advised and less necessary.

Morse, *A Preference for Liberty: The Case Against Involuntary Commitment of the Mentally Disordered*, 70 Cal.L.R. 54, 55 (1982).

With the passage of the Lanterman-Petris-Short Act (LPS), California became the first state to enact a highly restrictive civil commitment law which emphasized dangerousness as a necessary pre-condition for commitment. This legislation served as the model for other states which similarly amended their laws and restricted the grounds for commitment. *See* Schwitzgebel, *Survey of State Commitment Statutes*, in Civil Commitment and Social Policy 47, 53 (West Supp.1981). A series of decisions rendered by federal courts in various jurisdictions provided an additional impetus toward a tightening of standards. The case of *Lessard v. Schmidt*, 413 F.Supp. 1318 (E.D.Wis.1976), which found commitment laws to be unconstitutional was perhaps the most influential of these decisions.

By the late 1970s the pendulum had begun to swing back. The stringent standard which emphasized immediate dangerousness as the sole ground for commitment (as exemplified by the California LPS Act) was proving to be unworkable. *See* the materials in subsection II.4.c. *infra*. Several states including Washington, North Carolina, and Texas have recently amended their civil commitment laws to broaden the grounds for commitment. Revised Code of Washington, Chapter 71.05 (1982), General Statute of North Carolina—Chapter 122 (1981), and Senate Bill 435, An Act Reviewing Mental Health Code in Texas, effective September 1, 1983.

2. Proposals for the reform of the civil commitment laws have on several occasions been advanced in the form of model laws prepared by professional organizations or special commissions. An earlier effort at the design of a uniform law was jointly undertaken by the National Institute of Mental Health and the Federal Security Agency. *See, A Draft Act Governing Hospitalization of the Mentally Ill*, The Mentally Disabled and the Law (S. Brakel & R. Rock, revised ed. 1971), p. 454.

The most recent effort in this direction is the model law approved by the American Psychiatric Association (APA) in 1982. *See* Stromberg and Stone [APA Model Law] 20 Hav.J. on Legislation 275, 279 (1983). Selected provisions of this APA Model Law are considered later in this chapter.

B. THE "MENTAL ILLNESS" REQUIREMENT

1. Problems of Definition

DODD v. HUGHES

Supreme Court of Nevada, 1965.
81 Nev. 43, 398 P.2d 540.

THOMPSON, Justice.

By a habeas corpus application addressed to the Second Judicial District Court, Dodd sought his release from the Nevada State Hospital (NRS 433.040). He had been committed to that institution as a mentally ill person by order of the Fourth Judicial District Court. At the habeas hearing, the Superintendent of the Nevada State Hospital gave his opinion that Dodd, though a sociopath, was not psychotic, and therfore not "mentally ill" within the meaning of NRS 433.200. He suggested that Dodd be released from his confinement. Another doctor was of a different view. Though he agreed that Dodd was not psychotic, he believed that a sociopathic personality may be considered "mentally ill" as that term is used in the state. Additionally, he stressed Dodd's high potential for homicidal activity. At the conclusion of the hearing, the court directed the superintendent to apply to the board of the state prison commissioners for that board's consent to confine Dodd at the Nevada State Prison. The superintendent did as directed. The prison commissioners consented, and Dodd was delivered to the Nevada State Prison for confinement until further order of the court (NRS 433.310).[a]

The legislature did not define "mentally ill" when it passed the law governing the Nevada State Hospital (NRS 433.010–433.640). Its failure to do so supplies the basis for Dodd's appeal. It is his position that a person must exhibit one of the psychotic reactions as classified by the American Psychiatric Association before he may be considered mentally ill. Absent a classified psychosis, one may not be committed and confined. A sociopath (defined in the testimony as a disorder of personality affecting the ethical and moral senses) like Dodd, (and all the evidence is in accord that Dodd is, indeed, a sociopath), does

---

a. NRS 433.310 provides:

"1. Whenever a person legally adjudged to be mentally ill is deemed by the court or the superintendent to be a menace to public safety, and the court is satisfied that the facilities at the hospital are inadequate to keep such mentally ill person safely confined, the court may, upon application of the superintendent, commit such person to the Nevada state prison. The person shall be confined in the Nevada state prison until the further order of the committing court either transferring him to the hospital or declaring him to be no longer mentally ill.

not fall within any of the classified psychotic reactions and, therefore, may not be institutionalized. So it is that we are urged to fashion a definition for the words "mentally ill" and thereby fill the void in the statutory hospital law. It is suggested that we confine mental illness to the psychotic reactions as classified by the American Psychiatric Association. We are wholly unable to follow that suggestion. The record before us shows that the psychiatrists who testified do not agree on the statutory meaning of "mentally ill." Further, the record reflects that psychiatrists in general are at war over the propriety of the classifications of psychosis as specified by the American Psychiatric Association. We seriously doubt that the legislature ever intended medical classifications to be the sole guide for judicial commitment. The judicial inquiry is not to be limited so as to exclude the totality of circumstances involved in the particular case before the court. Recidivism, repeated acts of violence, the failure to respond to conventional penal and rehabilitative measures, and public safety, are additional and relevant considerations for the court in deciding whether a person is mentally ill. The assistance of medical examination and opinion is a necessary concomitant of the court hearing, but the court alone is invested with the power of decision. That power is to be exercised within the permissible limits of judicial discretion.

Here the record demonstrates a combination of things which should, and did, unquestionably, influence the lower court to enter the order it did. Dodd, an 18 year old, was shown, by testing, to have the intelligence quotient of a high grade moron. All agree that he is a sociopath almost devoid of moral sense. He has been proven, at least to date, wholly unresponsive to either penal or rehabilitative measures,[b] nor does he give promise of response to available probation services or psychiatric treatment. He possesses homicidal tendencies, and is dangerous. Finally, one of the testifying psychiatrists stated that Dodd is mentally ill within the intendment of the statute. In these circumstances the lower court did not abuse its discretion in denying habeas relief and ordering that Dodd be transferred to the Nevada State Prison for confinement.

Affirmed.

Questions and Comments

1. The *Dodd* decision rested on an interpretation of the phase of "mentally ill" as used in the Nevada statute. Not all jurisdictions, however, have adhered to this interpretation. The Supreme Court of

---

b. He experienced trouble with the police when eight years old. He was placed in the Elko Boys School from 1960–1962. While there he fought frequently. He escaped. While loose he hit an elderly man on the head with a crowbar, covered him with kerosene or gas, and set him on fire. He was then sent to Preston, California, a prison for hardcore youth criminals. In 1963 he was committed to the Nevada State Hospital, from which he "eloped" on four separate occasions.

Minnesota, for instance, recently held that an antisocial personality is not within the definition of a mental illness disorder *unless* in the absence of proof the individual has "lost the ability to control his actions." *Johnson v. Noot*, 323 N.W.2d 724, 727 (Minn.1982).

2. Like the Nevada statute in *Dodd*, most state commitment statutes do not attempt to provide any detailed definition of "mental illness" as that term is used in the statutes. However, some state legislatures have attempted to provide a limited definition. In Virginia "mentally ill" "means any person afflicted with a mental disease to such an extent that for his own welfare or the welfare of others, he requires care and treatment." Va.Code, § 37.1–1(15) (1976). Is this statute any more descriptive than one just using the term "mental illness"?

In Washington persons suffering from a "mental disorder" are subject to commitment. As used in the Washington statute, "mental disorder" means "any organic, mental, or emotional impairment which has substantial adverse effects on an individual's cognitive or volitional functions." West's Wash.Rev.Code Ann. 71.05.020(2) (1983). Michigan defines "mental illness" as "a substantial disorder of thought or mood which significantly impairs judgment, behavior, capacity to recognize reality, or ability to cope with the ordinary demands of life." Mich. Comp.Law Ann. § 330.1400a (West 1980).

Do the Washington and Michigan statutes represent an improvement over those statutes failing to offer any definition of "mental illness"? Does the focus on cognitive ability in those statutes better protect against labeling an individual mentally ill solely because of this deviant *behavior*? Would it be possible to legislate a definition of "mental illness" which would provide greater guidance to judges and juries than those provided by the Washington and Michigan statutes?

3. Some older commitment statutes used rather archaic descriptions of what is now the modern concept of "mental illness." Such statutes frequently allowed commitment of "lunatics" or "insane persons." It has been suggested that the use of such terminology in a commitment proceeding may itself impede the eventual recovery of the individual subject to commitment. One researcher has documented the resentment occurring in individuals subject to a charge of "lunacy" or "insanity." That researcher noted that a similar adverse reaction does not occur when terms such as "nervous breakdown" or "melancholy" are used to describe an individual's condition. Kerschbaumer, *A Patient's Reaction to a Lunacy Charge*, 101 J. Nervous and Mental Disease 378 (1945).

In some jurisdictions such as Iowa the necessary element is phrased in terms of a "serious mental impairment." *Matter of Oseing*, 296 N.W.2d 797 (Iowa 1980).

4. What are the implications for the legal system and particularly the civil commitment laws of the findings of behavioral science research concerning cult adherence? A report on some findings which appeared recently in the press include the following:

THE PSYCHOLOGY OF THE CULT EXPERIENCE

New York Times, March 15, 1982 at B5, col. 2.

A new understanding of the psychology of the cult experience is emerging from the work of researchers and clinicians who have studied current and former cult members. While stating that not all cults are necessarily psychologically damaging to their members, the researchers' findings offer insights about the proper treatment of those who have been harmed, as well as the techniques that cults use to hold the loyalty of old members and attract new ones.

Some researchers suggest that the study of the cult experience has important implications for theories about the functioning of the human brain.

"Many cult groups have developed basically similar and quite compelling conversion techniques for exploiting the vulnerabilities of potential converts," said John G. Clark Jr., an assistant clinical professor of psychiatry at the Harvard University Medical School.

THE MARKS OF A NEW DISEASE

Dr. Clark has, in his private practice and with colleagues in Boston, treated and studied more than 500 current and former cult members since 1974. "In some respects," he said, "the destructive effects of cult conversions amount to a new disease in an era of psychological manipulation."

"When kids come out of cults, they have symptoms you just don't normally see," said Stanley H. Cath, a psychoanalyst and associate professor of psychiatry at the Tufts University School of Medicine who has treated and studied 60 former cult members over the last decade. "But many practitioners are ignorant of this 'disease,' and don't know how to treat it."

Although the researchers said it is possible for those who have left cults to integrate their experience into their lives in healthy ways, many are unable to. Among the common negative characteristics exhibited by the former cult members studied, said Dr. Clark, are depression, guilt, fear, paranoia, slow speech, rigidity of facial expression and body posture, indifference to physical appearance, passivity and memory impairment.

Robert Jay Lifton, professor of psychiatry at Yale University Medical School, said that many in the psychological professions may not be aware of, or deny the existence of, clinical difficulties posed by cults. "There is a widespread misunderstanding of the phenomenon of persuasion that can bring about intense change in people," he said.

* * *

Dr. Cath defined a cult as a group of people joined together by a common ideological system fostered by a charismatic leader, where, he said, "the expectation is that they can transcend the imperfections and finitude of life."

He said: "Often they set up a we-they philosophy: We have the truth and you do not."

* * *

Dr. Clark is one of the founders of the Boston Personal Development Institute, a nonprofit group that treats former cult members and advises their families.

* * *

A typical manipulated conversion, Dr. Clark said, involves a vulnerable person—a student leaving home, or at exam time, or someone who has lost a friend or lover—who is enticed by some reward: companionship, peace of mind, a place to stay or an implied sexual offering. "Cult recruiters frequent bus stations, airports, campuses, libraries, rallies, anywhere that unattached persons are likely to be passing through," he said.

"Then they narrow the attention of the recruit, in controlled social situations," Dr. Clark said. "He or she is invited to attend a special function, or series of classes. Cult members are assigned to attend the prospect constantly. Eventually they keep the mark involved in group-ecstatic activities, or use meditation, obsessive praying, constant lecturing or preaching or lack of sleep to maintain the mind in a constantly debilitated state."

* * *

Several of the researchers believe that the studies of cult members may revise current theories about the workings of the brain. Dr. Cath and Dr. Clark, working independently, have been intrigued that the experiences described by cult members resemble personality changes regularly associated with disorders of the temporal lobe of the brain.

"The symptoms of temporal lobe epilepsy," said Dr. Clark, "are similar to those seen or reported as resulting from cult conversions: increased irritability, loss of libido or altered sexual interest; ritualism, compulsive attention to detail, mystical states, humorlessness and sobriety, heightened paranoia."

Dr. Cath said: "Keeping devotees constantly fatigued, deprived of sensory input and suffering protein deprivation, working extremely long hours in street solicitation or in cult-owned businesses, engaging in monotonous chanting and rhythmical singing, may induce psychophysiological changes in the brain. The rhythmical movement of the body can lead to altered states of consciousness, and changes in the pressure or vibration pattern of the brain may affect the temporal lobe."

Dr. Clark hypothesized that what he calls the "cult-conversion syndrome" represents an overload of the brain's ability to process information. He said: "The unending personalized attention given to recruits during the conversion experience works to overload the prospect's information-processing capacity. This has another important function: the induction of trancelike states. Cult proselytizers then exploit the recruit's suggestibility."

5. In some instances cult adherents have been subjected to the application of guardianship proceedings designed to allow the parents to

exercise control over an emancipated child. In this connection see *Katz v. Superior Court* at p. 497.

IN RE BEVERLY

Supreme Court of Florida, 1977.
342 So.2d 481.

ADKINS, Justice.

This is a direct appeal from the Circuit Court of Dade County which held that Section 394.467, Florida Statutes (1973), was constitutional. We have jurisdiction. Article V, Section 3(b)(1), Florida Constitution.

The pertinent portions of the statute under attack read as follows:

"394.467   *Involuntary hospitalization*

(1) *Criteria.*—A person may be involuntarily hospitalized if he is mentally ill and because of his illness is:

(a) Likely to injure himself or others if allowed to remain at liberty, or

(b) In need of care or treatment and lacks sufficient capacity to make a responsible application on his own behalf.

* * *

On June 20, 1975, the designee of the Administrator of the Jackson Memorial Hospital Institution filed a petition for the involuntary hospitalization of respondent. A hearing on the involuntary hospitalization petition was held on June 26, 1975, and resulted in an order requiring respondent to be hospitalized involuntarily. The judge specifically upheld the constitutionality of Section 394.467(1)(b), Florida Statutes (1973).

Appellant first says that the statute is so vague that persons of ordinary intelligence must guess at its meaning, and therefore violates the due process clause of the Fourteenth Amendment to the United States Constitution and Article I, Section 9, Florida Constitution. Specifically, appellant says that under the statute a person who is "mentally ill" may be involuntarily hospitalized, and that this term is unconstitutionally vague. Appellant argues that the vagueness impediment is not overcome by the definition in Section 394.455(3), Florida Statutes (1973), which reads:

" 'Mentally ill' means having a mental, emotional, or behavioral disorder which substantially impairs the person's mental health."

* * *

Appellant relies upon *Commonwealth ex rel. Finken v. Roop*, 234 Pa.Super. 155, 339 A.2d 764 (1975), which held that the language of the Pennsylvania involuntary hospitalization statute was unconstitutionally vague, in that it failed to give fair warning of the conduct proscribed by law and there was an absence of standard restricting the discretion of governmental authorities or courts in enforcing the law.

The Pennsylvania statute allowed a petition for commitment to be filed when "a person is believed to be mentally disabled and in need of care or treatment of such mental disability." The Pennsylvania statute defined "mentally disabled" as:

"[A]ny mental illness, mental impairment, mental retardation, or mental deficiency, which so lessens the capacity of a person to use his customary self-control, *judgment and discretion* in the conduct of his affairs and social relations as to make it necessary or advisable for him to be under care as provided in this act." 339 A.2d 764 at 775.

In holding that the definition was unconstitutionally vague, the Court said:

"Mental illness has been attacked as a criterion for commitment because it is usually defined in terms of deviation from the 'norm' and thus is dependent upon what the examining psychiatrist believes the 'norm' to be. If, however, the term 'mental illness" is given sufficient legal meaning so as not to be unconstitutionally vague, * * * the difference of opinion among psychiatrists as to what constitutes the 'norm' becomes much less important. Thus, if the statute has only a vague standard, the trier of fact must rely almost totally on the expert opinions. * * *

"The commitment procedure * * * has asked too much of psychiatrists. The psychiatrist is not merely asked to report his diagnosis and evaluation to the court, he is asked to draw legal conclusions—is the subject mentally ill and does he need confinement? These conclusions have severe legal consequences and should be answered by the judicial system. That can be accomplished by requiring a strict burden of proof, and by defining 'mental illness' in a manner which prevents the court from exercising unfettered discretion (i.e., blindly relying on the conclusion drawn by the examining psychiatrist) and which indicates the type of conduct for which commitment is an appropriate sanction. If the standards are sufficiently precise, confinement will be less dependent upon the examining psychiatrist's personal conception of normal social behavior.

"The narrow issue presented by appellant's vagueness argument, therefore, is whether the requirement that the subject's mental illness render him 'in need of care' is sufficient to withstand a constitutional attack of impermissible vagueness. Clearly it is not. 'In need of care' is so broad as to be virtually meaningless. Furthermore, once a finding of mental illness is made, it would be impossible not to find that the individual is in need of care." 339 A.2d 764 at 777–78.

It is elementary that statutes may properly authorize the involuntary commitment of the mentally ill when the term "mentally ill" is given a satisfactory *legal* meaning. Section 394.467(1), Florida Statutes, quoted above, imparts a sufficient *legal* meaning to the term "mental illness" by setting criteria. Under the statute the pertinent inquiry is whether the person is mentally ill and *because of his illness* is (1) likely to injure himself or others if allowed to remain at liberty, or (2) is in need of care or treatment and lacks sufficient capacity to make a reasonable application on his own behalf. These statutory standards are more precise than those discussed in *Commonwealth ex rel. Finken v. Roop, supra,* as the Florida statutory language is adequate to warn that a person is subject to involuntary hospitalization only if he or she is likely to harm himself or others, or if he or she requires treatment and does not have the capacity to decide for himself. The appellant's vagueness challenge to the statute is without merit.

[While the constitutionality of the statute was upheld, the trial court's commitment decision was reversed on the ground that the evidence presented did not meet the statutory standard by clear and convincing evidence.]

Questions and Comments

1. Due process under the Fourteenth Amendment requires that laws which impinge on protected rights such as speech or liberty contain "reasonably clear guidelines" as to their reach. *See generally, Smith v. Goguen,* 415 U.S. 566, 572–573, 94 S.Ct. 1242, 1246–1247, 39 L.Ed.2d 605 (1974). In *Commonwealth ex rel. Finken v. Roop,* 234 Pa.Super. 155, 339 A.2d 764 (1975), cited in the *In re Beverly* opinion above, the Pennsylvania Supreme Court found the language of Pennsylvania's involuntary hospitalization statute unconstitutionally vague. At the same time the language of the Florida statute was found to be sufficiently certain to meet constitutional standards. What distinguished the Florida and Pennsylvania definitions of mental illness? In this connection, note that the Florida statute defined mental illness as "having a mental, emotional, or behavioral disorder which substantially impairs the person's mental health." What was the basis for the court's conclusion that this definition "imparts sufficient legal meaning to the term 'mental illness' "?

2. Application of the "mental illness" requirement in commitment proceedings calls for a diagnostic judgment by experts. What is the capacity of psychiatrists or other model health professionals to render valid assessments as to the presence of mental illness or other diagnostic catalogues? In the connection consider the following commentaries:

> This is the fundamental reason why the importance of diagnosis is not self-evident in psychiatry in the way that it is in the other branches of medicine[:] because the therapeutic and prognostic implications of psychiatric diagnoses are relatively weak, and the diagnoses themselves relatively unreliable. * * * Most psychiatric illnesses are still defined by their syndromes, their typical clinical features, and necessarily so because we know too little of their antecedents to define them at any other level. Many of these clinical features, like depression and anxiety, are graded traits present to varying extents in different people and at different times. Further-

more, few of them are pathognomonic [sufficient conditions] of individual illnesses. In general, it is the overall pattern of symptomatology and its evolution over time that distinguishes one category of illness from another, rather than the presence of key individual symptoms. To put it in technical language, the defining characteristics of psychiatric illnesses are generally both polythetic and inexact." (A "polythetic concept" is a "cluster concept", *i.e.*, one that cannot be defined by reference to necessary or sufficient conditions alone, and can only be interpreted in terms of a cluster of factors, all of which are relevant; few (or none) of which are necessary or sufficient; and none of which is both. Both physical and mental disease seem to be cluster concepts.)

Kendell, *The Role of Diagnosis in Psychiatry*, 2, 25 (1975).

Diagnosis of mental condition depends to a large extent upon the psychiatrist's perception of the patient's overt behavior and nonverbal communication during interviews, and on additional information concerning the patient's background and conduct which the psychiatrist obtains from collateral sources. The diagnostic function is highly subjective; various characteristics of the examining psychiatrist or clinician may affect his perception of the patient and the integration of the observed data into a diagnostic formulation.

* * *

A further problem with diagnosis is that there is no general agreement that a particular symptom or group of symptoms evidences a particular diagnostic group, such as schizophrenia or manic-depressive reaction. One major study examining the relationship between symptom manifestation and inclusion in a particular diagnostic group concluded that "although relationships exist between symptoms and diagnosis, the magnitude of these relationships is generally so small that membership in a particular diagnostic group conveys only minimal information about the symptomatology of the patient." This finding led the author to observe: "Since the basis for diagnostic classification is ostensibly symptom manifestation, the question arises as to why such classification has been found to be reliable in spite of the fact that symptoms tend to occur with surprisingly comparable frequency across diagnostic groupings."

The significance of bias and lack of clear definition of diagnostic categories may be examined in terms of the reliability of the diagnostic process. Reliability in this sense refers to the degree of concurrence among clinicians on the diagnosis of the same patient. In one of the few systematic studies of diagnostic reliability, Ash compared diagnoses made by three psychiatrists on the same patients at a government clinic. The patients were examined by the psychiatrists jointly, but the diagnoses were recorded independently. The three agreed on the specific diagnostic category in only 20 percent of the cases; two psychiatrists agreed on a diagnosis in another 49 percent of the cases. When only a general diagnostic category was considered, agreement was higher. All three psychiatrists agreed in 46 percent of the cases; two psychiatrists agreed in another 51 percent of the cases; in only three percent of the cases did all three disagree. Ash made another rather sobering finding: In fully one-third of the cases, one psychiatrist found serious pathology, while the other two found the patient to be, with some qualifications, a normal individual. Moreover, the joint examinations may have inflated the levels of agreement by allowing tacit communication among the psychiatrists.

The findings of later researchers have generally been consistent with Ash's findings. In general, researchers have found that the level of reliability, as measured by inter-psychiatrist agreement on specific diagnostic categories, is quite low, typically in the neighborhood of 32 percent. An important exception is that the rate of agreement on organic disorders is generally quite high, roughly 80 to 90 percent, because these usually involve brain damage which can be detected by physical tests with proven high reliability. Reliability for general diagnoses falls in between, with any two psychiatrists agreeing only about 55 percent of the time.

Reisner and Semmel, *Abolishing the Insanity Defense: A Look at the Proposed Federal Criminal Code Reform Act in Light of the Swedish Experience,* 62 Cal.L.Rev. 773, 776 (1974).

From the preceding studies it is possible to draw the following conclusions. Psychiatric diagnoses are quite unreliable. Psychiatrists are more likely to disagree than to agree about specific diagnoses such as psychotic depression, paranoid schizophrenia, or passive-agressive personality; and while diagnoses limited to the broad categories of functional disorder are more reliable, in actual practice psychiatrists are almost as likely to disagree about such diagnoses as they are to agree. Although the validity of psychiatric diagnoses has not yet been carefully studied, the relevant evidence suggests that it is quite limited.

Ennis and Litwack, *Psychiatry and the Presumption of Expertise: Flipping Coins in the Courtroom,* 62 Cal.L.Rev. 693, 734, 735 (1974).

In connection with the preceding commentaries, consider the remarks of a leading forensic psychiatrist:

[E]arlier courts considering *parens patriae*-oriented statutes were troubled by the apparent inconsistencies in psychiatric diagnosis. To a large extent, this problem with reliability has been resolved with the introduction of clear-cut criteria for diagnosis, exemplified by the Third Edition of the American Psychiatric Association's Diagnostic and Statistical Manual. Studies of comparative diagnostic processes using these and related criteria have demonstrated a strong likelihood of diagnostic agreement among different raters. Mental illness need no longer be an idiosyncratic determination.

Appelbaum, *Is Need for Treatment Constitutionally Acceptable as a Basis for Civil Commitment,* Paper presented at the annual meeting of the Association of American Law Schools, San Francisco, CA, January 5, 1984.

In view of some behavioral scientists, diagnostic reliability could be materially improved by the utilization of controlled pooled rating methods which subsequently would be admissible as evidence. In this connection, consider the comments of Professor Paul Meehl, a renowned scholar and former President of the American Psychological Association:

I find—even in the academy, where intellectual responsibility is supposedly a top virtue—a depressing reliance on anti-nosologic clichés, such as "everyone knows that psychiatric diagnoses are completely unreliable."

This was not an empirically validated statement even before the reliability oriented interview developments of recent years, and I am amazed at psychologists who cite, say, Schmidt and Fonda's classic study as anti-nosological evidence, when the interjudge reliability of the "schizophrenia/non-schizophrenia" dichotomy was tetrachoric.95. The careful recent studies show that diagnostic reliability in psychiatry is at least as good as that of organic medicine.

* * *

The Spearman Brown Prophecy Formula has been in our psychometric tool kit for over 70 years. Why don't we use it? The fact that human ratings behave like test items in closely following this old equation has been known since the 1920s. So if clinician's ratings on "paranoid delusion" had a pairwise interjudge reliability of only .70 (we can do better than that) the old Formula tells us that we need 4 clinicians to get a pooled rating reliability of .90, and 6 raters would yield .933 (permitting, if content-valid, a net attenuated construct validity of .97, which should satisfy anybody !).

This sounds like a lot of clinical raters, but 2–4 clinicians independently viewing say, two videotaped standardized mental status interviews conducted by 2 others would cost less than the usual 4 "experts" (2 on each side) being put through their courtroom paces as we now do it. I admit that persuading lawyers to accept the fact that statistically combined numerical ratings are superior to unformalized talk would be a difficult educational task, especially since I have thus far had negligible success in educating supposedly scientific psychologists in such matters.

* * *

Meehl, The Insanity Defense, Minn. Psychologist, Summer 1983, 11, 14.

3. What are the implications of the findings which point to limitations in the ability of psychiatrists to diagnose and predict atypical behavior reliably? Do they, for instance, call for the rejection of civil commitment when it is based on nothing more than clinical perceptions of mental illness and predictions of dangerousness? Isn't the answer to this question dependent, at least in part, on the role of experts in the commitment process? For instance, a recent empirical study of commitment in North Carolina found a "significant difference between physician recommendations and final court disposition." Miller and Fiddleman, *Involuntary Civil Commitment in North Carolina: The Results of the 1979 Statutory Changes,* 60 N.C.L.Rev. 985, 1000 (1982). (During one six-month period only 67% of those recommended for commitment were, in fact, committed; in another six-month period 89% of

those recommended for commitment were committed.) Do these results suggest that judges and juries do not give conclusive weight to the opinion of experts and, in fact, exercise an independent judgment as to whether there is a need to commit?

The disagreement with experts may reflect either the court's doubt about the expert's clinical judgment or the application of independent nonclinical variables such as the court's perceptions of the community's tolerance for certain forms of abnormal behavior. To the extent that the disagreement reflects the former, is the judgment of judges and juries likely to result in a more accurate assessment of the condition of the patient in terms of the statutory standard? If the disagreement reflects the latter, is it appropriate for civil commitment decisions to take extraneous factors such as community tolerance into account?

4. Recent studies suggest that limitations on the predictions of dangerous behavior can be overcome at least in part by basing the prediction on a multiplicity of variables, including in particular a history of recent violent behavior. See, Appelbaum, *Civil Commitment* (to appear in Klerman, G. (ed.), *Psychiatry, Vol. 5, Epidemiology, Legal and Social Psychiatry.* Philadelphia, J.B. Lippincott, and New York, Basic Books). Would the imposition of an overt act requirement to the legal standards governing civil commitment make clinical predictions a more trustworthy basis for the commitment decision? For an expanded discussion of the overt act requirement imposed by some jurisdictions, see p. 353 n. 3, *infra*.

2. Mental Illness as the Sole Basis for Commitment

O'CONNOR v. DONALDSON

Supreme Court of the United States, 1975.
422 U.S. 563, 95 S.Ct. 2486, 45 L.Ed.2d 396.

Mr. Justice STEWART delivered the opinion of the Court.

The respondent, Kenneth Donaldson, was civilly committed to confinement as a mental patient in the Florida State Hospital at Chattahoochee in January 1957. He was kept in custody there against his will for nearly 15 years. The petitioner, Dr. J.B. O'Connor, was the hospital's superintendent during most of this period. Throughout his confinement Donaldson repeatedly, but unsuccessfully, demanded his release, claiming that he was dangerous to no one, that he was not mentally ill, and that, at any rate, the hospital was not providing treatment for his supposed illness. Finally, in February 1971, Donaldson brought this lawsuit under 42 U.S.C. § 1983, in the United States District Court for the Northern District of Florida, alleging that O'Connor, and other members of the hospital staff named as defendants, had intentionally and maliciously deprived him of his constitutional right to liberty. After a four-day trial, the jury returned a verdict assessing both compensatory and punitive damages against O'Connor and a codefendant. The Court of Appeals for the Fifth Circuit affirmed the judgment, 493 F.2d 507. We granted O'Connor's petition for certiorari, 419 U.S. 894, 95 S.Ct. 171, 42 L.Ed.2d 138, because of the important constitutional questions seemingly presented.

I

Donaldson's commitment was initiated by his father, who thought that his son was suffering from "delusions." After hearings before a county judge of Pinellas County, Fla., Donaldson was found to be suffering from "paranoid schizophrenia" and was committed for "care, maintenance, and treatment" pursuant to Florida statutory provisions that have since been repealed. The state law was less than clear in specifying the grounds necessary for commitment, and the record is scanty as to Donaldson's condition at the time of the judicial hearing. These matters are, however, irrelevant, for this case involves no challenge to the initial commitment, but is focused, instead, upon the nearly 15 years of confinement that followed.

The evidence at the trial showed that the hospital staff had the power to release a patient, not dangerous to himself or others, even if he remained mentally ill and had been lawfully committed. Despite many requests, O'Connor refused to allow that power to be exercised in Donaldson's case. At the trial, O'Connor indicated that he had believed that Donaldson would have been unable to make a "successful adjustment outside the institution," but could not recall the basis for that conclusion. O'Connor retired as superintendent shortly before this suit was filed. A few months thereafter, and before the trial, Donaldson secured his release and a judicial restoration of competency, with the support of the hospital staff.

The testimony at the trial demonstrated, without contradiction, that Donaldson had posed no danger to others during his long confinement, or indeed at any point in his life. O'Connor himself conceded that he had no personal or secondhand knowledge that Donaldson had ever committed a dangerous act. There was no evidence that Donaldson had ever been suicidal or been thought likely to inflict injury upon himself. One of O'Connor's codefendants acknowledged that Donaldson could have earned his own living outside the hospital. He had done so for some 14 years before his commitment, and immediately upon his release he secured a responsible job in hotel administration.

* * *

The evidence showed that Donaldson's confinement was a simple regime of enforced custodial care, not a program designed to alleviate or cure his supposed illness. Numerous witnesses, including one of O'Connor's codefendants, testified that Donaldson had received nothing but custodial care while at the hospital. O'Connor described Donaldson's treatment as "milieu therapy." But witnesses from the hospital staff conceded that, in the context of this case, "milieu therapy" was a euphemism for confinement in the "milieu" of a mental hospital. For substantial periods, Donaldson was simply kept in a large room that housed 60 patients, many of whom were under criminal commitment. Donaldson's requests for ground privileges, occupational training, and an opportunity to discuss his case with O'Connor or other staff members were repeatedly denied.

At the trial, O'Connor's principal defense was that he had acted in good faith and was therefore immune from any liability for monetary damages. His position, in short, was that state law, which he had believed valid, had authorized indefinite custodial confinement of the "sick," even if they were not given treatment and their release could harm no one.

The trial judge instructed the members of the jury that they should find that O'Connor had violated Donaldson's constitutional right to liberty if they found that he had

"confined [Donaldson] against his will, knowing that he was not mentally ill or dangerous or knowing that if mentally ill he was not receiving treatment for his alleged mental illness * * *"

* * *

The jury returned a verdict for Donaldson against O'Connor and a codefendant, and awarded damages of $38,500, including $10,000 in punitive damages.

The Court of Appeals affirmed the judgment of the District Court.

II

We have concluded that the difficult issues of constitutional law dealt with by the Court of Appeals are not presented by this case in its present posture. Specifically, there is no reason now to decide whether mentally ill persons dangerous to themselves or to others have a right to treatment upon compulsory confinement by the State, or whether the State may compulsorily confine a nondangerous, mentally ill individual for the purpose of treatment. As we view it, this case raises a single, relatively simple, but nonetheless important question concerning every man's constitutional right to liberty.

The jury found that Donaldson was neither dangerous to himself nor dangerous to others, and also found that, if mentally ill, Donaldson had not received treatment. That verdict, based on abundant evidence, makes the issue before the Court a narrow one. We need not decide whether, when, or by what procedures, a mentally ill person may be confined by the State on any of the grounds which, under contemporary statutes, are generally advanced to justify involuntary confinement of such a person—to prevent injury to the public, to ensure his own survival or safety, or to alleviate or cure his illness. For the jury found that none of the above grounds for continued confinement was present in Donaldson's case.

Given the jury's findings, what was left as justification for keeping Donaldson in continued confinement? The fact that state law may have authorized confinement of the harmless mentally ill does not itself establish a constitutionally adequate purpose for the confinement. Nor is it enough that Donaldson's original confinement was founded upon a constitutionally adequate basis, if in fact it was, because even if his involuntary confinement was initially permissible, it could not constitutionally continue after that basis no longer existed.

A finding of "mental illness" alone cannot justify a State's locking a person up against his will and keeping him indefinitely in simple custodial confinement. Assuming that that term can be given a reasonably precise content and that the "mentally ill" can be identified with reasonable accuracy, there is still no constitutional basis for confining such persons involuntarily if they are dangerous to no one and can live safely in freedom.

May the State confine the mentally ill merely to ensure them a living standard superior to that they enjoy in the private community? That the State has a proper interest in providing care and assistance to the unfortunate goes without saying. But the mere presence of mental illness does not disqualify a person from preferring his home to the comforts of an institution. Moreover, while the State may arguably confine a person to save him from harm, incarceration is rarely if ever a necessary condition for raising the living standards of those capable of surviving safely in freedom, on their own or with the help of family or friends.

May the State fence in the harmless mentally ill solely to save its citizens from exposure to those whose ways are different? One might as well ask if the State, to avoid public unease, could incarcerate all who are physically unattractive or socially eccentric. Mere public intolerance or animosity cannot constitutionally justify the deprivation of a person's physical liberty.

In short, a State cannot constitutionally confine without more a nondangerous individual who is capable of surviving safely in freedom by himself or with the help of willing and responsible family members or friends. Since the jury found, upon ample evidence, that O'Connor, as an agent of the State, knowingly did so confine Donaldson, it properly concluded that O'Connor violated Donaldson's constitutional right to freedom.

[The Court next considered defendant O'Connor's contention that even though Donaldson's confinement may have been illegal, the defendant could not be held personally liable under Section 1983 if his actions were taken in "good faith." Finding that the issues raised by the defendant as to the scope of qualified immunity of a public official under 42 U.S.C. § 1983 had not been considered by the lower courts, the case was remanded to the Court of Appeals for further consideration of these issues, particularly in the light of a case recently decided by the Supreme Court which construed the immunity provisions of this section.]

Questions and Comments

1. The holding in *Donaldson* is limited to the proposition that "[a] finding of 'mental illness' alone cannot justify a State's locking a person up against his will and keeping him indefinitely in simple custodial confinement." Thus, the case merely establishes the principle that mental illness without a finding of dangerousness or some other allowable ground, such as the need to protect the individual from harm, cannot serve as the basis for involuntary commitment. It is also important to note that the court expressly declines to decide whether confinement for the purpose of treatment is constitutionally allowable. Thus, the opinion is of limited scope and leaves numerous issues undetermined by the Supreme Court.

2. While the issue in *Donaldson* focused on the unlawfulness of the plaintiff's detention over a fifteen-year period, the principle of the case that mental illness standing by itself cannot serve as the grounds for commitment is equally applicable to the initial commitment decision.

3. The majority's opinion in *Donaldson* holds that psychiatric incarceration cannot be justified by an interest in isolating from the public those of its citizens "whose ways are different." It is, however, not entirely clear what the court means by the phrase "those whose ways are different." Does this include individuals whose behavior could constitute a disturbance of the peace or who by their inactivity would bring them within the definition of a vagrant, a criminally punishable condition in some jurisdictions. Is the court attempting to draw a line between those who simply look different from those manifesting behavior which is irrating or annoying to others? For instance, may the state constitutionally hospitalize a mentally ill person who screams in public or who disturbs others by ringing doorbells or randomly telephoning people at odd hours? Presumably persons who manifest this type of behavior can be criminally prosecuted under disorderly conduct statutes. Is there any reason why the state should be able to incarcerate in the one situation (following a criminal conviction) and not in the other (through psychiatric hospitalization)? Is the distinction that a criminal conviction requires a higher standard of proof (beyond a reasonable doubt rather than by "clear and convincing evidence")? Or more significantly is it that incarceration following conviction is for a definite and established term, whereas confinement associated with psychiatric hospitalization is of indefinite duration?

C. THE PREDICTION OF ADVERSE CONSEQUENCES REQUIREMENT

1. Introduction

As previously noted, a commitment statute typically requires proof of two elements: mental illness and some adverse consequences that would be avoided by the commitment of the afflicted individual. Draftsmen of legislation have encountered significant problems in designating with any degree of precision the types of adverse consequences which authorize commitment. Most common-ly, the standards that are used are rather general in nature and employ such terminology as "dangerousness to others" or "danger-ousness to him or herself." But the difficulties inherent in applying a standard framed in terms of dangerousness go beyond the defini-tion of *what consequences* should be deemed dangerous. There is the additional problem of establishing the degree of probability of the predicted event occurring. As illustrated by the materials that follow, an assessment of probability is inherent in every instance where a civil commitment statute is being applied. Thus if the commitment standard is framed in terms of "dangerousness to others," the trier of fact must first determine whether some predict-ed act or behavior is dangerous, and second, what is the likelihood of it occurring. The interrelationship of these elements and the difficul-ties posed by their application is explored in the materials which follow.

2. *Commitment for the Protection of Others*

a. *Physical Injury of Others*

JONES v. COUNTY BOARD OF MENTAL HEALTH, ETC.

Supreme Court of Nebraska, 1979.
203 Neb. 618, 279 N.W.2d 841.

HASTINGS, Justice.

Although docketed separately, by agreement of the parties this case was consolidated for argument with *Hill v. County Board of Mental Health*, 203 Neb. 610, 279 N.W.2d 838 (1979), and is con-trolled by that case. Myrtle Jones has appealed from an order of the District Court for Douglas County affirming the action of the Doug-las County board of mental health finding her to be a mentally ill dangerous person in need of board-ordered treatment. Error is assigned in that it is claimed the evidence was insufficient as a matter of law to establish these findings by clear and convincing proof.

The hearing was held before the mental health board on January 23, 1978, and arose out of a written complaint signed by the subject's mother, Mosie Lee Jones, who claimed that Myrtle Jones talked about killing her "kids and mother on New Years." Myrtle Jones was represented by counsel throughout all of the proceedings.

Dr. David J. Goldberg, a physician and psychiatrist, testified he had examined the subject on January 19, 1978, consisting of a clinical interview and review of the available records. She was initially incoherent, but as the interview progressed she became most pleas-ant. She described a series of incidents occurring during the immedi-ately preceding few weeks wherein she felt mistreated at home and reacted against her mother and stepfather, sometimes by hitting them in anger. On one occasion she told Dr. Goldberg her son was misbehaving and she said "I will kill you," and that it just came out in the heat of trying to reprimand the child. It was claimed by her to be merely a figure of speech since she didn't mean to kill him.

The diagnosis of Dr. Goldberg was as follows: "The diagnostic impression I have on this patient is one of a schizophrenic illness and I have contemplated two subtypes. One is a chronic undifferentiated. It is based mostly on the history this patient forwarded. It seems that the history of this illness goes back three or four years now in time. Second, of course, was schizophrenia, schizo-affective, agitated type because the affective component of this illness is quite noticeable. In any case, these are subtypes of the same illness, which is basically a schizophrenic process. My recommendation at this time is to continue psychiatric treatment * * * I certainly would recommend to continue in-patient treatment at this time." The witness defined schizophrenia as a mental illness. Another witness, a one-time fiance, testified he had heard the subject threaten to reprimand her children if they disobeyed her; and that he observed her spank the children from time to time, but none of them, to his knowledge, ever required medical attention because of the spankings.

Myrtle Jones testified in her own behalf and admitted she made the statement "if you don't obey me I'm going to kill you" to her 10-year-old girl and 11-year-old son. She went on to say, presumably concerning the same incident, "Because one night we were going to a friends of mine and they were going into the house and on the way into the house my little girl fell down on the ground. She turned around and she goes back to the car and goes back to where my mother is and then I said mother, when I get those kids I'm going to kill them and she said don't be hasty and I said if you can whip them, why can't I. Those are my exact words."

Perhaps some further insight into the mental state of the subject can be found in her statement in open hearing immediately after the board chairman announced the order of commitment. She said: "Simply because I said I was going to kill my God Damn kids? God Damn, Mama, you put me in a bad situation. You take me out of here."

The board found there was clear and convincing evidence of mental illness and dangerousness as manifested by the threats to the children. The District Court, hearing the appeal de novo on the record, affirmed the action of the board of mental health. We in turn must affirm unless we find as a matter of law that the order of the District Court is not supported by clear and convincing proof.

Again, as in *Hill v. County Board of Mental Health, supra* and *Petersen v. County Board of Mental Health,* 203 Neb. 622, 279 N.W.2d 844, the medical evidence establishes by clear and convincing proof that Myrtle Jones is suffering from a mental illness. That fact is not contested. Also, the threat, if in fact it qualified as a threat under the Nebraska Mental Health Commitment Act, was recent, having been made only 12 days prior to the filing of the petition. This, too, is not questioned.

The only question on appeal is whether the evidence establishing the threat demonstrates by clear and convincing proof that it manifested a "substantial risk of serious harm to another person." Myrtle Jones described the death threat as a "figure of speech." Her counsel, in appellant's brief, dismisses it as "common usage by angry parents of meaningless 'death threats' in discipling their misbehaving children." We think the matter cannot be dismissed that lightly. The existence of mental illness and the presence of a threat of violence cannot be examined in isolated vacuums of semantics. An extant mental illness with no manifestations of anger or violence, either verbal or physical, hardly presents a commitable situation. Likewise, a "death threat" by a parent with no demonstrable mental illness, following an episode with a rebellious child, very probably should give no cause for concern. However, the two together, under the circumstances then existing, may very well require immediate action rather than additional time to change the threat into an act.

From an examination of all of the evidence we cannot say as a matter of law that the District Court was wrong in finding the proof to be clear and convincing that Myrtle Jones was a mentally ill dangerous person as defined by law, and its judgment is affirmed.

Affirmed.

Questions and Comments

1. In *In re Graham*, 40 Ill.App.3d 452, 352 N.E.2d 387 (1976), the woman who was subject to commitment allegedly said to her mother, "You have to be eliminated. I haven't decided by what method, but you have to be eliminated." On another occasion, she told her mother and brother that "I would like to murder all of you. It wouldn't be murder; it would be a pleasure. I could tear you limb from limb and I wouldn't bat an eyelash." The woman herself testified she told her mother that "I could just kill you," but added that the statement was made under long-term, extreme provocation; that she was not serious about killing her mother; and that she was capable of confining herself. A psychiatrist testified that the woman was a paranoid schizophrenic and "in need of mental treatment." The decision committing the petitioner was affirmed on appeal with the court noting that a judge "is not required to wait until someone is harmed before entering a commitment order." At the time that the case was heard, Illinois authorized commitments where it is "reasonably expected at the time of the determination [that the individual] will intentionally or unintentionally physically injure another." Ill.Rev.Stat. Ch. 91½ § 1–119(1) (1979). In 1979 the requirement that the physical harm occur in the "near future" was added. Had the change been in effect when *In re Graham* was decided, is it likely that the result would have been the same?

2. Essential to the application of the commitment laws is the prediction of dangerousness or of some other adverse consequence. In this connection consider the implications of the following commentaries:

Diamond, *The Psychiatric Prediction of Dangerousness*, 123 Univ. of Penn.L.Rev. 439, 440, 447 (1974):

> Can psychiatrists predict danger with reasonable accuracy? Are there well-established clinical symptoms which, if present, can be relied upon to indicate potential danger? Can one be reasonably sure that persons who are not dangerous will not be labeled as such and unnecessarily confined? I believe the answer to all these questions is an emphatic "no."
>
> * * *
>
> [I]t is clear from the *Baxstrom* studies that of these 967 persons who had been convicted at one time of serious crimes, and who were designated as mentally ill and dangerous to others in order to justify their further confinement, only a very few were actually dangerous. One can only conclude that psychiatrists who make such judgments tended to over-predict dangerousness greatly, by a factor somewhere between ten and a hundred times the actual incidence of dangerous behavior. It is understandable why this should be so. If the psychiatrist under-predicts danger, and clears a patient who later commits a violent act, he will be subjected to severe criticism. If, on the other hand, he over-predicts danger, he will suffer no consequence from such faulty prediction, for his prediction might have come true had there been no intervention (such as institutionalization).

Ennis and Litwack, *Psychiatry and the Presumption of Expertise: Flipping Coins in the Courtroom*, 62 Cal.L.Rev. 693, 711–712 (1974).

> Perhaps the most important judgment psychiatrists make is whether or not an individual is "dangerous:"
>
>> [A]pproximately 50,000 mentally ill persons per year are predicted to be dangerous and preventively detained. * * * In addition, about 5% * * * of the total mental * * * hospital population of the United States * * * are kept in maximum security sections on assessment of their potential dangerousness.
>
> There is evidence that the perception of dangerousness is the single most important determinant of judicial decisions to commit individuals or to release patients requesting discharge from a hospital. Psychiatrists commonly testify at civil commitment proceedings that a given individual is "dangerous" to himself or others. How valid are these predictions? First let us consider the research results on dangerousness to others.
>
> In early 1969 Dershowitz reviewed the few studies in the literature on the prediction of anti-social conduct and concluded:
>
>> * * * that psychiatrists are rather inaccurate predictors—inaccurate in an absolute sense—and even less accurate when compared with other professionals, such as psychologists, social workers and correctional officials and when compared to actuarial devices, such as prediction or experience tables. Even more

[handwritten marginalia: "IN N.Y. PEOPLE HAD BEEN (ABOUT 1,000 PEOPLE) CONFINED AS DANGEROUSLY MI, BEC. OF RED TAPE HAD TO BE LET GO / NOTHING TERRIBLE HAPPENED"]

significant for legal purposes, it seems that psychiatrists are particularly prone to one type of error—overprediction. They tend to predict antisocial conduct in many instances where it would not, in fact, occur. Indeed, our research suggests that for every correct psychiatric prediction of violence, there are numerous erroneous predictions. That is, among every group of inmates presently confined on the basis of psychiatric predictions of violence, there are only a few who would, and many more who would not, actually engage in such conduct if released.

[E]ven with "the most careful, painstaking, laborious, and lengthy clinical approach to the prediction of dangerousness, false positives may be a minimum of 60 to 70%." In other words, even under controlled conditions, at least 60 to 70 percent of the people whom psychiatrists judge to be dangerous may, in fact, be harmless. (at 714).

3. Because of the problems inherent in predicting future conduct, a number of states now require that "dangerousness" in the context of commitment must be evidenced by a recent overt act before a finding of dangerousness is allowed. Thus, in Alabama, before commitment can occur the judge or jury must find "[t]hat the threat of substantial harm has been evidenced by a recent overt act." Ala.Code § 22–52–10(a)(3) (1982 Supp.). Similarly, in Michigan the judge or jury must find that the prospective patient "has engaged in an <u>act or act</u>s or made significant threats that are substantially supportive of the expectation" of dangerousness. Mich.Comp.Laws.Ann § 330.1401(a) (West 1980). In Arizona a finding of "danger to others" must be "based upon a history of either:

"(a) Having seriously threatened in the recent past by verbal or both, to engage in behavior which will likely result in serious physical harm to another person, * * * [or]

(b) Having inflicted or having attempted to inflict serious physical harm upon another person within one hundred eighty days preceding the fixing of the petition." Ariz.Rev.Stat.Ann. § 36–501(3) (West Supp.1983).

The Arizona statute further provides for extension of the 180 day period if the incident was followed by preventive confinement or supervision, or if the harm inflicted or attempted to be inflicted was "grievous or horrendous." Ariz.Rev.Stat.Ann. §§ 36–501(3)(b)(i) and (ii) (West Supp. 1983).

The courts have split on the issue of whether a finding of a recent overt act is constitutionally required in order to commit an individual. In *Lynch v. Baxley*, 386 F.Supp. 378, 391 (M.D.Ala.1974), the court held that it was, stating: "To confine a citizen against his will because he is likely to be dangerous in the future, it must be shown that he has actually been dangerous in the recent past and that such danger was manifested by an overt act, attempt, or threat to do substantial harm to himself or to another." The court in *In re Mary Louise Salem*, 31 N.C. App. 57, 228 S.E.2d 649 (1976), disagreed, stating: "An overt act may be clear, cogent and convincing evidence which will support a finding of imminent danger, but we cannot agree that there must be an overt act to establish imminent dangerousness."

Is it relevant that there is little data to support the view that a recent overt dangerous act enhances the reliability of a prediction of future dangerous acts in the forseeable future? In the absence of such evidence what is the rationale for requiring an overt act as a condition for commitment?

Neither cases nor the statutes have defined the phrase "overt act." What constitutes an "overt act"? Need it be the actual infliction of harm, or might a preparatory act such as the purchase of a gun coupled with a threat be sufficient?

4. As noted earlier the application of dangerousness as a standard involves both a definition of what consequences will be deemed to be dangerous and also the degree of probability of the predicted event occurring. How likely should it be that an act might occur before it is considered dangerous? 50%? 80%? 90%? More or less? Should your answer depend on the nature of act involved? If you were writing a commitment statute, how would you express the probability element of dangerousness?

In the District of Columbia a person is commitable if he is mentally ill and as a result of that illness "likely to injure himself or other persons if allowed to remain at liberty." D.C.Code Ann. § 21–541 (1981). In Washington dangerousness depends on a finding of "substantial risk" that physical harm will be inflicted by an individual on himself or another. West's Wash.Rev.Code Ann. 71.05.020 (1983). Do terms such as "likely," "reasonably expected," or "substantial risk" adequately reflect the probability of occurrence element of dangerousness? Would a requirement of finding an "imminent" or "certain" likelihood of harm be better? Is it possible that other phrases would make a difference in a jury's conclusion as to commitment?

5. Should the expert witness be required to estimate the probability that the predicted behavior will occur? Consider in this regard the following statement by the District of Columbia Court of Appeals:

> Psychiatrists should not be asked to testify, without more, simply whether future behavior or threatened harm is "likely" to occur. For the psychiatrist may—in his own mind—be defining "likely" to mean anything from virtual certainty to slightly above chance. And his definition will not be a reflection of any expertise, but of his own personal preference for safety or liberty. Of course, psychiatrists may be unable or unwilling to provide a precise numerical estimate of probabilities, and we are not attempting to so limit their testimony. But questioning can and should bring out the expert witness's meaning when he testifies that expected harm is or is not "likely." Only when this has been done can the court properly separate the factual question—what degree of likelihood exists in a particular case—from the legal one—whether the degree of likelihood that has been found to exist provides a justification for commitment. *Cross v. Harris,* 418 F.2d 1095, 1100–01 (D.C.Cir.1969).

6. Under the APA Model Law mental illness coupled with dangerousness is one of the grounds for commitment. However, in contrast to existing laws any individual committed on the grounds of dangerousness must in addition lack "capacity to make an informed decision concerning treatment." Stromberg and Stone, *A Model State Law on Civil Commitment of the Mentally Ill*, 20 Hav.J. on Legislation 275, 301 (1982). Under the model law a lack of "capacity to make an informed decision concerning treatment" is defined in terms of an inability by reason of mental disorder to "understand basically the nature and effects of hospitalization or treatment or is unable to engage in a rational decision making process." *Id.* at 301. This criterion thus precludes the involuntary commitment of a mentally ill person who is dangerous to others but is not impaired in terms of making an informed hospitalization or treatment decision. The Model Code does not provide any guidance on what disposition should be made of the class of persons where detention is required. Some adjustment in the APA standards seem to be called for as long as the insanity defense operates to remove the dangerous mentally ill from the reaches of the criminal correction system. This question of the disposition of the mentally ill offenders who are acquitted on grounds of insanity is considered in Chapter Eight.

The APA Model Law also bars the commitment of any individual including those who are dangerous unless "there is reasonable prospect that his disorder is treatable." *Id.* at 330. Neither the APA Model Law nor the commentaries of one of the drafters suggests what disposition should be made of those who are mentally ill and dangerous but not treatable.

COMMONWEALTH v. NASSAR

Supreme Judicial Court of Massachusetts, 1980.
380 Mass. 908, 406 N.E.2d 1286.

KAPLAN, Justice.

On May 15, 1979, after a bench trial in Superior Court, Berkshire County, the present respondents James John Nassar, III, and his wife Patricia Anne Nassar were found not guilty by reason of mental illness of the crimes of child abandonment and manslaughter incident to the death of their sixteen month old, third child Joshua. Under the provisions of G.L. c. 123, § 16(*a*), the judge ordered the respondents to be committed to the Department of Mental Health (Department) and hospitalized for observation. That observation having taken place, the district attorney petitioned the court under § 16(*b*) for the involuntary commitment of the respondents to a facility. After hearing, at which there was psychiatric testimony for the Commonwealth and for the respondents, the judge (who had not presided at the criminal trial) held that the respondents should be released from commitment, but, being doubtful about his decision involving the interpretation of the statute, he stayed entry of judgment and reported the case to the Appeals Court.

* * *

A. We present an outline of the psychiatric testimony, first describing how these witnesses reconstructed the respondents' impulsions leading to the death. The respondents, twenty-five years (James) and twenty-four years old at the time of hearing, had been married some six years and had led a seminomadic, reclusive life, relying largely on handouts from others to keep themselves going. They believe they were sanctified and among those selected to be saved. Through prayers they communicated in a telepathic way with God and were given instructions what to do; but they had to be wary to sense which of the messages were truly from God. Any true instructions were to be obeyed without question. Since the respondents had to be available at all times to do God's bidding, they could not undertake to work for a living, although James occasionally did odd jobs. Nor would they accept welfare help or have dealings with any government agency.

The respondents had had four children. Two of them were born at home and their births were unrecorded. Because of the respondents' manner of life, the care of children was burdensome for them. But they regarded the children as also sanctified. On occasion, in response to God's instructions, the respondents evidently ceased to feed their children, in the belief that the children's fast would help the unfortunate in India. The respondents no longer have custody of the two older children; it is understood that Sarah was given up for adoption in 1974 and Johanna was taken from the respondents in August, 1978, and placed in a foster home.

In September, 1977, the respondents received instructions to abandon Joshua; probably they had some expectation that he would be picked up and cared for by strangers. They believed they had left him at a church in Vermont and not on the steps of a church in North Adams where in fact he was found. When found, Joshua was dead; although no single cause could be ascribed, it was clear that the child was extremely malnourished. The respondents indicated they did not believe the dead child was Joshua. At the time of the abandonment of Joshua, Patricia was pregnant with Elizabeth. According to the respondents, this child, less than a year old, expired in her sleep, and it appears the respondents disposed of the body as garbage. Criminal proceedings against the respondents regarding this event were in process at the time of the § 16(*b*) hearing.

To turn to the psychiatric analyses. The witnesses agreed that the respondents were gravely ill, suffering from chronic schizophrenia, paranoid type. Their divorce from reality was in the form of a strong shared delusional system, originating in religious belief but now corrupted or distorted. In following the will of God as communicated to them, the respondents felt no personal responsibility, and therefore they evinced no emotion about the two deaths or the fate of their other children. Their "affect" was flat. To restore the respondents to normality or something approaching it would require extensive psychotherapy and likely a separation of the pair to break up their mutually reinforcing mental patterns.

What could be expected if the respondents were released? It was common ground among all the witnesses that any children born to the respondents—and they were a fecund couple—would be in serious peril from them, and there was some inferential suggestion that this might apply to other children as well, at least if they should fall into the respondents' custody over a period of time. There was also agreement that at a stage in treatment where either respondent or both began to overcome the delusional system and started to recognize a responsibility for what had happened to their children, suicidal or aggressive behavior toward others might burst out. With respect to Patricia, in particular, there was testimony of powerful repressed rage and hostility.

These forecasts were contingent—on eventual access to children or breakdown of the paranoid system. As to more immediate prognosis, the testimony diverged.

On one side, it was suggested that the divine instructions might call for acts of omission or commission as serious as those in the case of Joshua, or worse, and not limited in object to a child. The orders if "true" would be followed by the respondents in automatic fashion, for they were relieved of any sense of individual responsibility or guilt. Especially if released together, the respondents would continue as prisoners of their delusional system. The Commonwealth, basing itself on this line of testimony, said it would be foolhardy to allow at large persons who had caused one death and were possibly involved in another, had escaped criminal punishment thus far only by reason of mental incapacity at the time, and were still sick and prepared to answer wayward instructions that might be projected by their own diseased imaginations.

On the other side, witnesses suggested that the respondents if released would resume their isolated existence and a way of life that had been recessive rather than aggressive. The instructions they had received about Joshua reflected their inability to meet a child's needs and their response of abandonment was essentially negative. These witnesses were willing to extrapolate narrowly from Joshua's case to forecast danger to siblings, but they could see no significant current probability of peril to others or to the respondents themselves.

B. The legal question for the judge was posed by G.L. c. 123, § 8(a), as appearing in St.1976, c. 356, § 3, which, to justify involuntary commitment, requires findings that "(1) such person is mentally ill, and (2) the discharge of such person from a facility would create a likelihood of serious harm." "Likelihood of serious harm" is defined by § 1:

Likelihood of serious harm (1) [includes] * * * (2) a substantial risk of physical harm to other persons as manifested by evidence of homicidal or other violent behavior or evidence that others are placed in reasonable fear of violent behavior and serious physical harm to them *   *   *

*   *   *

There was no question about the mental illness which had manifested itself in the conduct fatal to Joshua, and which continued. As to "likelihood," each subdivision of the definition is predicated or conditioned on the manifestation of described "evidence." It will be seen in the following discussion that subdivision (2) is the critical one, and that there is doubt whether the judge interpreted it as we hold it should have been. Thus the case will be remanded for further proceedings. We subjoin a few other brief comments about the case.

*   *   *

Subdivision (2) deals with the prospect of harm to others. It calls for "evidence of homicidal or other violent behavior" or "evidence that others are placed in reasonable fear of violent behavior and serious physical harm to them." These are two alternative predicates, and we concentrate on the first. We are of the opinion that that predicate was established by trial of the respondents for involuntary manslaughter. The judge was prepared to concede that the respondents' behavior toward Joshua, resulting in his death, would be considered wanton or reckless conduct in sane persons, amounting to involuntary manslaughter; and it is plain enough that manslaughter (whether of the voluntary or involuntary type) is homicide. Nevertheless the judge appears to have taken the view—although not with complete clarity—that the first alternative clause was not satisfied because the homicide referred to had to be a "violent" one, whereas here the death came about through omissions or at any rate without a physical blow or other such impact. In other words, the judge read the words "homicidal or other violent behavior" as if "homicidal" was qualified by "violent." Without pausing to argue the question of the substantiality of a difference between omission and commission, especially as it might be apprehended by the victim, we take the position in the present context that homicide of any category is to be understood as in itself a violent crime, and "homicidal * * * behavior" should be read in the same manner. It seems reasonable that a recent episode of manslaughter combined with severe mental illness should qualify a person for consideration for commitment—although, as we shall see, it does not conclude the question.

*   *   *

That the first of the alternative conditions of subdivision (2) is found to exist does not in itself mean that the person should be committed. For the question remains whether his release would create "a substantial risk of physical harm to other persons." This is a determination to be made in the first instance by the trial judge, and in the present case we apprehend that the issue—a probabilistic one—was not faced squarely because of the threshold difficulty with "homicidal behavior."

* * *

[The case was remanded from the trial court for "such further hearings as * * * may seem advisable."]

Questions and Comments

1. Was it clear from the statute in *Nassar* whether the behavior in question met the statutory standards? What exactly was the issue of interpretation that was before the Court?

2. The court found that the Nassars to be committable in that they presented a "substantive risk of physical harm to other persons." Since the Nassar's two living children had been removed from their custody, what persons were at risk if the Nassars were not committed?

3. In a part of the opinion which was not reproduced above the *Nassar* court made the following observation:

> The case of *Lessard v. Schmidt* [349 F.Supp. 1078 (E.D.Wis.1972)] is cited on behalf of the respondents for the proposition that involuntary commitment must be supported by a showing by the State of imminent danger of harm; this to assure that the individual's "potential for doing harm, to himself or to others, is great enough to justify such a massive curtailment of liberty." "Immediacy" is linked to the requirement of an enhanced standard of proof in the sense that the forecast of events tends to diminish in reliability as the events are projected ahead in time. We may accept, further, that in the degree that the anticipated physical harm is serious—approaches death— some lessening of a requirement of "imminence" seems justified. It is perfected true that the assessments called for all along the line may be difficult; nevertheless there is no escape from making them under our statutory scheme.

At 1291.

Under this analysis the prediction called for in a civil commitment hearing entails a determination of, first, whether certain specific acts are likely to occur and, second, whether they are likely to occur within a *particular time frame*. What is the utility of including such a requirement? Further, can it be applied in a meaningful fashion? Does the statement also suggest that "imminency" is a constitutional requirement which, however, is variable depending on the severity of the anticipated harm?

b. Non-physical Injury to Others

CARRAS v. DISTRICT OF COLUMBIA

Municipal Court of Appeals for the District of Columbia, 1962.
183 A.2d 393.

HOOD, Chief Judge.

Appellant was arrested for an indecent exposure in a local bus terminal. He pleaded guilty to the charge, and on a showing to the court that appellant had twice before been committed to St.

Elizabeths Hospital for similar offenses and that he had been released from that institution only two months before the latest offense, proceedings were had under our sexual psychopath statute. After a hearing he was found to be a sexual psychopath and committed to St. Elizabeths Hospital. On this appeal appellant's chief argument is that the evidence did not sustain the finding that he was a sexual psychopath within the statutory definition, which reads as follows:

> "The term 'sexual psychopath' means a person, not insane, who by a course of repeated misconduct in sexual matters has evidenced such lack of power to control his sexual impulses as to be dangerous to other persons because he is likely to attack or otherwise inflict injury, loss, pain, or other evil on the objects of his desire." Code 1961, § 22–3503(1).

The basis for this argument is the preliminary report of the two psychiatrists who examined appellant and the testimony of one of those psychiatrists at the hearing. In the preliminary report the psychiatrists concluded that appellant was a sexual psychopath within the definition of the statute, but added: "Mr. Carras is not dangerous to others in spite of offensive inclinations. It is our recommendation that he receive ambulatory treatment (psychotherapy) for his condition."

The psychiatrist who testified at the hearing stated that appellant was of sound mind but had a compulsion to expose himself which he could not resist. He further said he did not believe appellant was dangerous in that he would physically attack anyone in any manner. He conceded there could be possible psychological damage to a minor child or sensitive adult should such a person observe an indecent exposure, but he repeated that appellant would not physically harm other persons and would be helped by ambulatory treatment.

The gist of appellant's argument is that in order to come within the statutory definition of sexual psychopath, one must be dangerous to others, and that this means likely to inflict physical injury to another; and that, absent the likelihood of physical danger to others, one cannot be classified under the statute as a sexual psychopath, no matter how disgusting and offensive his conduct may be to others.

It is our opinion that the words of the statute, "likely to attack or otherwise inflict injury, loss, pain, or other evil," are not to be restricted to physical injury alone. In the common understanding of the words, injury includes injury to the feelings, and pain includes mental suffering. The psychiatrists conceded, and without that concession we would hold as a matter of common sense, an exhibition of the sort here described might result in a painful reaction on the part of the observer and might produce a psychological injury. Much, of course, would depend upon the age, sex, sensitivity and experience of the observer, but the statute requires only a likelihood and not a certainty. * * *

We hold that the evidence justified the trial court in finding appellant to be a sexual psychopath and in ordering his commitment.

Affirmed.

Questions and Comments

1. Note that *Carras* did not deal specifically with commitment under a typical involuntary hospitalization statute. Rather it dealt with the commitment of an individual under the sexual psychopath laws of the District of Columbia. Nevertheless, the case is instructive as to the definition given to the term "dangerousness" as used in a non-criminal statute.

2. Six years after *Carras*, the Court of Appeals of the District of Columbia had occasion to review a similar case also brought under the sexual psychopath laws. In *Millard v. Harris*, 406 F.2d 964 (D.C.Cir. 1968), there was substantial evidence that Millard had, on a number of occasions including once when he was on leave from the hospital, exhibited himself in public. The court invalidated the commitment since the government had failed to show that Millard was likely to expose himself to "sensitive adult women and small children." It concluded that in the absence of this type of proof the government had failed to show dangerousness.

3. The implication of both the *Carras* and *Millard* cases is that infliction of psychic injury (*i.e.*, being confronted by an act of exhibitionism) can constitute a "danger to others." This view is the rule in a vast majority of states, as is exemplified by this ruling by a California court: "We have no hesitancy in holding that the threat of psychological trauma is quite as much a 'menace to the health or safety of others' as is probable physical injury." *People v. Stoddard*, 227 Cal.App.2d 40, 42, 38 Cal.Rptr. 407, 408 (1964). Should the probability and magnitude of harm to the exhibitionist resulting from institutionalization be weighed against the probability of harm to his potential victim in considering this question? Should the *Millard* court's assumption that only a minority consisting of "supersensitive women and small children are likely to suffer serious harm from isolated instances of exhibitionism" deserve the weight accorded it in the decision to let Millard go free?

4. Note that in some jurisdictions the infliction of serious emotional injury on others is made explicit grounds for civil commitment. In Iowa the law authorizes the commitment of a mentally ill individual who is "likely to inflict serious emotional injury on members of his or her family or others who lack reasonable opportunity to avoid contact with the afflicted person if the afflicted person is allowed to remain at liberty without treatment." Iowa Code Ann. § 229.1[2][b] (West Supp.1983).

5. Many jurisdictions such as Illinois require a finding that the individual is expected to "inflict serious physical harm * * * upon another" [Ill.Rev.Stat., ch. 91½ § 1–119 (1979)] in place of a "likely to inflict injury or dangerous" standard. Would commitment of a mentally

ill person be possible under any of the following situations in a jurisdiction which follows the Illinois model?

1. Exhibitionistic behavior of the type described in the *Carras* case?

2. A 45-year-old woman suffering from schizophrenia who repeatedly abducts unattended toddlers from shopping centers and takes them to her home. Assume further that the abducted children are always well cared for and that the woman in question is suffering from a delusion that the abducted children are her own.

6. Would committment be possible under the following circumstances in a jurisdiction which authorizes committment by a mentally ill person "who is likely to inflict serious emotional injury on another who lacks reasonable opportunity to avoid contact with the afflicted individual":

1. The shouting of loud hog calls on the street in the daytime and also late at night. *See, In re Perry,* 137 N.J.Eq. 161, 43 A.2d 885 (1945)?

2. Obscene phone calls placed on a random basis?

c. *Injury to Property*

The preceding section has explored the concept of dangerousness in terms of harm to the physical or psychological integrity of other persons. There is also an interest on the part of society in the protection of property. Consequently a number of statutes expressly provide that harm to property when coupled with the other necessary elements is an appropriate basis for commitment. Nevertheless, there always remains the question of how far such statutes should be taken. Should any and all harm to property regardless of value be encompassed by them? Aside from the problem of statutory interpretation, there is the possibility that notions of due process may limit the extent to which harm to property may be made the basis for commitment. The materials in this section address these issues.

SUZUKI v. YUEN

United States Court of Appeals, Ninth Circuit, 1980.
617 F.2d 173.

EUGENE A. WRIGHT, Circuit Judge.

I. DANGER TO PROPERTY

The district court held unconstitutional that part of the statute which allows the state to commit a mentally ill person who is dangerous only to property, but not to himself or others. The court reasoned that the state's interest in protecting property is not sufficiently compelling to warrant the curtailment of liberty brought about by involuntary civil commitment.

The statute allows the state to commit a mentally ill person who is "dangerous to property." The term "dangerous to property" is defined as

> inflicting, attempting or threatening imminently to inflict damage to *any property* in a manner which constitutes a crime, as evidenced by a recent act, attempt or threat.

H.R.S. § 334–1. (Emphasis supplied)

We need not decide whether a state may ever commit one who is dangerous to property. This statute would allow commitment for danger to any property regardless of value or significance. Because it would permit the state to deprive one of his liberty when he threatens harm to *any* property, it is too broad and is unconstitutional.

It is settled that a state may not commit one to a mental hospital unless: his potential for doing harm, to himself or to others, is great enough to justify such a massive curtailment of liberty.

More recently, the [Supreme] Court has stated that:

> The individual should not be asked to share equally with society the risk of error when the possible injury to the individual [from commitment] is significantly greater than any possible harm to the state.

Addington v. Texas, 441 U.S. 418, 99 S.Ct. 1804, 1810, 60 L.Ed.2d 323 (1979).

Under the current Hawaii definition of "danger to property," a person could be committed if he threatened to shoot a trespassing dog. The state's interest in protecting animals must be outweighed by the individual's interest in personal liberty.

In drafting involuntary commitment statutes, states should be cognizant of the "significant deprivation of liberty," *Addington, supra*, 441 U.S. at p. 424, 99 S.Ct. at p. 1809, and of the requirement that the countervailing state interest be equally significant. We express no opinion as to whether protecting property might ever be significant enough to permit involuntary commitment. The protection of just any property is not. This portion of the decision below is affirmed.

Questions and Comments

1. Note that the U.S. Court of Appeals in *Suzuki v. Yuen* expressly declines to rule whether the protection of property might ever be significant enough to constitutionally justify involuntary commitment. Why should injury to property be sufficient to justify incarceration following a criminal conviction but not sufficient for involuntary commitment? Is it the indeterminate nature of civil commitment which justifies the distinction?

2. To the extent that injury to property can be the basis for involuntary civil commitment, what type of injury will suffice? Are there some injuries, such as the writing of graffiti on subway walls, that

are too trivial to justify indefinite commitment? On the other hand, should acts of major vandalism or repeated writing of bad checks suffice? At what point does the property injury meet constitutional standards? How can an appropriate constitutional rule be framed? Or must each decision be an *ad hoc?*

3. In *Overholser v. Russell,* 283 F.2d 195 (D.C.Cir.1960), Russell was hospitalized involuntarily because of his undisputed mental illness and because of his proclivity to write checks without sufficient funds because of his illness. On appeal, the court affirmed, finding that Russell "would be dangerous to society because of his check-writing proclivity." The court explained that "we think [that] danger to the public need not be possible physical violence or a crime of violence. It is enough if there is competent evidence that he may commit any criminal act, for any such act will injure others and will expose the person to arrest, trial and conviction. There is always the additional possible danger—not to be discounted even if remote—that a non-violent criminal act may expose the perpetrator to violent retaliatory acts by the victim of the crime."

Should the possibility of retaliatory violence of the *victim* of some *non*-violent act be a relevant factor in considering the dangerousness *of the prospective patient?* If the retaliation theory is accepted, could it also be applied to a variety of other antisocial behaviors as well as to such quasi-"dangerous" acts as passing bad checks? This issue is considered in greater detail in the materials which follow.

3. Commitment for the Protection of the Afflicted Individual

a. Avoidance of Serious Injury

HILL v. COUNTY BOARD OF MENTAL HEALTH, Etc.

Supreme Court of Nebraska, 1979.
203 Neb. 610, 279 N.W.2d 838.

HASTINGS, Justice.

This is an appeal from an order of the District Court for Douglas County, affirming the order of the county mental health board. That board found that Richard Hill was a mentally ill dangerous person and committed him to the Lincoln Regional Center for treatment.

Upon appeal to this court it is assigned as error that the evidence was insufficient to support the finding that Richard Hill was a mentally ill dangerous person in need of board-ordered treatment.

* * *

The hearing before the mental health board was held on February 14, 1978, and Hill was represented throughout by counsel. Two psychiatrists, Dr. David Goldberg and Dr. Frank Menolascino, testified, the latter having been called by Hill. Without going into a great amount of detail, the histories obtained by the two physicians indicated a 25-year-old male Caucasian who was first committed to the Lincoln Regional Center in 1959 at the age of 6 years. Since 1965 he has been institutionalized, sometimes on leave, until the present time with the exception of approximately 3 to 4 years. Dr. Goldberg diagnosed him as having a personality disorder of an explosive type which he said carried with it the possibility of "dangerousness" as in a true psychotic personality. Dr. Menolascino essentially agreed with the findings and diagnosis of Dr. Goldberg, agreed that Mr. Hill was suffering from a form of mental illness, and gave as his opinion that Hill could not function outside of a structured institutional setting. Both physicians testified that the "personality disorder" of the type from which Mr. Hill is suffering is classified by the Diagnostic and Statistical Manual edited by the American Psychiatric Association as a mental illness, and that this manual is used as a handbook by psychiatrists in determining the existence of mental illnesses.

It appears obvious that the evidence presented by the two medical witnesses clearly and convincingly establishes that Hill is "mentally ill".

In making the findings that Hill presented a substantial risk of serious harm to another or to himself as evidenced by recent acts or threats of violence, the board and the District Court considered several incidents.

On May 24, 1977, while an inmate in the Douglas County jail, Hill was found sitting on his bunk with a rope, braided from torn strips of bedsheets, fastened around his neck. Sergeant Podjenski of the Douglas County sheriff's department testified that the rope was, in his opinion, of sufficient strength to hold a man's body and there was a shelf approximately 7 feet off the floor to which the rope could be tied. Hill stated to the sergeant that he wanted to kill himself.

On October 13, 1977, Sergeant Richard Lubash, also of the Douglas County sheriff's department, after receiving information of an alleged overdose of self-administered medicine, talked to Hill who admitted he had been saving up 200-milligram Thorazine pills and had taken seven of them all at once. There is no direct evidence of the possible effect of such a dosage. However, Dr. Menolascino in his testimony referred to them as tranquilizers and that his regular dosage was 200 milligrams a day. This must be viewed against additional testimony of Dr. Menolascino that in the past, while at the Regional Center, Hill had used staples and other sharp instruments to stick in his arm and pump ink from ink refills into his veins which required periods of hospitalization at Lincoln General Hospital. Although the witness testified that Hill's actions were not deliberately suicidal, but rather an attempt at recognition and change of environment, they would have endangered his life if not discovered in time and met with medical attention.

The point is, of course, that although Hill may not be suicidal in the true sense, he is capable of taking extreme steps which admittedly could endanger his life or health.

Deputy Sheriff Clemens testified that on January 5, 1978, Hill told him that he would gladly blow up his car for $50 and if he, Clemens, tried to stop him, he would blow him up for free. Hill had also told this same deputy on several occasions that it didn't bother him to hurt people.

The violent acts described above occurred within periods of 9 months, 4 months, and 6 weeks, respectively, of the hearing. The question presented by this appeal is whether they were sufficiently "recent" within the meaning of the law. It should be said at the outset that they all happened while Hill was in custody.

Furthermore, the court can not blindly disregard other incidents more remote in time which give some insight into this man's mental state. The incidents with the ink have been previously mentioned. In addition, in 1970, while Hill was working for a used car dealer, he became angry at his employer over a wage dispute and set fire to one of his vehicles. This incident led to a mental commitment.

*   *   *

The final question: Does he present a substantial risk of serious harm to another or himself as manifested by recent acts or threats of violence? Looking at his entire psychiatric background it appears obvious that he presents a potentially substantial risk of harm both to others and to himself. What, then, is a recent act? There is no way to establish a definite time-oriented period such as 1 week or 1 month, or for that matter, 1 year. Each case must be decided on the basis of the surrounding facts and circumstances. If a person commits an act and nothing at all is done for 1 year, we would be hard pressed to define that as a "recent act." On the other hand, if a person kills another and is tried for murder and a year later, after having been held in custody all that time, is finally adjudged innocent by reason of insanity, it would be ridiculous to say that the killing was not a "recent violent act."

*   *   *

The term recent should be given a reasonable construction. We hold that an act or threat is "recent" within the meaning of section 83–1009, R.S.Supp., 1978, if the time interval between it and the hearing of the mental health board is not greater than that which would indicate processing of the complaint was carried on with reasonable diligence under the circumstances existing, having due regard for the rights and welfare of the alleged mentally ill dangerous person and the protection of society in general.

The acts and threats in this case were "recent" and the judgment of the District Court was correct and is affirmed.

Affirmed.

Questions and Comments

1. Was the commitment of Hill based on his danger to self or to others? What was the specific evidence that he constituted a danger to himself? What was the evidence that he might pose a danger to others?

2. Quite aside from the appropriateness of Hill's initial commitment, what criteria should be applied to determine whether he is to be released? Specifically, if subsequent to his commitment Hill does not engage in conduct which is dangerous to himself or others, when does the presumption of dangerousness established by the initial commitment evaporate?

3. Commitment decisions may be based on a prediction that the individual is likely to commit suicide. What is the accuracy of suicide predictions? In this connection consider the following assessments:

* * * How accurate can any subjective, clinical assessment of likelihood of suicide be? At first sight, the accuracy of clinical predictions of suicide reported in the literature seems surprisingly high—much higher, in fact, than passages like the one just quoted might suggest. In one study, for example, 43 Veterans Administration hospital patients diagnosed as suffering from anxiety or depression who committed suicide were matched on the basis of age, sex, race, religion and psychiatric diagnosis with 43 other patients who did not commit suicide. Five raters were asked to predict which of the 86 patients had committed suicide on the basis of case records compiled before the suicides had taken place; they correctly identified 79% of the suicides and 64% of the controls.

Most of the research on suicide prediction, however, has been actuarial, not clinical. * * * [A] few examples will illustrate the present state of the art. Psychiatric diagnosis of mental illness alone provides a very poor basis for distinguishing the suicidal from the non-suicidal.

* * *

Record of a prior suicide attempt allows somewhat better differentiation, but since the suicide rate is still small among survivors of suicide attempts, the improvement is not very substantial. In the one-year follow-up of Philadelphia attempters, 1.44% committed suicide; analysis of the data permitted the identification of a high risk sub-group, but even for this high risk subgroup, the suicide rate was only 6%, * * * The seriousness of a suicide attempt also seems to be unreliable as a predictor of the probability of a later suicide.

* * *

Both clinical and actuarial studies may be quite misleading as an assessment of the usefulness of a prediction instrument. The customary procedure in such studies is to ask predictors to distinguish suicidal from non-suicidal individuals in a population in which the number of suicidal individuals is extremely high. The results appear much less impressive when applied to a population in which the suicide rate is low, as would be the case in actual practice.

* * *

Consider a medium-sized city, in which 1,000 persons survive a suicide attempt during the course of a year. Roughly 1% of these, or 10 persons, can be expected to kill themselves within the next year. Suppose predictions of a future suicide were made through a procedure (whether clinical or actuarial is immaterial) that was 80% efficient, *i.e.*, that correctly identified 80% of the suicidal individuals, while misidentifying only 20% of those who were not suicidal.

What would be the consequences of a decision to commit made on the basis of this prediction? Of the 10 suicidal persons, eight will have been identified correctly. Moreover, of the 794 persons predicted to be non-suicidal, only two actually will commit suicide. Thus far the accuracy seems remarkably high. However, of the 206 persons predicted to be suicidal, only eight actually will commit suicide. This is an accuracy of only 4%. In other words, *for every person correctly deprived of liberty, 24 persons will be deprived of liberty erroneously.* * * * In order that predictions of suicidal behavior be right more often than wrong for a population in which the suicide rate was as low as 1%, it would be necessary for the efficiency of the prediction to be as high as 99%, while if one required that they be right as often as nine times out of 10, an efficiency of approximately 99.9% would be required.

* * *

These figures demonstrate that a method for distinguishing persons who will commit suicide from those who will not with a measure of accuracy sufficiently high to permit its use in psychiatric commitments simply does not exist at present.

* * *

Greenberg, *Involuntary Psychiatric Commitments To Prevent Suicide*, 49 N.Y.U.L.Rev. 227, 259–62 (1974).

4. What is the relationship between mental illness and suicide? Does the presence of mental illness and particularly depressive psychosis increase the potential for suicide? A survey of various studies has led one commentator to conclude:

The popular stereotype linking suicide and mental illness is reflected in the emphasis in psychiatric research on suicide on the determination of suicide rates among patients with various psychiatric diagnoses. Possible links between suicide and depression have been particularly stressed. It has been estimated that anywhere between 10 and 40 percent of all suicides suffer from depression. Yet, as Kobler and Stotland point out, a distinction must be made between the presence of *symptoms* of depression and the presence of a depressive psychosis. As an unusual degree of unhappiness is a symptom of depression, investigators may mistakenly infer the presence of depressive illness from evidence that someone who committed suicide had been unhappy.

* * *

In fact, a study of suicide attempts among depressive patients found the attempt rate to be quite a bit lower among depressed persons who had persistent obsessions than among those whose obsessions were transient or who had no obsessions at all. Apparently, patients with obsessions were kept so preoccupied thinking about their obsessions that they were unable to think about other matters, such as killing themselves. To plan and carry through a suicide attempt may require more ability to think coherently and to act in a realistic, organized fashion than a patient with delusions or obsessions possesses. Among both schizophrenics and depressives it has been observed that suicide tends to occur not in the acute phase (in response to hallucinations, delusions or panic) but rather when the patient is improving and unable to cope with problems.

Greenberg, *Involuntary Psychiatric Commitments to Prevent Suicide*, 49 N.Y.U.L.Rev. 227, 234–36 (1974).

5. Aside from the prediction issues that pertain to the initial commitment, there are questions pertaining to the effectiveness of hospitalization in reducing the risk of subsequent suicide. To what extent, for instance, does treatment reduce the risk of suicide following the patient's release? Unfortunately, there have been few studies of this question and the results of those that have been conducted are inconclusive. *See* Greenberg at 256, 259.

Compulsory hospitalization of suicidal patients has also been defended on the grounds that persons who are suicidal remain so for only limited periods of time. Hospitalization is seen as incapacitating these individuals during critical periods, thereby reducing the overall potential of risk. These clinical impressions, however, have not been validated by any controlled studies. *See* Greenberg.

6. In determining whether an individual is dangerous to himself, is it appropriate to include nonviolent behavior by the afflicted individual which may provoke violence in others? This issue is graphically illustrated in the case of those suffering from Gilles La Tourette syndrome. A characteristic of this disorder is the uncontrollable uttering of obscenities. Suppose that a person suffering from the syndrome has the tendency to walk down streets shouting "fuck, fuck, fuck" in the presence of passerbys. Should the fact that such individual may be subject to violent retaliation by others be a permissible basis for commitment? Is it relevant to the resolution of this question that the treatment of Gilles La Tourette syndrome either in or out of hospitals has not been particularly effective?

b. Avoidance of Harm Due to Self-neglect

IN RE SCIARA

Appellate Court of Illinois, First District, Fifth Division, 1974.
21 Ill.App.3d 889, 316 N.E.2d 153.

SULLIVAN, Presiding Justice:

This appeal arises from an order finding respondent in need of mental treatment and placing her in the care and custody of her husband for one year, with authority to commit her to the Chicago Lake Shore Hospital.

This matter began with the filing of a petition by respondent's husband for her hospitalization, which was supported by Certificates of Need for Hospitalization by two doctors. At the hearing on the petition, the Public Defender, appointed to represent respondent, informed the court, "We are ready for hearing, Your Honor. Jury is waived." Thereupon, a psychiatrist, Dr. Dushkin, testified he had examined respondent several times in the past and found "she presents all of the symptoms of a severe schizophrenic, paranoid type." He also testified she was "psychotic, delusional, hallucinatory, autistic, and unpredictable in her ability to care for herself or her children." She had delusions that "if she were to be touched by individuals she would dissolve into nothing or die and that all meat is representative of death, not to be eaten, not only by herself or by her children." He stated her hallucinations were manifested by the fact that before answering questions "she would look to the side and always to the same area and then either answer or refuse to answer as if she was being warned." When he inquired whether she was being warned not to answer, she "smiled a little bit in a knowingly fashion." The doctor stated she demonstrated her autism (thinking based on wishes rather than on reality) by "her feeling that nothing actually that was happening really meant anything, that she should be able to be permitted to leave the hospital and go into a full life, that if her husband were to come back everything would be nice and happy."

According to the witness, her unpredictability with reference to the care of herself and her children was indicated by her inability to handle her affairs at home or to take care of herself in the hospital. He admitted that his opinion concerning her inability to care for her children was based on a report by her pediatrician, but that his opinion that she could not care for herself was based on his own observation of her. He also admitted that she was not a violent person and was not a threat to others, other than to her child and then only because of her inability to care for said child. He admitted also that his opinion that she could not take care of her affairs at home was based on the fact that others described her as "not too good of a housekeeper", and on her pediatrician's report that "her infant was not doing or thriving as well as he should."

*   *   *

The husband of respondent testified they had been separated for six months and he petitioned for her hospitalization because "she seemed to me at that time to be in a deep need of help." He based this belief on the fact that their 18 month old boy had his chin split open and a burn on his leg, had recently lost a little over a pound in weight and was being fed bread, rice and beans instead of a "normal balanced diet" and was being neglected by respondent "but not like she wanted to hurt him or anything like that" but that "nine times out of ten he'd be naked on the floor." He stated that the older child, six years of age, was allowed to play outside as late as 10:00 P.M. and that respondent was not giving milk to her children. He also stated that respondent told him she heard voices which told her there was rat poison on the floor and that she said on one occasion, "We are turning into cannibals and we are going to start eating one another" and on another occasion told him that meat would kill him. He testified that he worried about her when she was on the street because "she gets so wrapped up into these things that she doesn't know what she is doing and doesn't know what street she is on." He stated that before her marriage she tried to slit her wrists and that she had been in hospitals on other occasions for mental problems, the last time being nine months earlier for a few weeks. He stated her condition had "worsened" in the last six months and that he was presently living with the children and that he was giving respondent $15.00 a week for clothing and groceries and that he also "paid all the bills of every nature." He admitted respondent never threatened to harm him.

Respondent testified she had not been helped during her previous hospitalization and during her current three week stay at Lake Shore Hospital she was being tormented. She does not eat meat and "they (the staff) insist that I have meat." The staff seemed "a little bit demented."

  * * * She did not agree with Dr. Dushkin that she should go to the hospital because "I feel that they are infringing too much on my rights, my mind. I have a right to—I am not a dangerous person. I wanted to start painting or—I sketch and—I feel that—like they might destroy my mind with insulin shock treatments." She further stated she could take care of herself and needed work, suggesting she could be a housekeeper, babysitter or a waitress at night. When asked if she heard "any other voices of persons or things that are not present in the room at the time," she responded, "I did on one occasion close to a year ago." She stated her only other hallucinatory experience since then was to see a ghost once in a while. * * * We have examined the record here in the light of that standard, and initially we note that Section 1–11 of the Mental Health Code (Ill.Rev. Stat.1971, ch. 91½, par. 1–11) requires that the petitioner first establish that respondent was a person afflicted with mental illness. * * *

After establishing respondent was a person afflicted with mental illness, petitioner then was required to prove that, as a result of such mental illness (a) she was reasonably expected, at the time the determination was being made or within a reasonable time thereafter, to intentionally or unintentionally physically injure herself or other persons; or (b) she was unable to care for herself so as to guard herself from physical injury or to provide for her own physical needs.

It appears to us that the evidence clearly and convincingly established that respondent was afflicted with mental illness. Dr. Dushkin testified respondent "presents all of the symptoms of a severe schizophrenic, paranoid type", and that "she is psychotic, delusional, hallucinatory, autistic and unpredictable in her ability to care for herself or her children." Both he and Dr. Maltz, in their Certificates of Need for Hospitalization, gave opinions that respondent was in need of mental treatment.

Concerning the requirement that petitioner establish respondent was reasonably expected to intentionally or unintentionally physically injure herself or others, we are of the opinion that the only testimony having relation thereto is clearly to the contrary.

We turn now to the remaining question of whether or not there was clear and convincing proof of the requirement of the Code that, as a result of her mental illness, she was unable to care for herself so as to guard herself from physical injury or to provide for her own personal needs. The only testimony appearing in the record is in the testimony of Dr. Dushkin and respondent's husband. The doctor testified "she is unpredictable in her ability to care for herself—", and he stated this opinion was based upon his observation of her at the hospital. Her husband testified, "I am a little afraid for her when she is on the street because she gets really so wrapped up into these things that she doesn't know what she is doing. She will be walking down the street and she doesn't know what street she is on." In addition, he testified that before they were married she had slit her wrists. We note that Dr. Dushkin was not asked and did not provide any facts which were the basis of his statement of unpredictability. Neither was any inquiry made to him as to the possible significance of respondent's wrist slitting experience to her mental condition as he described it at the hearing. In any event, Dr. Dushkin gave no testimony indicating that respondent was unable to care for herself so as to guard herself from physical injury or that she was not able to attend to her own physical needs. The testimony of respondent's husband that sometimes "she doesn't know what street she is on" falls far short of the proof required to establish that she is unable to guard herself from physical injury. Furthermore, we have found no evidence in the record concerning any inability on her part to provide for her own physical needs.

For the reasons stated, it is our opinion that petitioner failed to clearly and convincingly establish that respondent was a person in need of mental treatment.

*   *   *

The order finding respondent to be a person in need of mental care is reversed.

Reversed.

BARRETT and DRUCKER, JJ., concur.

Questions and Comments

1. Some courts have applied standards similar to that which governed the disposition of *In re Sciara* in a more expansive fashion. For instance, in *In re Medlin*, 59 N.C.App. 33, 295 S.E.2d 604 (1982) the appellate court affirmed the order of commitment on the following record:

> * * * [A]t the time of the commitment hearing the respondent had been unemployed for almost one year, having left her job because she felt she was being harassed by a married man at work. There was no evidence presented that she had thereafter attempted to seek other employment. The respondent had been living in her car for two weeks prior to the hearing and it appeared that the only sustenance which respondent received was that which her daughter brought to the car for her. The record also revealed the fear of respondent's daughter that respondent would die of carbon monoxide poisoning if she were to continue to live in her car through the rest of the winter months.

At 606.

2. The civil commitment laws of many states expressly authorize commitment where the harm to the individual is a result of self-neglect. Representative provisions include the following:

New York: "in need of involuntary care and treatment" means that a person has a mental illness for which care and treatment as a patient in a hospital is essential to such person's welfare and whose judgment is so impaired that he is unable to understand the need for such treatment and care. N.Y. Mental Hygiene Law. Art. 9, § 9.01 (Consol 1979).

Illinois: "Person subject to involuntary admission" means * * * A person who is mentally ill and who because of his illness is unable to provide for his basic physical needs so as to guard himself from serious harm. Ill.Rev.Stat. ch. 1, § 1–119 (Supp.1979).

Michigan: A "person requiring treatment" means: A person who is mentally ill, and who as a result of that mental illness is unable to attend to those of his basic physical needs such as food, clothing, or shelter that must be attended to in order for him to avoid serious harm in the near future, and who has demonstrated that inability by failing to attend to those basic physical needs. * * * Mich.Comp. Laws Ann. § 330.1401 (1980).

3. A disproportionate number of those who are committed on the grounds that they cannot provide for their own physical needs are also incapacitated to a greater or lesser extent in their ability to consent to express opposition to hospitalization. Where the disability is substantial, they may be judicially declared incompetent and institutionalized pursuant to the special rules which apply to this class. [The procedures involving the hospitalization of incompetent persons are treated in greater detail in Chapter Seven]. The disability may, however, be less than that required for legal incompetency. At the same time, the

individual may lack the capacity to consent to admission as a voluntary patient. Those falling in this gray area are sometimes committed as "nonprotesting" patients. Even opponents of involuntary commitment seem to permit the forced hospitalization of "nonprotesting" individuals. *See* Morse, *A Preference for Liberty: The Case Against Involuntary Commitment of the Mentally Disordered,* 70 Cal.L.R. 54, 85 n. 137 (1982).

4. In *O'Connor v. Donaldson,* considered previously, the Court's opinion includes the following paragraph:

> May the State confine the mentally ill merely to ensure them a living standard superior to that they enjoy in the private community? That the State has a proper interest in providing care and assistance to the unfortunate goes without saying. But the mere presence of mental illness does not disqualify a person from preferring his home to the comforts of an institution.

422 U.S. 563, 575, 95 S.Ct. 2486, 2493, 45 L.Ed.2d 396 (1975). At what point, involving what kinds of predicted injuries to the individual resulting from neglect, may the state commit an individual? Where is the dividing line between raising the living standards of an individual and protecting that individual from physical deterioration which would result from a severe case of malnutrition? In other words, how much of a health hazard must be found before the state is free to intervene?

5. The mental health laws of most states permit, under appropriate circumstances, the involuntary institutionalization of non-dangerous but chronically mentally ill individuals. Institutionalization can be effected by one of two mechanisms. One involves a judicial procedure whereby the individual is declared incompetent. This is followed by the appointment of a guardian who may then seek court-authorized institutionalization by demonstrating that institutional care is in his ward's best interest. These procedures are described in greater detail in Chapter Seven. In the absence of an adjudication of incompetence, many commitment statutes authorize commitment upon a showing that the individual is unable to meet his basic physical needs and would suffer serious injury in the absence of hospitalization. California, for instance, permits the commitment of a person who is "gravely disabled," defined as one who "as a result of a mental disorder, is unable to provide for his basic personal needs for food, clothing, or shelter." West's Ann.Cal.Welf. & Inst.Code §§ 5150, 5008(h) (1984).

While the non-dangerous mentally ill once constituted a significant percentage of the institutionalized population, the current policy of deinstitutionalization has facilitated the massive discharge of these individuals. For many of these former mental patients, as pointed out by one critic of deinstitutionalization, discharge "has meant that they have been left to rot and decay, physically and otherwise, in broken down welfare hotels or in what are termed, with Orwellian euphemism, "personal-care" nursing homes. For thousands of younger psychotics discharged into the streets, it has meant a nightmare existence in the blighted centers of our cities, amidst neighborhoods crowded with prostitutes, ex-felons, addicts, alcoholics, and the other human rejects now repressively tolerated by our society.   Here they eke out a precarious existence, supported by welfare checks they may not even know how to cash." Andrew Scull, *Decarceration* (Englewood Cliffs, N.J.: Prentice-Hall, Inc., 1977), pp. 1–2.

See also note 3 at p. 383.

Deinstitutionalization has not only resulted in the wholesale discharge of mental patients but has also made it increasingly difficult for the non-dangerous mentally ill to be *admitted* into institutions, either voluntarily or involuntarily.   Thus, some of the past concerns of civil liberterians, whose objection to civil commitment stemmed from its intrusion on personal freedom, have been alleviated by the matrix of pressures which has brought about these developments.   The distressing alternatives to institutionalization, however, are giving rise to growing public concern over the plight of the chronically mentally ill.   With time this may bring about a reallocation of resources in order to establish appropriate care and treatment facilities for these individuals.   To facilitate such an effort, the legal system must address a number of outstanding issues, including:

> (a) What degrees of disability, involving what kinds of attendant risks, should be the basis for the institutionalization of the non-dangerous mentally ill?

> (b) How much deference should be given to the expressed intent of an individual confronting commitment who has not been adjudicated legally incompetent but who suffers some impairment of his ability to assess his situation?   Do current civil commitment laws make adequate provisions for a determination of competency to make a treatment or hospitalization decision?

> (c) What is the minimum level of treatment that must be provided to the non-dangerous chronically mentally ill in an institution?   Can institutionalization be justified by the providing of basic care and activity programs designed to enhance the functioning of the individual rather than treatment in the medical sense?

c. For the Purpose of Treatment

Whether the state may commit an individual who is not dangerous to himself or others for the sole purpose of providing that individual with treatment remains unresolved.   A minority of states explicitly authorize commitment for this specific purpose, and others have it as an unarticulated basis for commitment.

Some lower courts have expressed doubt about whether commitment for the purpose of treatment is constitutionally permissible. For instance in *Doremus v. Farrell*, 407 F.Supp. 509, 514 (N.D.Neb. 1975), the court noted:

> The "State may [not] lawfully confine an individual thought to need treatment and justify that deprivation of liberty solely by providing treatment.   Our concepts of due process would not tolerate such a 'trade-off.' " *O'Connor v. Donaldson*, 422 U.S. at 589, 95

S.Ct. at 2500, Chief Justice Burger concurring. Considering the fundamental rights involved in civil commitment, the *parens patriae* power must require a compelling interest of the state to justify the deprivation of liberty. In the mental health field, where diagnosis and treatment are uncertain, the need for treatment without some degree of imminent harm to the person or dangerousness to society is not a compelling justification.

* * *

To permit involuntary commitment upon a finding of "mental illness" and the need for treatment alone would be tantamount to condoning the State's commitment of persons deemed socially undesirable for the purpose of indoctrination or conforming the individual's beliefs to the beliefs of the State.

Notwithstanding the dictum found in some lower court opinions, the constitutionality of commitment for the sole purpose of treatment has not been authoritatively resolved. In fact, in *O'Connor v. Donaldson*, the court expressly refused to rule on the issue. In the words of Mr. Justice Stewart, "We need not decide whether, when, or by what procedures, a mentally ill person will be confined by the state on any of the grounds which, under contemporary statutes, are generally advanced to justify involuntary confinement of such a person—to prevent injury to the public, to insure his own survival or safety, *or to alleviate or cure his illness*" (emphasis added) at 573.

Questions and Comments

1. A Texas statute (Senate Bill 435, An act revising the Mental Health Code in Texas, effective September 1, 1983) that permits commitment of a person who "will, if not treated, continue to suffer severe and abnormal mental, emotional, or physical distress and will continue to experience deterioration of his ability to function independently and is unable to make a rational and informed decision as to whether or not to submit to treatment" is representative of state laws that authorize commitment for the sole purpose of treatment. It is noteworthy that the Texas language was taken from the recently publicized APA Model Law on Civil Commitment. *See Stromberg* and *Stone: A model state law on civil commitment of the mentally ill.* 20 Harv.J. on Legis. 275, 302–03 (1983).

2. Aside from the broader constitutional question other issues arise where commitment has as its sole purpose treatment. First, one might ask whether there is any difference between the treatment of the individual who suffers from a static rather than a deteriorating mental disorder. One may question whether the state has any substantial interest in imposing treatment merely to make an individual happier or less anxious. But, where the disease is progressive and treatment is necessary to arrest further deterioration, the state's interest may be somewhat greater.

3. Generally society allows an individual to elect or reject *medical* treatment. In psychiatric hospitalization, where the purpose behind

commitment is to protect the individual from self-inflicted harm, society disregards his individual preferences as to treatment. Presumably, this is because a mentally ill individual is conclusively deemed to lack the ability to make an informed and rational choice. Is the underlying assumption of these laws that mentally ill individuals lack the capacity to make a rational choice grounded on empirical fact? It is an assumption that has been questioned by some lower federal courts. In *Colyar v. Third Judicial District*, 469 F.Supp. 424 (D.Utah 1979) the court held:

> Given that in order to be involuntarily committed a mentally-ill person must be shown to be a danger to himself or others, and that such danger may include the incapacity to provide the basic necessities of life, the court feels constrained to hold that the state must also show that the individual is incapable of making a rational choice regarding the acceptance of care or treatment. As stated, a finding of mental illness does not necessarily mean that an individual is deprived of all of his capacity to make rational decisions.

> * * * [T]he involuntary commitment of the mentally ill under the parens patriae power must reflect the following considerations: The committing authority must find, as a threshold requirement, that the proposed patient is incapable of making a rational treatment decision. The purpose of this requirement is to require the committing court to "distinguish between those persons whose decisions to refuse treatment must be accepted as final from those whose choices may be validly overridden through parens patriae commitment."

at pp. 433–34.

See also *Lynch v. Baxley*, 386 F.Supp. 378, 391 (M.D.Ala.1974).

To what extent does the rationale of the *Colyar* case, which focuses on the individual's capacity to make a rational choice, apply where commitment is for the protection of others? Should a similar finding be required when commitment is based on dangerousness to others? Recall that the APA Model Law would in both the police power and *parens patriae* commitment require a finding that the individual lacks capacity to make an informed decision concerning hospitalization and treatment. Stromberg & Stone, *A Model State Law on Civil Commitment of the Mentally Ill*, 20 Harv.J. on Legis. 275–296 (1983). What justification is there for this requirement when the individual is committed because he poses a risk of physical injury to others? The APA Model Law provides no guidance on what disposition should be made where the dangerous mentally ill person does not lack capacity to make an informed decision. Is the underlying theory behind the APA proposal abolition of the insanity defense and disposition through the criminal process? But, even if this is so, why should the capacity of the individual to make a choice be relevant to the question of commitment under the police power?

4. What weight should be given to expressions of intent during periods of lucidity? In this connection, distinguish between these hypothetical problems excerpted from Livermore, Malmquist and Meehl, *On the Justifications for Civil Commitment*, 117 U.Pa.L.Rev. 75, 94 (1968):

(a) A distinguished law school professor, known for a series of brilliant articles, is suffering from an involutional depression. His scholarship has dried up, and, while he is still able to teach, the spark is gone and his classes have become extremely depressing. There is a chance, though probably not more than twenty-five per cent, that he will commit suicide. He has been told that he would recover his old elan if he were subjected to a series of electro-shock treatments but this he has refused to do. In fact, in years past when he was teaching a course in law and psychiatry, he stated that if he ever became depressed he wanted it known that before the onset of depression he explicitly rejected such treatment.

(b) A woman suffers from a severe psychotic depression resulting in an ability to do little more than weep. Again shock treatment is recommended with a reasonable prospect of a rapid recovery. The woman rejects the suggestion saying that nothing can make her a worthy member of society. She is, she claims, beyond help or salvation.

4. Limitations on the Power to Commit: The Least Restrictive Alternative Doctrine

a. Genesis of the Least Restrictive Alternative Doctrine

LAKE v. CAMERON

United States Court of Appeals, District of Columbia Circuit, 1966.

364 F.2d 657.

BAZELON, Chief Judge: *you put person in setting which is least restrictive*

Appellant is confined in Saint Elizabeths Hospital as an insane person and appeals from denial of release in habeas corpus. On September 29, 1962, when she was sixty years old, a policeman found her wandering about and took her to the D.C. General Hospital. On October 11, 1962, she filed in the District Court a petition for a writ of habeas corpus. The court transferred her to St. Elizabeths Hospital for observation in connection with pending commitment proceedings, allowed her to amend her petition by naming the Superintendent of Saint Elizabeths as defendant, and on November 2, 1962, dismissed her petition without holding a hearing or requiring a return.

After she filed her appeal from denial of habeas corpus, she was adjudged "of unsound mind" and committed to Saint Elizabeths. At the commitment hearing two psychiatrists testified that she was mentally ill and one of them that she was suffering from a "chronic brain syndrome" associated with aging and "demonstrated very frequently difficulty with her memory * * *. Occasionally, she was unable to tell me where she was or what the date was." Both psychiatrists testified to the effect that she could not care for herself adequately. She did not take a timely appeal from the commitment order. We heard her appeal from the summary dismissal of her petition for habeas corpus and remanded the case to the District Court with directions to require a return and hold a hearing.

At the hearing on remand, the sole psychiatric witness testified that appellant was suffering from a senile brain disease, "chronic brain syndrome, with arteriosclerosis with reaction." The psychiatrist said she was not dangerous to others and would not intentionally harm herself, but was prone to "wandering away and being out exposed at night or any time that she is out." This witness also related that on one occasion she wandered away from the Hospital, was missing for about thirty-two hours, and was brought back after midnight by a police officer who found her wandering in the streets. She had suffered a minor injury which she attributed to being chased by boys. She thought she had been away only a few hours and could not tell where she had been. The psychiatrist also testified that she was "confused and agitated" when first admitted to the Hospital but became "comfortable" after "treatment and medication."

At both the commitment hearing and the habeas corpus hearing on remand, appellant testified that she felt able to be at liberty. At the habeas corpus hearing her husband, who had recently reappeared after a long absence, and her sister said they were eager for her release and would try to provide a home for her. The District Court found that she "is suffering from a mental illness with the diagnosis of chronic brain syndrome associated with cerebral arteriosclerosis"; that she "is in need of care and supervision, and that there is no member of the family able to give the petitioner the necessary care and supervision; and that the family is without sufficient funds to employ a competent person to do so"; that she "is a danger to herself in that she has a tendency to wander about the streets, and is not competent to care for herself." The District Court again denied relief in habeas corpus, but noted appellant's right "to make further application in the event that the patient is in a position to show that there would be some facilities available for her provision." The court thus recognized that she might be entitled to release from Saint Elizabeths if other facilities were available, but required her to carry the burden of showing their availability.

Appellant contends in written and oral argument that remand to the District Court is required for a consideration of suitable alternatives to confinement in Saint Elizabeths Hospital in light of the new District of Columbia Hospitalization of the Mentally Ill Act, which came into effect after the hearing in the District Court. Indeed, her counsel appointed by this court, who had interviewed appellant, made clear in answer to a question from the bench on oral argument that although appellant's formal pro se pleading requests outright release, her real complaint is total confinement in a mental institution; that she would rather be in another institution or hospital, if available, or at home, even though under some form of restraint.

* * *

We are not called upon to consider what action we would have taken in the absence of the new Act, because we think the interest of justice and furtherance of the congressional objective require the application to the pending proceeding of the principles adopted in that Act. It provides that if the court or jury finds that a "person is mentally ill and, because of that illness, is likely to injure himself or other persons if allowed to remain at liberty, the court may order his hospitalization for an indeterminate period, or order any other alternative course of treatment which the court believes will be in the best interests of the person or of the public." D.C.Code § 21–545(b) (Supp. V, 1966). This confirms the view of the Department of Health, Education and Welfare that "the entire spectrum of services should be made available, including outpatient treatment, foster care, halfway houses, day hospitals, nursing homes, etc." The alternative course of treatment or care should be fashioned as the interests of the person and of the public require in the particular case. ⁋Deprivations of liberty solely because of dangers to the ill persons themselves should not go beyond what is necessary for their protection.

The court's duty to explore alternatives in such a case as this is related also to the obligation of the state to bear the burden of exploration of possible alternatives an indigent cannot bear. This appellant, as appears from the record, would not be confined in Saint Elizabeths if her family were able to care for her or pay for the care she needs. Though she cannot be given such care as only the wealthy can afford, an earnest effort should be made to review and exhaust available resources of the community in order to provide care reasonably suited to her needs.

At the habeas corpus hearing, the psychiatrist testified that appellant did not need "constant medical supervision," but only "attention"; that the psychiatrist would have no objection if appellant "were in a nursing home, or a place where there would be supervision." At the commitment hearing one psychiatrist testified that "Mrs. Lake needs care, whether it be in the hospital or out of the hospital," and did not specify what, if any, *psychiatric* care she needs. The second psychiatrist testified that she "needs close watching. She could wander off. She could get hurt and she certainly needs someone to see that her body is adequately cared for * * *. [She] needs care and kindness * * *." It does not appear from this testimony that appellant's illness required the complete deprivation of liberty that results from commitment to Saint Elizabeths as a person of "unsound mind."

* * *

We remand the case to the District Court for an inquiry into "other alternative courses of treatment." The court may consider, *e.g.*, whether the appellant and the public would be sufficiently protected if she were required to carry an identification card on her person so that the police or others could take her home if she should wander, or whether she should be required to accept public health nursing care, community mental health and day care services, foster care, home health aide services, or whether available welfare payments might finance adequate private care. Every effort should be made to find a course of treatment which appellant might be willing to accept.

* * *

We express no opinion on questions that would arise if on remand the court should find no available alternative to confinement in Saint Elizabeths.

* * *

Remanded for further proceedings in accordance with this opinion.

[The concurring opinion of J. Skelly Wright is omitted.]

BURGER, Circuit Judge, with whom DANAHER and TAMM, Circuit Judges, join (dissenting).

We disagree with remanding the case to require the District Court to carry out an investigation of alternatives for which Appellant has never indicated any desire. The only issue before us is the legality of Mrs. Lake's confinement in Saint Elizabeths Hospital and the only relief she herself has requested is immediate unconditional release. The majority does not intimate that Appellant's present confinement as a patient at Saint Elizabeths Hospital is illegal, or that there is anything wrong with it except that she does not like it and wishes to get out of any confinement. Nevertheless, this Court now orders the District Court to perform functions normally reserved to social agencies by commanding search for a judicially approved course of treatment or custodial care for this mentally ill person who is plainly unable to care for herself. Neither this Court nor the District Court is equipped to carry out the broad geriatric inquiry proposed or to resolve the social and economic issues involved.

* * *

Although proceedings for commitment of mentally ill persons are not strictly adversary, a United States court in our legal system is not set up to initiate inquiries and direct studies of social welfare facilities or other social problems. This Court exists to decide questions put before it by parties to litigation on the basis of issues raised by them in pleadings and facts adduced by those parties. D.C. CODE § 21–545 (Supp.1966) does not transmute the United States District Court for the District of Columbia into an administrative agency for proceedings involving the mentally ill. This statute provides only that "the court may order [a mentally ill person's] * * * hospitalization for an indeterminate period, or order any other alternative course of treatment which *the court believes* will be in the best interests of the person or of the public." (Emphasis added.) All this section does, or was intended to do, is authorize the court to order alternative courses of treatment, provided the evidence presented to it leads it to believe that some alternative is preferable to confinement in Saint Elizabeths Hospital. This appellant seeks only her release, not a transfer. We cannot find anything in this statute which even vaguely hints at a requirement that the court conduct broad inquiries into possible treatment facilities. In the absence of such language, we must interpret the statute as not enlarging the role of the court beyond its normal judicial function of deciding issues presented by the parties on the basis of such facts as the parties present.

* * *

What the majority has done here is first rewrite Mrs. Lake's petition for her, to demand something which she has never requested, then it has proceeded to remand, ordering the District Court to consider this new "petition" written by this court.

* * *

To show that Appellant really does object to the *place* of her confinement, the majority is forced to rely on the response of her appointed counsel to a question from the bench at oral argument. Counsel said that Appellant's major objection was that she was confined in a mental institution, and he intimated that possibly she might not be so unhappy with confinement in some other institution. This indicates that a large part of what troubles both Appellant and the majority is the fact that she is being confined in a *mental* institution and not some type of home for the aged which would provide essentially the same care but would not have attached to it the "onus" of being associated with a mental institution.

If Appellant were to receive precisely the same care she is presently receiving in the geriatrics ward of St. Elizabeths at an institution elsewhere with a name like Columbia Rest Haven, it does not appear that there would be much disagreement over the propriety of her confinement. However, a person's freedom is no less arrested, nor is the effect on him significantly different, if he is confined in a rest home with a euphemistic name rather than at St. Elizabeths Hospital.

* * *

We can all agree in principle that a series of graded institutions with various kinds of homes for the aged and infirm would be a happier solution to the problem than confining harmless senile ladies in St. Elizabeths Hospital with approximately 8000 patients, maintained at a great public expense. But it would be a piece of unmitigated folly to turn this appellant loose on the streets with or without an identity tag; and I am sure for my part that no District Judge will order such a solution. This city is hardly a safe place for able-bodied men, to say nothing of an infirm, senile, and disoriented woman to wander about with no protection except an identity tag advising police where to take her. The record shows that in her past wanderings she has been molested, and should she be allowed to wander again all of her problems might well be rendered moot either by natural causes or violence.   *   *   *

Questions and Comments

1. Note that in *Lake* the court found the requirement that there be an exploration for the least restrictive alternative grounded in the District of Columbia *statute* rather than the U.S. Constitution. Since *Lake* numerous states have by legislation imposed a similar requirement, which compels committing courts to consider less restrictive alternatives. *See*, for instance, Ala.Code § 22–52–10(a)(5) (1982 Supp.); Va.Code §§ 37.1–84.1(6) (1976) (c); West's Wash.Rev.Code Ann. 71.05.320(1) (1983); Mich.Comp.Laws § 330.1468(2)(c) (West Supp.1982); Ariz.Rev. Stat.Ann. § 36–540 (West Supp.1983); Ill.Rev.Stat. Ch. 91½, § 3–812 (1979).

2. Consider the history of Ms. Lake following the decision in *Lake v. Cameron, supra:*

> "Catherine Lake, the senile petitioner in the District of Columbia case establishing the obligation of courts there to examine less restrictive alternatives, spent the remaining five years of her life in a public mental hospital. In the committing judge's view, a nursing home or similar residential facility providing some substantial measure of supervision, but not totally preventing access to the outside world, would have been sufficient. Such facilities—even ones of the sort the Nader study exposed—were simply unavailable in the District of Columbia for most aged people as poor as Ms. Lake ∗   ∗   ∗ "

Chambers, *Alternatives to Civil Commitment of the Mentally Ill: Practical Guides and Constitutional Imperatives,* 70 Mich.L.Rev. 1107, 1189 (1972). The decision of the District Court finding that no suitable alternative existed is reported in 267 F.Supp. 155 (D.D.C.1967).

3. As made clear by numerous reports and commentaries deinstitutionalization has reduced the number of persons in institutions from 500,000 in the mid-1950s to approximately 190,000 twenty years later. One study has summarized the dimensions of this phenomenon as follows:

> Recent research has demonstrated that "of the state hospital patients admitted with 'major' psychiatric disorders (organic brain syndrome, schizophrenia, other neuroses [sic], and mental retardation) a surprisingly large percentage (about 60%) were, during the period 1969–73, either referred to outpatient clinics or discontinued without any referral. Another 10 percent were referred to nursing homes or homes for the aged."

> In some cases, the break with the past has been dramatically sudden, with transfers and ward closures sometimes ordered literally overnight. In Wisconsin, for example, new legislation authorizing an 80 percent reduction of psychiatric beds in the 35 county hospitals produced a 77 percent decline in inpatient population during fiscal year 1974. And in New York State, a 1968 memorandum from the Deputy Commissioner of Mental Hygiene ordering the implementa-

tion of a more selective admissions policy was followed by a fall in the state hospital cases from 78,020 in 1968 to 47,739 in 1971, and to 34,000 by 1973, a decline of some 64 percent in five years. In a few states, the cutback in patient population is now almost complete: Thus in California the inpatient census fell from 50,000 in 1955 to 22,000 by 1967, and to only 7,000 by 1973. Announcing that so far as the state government was concerned, "twenty-four hour hospitalization is the least acceptable for of treatment. Locally provided outpatient care is the most acceptable * * *," the Reagan administration unveiled a plan to phase out the remaining state hospitals before the end of the decade. And on a national basis, recent estimates have suggested that the population of state hospitals will be no more than 100,000 by 1980, or less than a fifth of what it was in 1955.

Andrew T. Scull, *Decarceration* (Englewood Cliffs, N.J.: Prentice-Hall, Inc., 1977), pp. 68–69.

Significantly, deinstitutionalization has not been accompanied by a parallel development of community mental health facilities. As a result, "thousands of former mental patients [are] living in squalid flop houses or wandering about the nations skidrows." Sheppard, "Community Mental Health Care Getting Second Thoughts," *New York Times*, July 23, 1979, p. A–13. Dramatic reduction in the numbers of persons kept in institutional care has meant that there has been a forced eviction in many states of all except those who are either seriously dangerous or so incapacitated that they can survive only in a mental hospital. *See Revised Rules Reduce Involuntary Confinement of Involuntary Patients, Wall Street Journal*, January 24, 1978, p. 1, col. 1. As a result, today it is unlikely that persons like Mrs. Lake would even be accepted for care in a state institution.

4. *Lake v. Cameron* merely requires a search for alternatives to total institutional care. If such alternatives do not exist, as proved to be the case in *Lake v. Cameron*, the court's duty is discharged. The utility of the principle is, therefore, limited unless courts themselves are at liberty to order the creation of alternate opportunities. *See* Reisner, *Psychiatric Hospitalization and the Constitution: Some Observations on Emerging Trends*, 1973 U. of I Law Forum 9, 11 (1973). There is little basis, moreover, for believing that courts have any authority in the absence of a legislative mandate to order the creation of community facilities. Decisions of the Supreme Court make it clear that the state does not have a constitutional obligation to provide basic services such as food, shelter, clothing, and schooling. *See, e.g., San Antonio Independent School District v. Rodriguez*, 411 U.S. 1, 93 S.Ct. 1278, 36 L.Ed.2d 16 (1973); *Dandridge v. Williams*, 397 U.S. 471, 90 S.Ct. 1153, 25 L.Ed. 2d 491 (1970); *Harris v. McCrae*, 448 U.S. 297, 100 S.Ct. 2671, 65 L.Ed.2d 784 (1980).

Judicial enforcement of rights is thus limited to ensuring that where the state has made specific benefits or entitlements available, they must be allocated in a rational and non-discriminatory manner. There is, thus, very little reason to believe that courts have any power to order the creation of community facilities in the absence of an affirmative decision by the state.

b. Constitutional Dimensions of the Least Restrictive Alternative Doctrine

In *Lake v. Cameron* the court of appeals drew on a statute to find a duty on the part of committing courts to search for the least restrictive alternative. In many jurisdictions, however, the legislature has neither expressed nor implied such a duty. As a result, one basis for contesting commitment in these jurisdictions has been the assertion that the least restrictive alternative doctrine is a constitutional requirement.

The view that the least restrictive alternative doctrine is of constitutional dimension and applicable in the absence of a state statute has been espoused by several lower federal courts. For instance, the opinion of the court in *Lessard v. Smith*, 349 F.Supp. 1078 (E.D.Wis.1972), vacated, 414 U.S. 473, 94 S.Ct. 713, 38 L.Ed.2d 661 (1974), included the following passage:

> Even if the standard for an adjudication of mental illness and potential dangerousness are satisfied, a court should order full-time involuntary hospitalization only as a last resort. A basic concept in American justice is the principle that "even though the governmental purpose be legitimate and substantial, that purpose cannot be pursued by means that broadly stifle fundamental personal liberties when the end can be more narrowly achieved. The breadth of legislative abridgment must be viewed in the light of less drastic means for achieving the same basic purpose." Shelton v. Tucker, 364 U.S. 479, 488, 81 S.Ct. 247, 252, 5 L.Ed.2d 231 (1960).

> * * * Perhaps the most basic and fundamental right is the right to be free from unwanted restraint. It seems clear, then, that persons suffering from the condition of being mentally ill, but who are not alleged to have committed any crime, cannot be totally deprived of their liberty if there are less drastic means for achieving the same basic goal. (at 1096.)

[The opinion of the District Court in Schmidt v. Lessard reprinted in part above, was appealed to the United States Supreme Court which vacated the judgment of the District Court on procedural grounds and remanded the case for further proceedings. Schmidt v. Lessard, 414 U.S. 473, 94 S.Ct. 713, 38 L.Ed.2d 661 (1974). On remand, the District Court entered another order providing declaratory and injunctive relief. 379 F.Supp. 1376 (E.D.Wis.1974). On appeal the Supreme Court again vacated the judgment and remanded the case to the District Court to determine whether the petitioner had exhausted his state appellate remedies. Schmidt v. Lessard, 421 U.S. 957, 95 S.Ct. 1943, 44 L.Ed.2d 445 (1975).]

Similarly, in *Lynch v. Baxley*, 386 F.Supp. 378 (M.D.Ala.1974), the court held that the state bears the burden of "demonstrating that the proposed commitment is to the least restrictive environment consistent with the needs of the person to be committed." At 394. At the same time, other courts such as the Supreme Court of New Mexico have rejected the contentions that due process requires the state to demonstrate that there is no alternative to "total institutionalization." *State v. Sanchez*, 80 N.M. 438, 457 P.2d 370 (1968).

The *Sanchez* decision was subsequently appealed to the Supreme Court which, however, rejected the appeal. This disposition, according to one federal court, suggests a rejection by the Supreme Court of the claim that the least drastic means principle applies to civil commitment. *Lynch v. Baxley*, 386 F.Supp. 378, 392 n. 10 (M.D.Ala. 1974). Notwithstanding its ambiguous constitutional status the least restrictive alternative doctrine has had a significant impact on the administration of civil commitment laws. The implications of this movement, which favors community treatment over institutionalization, are explored in the section which follows.

c. Deinstitutionalization: The Least Restrictive Alternative in Operation

The least restrictive alternative doctrine announced in cases such as *Lake v. Cameron* provided the legal impetus for a deinstitutionalization movement already enjoying strong support both within and outside the mental health professions. Advocates of deinstitutionalization pointed to the dehumanizing effects of overcrowded mental hospitals and suggested that any alternative would benefit the mentally ill. Treatment that would allow the patient to remain as part of the community was "perceived as positively therapeutic: as tending to nurture and sustain the mentally ill's social skills, rather than breaking them down; as providing social integration rather than social isolation; and, with assistance from community based mental health programs, as encouraging independent rather than dependent behavior." [Scull, *Deinstitutionalization and the Rights of the Deviant*, Journal of Social Issues, Summer 1981, at 6, 8.] Deinstitutionalization also became attractive to state policy makers and legislatures, which saw an opportunity to capitalize on federal funding opportunities for the establishment of community-based facilities. At the same time the shift of federally funded local programs served to reduce the financial burden associated with the maintenance of state hospitals.

Whether motivated by therapeutic or fiscal objectives, deinstitutionalization has had a dramatic impact on the care and treatment of the mentally ill. Between 1955 and 1978 the population of state mental hospitals declined from a high of 558,992 to a low of 148,533 (H.S. Wilson, *Deinstitutionalized Residential Care for the Mentally Disordered* [Grune and Stratton: New York, 1982], p. xviii). In qualitative terms the results of deinstitutionalization have been mixed. On the one hand, some model programs have reported positive results in terms of reducing the need for medication, promoting the capacity of former patients to live independently, and enhancing patients' occupational levels. Wilson at 111. At the same time, there is overwhelming evidence that deinstitutionalization has had castratrophic effects on the lives of many patients. It is clear, for instance, that community-based facilities simply do not exist in many areas of the country. *See, New York Times*, Nov. 18, 1979, p. 1.

Even where local treatment programs have been established, the operation of the system has proven to be far from ideal. All too often the systems depend upon the initiative of the former patient to seek counseling and treatment rather than establishing outreach programs capable of monitoring the condition of the former hospitalized patients and of bringing care into the home. These limitations can be attributed largely to budgetary constraints. As a result, there is a growing realization that "effective treatment in the community is at least as costly as in patient care." Miller, *The Least Restrictive Alternative: Hidden Meanings and Agendas*, Community Mental Health Journal, Spring 1982, at 46, 50.

While no comprehensive study of community treatment programs has been undertaken, there is growing evidence pointing to a virtual breakdown in the system of care available to the mentally ill in many communities. The following excerpts are illustrative of recent reports in both the media and in professional journals:

> *The New Snake Pits*, Newsweek, May 15, 1978 at 93.
>
> Just fifteen years ago, the U.S. embarked on a bold new approach to the care of the mentally ill. No longer would patients be locked away in the ilogarthian wards of bleak, overcrowded and often badly staffed state mental hospitals. Instead, they would return to their own cities and towns, to be treated at community mental-health centers and trained to become productive members of society once more.
>
> But the bright hope for a new era in mental health has dimmed. True, many of the state hospital wards stand empty. But vast numbers of their former inmates are worse off than they were before. Because of poor planning at all levels of government, lack of funds and the hostility of the healthy members of communities, expatients wander desolutely in inner-city ghettos and live in squalid single rooms or nursing homes that are ill-prepared to render the care they need. For some of them, "deinstitutionalization" has been tragic.
>
> * * *
>
> While the plan was noble in concept, most mental-health experts agree that it was disastrous in execution. Patients were released from state hospitals in droves, but neither Federal nor local governments had worked out plans to take care of them. As originally intended, the number of patients in state hospitals did drop sharply, from 550,000 in 1955 to 191,000 in 1975—a decrease of more than 65

percent. But these hopeful statistics are offset by the disturbing fact that about half the patients are readmitted, at least temporarily, to state hospitals within a year of their release. "All we're very good at," says Los Angeles psychiatrist Dr. Michael Levine, "is processing people through a revolving door."

Scull, *"A New Trade in Lunacy: The Recommodification of the Mental Patient,"* 24 American Behavioral Scientist 724 (1981) pp. 743–44, 748–49 (citations omitted).

What tended to be overlooked in the midst of all the excitement about the replacement of the mental hospital and elaborate theoretical proclamations about the virtues of the community was the degree to which the new programs remained castles in the air, figments of their planners' imaginations.   *   *   *

*   *   *   As efforts have at last been made to compare "the intentions and hopes of community mental health [with] the uncomfortable realities", so the magnitude of the discrepancies has become all too apparent. At every stage, deinstitutionalization has been characterized by ignorance, confusion, and inaction; and at every level of government, there has been a singular "lack of a planned, well-managed, coordinated and systematic approach" to the resultant problems. Even the simplest forms of official accounting—follow-up studies of the fate of expatients—are "generally haphazard, fragmented, or non-existent". One thing is certain, however: with few exceptions, they are not being served by the new community mental health centers. Quite apart from the centers' uneven geographical distribution and their current fiscal problems, "both their ideology and their most common services are not directed at the needs of those who have traditionally resided in state psychiatric institutions".

*   *   *

Questions and Comments

1. For additional media reporting of the effects of deinstitutionalization, *see:* Nelson, "Studies Report Mental Illness in Most Homeless in 2 Cities," *New York Times*, Oct. 2, 1983, p. 17; Herman, "Policy to Release Mental Patients Leaves Many to Face Harsh Fate," *New York Times*, Nov. 18, 1979, p. 1; Sheppard, "Community Mental Health Care Getting Second Thoughts," *New York Times*, July 23, 1979, p. 13; Schumach, "Mental Care Is Called Revolving Door," *New York Times*, March 18, 1974, p. 1. See also, Boffey, "Failure Is Found In the Discharge of Mentally Ill," *New York Times*, Sept. 13, 1984, p. 1, col. 2 [Summarizing a report by the American Psychiatric Association concluding that "the practice of discharging mentally ill patients from state hospitals into ill-prepared local communities had been a failure and 'a major societal tragedy.'"]

2. One striking result of deinstitutionalization is the shift from state-operated facilities to private ones. This phenomenon has, in fact,

facilitated the development of new industry. As described by one commentator:

> The massive outflow of people produced in the wake of the run-down and even the closure of state hospitals has created a sizeable market for private entrepreneurs offering "care" for ex-patients in the community, a development some states concede they are actively encouraging (*see* Indiana Department of Health 1975: 130). There has even emerged whole chains of "convalescent hospitals" and halfway houses run on a profit making basis. For example, one major chain known as "Beverly Enterprises," which began with three convalescent facilities in 1964, now owns 63 board and care facilities and sanitariums in the United States (38 in California alone), and had net revenues of $79.5 million in 1972 (*See* Chase 1973: 17).

Andrew Scull, *Decarceration* (Englewood Cliffs, N.J.: Prentice-Hall, Inc., 1977), p. 74 note 17.

3. The movement toward private institutional care has several important implications. First, it frequently leads to a shift of responsibility among governmental units in a state. In many states, for instance, once a patient is released and placed in a nursing or shelter care home the department of mental health is relieved of direct supervisory or financial responsibility for the care of the patient. Instead, the former patient becomes a dependent of the department of public aid. As a result, reimbursement for care is limited to the schedule that applies to public aid recipients, which is usually lower than the schedule for reimbursement for services contracted for by the department of mental health. The shift to *private* care can also impinge on the legal rights of the recipients of care. Most important, patients may no longer have the protections of the Constitution, since its provisions only cover actions of government or those operating under "color of law." This removal from constitutional protection, moreover, also serves to limit the protection available under federal civil rights laws. The scope of the available remedies under the Civil Rights Laws is discussed in Chapter II, Section III.B.

4. In view of the current and projected limitations in community mental health care facilities, what should be the attitude of the judiciary in applying the civil commitment laws? Is it clear that courts should apply the least restrictive alternative doctrine even where the quality of community care is only marginal? Is it clear that the presumption against institutional care of the mentally ill promotes their best interest under current conditions?

5. Among the grounds that have been advanced in favor of abolishing involuntary commitment are the limited resources available to treat the institutionalized mentally ill. As noted by one commentator:

> If involuntary commitment and treatment were abolished, mental health professionals would still be faced with more voluntary patients than they could treat adequately. It may reasonably be estimated that roughly five million persons in our society suffer from severe mental disorders (somewhat over two million of whom are chronically and severely disabled) and could benefit from treatment. If all

"pedigreed" mental health professionals (psychiatrists, psychologists, psychiatric social workers, psychiatric nurses) were to ignore all other client populations and treat only severely disordered persons, there would still be far too few professionals to provide even moderately good treatment to all the members of that group.

Stone, *The Preference for Liberty: The Case Against Involuntary Commitment of the Mentally Disordered*, 70 Cal.L.Rev. 54, 99 (1982). The statistics cited by Professor Stone on the incidence of severe mental illness are based in part on a Report of the Task Panel on the Nature and Scope of the Problems, in 2 Task Panel Reports Submitted to the President's Commission on Mental Health, at 19 (1978). *See*, Stone *id.* note 178.

In concluding that there are insufficient personal resources to treat the institutionalized mentally ill, Professor Stone tabulated the number of psychiatrists at 33,000 and of clinical psychologists at 24,000. See note 179. Are psychiatrists and clinical psychologists necessarily the only resources for the carrying out of treatment? Is it possible that treatment of severely disordered persons might appropriately involve greater use of nonclinical modalties, such as activity therapy supervised by specialized therapists, with the limited aim of enhancing the functioning of the individual?

d. *Role of the Judiciary in Implementing the Least Restrictive Alternative Doctrine*

If application of the least restrictive alternative principle is dependent on other community facilities the state has chosen to provide, the utility of the doctrine is likely to be limited. As was made clear earlier, most state and local legislative bodies have simply been unwilling to make the appropriations necessary to establish viable community treatment systems. Thus, the critical issue becomes the authority of courts to force the expenditures of funds for the development of community treatment facilities when a legislative body has failed to act. The power of courts to mandate increased governmental expenditures has been the subject of considerable debate among legal scholars. The majority view casts doubt on the constitutional power of federal courts to force expenditures where legislatures have been unwilling to make the needed appropriations. The rationale behind these perceived limits on judicial power has been analyzed by one commentator as follows:

> If the courts invite confrontation, [by imposing excessive financial requirements on legislative bodies], they will face a practical impediment to effectuating their orders more important than any yet mentioned. These judicial orders are unenforceable. Only the legislature can provide the necessary money, and only the executive can administer the spending of that money. The courts cannot imprison the legislature for contempt unless it raises or reallocates the necessary money, nor jail an executive official to ensure implementation of a government program. Courts ultimately lack the power to force

state governments to act. Unless the courts are willing to do what no responsible government official would do—close the institutions, and let the prisoners and the mentally ill, dangerous or otherwise, go free—if the courts are unwilling to play a game of "chicken" with state officials, as they should be, they should face the fact that these orders will be complied with, if at all, voluntarily, absent federal executive action to enforce them. Recognition of this practical limit on judicial power does not render the courts powerless to enforce the Constitution. It merely restricts them to their real, and not their imagined, power. "The Court's authority—possessed of neither the purse nor the sword—ultimately rests on sustained public confidence in its moral sanction."

Frug, *The Judicial Power of the Purse*, 126 U.Pa.L.Rev. 715, 792 (1978).

Questions and Comments

1. As noted above, traditional legal doctrine holds that when the legislature has failed to act, courts lack authority to order the expenditure of public funds necessary for the creation of community facilities. Some commentators have nonetheless argued that various constitutional provisions could be construed to provide authority for judicial action ordering the creation of such facilities. *See* Chambers, *Alternatives to Civil Commitment of the Mentally Ill: Practical Guides and Constitutional Imperatives*, 70 Mich.L.Rev. 1192, 1189–1194 (1972).

2. The judiciary may play a role in the establishment of community facilities quite apart from the evaluation of *constitutionally* based claims. For instance, the legislature may enact legislation which calls for community residential placement of mental patients, but fail to make it clear whether there is an absolute right to community placement or whether the right is contingent on the availability of facilities. Here the role of courts is to construe the intent of the legislature. Moreover, when legislation directs the state to provide specific services to individuals, courts are empowered to order the appropriate official to provide those services. A claim of this nature was the subject of a case recently decided by the Court of Appeals of New York, *Klostermann v. Cuomo*, Slip Opinion, March 27, 1984, Court of Appeals of New York. (Case # 87 and # 88.) The action in *Klostermann* was brought by nine persons who, having been discharged from a mental institution became among the "homeless wandering the streets of New York City. Efforts to receive assistance from State and municipal agencies were unavailing or, at best, resulted in only minimal, periodic assistance." *Id.* at 2.

The plaintiff's complaint was based upon "an asserted right under State law to receive residential placement, supervision, and care upon release from a State institution. Their claims [were] grounded in the provisions of * * * the Mental Hygiene Law, which prescribe certain acts that must be undertaken when a patient in a State psychiatric institution is to be discharged or conditionally released into the community." *Id.* at 3. The Court of Appeals held that the plaintiffs had asserted a justifiable claim and to the extent that the plaintiffs could "establish that defendants are not satisfying *nondiscretionary* obligations to perform certain functions, they are entitled to orders directing defendants to discharge those duties." *Id.* at 15 (emphasis added) At the same time, however, the court noted that "the courts must be careful to avoid * * * the fashioning of orders or judgments that go beyond any mandatory directives of existing statutes and regulations and intrude upon the policy-making and discretionary decisions that are reserved to the Legislative and Executive branches." *Id.*

III.   COMMITMENT PROCEDURES

A.   OVERVIEW OF THE COMMITMENT PROCESS

This chapter has thus far examined the substantive criteria governing involuntary commitment. We now need to address the process by which an individual can be taken against his will from his surroundings and transferred to a psychiatric facility, which is then authorized to detain and examine him. Nearly all states provide for two basic methods of achieving involuntary commitment. One is the emergency form of commitment, which authorizes, under appropriate circumstances, the transfer and admission of an individual into a facility without any prior formal hearing or adjudication. Such a hearing or adjudication generally is held, but not for several days or even weeks after admission. The second method of involuntary commitment is based on a court order that follows a formal hearing held prior to the detention of the individual. Thus, the principal distinction between these two methods is the timing of a formal hearing, before or after commitment.

The processes detailed below are designed to illustrate the general form of the two methods available in most jurisdictions. It should be noted at the outset that, although the required procedures are usually spelled out in considerable detail by statutory law, the precise requirements vary from state to state. Accordingly, the following descriptions are intended only to point out the salient features of the procedures available in most jurisdictions and do not purport to include *all* the procedural requirements that are likely to be found in any given jurisdiction.

1.   Emergency Commitment Procedures

The emergency commitment process can generally be initiated by any adult who signs a petition under oath asserting that immediate treatment is needed for the protection of an individual or other persons. The petition must generally be accompanied by a certificate executed by a "qualified examiner" attesting to the subject's need for immediate treatment. Persons designated to act as "qualified examiners" typically include such mental health professionals as psychiatrists, physicians, clinical psychologists, psychiatric social workers, or psychiatric nurses. The executed petition and certificate, which may be presented to either the police or a mental health facility, provide the sole basis for the individual's being taken into custody and transported to the psychiatric facility.

A more abbreviated procedure is available in many jurisdictions. It allows a police officer who believes that immediate hospitalization is necessary to take a person into custody and secure his admission into a psychiatric facility. These laws, which dispense with the requirement of an evaluation by a "qualified examiner," serve to invest the police with total discretion to commit an individual on an emergency basis. However, an individual admitted under these conditions may, under the law of most jurisdictions, be detained for no more than one day unless a certificate is subsequently executed by a qualified examiner who may be a staff member of the institution holding the individual. In any event, all individuals detained under emergency procedures must be afforded a judicial type hearing within a specific time, which may be as little as two or as long as six weeks.

2. Commitment by Court Order

In the absence of an emergency most state laws provide for a more formal and elaborate admissions process. This procedure, commonly known as admission by court order, may also be initiated by any adult who has reason to believe that an individual is in need of treatment. The petition is then filed with a court. In some cases the petition is accompanied by a certificate executed by a "qualified examiner." The petition, whether submitted with or without an accompanying certificate, empowers the court to order the individual in question to undergo a psychiatric examination by a psychiatrist or other examiner designated by the court. If necessary, the individual may be taken into custody by the police to ensure his presence at the place of examination. If the examination confirms that the individual is in "need of treatment," a formal hearing or trial to adjudicate the individual's commitability will be scheduled. The hearing, which will be considered in detail in a subsequent section, serves to adjudicate whether the individual's condition meets the substantive legal standards required by the commitment laws of the state. The court determination or jury verdict on these questions determines whether the individual is to be committed.

Questions and Comments

1. As noted above, the commitment laws of numerous jurisdictions give police officers discretion to apprehend and detain an individual who an officer deems to require emergency psychiatric treatment. In most cases the behavior which leads to apprehension could also be the basis of an arrest for the violation of a criminal offense, such as disturbing the peace. In fact, the initial apprehension is frequently associated with an arrest. It is only after the individual is in custody that the officer may elect to treat the offender as a psychiatric case and effect emergency commitment.

Among the issues raised by these procedures is the basis upon which the police are legally justified in apprehending and arresting an individual. Must the police, for instance, actually witness the criminal conduct, or can they rely on a citizen's complaint? These questions were addressed in *McKinney v. George*, 556 F.Supp. 645 (N.D.Ill.1983). The plaintiff, who had been psychiatrically hospitalized following his arrest for disorderly conduct, alleged a violation of his constitutional rights. In rejecting the plaintiff's claim the court held that the requirement of probable cause to arrest may be satisfied when the information providing the basis for the officer's decision to arrest comes from a credible third party. "It is not required by statute or case law that the arresting officer personally observe erratic behavior in the case of a person who needs hospitalization for mental illness" at 650. *See also* Monahan, Caldeira, and Friedlander, *Police and the Mentally Ill: A Comparison of Committed and Arrested Persons*, 2 Intl.J. of Law and Psychiatry 509, 515 (1979) (an empirical study of the police decision making process in the channeling of the mentally ill).

B. ISSUES PERTAINING TO EMERGENCY COMMITMENT

1. *Introduction*

Emergency commitment is arguably justified by the state's compelling interests in protecting the individual or others from an immediate threat of injury. Once the individual has been retained for observation and treatment, however, the emergency which justified summary commitment has passed. At this point the individual's constitutional interests in due process reemerge, and the issue to be confronted is how soon after the initial admission is the individual entitled to a judicial type hearing. Beyond this is the question of the kind of hearing to which the individual is entitled at this early stage. These issues are discussed in the materials which follow.

2. *Probable Cause Hearings*

a. *The Purpose of the Probable Cause Hearing*

The circumstances of those committed under emergency procedures are quite similar to those of individuals who have been arrested without a warrant and are detained on the basis of a charge placed by the police. In both cases there has been a deprivation of liberty without hearing. In the criminal context the Constitution has been construed to require some form of prompt initial hearing following the accused person's detention. This rule is based on the following considerations:

> [A] policeman's on-the-scene assessment of probable cause provides legal justification for arresting a person suspected of crime, and for a brief period of detention to take the administrative steps incident to arrest. Once the suspect is in custody, however, the reasons that justify dispensing with the magistrate's neutral judgment evaporate. There no longer is any danger that the suspect will escape or commit further crimes while the police submit their evidence to a magistrate.

And, while the State's reasons for taking summary action subside, the suspect's need for a neutral determination of probable cause increases significantly. * * * When the stakes are this high, the detached judgment of a neutral magistrate is essential if the Fourth Amendment is to furnish meaningful protection from unfounded interference with liberty. *Gerstein v. Pugh,* 420 U.S. 103, 114–115, 95 S.Ct. 854, 863–864, 43 L.Ed.2d 54 (1975).

These considerations calling for a review of the detention decision by a neutral and detached decision maker arguably apply with equal force where the police action leads to a psychiatric commitment. As a result, numerous courts have recognized a constitutional right to a probable cause hearing on the part of those who are committed on an emergency basis. At the same time there are significant variations among the various states as to both the timing and procedural requirements of these preliminary hearings.

b. Timing of the Hearing

Statutory provisions governing the timing and circumstances that trigger a probable cause hearing vary greatly from state to state. Under some state statutes, only a short emergency detention period (from 24–72 hours) is authorized, but extensions of 14 to 30 days may be obtained by petition prior to any court hearing. Other statutes call for a probable cause hearing only when it is specifically requested by the patient or a relative or friend. Although such hearings are generally provided within three to five days of the initial detainment, invocation of the hearing may be dependent on the ability of the individual, who is quite often heavily medicated, and the willingness of the relative, who may have initiated the commitment process, to request such a hearing. Still other statutes require that the individual be released if a probable cause hearing is not conducted within 72 hours of detention.

As noted earlier, even in the absence of statutory provisions courts have recognized a constitutional right to a probable cause hearing for those committed on an emergency basis. Courts do disagree on how promptly a hearing must be provided. Some have found that a hearing is constitutionally required within two to five days. Those tolerating longer periods have emphasized the desirability of allowing sufficient time to permit the state to diagnose the condition of the detained individual. Courts that have required a prompt hearing have noted that the state need not "prove its case" at the hearing, but merely demonstrate probable cause to believe the individual is in need of treatment. Thus an observation period of two to three days has been deemed to provide a sufficient basis for the initial evaluation. *See Luna v. Van Zandt,* 554 F.Supp. 68, 72 (S.D. Tex.1982), for a discussion of earlier decisions.

c. Elements of the Probable Cause Hearing

As noted earlier, the initial probable cause hearing need not be a formal hearing. Although the complexity of these hearings and the procedural safeguards provided vary from state to state, several elements are essential. First, the individual and his attorney—most states provide for the appointment of counsel to indigent persons—must receive adequate notice of the hearing. What is meant by "adequate notice" is not entirely clear, however, and often the attorney will have no more than 24 hours to meet with his client, interview any physicians involved in his hospitalization, and prepare for the hearing. The adequacy of the notice, as well as the overall complexity of the hearing itself, is to some extent a function of how soon after detention the hearing is held.

The hearing itself must provide the individual with an opportunity to refute the state's claims. Generally, the hearing is conducted by a judicial official, often a judge of the Probate Court, but the cases suggest that any neutral decision maker would satisfy due process, rendering a county mental health officer equally appropriate. Similarly, the hearing need not take place in a courtroom and will often be conducted at the mental health facility itself. The individual generally does not have the right to confront witnesses or assert Fifth Amendment protections against self-incrimination. Often the hearing consists of no more than the reading of affidavits and counteraffidavits by mental health professionals or the presentation of testimony concerning the individual's condition and conduct.

C. PROCEDURAL REQUIREMENTS FOR THE FULL HEARING

1. Introductory Comments: Right to a Fair Hearing

The authority which federal and state governments may exert over individuals is limited by provisions in the Fifth and Fourteenth Amendments, which prohibit deprivations of "life, liberty, or property, without due process of law." The obligation imposed upon government by the due process clause does not lend itself to rigid formulation. In the context of administrative or judicial action that threatens a protected interest due process has been construed to require "an opportunity to be heard." *Londoner v. Denver*, 210 U.S. 373, 28 S.Ct. 708, 52 L.Ed. 1103 (1908). As observed by Mr. Justice Frankfurter:

> No better instrument has been devised for arriving at truth than to give a person in jeopardy of serious loss notice of the case against him and opportunity to meet it. Nor has a better way been found for generating the feeling, so important to popular government, that justice has been done.

Joint Anti-Fascist Refugee Committee v. McGrath, 341 U.S. 123, 171–172, 71 S.Ct. 624, 648–649, 95 L.Ed. 817 (1951).

Essential to the application of this principle is the identification of those interests that give rise to protection. Since at a minimum these interests involve freedom from physical restraint, governmental authority may not impose any significant physical restraint on an individual without affording the person some procedural safeguards. In the context of the criminal process, due process requires a judicial hearing, the right to a jury trial, the right to be represented by counsel at all stages, the right to confront adverse witnesses, the right to invoke constitutional protection against self-incrimination, and, finally, the right to have the issue of guilt resolved in terms of the "beyond the reasonable doubt" standard. At the other end of the spectrum, when governmental action affects a lesser interest such as welfare benefits or the opportunity to practice a profession, due process may be satisfied by a relatively informal administrative hearing. Moreover, while the claimant may have a right to adequate notice and the opportunity to confront adverse witnesses, the decision maker may be an official of the welfare agency rather than a judge or jury. Also, although the individual has the right to secure legal assistance if he desires, there is no requirement that the government provide counsel to indigent claimants.

The type of hearing required for civil commitment under the due process provisions of the Constitution has not been authoritatively delineated by the Supreme Court. While most states require a judicial hearing, presided over by a judicial officer, and many authorize a jury trial, a very limited number of states permit commitment to be ordered by an administrative board. Most states today guarantee counsel for an individual faced with commitment. Many states do not, however, provide an independent psychiatric expert to indigent persons confronted by the commitment process.

The procedures used to commit individuals have been challenged more and more often in recent years. In the absence of clear constitutional mandates, the courts and legislatures have looked to existing models of due process hearings for guidance. The procedures that have been developed are the result of a combination of procedures taken from the judicial criminal law model and the administrative model mentioned above. The similarity of effect on the individual's liberty by both processes makes analogy to criminal procedures singularly appropriate. Significant differences in these processes must be recognized, however. Under criminal law the government cannot generally deny liberty to an individual unless an overt act has been committed. Punishment follows only after the commission of the act has been shown within the constitutionally required procedural framework, including the requirement of proof beyond a reasonable doubt. While it may lead to a similar deprivation of liberty, the civil commitment process is generally concerned with the prediction of undesired behavior rather than the demonstration that a prescribed act has been committed by the individual. The focus of the process is prospective in that civil commitment may be used in anticipation of the commission of an act.

Moreover, civil commitment differs from the criminal process in terms of the dominant societal purpose behind the exercise of the state's power. A fundamental ingredient in the criminal process is the imposition of punishment to achieve deterrence. In contrast, the principal purpose of civil commitment is treatment and protective isolation of the individual. Thus the government is not merely exercising police power in civilly committing an individual, but there is also a strong element of *parens patriae* power involved. These differences in basic purpose and sources of power conceivably justify taking an approach to procedures that lies somewhere between the criminal model and the less formalized administrative model.

The approach that will ultimately be adopted by the U.S. Supreme Court remains to be determined. In the meantime, the decision of state and lower federal courts reflect current judicial tendencies in approaching due process issues in civil commitment situations. The materials which follow focus on some of these decisions.

2. Right to Notice

Whether a hearing is held before or after admission, it has been viewed as an essential part of due process that the individual who is threatened with a loss of liberty be advised of his rights to a hearing and notice of other ancillary rights, such as a right to be represented by counsel. The manner in which this information is transmitted to the individual varies depending on the circumstances. Normally, if the individual is still at liberty, written notice is generally served on the person facing commitment by an individual functioning under the authority of the courts. If the individual is already in detention following an emergency commitment, the formal notice is usually given to the individual by one of the facility staff. Generally, the notice must include "the time and location of the hearing * * * the reasons for his detention, [and] the standards for commitment." *Doremus v. Farrell,* 407 F.Supp. 509, 515 (D.Neb.1975).

It is essential, moreover, that to comply with due process the notice of any scheduled hearing "must be given sufficiently in advance of the proceeding to afford one a reasonable opportunity to prepare." *Id.* at 515.

Questions and Comments

1. While giving notice appears to be a constitutional requirement, it is also mandated by most state commitment statutes. Exactly what information should be encompassed by the notice has not been authoritatively resolved. The prevailing view is one of flexibility and so constitutional requirements are satisfied if the notice "is reasonably calculated to inform the person to whom it is directed of the nature of the proceeding." *French v. Blackburn,* 428 F.Supp. 1351, 1356 (M.D.N.C.1977).

2. Whether notice to the individual who is the subject of a civil commitment proceeding may be dispensed with on the grounds that it may be medically or psychiatrically damaging is considered in subsection 4, *infra*.

3. Little attention has been paid to the problem of providing adequate notice to individuals who, because of either temporary or permanent disability, may not be able to comprehend written communications fully. Whether due process requires anything more than a formal written notice has not been addressed by judicial authorities.

3. The Nature of the Hearing—Must It Be Before a Judicial Officer?

It is fundamental to our constitution that deprivation of liberty may only occur after a hearing which accords with due process. As noted in a previous section, however, emergency commitment can precede the hearing. While most jurisdictions provide for a hearing before a *judicial officer*, few jurisdictions permit commitment hearings to be held before an administrative panel. The permissibility of this approval is the issue addressed here.

DOREMUS v. FARRELL

United States District Court, Northern District of Nebraska, 1975.
407 F.Supp. 509.

Plaintiffs contend that due process requires the final commitment hearing to be a judicial determination, rather than an administrative one [as authorized by Statute in Nebraska]. Although a judicial determination would be desirable, since courts can more effectively preserve procedural due process and constitutional rights, as well as rule more proficiently on evidentiary questions, we do not believe that due process or equal protection mandates a judicial hearing. The Supreme Court has recognized the power of administrative boards to revoke parole and probation. The deportation of aliens has long been considered a proper function for executive commissions. The procedural safeguards guaranteed by due process, the standards for commitment and the availability of prompt de novo review by the district court after the finding of mental illness by the county board, convinces the Court that an administrative determination is not constitutionally objectionable.

Questions and Comments

1. At least four states, Nebraska, Iowa, Rhode Island, and Mississippi, have statutory provisions that authorize commitment hearings to be conducted by an administrative board rather than a judicial officer. Note, however, that the Nebraska statute, which was challenged in the *Doremus* case, allowed an appeal by the committed person and a *de novo* determination by court. It is not altogether clear whether an administra-

tive hearing is constitutionally allowable if a right to a *de novo* hearing is not included.

2. While the U.S. Supreme Court had not passed on the constitutionality of non-judicial hearings in the standard commitment process, it has addressed the issue in the context of the transfer to psychiatric hospitals of persons incarcerated in correctional facilities. In *Vitek v. Jones*, 445 U.S. 480, 100 S.Ct. 1254, 63 L.Ed.2d 552 (1981), the Court held that a person confronting transfer from a prison to a mental hospital was constitutionally entitled to an adversary type hearing before "an independent decisionmaker." *Id.* 445 U.S. at 495, 100 S.Ct. at 1264. At the same time, the Court held that the decisionmaker did not need to be a judicial officer and could, in fact, be an employee or affiliated with either "the prison or hospital administration." *Id.* 445 U.S. at 496, 100 S.Ct. 1265.

3. As noted in the previous section, a probable cause hearing must be held promptly after a civil commitment under state's emergency commitment provisions. How much time must elapse before a final hearing? This issue has only rarely been addressed, though one court adopted the following rule:

> Just as emergency detention is justified only until a probable cause hearing can be conducted, temporary detention following a finding of probable cause to believe that confinement is necessary can be justified only for the length of time required to arrange a full hearing on the need for commitment. Due process requires that such hearing be held within a reasonable time following initial detention, but in no event sooner than will permit adequate preparation of the case by counsel or later than thirty (30) days from the date of the initial detention.

Lynch v. Baxley, 386 F.Supp. 378, 388 (M.D.Ala.1974).

4. Confrontation of Witnesses and the Right to Be Present

The right of a person to confront his accusers is an essential part of due process. At the heart of this notion is the idea that an individual should not be subjected to a loss of liberty on the basis of anonymous accusations. In legal terms the implementation of this concept entails various rights, including the opportunity to be present at the hearing and the right to cross examine witnesses.

As previously noted, the commitment process may be triggered by observations or reports of private individuals, the observations of public officials, and the evaluations and statements of mental health professionals. It is at the adversary hearing that the individual threatened with commitment is guaranteed the opportunity, with the assistance of counsel, to challenge the accuracy or validity of any statement that is being relied on by the state, which is the moving party in a commitment proceeding.

Closely related to the right to cross examine adverse witnesses is the ability to offer evidence and to participate in the presentation of the defense. *See Stamus v. Leonhardt*, 414 F.Supp. 439, 447 (S.D. Iowa 1976). As a consequence, the right to confront witnesses encompasses not only the opportunity to question witnesses under oath but also the right to subpoena witnesses whose testimony could be used to impeach the state's witnesses.

While these rights have generally been viewed as an integral part of the rights constitutionally guaranteed to an individual threatened by a loss of liberty, some states have commitment laws that allow the subject of the commitment proceeding to be excluded from the hearing. Typically, such states authorize exclusion when the subject's presence would "probably be injurious to the subject." 414 F.Supp. at 447. While the permissibility of such provisions have not been passed on by the U.S. Supreme Court, a number of lower federal courts have found that these exceptions violate due process. In passing on the constitutionality of this type of provision, contained in an earlier version of the Iowa commitment statute, the court in *Stamus v. Leonhardt*, 414 F.Supp. 439 (S.D.Iowa 1976) held:

> Section 229.4 of the Code accorded the subject the right to be present at hearings unless the hospitalization commission found that the subject's presence would "probably be injurious" to the subject "or attended with no advantage." Pursuant to this provision, Dorothy Stamus was taken before the hospitalization commission during her hearing and questioned. However, as was the general practice in Polk County, she was excluded from the hearing room preceding and after her questioning period. This restriction on the plaintiff's right to be present was an unconstitutional deprivation of her right to due process.

> The Supreme Court has required the presence of the person proposed to be involuntarily committed under a Sex Offender Act at all proceedings conducted for that purpose unless the right was knowingly and intelligently waived by the subject of the proceeding or his or her attorney.

> Although this right is explicitly preserved for criminal defendants in the Sixth Amendment to the Constitution, courts have required the same right in the civil commitment context. The same purposes for requiring the person's presence exist in both the civil and criminal context: to allow the individual to assure that his or her interests are being protected and to give the fact-finder an opportunity to speak with the person and observe his or her demeanor. The results of the hearings, confinement in an institution and a loss of personal liberty, are often the same in the civil commitment and criminal context. Thus, there must be a right for the individual under discussion to be present at all proceedings for civil commitment. The hospitalization commission in Polk County transgressed this right as applied to Dorothy Stamus by not permitting her to be present throughout her hearing, and thereby deprived her of procedural due process. Further, as recognized by the Court in *Lynch v. Baxley*, "The right to be present at the hearing necessarily includes the right to participate therein to the extent of the subject's ability." 386 F.Supp. at 389. To the extent Dorothy Stamus was excluded from the hearing, this right was clearly transgressed.

At 447.

5. Is There a Right to a Trial by Jury?

MARKEY v. WACHTEL

Supreme Court of Appeals of West Virginia, 1979.
264 S.E.2d 437.

MILLER, Justice:

In *State ex rel. Hawks v. Lazaro*, W.Va., 202 S.E.2d 109 (1974), we set forth a number of due process rights which must be accorded adults who are faced with involuntary commitment to mental hospitals. In the four consolidated cases now before us, we are asked to further hold that such persons shall be accorded the right to a jury trial. We decline to do so.

* * *

In *Hawks*, we assimilated the test of *Specht v. Patterson*, 386 U.S. 605, 87 S.Ct. 1209, 18 L.Ed.2d 326 (1967), and enhanced its safeguards for those faced with involuntary mental commitment, and fastened this protection to Article III, Section 10 of our own (state) Constitution. We believe that it comports with or surpasses any federal due process procedure that may ultimately be found to be applicable.

* * *

We are reinforced in this view by the fact that the United States Supreme Court has held that, despite the criminal overtones in a juvenile delinquency proceeding, the Sixth Amendment right to jury trial in a criminal case does not require the states, under the Due Process Clause of the Fourteenth Amendment, to accord a jury trial in a juvenile delinquency hearing. Furthermore, it is not without significance that *Addington*, a unanimous opinion (of the U.S. Supreme Court), took great pains to delineate the "civil" aspect of the involuntary commitment proceeding and distinguish it from a criminal sentence.

In the final analysis, our procedural due process standard set in *Hawks* is predicated on the fact that we recognize that an important liberty interest is involved in an involuntary commitment proceeding which requires substantial due process protection. Weighed against this private interest is society's interest, acting through the governmental process, to require those who are found to be dangerous by reason of mental disorder to undergo treatment.

The heart of the adversarial issue is the mental condition of the individual which, as *Addington* recognizes, is a technically complex question based on the testimony of experts which a lay jury has difficulty understanding. We are unwilling to hold as a constitutional principle that the resolution of this issue can only be accomplished by a jury. Neither historical precedent nor the requisite due process procedural balance mandates such a conclusion.

We, therefore, conclude that Article III, Section 10 of the West Virginia Constitution cannot be interpreted to require a constitutional right to jury trial in a proceeding for the involuntary commitment of an adult to a mental health facility.

Questions and Comments

1. Some lower federal courts have suggested a jury trial is desirable even if not constitutionally required. For instance, in *Lynch v. Baxley*, 386 F.Supp. 378 (M.D.Ala.1974) the court observed:

> It has been generally assumed that there is no common law right to trial by jury in traditionally equitable probate court proceedings.

> Moreover, the Supreme Court of the United States has held that trial by jury is neither a necessary element of the "fundamental fairness" guaranteed litigants by the Due Process Clause, nor an essential component of accurate factfinding. Plaintiffs have cited no case, and independent research has disclosed no case, holding that trial by jury is constitutionally required in civil commitment proceedings.

> Although there may be no such constitutional right, we believe that in most, if not all, instances a jury is desirable.

at 394.

2. In what way does a jury provide persons confronting commitment with greater protection against the abuse or misapplication of the laws? If a jury does provide such protection, is it because the traditional requirement of unanimity makes it less likely that whatever decision is reached will be free of prejudicial error?

3. To some extent the commitment laws undoubtedly serve to remove from the community individuals whose behavior is generally deemed to be objectionable. To what extent does the jury rather than a judge serve as an appropriate litmus test for the tolerance of the community? Would a trial before a judge better insulate the commitment process from considerations of community tolerance?

4. Even though the Constitution has not been construed to guarantee a jury trial to persons facing commitment, the laws of most states give individuals that right. In a number of these states the jury trying commitment cases may be made up of only six persons rather than the twelve used in criminal cases.

6. Right to Legal and Psychiatric Assistance

a. Legal Assistance

ELKIN, *LEGAL REPRESENTATION OF THE MENTALLY ILL*
82 W.Va.L.Rev. 157–58 (1979).

One of the rights now afforded individuals subject to involuntary civil commitment is representation by legal counsel. By one count, forty-two of the states now provide for legal representation, and the presence of defense counsel or a guardian ad litem in civil commitment proceedings is now routine. By statute, the majority of states require that legal counsel be appointed for individuals subject to

involuntary commitment. Where statutes fail to provide for counsel, counsel may still be required as a matter of constitutional right.
* * *

While the right to counsel in civil commitment hearings is now secured by statutory provision buttressed by judicial suggestion that counsel is constitutionally required, there remains a question concerning the appropriate role of an attorney in representing the mentally ill. * * *

Questions and Comments

1. Whether a person confronting civil commitment has the right to appointed counsel has not been authoritatively decided by the U.S. Supreme Court. However, a number of lower court decisions have suggested that there is such a right. The only Supreme Court decision to date which has considered this question is *Vitek v. Jones*, 445 U.S. 480, 100 S.Ct. 1254, 63 L.Ed.2d 552 (1980). In *Vitek* the Supreme Court was called upon to define the procedural rights of a convicted felon in a correctional institution, whom the state seeks to transfer to a psychiatric hospital. A majority of the Supreme Court justices held that while a prisoner confronting transfer to a psychiatric facility has a right to "qualified and independent assistance" at the hearing, it need not necessarily be a licensed attorney who renders the assistance. The concurring opinion of Mr. Justice Powell, which controlled the disposition of this issue in the case, resolved the question in the following terms:

> * * * Our decisions defining the necessary qualifications for an impartial decisionmaker demonstrate that the requirements of due process turn on the nature of the determination which must be made. "Due Process has never been thought to require that the neutral and detached trier of fact be law-trained or a judicial or administrative officer." *Parham v. J.L.*, 442 U.S. 584, 99 S.Ct. 2493, 61 L.Ed.2d 101 (1979). In that case, we held that due process is satisfied when a staff physician determines whether a child may be voluntarily committed to a state mental institution by his parents. That holding was based upon recognition that the issues of civil commitment "are essentially medical in nature," and that " 'neither judges nor administrative hearing officers are better qualified than psychiatrists to render psychiatric judgments.' "

> In my view, the principle that due process does not always require a law-trained decisionmaker supports the ancillary conclusion that due process may be satisfied by the provision of a qualified and independent advisor who is not a lawyer. As in *Parham v. J.L.*, the issue here is essentially medical. Under state law, a prisoner may be transferred only if he "suffers from a mental disease or defect" and "cannot be given proper treatment" in the prison complex. Neb.Rev. Stat. § 83–180(1). The opinion of the Court allows a non-lawyer to act as the impartial decisionmaker in the transfer proceeding. *Ante*, at 1265.

The essence of procedural due process is a fair hearing. I do not think that the fairness of an informal hearing designed to determine a medical issue requires participation by lawyers. Due process merely requires that the State provide an inmate with qualified and independent assistance. Such assistance may be provided by a licensed psychiatrist or other mental health professional. Indeed, in view of the nature of the issue involved in the transfer hearing, a person possessing such professional qualifications normally would be preferred. As the Court notes, "[t]he question whether an individual is mentally ill and cannot be treated in prison 'turns on the meaning of the facts which must be interpreted by expert psychiatrists and psychologists.'" I would not exclude, however, the possibility that the required assistance may be rendered by competent laymen in some cases. The essential requirements are that the person provided by the State be competent and independent, and that he be free to act solely in the inmate's best interest.

445 U.S. at 498, 100 S.Ct. 1266.

2. To what extent are the circumstances of a prisoner who is serving a sentence and is threatened with transfer to a psychiatric facility similar to those of an individual facing civil commitment? Does it make a difference if the former has already lost his right to liberty and therefore only faces an injury in the sense that he may be stigmatized by being characterized as a psychiatric patient? Does this distinction call for a difference in the scope of procedural due process protection accorded to these different situations?

3. Frequently the appointment of counsel occurs only a short time before the hearing; such procedures raise questions as to the adequacy of representation. In *Stamus v. Leonhardt*, 414 F.Supp. 439 (S.D.Iowa 1976), this problem has been addressed in the following terms:

It is next asserted that Dorothy Stamus was denied the *presence of effective counsel at the hearing.* * * * Plaintiffs contend that the subject must be fully advised of his or her right to counsel at all significant stages of the commitment process and that counsel will be appointed if the person is unable to afford counsel. Plaintiffs also assert that counsel must be made available far enough in advance to permit adequate opportunity to prepare for the hearing. The Court agrees. "The subject of an involuntary civil commitment proceeding has the right to the effective assistance of counsel at all significant stages of the commitment process. Further, he has the right to be advised of his right to counsel, and to the appointment of counsel if indigent." *Lynch v. Baxley*, 386 F.Supp. at 389.

4. The functions of counsel in a commitment proceeding have been described by one court:

Inherent within the requirement of affirmative advocacy is the duty of the guardian ad litem to actively investigate the charges against the accused and the facts upon which they are based. In preparation for the commitment hearing, the duty to investigate contemplates the following:

> Prior to the hearing the attorney must make a thorough study of all the records that are available to him through the court, the hospital, and, at times, social agencies. He must always communicate with the proposed patient and, where possible, family and friends. The attorney should work toward an understanding of the events that led up to and contributed to the filing of the petition. Only in this way can he attempt to develop possible alternatives to hospitalization.

Cohen, supra, 44 Tex.L.Rev. at 452. As noted immediately above, a full investigation necessarily entails a meaningful consultation with the client, explaining the legal consequences of commitment and exploring all relevant factors in his defense.

Quesnell v. State, 83 Wn.2d 224, 517 P.2d 568 (1974).

Note that the defendant in a civil commitment proceeding may waive the right to counsel. However, any waiver must be knowing and informed. *See generally* Brunetti, *The Right to Counsel, Waiver Thereof, and Effective Assistance and Counsel in Civil Commitment Proceedings,* 29 Sw.L.J. 684 (1975).

5. Various studies suggest that appointed counsel have all too often carried out their defense functions very perfunctorily. *See* Cohen, *The Function of the Attorney and the Commitment of the Mentally Ill,* 44 Tex.L.Rev. 424 (1966); Wexler & Scoville, *Special Project—The Administration of Psychiatric Justice: Theory and Practice in Arizona,* 13 Ariz.L.Rev. 1, 51–60 (1971): Note, *Involuntary Hospitalization of the Mentally Ill Under Florida's Baker Act: Procedural Due Process and the Role of the Attorney,* 26 U.Fla.L.Rev. 508 (1974). *See also,* Andalman and Chambers, *Effective Counsel for Persons Facing Civil Commitment: A Survey, A Polemic and A Proposal,* 45 Miss.L.J. 43 (1974).

Various factors may account for these findings. First, some attorneys may erroneously perceive that their role is "limited to insure that the patient's statutory and constitutional rights are not violated during the legal process of the commitment." Elkins, *Legal Representation of the Mentally Ill,* 82 W.Va.L.Rev. 157, 181 (1979). Second, attorneys who themselves lack clinical training or experience in dealing with law and psychiatric cases are frequently reluctant to challenge what they regard as authoritative medical opinions. *Id.* at 185. Third, the system of compensation does not encourage significant expenditures of time and effort on the part of appointed counsel. Finally, attorneys may perceive their role in non-traditional legal terms. For instance, some attorneys may at least explicitly accept the need for compelled treatment when their client is obviously disordered and the attorney feels that the client may be placed at risk without treatment.

6. Are there any circumstances where an attorney is justified in providing less than a full and vigorous defense of the client confronting commitment? What if the attorney is convinced that the client is

mentally disordered and highly suicidal? *See generally*, Litwack, *The Role of Counsel in Civil Commitment Proceedings: Emerging Problems*, 62 Cal.L.Rev. 816 (1974).

b. *Psychiatric Assistance*

IN RE GANNON

Superior Court of New Jersey, 1973.
123 N.J.Super. 104, 301 A.2d 493.

MEREDITH, J.C.C.

Movant is an indigent patient at the Veterans Administration Hospital, Lyons, New Jersey. He had entered the hospital voluntarily and later expressed a desire to be released. After his release was denied by the hospital staff, commitment proceedings pursuant to N.J.S.A. 30:4–23 et seq. were begun in the Somerset County Court. The instant motion has been brought to secure an independent psychiatric examination.

Commitment to a psychiatric hospital obviously entails a significant loss of liberty which, as in a criminal proceeding, must be under due process of law. It is the opinion of this court that in a commitment proceeding due process of law includes the right to an independent psychiatric examination.

The right of an indigent patient to have counsel appointed has already been established, but the presence of a lawyer at the commitment hearing is not a sufficient safeguard for the patient's rights. No matter how brilliant the lawyer may be, he is in no position to effectively contest the commitment proceedings because he has no way to rebut the testimony of the psychiatrist from the institution who has already certified to the patient's insanity under N.J.S.A. 30:4–29.

This court has had enough experience to know that psychiatrists differ very definitely in their evaluations and diagnoses of mental illness. In a commitment proceeding where the court is in effect bound by the expertise of the psychiatrist, the right to counsel is of little value without a concurrent right to an independent psychiatric examination.

In addition to the due process basis for appointment of an independent psychiatrist, there is an inferential basis in N.J.S.A. 30:4–42, which provides that the hearing court has the power to order, at the county's expense, taking and transcription of testimony at a commitment hearing. Such a hearing is of little value, if not actually a sham, when the only testimony is that of the certifying psychiatrist. The court is of the opinion that N.J.S.A. 30:4–42 impliedly authorizes the appointment of an independent psychiatrist to examine the patient at the county's expense where his testimony is necessary to make the hearing effective.

The appointment of independent psychiatrists for indigents has been approved in our sister states of New York and Pennsylvania, and has been long established in the District of Columbia.

The right to counsel has not been construed to allow an indigent to choose his own lawyer. Similarly, an indigent in a commitment proceeding should not have the right to "shop around" for a psychiatrist who agrees with him. The independent psychiatrist is to assist the court, not the patient; all he need do is render his best judgment and make all relevant information available both to the court and to the defense.

Therefore, the court will entertain an order for the appointment of an independent psychiatrist to examine the movant, such psychiatrist to be designated by the court and paid by the county.

Motion granted.

Questions and Comments

1. In a sense there is always an absolute right to an independent psychiatric evaluation, since the defendant has a constitutional right to introduce any relevant evidence, including expert testimony. The real issue pertains to access to an independent psychiatric expert when the individual is indigent or has limited financial means. Only a minority of states have enacted specific statutory provisions authorizing the appointment of an independent psychiatric expert if the defendant makes such a request.

Generally, these statutes stipulate that the expert appointed to perform the mental examination must be medically trained. The current tendency, however, is to authorize the appointment of any "qualified expert," which is defined to include clinical psychologists. *See,* West's Ann.Cal.Welf. & Instit.Code §§ 5251, 6507 (1972), Ill.Rev.Stat. (Section 3804) 1979. On the use of psychologists in civil commitment proceedings, *see* Miller, Lower and Bleechmore, *The Clinical Psychologist as an Expert Witness on Questions of Mental Illness and Competency,* 4 Law and Psych.Rev. 115 (1978).

2. The value of a psychiatric examination is discussed in Perr, *Independent Examination of Patients Hospitalized Against Their Will,* 131 American Journal of Psychiatry 765 (1974). *Also see* Special Project, *The Administration of Psychiatric Justice: Theory and Practice in Arizona,* 13 Ariz.L.Rev. 1, 60 n. 195 (1971).

7. Standard of Proof in Commitment Proceedings

It is the state which must prove that an individual is committable. The central problem is determining what quantum of evidence is required for the state to have proven its case.

The law has established various standards of proof; their use depends on the nature of the particular proceeding. The most familiar is the standard of "proof beyond a reasonable (*i.e.,* well-founded) doubt," which is used in criminal cases. This most stringent burden is thought necessary because of the possible deprivation of liberty a person confronted with a criminal charge faces.

A lesser standard is typically used for non-criminal civil cases, such as contract disputes or negligence cases (e.g., malpractice). In such a case, the plaintiff must prove his case by a "preponderance of the evidence" in order to prevail. Technically, this standard means that the plaintiff must present more evidence favorable to his position than there is against it.

A third, intermediate standard is proof by "clear and convincing evidence." This standard is more demanding than the preponderance standard but less so than the reasonable doubt standard. All of these standards, however, are general guidelines, not litmus-paper tests in the actual fact-finding process. The credibility and weight given to any evidence remain subject to the deliberative process of the individual judge or juror.

ADDINGTON v. TEXAS

Supreme Court of the United States, 1979.
441 U.S. 418, 99 S.Ct. 1804, 60 L.Ed.2d 323.

Mr. Chief Justice BURGER delivered the opinion of the Court.

The question in this case is what standard of proof is required by the Fourteenth Amendment to the Constitution in a civil proceeding brought under state law to commit an individual involuntarily for an indefinite period to a state mental hospital.

I

On seven occasions between 1969 and 1975, appellant was committed temporarily to various Texas state mental hospitals and was committed for indefinite periods to Austin State Hospital on three different occasions. On December 18, 1975, when appellant was arrested on a misdemeanor charge of "assault by threat" against his mother, the county and state mental health authorities therefore were well aware of his history of mental and emotional difficulties.

Appellant's mother filed a petition for his indefinite commitment in accordance with Texas law. The county psychiatric examiner interviewed appellant while in custody and after the interview issued a Certificate of Medical Examination for Mental Illness. In the certificate, the examiner stated his opinion that appellant was "mentally ill and require[d] hospitalization in a mental hospital."

Appellant retained counsel and a trial was held before a jury to determine in accord with the statute:

"(1) whether the proposed patient is mentally ill, and if so

"(2) whether he requires hospitalization in a mental hospital for * * * the protection of others. * * *

The trial on these issues extended over six days.

The State offered evidence that appellant suffered from serious delusions, that he often had threatened to injure both of his parents and others, that he had been involved in several assaultive episodes while hospitalized and that he had caused substantial property damage both at his own apartment and at his parents' home. From these undisputed facts, two psychiatrists, who qualified as experts, expressed opinions that appellant suffered from psychotic schizophrenia and that he had paranoid tendencies. They also expressed medical opinions that appellant was probably dangerous both to himself and to others. They explained that appellant required hospitalization in a closed area to treat his condition because in the past he had refused to attend outpatient treatment programs and had escaped several times from mental hospitals.

* * *

The trial judge submitted the case to the jury with the instructions in the form of two questions:

"1. Based on clear, unequivocal and convincing evidence, is Frank O'Neal Addington mentally ill?

"2. Based on clear, unequivocal and convincing evidence, does Frank O'Neal Addington require hospitalization in a mental hospital for his own welfare and protection or the protection of others?"

Appellant objected to these instructions on several grounds, including the trial court's refusal to employ the "beyond a reasonable doubt" standard of proof.

The jury found that appellant was mentally ill and that he required hospitalization for his own or others' welfare. The trial court then entered an order committing appellant as a patient to Austin State Hospital for an indefinite period.

Appellant appealed that order to the Texas Court of Civil Appeals, arguing, among other things, that the standards for commitment violated his substantive due process rights and that any standard of proof for commitment less than that required for criminal convictions, *i.e.*, beyond a reasonable doubt, violated his procedural due process rights. The Court of Civil Appeals agreed with appellant on the standard-of-proof issue and reversed the judgment of the trial court.

* * *

On appeal, the Texas Supreme Court reversed the Court of Civil Appeals' decision.

II

The function of a standard of proof, as that concept is embodied in the Due Process Clause and in the realm of factfinding, is to "instruct the factfinder concerning the degree of confidence our society thinks he should have in the correctness of factual conclusions for a particular type of adjudication." The standard serves to allocate the risk of error between the litigants and to indicate the relative importance attached to the ultimate decision.

Generally speaking, the evolution of this area of the law has produced across a continuum three standards or levels of proof for different types of cases. At one end of the spectrum is the typical civil case involving a monetary dispute between private parties. Since society has a minimal concern with the outcome of such private suits, plaintiff's burden of proof is a mere preponderance of the evidence. The litigants thus share the risk of error in roughly equal fashion.

In a criminal case, on the other hand, the interests of the defendant are of such magnitude that historically and without any explicit constitutional requirement they have been protected by standards of proof designed to exclude as nearly as possible the likelihood of an erroneous judgment. In the administration of criminal justice, our society imposes almost the entire risk of error upon itself. This is accomplished by requiring under the Due Process Clause that the state prove the guilt of an accused beyond a reasonable doubt.

The intermediate standard, which usually employs some combination of the words "clear," "cogent," "unequivocal," and "convincing," is less commonly used, but nonetheless "is no stranger to the civil law." One typical use of the standard is in civil cases involving allegations of fraud or some other quasi-criminal wrongdoing by the defendant. The interests at stake in those cases are deemed to be more substantial than mere loss of money and some jurisdictions accordingly reduce the risk to the defendant of having his reputation tarnished erroneously by increasing the plaintiff's burden of proof. Similarly, this Court has used the "clear, unequivocal and convincing" standard of proof to protect particularly important individual interests in various civil cases. [*i.e.*, deportation and denaturalization.]

Candor suggests that, to a degree, efforts to analyze what lay jurors understand concerning the differences among these three tests or the nuances of a judge's instructions on the law may well be largely an academic exercise; there are no directly relevant empirical studies. Indeed, the ultimate truth as to how the standards of proof affect decisionmaking may well be unknowable, given that factfinding is a process shared by countless thousands of individuals throughout the country. We probably can assume no more than that the difference between a preponderance of the evidence and proof beyond a reasonable doubt probably is better understood than either of them in relation to the intermediate standard of clear and convincing evidence. Nonetheless, even if the particular standard-of-proof catchwords do not always make a great difference in a particular case, adopting a "standard of proof is more than an empty semantic exercise."

III

In considering what standard should govern in a civil commitment proceeding, we must assess both the extent of the individual's interest in not being involuntarily confined indefinitely and the state's interest in committing the emotionally disturbed under a particular standard of proof. Moreover, we must be mindful that the function of legal process is to minimize the risk of erroneous decisions.

A

This Court repeatedly has recognized that civil commitment for any purpose constitutes a significant deprivation of liberty that requires due process protection. Moreover, it is indisputable that involuntary commitment to a mental hospital after a finding of probable dangerousness to self or others can engender adverse social consequences to the individual. Whether we label this phenomena "stigma" or choose to call it something else is less important than that we recognize that it can occur and that it can have a very significant impact on the individual.

The state has a legitimate interest under its *parens patriae* powers in providing care to its citizens who are unable because of emotional disorders to care for themselves; the state also has authority under its police power to protect the community from the dangerous tendencies of some who are mentally ill. Under the Texas Mental Health Code, however, the State has no interest in confining individuals involuntarily if they are not mentally ill or if they do not pose some danger to themselves or others. Since the preponderance standard creates the risk of increasing the number of individuals erroneously committed, it is at least unclear to what extent, if any, the state's interests are furthered by using a preponderance standard in such commitment proceedings.

The expanding concern of society with problems of mental disorders is reflected in the fact that in recent years many states have enacted statutes designed to protect the rights of the mentally ill. However, only one state by statute permits involuntary commitment by a mere preponderance of the evidence, Miss.Code Ann. § 41–21–75 (1978 Supp.), and Texas is the only state where a court has concluded that the preponderance-of-the-evidence standard satisfies due process. We attribute this not to any lack of concern in those states, but rather to a belief that the varying standards tend to produce comparable results. As we noted earlier, however, standards of proof are important for their symbolic meaning as well as for their practical effect.

At one time or another every person exhibits some abnormal behavior which might be perceived by some as symptomatic of a mental or emotional disorder, but which is in fact within a range of conduct that is generally acceptable. Obviously, such behavior is no basis for compelled treatment and surely none for confinement.

However, there is the possible risk that a factfinder might decide to commit an individual based solely on a few isolated instances of unusual conduct. Loss of liberty calls for a showing that the individual suffers from something more serious than is demonstrated by idiosyncratic behavior. Increasing the burden of proof is one way to impress the factfinder with the importance of the decision and thereby perhaps to reduce the chances that inappropriate commitments will be ordered.

The individual should not be asked to share equally with society the risk of error when the possible injury to the individual is significantly greater than any possible harm to the state. We conclude that the individual's interest in the outcome of a civil commitment proceeding is of such weight and gravity that due process requires the state to justify confinement by proof more substantial than a mere preponderance of the evidence.

B

Appellant urges the Court to hold that due process requires use of the criminal law's standard of proof—"beyond a reasonable doubt."

* * *

There are significant reasons why different standards of proof are called for in civil commitment proceedings as opposed to criminal prosecutions. In a civil commitment state power is not exercised in a punitive sense. Unlike the delinquency proceeding in *Winship*, a civil commitment proceeding can in no sense be equated to a criminal prosecution.

In addition, the "beyond a reasonable doubt" standard historically has been reserved for criminal cases. This unique standard of proof, not prescribed or defined in the Constitution, is regarded as a critical part of the "moral force of the criminal law," and we should hesitate to apply it too broadly or casually in noncriminal cases.

The heavy standard applied in criminal cases manifests our concern that the risk of error to the individual must be minimized even at the risk that some who are guilty might go free. The full force of that idea does not apply to a civil commitment. It may be true that an erroneous commitment is sometimes as undesirable as an erroneous conviction * * *. However, even though an erroneous confinement should be avoided in the first instance, the layers of professional review and observation of the patient's condition, and the concern of family and friends generally will provide continuous opportunities for an erroneous commitment to be corrected. Moreover, it is not true that the release of a genuinely mentally ill person is no worse for the individual than the failure to convict the guilty. One who is suffering from a debilitating mental illness and in need of treatment is neither wholly at liberty nor free of stigma.

It cannot be said, therefore, that it is much better for a mentally ill person to "go free" than for a mentally normal person to be committed.

Finally, the initial inquiry in a civil commitment proceeding is very different from the central issue in either a delinquency proceeding or a criminal prosecution. In the latter cases the basic issue is a straightforward factual question—did the accused commit the act alleged? There may be factual issues to resolve in a commitment proceeding, but the factual aspects represent only the beginning of the inquiry. Whether the individual is mentally ill and dangerous to either himself or others and is in need of confined therapy turns on the *meaning* of the facts which must be interpreted by expert psychiatrists and psychologists. Given the lack of certainty and the fallibility of psychiatric diagnosis, there is a serious question as to whether a state could ever prove beyond a reasonable doubt that an individual is both mentally ill and likely to be dangerous.

The subtleties and nuances of psychiatric diagnosis render certainties virtually beyond reach in most situations. The reasonable-doubt standard of criminal law functions in its realm because there the standard is addressed to specific, knowable facts. Psychiatric diagnosis, in contrast, is to a large extent based on medical "impressions" drawn from subjective analysis and filtered through the experience of the diagnostician. This process often makes it very difficult for the expert physician to offer definite conclusions about any particular patient. Within the medical discipline, the traditional standard for "factfinding" is a "reasonable medical certainty." If a trained psychiatrist has difficulty with the categorical "beyond a reasonable doubt" standard, the untrained lay juror—or indeed even a trained judge—who is required to rely upon expert opinion could be forced by the criminal law standard of proof to reject commitment for many patients desperately in need of institutionalized psychiatric care. Such "freedom" for a mentally ill person would be purchased at a high price.

* * *

That some states have chosen—either legislatively or judicially— to adopt the criminal law standard gives no assurance that the more stringent standard of proof is needed or is even adaptable to the needs of all states. The essence of federalism is that states must be free to develop a variety of solutions to problems and not be forced into a common, uniform mold. As the substantive standards for civil commitment may vary from state to state, procedures must be allowed to vary so long as they meet the constitutional minimum. We conclude that it is unnecessary to require states to apply the strict, criminal standard.

C

Having concluded that the preponderance standard falls short of meeting the demands of due process and that the reasonable-doubt standard is not required, we turn to a middle level of burden of proof that strikes a fair balance between the rights of the individual and the legitimate concerns of the state. We note that 20 states, most by statute, employ the standard of "clear and convincing" evidence; 3 states use "clear, *cogent*, and convincing" evidence; and 2 states require "clear, *unequivocal* and convincing" evidence.

We have concluded that the reasonable-doubt standard is inappropriate in civil commitment proceedings because, given the uncertainties of psychiatric diagnosis, it may impose a burden the state cannot meet and thereby erect an unreasonable barrier to needed medical treatment. Similarly, we conclude that use of the term "unequivocal" is not constitutionally required, although the states are free to use that standard. To meet due process demands, the standard has to inform the factfinder that the proof must be greater than the preponderance-of-the-evidence standard applicable to other categories of civil cases. * * *

[We] remand the case for further proceedings not inconsistent with this opinion.

Vacated and remanded.

Mr. Justice POWELL took no part in the consideration or decision of this case.

Questions and Comments

1. One commentator has suggested that the results in *Addington v. Texas* and the Court's decision in *Parham v. J.R.*, 442 U.S. 584, 99 S.Ct. 2493, 61 L.Ed.2d 101 (1979), indicate that "the court is unwilling to curb the power of institutional psychiatry through the creation of additional procedural safeguards for the mentally ill. The court may be signaling that the spill over of the rights from the criminal justice system to the mental health system has ended." Elkins, *Legal Representation of the Mentally Ill*, 82 W.Va.L.Rev. 157, 157 n. 1 (1979).

2. Does the standard announced in *Addington v. Texas* apply to a commitment hearing that follows an acquittal of a crime on the grounds of insanity? A number of states have enacted special commitment provisions for this class of persons. Some states such as Connecticut provide that where a person has been acquitted on grounds of insanity and is deemed to be dangerous, the state must prove his dangerousness by only a *preponderance of the evidence* rather than by clear and convincing evidence. The constitutionality of a different standard of proof for commitment following an acquittal on grounds of insanity was addressed by the Supreme Court in *Jones v. United States*, — U.S. —, 103 S.Ct. 3043, 77 L.Ed.2d 694 (1983), which appears at p. 648 *infra*.

3. Is there any basis for applying different procedural rules and standards of proof where the commitment is for the protection of the individual rather than for the protection of society? Are the purposes of the state in the latter instance more like those that apply in the administration of criminal laws?

8. *Privilege Against Self-Incrimination*

WESSON, *THE PRIVILEGE AGAINST SELF–INCRIMINA-TION IN CIVIL COMMITMENT PROCEEDINGS*
1980 Wis.L.Rev. 697, 698–700 (1980).

One who attends, or reads accounts of, many civil commitment proceedings will be struck by the extent to which the evidence presented at the hearings commonly has a single source—the respondent. The state's principal witness is almost always a psychiatrist or other mental health professional who has examined the respondent, frequently while he or she was involuntarily in the examiner's custody. The state may also present, either directly or as a basis for the examiner's testimony, observations of the respondent made by nursing staff, aides, clinical psychologists, and even custodial personnel. The perceptions of these individuals are often available only because the state has used its coercive powers to require the respondent to submit to observation.

The use of respondent-generated evidence is surprising to lawyers brought up in the Anglo-American tradition, who expect that the state will not be permitted to exact one's cooperation in his or her own imprisonment—a traditional value finding constitutional expression in the fifth amendment's privilege against self-incrimination.

*   *   *

The fifth amendment's protection against compelled self-incrimination offers the individual accused of a crime several important advantages. In the courtroom, it offers the defendant not only the option to decline to answer questions the answers to which might be incriminating, but also the option to decline to take the stand. It prohibits the prosecution from calling the jury's attention to the defendant's failure to testify, and prohibits the judge from instructing the jury that it may take account of the defendant's silence. It also forbids the jury, to the extent that its deliberations can be policed, from drawing any unfavorable inferences from that silence.

Outside the courtroom, the privilege against self-incrimination contains several important limitations on the conduct of state agencies—usually the police—in questioning any suspect in custody. Suspects have an absolute right to remain silent, and must be informed of that right. Suspects must be told that their statements may be used against them. Any statement a suspect makes in response to interrogation before having been advised of the right to silence is inadmissible at any later judicial proceeding except for purposes of impeachment. In addition, the privilege against self-incrimination requires that suspects be informed of the right to counsel; if a suspect requests counsel, either the request must be granted or all interrogation must cease. Once the required advice is given, a suspect's silence in response to interrogation cannot be the basis of later comment at a trial or hearing—even for purposes of impeaching a defense or alibi later articulated.

In addition to the complicated network of warnings and rules that it erects for the accused criminal in pretrial stages, the privilege against self-incrimination assures that involuntary statements—statements that are the results of official coercion, force, or trickery, rather than willing acts of the accused—may not be used against the accused for any purpose. * * *

The situation of one taken into custody because he is suspected of mental illness presents a stark contrast to the situation of the accused criminal. Accused criminals are not, at least in theory, taken into custody to make it convenient for the police to use them as sources of evidence. They are supposed to be detained in most cases merely for completion of appropriate charging routines and for some expeditious proceeding to assure, through the mechanism of bail, that the accused will appear for trial. Persons suspected of being mentally disturbed are, on the other hand, commonly confined for days or weeks for the express purpose of giving the state's experts an opportunity to "investigate" their mental states, propensities for violence, and need for treatment—precisely the characteristics that may form the basis for their eventual involuntary confinement in an institution. The mental health respondent will probably not be advised of any right to remain silent during the psychiatric examination, or that his or her statements may be the basis for involuntary commitment proceedings. Even if the respondent is told of the right to counsel and indicates he or she wishes to exercise that right, observation and testing will most likely continue until counsel's arrival. Should the respondent refuse to speak to the examiner, he or she still will not escape psychiatric probing. The professional will analyze the respondent's demeanor and nonverbal attitudes, as well as the specific words used to express the refusal to speak. Mental health professionals have been trained to overcome the reluctance of their subjects. Any communications eventually made will probably be the product of the interviewer's skill rather than the freely chosen disclosures of the respondent.

The mental health respondent's situation in court is less clear. Since few mental health proceedings are jury trials, the questions of comment upon and inference from a respondent's silence have not been fully litigated. It is unlikely that an objection to an expert witness's account of the respondent's refusal to cooperate would be sustained on self-incrimination grounds. Some courts have held that there is no prohibition against the state's calling the respondent to the stand at a civil commitment proceeding, although this question is also seldom litigated.

How can these dramatic differences in the situation of the criminal defendant and the mental health respondent be explained? * * * The most significant explanation, * * * is the characterization of commitment proceedings as "civil" in nature and hence inappropriate forums for the invocation of protections designed for the accused criminal.

LESSARD v. SCHMIDT

United States District Court, Eastern District of Wisconsin, 1972.
349 F.Supp. 1078, vacated on other grounds, 421 U.S. 957, 95 S.Ct. 1943, 44 L.Ed.2d 445 (1975).

J. SPRECHER, Circuit Judge.

Plaintiffs assert that the privilege against self-incrimination is applicable to civil commitment proceedings. As may readily be seen, application of the privilege involves conflicting considerations. On the one hand, statements made by a prospective mental patient may well be the basis for total involuntary loss of freedom, and thus it will not do to simply label these proceedings civil. In this respect at least the Supreme Court's opinion in In re Gault, 387 U.S. 1, 49, 50, 87 S.Ct. 1428, 1455, 1456, 18 L.Ed.2d 527 (1967), is directly applicable:

> "It is true that the statement of the privilege in the Fifth Amendment, which is applicable to the States by reason of the Fourteenth Amendment, is that no person 'shall be compelled in any *criminal case* to be a witness against himself.' However, it is also clear that the availability of the privilege does not turn upon the type of proceeding in which its protection is invoked, but upon the nature of the statement or admission and the exposure which it invites. The privilege may, for example, be claimed in a civil or administrative proceeding, if the statement is or may be inculpatory.

> * * *

> * * * "[C]ommitment is a deprivation of liberty. It is incarceration against one's will, whether it is called 'criminal' or 'civil.' And our Constitution guarantees that no person shall be 'compelled' to be a witness against himself when he is threatened with deprivation of his liberty—a command which this Court has broadly applied and generously implemented in accordance with the teaching of the history of the privilege and its great office in mankind's battle for freedom."

* * *

We find Justice Douglas' opinion and the underlying decision in *Gault* persuasive. Wisconsin may not, consistent with basic concepts of due process, commit individuals on the basis of their statements to psychiatrists in the absence of a showing that the statements were made with "knowledge" that the individual was not obliged to speak. We do think, however, that the safeguards of the privilege may be obtained without the presence of counsel in the psychiatric interview. The patient should be told by counsel and the psychiatrist that he is going to be examined with regard to his mental condition, that the statements he may make may be the basis for commitment, and that he does not have to speak to the psychiatrist. Having been informed of this danger the patient may be examined if he willingly assents. It may be expected that most patients, like Miss Lessard in the present case, will desire to talk to a person they believe they can trust. Basic fairness requires, though, that they be given notice of the fact that their statements may indeed tend to incriminate them in the eyes of the psychiatrist and the trier of fact in a civil commitment proceeding.

*   *   *

MOSS v. STATE

Court of Civil Appeals of Texas, 1976.
539 S.W.2d 936.

GUITTARD, Justice.

*   *   *

The most difficult question presented is that raised by appellant's sixth ground, which attacks the provision of § 32 of the Code authorizing the judge to order the proposed patient to submit to a psychiatric examination. This section provides:

(a) Before a hearing may be had on an Application for Temporary Hospitalization there must be filed with the county court Certificates of Medical Examination for Mental Illness by two (2) physicians who have examined the proposed patient within five (5) days of the filing of the Certificate, each stating that the proposed patient is mentally ill and requires observation and/or treatment in a mental hospital.

(b) If the Certificates of two (2) physicians are not filed with the Application, the county judge shall appoint the necessary physicians, at least one of whom shall be a psychiatrist if one is available in the county, to examine the proposed patient and file Certificates with the county court. *The judge may order the proposed patient to submit to the examination.* [Emphasis added.]

Acting pursuant to this section, the probate judge appointed two physicians to examine appellant and ordered her to submit to such examinations. The examinations proceeded notwithstanding notice by appellant's counsel that appellant did not consent. The examining physicians were permitted to testify at the hearing, over appellant's objection, concerning their diagnosis and recommendations based on information obtained from appellant in these examinations.

Appellant argues that since involuntary hospitalization is a deprivation of liberty, the proposed patient has the same privilege to refuse to give evidence against himself as a person accused of a crime. Consequently, she insists, to order a person to submit to the interrogation involved in a psychiatric examination, as implied by § 32(b), requires him to give evidence against himself, thus depriving him of his liberty contrary to the fifth and fourteenth amendments to the Constitution of the United States.

We are not concerned with whether a person ordered to submit to a psychiatric examination under § 32(b) may refuse to divulge information that might be used against him in a criminal prosecution. For the purpose of this opinion, we assume that he may claim the privilege to this extent. Our question is whether he may refuse to answer any or all questions put to him by the appointed psychiatrist or other physician on the ground that his answers may be used against him in a civil commitment proceeding.

We have found only one decision holding that the privilege against self-incrimination applies in this situation. In *Lessard v. Schmidt*, 349 F.Supp. 1078, 1100–02 (E.D.Wis.1972), *vacated on other grounds*, 421 U.S. 957, 95 S.Ct. 1943, 44 L.Ed.2d 445 (1975), a three-judge federal district court made a broad review of the Wisconsin commitment procedure and held that statements to a psychiatrist, unless made voluntarily after notice of the possible consequences, cannot be the basis for an order of commitment, since such statements are incriminating in effect. Other authorities have seen a distinction between criminal prosecutions and civil commitment proceedings, in that the principal issue in a civil commitment proceeding is present mental condition rather than past anti-social activity, and have adopted the view that to recognize the privilege in this situation would deprive the court of the best and most reliable evidence,

*   *   *

The Supreme Court's unwillingness to apply criminal due process requirements inflexibly to all proceedings involving involuntary incarceration is demonstrated in *McKeiver v. Pennsylvania*, 403 U.S. 528, 91 S.Ct. 1976, 29 L.Ed.2d 647 (1971), in which the Court held that due process does not require trial by jury in a juvenile delinquency case. Likewise, in *Morrissey v. Brewer*, 408 U.S. 471, 481, 92 S.Ct. 2593, 2600, 33 L.Ed.2d 484 (1972), which involved the application of due process guarantees to proceedings for revocation of parole, the Court reaffirmed previous declarations that due process is flexible and calls for such procedural protection as the particular situation demands, and that a determination of what process is due requires a determination of the precise nature of the governmental function involved and the private interest affected.

We are persuaded that the balance of the competing public and private interests with respect to the privilege of withholding information from the court in a civil commitment proceeding differs substantially from the balance struck in *Gault* for juvenile delinquency proceedings. In *Gault*, the Court emphasized the possibility that the juvenile's admissions of guilt might be used against him in a criminal prosecution if the juvenile court should exercise its discretion to relinquish its jurisdiction to the ordinary criminal courts. 387 U.S. at 50–51, 87 S.Ct. at 1456.

* * *

The major ground of the decision, however, appears to rest on the Court's analysis of the rationale underlying the privilege against self-incrimination. According to the prevailing opinion by Justice Fortas, the privilege is based on the assumption that the confession of a criminal act is basically untrustworthy unless shown to be entirely voluntary. The Court reasons that if a confession of crime is untrustworthy in the case of an adult, it is even more so in the case of a child, as illustrated by the examples cited of children who confessed to crimes they did not commit. 387 U.S. 44–56, 87 S.Ct. 1453–59.

In our opinion the considerations deemed controlling in *Gault* do not apply with the same force when the issue is not a past act, which can be established by the testimony of an ordinary witness, but a present mental condition, which can be adequately described and evaluated only with the assistance of experts. There is little danger that the statements of the proposed patient to the examiner will be taken as evidence in a subsequent criminal proceeding, since the privilege is admittedly applicable to that extent. So far as untrustworthiness is concerned, the opinion of a physician based on the patient's statements to him is likely to be more reliable than the opinion of the same physician if based on the statements of other witnesses who must rely on their own casual and untrained observation. Although an examination ordered by the court may be coercive to some extent, particularly if the patient is under detention, no particular answer is as likely to be coerced as when the inquiry is whether the person in question committed a particular criminal act. Consequently, we do not consider such a compelled examination inhumane or likely to produce an untrustworthy result to the same extent as a confession of crime elicited by interrogation of an accused person in custody of the police.

Indeed, a mental examination by a psychiatrist or other physician may properly be regarded as a protection for a person alleged to be mentally ill. The people of Texas have recognized this protection by including in their Bill of Rights a provision that "no person shall be committed as a person of unsound mind except on competent medical or psychiatric testimony." Tex.Const. art. I, § 15–a. This provision is a strong declaration of the public policy of this state concerning the necessity of expert testimony in a civil commitment proceeding. Without this guarantee, a person who is merely eccentric may be committed to an institution against his will on the basis of testimony by misguided or unscrupulous persons who are neither enlightened nor restrained by the training, experience, and standards of the medical profession. This guarantee would be substantially weakened, and perhaps nullified, if the physician or psychiatrist is provided no opportunity to employ the procedures recognized in the profession for diagnosing the problems of the mentally disturbed patient.

The psychiatric interview, as we understand it, is highly important to proper diagnosis and treatment of a mentally disturbed patient. In a case of physical illness, the physician consulted would be at a serious disadvantage if he is required to make a diagnosis and prescribe a treatment without examining the patient and hearing at first hand the patient's own account of his history and complaints. A psychiatrist or other physician consulted about suspected mental illness is at an equal if not greater disadvantage if he is required to make a diagnosis and recommendation without a direct interview with the patient, since the only manifestation of mental illness may be the patient's revelation of his own mental processes. An opinion based on an interview is likely to be more reliable than one based entirely on information related to the physician by the patient's family or other related persons or one expressed in court in response to a hypothetical question based on the testimony of other witnesses. Thus the [state] constitutional guarantee of "competent medical or psychiatric testimony," reasonably implies a proper opportunity to examine the patient and affords substantial protection against deprivation of liberty, even to a person unwilling to submit to such examination. Certainly a proposed patient who may be dangerous to himself or others should not be able to avoid restraint by refusing to submit to the examination necessary to satisfy the requirements of the Texas Constitution and Mental Health Code.

We recognize, of course, that the fourteenth amendment right of due process takes precedence over the provision of our Texas Bill of Rights, but, as the Supreme Court of the United States has recognized in the cases above discussed, due process is a flexible concept requiring a balancing of interests. The interest of the individual in maintaining his liberty must be balanced against the interest of the state in protecting its citizens against injury from mentally disturbed persons, and also against the state's interest in providing care and treatment for mentally disturbed persons unable to appreciate the necessity for hospitalization. On striking that balance in the light of the foregoing considerations, we conclude that due process does not require an absolute privilege against providing information in a psychiatric interview that may be used by the interviewer as basis for his recommendation for hospitalization, but rather requires safeguards to assure that such interviews are not employed as instruments of abuse or oppression.

Questions and Comments

1. Most courts, following *Moss v. State*, have found that the privilege against self-incrimination cannot be invoked to preclude the admission of the testimony of examining experts. For instance, *see In re Beverly*, 342 So.2d 481, 488 (Fla.1977), and *Tippett v. Maryland*, 436 F.2d 1153 (4th Cir.1971), both holding that the privilege against self-incrimination does not require advising the subjects of commitment proceedings that their statements may be used in such proceedings. The

Supreme Court granted certiorari *sub nom. Murel v. Baltimore City Criminal Court*, 404 U.S. 909, 92 S.Ct. 567, 30 L.Ed.2d 552 (1971), but later dismissed it as improvidently granted, 407 U.S. 355 (1972). Note, however, that psychiatric testimony can, in some instances, be excluded on other grounds. For instance, the "psychotherapist/patient" privilege, which is recognized by various states, could be used to exclude testimony if the psychiatrist or psychologist who is called upon to testify was acting as the defendant's therapist *at the time of the examination. See* Note, *Application of the Fifth Amendment Privilege Against Self-Incrimination to the Civil Commitment Proceeding*, 1973 Duke L.J. 729, Note 33 (1979). This issue is discussed in detail in Chapter Four.

2. Some states have by statute restricted the use of evidence provided by the subject in the course of a psychiatric examination. The Wisconsin statute, for instance, provides:

> Prior to the examination the subject individual shall be informed that his or her statements can be used as a basis for commitment and that he or she has the right to remain silent, and that the examiner is required to make a report to the court even if the subject individual remains silent. Wis.Stat. § 51.20(9) (1977).

It may also be the practice of some mental health facilities to provide similar warnings even when not statutorily required to do so. Such warnings, even when given, may be delivered in ambiguous terms. See, *e.g., Gibson v. Zahradnick*, 581 F.2d 75, 78 (4th Cir.1978) (defendant committed for restoration of competency told that he "had a right to refuse to talk" to psychiatrist but that it "would be helpful" if he would talk). They may also be dictated by nonconstitutional considerations. *See Commonwealth v. Lamb*, 365 Mass. 265, 311 N.E.2d 47 (1974) (patient must be warned that statutory physician-patient privilege does not apply and that the patient's statements may be used at commitment hearings). *See* generally, Wesson, *The Privilege against Self-Incrimination in Civil Commitment Proceedings*, 1980 Wis.L.Rev. 697, Note 18 (1980).

3. Whether other constitutional protections such as the Fourth Amendment (which prohibits unreasonable search and seizure) are applicable to civil commitment proceedings has not been addressed in any reported decision. See generally Wayne R. LaFave, Search and Seizure: A Treatise on the Fourth Amendment, (St. Paul, Minn.: West Publishing Co., 1978), pp. 88–89.

D. REVOCATION OF CONDITIONAL RELEASE: PROCEDURAL REQUIREMENTS

The commitment laws of numerous states permit institutionalized patients to be given convalescent leave or to be released from the institution on a conditional basis. Such release is provisional, however, and under appropriate circumstances the patient may be summarily readmitted, thereby circumventing the usual commitment procedures.

Laws authorizing convalescent leaves or conditional releases are designed to facilitate the recovery of the patient and promote his reentry into the outside community. This approach, as described by one authority, calls for the placement of the patient upon his release in one of a range of residential settings that have varying degrees of supervision. Note, *Constitutional Law: The Summary Revocation of an Involuntary Mental Patient's Convalescent Leave—Is It Unconstitutional?*, 33 Okla.L.Rev. 366, 369 (1980). In this way "the patient makes a transition from the acute treatment facility to resumption of his normal life through a series of steps." *Id.* at 369.

As a practical matter, however, such transitional facilities rarely exist, and in most cases conditional release programs operate on a much more basic level. Typically, upon release the patient returns directly to his former community, living either at home or in a half-way house or shelter care home. At the same time, he is generally referred to a local community mental health center, which is to provide medication and general supervision.

A central feature of most laws authorizing the conditional release of patients is the authority of the head of the facility where the patient was originally confined to revoke the conditional release whenever he believes "the conditions justifying hospitalization continue to exist." *Application of True*, 103 Idaho 151, 645 P.2d 891, 893 (1982). Moreover, this authority to revoke conditional release is generally absolute and the patient is denied any right to a hearing. This authority may be exercised for as long as the conditional release is in effect, which in many states may be up to twelve months.

These provisions giving summary revocation power to a facility's director have come under increasing attack in recent years. On the one hand, these provisions are seen as unconstitutionally infringing on the patient's liberty by denying the patient any right to a hearing before or after his readmission. From the standpoint of the institution the authority of summary revocation is seen as a necessary adjunct to a policy which emphasizes the integration of patients into the community at the earliest possible time. Without such authority, it is argued, the institution would be less able to extend its authority over the patient and ensure that the patient continues treatment during the transitional period. These conflicting interests and how they relate to the procedural aspects of the revocation decision are explored in the case which follows:

APPLICATION OF TRUE v. DEPARTMENT OF HEALTH AND WELFARE

Supreme Court of Idaho, 1982.
103 Idaho 151, 645 P.3d 891.

McFADDEN, Justice.

*   *   *

Helen True appeals from an order entered by the district court quashing a writ of habeas corpus. The return on the writ of habeas corpus discloses that the appellant is a patient at State Hospital South in the custody of the Idaho Department of Health and Welfare pursuant to a judicial hospitalization order dated December 30, 1971. It is undisputed that at some point in time following the appellant's being placed in the custody of the [Idaho Department of Health and Welfare] she was placed on conditional release (outpatient) status, but was then summarily returned to State Hospital South for rehospitalization on August 22, 1974.

The appellant subsequently instituted the instant habeas corpus proceedings on August 31, 1978, challenging the constitutionality of her rehospitalization. The issue before us is whether due process principles enunciated by the United States Supreme Court in *Morrissey v. Brewer*, 408 U.S. 471, 92 S.Ct. 2593, 33 L.Ed.2d 484 (1972), dictate that a patient committed to the custody of the Department of Health and Welfare but who has been conditionally released from institutional hospitalization must be afforded written notice and a hearing prior to the revocation of his conditional release status.

At the time the appellant was rehospitalized, then in effect I.C. §§ 66–338 and 339 (1974), governed the conditional release of those persons committed to the custody of the Department of Health and Welfare. I.C. § 66–338(a) (1974) authorized the director of the department or his designated representative to "release an improved patient on the condition that he receive outpatient treatment or on such other reasonable conditions as may be specified." However, an improved patient's conditional release status could be revoked in two situations. First, a conditionally released patient could be immediately rehospitalized in the event the patient had failed to fulfill the conditions of his release and the director of the department or his designated representative "ha[d] reason to believe that conditions justifying hospitalization continue[d] to exist." Second, the director of the department or his designated representative could order the immediate rehospitalization of a conditionally released patient in the event it was reported "by any two (2) persons who are either licensed physicians, health officers, designated examiners or peace officers, the prosecuting attorney or a judge of a court * * * [that the patient] ha[d] relapsed and [was] again in need of hospitalization. Inherent to both situations was a determination that the conditions warranting hospitalization of the patient in the first instance were again present, *i.e.*, the patient was mentally ill or mentally retarded and because of his ailment was likely to injure himself or others. In both situations the order of rehospitalization was *ex parte*, and when indorsed by a judge authorized the immediate detention of the patient.

*   *   *

I

The United States Supreme Court has settled on a two-step analysis in determining the dictates of due process: (1) is the specific interest threatened by government action within the contemplation of the liberty or property language of the Fourteenth Amendment; and (2) assuming the existence of such an interest, what process is due. * * * The initial determination of whether an individual is entitled to any procedural protection involves an examination of the extent to which the person "will be 'condemned to suffer grievous loss' * * * by the allegedly arbitrary action of the state. This determination necessarily entails inquiring whether the asserted interest being threatened by state action is within the scope of the liberty or property language of the Fourteenth Amendment. * * *

"[O]nce it is determined that due process applies, the question remains what process is due."

* * *

In summary, the approach is utilitarian, requiring a preliminary showing that the asserted interest is a cognizable interest under the Fourteenth Amendment, and then requiring a balancing of the relative interests of the individual and the state. * * *

II

Applying the first level of the test and scrutinizing the interest of a conditionally released mental health patient, the court in *Meisel v. Kremens*, 405 F.Supp. 1253, 1256 (E.D.Pa.1975) concluded that:

"At issue in the instant case is not the absolute liberty a person alleged to be mentally ill enjoys prior to his initial commitment to a mental institution, but rather the 'conditional liberty' enjoyed by a person who, after commitment to a mental institution, is then released on parole. * * * The liberty at stake in a civil commitment proceeding is as valuable an interest as the liberty at stake in a criminal trial. * * * [T]he Supreme Court has unanimously held that the 'conditional liberty' of the paroled criminal falls within the scope of the Fourteenth Amendment and is entitled to the protection of the Due Process Clause. *Morrissey v. Brewer, supra*, 408 U.S. at 482, 92 S.Ct. 2593 [at 2600]. * * *

The rationale of the *Meisel* decision was followed by another federal district court in the case of *Lewis v. Donahue*, 437 F.Supp. 112 (M.D. Okla.1977). In *Lewis*, the plaintiff was involuntarily committed to an Oklahoma state mental hospital, and eight days later she was released and placed on outpatient aftercare status. Two and one half months later she was rehospitalized pursuant to Section 73 of Title 43A of the Oklahoma statutes, which provided for the revocation of outpatient aftercare status by way of judicial order, issued summarily, upon *ex parte* application. The court held that the patient in question had a constitutionally protected interest in her conditional liberty, and that the statutory scheme for rehospitalization denied due process because it permitted revocation without notice or opportunity to be heard before rehospitalization.

* * *

The views expressed in the cases of *Meisel* and *Lewis*, are not universally shared by other courts. In *Dietrich v. Brooks*, 27 Or. App. 821, 558 P.2d 357 (1976), the Oregon Court of Appeals did not find that state's conditional release statute unconstitutional. In *Dietrich* the appellant was involuntarily committed to an Oregon state mental hospital, and several months later conditionally released on a "trial visit." Thereafter, he was returned to the hospital after two persons signed an affidavit requesting revocation of the patient's leave. The patient challenged the statute and his rehospitalization as violating due process. The court impliedly recognized that a mental health patient while on conditional release has a protectible "conditional liberty" interest under the Fourteenth Amendment. However, the court opined that there were "profound differences of nature, degree and function between [parole and conditional release] which [made] * * * different due process considerations appropriate." * * * Thus, the court held that when looking at the overall statutory scheme of involuntary commitment, the procedural protections afforded the patient upon summary revocation of conditional release were adequate.

* * *

A synthesis of the above cases leads us to conclude that the better view is the one reflected in the holdings of *Meisel* and *Lewis*. A mental health patient committed to the custody of the Department of Health and Welfare who is conditionally released from hospitalization has a liberty interest in that status which cannot be terminated without due process of law.

* * *

Before turning to the question of what process is due a mental health patient whose conditional release status is subject to revocation, we turn our attention to the Department of Health and Welfare's contention that the post-rehospitalization judicial review procedure as well as the provision for habeas corpus review withstand constitutional scrutiny.

* * *

Both statutory provisions enable a mental health patient to seek an after the fact determination of the propriety of an order of rehospitalization. The United States Supreme Court has recognized that provisions for subsequent judicial inquiry into the propriety of governmental deprivations of liberty or property interests will withstand constitutional scrutiny in limited circumstances, *i.e.*, the opportunity for ultimate judicial determination must adequately protect the interests of the individual affected by the summary action and there must be an overriding state interest in postponing inquiry. In the instant case, however, it cannot be said that [the statutory provisions] adequately protect the interests of a mental health patient whose conditional release status has been revoked. Review under either provision is not mandatory. Neither provision requires that the patient be apprised of the reasons for his rehospitalization. Under these circumstances, there can be no assurances of meaningful review. But more importantly, both provisions are infirm because they place the burden on the patient to bring forth sufficient facts to justify relief from an order of rehospitalization. It is the state, in cases where it seeks to deprive an individual of a protectible liberty or property interest, which must bring forth sufficient facts justifying its summary action.

* * *

Although the United States Supreme Court has not addressed the due process implications of the revocation of a mental health patient's conditional release, it is apparent from the foregoing cases that reliance upon the criminal analogy is suspect in determining what process is due such an individual. * * * It is to be recalled that a decision to revoke a mental health patient's conditional release status and to rehospitalize the patient must be accompanied by a determination that the conditions warranting hospitalization in the first instance are again present. The governmental interest therefore involved when a decision is made to rehospitalize a mental health patient on conditional release status is of significant magnitude: the protection of society from the patient and/or the protection of the patient from himself. Thus viewed, timing becomes more critical in the instant case than it is in the parole setting.

* * *

The great weight we accord the Department's need for immediate rehospitalization of a conditionally released mental health patient suspected of remission is such that the general rule that an individual be given an opportunity for a hearing before he is deprived of a protectible interest is inapplicable. The situation present when a decision is made to revoke the conditional release status of the patient is extraordinary: the patient because of a suspected remission in his mental condition possibly poses a danger to others and/or to himself.

* * * In order to militate against the possibility of an erroneous decision that rehospitalization is warranted, the court is also of the opinion that a mental health patient whose conditional release status is subject to revocation is entitled to mandatory notice and a hearing to follow as soon as is reasonably possible after the patient's return to the hospital.

Specifically, the minimal due process requirements are: (1) prompt written notice to the patient of the reasons for and evidence relied on justifying rehospitalization as well as notice of the right to challenge the allegations and (2) a hearing before a neutral hearing body to be held as soon as is reasonably possible following the patient's rehospitalization, at which time the patient is to be afforded the right to counsel, the right to present evidence and examine witnesses, and upon a decision sustaining the order of rehospitalization, the right to a written statement by the fact-finding body as to the reasons for revocation of the patient's conditional release status. We stress that these are minimal requirements.

* * *

BISTLINE and DONALDSON, JJ., concur.

* * *

Questions and Comments

1. *Meisel v. Kremens* and *Lewis v. Donahue* cited in the court's opinion in *Application of True* serve, of course, to limit the discretion of institutions to revoke conditional releases by requiring a hearing either before or after the patient's readmission. To what extent might the imposition of these procedural requirements discourage institutions from releasing patients where there is some doubt concerning the individual's ability to function outside of the institution?

2. Are there any substantive constitutional limits on the conditions which may be imposed as a condition for release? For instance, in a state where committed patients have the right to decline antipsychotic medication may release be conditional on the patient's agreement to accept medication as an outpatient?

3. According to the court in *Application of True*, due process requires a hearing "before a neutral hearing body to be held as soon as reasonably possible following the patient's rehospitalization." Would a hearing conducted before a hearing officer who is an employee of the institution meet the court's test? In this connection, consider the hearing requirements imposed by the Supreme Court in different but related situations such as the Voluntary Admission of Minors, *See Parham v. J.R.*, at p. 296, and the transfer of prisoners from a commitment institution to a psychiatric facility. *See Vitek v. Jones*, at p. 404 n. 1.

IV. RIGHTS OF INVOLUNTARILY COMMITTED PERSONS

The preceding materials have placed a major emphasis—either directly or indirectly—on the commitment process. This has involved examination of the problems surrounding application of the standards governing commitment as well as the process by which the commitment determination takes place. The final section of this chapter explores the rights of the individual *after* the commitment order has been entered and confinement begins.

A patient in a psychiatric facility retains a variety of legal rights. These rights can arise out of the general laws of the state as well as from federal statutory law. In some instances, as the cases in this section will demonstrate, the source of a patient's rights will often be the United States Constitution itself. Because of the express wording of the Fourteenth Amendment, however, constitutional rights attach only in instances where a patient asserts these rights against an action *by the State or one of its entities*. Resolution of the "state action" question is thus essential to the definition of patient rights. Unless the administration of a psychiatric facility is brought within the ambit of "state action", that facilities' methods of caring for the mentally ill will not be subject to constitutional restraints.

As a result of various court decisions defining "state action", there has been a gradual modification of the public/private dichotomy and a corresponding change in the reach of constitutional protections. These decisions have established the rule that in certain instances, state involvement in a private enterprise converts what would otherwise be private action into "state action". The requirement for such a conversion is a sufficiently close nexus between the State and the challenged action of the private entity "* * * so that the actions of the latter may fairly be treated as that of the State itself." *Blum v. Yaretsky*, 457 U.S. 991, 102 S.Ct. 2777, 2786, 73 L.Ed.2d 534 (1982).

In general, the necessary nexus is established by showing the existence of one of the two following conditions. The first entails a finding that the State "has exercised coercive power or has provided such significant encouragement, either overt or covert, that the choice must in law be deemed to be that of the State." *Blum* at 2786. Alternatively, a sufficient nexus may be established if "the private entity has exercised powers that are traditionally the exclusive perogative of the State." *Blum* at 2786.

The parameters of the "state action" requirement are likely to receive increasing scrutiny in the coming years as states continue to increase the role of privately operated facilities in providing for the care and treatment of the mentally ill. Through a variety of devices, state agencies are endeavoring to promote the establishment of such private facilities. In Illinois, agencies of the State have promoted the establishment of private facilities by offering long term contracts to private interests which provide for State reimbursement for the services rendered to patients. These contracts are then utilized by private operators to obtain financing for the construction of special rehabilitation facilities for the mentally ill, which typically provide care for 100 to 150 patients each when operational.

What remains to be seen is whether such facilities will be characterized as private or as extensions of the State. If the latter view prevails, then the operations of these facilities will be subjected to constitutional limitations and restraints. While higher federal courts have not yet addressed this question directly, the Supreme Court recently expressed a restrictive view of the "state action" concept in *Blum v. Yaretsky*, 457 U.S. 991, 102 S.Ct. 2777, 2786, 73 L.Ed.2d 534 (1982). In *Blum* the Court held that medicaid residents of a private nursing home had failed to establish "state action" in the decision of the nursing home to transfer them to a lower-level facility. Neither the fact that State funds paid for more than 90 percent of the cost of the patient's care nor the fact that the facility was extensively regulated by State agencies was deemed sufficient to establish "state action". Significantly, however, the Court noted that the privately owned nursing homes were not performing "a function that has traditionally been the exclusive perogative of the State." *Blum*, 102 S.Ct. at 2789. The decision in *Blum* thus leaves room to distinguish *psychiatric* facilities, whose operations have traditionally been largely a function of the State.

A. THE RIGHT TO TREATMENT

The phrase "right to treatment" has become prominent in recent years as a result of numerous court decisions that have held that involuntarily hospitalized individuals have a "right to treatment" or, in the case of the developmentally disabled, a "right to habilitation." In some jurisdictions this right was the product of legislative action. Just as frequently, however, the right to treatment has been judicially imposed as a matter of constitutional principle. Whatever its source, the doctrine has provided the legal basis for judicial mandates increasing state expenditures for the operation of psychiatric institutions. Decrees implementing the doctrine typically required extensive changes in the operation of an institution and its programs, including changes in the physical condition of the facility, its staffing, and the quality of the treatment provided.

Undoubtedly the most prominent of the institutional cases implementing the right to treatment was *Wyatt v. Stickney*, 325 F.Supp. 781 (M.D.Ala.1971), *hearing on standards ordered* 334 F.Supp. 1341 (M.D.Ala.1971), *enforced* 344 F.Supp. 373 (M.D.Ala.1972); 344 F.Supp. 387 (M.D.Ala.1972), *affirmed sub nom.* The circumstances giving rise to this landmark litigation and the consequences of the court's decision have been summarized as follows:

> The suit was precipitated by a reduction in the budget of Alabama's Bryce Hospital, a mental institution. A group of patients and discharged employees sued, alleging that conditions at the hospital—even before they were exacerbated by the budget cuts—were unconstitutional. Substantively, the suit turned on the recognition of the right of mental patients to some minimal level of medical treatment.

> *   *   *

> Although the court recognized a right to treatment, it initially declined to determine the standards "to be used in effectuating [that] right."

> *   *   *

> Nine months later the court found that the defendants had failed to comply with their obligation to design and implement new treatment programs. It was still, however, reluctant to remove primary responsibility from the state officials. Rather than turning over the

operation of the state's mental hospitals to a panel of masters, the court scheduled a hearing to allow the parties and *amici* to propose standards that would meet constitutional requirements. Eighteen months after the suit was filed, on the basis of this hearing, the court issued an interim emergency order relating to conditions at one of the institutions. A month later it issued a more extensive order detailing minimum treatment and care standards. This later order contained the elaborate detail that is one hallmark of the "new" institutional litigation: it specified such aspects of institutional life as clothing allotments, linen, telephone and mail privileges, food expenditures for residents, and staff qualifications. Even this detailed system of supervision, however, produced no magical solutions, and the *Wyatt* litigation required many more decisions by the court.

Eisenberg and Yeazell, *The Ordinary and Extraordinary in Institutional Litigation*, 93 Harv.L.Rev. 465, 468–70 (1980).

The order in *Wyatt v. Stickney* set a model for other decrees concerning the operation of institutions for the mentally ill or the developmentally disabled. As of 1978, federal court action had prompted at least 11 states to overhaul their institutional mental health facilities. *See* Frug, *Judicial Power of the Purse*, 126 Pa.L. Rev. 715, 718 (1978). Significantly, however, none of these decisions was the subject of review by the U.S. Supreme Court. As a result, there remained some uncertainty both as to the existence of a right to treatment and its scope. Finally, in *Youngberg v. Romero*, the Supreme Court agreed to review a plaintiff's assertion of a right to habilitation. Although the decision focuses on the rights of the developmentally disabled to habilitation, the principles should be equally applicable to institutions providing treatment to the mentally ill.

YOUNGBERG v. ROMEO

Supreme Court of the United States, 1982.
457 U.S. 307, 102 S.Ct. 2452, 73 L.Ed.2d 28.

Justice POWELL delivered the opinion of the Court.

The question presented is whether respondent, involuntarily committed to a state institution for the mentally retarded, has substantive rights under the Due Process Clause of the Fourteenth Amendment to (i) safe conditions of confinement; (ii) freedom from bodily restraints; and (iii) training or "habilitation." Respondent sued under 42 U.S.C. § 1983 three administrators of the institution, claiming damages for the alleged breach of his constitutional rights.

I

Respondent Nicholas Romeo is profoundly retarded. Although 33 years old, he has the mental capacity of an eighteen-month old child, with an I.Q. between 8 and 10. He cannot talk and lacks the most basic self-care skills. Until he was 26, respondent lived with his parents in Philadelphia. But after the death of his father in May 1974, his mother was unable to care for him. Within two weeks of the father's death, respondent's mother sought his temporary admission to a nearby Pennsylvania hospital.

Shortly thereafter, she asked the Philadelphia County Court of Common Pleas to admit Romeo to a state facility on a permanent basis. Her petition to the court explained that she was unable to care for Romeo or control his violence. As part of the commitment process, Romeo was examined by a physician and a psychologist. They both certified that respondent was severely retarded and unable to care for himself. On June 11, 1974, the Court of Common Pleas committed respondent to the Pennhurst State School and Hospital, pursuant to the applicable involuntary commitment provision of the Pennsylvania Mental Health and Mental Retardation Act.

At Pennhurst, Romeo was injured on numerous occasions, both by his own violence and by the reactions of other residents to him. Respondent's mother became concerned about these injuries. After objecting to respondent's treatment several times, she filed this complaint on November 4, 1976, in the United States District Court for the Eastern District of Pennsylvania as his next friend. The complaint alleged that "[d]uring the period July, 1974 to the present, plaintiff has suffered injuries on at least sixty-three occasions." The complaint originally sought damages and injunctive relief from Pennhurst's director and two supervisors, it alleged that these officials knew, or should have known, that Romeo was suffering injuries and that they failed to institute appropriate preventive procedures, thus violating his rights under the Eighth and Fourteenth Amendments.

Thereafter, in late 1976, Romeo was transferred from his ward to the hospital for treatment of a broken arm. While in the infirmary, and by order of a doctor, he was physically restrained during portions of each day. These restraints were ordered by Dr. Gabroy, not a defendant here, to protect Romeo and others in the hospital, some of whom were in traction or were being treated intravenously. Although respondent normally would have returned to his ward when his arm healed, the parties to this litigation agreed that he should remain in the hospital due to the pending law suit. Nevertheless, in December 1977, a second amended complaint was filed alleging that the defendants were restraining respondent for prolonged periods on a routine basis. The second amended complaint also added a claim for damages to compensate Romeo for the defendants' failure to provide him with appropriate "treatment or programs for his mental retardation." All claims for injunctive relief were dropped prior to trial because respondent is a member of the class seeking such relief in another action.

An eight-day jury trial was held in April 1978. Petitioners introduced evidence that respondent participated in several programs teaching basic self-care skills. A comprehensive behavior-modification program was designed by staff members to reduce Romeo's aggressive behavior, but that program was never implemented because of his mother's objections. Respondent introduced evidence of his injuries and of conditions in his unit.

At the close of the trial, the court instructed the jury that "if any or all of the defendants were aware of and failed to take all reasonable steps to prevent repeated attacks upon Nicholas Romeo," such failure deprived him of constitutional rights. The jury also was instructed that if the defendants shackled Romeo or denied him treatment "as a punishment for filing this lawsuit," his constitutional rights were violated under the Eighth Amendment. Finally, the jury was instructed that only if they found the defendants "deliberately indifferent to the serious medical [and psychological] needs" of Romeo could they find that his Eighth and Fourteenth Amendment rights had been violated. The jury returned a verdict for the defendants, on which judgment was entered.

The Court of Appeals for the Third Circuit, sitting en banc, reversed and remanded for a new trial. The court held that the Eighth Amendment, prohibiting cruel and unusual punishment of those convicted of crimes, was not an appropriate source for determining the rights of the involuntarily committed. Rather, the Fourteenth Amendment and the liberty interest protected by that amendment provided the proper constitutional basis for these rights. In applying the Fourteenth Amendment, the court found that the involuntarily committed retain liberty interests in freedom of movement and in personal security. These were "fundamental liberties" that can be limited only by an "overriding, non-punitive" state interest. It further found that the involuntarily committed have a liberty interest in habilitation designed to "treat" their mental retardation.

The en banc court did not, however, agree on the relevant standard to be used in determining whether Romeo's rights had been violated. Because physical restraint "raises a presumption of a punitive sanction," the majority of the Court of Appeals concluded that it can be justified only by "compelling necessity." A somewhat different standard was appropriate for the failure to provide for a resident's safety. The majority considered that such a failure must be justified by a showing of "substantial necessity." Finally, the majority held that when treatment has been administered, those responsible are liable only if the treatment is not "acceptable in the light of present medical or other scientific knowledge."

Chief Judge Seitz, concurring in the judgment, considered the standards articulated by the majority as indistinguishable from those applicable to medical malpractice claims. In Chief Judge Seitz's view, the Constitution "only requires that the courts make certain that professional judgment in fact was exercised." He concluded that the appropriate standard was whether the defendants' conduct was "such a substantial departure from accepted professional judgment, practice or standards in the care and treatment of this plaintiff as to demonstrate that the defendants did not base their conduct on a professional judgment."

We granted the petition for certiorari because of the importance of the question presented to the administration of state institutions for the mentally retarded.

II

We consider here for the first time the substantive rights of involuntarily-committed mentally retarded persons under the Fourteenth Amendment to the Constitution. In this case, respondent has been committed under the laws of Pennsylvania, and he does not challenge the commitment. Rather, he argues that he has a constitutionally protected liberty interest in safety, freedom of movement, and training within the institution; and that petitioners infringed these rights by failing to provide constitutionally required conditions of confinement.

The mere fact that Romeo has been committed under proper procedures does not deprive him of all substantive liberty interests under the Fourteenth Amendment. Indeed, the state concedes that respondent has a right to adequate food, shelter, clothing, and medical care. We must decide whether liberty interests also exist in safety, freedom of movement, and training. If such interests do exist, we must further decide whether they have been infringed in this case.

A

Respondent's first two claims involve liberty interests recognized by prior decisions of this Court, interests that involuntary commitment proceedings do not extinguish. The first is a claim to safe conditions. In the past, this Court has noted that the right to personal security constitutes an "historic liberty interest" protected substantively by the Due Process Clause. And that right is not extinguished by lawful confinement, even for penal purposes. If it is cruel and unusual punishment to hold convicted criminals in unsafe conditions, it must be unconstitutional to confine the involuntarily committed—who may not be punished at all—in unsafe conditions.

Next, respondent claims a right to freedom from bodily restraint. In other contexts, the existence of such an interest is clear in the prior decisions of this Court. Indeed, "[l]iberty from bodily restraint always has been recognized as the core of the liberty protected by the Due Process Clause from arbitrary governmental action." This interest survives criminal conviction and incarceration. Similarly, it must also survive involuntary commitment.

B

* * * [Respondent] asserts a "constitutional right to minimally adequate habilitation." This is a substantive due process claim that is said to be grounded in the liberty component of the Due Process Clause of the Fourteenth Amendment. The term "habilitation," used in psychiatry, is not defined precisely or consistently in the opinions below or in the briefs of the parties or the amici. As noted previously, the term refers to "training and development of needed skills." Respondent emphasizes that the right he asserts is for "minimal" training, and he would leave the type and extent of training to be determined on a case-by-case basis "in light of present medical or other scientific knowledge."

In addressing the asserted right to training, we start from established principles. As a general matter, a State is under no constitutional duty to provide substantive services for those within its border. When a person is institutionalized—and wholly dependent on the State—it is conceded by petitioner that a duty to provide certain services and care does exist, although even then a State necessarily has considerable discretion in determining the nature and scope of its responsibilities. Nor must a State "choose between attacking every aspect of a problem or not attacking the problem at all."

Respondent, in light of the severe character of his retardation, concedes that no amount of training will make possible his release. And he does not argue that if he were still at home, the State would have an obligation to provide training at its expense. The record reveals that respondent's primary needs are bodily safety and a minimum of physical restraint, and respondent clearly claims training related to these needs. As we have recognized that there is a constitutionally protected liberty interest in safety and freedom from restraint, training may be necessary to avoid unconstitutional infringement of those rights. On the basis of the record before us, it is quite uncertain whether respondent seeks any "habilitation" or training unrelated to safety and freedom from bodily restraints. In his brief to this Court, Romeo indicates that even the self-care programs he seeks are needed to reduce his aggressive behavior. And in his offer of proof to the trial court, respondent repeatedly indicated that, if allowed to testify, his experts would show that additional training programs, including self-care programs, were needed to reduce Romeo's aggressive behavior. If, as seems the case, respondent seeks only training related to safety and freedom from restraints, this case does not present the difficult question whether a mentally retarded person, involuntarily committed to a state institution, has some general constitutional right to training *per se*, even when no type or amount of training would lead to freedom.

* * *

* * * [W]e agree that respondent is entitled to minimally adequate training. In this case, the minimally adequate training required by the Constitution is such training as may be reasonable in light of respondent's liberty interests in safety and freedom from unreasonable restraints. In determining what is "reasonable"—in

this and in any case presenting a claim for training by a state—we emphasize that courts must show deference to the judgment exercised by a qualified professional. By so limiting judicial review of challenges to conditions in state institutions, interference by the federal judiciary with the internal operations of these institutions should be minimized. Moreover, there certainly is no reason to think judges or juries are better qualified than appropriate professionals in making such decisions. (Courts should not " 'second-guess the expert administrators on matters on which they are better informed.' "). For these reasons, the decision, if made by a professional, is presumptively valid; liability may be imposed only when the decision by the professional is such a substantial departure from accepted professional judgment, practice or standards as to demonstrate that the person responsible actually did not base the decision on such a judgment. In an action for damages against a professional in his individual capacity, however, the professional will not be liable if he was unable to satisfy his normal professional standards because of budgetary constraints; in such a situation, good-faith immunity would bar liability.

* * *

In this case, we conclude that the jury was erroneously instructed. * * * Accordingly, we vacate the decision of the Court of Appeals and remand for further proceedings consistent with this decision.

So ordered.

Justice BLACKMUN, with whom Justice BRENNAN and Justice O'CONNOR join, concurring.

I join the Court's opinion. I write separately, however, to make clear why I believe that opinion properly leaves unresolved * * * important issues.

* * *

The * * * difficult question left open today is whether respondent has an independent constitutional claim, grounded in the Due Process Clause of the Fourteenth Amendment, to that "habilitation" or training necessary to preserve those basic self-care skills he possessed when he first entered Pennhurst—for example, the ability to dress himself and care for his personal hygiene. In my view, it would be consistent with the Court's reasoning today to include within the "minimally adequate training required by the Constitution," such training as is reasonably necessary to prevent a person's pre-existing self-care skills from *deteriorating* because of his commitment.

The Court makes clear that even after a person is committed to a state institution, he is entitled to such training as is necessary to prevent unreasonable losses of additional liberty as a result of his confinement—for example, unreasonable bodily restraints or unsafe institutional conditions. If a person could demonstrate that he entered a state institution with minimal self-care skills, but lost those skills after commitment because of the State's unreasonable refusal to provide him training, then, it seems to me, he has alleged a loss of liberty quite distinct from—and as serious as—the loss of safety and freedom from unreasonable restraints. For many mentally retarded people, the difference between the capacity to do things for themselves within an institution and total dependence on the institution for all of their needs is as much liberty as they ever will know.

Although respondent asserts a claim of this kind, I agree with the Court that "[o]n the basis of the record before us, it is quite uncertain whether respondent [in fact] seeks any 'habilitation' or training unrelated to safety and freedom from bodily restraints." Since the Court finds respondent constitutionally entitled at least to "such training as may be reasonable in light of [his] liberty interests in safety and freedom from unreasonable restraints," I accept its decision not to address respondent's additional claim.

If respondent actually seeks habilitation in self-care skills not merely to reduce his aggressive tendencies, but also to maintain those basic self-care skills necessary to his personal autonomy within Pennhurst, I believe he is free on remand to assert that claim. Like the Court, I would be willing to defer to the judgment of professionals as to whether or not, and to what extent, institutional training would preserve respondent's pre-existing skills. As the Court properly notes, "[p]rofessionals in the habilitation of the mentally retarded disagree strongly on the question whether effective training of all severely or profoundly retarded individuals is even possible."

If expert testimony reveals that respondent was so retarded when he entered the institution that he had no basic self-care skills to preserve, or that institutional training would not have preserved whatever skills he did have, then I would agree that he suffered no additional loss of liberty even if petitioners failed to provide him training. But if the testimony establishes that respondent possessed certain basic self-care skills when he entered the institution, and was sufficiently educable that he could have maintained those skills with a certain degree of training, then I would be prepared to listen seriously to an argument that petitioners were constitutionally required to provide that training, even if respondent's safety and mobility were not imminently threatened by their failure to do so.

The Court finds it premature to resolve this constitutional question on this less-than-fully-developed record. Because I agree with that conclusion, I concur in the Court's opinion.

Chief Justice BURGER, concurring in the judgment.

* * *

I agree with the Court that some amount of self-care instruction may be necessary to avoid unreasonable infringement of a mentally-retarded person's interests in safety and freedom from restraint; but it seems clear to me that the Constitution does not otherwise place an affirmative duty on the State to provide any particular kind of training or habilitation—even such as might be encompassed under the essentially standardless rubric "minimally adequate training," to which the Court refers.

*   *   *

Questions and Comments

1. To what extent does *Youngberg v. Romeo* validate the broad right to treatment mandated by decisions such as *Wyatt v. Stickney* discussed above? In this connection consider the following analysis of the *Romeo* decision:

> The Court's formulation of Romeo's right to training explicitly left unresolved the disagreement in the lower federal courts concerning the existence and scope of broader rights to treatment. Some lower federal courts have established, by analogy to first amendment doctrine, a constitutional right to be confined in the "least restrictive environment" or to be given a treatment program that is the "least restrictive alternative." Other courts have held that due process requires states to provide habilitation as a quid pro quo for imposing confinement without the rigorous procedural prerequisites of criminal conviction. Finally, some courts have enunciated a right to the treatment necessary to afford a realistic opportunity to improve patients' capabilities, on the ground that such improvement is the only legitimate purpose of involuntary commitment. Numerous courts have rejected these rulings, however, and have criticized the right to treatment as a theoretically unsound and nonjusticiable right. Justice Powell refused to endorse—or to reject—any of these theories, and instead established a right to training as a "liberty interest" born of and limited by the need to protect other traditionally recognized freedoms.

Comment, *The Supreme Court 1981 Term*, 96 Harv.L.Rev. 62, 80–81 (1982).

2. Is it significant that the court limited the right of patients in *Romeo* to "minimally adequate or reasonable training to ensure safety and freedom from undue restraint," 102 S.Ct. at 2460, rather than the right originally claimed by petitions to "such treatment as will afford a reasonable opportunity to acquire and maintain life those skills necessary to cope as effectively as [his] capacities permit"? *See* Comment, *The Supreme Court 1981 Term*, 96 Harv.L.Rev. 67, 79 (1982).

3. To what extent is compliance with the requirements of *Youngberg* likely to be affected by the Court's decision that even where there is a violation the plaintiff is only entitled to injunction relief instead of damages?

4. The *Romeo* decision also leaves unresolved the problem of judicial enforcement where compliance with the court's decree involves additional expenditures which the state legislature refuses to appropriate. In all past right-to-treatment cases, courts have been able to avoid a direct clash with legislative bodies by securing voluntary compliance. *Case*

Comment, "Wyatt v. Stickney" and The Right of Civilly Committed Mental Patients to Adequate Treatment, 86 Harv.L.Rev. 1282, 1303 (1973).

For an example of the judicial/legislative "negotiations" that may accompany implementation to the right to treatment doctrine see *Welsch v. Likins,* 550 F.2d 1122 (8th Cir.1977). For a commentary on the problems of the implementation of the right to treatment, *see The "Wyatt" Case: Implementation of a Judicial Decree Ordering Institutional Change,* 84 Yale L.J. 1338 (1975).

5. Cases such as *Youngberg v. Romeo* involve the assertion of rights to habilitation or treatment on the part of those who are involuntarily confined. A different but related question concerns the power of the state to enact laws which interfere with the individual's access to treatment which would otherwise be available. One of the few cases which has addressed this issue in the psychiatric treatment context is *Aden v. Younger,* 57 Cal.App.3d 622, 129 Cal.Rptr. 535 (1976). In *Aden* the challenged law sought to regulate the conditions under which psychosurgery and electroconvulsive therapy could be administered to institutionalized patients. The petitioners, who had consented to electroconvulsive therapy, challenged the provisions of the statute calling for mandatory notification of a relative and review and approval by a panel of physicians prior to the administration of treatment. On appeal, these provisions were found to infringe the patients' constitutional right to privacy in selecting and consenting to treatment.

Similar reasoning led to the issuance of a court injunction against the application of a Berkeley, California municipal law which banned the administration of electroshock therapy within the city limits. The ordinance was a result of a city-wide referendum which was voted on by the residents of Berkeley in the November 1983 election. In striking down the ordinance the presiding judge observed that "[t]he ultimate right is the citizen's right to have his healer unobstructed." "Judge Voids Ban by Berkeley on Electroshock Treatment," *New York Times,* January 15, 1983, p. 8, col. 4.

B. THE RIGHT TO DECLINE TREATMENT

1. Introduction

An issue that has been raised with increasing persistence in recent years is the right of involuntarily hospitalized patients to refuse psychiatric treatment. Currently no authoritative delineation of the scope of this right has emerged. In some states committed patients who are not legally incompetent enjoy significant rights to refuse treatment. In others all involuntarily committed patients remain subject to forced treatment. As the materials that follow illustrate, no uniform constitutional standard is yet available. Thus, whether and under what conditions a patient may be compelled to accept treatment are questions that are now decided on a state by state basis.

What accounts for this remarkable lack of certainty and uniformity in this field of regulation? Perhaps more than anything else it is the profound and rapid changes which have enveloped the entire mental health system in recent years. Until the early 1950's committed persons were generally disqualified from any meaningful participation in treatment decisions. In fact, under the law of a number of states the commitment decision automatically rendered the person legally incompetent, leaving the individual with no legal power to either consent to or refuse treatment. In other states, the finding that the individual was commitable merely presented a rebuttable presumption of incompetency. But even in those states where the committed patient was not automatically rendered legally incompetent, those who had been involuntarily committed were as a matter of policy subject to compelled treatment. As noted by one court, "[I]nherent in an adjudication that an individual should be committed under the state's *parens patriae* power is the decision that he can be forced to accept the treatments found to be in his best interest; it would be incongruous if an individual who lacks capacity to make a treatment decision could frustrate the very justification for the state's action by refusing such treatments." *Price v. Sheppard*, 307 Minn. 250, 239 N.W.2d 905, 911 (1976). Implicit in this view was the notion that mental patients are generally incapable of assessing their own situation and making a rational decision about treatment.

Recent years have witnessed marked changes in the attitude of both courts and legislatures toward the institutionalized mentally ill. Numerous states have revamped their commitment laws and at the same time have enacted specific provisions giving mental patients an explicit right to decline treatment. In other states limitations on compelled treatment have come about as a result of court decisions. However, both statutes and court decisions have tended to draw a distinction between intrusive and less intrusive treatment modalities. Frequently, only the more intrusive interventions such as ECT or psychosurgery have been the subject of special legislative or judicial protection.

While there is a definite movement toward increased patient authority to control treatment decisions, broad variations continue to exist across the nation. In terms of constitutional adjudication which could serve to establish a uniform minimum standard, the Supreme Court has to date provided only minimal guidance. As a consequence, in those jurisdictions that have *not* adopted comprehensive legislation the right of institutionalized patients to decline various treatment modalties remains unresolved. The materials which follow seek both to chart the developments to date and also to highlight the issues which remain to be resolved.

Questions and Comments

1. As noted above, in a number of states explicit statutory provisions govern the administration of treatment to mental patients. In the

absence of such statutes it has been up to the courts to establish guidelines on the basis of constitutional principles. An issue to be addressed in this connection is the capacity of courts to make these judgments. To what extent, for instance, do constitutional principles lend themselves to the resolution of specific issues such as the degree of intrusiveness of a particular therapy which in turn calls for either patient consent or special judicial authorization. *See, e.g., Price v. Sheppard*, at pg. 456 *infra*.

2. There are two possible approaches to limiting the authority of institutions to compel psychiatric treatment. One is to allocate exclusive decision-making power to the patient. The other is to require the institution to seek judicial approval as a substitute for the patient's consent. Arguably, the latter is only appropriate where the patient is incapacitated in terms of his decision-making ability. Thus, a threshold issue is the degree of incapacitation which justifies taking the decision away from the patient. The cases which follow explore this issue in greater detail.

3. Committed patients who have not been found legally incompetent have traditionally had the legal right to consent to non-psychiatric medical treatment, in contrast to psychiatric treatment, which was traditionally imposed. In particular, however, even general medical treatment was provided without much attention to the requirements of informed consent. The legal regulations which apply to the treatment of incompetent persons are considered in Chapter Seven.

2. Psychotropic Medication

a. Clinical Application

PLOTKIN, *"LIMITING THE THERAPEUTIC ORGY: MENTAL PATIENTS' RIGHT TO REFUSE TREATMENT"*
72 N.W.L.Rev. 461, 474–79 (1978).

In 1952, Delay, Deniker, and Harl began a new era in the treatment of psychiatric disorders by discovering the "remarkable" effectiveness of chlorpromazines in aborting acute psychotic episodes. The later confirmation of these reports resulted in rapidly increasing use of these drugs throughout the world and stimulated an intensive search for related families of compounds. As a consequence of this effort, a new class of drugs known as *major tranquilizers* was developed. They remain the most firmly established of all the pharmacotherapies in the treatment of mental disorders.

Of the different types of major tranquilizers, the most commonly prescribed are phenothiazines. Although extensive clinical research has attempted to document the effectiveness of these drugs—particularly in ameliorating the symptoms of schizophrenia—clinicians have encountered great difficulty in scientifically predicting a particular individual's response to a particular drug, and the results frequently appear paradoxical or idiosyncratic.

Similarly, researchers have been unable to conclude with any certainty which drugs to prescribe for specific conditions. Various attempts have been made to pair particular phenothiazines with individual symptoms, but the results have been inconclusive. Thus, only minor differences appear to exist among these drugs. Even after a drug is selected, the specific dosage must still be determined by trial and error. Any efficacy of drug therapy is fortuitous in light of current practices: "Drugs are chosen by custom and rumored repute, and dosage is commonly adjusted upward until the patient either responds or develops toxic symptoms."

Unfortunately, rather unpleasant "toxic" effects regularly accompany the use of antipsychotic drugs to ameliorate schizophrenic symptoms. The most common results are the temporary, muscular side effects (extra-pyramidal symptoms) which disappear when the drug is terminated; dystonic reactions (muscle spasms, especially in the eyes, neck, face, and arms; irregular flexing, writhing or grimacing movements; protrusion of the tongue); akathesia (inability to stay still, restlessness, agitation); and Parkinsonisms (mask-like face, drooling, muscle stiffness and rigidity, shuffling gait, tremors). Additionally, there are numerous other nonmuscular effects, including drowsiness, weakness, weight gain, dizziness, fainting, low blood pressure, dry mouth, blurred vision, loss of sexual desire, frigidity, apathy, depression, constipation, diarrhea, and changes in the blood. Infrequent, but serious, nonmuscular side effects, such as skin rash and skin discoloration, ocular changes, cardiovascular changes, and, occasionally, sudden death, have also been documented.

The most serious threat phenothiazines pose to a patient's health is a condition known as tardive dyskinesia. This effect went unrecognized for years because its symptoms are often not manifested until late in the course of treatment, sometimes appearing after discontinuation of the drug causing the condition. Tardive dyskinesia is characterized by involuntary muscle movements, often in the oral region. The associated rhythmic movements of the lips and tongue (often mimicking normal chewing, blowing, or licking motions) may be grotesque and socially objectionable, resulting in considerable shame and embarrassment to the victim and his or her family. Additionally, hypertrophy of the tongue and ulcerations of the mouth may occur, speech may become incomprehensible, and, in extreme cases, swallowing and breathing may become difficult. To date, tardive dyskinesia has resisted curative efforts, and its disabling manifestations may persist for years.

There is little doubt that prolonged administration of psychoactive drugs plays a major role in the development of tardive dyskinesia. Individual susceptibility to the condition depends upon a variety of factors, including increasing age, sex, and the existence of organic brain syndromes. Despite this potential danger of serious complications, psychiatrists remain reluctant to withdraw or reduce drug usage for fear of risking a relapse.

b. Legal Perspectives

ROGERS v. OKIN

United States Court of Appeals, First Circuit, 1980.
634 F.2d 650, *vacated and remanded, sub nom.* Mills v. Rogers, 457 U.S. 291, 102
S.Ct. 2442, 73 L.Ed.2d 16 (1982).

COFFIN, Chief Judge.

These appeals are the latest stage in a lengthy and complex civil rights action concerning the practices at Massachusetts state mental health facilities. Plaintiffs are voluntary and involuntary psychiatric patients at Massachusetts state mental health facilities. Defendants are the state Commissioner of Mental Health and various hospital officials and physicians responsible for plaintiffs' care. The full factual background and procedural history are set forth in the published opinion of the district court, *Rogers v. Okin*, 478 F.Supp. 1342 (D.Mass.1979), and will not be repeated here. Two chief issues are raised in these cross-appeals from the district court judgment: I. Under what circumstances may state officials forcibly administer antipsychotic drugs to mental health patients without violating the Fourteenth Amendment? II. Did the district court correctly find that an award of monetary damages to plaintiffs under 42 U.S.C. § 1983 or various state causes of action was not warranted? On the latter issue, we fully concur with the judgment of the district court. With regard to the former, we are in substantial agreement with portions of the district court's reasoning, but find that several important aspects of the court's ruling require modification.

I.

A. Nature of the Individual Right

We begin our analysis with what seems to us to be an intuitively obvious proposition: a person has a constitutionally protected interest in being left free by the state to decide for himself whether to submit to the serious and potentially harmful medical treatment that is represented by the administration of antipsychotic drugs. The precise textual source in the Constitution of the protection of this interest is unclear, and the authorities directly supportive of the proposition itself are surprisingly few. Nevertheless, we are convinced that the proposition is correct and that a source in the Due Process Clause of the Fourteenth Amendment for the protection of this interest exists, most likely as part of the penumbral right to privacy, bodily integrity, or personal security.

* * *

None of the parties or *amici* in this suit contest the correctness of this general proposition. With regard to the treatment of the mentally ill in state run institutions, however, defendants point to several state interests that, they claim, override the individual's protected interest and justify the forced administration of drugs. Additionally, defendants contend that within this context, the interests of the individuals to whom the state wishes to administer drugs are fundamentally different from those of individuals who are not mentally ill, and are not in fact inconsistent with the interests of the state. Plaintiffs, on the other hand, while conceding that the interests of the individual are not absolute and can be overridden in certain circumstances, argue that the mere fact that an individual suffers from mental illness and resides in a mental health facility does not constitute such a circumstance. In order to resolve this dispute between the parties, we first examine the various state interests involved.

B. STATE INTERESTS

As we have indicated, neither defendants nor their *amici* argue that the state could forcibly administer antipsychotic drugs to a randomly selected "normal" individual. Unfortunately, the plaintiffs in this suit are far from "normal". Instead, suffering from various mental illnesses, they are in the words of the district court "victims of fate shortchanged by life." As a result of their afflictions, they are in many instances in desperate need of care and treatment, and, in some cases, are dangerous to either themselves or others. Because of their illnesses, some of these individuals are unable to make any meaningful choice as to whether they should accept treatment, including the administration of drugs. Given these circumstances, the state asserts primarily its police power and its *parens partiae* power as justifications for the forcible administration of antipsychotic drugs to those individuals who are in state run hospitals as a result of mental illness.

1. *Police Power.* The parties agree that the state has a legitimate interest in protecting persons from physical harm at the hands of the mentally ill. They also agree that this interest can justify the forcible administration of drugs to a mentally ill person whether or not that person has been adjudicated incompetent to make his own treatment decisions. The district court accordingly held that "a committed mental patient may be forcibly medicated in an emergency situation in which a failure to do so would result in a substantial likelihood of physical harm to that patient, other patients, or to staff members of the institution." Plaintiffs have no complaint with this ruling. * * *

Defendants' . . . basic complaint is that the necessity of finding a "substantial likelihood of physical harm * * *" is an overly rigid and unworkable requirement. Defendants argue that some mentally ill patients have an identifiable capacity for spontaneous acts of violence but that it is not always possible to determine beforehand whether a specific patient is likely to commit such acts. This problem of prediction is increased, defendants claim, by the prospect that doctors will be second-guessed in section 1983 suits for damages. In sum, defendants assert that the overall effect of following the district court's standard is to increase the incidence of violent acts that otherwise would not occur had a less restrictive standard been used.

* * *

For example, at one point during the trial, defendant Gill, director of the Austin Unit of the state hospital, testified that a particular patient on one occasion displayed indications of a possible proclivity towards violence. Defendant, who was aware of the patient's previous favorable medical reaction to the administration of drugs, testified that he would have forcibly medicated the patient as a precaution had he been free to do so. He stated, however, that the indications were not sufficiently clear to enable him to predict that the patient would be likely to commit violence without the medication. He therefore did not medicate the patient, who subsequently seriously injured a staff member during a spontaneous violent outburst. The district court dismissed this incident simply by finding that the defendant doctor had erred in his medical prognosis: he should have realized that violence was likely to occur.

This rather typical dialogue reveals, we think, the inaptness in this context of a clear-cut unitary standard of quantitative likelihood that violence would occur if no medication is administered. In the first place, a unitary standard assumes that there is only one kind of probability to be tested. * * * Here, however, there are two sets of interests, each capable of being compelling and, most importantly, each capable of varying from case to case. On the institutional side, we deal with an institution to which many individuals are involuntarily committed because of a demonstrated proclivity for committing acts of violence outside the hospital community, a proclivity that the record shows often carries over after commitment. The volatility of a large concentration of such individuals adds substance and immediacy to the state's concern in preventing violence. This concern takes on an added dimension when we consider that patients themselves are the likely victims of any violence. These mental patients are persons who, as we have noted, have "a right, under the Fourteenth Amendment, to be secure in [their] life and person while confined under state authority." On the individual's side, we deal with the concededly substantial right of competent patients to be free from the forcible administration of antipsychotics, the violation of which right may not only occasion temporary distress but possibly aftereffects as well.

The professional judgment-call required in balancing these varying interests and determining whether a patient should be subjected to forcible administering of antipsychotic drugs demands an *individualized* estimation of the possibility and type of violence, the likely effects of particular drugs on a particular individual, and an appraisal of alternative, less restrictive courses of action. Thus, for example, if the violence feared is potentially life-threatening, and the patient's prior experience with antipsychotics favorable, it would be patently unreasonable to require that defendants determine that the probability of the feared violence occurring is greater than fifty percent before they can act. By contrast, if the patient has experienced severe adverse side-effects from antipsychotics, it would be only reasonable to expect defendants to explore less harmful alternatives much more vigorously than in the former case.

Not only do we deem out of place a simplistic unitary standard for police power emergency drug administration, but we see particular problems in adopting such a standard that can be interpreted as requiring a prediction of more-probable-than-not violent behavior. While lawyers and judges may assure themselves that such a standard allows adequate scope for discretion, the important fact is that trained psychiatrists, who possess expert qualifications and experience that the judge lacks, find that in many situations they cannot make predictions that, to their science oriented minds, meet a quantitative level of probability. Instead of second-guessing defendants, the court should have taken as true their asserted difficulties in applying the court's general formulation (at least in the absence of a finding that defendants were lying), and fashioned a ruling that took these difficulties into consideration. "[N]either judges nor administrative hearing officers are better qualified than psychiatrists to render psychiatric judgments." *Parham v. J.R.*, 442 U.S. 584, 607.

*   *   *

*   *   * [W]e do not imply that the Constitution places no limits on the discretion of the defendants. The state's purpose in administering drugs forcibly must be to further its police power interests, i.e., the decision must be the result of a determination that the need to prevent violence in a particular situation outweighs the possibility of harm to the medicated individual.

*   *   *

*   *   * [G]iven the interests involved, the Fourteenth Amendment requires the imposition of procedures whereby the necessary determinations can be made with due process. Thus, for example, it would seem that at a minimum the determination that medication is necessary must be made by a qualified physician as to each individual patient to be medicated.

*   *   *

In sum, we hold that the district court should not attempt to fashion a single "more-likely-than-not" standard as a substitute for an individualized balancing of the varying interests of particular patients in refusing antipsychotic medication against the equally varying interests of patients—and the state—in preventing violence. Because we recognize the legitimacy of both of these interests, we conclude that neither should be allowed necessarily to override the other in a blanket fashion. Instead, the court should leave this difficult, necessarily *ad hoc* balancing to state physicians and limit its own role to designing procedures for ensuring that the patients' interests in refusing antipsychotics are taken into consideration and that antipsychotics are not forcibly administered absent a finding by a qualified physician that those interests are outweighed in a particular situation and less restrictive alternatives are unavailable.

2. PARENS PATRIAE POWERS

* * * There is no doubt that "[t]he state has a legitimate interest under its *parens patriae* powers in providing care to its citizens who are unable to care for themselves * * *." * * * However, for the state to invoke this interest as a justification for the administration of treatment that could represent substantial intrusions upon the individual, the individual himself must be incapable of making a competent decision concerning treatment on his own. Otherwise, the very justification for the state's purported exercise of its *parens patriae* power—its citizen's inability to care for himself would be missing. Therefore, the *sine qua non* for the state's use of its *parens patriae* power as justification for the forceful administration of mind-affecting drugs is a determination that the individual to whom the drugs are to be administered lacks the capacity to decide for himself whether he should take the drugs.

For the most part, the parties do not contest this conclusion. Instead, their dispute concerns whether or not such a determination has in fact been properly made with respect to the plaintiffs. Defendants assert that the judicial commitment proceedings conducted under Massachusetts law, Mass.Gen.Laws Ann. ch. 123 (1979), constitute the determination of incapacity necessary for the state to provide treatment over the objections of the patient. "Given that these patients have already been recognized as so mentally ill that their decision to reject voluntary hospitalization and its treatment has been overridden, it is illogical to accept the patient's same objections to treatment once hospitalized." To demonstrate why the district court was correct in rejecting this assertion, we turn our focus to the Massachusetts commitment scheme.

* * *

When we scrutinize this statutory scheme in search of a judicial determination of *incapacity*, we find no direct inference of such. We can conceive of a logical step that could be taken—inferring from an adjudication that an individual was incompetent to make a decision concerning his commitment that he was incompetent to make decisions concerning his treatment.

* * *

Defendants contest the correctness of this conclusion by pointing to the fact that the statutory scheme does require a finding that the committed individual suffers from mental illness. This finding, defendants argue, is a sufficient predicate to state action based on its *parens patriae* power. Nothing in the statutory scheme, however, suggests that a finding of mental illness is equivalent to a finding that the individual is incapable of deciding for himself whether commitment and treatment are in his own best interest. Indeed, as the district court noted, the fact that Massachusetts law provides for a separate proceeding for determinations of legal incompetency, Mass.Gen.Laws Ann. ch. 123 § 25, strongly implies that the commitment proceeding itself is not intended to be a determination that the individual lacks the capacity to make his own treatment decisions.

* * *

The foregoing analysis is not intended to suggest that the Massachusetts commitment scheme is unconstitutional. To the contrary, in many respects the Massachusetts scheme goes well beyond the minimum requirements mandated by the Fourteenth Amendment. The point of our analysis is instead to demonstrate that the commitment decision itself is an inadequate predicate to the forcible administration of drugs to an individual where the purported justification for that action is the state's *parens patriae* power.

In so ruling, we recognize that there is a need for some procedure whereby the state can provide needed treatment to an objecting individual who lacks the capacity to make meaningful treatment decisions on his own. The district court, pointing to the powers and proceedings of the Massachusetts Probate Courts, Mass.Gen.Laws Ann. ch. 123 § 25; * * * The court did not hold that fullblown probate proceedings are constitutionally required. Rather, the court held that some determination of incompetency must be made, and found that probate proceedings under section 25 of chapter 123 sufficed. * * *

We do agree with defendants, however, that there are two aspects of the district court's ruling that require some modification. First, the district court held that absent an "emergency" defendants can never forcibly medicate an individual without an adjudication of incompetency and approval by the appointed guardian. The court defined an emergency as "circumstances in which a failure to [forcibly medicate] would bring about a substantial likelihood of physical harm to the patient or others." In so restricting the definition to instances in which immediate action is required to prevent physical harm the district court rejected defendants' claim that an emergency should also include situations in which the immediate administration of drugs is reasonably believed to be necessary to prevent further deterioration in the patient's mental health.

* * *

* * * [I]n the particular situation presented here, it cannot be said that the interests of the patient himself would be furthered by requiring responsible physicians to stand by and watch him slip into possibly chronic illness while awaiting an adjudication of incompetency. Instead, the interests of the individual in such a situation coincide with those of the state and mandate decisive, immediate

action. We therefore vacate the district court's limited definition of the emergency circumstances in which adjudications are not required and remand the case for consideration of alternative means for making incompetency determinations in situations where any delay could result in significant deterioration of the patient's mental health.

* * *

[The court next concluded that contrary to the finding of the trial court, the treatment of incompetent persons did not in every instance require that "state officials must receive guardian approval for individual treatment decisions."]

Second, it is possible to read the district court's opinion as implying that once a determination of incompetency has been made, a traditional, individual guardian must make all treatment decisions involving the use of antipsychotic drugs. To the extent that the district court's opinion might be so read, we reject that part of its holding.

* * *

Of course the mere fact that it would be impractical to have a guardian make all significant treatment decisions for an incompetent patient does not itself indicate that it is undesirable to have a guardian make those decisions that can be made practically. Our concern, however, is that the requirement of individualized guardian review on only some aspects of significant treatment decisions might in the long run create a tendency for patients to receive other treatment, *i.e.*, no treatment, in situations where the best interests of the patient would dictate otherwise.

* * * [we] think that the nature of the problem presented is such that it is unwise to declare that the Constitution requires that state officials must receive guardian approval for individual treatment decisions simply because the administration of drugs is recommended.

* * *

Judgment affirmed in part, reversed in part, and vacated and remanded for further proceedings in accordance with this opinion.

Questions and Comments

1. Note that in *Rogers* the court draws a clear distinction between commitments effected under the police power, *i.e.*, for the protection of other persons, and those which have a *parens patriae* purpose, *i.e.*, protection of the committed individual. In the case of the former, psychotropic treatment may be compelled where a qualified physician makes a determination that "the need to prevent violence in a particular situation outweighs the possibility of harm to the medicated individual." In the instance of *parens patriae* commitments, treatment may only be compelled where there is an emergency or there has been a judicial determination that the individual "lacks the capacity to make a meaningful treatment decision." An "emergency" as defined by the Court of

Appeals in *Rogers* encompasses those situations where immediate action is required to prevent either physical harm to the individual or a "deterioration of the patient's mental health."

2. The *Rogers* decision serves to allocate substantial decision making authority to professionals, most notably the supervising physician, particularly in the case of persons detained under the police power. Is this development consistent with cases decided by the Supreme Court such as *Parham v. J.R.* (p. 296) and *Youngberg v. Romeo* (p. 432)? Do these cases signal a shift away from the judicial "legalization" of patient rights characterized by the due process cases of the 1970's and the reallocation of authority to medical or professional personnel affiliated with institutions?

3. The opinion of the Court of Appeals in *Rogers v. Okin* set out above was vacated by the U.S. Supreme Court on June 18, 1982 *sub nom. Mills v. Rogers*, 457 U.S. 291, 102 S.Ct. 2442, 73 L.Ed.2d 16 (1982). In vacating the decision, however, the Court failed to reach the substantive issues presented by the case. Speaking through Justice Powell, the Court noted that after the First Circuit had handed down its judgment, the Supreme Judicial Court of Massachusetts held in *In the Matter of Guardianship of Richard Roe III*, 383 Mass. 415, 421 N.E.2d 40 (1981), that a person has a protected liberty interest in "decid[ing] for himself whether to submit to the serious and potentially harmful medical treatment that is represented in the administration of antipsychotic drugs." While the Massachusetts decision was limited to cases involving non-institutionalized mental patients, the Supreme Court nevertheless concluded that "it is distinctly possible that Massachusetts recognizes liberty interests of persons adjudged incompetent that are broader than those protected directly by the Constitution of the United States." 102 S.Ct. at 2450. Thus, the Court concluded that the issues presented by *Rogers v. Okin* could possibly be decided by state law alone, thereby avoiding the necessity of reaching the federal constitutional question.

4. Upon remand, the U.S. Court of Appeals for the First Circuit certified nine questions to the Supreme Judicial Court of Massachusetts. Among the certified questions were the following:

> 1. Under state law, does the involuntary civil commitment of a person to a mental institution constitute a determination of incompetency to make treatment decisions?
>
> 2. If not, does state law, in the absence of an emergency * * * require a judicial finding of incompetence and appointment of a guardian as the exclusive method for determining incompetency to make treatment decisions?

In response to the First Circuit request, the Supreme Judicial Court of Massachusetts answered the certified questions in *Rogers v. Commissioner* which is set out at page 453, *infra*.

5. In spite of the latitude that *Rogers* gives to a professional to administer psychotropic medication in emergency situations or where necessary to prevent violence, some commentators have criticized *Rogers* and similar decisions (*see, e.g., Davis v. Hubbard*, 506 F.Supp. 915 (N.D.

Ohio 1980), *In re K.K.B.*, 609 P.2d 747 (Okl.1980)) as being overly restrictive on the following grounds:

> First, antipsychotic medications benefit many patients and permit them to leave the hospital sooner. In one major study, seventy-five percent of the patients treated with antipsychotic drugs showed marked to moderate improvement within six weeks of hospital admission, while only twenty-three percent of the placebo group achieved such improvement.
>
> Second, most patients need involuntary medication only infrequently, and patients usually come to accept the medication. Voluntary acceptance by an involuntary patient, of course, may be flawed. But it is striking that about two-thirds of involuntary patients continue voluntary treatment following a period of involuntary confinement, frequently with drug therapy.
>
> Third, many or most committed patients lack capacity to make reasoned treatment decisions, and therefore probably lack capacity to make reasoned refusals. Moreover, many patients state reasons for refusing that are verbally incomprehensible, obvious manifestations of their disease (for example, "the CIA wants you to use this drug to kill me"), or manifestly ambivalent.
>
> Fourth, although there is considerable controversy over the frequency and seriousness of adverse side effects of antipsychotic medication, such as tardive dyskinesia, most research suggests that few cases develop from drug treatment lasting less than three months, and most cases occur only after use of antipsychotic drugs for more than two years. The possibility of such side effects should not be minimized, and patients on such medications should be monitored carefully. Fortunately, medical means to avoid and to treat such effects are improving.
>
> Fifth, the impact of treatment refusals must be considered. One study of the impact in Massachusetts following the *Rogers* decision found that more than half (89 of 159) of the patients who persistently refused treatment deteriorated.

Stromberg and Stone, *A Model State Law on Civil Commitment of the Mentally Ill,* 20 Harv.J. on Legis. 265, 353 (1983).

Other commentators would favor a rule more restrictive than that announced by the court in *Rogers* and would require the informed consent of the patient in all instances on the grounds that:

> Regardless of whether the benefits of phenothiazines outweigh their side effects, the primary reason for the continuing extensive use of these drugs is not so much their therapeutic benefits as it is the control of institutional patients' behavior. Indeed, management of "combatant, hyperactive, destructive, and hostile patients" is "one of the difficult problems in hospital psychiatry," and "control of such behavior in these patients is the first order of treatment."

Plotkin, *Limiting the Therapeutic Orgy: Mental Patients' Right to Refuse Treatment,* 72 N.W.L.Rev. 461, 478 (1978).

ROGERS v. COMMISSIONER

Supreme Judicial Court of Massachusetts, Suffolk, 1983.
390 Mass. 489, 458 N.E.2d 308.

ABRAMS, J. We are asked to respond to nine questions certified by the United States Court of Appeals for the First Circuit which focus on the right of involuntarily committed mental patients to refuse treatment, and the standards and procedures which must be followed to treat those patients with antipsychotic medication.

*Questions 1, 2, and 3. Competence of involuntarily committed patients to make treatment decisions * * **

* * * The right of an individual "to manage his own person" necessarily encompasses the right to make basic decisions with respect to "taking care of himself," including decisions relating to the maintenance of physical and mental health. We think it clear that the right to make treatment decisions is an essential element of the patient's general right "to manage his affairs." G.L. c. 123, § 25. "[A] finding [of incompetence], apart from evidence as to mental illness, should consist of facts showing a proposed ward's inability to think or act for himself as to matters concerning his personal health, safety, and general welfare. * * *" Absent such a finding, a person is competent to "act for himself as to matters concerning his personal health," including acceptance or refusal of medication. Thus, a person diagnosed as mentally ill and committed to a mental institution is still considered to be competent to manage his personal affairs.

We conclude that a mental patient has the right to make treatment decisions and does not lose that right until the patient is adjudicated incompetent by a judge through incompetence proceedings.

The defendants argue that they, as doctors, should be responsible for making treatment decisions for involuntarily committed patients, whether competent or not. We do not agree. "Every competent adult has a right 'to forego treatment, or even cure, if it entails what for him are intolerable consequences or risks however unwise his sense of values may be in the eyes of the medical profession.'" This right has constitutional and common law origins, which protect each person's "strong interest in being free from nonconsensual invasion of his bodily integrity." Since by statute and by common law, involuntarily committed patients are competent until adjudicated incompetent and because we have held that competent individuals have a right to refuse treatment, the defendants' argument fails.

We conclude that a distinct adjudication of incapacity to make treatment decisions (incompetence) must precede any determination to override patients' rights to make their own treatment decisions.

* * *

[Questions 4 and 5 concerned the procedures required for the medication of incompetent patients.]

Questions 6 and 7. *"Police power" and the use of antipsychotic drugs.* The defendants assert that if they are unable to medicate, hospital administration becomes more difficult, lengths of stay increase, fewer patients can be treated, staff turnover increases and new personnel become more difficult to attract. The defendants also argue that the illness of one patient on a ward may be provocative, exacerbating the illness of other patients, and adversely affecting the doctors' ability to treat.

In addition, they claim it is more difficult to conduct group therapy in an environment in which they cannot medicate with antipsychotic drugs. However, governmental interest "in permitting hospitals to care for those in their custody [is] not controlling, since a patient's right of self-determination [is] normally * * * superior to such institutional considerations."

In *Guardianship of Roe,* 383 Mass. 415, 421 N.E.2d 40 (1981), we noted that "[c]ommentators and courts have identified abuses of antipsychotic medication by those claiming to act in an incompetent's best interests." In *Davis v. Hubbard,* 506 F.Supp. 915, 926 (N.D. Ohio 1980), the judge found that seventy-three per cent of the patients of Lima (Ohio) State Hospital received psychotropic drugs, and that the high prescription rate "can be justified only for reasons other than treatment—namely, for the convenience of the staff and for punishment."

* * *

[An extensive compilation of cases and authorities that have found that psychotropic drugs have frequently been used for the purpose of control rather than treatment are omitted.]

Nevertheless, psychiatric institutions must offer protection to third persons, whether staff members or patients, and must preserve security within the institution. However, when public safety and security are a consideration in the decision to administer antipsychotic drugs over a patient's objection, the "antipsychotic drugs function as chemical restraints forcibly imposed upon an unwilling individual who, if competent, would refuse such treatment." In such circumstances, the antipsychotic drug treatment is administered for the benefit of others, and the statutory and regulatory conditions for the use of chemical restraints must be followed.

General Laws c. 123, § 21, as amended by St.1978, c. 367, § 71F, requires that State mental health patients may be restrained "only in cases of emergency such as the occurrence of, or serious threat of, extreme violence, personal injury, or attempted suicide." In no case may chemical means of restraint be used without "written authorization * * * in advance by the superintendent or director of the I.C.U. or by a physician designated by him for this purpose."

* * *

The use of chemicals to restrain State mental patients is limited to emergencies in which the patient harms, or threatens to harm, himself or others.

* * *

We conclude that only if a patient poses an imminent threat of harm to himself or others, and only if there is no less intrusive alternative to antipsychotic drugs, may the Commonwealth invoke its police powers without prior court approval to treat the patient by forcible injection of antipsychotic drugs over the patient's objection. No other State interest is sufficiently compelling to warrant the extremely intrusive measures necessary for forcible medication with antipsychotic drugs. Any other result also would negate the Legislature's decision to regulate strictly the use of mind altering drugs as restraints.

Questions 8 and 9. Forcible antipsychotic medication essential to prevent "immediate, substantial, and irreversible deterioration of a serious mental illness." We have rejected the broad, traditional parens patriae power invoked by a State to do what is best for its citizens despite their own wishes,

However, the State may, in rare circumstances, override a patient's refusal of medication under its so called "parens patriae" powers, even though no threat of violence exists. A patient may be treated against his will to prevent the "immediate, substantial, and irreversible deterioration of a serious mental illness," in cases in which "even the smallest of avoidable delays would be intolerable."

In such a situation, interim treatment may be given to an incompetent patient, or to one whom doctors, in the exercise of their professional judgment, believe to be incompetent. If a patient is medicated in order to avoid the "immediate, substantial, and irreversible deterioration of a serious mental illness," and the doctors determine that the antipsychotic medication should continue and the patient objects, the doctors must seek an adjudication of incompetence and if, after hearing, the patient is found to be incompetent, the judge should make a substituted judgment treatment plan determination.

* * *

Questions and Comments

1. Note that the decision of the Supreme Judicial Court of Massachusetts is based on state law. Since it relies in part on an interpretation of a Massachusetts statute, the decision has no binding effect on any other state. Nevertheless, the decision may serve as a model for the courts of other jurisdictions that have similar statute enactments.

2. What are the differences in the scope of institutional authority to compel the administration of psychotropic drugs under *Rogers v. Okin* which appears at p. 444 and *Rogers v. Commissioner* decided by the

Massachusetts court? Do these differences extend to both the police power as well as the *parens patriae* types of commitment?

3. The Massachusetts Supreme Judicial Court's decision in *Rogers v. Commissioner* will probably allow the Circuit Court of Appeals to find for the plaintiff in the pending case of *Rogers v. Okin* on the basis of Massachusetts *state law.* If so, the existence of a federal constitutional right to refuse treatment, an issue that was at one point before the Supreme Court, will again escape resolution.

4. For a survey of laws governing patients rights to decline psychotropic medication see, Callahan and Longmire, Psychotropic Patients' Right to Refuse Psychotropic Medication: A National Survey, 7 Mental Disability Law Rep. 494 (December 1983).

3. *Electroconvulsive Therapy*

a. *Clinical Application*

NOTE, *REGULATION OF ELECTROCONVULSIVE THERAPY*
75 Mich.L.Rev. 363 (1976).

ECT is the term generally used to describe several types of psychiatric treatment, all of which involve inducing in the patient a convulsive seizure similar to a grand mal epileptic attack. The patient does not eat for four hours prior to the convulsion. Sedatives may be provided before treatment, but usually no drug therapy occurs. One-half hour before the convulsion, atropine, a preanesthetic medication that reduces the risk of suffocation by decreasing the production of saliva, is furnished. A fast-acting barbiturate anesthetic is then injected so that the patient will feel neither the muscle contractions that precede muscle relaxation nor the unpleasant sensation of respiratory arrest. Electrodes are attached to the patient's temples and a current that ranges between seventy and 130 volts is administered for 0.1 to 0.5 seconds. The seizure, the therapeutic agent, lasts between thirty and fifty seconds. The patient remains totally unconscious for a few minutes after the convulsion; full consciousness is regained in five to thirty minutes.

This procedure is most widely used to treat severe depression and schizophrenia. Although there is evidence, albeit disputed, that it has at least some positive effect, there is little agreement as to the process by which ECT ameliorates these conditions.

b. *Legal Perspectives*

PRICE v. SHEPPARD
Supreme Court of Minnesota, 1976.
307 Minn. 250, 239 N.W.2d 905.

YETKA, Justice.

This appeal from a summary judgment entered in the Ramsey County District Court involves an action against the medical director of the Minnesota Security Hospital at St. Peter, Dr. Charles G. Sheppard, for (1) assault and battery, and (2) violation of plaintiff Dwight Price's civil rights under 42 U.S.C.A. § 1983. The claims arise out of the administration of a series of 20 electroshock treatments, given against the express wishes of plaintiff Willa Mae Price, Dwight's mother and natural guardian, while Dwight, a minor, was under involuntary commitment in the Minnesota Security Hospital at St. Peter.

* * *

Dwight Price was committed to the Hastings State Hospital September 8, 1971, by order of the Ramsey County Probate Court, which found Dwight to be "mentally ill-inebriate." The commitment petition was brought by Dwight's mother, Willa Mae Price, apparently in order to secure treatment for Dwight for a developing drug and alcohol problem. Several attempts at voluntary treatment, prior to the commitment proceedings, had proved unsuccessful.

Shortly after being admitted to Hastings, Dwight allegedly attempted to strangle one of the hospital staff. Because Hastings was not equipped to handle dangerous patients, Dwight was transferred to the Security Hospital at St. Peter on September 11, 1971.

Dwight's condition, upon his admission at St. Peter was diagnosed as simple schizophrenia. He was treated with tranquilizing and antidepressant medications, but apparently failed to respond and continued to be aggressive and assaultive to the staff and other patients. For this reason, Dr. Sheppard prescribed electroshock therapy.

He sought Mrs. Price's consent to administer the electroshock treatments. Through her attorney Mrs. Price arranged for an independent medical examination by Dr. William Chalgren, a Mankato psychiatrist, for the purpose of determining the advisability of the proposed treatment. Dr. Chalgren examined Dwight November 27, 1971, and recommended that drug treatment continue but that if Dwight did not respond favorably, electroshock treatment be given.

Dr. Chalgren's recommendations were followed by the staff at St. Peter, but Dwight's condition did not improve. Accordingly, on December 22, 1971, without the consent of Mrs. Price, electroshock therapy began and was continued to February 11, 1972. Dwight was released from St. Peter June 19, 1972.

The issues raised on this appeal are:

(1) Does the administration of electroshock therapy to an involuntarily committed minor patient of a state mental hospital, without the consent of the minor's guardian, violate his rights (a) to be free from cruel and unusual punishment, and (b) of privacy?

(2) Is a state official entitled to immunity from an action for damages for acts performed by him in good faith and which he could

not reasonably have known would violate the constitutional rights of another?

1. We do not agree with the claim that the electroshock therapy was cruel and unusual punishment for the reason that the record does not suggest, nor have plaintiffs demonstrated, how those treatments, under the circumstances of this case, can be regarded as "punishment." While plaintiffs are certainly correct in the statement that the characterization of electroshock therapy by defendant as "treatment" does not insulate it from Eighth Amendment scrutiny, that alone does not establish that the treatments were "punishment."

*   *   *

2. Plaintiffs second claimed violation of the minor's civil rights— the right of privacy—is more troublesome, primarily because that emerging right is currently so ill-defined.

*   *   *

We recognize that it is far too early in the evolution of the right of privacy to offer any single definition or rule of what the right entails. Only its broadest contours have been sketched. We do feel, however, because of the importance of that emerging right, it is appropriate for us, at this time, to set forth more than our bare conclusion that the right of privacy is or is not involved.

At the core of the privacy decisions, in our judgment, is the concept of personal autonomy—the notion that the Constitution reserves to the individual, free of governmental intrusion, certain fundamental decisions about how he or she will conduct his or her life. Like other constitutional rights, however, this right is not an absolute one and must give way to certain interests of the state, the balance turning on the impact of the decision on the life of the individual. As the impact increases, so must the importance of the state's interest. Some decisions, we assume, will be of little consequence to the individual and a showing of a legitimate state interest will justify its intrusion; other decisions, on the other hand, will be of such major consequence that only the most compelling state interest will justify the intrusion.

But once justified, the extent of the state's intrusion is not unlimited. It must also appear that the means utilized to serve the state's interest are necessary and reasonable, or, in other words, in light of alternative means, the least intrusive.

*   *   *

The question in the case before us is whether the state, consistent with Dwight Price's right of privacy, can assume the decision of whether Dwight, an involuntarily committed mental patient, will undergo psychiatric treatment. We observe that the more fundamental decision, whether he was to undergo hospitalization, was assumed by the state at the commitment proceeding, the validity of which is not contested.

The impact of the decision on the individual is unquestionably great, for the result is the alteration of the patient's personality. The state's interest in assuming the decision is in acting as *parens patriae*, fulfilling its duty to protect the well-being of its citizens who are incapable of so acting for themselves. Under the circumstances of this case, that interest can be articulated as the need for the state to assume the decision-making role regarding the psychiatric treatment for one who, presumptively, based on the fact of commitment on the ground of mental illness, is unable to *rationally* do so for himself. If that interest of the state is sufficiently important to deprive an individual of his physical liberty, it would seem to follow that it would be sufficiently important for the state to assume the treatment decision. We hold that it is.

"Under the *parens patriae* rationale, an individual may be committed when he lacks capacity to make a rational decision concerning hospitalization, and the treatment or custodial care available would be beneficial enough to outweigh the deprivations which commitment would impose on him. Inherent in an adjudication that an individual should be committed under the state's *parens patriae* power is the decision that he can be forced to accept the treatments found to be in his best interest; it would be incongruous if an individual who lacks capacity to make a treatment decision could frustrate the very justification for the state's action by refusing such treatments." Note, *Developments in the Law—Civil Commitment of the Mentally Ill*, 87 Harv.L.Rev. 1190, 1344 (1974).

The more important question, we believe, involved in the state's assumption of the treatment decision is the necessity and reasonableness of the means utilized by the state in treating an involuntarily committed patient. The techniques generally available to treat psychological disorders range in degree of severity and coerciveness from the least intrusive forms such as milieu therapy (behavior changes produced by manipulation of the patient's environment) and psychoanalysis, to drug, aversion, or electroconvulsive therapy, and ultimately to psychosurgery. Some of these techniques require the voluntary participation of the patient in order to be effective, while others can be effective when involuntarily imposed. As the techniques increase in severity, so do the risks of serious and long-lasting psychological or neurological damage.

Whether the administration of electroshock treatments, one of the most intrusive forms of treatment, was necessary and reasonable in the treatment of Dwight Price is a question we cannot reach. We believe, and so hold, that whatever the answer to that question may be, on the record before us the defendant is immune from liability under 42 U.S.C.A. § 1983.

* * *

[Under § 1983 liability can only be imposed if the state official knew or reasonably should have known that his actions would violate the constitutional right of another.]

*   *   *   It seems abundantly clear, given the vagueness of the constitutional right of privacy, that the defendant could not reasonably have known that the administration of electroshock treatments to Dwight Price violated a "clearly established" constitutional right.

*   *   *

Because the potential impact of the more intrusive forms of treatment is so great, we are reluctant in those cases where the patient or guardian refuse their consent, to leave the imposition of the more intrusive forms of treatment solely within the discretion of medical personnel at our state hospitals. For that reason, we adopt the following procedure for future cases:

> (1) If the patient is incompetent to give consent or refuses consent or his guardian other than persons responsible for his commitment also refuses his consent, before more intrusive forms of treatment may be utilized, the medical director of the state hospital must petition the probate division of the county court in the county in which the hospital is located for an order authorizing the prescribed treatment;

> (2) the court shall appoint a guardian ad litem to represent the interests of the patient;

> (3) in an adversary proceeding, pursuant to the petition, the court shall determine the necessity and reasonableness of the prescribed treatment.

In making that determination the court should balance the patient's need for treatment against the intrusiveness of the prescribed treatment. Factors which should be considered are (1) the extent and duration of changes in behavior patterns and mental activity effected by the treatment, (2) the risks of adverse side effects, (3) the experimental nature of the treatment, (4) its acceptance by the medical community of this state, (5) the extent of intrusion into the patient's body and the pain connected with the treatment, and (6) the patient's ability to competently determine for himself whether the treatment is desirable.

We cannot draw a clear line between the more intrusive forms of treatment requiring this procedural hearing and those which do not. Certainly this procedure is not intended to apply to the use of mild tranquilizers or those therapies requiring the cooperation of the patient. On the other hand, given current medical practice, this procedure must be followed where psychosurgery or electroshock therapy is proposed.

Affirmed.

Questions and Comments

1. While the patient in *Price* was a minor, the reasoning of the court which limits the state's authority to impose ECT without either judicial

authorization or the consent of the guardian would apply equally to an adult patient.

2. On what basis did the court distinguish the constitutional limitations which apply to psychosurgery and electroshock therapy from other therapies such as mild tranquilizers which, according to the court, require special authorization? Would psychotropic medication also be subject to the special procedures applicable to ECT?

3. Various commentators and court decisions distinguish between "intrusive" and "non-intrusive" therapies, with the former category being subject to special regulation or control. What criteria serve to distinguish these two categories? Presumably, intrusiveness in the psychiatric sense involves physical interference with the patient for the purpose of altering his thought or behavior processes.

According to one commentator both the physical and psychological invasion appear necessary for a treatment to be characterized as "intrusive." The six criteria which make up the concept include:

(i) the extent to which the effects of the therapy upon mentation are reversible;

(ii) the extent to which the resulting psychic state is "foreign," "abnormal," or "unnatural" for the person in question, rather than simply a restoration of his prior psychic state (this is closely related to the "magnitude" or "intensity" of the change);

(iii) the rapidity with which the effects occur;

(iv) the scope of the change in the total "ecology" of the mind's functions;

(v) the extent to which one can resist acting in ways impelled by the psychic effects of the therapy; and

(vi) the duration of the change.

Shapiro, *Legislating the Control of Behavior Control: Autonomy and the Coercive Use of Organic Therapies*, 47 S.Cal.L.Rev. 237, 256 n. 51 (1974). *See also*, Note, *Regulation of Electroconvulsive Therapy*, 75 Mich.L.Rev. 363, 375 n. 81 (1976).

How satisfactory are these criteria? Would their application lead to a reasonable degree of predictability so that therapists can be on notice as to whether a particular treatment is intrusive and, therefore, subject to special procedures before the matter is litigated?

4. *Price v. Sheppard* is one of a limited number of appellate decisions which, in the absence of any statutory restrictions, have recognized a constitutional limitation on the administration of ECT. See also, *Gundy v. Pauley*, 619 S.W.2d 730 (Ky.App.1981). It is questionable whether the constitutional holding of the Price court will gain general acceptance. However, numerous states have regulated the application of ECT through legislation, though statutes vary widely. In some cases the patient is merely given the *right to refuse* ECT. In states such as California, Illinois, and eleven others the individual must give "informed consent" before ECT can be administered. A dozen other states provide mental patients with a general right to refuse medication and other

forms of treatment. Mental Disability Law Reporter, No. 7, p. 151 (1983). What is the distinction between the *right to refuse* treatment and the requirement of *informed consent?* Does the former allow the administration of the treatment when the patient merely acquiesces, whereas in the latter the patient must have sufficient understanding to give his consent?

5. What criteria should courts use in determining whether the individual is capable of making an informed decision in the hearings called for by *Price v. Sheppard?* What degree of insight should be required? These issues are explored in greater detail in Chapter Four.

4. *Psychosurgery*

a. *Clinical Application*

PLOTKIN, *LIMITING THE THERAPEUTIC ORGY: MENTAL PATIENTS' RIGHT TO REFUSE TREATMENT*
72 Nw.L.Rev. 461, 466–71 (1978).

The earliest example of psychosurgery dates back to the Incacivilization where the perforation of the skull was used to "cure" mental illness by supposedly releasing evil spirits from the brain. Now, as then, psychosurgery is simply "[b]rain surgery performed for the relief of mental and psychic symptoms." The difference between psychosurgery and routine brain surgery is that psychosurgery is used to alter behavior.

After early research by Fulton and Jacobsen catalogued the disappearance of frustration, temper tantrums, and anxiety toward learning tasks following frontal cortex ablation in two chimpanzees, modern surgeons began to contemplate psychosurgery as a viable treatment technique. The Portuguese team of Moniz and Lima introduced bilateral prefrontal lobotomy on humans in 1936. They hypothesized that "by interrupting some of the connections between the prefrontal lobes and other parts of the brain, some modifications might be brought about in the mental processes of psychotic individuals."

In 1936, on the strength of Moniz's results, Freeman and Watts, the American "pioneers" of psychosurgery, performed the first "standard" lobotomy in the United States. They were able to achieve a bleaching of emotional tone and a quieting of anxiety in psychotic patients. They reported that:

> [patients] are not apathetic, lacking all emotion, after lobotomy; rather, the emotion attaches itself to external happenings rather than to inner experiences. Patients * * * are usually cheerful, responsive, affectionate and unreserved. They are outspoken, often critical of others and lacking in embarrassment. * * * Some patients are distractible, others have single track minds; some are indolent, others are human dynamos. The most striking and constant change from the pre-operative personality lies in a certain unselfconsciousness.

* * * The patient emerges from operation with an immature personality that is at first poorly equipped for maintaining him in a competitive society; but with the passage of time there is progressive improvement, so that in about one-half of the cases earning a living again becomes possible.

* * *

Other authors have been less charitable toward this treatment modality. Lobotomized patients have been termed "postoperative vegetables," and a definite stereotyped "lobotomy personality," manifested by either torpidity or euphoria, has been identified. In fact, it appears that any attempt at achieving a satisfactory result represents a "tenuous balance between failure to achieve any effect and unacceptable personality change."

A wide variety of bodily effects have been observed in lobotomized patients. Freeman and Watts noted increased appetite, "mask-like" face, incontinence, stupor, aphasia, hemiplegia, reflex grasping, and positive Babinski reflex. Convulsive seizures, a significant postoperative complication, have frequently been reported. Mortality, primarily caused by cerebral hemorrhage, has ranged from 2 to 3 percent in the larger studies.

* * *

As a result of both the frequency of psychosurgery's negative effects and the increasing availability of psychotropic drugs, a significant decline in the use of psychosurgery occurred during the 1950's, especially in state hospitals. Nevertheless, psychosurgery, while dormant, did not disappear; in fact, it has rallied in the last decade. A small group of neurosurgeons are struggling to devise methods for increasing the specificity of therapeutic results, while diminishing the unfavorable personality effects associated with classical lobotomies.

Current procedures, allegedly aiming only at specific sites in the brain, emphasize extremely precise localization and limitation of the operation to achieve therapeutic benefit without use of extensive cutting techniques. Generally, more favorable results have been reported with these localized procedures. The severe emotional blunting, impaired intellectual functioning, and extensive somatic side effects which accompanied the older techniques are today reported to occur with less frequency.

Many of these modern studies also indicate that psychosurgery's use has obtained "positive" results in depression, neurosis, and phobias. Conversely, psychosurgery has not achieved favorable results in schizophrenics. This is a particularly noteworthy finding since treatment of schizophrenia remains a major problem in state mental hospitals.

While the proponents of psychosurgery contend that their procedures have developed beyond the experimental stage, few, if any, advocate its use without qualification. Because irreversible brain destruction is implicit, "[a] patient should have been proven to be unresponsive to all other appropriate psychiatric treatment modalities and he should be disabled to the point that any potential hazards from the operation are felt to be equal to or less than the disability suffered as a result of his illness."

b. Legal Perspectives

Undoubtedly the most controversial of all psychiatric treatment is psychosurgery, which may be broadly defined to include any procedure that removes, destroys, or interrupts the continuity of the brain tissue. This includes not only radical alterations, such as were practiced in the 1950's, but also the newer stereotachtic procedures which destroy minute amounts of brain tissue. The widespread abuses which have been reported and the use of these procedures has led many states to enact legislation regulating psychosurgery. *See* Stromberg and Stone, *A Model State Law on Civil Commitment of the Mentally Ill*, 20 Harv.J. on Legis. 275, 311, n. 108 (1983). In essence, these laws require both the informed consent of the patient and, of equal importance, a very detailed and comprehensive review of the treatment decision process.

Even in those states where the legislature has not enacted comprehensive regulations on psychosurgery, there is today little doubt that these procedures may not be applied to involuntarily committed patients without either informed consent of the patient or court approval. For instance, the influential National Commission for the Protection of Human Subjects of Biomedical and Behavior Research in its report concluded that psychosurgery must be closely regulated and in the case of involuntarily committed patients should only be performed with the informed consent of the patient and review by both the institutional review board and a national psychosurgery advisory board. Stromberg and Stone, at 311. One lower court decision, moreover, has held that an involuntary patient cannot give truly informed consent to psychosurgery. *See, Kaimowitz v. Department of Mental Health for the State of Michigan*, at p. 176 *supra*.

Questions and Comments

1. California was the first state to regulate psychosurgery. The following provisions were included:

(1) that the treatment (psychosurgery) be "critically needed for the welfare of the patient";

(2) that the prospective patient give his written informed consent;

(3) that a relative be notified of the proposed procedure; and

(4) that a Board of three medical specialists review the medical record and unanimously agree both as to the necessity of the treatment and the capacity of the patient to consent.

These provisions were challenged in *Aden v. Younger,* 57 Cal.App.3d 662, 129 Cal.Rptr. 535 (1976), as an infringement of the consenting patients' right to privacy.

The California Appellate Court upheld the overall validity of the law but found several of its provisions unconstitutional. Among these were the requirement that the treatment be "critically needed for the welfare of the patient" was found unconstitutionally vague. The requirement that a relative be notified was deemed to constitute an infringement of the patients' right to privacy.

2. Regulation of psychosurgery only covers those surgical procedures which have as their primary purpose the treatment of mental disease or the alteration of behavior. Thus, surgeries designed to ameliorate the effects of such disorders as epilepsy or Parkinsonism or the excision of brain tumors would not be subject to the limitations of the laws regulating psychosurgery. *See,* Stromberg and Stone, at 312, n. 116.

3. There is a sizeable and vocal minority who believe that the use of psychosurgery should be abolished. The leading advocate of abolition, Dr. Peter Breggin asserts: "[T]here can be no rationale for 'helping' an individual by blunting his highest adaptive mechanisms * * * [I]mprovement in function cannot follow mutilation of the functioning brain." Plotkin, *Limiting the Therapeutic Orgy: Mental Patients' Right to Refuse Treatment,* 72 Nw.L.Rev. 461, 466–71 (1978).

5. *Behavior Modification Therapy*

a. *Clinical Application*

PLOTKIN, *LIMITING THE THERAPEUTIC ORGY: MENTAL PATIENTS' RIGHT TO REFUSE TREATMENT*
72 Nw.L.Rev. 461, 479–81 (1978).

Behavior therapy is the application of systematically-obtained empirical data and theoretical concepts to describe and remedy abnormal patterns of behavior. It is, in other words, a systematic means of controlling human behavior based on the assumption, drawn from research upon animal and human subjects, that a person's maladaptive behavior is an effort to reduce or avoid problems by escape.

Pavlov's classical animal conditioning experiments stirred other behavioralists to apply his experimental procedures to the study of human behavior. Although there has yet to evolve a single, universally accepted technique, most practitioners subscribe to one of three common methods of behavior therapy: desensitization, aversion therapy, and operant conditioning.

Desensitization is a counterconditioning technique in which a person is exposed to an unpleasant or feared experience in gradual steps. During this gradual exposure, the therapist attempts to elicit responses from the person that are antagonistic to the anxiety usually provoked by the unpleasant stimulus. It is hoped that this will desensitize the patient by weakening his or her association between the anxiety and the stress-inducing situation.

Aversion therapy is used to eliminate various forms of undesirable behavior by punishing the person each time the specified behavior occurs. The punishment, or aversive stimulus, may occur at the same time as the undesired behavior, or it may closely follow after exhibition of the behavior.

Operant conditioning attempts to control behavior by reinforcing only desired behaviors. The principle "is that behavior is primarily influenced by what follows it—its consequences—and that in order to change behavior the consequences of that behavior should be altered." Rather than punishing, or negatively reinforcing maladaptive behavior, the principle of operant conditioning is to withhold approval for such actions so that the unwanted behavior will ultimately become "extinct."

Behavior therapies, in one form or another, have been extensively used in institutions. One estimator suggested that "half the nation's public mental hospitals have projects based on behavior therapy concepts." On the basis of such experience, behaviorists claim that they now have reliable scientific data proving that their techniques are effective.

b. Legal Perspectives

KNECHT v. GILLMAN

United States Court of Appeals, Eighth Circuit, 1973.
488 F.2d 1136.

ROSS, Circuit Judge.

This is an action by Gary Knecht and Ronald Stevenson, both in the custody of the State of Iowa, against officials of that state, under 42 U.S.C. § 1983. Their complaint alleged that they had been subjected to injections of the drug apomorphine at the Iowa Security Medical Facility (ISMF) without their consent and that the use of said drug by the defendants constituted cruel and unusual punishment in violation of the eighth amendment. The trial court dismissed their complaint for injunctive relief. We reverse with directions to enjoin the defendants from further use of the drug except pursuant to specific guidelines hereinafter set forth.

* * * [T]he evidence contained in the report of the magistrate showed that apomorphine had been administered at ISMF for some time prior to the hearing as "aversive stimuli" in the treatment of inmates with behavior problems. The drug was administered by intra-muscular injection by a nurse after an inmate had violated the behavior protocol established for him by the staff. Dr. Loeffelholz testified that the drug could be injected for such pieces of behavior as not getting up, for giving cigarettes against orders, for talking, for swearing, or for lying. Other inmates or members of the staff would

report on these violations of the protocol and the injection would be given by the nurse without the nurse or any doctor having personally observed the violation and without specific authorization of the doctor.

When it was determined to administer the drug, the inmate was taken to a room near the nurses' station which contained only a water closet and there given the injection. He was then exercised and within about fifteen minutes he began vomiting. The vomiting lasted from fifteen minutes to an hour. There is also a temporary cardio-vascular effect which involves some change in blood pressure and "in the heart." This aversion type "therapy" is based on "Pavlovian conditioning."

The record is not clear as to whether or not the drug was always used with the initial consent of the inmate. It has apparently been administered in a few instances in the past without obtaining written consent of the inmate and once the consent is given, withdrawal thereof was not permitted. Apparently, at the time of trial apomor-phine was not being used unless the inmate signed an initial consent, but there is no indication that the authorities now permit an inmate to withdraw his consent once it is given. Neither is there any indication in the record that the procedure has been changed to require the prior approval of a physician each time the drug is administered. Likewise there is no indication that there has been any change in the procedure which permits the administration of the drug upon reports of fellow inmates despite a recommendation by the magistrate that this practice should be avoided.

The testimony relating to the medical acceptability of this treatment is not conclusive. Dr. Steven Fox of the University of Iowa testified that behavior modification by aversive stimuli is a "highly questionable technique" and that only a 20% to 50% success is claimed. He stated that it is not being used elsewhere to his knowledge and that its use is really punishment worse than a controlled beating since the one administering the drug can't control it after it is administered.

On the other hand, Dr. Loeffelholz of the ISMF staff testified that there had been a 50% to 60% effect in modifying behavior by the use of apomorphine at ISMF. There is no evidence that the drug is used at any other inmate medical facility in any other state.

The Iowa Security Medical Facility is established by Section 223.1, Code of Iowa, 1973. It is an institution for persons displaying evidence of mental illness or psychological disorders and requiring diagnostic services and treatment in a security setting.

* * *

* * * [T]he purpose of confinement at ISMF is not penal in nature, but rather one of examination, diagnosis and treatment. Naturally, examination and diagnosis, by their very definition, do not

encompass the administration of drugs. Thus, when that course of conduct is taken with respect to any particular patient, he is the recipient of treatment.

The use of apomorphine, then, can be justified, only if it can be said to be treatment. Based upon the testimony adduced at the hearing and the findings made by the magistrate and adopted by the trial court, it is not possible to say that the use of apomorphine is a recognized and acceptable medical practice in institutions such as ISMF. Neither can we say, however, that its use on inmates who knowingly and intelligently consent to the treatment, should be prohibited on a medical or a legal basis. The authorities who testi- fied at the evidentiary hearing indicate that some form of consent is now obtained prior to this treatment. The only question then is whether, under the eighth amendment, its use should be prohibited absent such consent; and if so what procedure must be followed to prevent abuses in the treatment procedures and to make certain the consent is knowingly and intelligently made.

At the outset we note that the mere characterization of an act as "treatment" does not insulate it from eighth amendment scrutiny.

* * *

Here we have a situation in which an inmate may be subjected to a morphine base drug which induces vomiting for an extended period of time. Whether it is called "aversive stimuli" or punishment, the act of forcing someone to vomit for a fifteen minute period for committing some minor breach of the rules can only be regarded as cruel and unusual unless the treatment is being administered to a patient who knowingly and intelligently has consented to it. To hold otherwise would be to ignore what each of us has learned from sad experience—that vomiting (especially in the presence of others) is a painful and debilitating experience. The use of this unproven drug for this purpose on an involuntary basis, is, in our opinion, cruel and unusual punishment prohibited by the eighth amendment.

We turn then to the question of how best to prevent abuse in the treatment procedures of consenting participants and how to make certain that the consent is knowingly and intelligently given.

* * *

In this case the trial court should enjoin the use of apomorphine in the treatment of inmates at the ISMF except when the following conditions are complied with:

1. A written consent must be obtained from the inmate specifying the nature of the treatment, a written description of the purpose, risks and effects of treatment, and advising the inmate of his right to terminate the consent at any time. This consent must include a certification by a physician that the patient has read and under- stands all of the terms of the consent and that the inmate is mentally competent to understand fully all of the provisions thereof and give his consent thereto.

2. The consent may be revoked at any time after it is given and if an inmate orally expresses an intention to revoke it to any member of the staff, a revocation form shall be provided for his signature at once.

3. Each apomorphine injection shall be individually authorized by a doctor and be administered by a doctor, or by a nurse. It shall be authorized in each instance only upon information based on the personal observation of a member of the professional staff. Information from inmates or inmate aides of the observation of behavior in violation of an inmate's protocol shall not be sufficient to warrant such authorization.

The judgment of the district court is reversed with directions to grant the injunction under the terms hereinbefore set forth.

*   *   *

Questions and Comments

1. Note that the court's ruling in *Knecht* is based on the findings of the trial court that the administration of apomorphine is not a "recognized and acceptable medical practice." Is it conceivable that another court might find that the use of apomorphine is recognized and accepted as a medical practice? Would such use of the drug then be considered treatment rather than punishment? What other factors influenced the court's decision?

2. *Knecht v. Gilman* raises the broader question of how one can meaningfully distinguish between punishment and treatment. Can the distinction be found by defining the objectives of the two activities? Could the distinction turn on the subjective intent of the person administering the activity? Should the court have based its judgment on the ISMF staff's good faith belief that the drug was being used solely to "treat" behavioral disorders? Recall the claim of ISMF's doctor that the drug was 50–60% successful in modifying behavior. Should these results have been given more weight by the court?

Consider the court's suggestion that an individual's consent to the administration of apomorphine would take the practice out of the realm of cruel and unusual punishment and render it an acceptable form of treatment. What does this suggest about the nature of the distinction between punishment and treatment? Recall the testimony of Dr. Fox that the use of apomorphine was "punishment worse than a controlled beating." Could an inmate's consent to such a *beating* legitimatize corporal punishment as treatment?

3. Behavior modification can also be based on programs which use positive reinforcements or rewards. The following excerpt provides a description of the techniques commonly used in these programs:

*   *   *

[I]f certain behaviors occur naturally with a high frequency, then the opportunity to engage in those behaviors can be used as effective reinforcers to strengthen a low-frequency behavior. The psychologists determined the high frequency-behaviors empirically:

> It was noted that certain patients often hoarded various items under their mattresses. The activity in this case, in a general sense, consisted of concealing private property in such a manner that it would be inaccessible to other patients and the staff. Since this event seemed to be highly probable, it was formally scheduled as a reinforcer. Keys to a locked cabinet in which they could conceal their private possessions just as they had been doing with the mattresses were made available to patients.

> Another activity that was observed to be highly probable was the attempt of patients to conceal themselves in several locations on the ward in an effort to enjoy some degree of privacy. A procedure was therefore instituted whereby a patient could obtain a portable screen to put in front of her bed or access to a bedroom with a door. Another event that had a high probability of occurrence for some patients was a visit with the social worker or psychologist. This was used as a reinforcer by arranging appointments with either of these staff members.

> Ground privileges and supervised walks by the staff were also established as reinforcers by application of the Premack Principle, since patients were frequently observed to "stay at the exit to the ward and try to leave." The opportunity to attend religious services was also used as a reinforcer since several patients attended frequently when they were allowed to freely.

> Thus, personal cabinets, room dividers, visits with the professional staff, ground privileges, supervised walks, and religious services were all made contingently available to the patients: they could be purchased if the patient had performed a sufficient number of target responses to have earned the requisite tokens to purchase the reinforcers. They were otherwise unavailable. Other reinforcers in the Anna State Hospital program included a personal chair, writing materials and stationery, movies, television programs, and various commissary items.

*   *   *

David B. Wexler, *Mental Health Law* (New York: Plenum Press, 1981) p. 215–16.

To what extent may "rights" be withdrawn by an institution in order to implement a behavior modification program? Would patient consent be necessary to implement such program? If patient consent is a requirement, is it likely that behavior modification programs can, in fact, be implemented for large numbers of patients? Could the institution utilize reinforcers that have not been guaranteed as rights? What kinds of non-guaranteed incentives might be available? *See,* David B. Wexler, *Mental Health Law* (New York: Plenam Press, 1981) p. 226.

C. MISCELLANEOUS RIGHTS OF THE INSTITUTIONALIZED PATIENT

1. Freedom From Physical Restraints

The patient's freedom of movement within the institution can be limited either by placing the patient in seclusion or by use of mechanical devices designed to restrain the patient's mobility. Seclusion serves to remove the descriptive or disturbed patient from social contact by isolating him in a locked room. As described by the court in one recent case, "Seclusion * * * involves placing the patient in one of the individual sleeping rooms in the ward, usually furnished with only a a bed, and locking the door." *Eckerhart v. Hensley*, 475 F.Supp. 908, 926 (W.D.Mo.1979). Restraint is a means of restricting a patient's ability to react physically by temporarily limiting his freedom of body and limb movement by use of physical or mechanical restraints, such as cuffs, straps, mittens, or braces. *Id.*

Seclusion and the use of restraints are generally considered to be necessary and useful treatment devices under certain circumstances. Nevertheless, increasing criticism has been leveled against what are perceived to be abuses of these "treatment or control techniques." Some observers contend that mechanical restraints and isolation have been improperly used to punish problem patients or as a substitute for adequate supervision in an understaffed facility. *See* Schwitzgebel and Schwitzgebel, *Law and Psychological Practice* (1980) at 47. As a result, it has been urged that the use of these devices be the subject of legal regulation.

A number of states have responded to evidence of past abuses by enacting specific legislation regulating the use of both isolation and restraint. In Illinois seclusion and restraints may be used only pursuant to a physician's order or in the event of an emergency. The Illinois statute also requires that following an imposition of seclusion or restraints, the order must be reviewed, confirmed, and documented by a physician at least once every 72 hours. Ill.Rev.Stat. Ch. 91½ §§ 2–108, 2–109 (1979).

In the absence of legislative enactment, a number of courts have attempted to achieve regulation through the introduction of constitutional due process protection. One court, for instance, has imposed an absolute prohibition on the use of seclusion for the mentally retarded. *New York State Association for Retarded Children v. Rockefeller*, 357 F.Supp. 752, 768 (E.D.N.Y.1973). Another federal district court has held that seclusion, or "time out procedures," may be used only where it is "closely supervised and an integral part of the behavioral treatment program." *Wyatt v. Stickney*, 344 F.Supp. 387, 400 (M.D.Ala.1973), aff'd 503 F.2d 1305 (5th Cir. 1974). A recent decision by a federal district court in Missouri found that seclusion and restraint could only be imposed where the institution adheres to a comprehensive procedural scheme similar to that required by the Illinois statute. The procedures mandated by the court included a physician's authorization in non-emergency situations, close monitoring of the patient during the seclusion or restraint, and periodic review of the physician's order by a treatment team and a separate review committee. *Eckerhart v. Hensley*, 475 F.Supp. 908, 926–27 (W.D.Mo.1979).

The status of these cases is uncertain after the Supreme Court's decision in *Youngberg v. Romeo*, 457 U.S. 307, 102 S.Ct. 2452, 73 L.Ed.2d 28 (1982), the main body of which is set out at p. 432. One of the issues in *Youngberg* involved a challenge to the use of mechanical devices, described as "soft" restraints, which encumbered the patient's arms. Evidence introduced during the case indicated that restraints were employed because the patient had on numerous occasions suffered injuries as a result of his own violent behavior, 102 S.Ct. at 2455. While the Court acknowledged that an institutionalized patient retains a liberty interest, it also held that the interest is not absolute and that physical restraints could be imposed under appropriate circumstances. Moreover, the Court rejected the contention that physical restrictions on liberty should only be imposed in the face of a "compelling" or "substantial necessity." 102 S.Ct. at 2461. Instead, the Court limited judicial review of institutional decision to impose restraints or isolation to an inquiry as to whether the restrictions result from the exercise of professional judgment. Thus, restraints are permissible whenever "professional judgment deems [them] necessary to assume * * * safety or to provide needed training." 102 S.Ct. at 2462. As a result of *Youngberg* and in the absence of state statutes imposing additional regulation, institutions appear to have considerable latitude in the use of these devices so long as their use is authorized and closely monitored by a professional.

Questions and Comments

1. A related issue concerns the legal rights of a patient facing transfer to a maximum security facility. In *Jones v. Robinson*, 440 F.2d 249 (D.C.Cir.1971), the court found a right to procedural due process in the case of a patient who had been accused of rape and transferred from a less restrictive unit to a maximum security unit in the same hospital. While recognizing that "[t]he purpose of the hospital authorities in making their judgment is a limited one related to appropriate treatment for the accused and appropriate protection for the other patients," the court asserted its authority to review such internal administrative decisions in keeping with its *habeas corpus* power. In order to facilitate such review and to guarantee the patient procedural due process, the following procedures were held necessary when a patient is accused of committing a crime:

* * *

1. That the officer conducting the inquiry be neutral, in the sense that where possible he have no prior connection with the accused patient, his alleged victim, or the incident under investigation. A

doctor, an administrative assistant to the superintendent or similar personnel of the hospital could serve in this capacity.

2.   That the investigating officer interview all the witnesses himself, including those suggested by the accused patient, and make a written memorandum of each interview. In this way the same fact finder can judge the credibility of all witnesses.

3.   That copies of these memoranda be made available to the accused patient and that he be given an opportunity to respond to the allegations contained therein. *Compare* Goldberg v. Kelly, *supra,* 397 U.S. at 267–268, 90 S.Ct. 1011.

4.   Where the hospital authorities believe that confrontation and cross-examination will not adversely affect the patients involved, including the witnesses, confrontation and cross-examination to the extent indicated should be permitted.

5.   That a lawyer to represent the accused patient is not required, but the hospital authorities may conclude that a lay representative assigned to the accused patient may be in the interest of justice.

6.   No court reporter or transcript of the proceedings would ordinarily be necessary, but detailed informal memoranda should be kept by the investigating officer who shall also make findings and give reasons for his decision. These memoranda, together with his findings and reasons, should become a part of the permanent records of the hospital.

7.   That while the investigating officer may determine whether the evidence is sufficient to justify a transfer of the accused patient to John Howard, to be effective that judgment must be affirmed by the superintendent of the hospital after a review of the record. (440 F.2d at 251–52.)

2.   In reaching its result, the court in *Jones v. Robinson,* cited in note 1 above, did not characterize the transfer contemplated by hospital officials as punishment. If the sole purpose of the transfer was treatment or protection of others, why should procedural due process be required? Is transfer to a maximum security facility different from seclusion or restraint when used to treat the patient and protect others?

2.   *Mandatory Work Assignments*

WEIDENFELLER v. KIDULIS

United States District Court, Eastern District of Wisconsin, 1974.
380 F.Supp. 445.

*   *   *

REYNOLDS, Chief Judge:

This is an action brought under the thirteenth amendment of the United States Constitution and the Fair Labor Standards Act in which two mentally handicapped individuals seek monetary and declaratory relief against defendants for the productive labor which they were allegedly forced to perform without compensation at the defendants' mental institutions.

Plaintiff Joseph Weidenfeller is a forty-four year old male who was born in Milwaukee, Wisconsin. He suffers from mental retardation and has been in custodial treatment facilities his entire life. He is still receiving treatment and custodial care because of his mental disabilities. Plaintiff Edwin Kryszewski is a thirty-one year old male and was also born in Milwaukee. He suffers from mental retardation and has been in custodial treatment centers for most of his life. He is presently undergoing treatment for his mental disabilities. All the expenses of both Joseph Weidenfeller and Edwin Kryszewski have been paid for through grants from the Milwaukee County Department of Public Welfare. The named defendants in this action are owners and proprietors of the Kidulis Family Group Home and Yorkville Nursing Home. Each of these family boarding homes is thus privately owned and is operated for profit.

This case arose out of the following factual context. On July 9, 1965, the two plaintiffs were permanently discharged from the Wisconsin Department of Health and Social Services Southern Colony to the defendants for custodial care and treatment. Kryszewski remained in the defendants' custody until April 27, 1973. Weidenfeller remained under defendants' care and control until October 15, 1973. Both plaintiffs were transferred to another institution which is not a party to this suit.

During his stay at the Kidulis Family Group Home, Joseph Weidenfeller was employed on the premises. He mowed the grass, cleaned patients' rooms, and washed dishes in the kitchen. Edwin Kryszewski likewise worked during his stay at the home. His tasks included such endeavors as unloading various materials, cleaning toilets and sinks, and scrubbing the kitchen floor. Neither plaintiff was ever compensated for his work at the institution.

Plaintiffs ground their complaint in the United States Constitution, alleging that the labor they performed at the home was nontherapeutic, was solely for the economic benefit of the institution, and was physically coerced upon them. Plaintiffs consequently claim that their thirteenth amendment right against involuntary servitude has been abridged. Alternatively, plaintiffs base their allegations on the Fair Labor Standards Act which provides for the establishment of fair labor standards in employment in and affecting interstate commerce. * * *

* * *

It is clear that throughout the United States mentally handicapped or retarded residents of both private and public institutions are often required to perform tasks, for little or no compensation, which primarily benefit the needs of the institution and not the individual. The issue specifically posed by defendants' motion is what legal theories, if any, are present to aid the mentally retarded in gaining entry into a federal court so that they, the mentally retarded, might resolve various conflicts between institution administrators and themselves. In the instant matter, plaintiffs have presented me with several alternative theories. I shall examine each of these separately.

A. THE FAIR LABOR STANDARDS ACT

The Fair Labor Standards Act of 1938, creates a statutory scheme for the payment of minimum wages and overtime compensation to individuals covered by the Act. Among its provisions, § 6, provides for minimum wages; § 7, provides for maximum hours and payment of overtime; and § 11(c), states that employers covered by the Act shall keep records of wages paid and employment hours. It has been held by several courts that a right to compensation exists for residents of mental institutions under the Fair Labor Standards Act. The language of the Act supports this conclusion. * * * On the basis of these allegations, I find that plaintiffs have clearly stated a cause of action upon which relief may be granted.

B. THE THIRTEENTH AMENDMENT

The scope of the thirteenth amendment to the United States Constitution is manifest. It states:

"Section 1. Neither slavery nor involuntary servitude, except as a punishment for crime whereof the party shall have been duly convicted, shall exist within the United States, or any place subject to their jurisdiction.

"Section 2. Congress shall have power to enforce this article by appropriate legislation."

Although the immediate aim of the thirteenth amendment was the abolition of slavery, it has been construed to encompass or maintain a system of free and voluntary labor throughout the United States.

It has been held that forced labor of certain individuals, including the mentally disabled, amounts to involuntary servitude and therefore is violative of the thirteenth amendment. It, however, has never been held that the mere subjecting of the mentally retarded to any form of work program is *per se* unconstitutional under the thirteenth amendment. Plaintiffs who wish to allege a cause of action under the thirteenth amendment must confront two substantial hurdles. First, they must allege (and ultimately prove on the merits) that their labors were performed involuntarily. Plaintiffs in the instant matter, having alleged in their complaint that as a result of their mental conditions they were coerced into performing designated tasks, have satisfied this requirement.

Even upon a showing that labor was performed involuntarily, however, courts have held that such labor is not violative of the thirteenth amendment if it serves a compelling state interest. Thus, it has recently been held that " * * * the Thirteenth Amendment may be violated if a mental institution requires inmates to perform chores which have no therapeutic purpose or are not personally related, but are required to be performed solely in order to assist in the defraying of institutional costs * * *."

Secondly, therefore, plaintiffs must allege that the work they performed was not therapeutic. Plaintiffs have so alleged in the instant matter. I might add that the burden placed on the state in these matters is something more than merely concluding that all involuntary civil commitments serve the compelling state interest of protecting society from the mentally ill.

Likewise, the plaintiffs here will carry a heavy burden in demonstrating that any given task is not therapeutic.

* * *

For the purposes of this motion to dismiss, I find that the plaintiffs, in alleging that they have been forced to provide nontherapeutic labor for the institution in which they were detained, have in essence alleged that they possess a constitutional right to a level of therapy consistent with the expressed treatment objectives of civil commitment in Wisconsin, and that they have not received their constitutional right to treatment. I find this to be a viable theory upon which relief might be granted on the merits, and I cannot dismiss it for failure to state a claim upon which relief may be granted.

* * *

In conclusion, therefore, the plaintiffs have stated a cause of action based on several alternative legal theories: the Fair Labor Standards Act, the thirteenth amendment, and the constitutional right to treatment. All of these theories allow plaintiffs to survive defendants' motion to dismiss.

Questions and Comments

1. Different legal standards apply to each of the three legal theories recognized by the *Weidenfeller* court as supporting objections to mandatory work assignments. To sustain a claim for compensation under the Fair Labor Standards Act, the economic reality test discussed in *Souder v. Brennan*, 367 F.Supp. 808 (D.D.C.1973), requires the patient merely to demonstrate that the institution "derives * * * consequential economic benefit" from the services performed.

A patient seeking relief from forced work assignments must meet more burdensome standards if he proceeds under the Thirteenth Amendment. To demonstrate a Thirteenth Amendment violation, the court observes that a patient must demonstrate that the work performed was both involuntary and non-therapeutic. However, not all non-therapeutic work necessarily infringes the patient's rights. As noted by the court in *Jobson v. Henne*, 355 F.2d 129 (2d Cir.1966):

> The state is not * * * foreclosed from requiring that a lawfully committed inmate perform without compensation certain chores designed to reduce the financial burden placed on a state by its program of treatment for the mentally retarded, if the chores are reasonably

related to a therapeutic program, or if not directly so related, chores of a normal housekeeping type and kind. * * * Nevertheless, there may be some mandatory programs so ruthless in the amount of work demanded, and the conditions under which the work must be performed, and thus so devoid of therapeutic purpose, that a court justifiably could conclude that the inmate had been subjected to involuntary servitude.

Id., at 131–132.

Satisfying the standard proposed by the court in *Jobson* has generally proved difficult. Thus, in *Estate of Buzzelle v. Colorado State Hospital*, 176 Colo. 554, 491 P.2d 1369 (1971), the court found that over 6,000 hours of work "at several different jobs, varying from food preparation and service to . . . cleaning and maintenance of the physical plant of the hospital" were "related to a therapeutic program of rehabilitation." 176 Colo. 554 at 556, 559, 491 P.2d 1369 at 1370, 1371. Similarly, the court in *Krieger v. State of New York*, 54 Misc.2d 583, 283 N.Y.S.2d 86 (1966) found that a resident "required to mop floors, clean toilet bowls and other similar work "had no cause of action since the work was "of a normal housekeeping type and kind." 283 N.Y.S.2d 86 at 89.

Patients objecting to mandatory work assignments are likely to have more success if they seek to demonstrate a violation of their due process right to treatment. The operative legal standards in such actions are derived from the rules governing the constitutional rights of mentally retarded and mentally ill patients adopted in the *Wyatt v. Stickney* cases, 344 F.Supp. 373 and 344 F.Supp. 387 (M.D.Ala.1972), aff'd 503 F.2d 1305 (5th Cir. 1974). The *Wyatt* court provided that resident patients could not be required to perform labor involving the maintenance of the institution, but could do so voluntarily if compensated in accordance with the minimum wage laws. 344 F.Supp. at 381, 402. Further, residents may engage in voluntary therapeutic labor "for which the institution would otherwise have to pay an employee" only if the labor is (a) an integrated part of an approved plan of treatment; (b) supervised by a staff member; and (c) compensated in accordance with the minimum wage laws. *Id.* Resident patients may, however, be required to perform personal housekeeping tasks in addition to therapeutic or vocational training tasks which do not involve institutional operation or maintenance and are an integrated and supervised part of the patients treatment program. With respect to mentally ill patients, the *Wyatt* court provides that non-maintenance assignments of longer than three months are presumed not to be vocational training tasks.

2. One psychiatrist has offered the following observations based on his personal experience in using psychiatric patients for various institutional chores:

As a resident in psychiatry on the staff of a state hospital, I used four men to assist me in giving electric shock treatments. In contrast with the disharmony of the treatments, the men moved smoothly and effectively. They would escort the patients individually to the treatment area, reassure them, efficiently hold them during the seizures, and then watch over them in the recovery stage. These four men themselves were patients and had been for a long time. And as time went on they proved to be even more useful and made a real contribution to the ward life.

Ostensibly in the interest of esprit de corps, the four men were given armbands designating each as a "First Aider." Two unused rooms were fitted out with beds, chairs, and bureaus for their use and for a time they each received a token gratuity of a fifty-cent canteen card per week * * *

Only after I was away from the state mental hospital for a while, however, and could view my use of the First Aiders in some perspective did I come to realize that this really represented a gross abdication of my primary responsibility as a psychiatrist. The recompenses I arranged for the First Aiders may very well have led them to consider me a good guy. But as an integral part of the hospital, whose interests came first, I was actually being a very poor doctor to them: they were helping me with masses of other patients while their need for recovery and discharge was completely overlooked. Their role of institutional worker was so established and self-effacing and accepted that the question of their further recovery never came up * * *

Unfortunately, this exploitation can be accommodating to their illness and increase their dependency on the institution. Rather than getting well, they can become "good patients," and their hospital stays stretch into years. Tragically, without such institutional peonage on the part of its patients, the state mental hospital system would have to close down completely * * *

Patients become institutional workers if the work and the implicit symbolic payment gratify their dependency needs enough to make them useful and immobolize them. The non-working patient, unable to mobilize himself and hopefully kept inert, repeats his pre-institutional role of failure, this time in the still more destructive role of a public charge. This process is regressive for both groups: formerly skilled persons can become satisfied dishwashers; patients on the wards who are not working and who could benefit from learning to wash dishes are denied this opportunity * * *

Bartlett, *Institutional Peonage*, Atlantic Monthly, July 1964 at 116.

3. Communication With Persons Outside the Institution

The First Amendment protects all persons from unreasonable interference with the right to free communication. When a mentally ill patient is institutionalized, a tension develops between his First Amendment rights and the need to regulate his environment for purposes of treatment. For those confined in a mental institution the importance of free communication with friends, relatives, or legal advisors may be particularly vital. Protection from wrongful or abusive hospitalization is enhanced if the patient is free to contact persons outside the institution who may provide access to legal process. Moreover, a comprehensive therapy program should foster the patient's communicative skills and avoid unnecessary isolation, which may impede the patient's successful return to society. These interests must be weighed against the hospital's concern for maintaining an environment free of disruptive outside influences that might hinder the patient's treatment and rehabilitation. The hospital may also have a responsibility to prevent the patient from seeing communications that may be disturbing to him/her. Quite apart from the description of treatment, the power to regulate visitation and correspondence is necessary to maintain security and administrative order in the hospital.

The competing interests that surround the patient's right to communicate have long been recognized by both mental health professionals and lawmakers. Many states have some form of statutory provision concerning patient correspondence or visitation. Such provisions typically provide that hospitalized patients have the right to:

(1) receive visitors;

(2) communication with persons outside the hospital; and

(3) communicate by uncensored and sealed mail with legal counsel, the Board, the courts and the Attorney General of the State.

Vernon's Ann.Texas, Stat. Art. 5547.

At the same time, most statutes afford the hospital administration considerable discretion in determining whether correspondence or visitation privileges are in the patient's best interest. The Texas statute, for instance, authorizes the head of the hospital to impose restrictions on visitation and communication rights when it is necessary for the "welfare of the patient." *See* Vernon's Ann.Texas Stat. Art. 5547. Hospital discretion may be exercised by censoring incoming or outgoing mail to protect the patient from possibly injurious matter or to restrain the patient from sending out improper communications. Laws can deny visitation when the hospital administrator believes the visitor may be a harmful influence upon the patient.

Most statutes do not limit the patient's unfettered rights to communication with his/her physician, attorney, or a judicial or state officer. Thus, while the patient's general First Amendment rights are often subordinated to the needs of hospital administration and medical treatment, the patient's access to the legal system has been afforded greater protection.

Until recently, cases that have addressed the constitutionality of hospital regulation of patient communication also emphasized the right of access to legal protection. Where the courts have acted to overturn restrictions on free communication, they have done so most often to secure the patient's constitutional right to seek *habeas corpus* relief. Very few cases have involved challenges to hospital regulations on general First Amendment grounds. At the same time a number of recent decisions indicate an increasing readiness of courts to recognize freedom of communication as a substantive part of a patient's rights that cannot be abridged without proper justification.

In part, these decisions are extensions of legal developments in the correctional field and particularly the decision of the U.S. Supreme Court in *Procunier v. Martinez*, 416 U.S. 396, 94 S.Ct. 1800, 40 L.Ed.2d 224 (1974). There the Court considered for the first time the appropriate standard for testing the constitutionality of censorship regulations for prisoners' mail. Direct correspondence between inmates and persons with an interest in communicating with them, the Court held, involves more than the rights of prisoners. Whether the prisoner is the intended recipient or the transmitter of the letter, the First Amendment rights of both parties to the correspondence would be abridged by governmental interference. In a related vein, the Court, in *Developmental Disabilities Advocacy Center v. Melton*, 689 F.2d 281 (1st Cir.1982), held that a not-for-profit legal advocacy organization had a First Amendment interest in communicating with mentally retarded patients in a state institution and so had *standing* to object to that institution's visitation restrictions.

Although the Court in *Procunier* found that the prisoner's First Amendment interest in uncensored communication was a "liberty" interest and entitled to due process protection under the Fourteenth Amendment, the Court also recognized legitimate governmental interests. Certain restraints on correspondence could be justified if reasonably imposed to foster security, order, or the rehabilitation of a prisoner. The restraints employed, the Court held, could be "no greater than is necessary or essential to the protection of the particular governmental interest involved." 416 U.S. at 414, 94 S.Ct. at 1811.

In *Brown v. Schubert*, 389 F.Supp. 281 (E.D.Wis.1975), the ruling in *Procunier* was held to be equally applicable when the restrictions effected mental patients in a state hospital and involved patients who had been stripped of communication privileges and transferred to maximum security wards because they had mailed letters to a local newspaper reporter and an Urban League official. The Court ordered the privileges to be reinstated and enjoined further interference with the patients' correspondence except to inspect the mail for contraband.

The *Brown* case may be seen as the judicial response to a clear and egregious violation of First Amendment rights and where the institution's policy rested on no defensive state interest. It thus serves as little guidance to the disposition of cases where the restriction is based on some legitimate interest necessary to advance either the security of the institution or the therapeutic welfare of the patients. How these cases will be decided and what balance will be struck in weighing the competing interests of the patient's First Amendment rights against the other interests of the institution remains to be decided.

Questions and Comments

1. The potential danger to a mentally ill patient's rehabilitation posed by incoming mail of a non-legal nature may justify a degree of censorship in some cases. Does the same hold true for outgoing mail? What are the interests of the hospital in censoring mail leaving the institution? It has been suggested that the potential for distress or embarrassment caused by the patient's letters could be avoided merely by indicating on the unopened envelope that the author is an institutionalized patient. Would such a procedure be an appropriate balancing of the patient's First Amendment rights and the hospital's protective interest? Would this procedure solve the problem?

2. Presidential assailant John Hinckley, Jr., was confined to St. Elizabeth's Hospital in Washington, D.C., following a finding of not guilty by reason of insanity of the shooting of President Ronald Reagan and three others. Hinckley complained to the American Civil Liberties Union that the hospital refused to allow him to give interviews to reporters and that his outgoing mail was being intercepted and read. *New York Times.* Oct. 8, 1982, at 9, col 1.

What are Hinckley's rights with respect to interviews and press conferences? How do they weigh against the medical and administrative interests of St. Elizabeth's?

Hospital officials claimed that Hinckley's mail was read to protect him from sending letters that would be "detrimental to his interests." One of the letters read by hospital personnel contained a request for aid in killing actress Jodie Foster, with whom Hinckley was apparently obsessed when he attempted to assassinate President Reagan. The letter was turned over to the F.B.I. Whose interests are being protected by the censorship of Hinckley's mail? Are they medical interests?

3. A recent constitutional challenge to a hospital regulation, which had prohibited communication between a minor patient and her parents for over one month, resulted in a distinction between the rights of voluntary and involuntary patients. In *Doe v. Public Health Trust of Dade County*, 696 F.2d 901 (11th Cir.1983), the parents argued that their fundamental constitutional rights of familial association were violated unnecessarily under the hospital's rules. While acknowledging that voluntary patients retain some First Amendment communication rights, the court held that under the cumberance of the case, no constitutional violation had occurred. The test according to the court was whether the non-communication rule was "medically legitimate and therapeutic." 696 F.2d at 904.

D. THE RIGHT TO PERIODIC REDETERMINATION OF COMMITABILITY

FASULO v. ARAFEH

Supreme Court of Connecticut, 1977.
173 Conn. 473, 378 A.2d 553.

LONGO, Associate Justice.

The plaintiffs, Ann Fasulo and Marie Barbieri, alleging that they were illegally confined in the Connecticut Valley Hospital by the defendant superintendent, petitioned the Superior Court for writs of habeas corpus. The court denied the writs and the plaintiffs appealed.

Ann Fasulo was civilly committed to Connecticut Valley Hospital in 1951, as was Marie Barbieri in 1964. Both plaintiffs press two major claims in this appeal. First, they argue that since there is a requirement of periodic court review of the necessity for confinement of those individuals who have been acquitted of an offense on the grounds of mental disease or defect, but not for persons like themselves who are civilly committed, their continued confinement violates the equal protection guarantee of article first, § 20, of the Connecticut constitution. They also claim that because their commitments are of indefinite duration and there is no procedure for periodic court review of the necessity for their confinement, their confinement is in violation of the due process guarantee of article first, § 8, of the Connecticut constitution.

We consider the plaintiffs' due process claim. Though the plaintiffs do not challenge their initial involuntary commitments, the due process safeguards incorporated into that procedure help to illuminate the plaintiffs' grievances. Among the important requirements of General Statutes § 17–178 are a judicial hearing initiated by the state at which the state bears the burden of proving that involuntary commitment is necessary, testimony by independent physicians who have recently examined the subject, and the rights to be represented by counsel, to present a defense and to cross-examine witnesses. Under General Statutes § 17–178 the necessity for confinement is to be determined according to a legal standard as a conclusion of law. The due process clause of the Connecticut constitution shares but is not limited by the content of its federal counterpart. In *O'Connor v. Donaldson,* 422 U.S. 563, 580, 95 S.Ct. 2486, 2496, 45 L.Ed.2d 396, Mr. Chief Justice Burger in a concurring opinion spoke of the process due a person civilly committed to a mental institution: "There can be no doubt that involuntary commitment to a mental hospital, like involuntary confinement of an individual for any reason, is a deprivation of liberty which the State cannot accomplish without due process of law. Commitment must be justified on the basis of a legitimate state interest, and the reasons for committing a particular individual must be established in an appropriate proceeding. Equally important, confinement must cease when those reasons no longer exist.

As recognized by General Statutes § 17–178, the authority of the state to confine an individual is contingent upon the individual's present mental status, which must be one of mental illness amounting to a need for confinement for the individual's own welfare or the welfare of others or the community. The original involuntary commitment proceeding can only establish that the state may confine the individual at the time of the hearing and for the period during which the individual is subject to the requisite mental illness. As the United States Supreme Court has recognized, "At the least, due process requires that the nature and duration of commitment bear some reasonable relation to the purpose for which an individual is committed." *Jackson v. Indiana*, 406 U.S. 715, 738. Once the purpose of the commitment no longer exists, there is no constitutional basis for the state to continue to deprive the individual of his liberty. To satisfy due process, the procedure for releasing a civilly committed patient must be adequate to assure release of those who may no longer constitutionally be confined. Due process is a flexible concept, the content of which must be renewed each time it is used to measure the adequacy of challenged procedures. In general, "the thoroughness of the procedure by which [a] deprivation is effected must be balanced against the gravity of the potential loss and the interests at stake." It is significant to this case that the process afforded an individual must be "tailored to the capacities and circumstances of those who are to be heard." *Goldberg v. Kelly*, 397 U.S. 254, 268–69, 90 S.Ct. 1011, 1021, 25 L.Ed.2d 287.

These plaintiffs have been deprived of their liberty. Their loss is already great, but can be initially justified as a result of the legitimate exercise of the parens patriae power of the state. The plaintiffs, however, have been committed indefinitely and confined for periods of twenty-six and thirteen years respectively, thus requiring us to heed the warning of the United States Supreme Court that the longer the commitment, the greater the safeguards which are required to ensure that no one is deprived of liberty without due process. We must, therefore, review the plaintiffs' claims in light of the important interest at stake—liberty—and the great loss which its extended deprivation constitutes.

Any procedure to allow the release of involuntarily confined civilly committed individuals must take account of the controlled and often isolated environment of the mental hospital from which the confined individuals will seek release. It must calculate the possible incompetence of those confined, their limited knowledge of release procedures, the cost of pursuing review and the amount of effort necessary to pursue review. Further, the procedure must be adapted to the possible effect of drugs or other treatment on the patient's capacity and must be formulated with consideration of institutional pressures to rely on the *medical* judgments of the hospital staff rather than to pursue extrainstitutional *legal* remedies. See note, "Civil Commitment of the Mentally Ill," 87 Harv.L.Rev. 1190, 1398.

At present, Connecticut provides several routes by which a mental patient can challenge his confinement. General Statutes § 17–192 allows for release (1) by order of the Probate Court "upon application and satisfactory proof that such person has been restored to reason," or (2) "[i]f the officers, directors or trustees of a state hospital for mental illness are notified by the superintendent or other person in a managerial capacity of such institution that he has reason to believe that any person committed thereto by order of a probate court is not mentally ill or a suitable subject to be confined in such institution, such officers, directors or trustees may discharge such person." Under the second method the patient runs the risk of having his release prevented by a superintendent whose determination may later be found by a court to have been erroneous. Furthermore, the second procedure disregards the fundamental fact that the state's power legitimately to confine an individual is based on a legal determination under General Statutes § 17–178 "that the person complained of is mentally ill and dangerous to himself or herself or others or gravely disabled" and that the commitment shall only continue "for the period of the duration of such mental illness or until he or she is discharged in due course of law." The state's power to confine terminates when the patient's condition no longer meets the legal standard for commitment. Since the state's power to confine is measured by a legal standard, the expiration of the state's power can only be determined in a judicial proceeding which tests the patient's present mental status against the legal standard for confinement. That adjudication cannot be made by medical personnel unguided by the procedural safeguards which cushion the individual from an overzealous exercise of state power when the individual is first threatened with the deprivation of his liberty.

* * *

We also find the first method of release provided for in General Statutes § 17–192 constitutionally deficient. The method allows release of a patient after he has applied to the Probate Court for discharge and has proved that he has been "restored to reason." We find this procedure inadequate on two grounds. First, it places the burden of initiating review of his status on the patient, a requirement which suffers from conceptual as well as serious practical deficiencies. As we stated previously, since the state's power to confine is premised on the individual's present mental status, the original involuntary commitment proceeding can only establish that the state may confine the individual at the time of the hearing and for the foreseeable period during which that status is unlikely to change. Upon the expiration of that period, the state's power to deprive the patient of his liberty lapses and any further confinement must be justified anew. The state, therefore, must bear the burden of initiating recommitment proceedings.

This same reasoning applies to the burden of proof at the recommitment hearing. The burden should not be placed on the civilly committed patient to justify his right to liberty. Freedom from involuntary confinement for those who have committed no crime is the natural state of individuals in this country. The burden must be placed on the state to prove the necessity of stripping the citizen of one of his most fundamental rights, and the risk of error must rest on the state.

* * *

Furthermore, to require a patient to initiate judicial review of his confinement and to bear the burden of proving the nonexistence of the necessity for that confinement ignores the practical considerations discussed above which are inherent in the mental patient's situation. Briefly, these include the difficulties of overcoming an isolated environment to initiate and coordinate a challenge to one's confinement. For instance, we cannot assume that friends and allies will always be available to secure counsel and marshal evidence on the patient's behalf. Nor can we assume that even if a patient is notified of his right to pursue any of the available remedies, he will be adequately protected. The state has suggested that the procedure provided in General Statutes § 17–178, as amended by section 3(b) of 1976 Public Acts, No. 76–227, effective in March of 1977, met the constitutional arguments of the petitioners. That statute as amended is not now before us and we decline to rule prematurely on its provisions. We note, however, that many of the safeguards we have found necessary in this opinion are provided for in the new statute, particularly the right to a recommitment hearing with all the procedural safeguards of the initial commitment hearing at which the burden of proving the necessity for confinement rests on the state. Unfortunately, though the statute provides for annual notice to patients of their right to a hearing, the burden of requesting and, therefore, initiating review remains with the patient. The state seeks to justify this procedure by arguing that allowing the patient to choose whether to have a hearing will avoid unnecessary judicial proceedings. We doubt whether this rationale is adequate since it ignores the practical difficulties of requiring a mental patient to overcome the effects of his confinement, his closed environment, his possible incompetence and the debilitating effects of drugs or other treatment on his ability to make a decision which may amount to the waiver of his constitutional right to a review of his status.

* * *

We, therefore, hold that these plaintiffs have been denied their due process rights under the Connecticut constitution by the state's failure to provide them with periodic judicial review of their commitments in the form of state-initialed recommitment hearings replete with the safeguards of the initial commitment hearings at which the state bears the burden of proving the necessity for their continued confinement.

* * *

It is, therefore, ordered that the writs be granted and that the plaintiffs be afforded a hearing at which the state must justify their continued confinement.

There is error, and the case is remanded with direction to grant the writs in accordance with this opinion.

In this opinion SPEZIALE, J., concurs.

BOGDANSKI, Associate Justice (concurring).

* * *

[The dissenting opinion of Justice Loiselle in which Chief Justice House concurred was omitted.]

Questions and Comments

1. What time period would satisfy the requirement of periodic review mandated by the *Fasulo* court?

2. The court in *Fasulo* also considered an amended version of Connecticut's civil commitment laws which gave each patient an annual opportunity to a hearing. While the court declined to pass on the law as amended, the opinion of the majority suggests that the mere opportunity of a hearing might not be sufficient. Does this suggest that the majority would reject any provision allowing a waiver of the right to a hearing?

What policy considerations would support a rule permitting waivers? In this connection, consider the arguments advanced by one commentator:

> Problems regarding the recommitment process are only now beginning to surface. Previously, recommitment was relatively unknown, for civil commitment was typically of indefinite duration. Patient release ordinarily occurred only if and when hospital authorities believed it warranted. In particularly rare instances, knowledgeable and persistent patients triggered judicial review of the propriety of their continued confinement. Once in court, those persistent petitioners were often expected to carry the burden of persuasion regarding their readiness for release.
>
> Release patterns in mental health law are now, however, in the midst of a radical revision. The revision is attributable to a rapidly emerging conviction that, as a matter of sound social policy and quite probably as a matter of constitutional law, durational limits should be clamped on civil commitments.
>
> * * * The proper procedure for the state to employ to justify anew its basis for continued confinement, according to the *Fasulo* court, would be a state-initiated recommitment hearing. At that proceeding, the patient would be given the full panoply of protections

associated with commitment hearings generally, and the state would carry the burden of persuasion regarding the need for further confinement.

Fasulo is fully representative of the trend of case law and statutes requiring release or recommitment after the passage of a specified period. The trend is to be applauded. After a reasonable period of time, it is wise to authorize judicial review of a committed patient's status, and the patient ought not to bear the onus of initiating that review.

The problems of patient-initiated review were clearly noted in *Fasulo*. Though purporting to avoid ruling on the merits of an amended statute that was technically not before it, the *Fasulo* court nonetheless addressed the statute's patient-initiated review requirement   *   *   *

*   *   *

[The Court's] language surely—and rightly—rejects a scheme where review is available only to those patients who affirmatively request it. The problem with the language, however, resides in its clear-cut potential for overkill.

Fasulo was concerned with environmental and clinical conditions which may impair a patient's "ability to make a decision which may amount to a waiver of his constitutional right to a review of his status." That concern, therefore, may be interpreted as invalidating not only the requirement of *patient-initiation*, but as invalidating also the possibility of a patient *waiving* a state-initiated judicial review of the patient's status.

The broad interpretation of the *Fasulo* language—the suggestion that *nonwaivable* recommitment hearings may be constitutionally compelled—is strongly reinforced by the court's heavy reliance on a law review project which, for reasons identical to those noted in *Fasulo*, apparently concluded that waiver of recommitment hearings should be ruled impermissible. Fortunately, however, the interpretation is merely derived from inference and is dicta at that. The waivability of recommitment hearings is an emerging issue clouded by conceptual confusion, pragmatic considerations, and empirical uncertainties that need to be analyzed from many perspectives before closure is reached on the question.

*   *   *

Clearly, if mechanisms could be devised to eliminate the need for those, and only those, recommitment hearings that are truly unnecessary and truly unwanted by the patients, a host of considerations would favor a rule of waivability. A number of such considerations come quickly to mind.

There is, of course, the sheer economic consideration involving the depletion of judicial, mental health, and related resources. Courts sitting in the vicinity of state hospitals have terribly heavy commitment calendars. They assuredly would wish to be spared the time and expense of conducting unnecessary and unwanted recommitment hearings.

The judicial time-and-cost saving interest would be particularly evident, of course, if an appreciable number of patients wished to waive such hearings. At the moment, the percent of patients desiring waiver is an empirical unknown. It would not be at all surprising, however, for a rather large number of patients to desire waiver. The depressed and suicidal might well constitute one such patient category. So too, many elderly, "gravely disabled" patients might opt for waiver, were it available, rather than attend hearings only to learn what they already know: that their clinical and family situation is unchanged or has worsened, and that no facilities less restrictive than full-time hospitalization can yet be found for their placement.

Needless to say, physicians, nurses, and ward attendants would also prefer to treat than to testify. To the extent that they are called upon to testify in unnecessary and unwanted hearings, the patients and the public would be best served by those mental health witnesses playing instead a therapeutic role.

* * *

The interests of psychotherapists and of certain patients converge in their concern over the possible traumatic and anti-therapeutic effects of recommitment hearings. Unlike initial hearings, where the possible trauma to the patient is probably outweighed by the feedback to him of the impropriety of his behavior and by the presentation of convincing evidence that commitment is called for, the interests deserve to be balanced differently in the framework of recommitment.

By the time of recommitment, a patient may well be quite aware of what is objectionable about his behavior or of why alternative placement seems unsuitable. Moreover, whether hearing adverse testimony will prove traumatic or anti-therapeutic is no longer a matter of enormous abstract speculation: the patient will have already experienced one commitment hearing and may now be in a fairly good position to assess the relative costs and benefits of contesting recommitment. If recommitment is in any event likely, a number of patients may wish to avoid hearings at which testimony will be given regarding, for example, the persistence of their depressed and suicidal state, or the continuing unwillingness of families or of nursing homes to accept patients who act out conflicts or who are sometimes assaultive.

* * *

[I]t is possible, if and when an effective patient advocacy system is established, for a jurisdiction, even in the recommitment context, to mitigate considerably the influence of the *Fasulo* factors. After a patient has been involuntarily confined for a specified time, the state must, under the laudable emerging body of law, release the patient or initiate recommitment proceedings. Once a recommitment petition is filed, the patient should be consulted by an appointed attorney.

* * *

* * * [T]he concerns (*Fasulo* factors) that prompt a nonwaivability rule in the recommitment context can seemingly be reduced by conscientious and effective counsel. Waivability—consent to recommitment for up to a specified period—should probably be authorized if a lawyer playing an adversary role certifies to the court that he has investigated the case and has consulted with his client, that he has explained to the client the options and the right to contest recommitment, and that he has concluded that the client desires to consent to recommitment.

* * *

Wexler, *"The Waivability of Recommitment Hearings,"* 20 Ariz.L.Rev. 175, 175–80, 184–86 (1978).

Chapter Seven

INCOMPETENCY AND GUARDIANSHIP

Table of Sections

I. COMPETENCY PROCEEDINGS AND THE GUARDIANSHIP SYSTEM: AN OVERVIEW

A. INTRODUCTION

The Constitution guarantees every citizen equality under law. This right protects not only against the government's discriminatory application of laws to individuals, but also ensures that every person has equal enjoyment of the basic rights accorded to all citizens. These individual rights generally include the freedoms to contract, to seek legal redress of claims, and to invoke laws designed to preserve one's personal autonomy. The concept of personal autonomy, in turn, includes such matters as where one lives, determinations relating to procreation and marriage, and medical treatment decisions.

However, meaningful exercise of these rights assumes a physical and intellectual capacity on the part of the individual to make thoughtful choices. When a person's decision-making ability is significantly impaired, he may be unable to invoke his individual civil rights or may exercise them in ways injurious to his own interest. The need to protect those incapable of managing their personal affairs has led to the establishment of a system for the adjudication of competency and the appointment of a guardian to act on behalf of incapacitated persons.

Under the laws of most states two issues are generally addressed in an incompetency proceeding. One pertains to the competency of the individual to manage his *financial affairs*, the other focuses on the capacity of the individual to make decisions as to his *physical welfare*. An adjudication of incompetency, therefore, may render the person unable to exercise his legal rights over either his financial affairs, his person or both.

An ancillary result of a determination of incompetency is generally court appointment of a *guardian* to exercise authority on behalf of the incompetent. In some jurisdictions one person may be appointed to act as guardian of the person and another to manage the individual's financial assets. Guardians of the person generally have the authority to act on behalf of the incompetent as to those matters that pertain to the individual's physical well-being, which may include decisions pertaining to residential placement, education, and medical treatment. Guardians of the estate, known in some states as "conservators," are charged with the management of the incompetent's property and accordingly may enter into contracts on the ward's behalf and represent him in any necessary legal proceedings.

A growing minority of states have enacted statutes that provide for the appointment of a *limited* guardian. The key aim here is to appoint a guardian with the powers to provide only the degree of control, assistance, and advice that the ward requires. Thus, unlike the traditional system of guardianship, the powers of a limited guardian can be restricted to specific functions. Application of the principles underlying the system of limited guardianship are illustrated by the following example:

An individual may be able to understand monetary concepts up to fifty dollars but have no understanding of sums beyond that amount. That same individual may be able to understand time periods of up to one week or one month in duration, but not beyond that period. Limitations can be drawn to respect the areas of ability; for example, to respect the ability of the individual to spend up to fifty dollars on the weekly or monthly groceries, without the interference of a guardian. However, if expenditures over fifty dollars on a monthly basis are to be anticipated, such expenditures would be valid only with the consent of the limited guardian.

Dussault, *Guardianship and Limited Guardianship in Washington State: Application For Mentally Retarded Citizens*, 13 Gonzaga L.Rev. 585, 606 (1978).

Significant changes have occurred in the guardianship system in recent years. Most of these changes pertain to the authority of the guardian to authorize medical or biological intervention affecting the ward. These issues, which are the primary concern of this chapter, are taken up after a preliminary review of the standards employed to determine competency and of the procedures required in the guardianship system.

Questions and Comments

1. The question of competency is entirely distinct from the question of commitment. Until fairly recently, however, these issues have frequently been confused. Prior to the mid-1950's, a number of jurisdictions merged competency issues with the commitment decision. In these states an order for involuntary hospitalization was also an adjudication of incompetency. In other jurisdictions civil commitment created a rebuttable presumption of incompetency. *See* S. Brakel and R. Rock, *The Mentally Disabled and the Law* (Chicago: University of Chicago Press, 1971) at 253.

Another reason for the confusion between incompetency and civil commitment was the tendency of statutory language to use the term "insanity" to describe both concepts. Even today confusion continues. As noted by one study:

> Statutory terminology today shows some improvement, but the confusion persists. Most of the statutes still fail to make the proper distinctions. Many provisions still employ terms such as insane, lunatic, idiocy, and the like. Some of the incompetency statutes do not use the term "incompetent" at all, but simply state that a guardian may or shall be appointed for a person who suffers from a designated mental or physical disability. Such statutes thus predicate loss of the right to conduct one's business not on a finding of incapacity to do so, but on the determination of some medical-diagnostic condition.

Brakel and Rock, at 251.

2. The determination of competency and the related guardianship system have traditionally been controlled by state law, with individual states establishing their own standards and procedures. As a consequence, there has been little uniformity in this area. More recently, however, there has been a movement toward unification largely as a result of the work of the National Conference of Commissioners on Uniform State Laws, which formulated the Uniform Probate Code [U.P.C.]. Part 5 of the Code (Protection of Persons Under Disability and Their Property) establishes a comprehensive regulatory framework. As of 1981 several states had adopted versions of the U.P.C. Two others,

Illinois and Michigan, have amended their statutes along the lines of the U.P.C. principles. See Doussard, *The Effects of the Uniform Probate Code on Estate Administration and Tax Planning*, 8 Estate Planning 142 (May 1981).

B. HISTORICAL ANTECEDENTS

SAMUEL BRAKEL AND RONALD ROCK, *THE MENTAL-LY DISABLED AND THE LAW*

University of Chicago Press, p. 250 (1971).

Incompetency proceedings are of a much earlier origin than hospitalization proceedings. For example, in Rome at the time of Cicero elaborate provisions were made for the protection of the property of the mentally disabled, while none at all existed for their person. This pattern was followed in England and also in colonial America, where several of the colonies passed legislation designed to protect the estates of "insane persons" long before the colonial governments became concerned with the personal welfare of the mentally disabled.

No institution for the care of the mentally disabled existed in England until long after the Norman Conquest. Guardianship of the mentally disabled in medieval England was the function of the lord of the manor, who was to protect their proprietary and personal interests. This guardianship actually applied to both the person and the property of the "insane"; but the chief reason for its existence was apparently proprietary, stemming from the desire to prevent the mentally disabled from becoming a public burden or dissipating their assets to the detriment of their heirs.

It would seem that originally this guardianship, or tutorship as it was called, was applicable only to mentally deficient persons. By the beginning of the fourteenth century, however, guardianship was expanded to include mentally ill persons and was formally recognized as a duty of the Crown.

The king's guardianship was exercised through the Lord Chancellor, by virtue of a special commission issued to him by the Crown rather than by the general authority of the chancery court. In exercising the power, the Chancellor held an inquisition to inquire into the condition of the mentally disabled person and to appoint a committee for his person and property if he was adjudged an "idiot" or a "lunatic." It was the further duty of the chancery court to supervise and control the conduct of such a committee.

In the United States responsibility for incompetents was deemed to be vested in the people. Either by inheritance from the common law or by express constitutional and statutory provisions, jurisdiction over the person and property of incompetents was assumed by the courts of equity. Currently, other courts also exercise jurisdiction over incompetency proceedings.

C. STANDARDS GOVERNING THE COMPETENCY DETERMINATION

1. Illustrative Provisions

QUINN ESTATE

54 Pa.D. & C.2d 405 (Phila. County Orphans' Ct. 1971).

SILVERSTEIN, J., December 8, 1971.—By decree dated July 15, 1971, pursuant to petition filed by Manuel Kaufman, Deputy Welfare Commissioner of the City of Philadelphia, a citation issued directed to Kathryn M. Quinn to show cause why she should not be adjudged an incompetent and a guardian of her estate appointed. At the hearing on August 19, 1971, Francis I. Farley, Esquire, appeared on behalf of Kathryn M. Quinn. Kathryn M. Quinn was not present although Mr. Farley advised the court that he had written Miss Quinn two letters advising her to be present.

Sara Downey, a social worker in the Adult Services Department of Public Welfare, testified that she has visited Miss Quinn, who is 56 years old, once a week since February 1971. That from her observation, there was no heat in the house. The interior of the house is in poor condition. Miss Quinn keeps two dogs and two cats whose leavings cover the floors. Apparently, Miss Quinn makes no attempt to clean up the house. There are roaches and flies in abundance in the house. The plumbing is not operative and Miss Quinn uses a drain in the backyard as a toilet. Trash accumulates in the house and yard. An abatement crew from License and Inspection spent two days cleaning out the house and yard but trash is accumulating again.

Miss Quinn receives a welfare check of $101.60 each month. Frequently, Miss Quinn denies that the check has arrived. Miss Downey has been in touch with the Philadelphia Electric Company which has threatened to terminate service for nonpayment of its bills. The gas company has also threatened to terminate service and advises Miss Downey that Miss Quinn refuses entrance to their meter reader. There are outstanding bills from the telephone, gas and electric companies, as well as Graduate Hospital ($29.00), Wanamaker's ($330.72), water and sewer taxes ($37.28) and real estate taxes ($168.35). Miss Downey testified that from her observation Miss Quinn is incapable of making decisions concerning her day-to-day life. Sometimes she is lucid and at other times she has told Miss Downey that she feels she is living in a nightmare.

Miss Downey stated she had explained the nature of the guardianship proceedings to Miss Quinn, who had only laughed. It was Miss Downey's opinion that Miss Quinn did not understand the nature of the proceedings.

Mrs. John Lannutti, a niece of the alleged incompetent, confirmed Miss Downey's testimony concerning the conditions in which Miss

Quinn is living. She stated that when she had visited the house years past, it was always neat and clean. She had not been to the house for two years before her visit in March 1971. That in the intervening period Kathryn Quinn's physical condition had deteriorated markedly.

Dr. Alfred Duncan, a psychiatrist with the Mental Health and Retardation Unit of the City of Philadelphia, testified that he examined Kathryn Quinn at the request of Miss Downey on April 28, 1971. He found no organic deficit and found her general health to be unremarkable. He did, however, reach a diagnosis of residual schizophrenia. He stated that " * * * as one of the characteristics of residual schizophrenia, the likelihood of her being inclined to manage affairs to any degree is small." Dr. Duncan stated that the prognosis was that Miss Quinn's condition was likely to remain static. That she might improve if she would attend a mental health center and take medication, but she refused to do so.

* * *

In considering the evidence and the motion to dismiss, I am aware that the Incompetents' Estates Act of February 28, 1956, P.L. (1955) 1154, 50 P.S. § 3101, et seq., which empowers a court to declare a person mentally incompetent and to place such individual's business affairs in the hands of another for management is "a dangerous statute easily capable of abuse".

The Incompetents' Estates Act, as amended, provides under "Definitions": "(3) 'Incompetent' means a person who, because of mental infirmities of old age, mental illness, mental deficiency, drug addiction or inebriety, is unable to manage his property, or is liable to dissipate it or become the victim of designing persons": 50 P.S. § 3102.

The standard of proof in incompetency proceedings has been repeatedly set forth by the Supreme Court: "Mental capacity and competency <u>are to be presumed</u> and before any person shall be deprived of the right to handle his or her own property and manage his or her own affairs there must be <u>*clear*</u> and <u>*convincing*</u> proof of mental incompetency <u>and such proof</u> must be <u>*preponderating*</u>".

I am satisfied from the testimony that Kathryn Quinn is incompetent as defined in the act.

* * *

The uncontradicted testimony of the wretched conditions in which the alleged incompetent apparently willingly lives and of her personal habits is clear evidence of her inability to manage her own affairs.

For the above reasons, I enter the attached decree.

SUR EXCEPTIONS TO DECREE

KLEIN, Adm. J., March 13, 1972.—It is crystal clear that Kathryn Quinn is an elderly woman, suffering from schizophrenia, who without supervision might soon die of malnutrition and neglect. Judge

Silverstein, after a most careful study of the matter, wrote a comprehensive adjudication, in which he reviewed the factual situations and the applicable law and adjudged the respondent incompetent and appointed John L. Steward, Director of the Adult Services Division of the Department of Public Welfare of the City of Philadelphia, guardian of her estate.

Judge Silverstein's order was obviously correct and serves the best interests of this unfortunate woman.

* * *

Questions and Comments

1. The Pennsylvania law of incompetency, which the court was called upon to apply in the *Quinn* case, illustrates the lack of precision typifying many of these statutes. Under Pennsylvania's Incompetent's State Act of 1955 (which has since been amended), an incompetent person is defined as one who "because of mental infirmities of old age, mental illness, mental deficiencies, drug addiction, or inebriety, is unable to manage his property, or is liable to dissipate it or become the victim of designing persons." Incompetent's Estates Act of February 20, 1956 P.L. 1154, 50 P.S. § 3102 (1955). This definition, which focused on the ability of the individual to manage his *financial* affairs, would technically have authorized only the appointment of a guardian for Ms. Quinn's estate. However, as the evidence made clear, Ms. Quinn's problem was her inability to care for her physical needs, more than an inability to manage her financial affairs. In appointing a person to act as guardian of the person as well as guardian of the estate, the court order had to go beyond statutory authority.

2. The issue of incompetency arises most often in the case of persons suffering a developmental disability. The instance of mental retardation does not of itself, however, necessarily lead to legal incompetency. The basic issue, in every case, is the ability of the individual to care for himself or manage his everyday financial affairs.

The type of inquiry called for is illustrated by the following opinion:

> Considering all of the testimony, including that of Mary and the three physicians, we conclude that Mary M. Ferraro is mentally retarded, has received little formal education and needs assistance in making mathematical calculations. There is no evidence that she is suffering from any mental illness. The medical testimony describes her as retarded, but we find no proof that she is retarded to the degree of incompetence. She probably has a low intelligence quotient, although none of the physicians seem to have been aware of the necessity for an examination into this field. Low intelligence, limited ability, poor education, or even illiteracy is no evidence per se of incompetence. She is regularly employed, manages her own affairs within her limitations and saves her money. She is in no danger of dissipating or losing any of it. The burden of establishing incompetency is on the petitioner * * * and we conclude that that burden has not been met * * *

In re Ferraro, 63 Berks County L.M. 177, 179–80 (C.P.1972).

3. The incompetency of an individual may be limited to a particular activity or function, for instance, capacity of the individual to consent to medical treatment. The criteria governing competency in the medical treatment context are considered at p. 507 note 2.

4. The scope of legal disability that follows a determination of incompetency varies from one jurisdiction to another. Most commonly, however, the incapacity extends to the selling or purchase of property, entering into contracts, or suing or being sued. Additionally, in some states incompetency bars an individual from marrying, operating a motor vehicle, or consenting to medical treatment. Unless otherwise specified by statute, the scope of the disability is determined by the court order following the determination of incompetency.

In states which have adopted *limited* guardianship, the ward retains all civil and legal rights except those specifically restricted by the court. Similarly, modern conservatorship statutes typically provide that the appointment of a conservator cannot be used as evidence of incompetency and that the ward cannot be deprived of any civil rights based solely on such an appointment.

5. What is the effect of a contract entered into by a person adjudicated to be incompetent? Contracts, unless they are for necessities, are voidable even though the contract may have been partially or totally performed. In the absence of a judicial finding of incompetency the acts of a person who is, in fact, incompetent may under some circumstances be the basis for having the contract set aside and voided. Similarly, a person who the physician knows is incompetent to give knowing and informed consent lacks legal capacity to consent to biomedical treatment. The issue of informed consent to treatment is treated in greater detail in Chapter Three.

2. Emerging Limits

KATZ v. SUPERIOR COURT

Court of Appeals, First District, 1977.
73 Cal.App.3d 952, 141 Cal.Rptr. 234.

SIMS, Acting P.J.

[The parents of five adult children obtained court orders appointing them temporary conservators of the persons of their children * * * The petitions alleged that conservatorship was required because of mental illness or weakness and unsound mind of the children, and that they were unable to properly care for their personal property and were likely to be deceived by artful and designing persons. Declarations filed by the parents alleged that each of the children had become involved with a religious organization that placed psychological pressures on the children causing impairment of their physical and mental health and loss of their free will. There was testimony that as members of the religious organization, the children were subjected to coercive persuasion or "brainwashing."]

* * *

We first examine petitioners' contention that the provisions of section 1751 of the Probate Code, under which these proceedings were instituted were unconstitutionally vague. Those provisions must furnish guidance for the determination of the "good cause" required by section 2201 which authorizes the appointment of a temporary conservator. The record reflects that the petitions for appointment were entitled "Application For Appointment Of A Guardian (Conservator) Of The Person." Each alleged in pertinent part: "The appointment request for the proposed ward is required because of mental illness or weakness and unsound mind. The proposed ward is unable to property [sic] care for the person or the property of the proposed ward and is likely to be deceived by artful and designing persons."

* * *

We therefore are concerned only with those former provisions of section 1751 which provided that the court "shall appoint a conservator of the * * * person * * * [first] of any adult person who by reason of advanced age, *illness*, injury, *mental weakness*, intemperance, addiction to drugs or other disability, or *other cause* is unable properly to care for himself or his property, or [second] who *for said causes or for any other cause is likely to be deceived or imposed upon by artful or designing persons.*" (Emphasis added.)

The court's orders following the hearing, contain no findings of fact which would disclose the ground or grounds on which the orders were based. In announcing its decisions the trial court gave no clue to what facts he considered were established by the evidence. The petitioners point out that there is nothing to show that the petitioners were unable to care for themselves, and that there was only limited evidence to show that care of property was involved, and that issue was not directly raised. They conclude that [the second ground

a The applications for appointment of a temporary conservator were each accompanied by the following declaration:

"I HEREBY DECLARE that:

"I am the natural parent of the proposed ward.

"That during 1976, my child, the proposed ward, became involved with an association known as the Unification Church, headed by Rev. Sun Myung Moon.

"Based on my contacts with my child before and after the involvement with this group, and the changes I have observed in my child, I am concerned that my child is not now acting on free will, and that both the physical and mental health of the proposed ward are impaired. I am informed and believe and thereon allege that this is due to psychological pressures on my child in the present environment, and that these pressures are intentionally produced as a part of a system of mind control that is imposed upon the proposed ward by the Cult.

"In summary, that since the proposed ward's involvement with this Cult, during the above-mentioned period of time the following changes have taken place:

"1. Abrupt personality changes;

"2. Assets the proposed ward acquires is [sic] or has been [sic] transmitted to the leaders of the group.

"3. My child appears to be the victim of mind control through hypnosis, mesmerism, and/or brain washing."

* * *

contained in the statute] is unconstitutionally vague as applied in the circumstances of this case.

*   *   *

[A] statute which either forbids or requires the doing of an act in terms so vague that men of common intelligence must necessarily guess at its meaning and differ as to its application, violates the first essential of due process of law."

*   *   *

Although the words "likely to be deceived or imposed upon by artful or designing persons" may have some meaning when applied to the loss of property which can be measured, they are too vague to be applied in the world of ideas. In an age of subliminal advertising, television exposure, and psychological salesmanships, everyone is exposed to artful and designing persons at every turn. It is impossible to measure the degree of likelihood that some will succumb. In the field of beliefs, and particularly religious tenets, it is difficult, if not impossible, to establish a universal truth against which deceit and imposition can be measured.

*   *   *

In view of the values involved we conclude that the provisions of section 1751 as it read prior to July 1, 1977, were too vague to be applied in proceedings to deprive an adult of his freedom of action as proposed by the parents in this case.

*   *   *

As an alternative ground of decision we are asked to find that the temporary orders violated the conservatees' rights to freedom of religion and association under the federal and state Constitutions. (U.S. Const., 1st Amend., Cal.Const., art. I, §§ 1 and 4.) The parents claim that there is no freedom of action, freedom of religion, or freedom of assembly involved, that the sole issue is whether or not the conservatees have been deprived of their reasoning powers by artful and designing persons. On behalf of the conservatees it is urged that since an alleged religious group is involved, there can be no inquiry into the validity of the beliefs held by the members of that group, and the proceedings below trespassed into that field.

*   *   *

The test of interference with action * * * protected by the First Amendment, is a compelling state interest. * * * The cases reviewed demonstrate that the state may have a compelling state interest in preventing fraud under the guise of religious belief. If such is the case criminal sanctions may be imposed where there is no bona fide conviction on the part of the actors. * * * We also recognize that the state has an interest in the health of its citizens. * * * We conclude that in the absence of such actions as render the adult believer himself gravely disabled as defined in the law of this state, the processes of this state cannot be used to deprive the believer of his freedom of action and to subject him to involuntary treatment.

* * *

The petition is granted with respect to petitioners. Let a peremptory writ of mandate issue directing the respondent superior court to set aside and vacate its orders appointing temporary conservators for each of said petitioners and the letters of temporary conservatorship issued thereon.

Questions and Comments

1. What is the relevance of the court's statement that absent "such actions as render the adult believer himself gravely disabled * * * [t]he powers of the state cannot be used to deprive the believer of his freedom of action" at 256? Does the language suggest that even a redrafted statute could not permit the imposition of a guardian under the facts of this case?

2. To what extent can or should the guardianship process be used to permit families to "rescue" adult children from deviant lifestyles which are not immediately dangerous to the individual's physical well being? See Note: Cults, Deprogramming, and Guardianship: A Model Legislative Proposal, 17 Colum.J.L. & Soc.Prob. 163 (1982) (suggesting that guardianship should be imposed to allow deprogramming when the cult uses "coercive persuasion" which abridges the individual's autonomy). See also, Note: Religious Deprogramming: A Solution Through Judicially Appointed Guardians, 7 Nova L.Rev. 383 (1983).

In answering this question does it make any difference whether the condition is diagnosed by experts as a mental disorder? In this connection, consider the testimony of the defendant's expert in the Katz case:

> It is my opinion that all five of these well-meaning, well-intentioned young people—Jan Kaplan, Leslie Brown, John Hovard, Jacqueline Katz and Barbara Underwood—have several symptoms which are not present in the average individual of their ages and background.

> During my interviews with them, it was as though these individuals responded to a pre-set (i.e., there was an effort made to answer all questions out of a limited set of answers). This limited set of answers appeared to be alien or inconsistent with those of their non-cult peers.

> They all suffered from gross lack of information regarding current events; they all seemed to be preoccupied with a concern about their selfishness, but all reported that they worked as much as twenty hours a day.

> They all showed a moderate degree of memory impairment, especially about their childhoods; their functional vocabulary in terms of the words that they used during the interview was limited and constricted.

Their affects were blunted, emotionality frozen in a child-like inappropriate smile to all input, whether it be hostile or otherwise.

They were all wide-eyed, had short attention spans and a decreased ability to concentrate.

They were all vague, with limited ability towards abstractions; they were full of inconsistencies, contradictions and confabulations when pressured.

They uniformly held that the Unification Church was not responsible for anything unless it was positive.

They had very little concern for previous and future personal goals; they were paranoid about previous relationships, and had defensive attitudes toward id urges.

Their inner sense of authority was lost, and all responded as if they were influenced by an outside authority.

They all showed various degrees of regression and child-like attitudes, especially when stressed.

In general, they did not respond as one would expect from their background and personality types.

Katz, 141 Cal.Rptr. at 248. See also, note 4, p. 335 *supra* for a report of research findings concerning what has been labeled the "cult conversion syndrome."

3. Efforts to use the guardianship process to deprogram persons involved in cult activities have also been attacked on procedural grounds. For instance, in *Taylor v. Gilmartin*, 686 F.2d 1346 (10th Cir.1982), the judicial order authorizing the appointment of a guardian who then instituted the deprogramming was held to be void because of the judge's failure to comply with procedural requirements of the state law. The invalidity of the guardianship order was held to have stripped those who acted under it of any legal protection. As a result, the plaintiff was found to have stated a cause of action against the deprogrammers under one of the federal civil right statutes (42 U.S.C.A. § 1985(2) and (3)).

4. Guardianship statutes are increasingly being attacked on the ground of vagueness. For example, a Utah statute authorized appointment of a guardian when the individual is

impaired by reason of mental illness, mental deficiency, physical illness or disability, advanced age, chronic use of drugs, chronic intoxication, or other cause (except minority) to the extent that he lacks sufficient understanding or capacity to make or communicate responsible decisions concerning his person.

Utah Code Ann., § 75–1–201(18) (1953). The statute was challenged on the grounds that the words "capacity to make or communicate *responsible decisions* concerning his person" [emphasis added] would allow the appointment of a guardian for a person "who makes decisions regarded by some as irresponsible, even though he has sufficient capacity to make personal management decisions which allow him to function in a manner acceptable to himself and without any threat of injury to himself." *In re Boyer*, 636 P.2d 1085 (Utah 1981). According to the Utah Supreme

Court, the key phrase "responsible decisions" admits of such broad interpretation as to raise a serious question of unconstitutional vagueness. Id. at 1089.

The court was nevertheless able to avoid declaring the statute unconstitutional by construing the statute to require an impairment which renders the individual "unable to care for his personal safety or unable to attend to and provide for such necessities as food, shelter, clothing, and medical care." *Id.*

5. A number of state laws specifically make chronic alcoholism one of the conditions which permits a finding of incompetency. Wisconsin, for instance, provides for guardianship and protective placement of individuals who because of an "alcoholic condition" are incapable of caring for themselves.

This provision was, however, interpreted by one appellate court to require a specific finding that the individual "is not capable of making a knowing and voluntary choice about his drinking." *Guardianship of Shaw*, 87 Wis.2d 503, 275 N.W.2d 143, 148 (1979). The court, in other words, distinguished between an "involuntary" alcoholic and one who "continues to drink because [he] prefers an alcoholic life-style." The latter were found to be beyond the reach of the Wisconsin incompetency laws.

D. INCOMPETENCY PROCEEDINGS

SAMUEL BRAKEL AND RONALD ROCK, *THE MENTALLY DISABLED AND THE LAW*

(University of Chicago Press, 1971), 258.

INITIATION OF INCOMPETENCY PROCEEDINGS

The procedure governing a determination of incompetency is substantially similar to that used in judicial hospitalization proceedings. Although in a very few states a petition can be presented only by a relative or a friend, in most states it can be brought by any interested person. Notice to the alleged incompetent is a statutory requirement in a vast majority of states. Even where statutes do not make notice a requirement, the courts usually have held it to be essential on the theory that a statute which made notice unnecessary would be a violation of due process. However, in a few jurisdictions the judge may, if it is deemed necessary, dispense with notice altogether. In a few others the court has discretion to reduce, for good cause, the length of time between the service of notice and the holding of the hearing. About half the states require that notice be given to one or more relatives in addition to the notice served upon the alleged incompetent. In only some ten to twelve states do statutes require that a medical certificate of the incompetent's mental condition accompany the petition. However, some other states require medical evidence at the hearing or an investigation of the petition by a commission of doctors.

Hearing and Testimony

The person alleged to be incompetent is entitled to produce evidence and witnesses in order to dispute the allegations set out in the petition and the evidence against him. About half the states make some provision for the appointment of counsel or a guardian *ad litem*. In a number of these states such appointment is discretionary with the court. In some others the prosecuting attorney is to act as counsel for the alleged incompetent unless the latter is able to furnish his own. Because the proceedings may result in the loss of the person's civil rights as well as the loss of control over his property, representation by counsel would appear to be a necessary protection. Ordinarily the incompetent must be present at the hearing unless it is shown to the court's satisfaction that his presence should be dispensed with.

* * *

Under the federal Constitution, neither the due process clauses of the Fifth and Fourteenth Amendments nor the right to trial by jury in criminal cases guaranteed by the Seventh Amendment appear to give an alleged incompetent the right to demand a jury. Several state courts have held, however, that there was a right to trial by jury in incompetency proceedings at common law and that state constitutional guarantees of trial by jury consequently extend and preserve such a right; and some jurisdictions have held that even though the right did not exist at common law, it existed by statute before the adoption of the state constitution and was, therefore, incorporated in the constitutional provisions guaranteeing jury trials. Nonetheless, the states generally recognize no original or common-law right to trial by jury in incompetency cases. About one-third of the states presently provide by statute for either mandatory or optional juries in such cases; but as in most civil proceedings, the right to have a jury determine incompetency may be waived.

In some jurisdictions, the alleged incompetent's failure to demand a jury trial is deemed to be a waiver of his right. In this circumstance his right to a jury trial would not be effective unless he were informed of his right to demand such a procedure. This problem is not so acute in those states where the court is required to appoint counsel or a guardian *ad litem* for incompetency proceedings, but where the alleged incompetent is not represented by counsel, it is quite likely that he would not be cognizant of his right to a jury.

Questions and Comments

1. Incompetency determinations involve the application of the preponderance of the evidence standard generally applicable to civil cases. A minority of courts, however, have as a matter of state common law required the higher clear and convincing evidence test. *See In re Boyer,*

636 P.2d 1085 (Utah 1981). Still, most courts continue to adhere to the preponderance of the evidence test. As explained by one court:

> We do not feel that more harm will befall an individual who is erroneously subjected to guardianship than to an individual who is in need of a guardian but is erroneously denied one. If an individual is erroneously subjected to guardianship, then [state law] allows such a ward to file a petition for the removal of his guardian. *Guardianship of Roe*, 383 Mass. 415, 421 N.E.2d 40–47 (1981).

2. Legal incompetency can be terminated through a "restoration" proceeding. The judicial procedures followed in such restoration proceedings closely parallels those required by the initial incompetency hearing. However, "a few states have no specific restoration procedures but merely provide that the court is to discharge the guardian when the cause for which the guardianship was granted has ceased or is removed." Brakel and Rock, *The Mentally Disabled and the Law* at 262.

E. APPOINTMENT AND RESPONSIBILITIES OF THE GUARDIAN

SAMUEL BRAKEL AND RONALD ROCK, *THE MENTALLY DISABLED AND THE LAW*

(University of Chicago Press, 1971), 260.

When incompetency is determined independently of hospitalization, a guardian is usually appointed for the incompetent. * * *

Guardianship may be limited to guardianship of the person or guardianship of the estate, or may include both. In most states one guardian may be appointed for the person of the incompetent and another appointed for the estate. Corporations may act as guardians in about one-third of the states. In some jurisdictions the term "conservator," "curator," "committee," or "tutor" is used instead of "guardian." "Conservator" or "curator" are applied especially to guardians of the estate.

A guardian of the estate engages in the usual activities of property management, buys and sells on behalf of the ward, makes contracts for him, and represents him in legal proceedings. As an agent of the court, the guardian is answerable to it for the judicious use of the ward's funds. He must obtain the court's permission for certain activities, as would be required if he were the guardian of a minor, and must submit the same kind of accounts. In general, the guardian has greater powers over his ward's personal property than over his real property. Usually, a court order must be secured before a sale of the ward's real property can be consummated. A guardian of the person has essentially the same duties and obligations toward his ward as the person having the custody of a minor.

* * *

One of the primary aims of guardianship laws should be to assure that guardians or representatives are in fact appointed for those adjudicated or administratively designated as incompetent and that such appointments coincide temporally with the fact of incompetency. The statutes which formerly merged the issues of hospitalization and competency often failed to accomplish these objectives. The decline of merger in favor of separation of the issues in the great majority of jurisdictions has resolved only part of the problem. An independent judicial determination of incompetency assures virtually by definition the appointment of a guardian, but such a determination may never take place, or if it does it may occur long after the fact of hospitalization, while in the meantime the hospitalized patient remains de facto incompetent by virtue of institutionalization or by express administrative regulation. The hospitals themselves often manage patients' funds and may to some extent perform the functions of guardianship generally; the laws, however, need to make it clear that whichever agency or person acts as the representative of a de facto incompetent patient must comply with the standards of responsibility and disinterest that this fiduciary function implies.

It must be noted that the private court-appointed guardian— usually a friend or relative of the incompetent—is not the only and exclusive type of guardian. Limited guardianships are operative in the administration of veterans' benefits and social security. These types, in numbers alone, far surpass the traditional private guardian. Public guardians have been created in a number of states. The New York hospital system has its "Reimbursement Agent." State guardianship in Minnesota has come under intensive study, and its type has become known as the "Minnesota Plan."

* * *

Questions and Comments

1. An adjudication of incompetency does not necessarily lead to the appointment of a guardian for either the person or the estate. As a result, some individuals who have been found incompetent are in a type of legal limbo. They have no capacity to transact their affairs and, until a petitioner files for the appointment of a guardian, there is no one who is legally empowered to act on their behalf.

2. In the absence of a close relative or friend who is willing to act as a guardian, some states have adopted a system of public guardianship. The public guardianship system, however, is not well developed and does not exist in many jurisdictions. Moreover, institutions to which the incompetent may be committed are frequently reluctant to assume the responsibilities of a guardianship. Thus, it is not uncommon for incompetent persons who have been institutionalized to lack a guardian who may be needed to give consent for medical treatment. However, the supreme court of at least one state has held that where the legislature has not made provisions for such appointment, the state has a *legal obligation* to secure a guardian for the incompetent. *In the Matter of Gamble*, 118 N.H. 771, 394 A.2d 308 (1978).

II. TREATMENT AND BIOMEDICAL INTERVENTIONS INVOLVING INCOMPETENT PERSONS

A. INTRODUCTION

As noted in Chapter Three, all non-emergency administrations of biomedical interventions require the informed consent of the patient. As pointed out in Chapter Six, however, the requirement of consent is often set aside in the case of institutionalized patients when the treatment pertains directly to the individual's mental disorder. An even broader exception to the requirement of patient consent applies where there has been an adjudication of incompetency and the patient lacks legal capacity to give valid consent to medical treatment. In this situation most states provide some type of substituted consent mechanism. For instance, in those states that adhere to the Uniform Probate Code, the guardian or conservator has sole authority to consent to medical or professional care for the ward. In other states the spouse or next of kin of the incompetent patient may also have authority to provide proxy consent.

The powers of guardians to consent to customary medical treatment do not, however, extend equally to all biomedical procedures. The laws of a number of states, for instance, establish a different substituted consent procedure in four categories of biomedical intervention:

(1) *psychiatric* treatment modalities deemed particularly intrusive or hazardous;

(2) nontherapeutic sterilization and abortion;

(3) biomedical intervention for the benefit of others, *e.g.*, when the subject is a prospective organ donor;

(4) nontherapeutic research.

The scope of the guardian's authority to consent to these forms of biomedical intervention is often greatly curtailed or even replaced by judicial decision-making. Although fundamental distinctions between such intervention and traditional forms of medical treatment are widely recognized, there is no uniform approach to the creation of appropriate substituted consent mechanisms. In some states these categories of biomedical intervention have been, at least in part, legislatively regulated. In others, legal guidelines have been developed as a result of court decisions. In many states, however, when the intervention involves something other than customary medical treatment, neither statutory law nor judicial precedent is available to provide guidance to physicians or researchers.

Significantly, a number of fundamental issues remain largely unresolved. First, are there any constitutional limits which may altogether prohibit certain biomedical interventions involving incompetent persons? Second, what consent mechanisms must be employed to authorize specific categories of biomedical intervention? Finally, what standard must be applied by those legally authorized to make a decision on behalf of the incompetent? These issues are explored in the materials which follow.

Questions and Comments

1. What alternatives are available if the incompetent patient has no guardian or the guardian refuses to give consent to treatment deemed necessary by the treating physician? If no guardian has been appointed, the hospital or physician may petition the court to have a temporary or permanent guardian appointed. Where a guardian has been appointed but refuses to consent to the treatment, the physician or medical director of the facility may petition the appropriate court (which is usually the probate division of the county court in which the hospital or facility is located) for the appointment of a special guardian *ad litem*. The function of the guardian *ad litem* is to act as a representative of the patient in a special hearing before the court to determine the necessity and reasonableness of the proposed treatment. By this procedure the decision of the permanent guardian to forego treatment can be judicially overridden. See generally, *Price v. Sheppard*, 307 Minn. 250, 239 N.W.2d 905, 913 (1976).

2. The meaning of competency in the medical treatment context has not been articulated with any degree of precision. In the absence of guidance from legal institutions, two basic approaches have been advanced. One set of proposed guidelines would ask merely whether the patient "has sufficient mental capacity to understand what is proposed and to express an opinion as to his or her participation. *See* U.S. Department of Health, Education, and Welfare, Protection of Human Subjects: Proposed Policy, Federal Register 39:30647–30657, Aug. 23, 1974. Presumably this approach would emphasize *cognitive* comprehension.

Another approach to competency determination attempts to evaluate the "rationality" of the individual's decision. This approach would consider primarily the character of the decision's *outcome*, rather than the individual's capacity to understand the risks and alternatives involved in the decision. Thus, "the patient who fails to make a decision that is roughly congruent with the decision that a reasonable person in like circumstances would make is viewed as incompetent." *See* Roth, Meisel, and Lidz, *Tests of Competency to Consent to Treatment*, 134 Am.J.Psychiatry 279, 280–81 (1977). Clearly this test in contrast to the first would give less deference to individual choice and thus disqualify a broader class of individuals from retaining decision-making authority.

An even broader and more expansive test has been proposed by a number of psychiatric commentators. This test would inquire into both the "rational motivations" of the decision as well as the individual's "capacity to engage in the decision-making process." Applebaum and Batemont, *Competency to Consent to Voluntary Hospitalization: A Theoretical Approach*, Bulletin of the American Academy of Psychiatry and the Law (in press). The latter aspect explores the patient's emotional response to the decision-making situation. Presumably, incapacity could be found where the patient attaches an idiosyncratic meaning to the treatment that is being proposed. For instance, if a particular treatment or procedure might be "sufficiently provocative of anxiety and fear, the patient may be forced to revert to * * * primitive, even psychotic, levels of defense for coping with it. Thus the recommendation for the procedure itself may force the patient into an apparently incompetent state and may preclude the obtaining of competent consent." Applebaum and Roth, *Clinical Issues in the Assessment of Competency*, 138 Am.J. of Psych. 1462, 1463 (1981).

3. As the materials which follow make clear, once the individual has been adjudicated incompetent, courts are increasingly applying the "substituted judgment" doctrine, which compels the substituted decision-maker to take into account the preferences of the ward, including those which may be idiosyncratic. Thus, even irrational preferences of the ward may affect the ultimate treatment decision made by the guardian or court. If the ward's irrational preferences can be taken into account when substituting the court's judgment for an incompetent, is it consistent to require the individual's decision to pass a "rational(ity)" test when making the initial competency evaluation?

B. THERAPEUTIC TREATMENT

1. Overview

As noted earlier, the legal system has traditionally authorized third persons, such as relatives or guardians of an incompetent person, to consent to medical treatment on his behalf. For those incompetent persons who had neither a guardian nor a relative, physicians "customarily used their own best judgment, aided by the advice of colleagues and frequently the opinions of other health professionals." Baron, *Assuring "Detached but Passionate Investigation and Decision": The Role of Guardian Ad Litem in Saikewicz-type Cases*, 4 Am.J. of L. and Medicine, 111, 116 (1978).

More recently, however, with the expansion of the doctrine of informed consent (see Chapter III), both legislatures and courts have moved to ensure a more meaningful substituted consent mechanism. This has resulted in greater reliance on the guardianship system as the primary means of providing substituted consent to treatment. Under this system, "[t]he guardian of the mentally incompetent person [today] has the same powers and duties as does the managing conservator of a minor." *Little v. Little*, 576 S.W.2d 493, 495 (Tex. Civ.App.1979). Such authority does not generally extend, however, beyond the power to consent to *conventional* therapeutic treatment of the ward. *Id.* at 498.

The same concerns that have led to a greater reliance on the formal guardianship system to protect the interests of those who are incompetent have led to a narrowing of the guardian's authority. An increasing number of states, for instance, require *judicial* authorization for certain psychiatric treatment modalities. Similarly, most states currently require court review prior to the use of biomedical interventions that are not of direct therapeutic value to the ward. The consent procedures imposed in cases of noncustomary or nontherapeutic interventions are considered in the materials which follow.

2. *Consent to Therapeutic Medical Treatment: Emerging Limitations*

IN THE MATTER OF GUARDIANSHIP OF RICHARD ROE, III

Supreme Judicial Court of Massachusetts, 1981.
383 Mass. 415, 421 N.E.2d 40.

HENNESSEY, Chief Justice.

The ultimate question we address in this case is whether the guardian of a mentally ill person possesses the inherent authority to consent to the forcible administration of antipsychotic medication to his noninstitutionalized ward in the absence of an emergency.

* * *

We summarize the material facts found by the judgment following the hearings on appointment of a permanent guardian. We emphasize first that the guardian ad litem frankly conceded at oral argument that the ward is "substantially and severely mentally ill," and this is therefore not directly in issue.

The ward was born on December 28, 1958, and was twenty-one years of age at the time of both guardianship appointments. As a child, the ward had been a bright and popular student, elected twice as vice-president of his junior high school class in the public school system. In his freshman year of high school he entered a private, residential preparatory school located near his home. During his first year at this private school he began to abuse alcohol, marihuana, and LSD, and he became withdrawn and seclusive. The ward's academic performance deteriorated and, as a result of his drinking and other behavior, he was expelled from the private school. He subsequently returned to the public school system, but his performance was so poor that he left the school without graduating.

While at the public school the ward was evaluated and it was recommended that he be hospitalized in a psychiatric hospital. During this time he displayed violent behavior toward his sister and threatened to kill his mother. Subsequently, on August 21, 1979, he was committed to Northampton State Hospital for observation on a charge of receiving stolen property. He was diagnosed as mentally ill, suffering from schizophrenia, chronic undifferentiated type. After his release from Northampton State Hospital he continued to reside at home, where his family tried to protect him from stressful influences. The ward displayed bizarre behavior at home, wearing a fur coat for hours on extremely hot days and standing for prolonged periods of time with a water glass poised at his lips. On numerous occasions the ward's father tried to involve the ward in psychotherapy, but the ward refused to accept any treatment or therapy.

On February 19, 1980, the ward was committed for a second time to Northampton State Hospital for observation, as a result of being charged with attempted unarmed robbery and assault and battery. While so institutionalized, the ward attacked another patient for no apparent reason and had to be restrained by hospital attendants. He was diagnosed as suffering from schizophrenia, paranoid type, and it was recommended that he be treated with antipsychotic medication. The ward refused all drugs, as he had on many previous occasions, and refused as well to engage in psychotherapy. This refusal to accept antipsychotic medication was based on the ward's prior experiences with illicit drugs which, among other things, caused him to be involved in an automobile accident. The guardian ad litem strongly contends that another factor in this refusal was the ward's acceptance of certain tenets of the Christian Science faith, and there was evidence which might support such a contention, although the judge concluded otherwise.

While the ward was still hospitalized, his parents filed petitions seeking appointment of the father as both temporary and permanent guardian. * * * Finding, inter alia, that there was a strong likelihood that the ward would inflict serious injury upon the public or himself and that there was a need for the immediate appointment of a temporary guardian, the probate judge on April 1, 1980, granted the parents' petition seeking the father's appointment as temporary guardian. * * * The temporary guardian was appointed permanent guardian on July 30, 1980, with authority to consent to the challenged medical treatment * * *

* * *

We begin our discussion of the medical treatment decision by noting that we are directly presented with only one question. We must decide whether the substituted judgment determination to be made in cases such as this may be delegated to the guardian.

* * *

A. NEED FOR A COURT ORDER

The primary dispute in this case concerns the means by which the ward is to exercise his right to refuse treatment, a right which the ward possesses but is incapable of exercising personally. The guardian's position is that the power to exercise this right on behalf of the ward is vested in the guardian simply by virtue of his appointment as guardian. The ward claims that he is entitled to a judicial determination of substituted judgment. The question is, then, who ought to exercise this right on behalf of the ward? We think that this question is best resolved by requiring a judicial determination in accordance with the substituted judgment doctrine.

* * *

The question presented by the ward's refusal of antipsychotic drugs is only incidentally a medical question. Absent an overwhelming State interest, a competent individual has the right to refuse such treatment. To deny this right to persons who are incapable of exercising it personally is to degrade those whose disabilities make them wholly reliant on other, more fortunate, individuals. In order to accord proper respect to this basic right of all individuals, we feel that if an incompetent individual refuses antipsychotic drugs, those charged with his protection must seek a judicial determination of substituted judgment. No medical expertise is required in such an inquiry, although medical advice and opinion is to be used for the same purposes and sought to the same extent that the incompetent individual would, if he were competent.

* * *

There is no bright line dividing those decisions which are (and ought to be) made by a guardian, from those for which a judicial determination is necessary. The tension which makes such a line so difficult to draw is apparent. There is an obvious need for broad, flexible, and responsive guardianship powers, but simultaneously there is a need to avoid the serious consequences accompanying a well-intentioned but mistaken exercise of those powers in making certain medical treatment decisions.

We have recently identified the factors to be taken into account in deciding when there must be a court order with respect to medical treatment of an incompetent patient. "Among them are at least the following: the extent of impairment of the patient's mental faculties, whether the patient is in the custody of a State institution, the prognosis without the proposed treatment, the prognosis with the proposed treatment, the complexity, risk and novelty of the proposed treatment, its possible side effects, the patient's level of understanding and probable reaction, the urgency of decision, the consent of the patient, spouse, or guardian, the good faith of those who participate in the decision, the clarity of professional opinion as to what is good medical practice, the interests of third persons, and the administrative requirements of any institution involved." *Matter of Spring*, 405 N.E.2d 115. Without intending to indicate the relative importance of these and other factors in all cases, it is appropriate to identify some of those factors which are weighty considerations in this particular case. They are: (1) the intrusiveness of the proposed treatment, (2) the possibility of adverse side effects, (3) the absence of an emergency, (4) the nature and extent of prior judicial involvement, and (5) the likelihood of conflicting interests.

(1) *The intrusiveness of the purposed treatment.* We can identify few legitimate medical procedures which are more intrusive than

the forcible injection of antipsychotic medication. "In general, the drugs influence chemical transmissions to the brain, affecting both activatory and inhibitory functions. Because the drugs' purpose is to reduce the level of psychotic thinking, it is virtually undisputed that they are mind-altering."

* * * Because of both the profound effect that these drugs have on the thought processes of an individual and the well-established likelihood of severe and irreversible adverse side effects, we treat these drugs in the same manner we would treat psychosurgery or electroconvulsive therapy.

* * *

(2) *The possibility of adverse side effects.* Although, as we establish above, the intended effects of antipsychotic drugs are extreme, their unintended effects are frequently devastating and often irreversible.

* * *

(3) *The absence of an emergency.* The evidence presented in the proceedings below makes it quite clear that the probate judge was not presented with a situation which could accurately be described as an emergency.

* * *

(4) *The nature and extent of prior judicial involvement.*

* * *

In a case such as the one before us, some judicial involvement is unavoidable inasmuch as the judge must: (1) appoint the guardian, and (2) determine the ward's competency to make treatment decisions. This significant and inescapable prior judicial involvement eliminates much concern we might otherwise have about requiring a further judicial determination, since one of the factors we consider in deciding whether the guardian is to make the substituted judgment determination is the amount of additional time which will be needed to obtain a judicial determination. While this prior involvement is not conclusive in and of itself, it is a factor to be considered in determining whether a court order must be obtained.

(5) *The likelihood of conflicting interests.* Decisions such as the one the guardian wishes to make in this case pose exceedingly difficult problems for even the most capable, detached, and diligent decisionmaker. We intend no criticism of the guardian when we say that few parents could make this substituted judgment determination—by its nature a self-centered determination in which the decisionmaker is called upon to ignore all but the implementation of the values and preferences of the ward—when the ward, in his present condition, is living at home with other children. Nor do we think that the father was not a suitable person to be appointed guardian. Those characteristics laudable in a parent might often be a substantial

handicap to a guardian faced with such a decision but who might in all other circumstances be an excellent guardian.

A judicial determination also benefits the gaurdian [sic], who otherwise might suffer from lingering doubts concerning the propriety of his decision.

*   *   *

B. Relevant Factors in the Substituted Judgment Determination.

The immediate question confronting us is resolved by our conclusion that, when a timely determination needs to be made, it is to be made by a judge. However, because of the likelihood that a proper determination will be sought by these or other parties in the future, we set forth below guidelines to be followed in order to ensure accuracy and consistency in proceedings in the Probate Court.

The factors we identify below are to be considered by the probate judge in order to identify the choice "which would be made by the incompetent person, if that person were competent, but taking into account the present and future incompetency of the individual as one of the factors which would necessarily enter into the decision-making process of the competent person." *Superintendent of Belchertown State School v. Saikewicz*, 752–753, 370 N.E.2d 417 (1977). The determination must "give the fullest possible expression to the character and circumstances of that individual." We observe that this is a subjective rather than an objective determination. All persons involved in such an inquiry will readily admit that the bounds of relevance therefor are exceedingly broad. In this search, procedural intricacies and technical niceties must yield to the need to know the actual values and preferences of the ward. In this spirit we briefly identify the following relevant factors, cautioning that they are not exclusive, recognizing that certain of them may not exist in all cases, and declining to establish their relative weights in any individual case. They are: (1) the ward's expressed preferences regarding treatment; (2) his religious beliefs; (3) the impact upon the ward's family; (4) the probability of adverse side effects; (5) the consequences if treatment is refused; and (6) the prognosis with treatment.

(1) *The ward's expressed preferences regarding treatment.* If the ward has expressed a preference while not subjected to guardianship—and presumably competent—such an expression is entitled to great weight in determining his substituted judgment unless the judge finds that either: (a) simultaneously with his expression of preference the ward lacked the capacity to make such a medical treatment decision, or (b) the ward, upon reflection and reconsideration, would not act in accordance with his previously expressed preference in the changed circumstances in which he currently finds himself.

Even if the ward lacks capacity to make treatment decisions, his stated preference is entitled to serious consideration as a factor in the substituted judgment determination. "Although [the ward] failed to understand his mental condition and his need for treatment, we think his stated preference must be treated as a critical factor in the determination of his 'best interests.' " This respect for the ward's preference and the reasons for this deference have long been recognized in our cases. "A man may be insane so as to be a fit subject for guardianship, and yet have a sensible opinion and strong feeling upon the question who that guardian shall be. And that opinion and feeling it would be the duty as well as the pleasure of the court anxiously to consult, as the happiness of the ward and his restoration to health might depend upon it."

(2) *The ward's religious beliefs.* An individual might choose to refuse treatment if the acceptance of such treatment would be contrary to his religious beliefs. If such a reason is proffered by or on behalf of an incompetent, the judge must evaluate it in the same manner and for the same purposes as any other reason: the question to be addressed is whether certain tenets or practices of the incompetent's faith would cause him individually to reject the specific course of treatment proposed for him in his present circumstances.

* * *

(3) *The impact upon the ward's family.* An individual who is part of a closely knit family would doubtless take into account the impact his acceptance or refusal of treatment would likely have on his family. Such a factor is likewise to be considered in determining the probable wishes of one who is incapable of formulating or expressing them himself. In any choice between proposed treatments which entail grossly different expenditures of time or money by the incompetent's family, it would be appropriate to consider whether a factor in the incompetent's decision would have been the desire to minimize the burden on his family. If this factor would have been considered by the individual, the judge must enter it into the balance of making the substituted judgment determination. If an incompetent has enjoyed close family relationships and subsequently is forced to choose between two treatments, one of which will allow him to live at home with his family and the other of which will require the relative isolation of an institution, then the judge must weigh in his determination the affection and assistance offered by the incompetent's family. We note, however, that the judge must be careful to avoid examination of these factors in any manner other than one actually designed and intended to effectuate the incompetent's right to self-determination.

* * *

(4) *The probability of adverse side effects.* We have described the adverse side effects of antipsychotic medication. Clearly any competent patient choosing whether to accept such treatment would

consider the severity of these side effects, the probability that they would occur, and the circumstances in which they would be endured. The judge must also consider these factors in arriving at a determination of substituted judgment on behalf of an incompetent.

(5) *The consequences if treatment is refused.* If the prognosis without treatment is that an individual's health will steadily, inevitably and irreversibly deteriorate, then that person will, in most circumstances, more readily consent to treatment which he might refuse if the prognosis were more favorable or less certain. This general rule, however, will not always indicate whether an individual would, if competent, accept treatment. For example, in regard to the religious beliefs "even in a life-or-death situation one's religion can dictate a 'best interest' antithetical to getting well." This factor, as all the rest of the factors, must be utilized to reach an individual determination. While no judge need ignore the basic logic and common values which ordinarily underlie individual preference, he must reach beyond statistical factors and general rules to see "the complexities of the singular situation viewed from the unique perspective of the person called on to make the decision." *Saikewicz*, 370 N.E.2d 417.

(6) *The prognosis with treatment.* We think it can fairly be stated as a general proposition that the greater the likelihood that there will be cure or improvement, the more likely an individual would be to submit to intrusive treatment accompanied by the possibility of adverse side effects. Additionally, professional opinion may not always be unanimous regarding the probability of specific benefits being received by a specific individual upon administration of a specific treatment. Both of these factors—the benefits sought and the degree of assurance that they actually will be received—are entitled to consideration.

*   *   *

C. The Accommodation of Overriding State Interests

There are circumstances in which the fundamental right to refuse extremely intrusive treatment must be subordinated to various State interests.

(1) *The State interests involved.* Among the State interests which we have identified in our prior cases are: "(1) the preservation of life; (2) the protection of the interests of innocent third parties; (3) the prevention of suicide; and (4) maintaining the ethical integrity of the medical profession."

*   *   *

In the present case the judge found that the State had a vital interest in seeing that its residents function at the maximum level of their capacity and that this interest outweighed the rights of the individual. We disagree. While the State, in certain circumstances, might have a generalized parens patriae interest in removing obstacles to individual development, this general interest does not outweigh the fundamental individual rights here asserted.

The preservation of life, "the most significant of the asserted State interests," is not assertable in this case, as the proposed treatment is not intended to prolong life. There is no evidence that the ward is suicidal, nor is there evidence that medical ethics are seriously implicated. In the past we have interpreted the phrase "the protection of the interests of innocent third parties" as representing the State's interest in protecting minor children from the emotional and financial consequences of the decision of a competent adult to refuse life-saving or life-prolonging treatment. We have identified this as a State interest of considerable magnitude. Equally deserving of such regard is the State interest in preventing the infliction of violence upon members of the community by individuals suffering from severe mental illness. This is a second aspect of the State interest in protecting innocent third parties. Although few would question that this interest is capable of overriding the individual's right to refuse treatment, a substantial question remains as to the likelihood of violence which must be established in order to support forced administration of antipsychotic medication.

* * *

* * * [W]here the State's interest in preventing violence in the community has been found sufficient to override the individual's right to refuse treatment, two means are then available for protecting this State interest. In such cases, that lesser intrusive means of restraint which adequately protects the public safety is to be used. The right to the least intrusive means if derived from the right to privacy, which stands as a constitutional expression of the "sanctity of individual free choice and self-determination as fundamental constituents of life." In order to satisfy the least intrusive means test, the incompetent is entitled to choose, by way of substituted judgment, between involuntary commitment and involuntary medication. Such an extended substituted judgment proceeding differs from the substituted judgment determination we describe[d] *supra*, only in that the outcome is limited to involuntary commitment or involuntary medication.

* * *

Our guidelines make clear that if the guardian seasonably petitions the Probate Court for an order directing the administration of antipsychotic medication to the ward, then the petition should receive prompt and full consideration. Since no such request was before the probate judge, his order authorizing involuntary treatment was premature. We therefore vacate the order in so far as it allows the ward to be medicated over his objection. The remainder of the order, appointing Richard Roe, Jr., as guardian of his son, Richard Roe, III, is affirmed.

So ordered.

Questions and Comments

1. In *Guardianship of Roe III* the Massachusetts Supreme Judicial Court held that the guardian lacks power to authorize the administration of antipsychotic medication to an uninstitutionalized ward. Note, in this connection, that Massachusetts statutory law was silent as to the powers of guardians to consent to treatment. Would a legislature have the power to authorize the guardian to consent to the psychotropic medication? Does *Roe III* establish any constitutional barriers to such legislative authority?

2. What should be the duration of a court order directing administration of antipsychotic medication? In a footnote to *Roe III*, the Massachusetts court recognized that a "judge may appropriately authorize a treatment program which utilizes various specifically identified medications administered over a prolonged period of time." 421 N.E.2d at 59 n. 19. The court noted further that "the order should provide for periodic review to determine if the ward's condition and circumstances have substantially changed." *Id.* What kinds of changes in "conditions and circumstances" would necessitate a change in the judicial order? How often should the order be reviewed? The *Roe III* court suggests only that a "party with standing may seek modification of such an order at any reasonable time." *Id.*

3. Apparently the primary objective of the guardianship in *Roe III* was to provide the basis for parental consent for the medication of the son following his release from the institution. If continued medication is the only means by which some disordered individuals can function outside of an institutional setting, will not the *Roe III* ruling, which places procedural barriers to the subsequent administration of medication, discourage the willingness of guardians to seek the release of institutionalized individuals?

4. Is there a potential tension between the interests of individuals in freedom from *compelled medication* and their interest to be free from *confinement?* How should a court, called upon to pass on a petition for compelled medication on an *outpatient basis*, respond when the evidence indicates that the individual could not function outside an institutional setting without medication? Should the individual's interest in avoiding confinement override other competing interests including the avoidance of compelled medication and the risks normally associated with such medication?

5. There is a division among courts as to the appropriate standard that must be applied when a court is called upon to pass on noncustomary treatment. Some courts employ what is known as the "best-interest" test. Other courts, such as the court in *Roe III*, adhere to the "substituted judgment" standard. In applying the best-interest test the court attempts to seek an objective determination. The focus is on the best interest of the ward, given his general circumstances, an approach that excludes consideration of idiosyncratic factors or preferences particular to the individual. Thus any special preferences, including religious ones, that the ward might hold or have held prior to losing competency would

not necessarily be taken into account. The substituted judgment standard, in contrast, seeks to identify and apply the particular preferences of the individual, including those that the individual held prior to the loss of competency. Thus, as noted by one court, "[i]f an individual would, if competent, make an unwise or foolish decision, the judge must respect that decision so long as he would accept the same decision if made by a competent person in the same circumstances." *In the Matter of Roe*, 383 Mass. 415, 421 N.E.2d 40, 59 n. 20 (1981). See also, *In re Boyd*, 403 A.2d 744 (D.C.App.1980).

Some jurisdictions that adhere to the substituted judgment test call for its application even when the individual has been incompetent since birth. *Superintendent of Belchertown v. Saikewicz*, 373 Mass. 728, 370 N.E.2d 417, 430–431 n. 15 (1977). *See also, In the Matter of Roe III*, 383 Mass. 415, 421 N.E.2d 40, 56 n. 16 (1981). While these courts have acknowledged that in such cases it may be necessary to rely to a greater degree on objective criteria, they maintain that "the effort to bring the substituted judgment into step with values and desires the effected individual must not be abandoned." *Superintendent of Belchertown v. Saikewicz*, 373 Mass. 728, 370 N.E.2d 417, 430–431 (1977). These decisions, however, do not make clear how a substituted judgment approach, using "objective criteria," differs from the best-interest test.

Note that the application of the substituted judgment doctrine where the individual has been incompetent since birth has been criticized by some courts as being "unrealistic." *Matter of Storar*, 52 N.Y.2d 363, 438 N.Y.S.2d 266, 420 N.E.2d 64, 72 (1981). *See also*, Swazey, *Treatment and Nontreatment Decisions: In Whose Best Interests?*, in Dilemmas of Dying 95, 96–97 (C. Wong and J. Swazey, eds. 1981), cited in *In the Matter of Roe III*, 383 Mass. 415, 421 N.E.2d 40, 56–57 n. 16 (1981).

C. PSYCHIATRIC HOSPITALIZATION

F. LINDMAN AND D. McINTYRE, *THE MENTALLY DISABLED AND THE LAW*

(Chicago: American Bar Foundation, 1961), at 226.

A few guardianship statutes are so broad in their grant of authority that they might be construed as authorizing the guardian to hospitalize his ward despite the fact that the hospitalization statutes do not so provide. On the other hand, many states have provisions which imply that the hospitalization statutes provide the sole methods of hospitalizing persons.

The question remains whether a guardian should be permitted to hospitalize his ward against his will and without recourse to the normal statutory hospitalization procedure. If the guardian is permitted to do this, the incompetency determination assumes unusual importance in that it makes the incompetent subject to compulsory hospitalization at his guardian's discretion.

VON LUCE v. RANKIN

Supreme Court of Arkansas, 1979.
267 Ark. 34, 588 S.W.2d 445.

PURTLE, Justice.

This is an appeal from the denial of a Petition for a Writ of Habeas Corpus in the Pulaski County Chancery Court. Appellant was admitted to the state hospital as a voluntary patient by her guardian and subsequently sought release through a petition for habeas corpus. * * *

The question to be determined is whether a guardian may voluntarily confine her ward as a patient in the state hospital against the wishes of the ward and without the ward's consent or a probate court hearing. * * *

On May 10, 1979, Ute Patterson, the daughter of Anne Kay Von Luce, petitioned the Washington Probate Court for appointment of herself as guardian of her mother. On the same date an order appointing the daughter as temporary guardian was issued by the court. The order simply stated that petitioner was an "incompetent." There was an unverified letter from a doctor to the effect that in his opinion Mrs. Von Luce was an "incompetent."

* * * [Four] days after the order appointing the guardian she voluntarily admitted her mother into the state hospital in Little Rock. On June 6, 1979, the ward filed a petition in the Pulaski County Chancery Court seeking a writ of habeas corpus.

* * *

Mental illness alone is not justification for a guardian or a state to lock a person up. There must be a meaningful hearing in accordance with due process before such action is authorized. * * * In this case there has simply been no attempt on the part of anyone to comply with the provisions of any Arkansas law as it relates to involuntary commitment. Not even a mentally ill person may be confined against his will unless he is afforded due process of law. Act 817 provides that before a person may be committed for 30 days or more there must be a hearing at which clear and convincing evidence is presented to the effect that the ward or detainee is homicidal, suicidal or gravely disabled. We are not unaware of the problem of society and the mentally ill. The welfare of the people and the mental patient must both be given careful attention. The best interest of both must be weighed and taken into consideration when the question of confinement is at issue. If we were not to require at least substantial compliance with the law to fully protect the rights of incompetents it would be possible for an unscrupulous person to have himself appointed as guardian and then lock his ward in a mental institution and proceed to waste the ward's estate. If a state and the judiciary are not vigilant in the protection of the rights of incompetents it is likely to lead to the abuse of the person and estate of such incompetents. The mentally ill are unable to think and care for themselves in a normal manner and of necessity depend upon the state and the courts for protection. Although due process safeguards do not extend to the voluntary committee they most definitely extend to involuntary detainees. When a voluntary patient seeks relief he must be released or henceforth treated as an involuntary detainee in which case the due process safeguards must definitely apply. We have no choice on the record before us other than to treat petitioner as an involuntary detainee and must hold in this case that the ward was not afforded either procedural or substantive due process. Therefore, the court should have granted the petition for habeas corpus.

Reversed and remanded.

* * *

HICKMAN, Justice.

If the majority's position is that a "voluntary" commitment is with the consent of the ward, this ignores the fact that a ward has a guardian because the ward is incompetent, and his power to consent has been removed.

It is my judgment any commitment without a hearing violates due process of law.

Questions and Comments

1. Is Justice Hickman correct in his contention that due process is violated when a *non-protesting* incompetent person is institutionalized by action of the guardian? Should it make a difference whether the placement is into a nursing home or a psychiatric institution?

2. Some courts have refused on constitutional grounds to give effect to state laws which specifically authorize a guardian to "voluntarily admit" the ward into a psychiatric facility. *See Pima County Public Fiduciary v. Superior Court for Pima County*, 26 Ariz.App. 85, 546 P.2d 354 (1976) (holding that the guardian cannot waive the ward's due process rights to a hearing). *See also Matter of Guardianship of Anderson*, 17 Wash.App. 690, 564 P.2d 1190 (1977) (holding that the provision "any person * * * suitable * * * for care and treatment as mentally ill * * * who applies for admission * * * through their court appointed guardian" could not be construed to permit involuntary incarceration of the ward without a judicial hearing).

D. NONTHERAPEUTIC BIOMEDICAL INTERVENTIONS

1. Sterilization and Abortion

A number of recent appellate decisions, as exemplified by the cases which follow, have sought to restrict the discretion of courts to authorize the sterilization of incompetent individuals. It may be relevant to an understanding of these cases to consider briefly the related issue of eugenic sterilization, *i.e.*, sterilization having as the primary purpose the improvement of the quality of the population by control of childbearing. The following commentaries summarize the factual background for this issue:

> The use of sterilization for eugenic purposes was first suggested in the 19th century. However, at that time the only known surgical procedure for sterilization was castration. There were some incidents where castration was actually used for eugenic purposes. * * *

> Public resentment to castration was a great obstacle to the advocates of eugenic sterilization. Around 1900, the surgical procedures of vasectomy and salpingectomy were developed. There was very little public resentment toward these procedures. They accomplished complete sterilization without the many severe side effects of castration. However, the use of these procedures for eugenic purposes was not readily accepted and their use remained heavily criticized.

> At the advent of these new sterilization procedures there was no statutory authority for eugenic sterilizations. But the advocates of eugenic sterilization soon sought legislative sanction for their cause.

Comment, *Eugenic Sterilization Statutes: A Constitutional Re-Evaluation*, 14 J. of Fam.L. 280 (1975).

> State compulsory eugenic sterilization found its way into American law for the first time in Indiana in 1907. Until the famous case of *Buck v. Bell* in 1927, its constitutional status was still in doubt, but Mr. Justice Holmes and the United States Supreme Court left no doubts about either its constitutionality or its vitality as a proper exercise of state police powers. State laws and sterilization operations peaked in the 1930's. [An estimated 25,000 sterilizations were performed under these laws in the decade of the 1930's.] The war years brought a slowdown, and after World War II, a vastly larger and more articulate mental health movement, aided in part by Federal funding, took a new look at the origins and treatment of mental illness and mental retardation and the utility of eugenic sterilization laws. The result was a precipitous drop in operations, either because of a refusal to enforce the laws, or a shift from compulsory procedures, or even outright repeal of eugenic sterilization laws * * *

*   *   *

Julius Paul, "State Eugenic Sterilization History: A Brief Overview" in Robitscher, *Eugenic Sterilization* (Springfield, Ill.: Charles C. Thomas, 1973), at 25.

MATTER OF SALLMAIER

Supreme Court, Special Term, Queens County, Part 1, 1976.
85 Misc.2d 295, 378 N.Y.S.2d 989.

SIDNEY LEVISS, J. This is an application for an order authorizing the petitioner to consent to a sterilization procedure on behalf of her adult daughter, the respondent herein and a person alleged to be incapable of giving consent.

A guardian ad litem has been appointed to represent the rights and interests of respondent and has submitted a report of his findings and recommendation. Pursuant to an order of this court dated December 4, 1975, a psychiatrist was appointed to conduct an examination of respondent and to submit a report on his findings. Upon receipt of the reports of the guardian and the court-appointed psychiatrist, a hearing was held on December 12, 1975 during which the testimony of the examining psychiatrist and respondent's parents was taken. The court, in addition, interviewed respondent after determining that she could not be duly sworn.

The respondent was born September 1, 1952 at Jamaica Hospital and is the younger of two children. At the age of two she suffered a seizure which resulted in brain damage. After attending classes for brain damaged children, she attended the Institute for the Crippled and Disabled and now attends the Cerebral Palsy Center where she is employed at a nominal salary to do simple packing. Respondent resides in Queens County with her parents.

The condition from which the respondent suffers was diagnosed by the court-appointed psychiatrist as severe mental retardation with marked infantile thinking, behavior and attitudes. Her condition is not congenital, having resulted from organic brain damage, although it is irreversible. At her present age of 23 she is sexually mature, but has an I.Q. of 62 and functions at a six- or seven-year-old age level. She is unable to understand abstract concepts and does not know the difference between a man and a woman. Although respondent's vocabulary is good and she appears friendly and cooperative, she refuses all medication, has many phobias, and her personal hygiene and menstrual cycle must be handled by her mother. From all the evidence before the court as well as from its observations of respondent, the court has concluded that she is unable to knowingly consent or withhold consent to the proposed sterilization procedure.

The State of New York since 1918 does not have a statute authorizing the sterilization of individuals. * * * Other States, however, have statutes authorizing sterilization in a variety of cases.

The jurisdiction of the court in this proceeding arises not by statute, but from the common-law jurisdiction of the Supreme Court to act as *parens patriae* with respect to incompetents. * * * The decision to exercise the power of *parens patriae* must reflect the welfare of society, as a whole, but mainly it must balance the individual's right to be free from interference against the individual's need to be treated, if treatment would in fact be in his best interest.

The decision to authorize compulsory medical treatment for an individual is subject to a variety of factors and is an extremely difficult decision to make. In determining whether a sterilization procedure would be in respondent's best interest, the court has given great weight to the testimony of the court-appointed psychiatrist that in his expert opinion sterilization is recommended because pregnancy would have a substantial likelihood of causing a psychotic reaction in respondent. From this expert opinion, coupled with the recommendation by the guardian ad litem, the opinion of the family psychiatrist, respondent's proclivity for encounters with males and the testimony of respondent's parents, the court has concluded that it would be in the best interest of respondent to have a sterilization procedure performed.

Accordingly, the application is granted.

MATTER OF MOE

Supreme Judicial Court of Massachusetts, 1982.
385 Mass. 555, 432 N.E.2d 712.

LIACOS, Justice.

The Probate Court for Worcester County appointed Ann Moe the guardian of her mentally retarded daughter, Mary Moe, on July 28, 1978. On April 1, 1980, the guardian petitioned the court, seeking an order permitting an abdominal tubal ligation (sterilization) to be performed on her ward. The petition alleged that although the ward is of legal age, she "is a mentally retarded person, whose chronological age does not conform with her emotional, intellectual, or developmental age and, upon facts and circumstances in the knowledge of your petitioner, and in the knowledge of professionals in the Health Care Field, it would be in the best interest of the ward to have an abdominal tubal ligation."

On May 23, 1980, the probate judge appointed a guardian ad litem. The guardian ad litem filed an "objection to abdominal tubal ligation" on September 2, 1980, expressing his belief that, although sterilization would be in the ward's best interest, there was no apparent legal authority for the probate judge to authorize the requested procedure.

* * *

On March 16, 1981, the judge reported the matter, without decision, to the Appeals Court. Two questions were reported: "1. Can the probate and family court, absent specific statutory authority, order sterilization of an adult mentally retarded female; and 2. If the response to question one is in the affirmative, what procedures and standards should be followed and applied?"

* * *

The facts as they appear in the record are as follows.[a] The ward is a mentally retarded woman born on August 6, 1956. Her emotional, intellectual, and developmental age, however, does not conform to

---

a. The petitioner states additional facts in her brief, *e.g.*, that the ward is severely retarded, that she is institutionalized in a State institution, that she has previously suffered a "sexual incident" at the institution, that she is unable to effectively practice any other medically recognized method of birth control, and that she has no prospect of assuming normal parental duties and responsibilities should she give birth to a child.

* * *

her chronological age, and she currently functions at the level of a four year old. In the view of professionals in the health care field it would be in the best interest of the ward to have an abdominal tubal ligation.

Medical practitioners in the Commonwealth refuse to perform the abdominal tubal ligation procedure without a court order.

* * * In this case the ward's presumed inability to give her knowing consent regarding a sterilization operation, as a competent individual could, is said to require the aid of the court. The guardian argues that the method to ensure that the ward's best interests are thoroughly protected is judicial intervention.

There is no specific Massachusetts statute granting a guardian the power to authorize a sterilization operation on behalf of his or her ward. * * *

Although [Massachusetts General Laws] c. 201, § 12 confers the "care and custody" of a ward upon a duly appointed guardian, [other provisions] requires the knowledgeable consent of the individual to be sterilized. In addition, our prior cases have established that prior judicial approval is required before a guardian may consent to administering or withholding of proposed extraordinary medical treatment. Since sterilization is an extraordinary and highly intrusive form of medical treatment that irreversibly extinguishes the ward's fundamental right of procreative choice, we conclude that a guardian must obtain a proper judicial order for the procedure before he or she can validly consent to it. Guardians and parents, therefore, absent statutory or judicial authorization, cannot consent to the sterilization of a ward in their care or custody.

* * *

[In answer to the first question the appellate court held that in the absence of any limiting legislative enactment, the Probate Court has plenary power to exercise its jurisdiction to provide for the needs of the mentally incompetent person.]

* * *

Although G.L. c. 112, § 12W, which prohibits a physician from performing a sterilization unless the physician has the knowledgeable consent of the patient in writing, appears to be "limiting" legislation, this statute cannot be read to deny incompetent individuals the same procreative choices which competent persons may exercise. Because a competent individual has a right to be sterilized, "[t]o deny this right to persons who are incapable of exercising it personally is to degrade those whose disabilities make them wholly reliant on other, more fortunate, individuals." "To protect the incompetent person within its power, the State must recognize the dignity and worth of such a person and afford to that person the same panoply of rights and choices it recognizes in competent persons." *Superintendent of*

Belchertown State School v. Saikewicz, 373 Mass. 728, 746, 370 N.E.2d 417 (1977).

This is accomplished through the doctrine of substituted judgment determined by proceedings in a court of competent jurisdiction. See *Guardianship of Roe,* 421 N.E.2d 40.

Procedure. (a) *Substituted judgment.* In utilizing the doctrine of substituted judgment, this court seeks to maintain the integrity of the incompetent person by giving the individual a forum in which his or her rights may be exercised. The court dons "the mental mantle of the incompetent" and substitutes itself as nearly as possible for the individual in the decision making process. In utilizing the doctrine the court does not decide what is necessarily the best decision but rather what decision would be made by the incompetent person if he or she were competent. "In short, if an individual would, if competent, make an unwise or foolish decision, the judge must respect that decision as long as he would accept [or be bound to accept] the same decision if made by a competent individual in the same circumstances."

*   *   *

We are aware of the difficulties of utilizing the substituted judgment doctrine in a case where the incompetent has been mentally retarded since birth. The inability, however, of an incompetent to choose, should not result in a loss of the person's constitutional interests. To speak solely in terms of the "best interests" of the ward, or of the State's interest, is to obscure the fundamental issue: Is the State to impose a solution on an incompetent based on external criteria, or is it to seek to protect and implement the individual's personal rights and integrity? We reject the former possibility. Each approach has its own difficulties, but the use of the doctrine of substituted judgment promotes best the interests of the individual, no matter how difficult the task involved may be. We admit that in this case we are unable to draw upon prior stated preferences the individual may have expressed. An expression of intent by an incompetent person while competent, however, is not essential. "While it may thus be necessary to rely to a greater degree on objective criteria *   *   * the effort to bring the substituted judgment into step with the values and desires of the affected individual must not, and need not, be abandoned." The courts thus must endeavor, as accurately as possible, to determine the wants and needs of this ward as they relate to the sterilization procedure.

b. *Applicable standards.* We now consider the standards the Probate Court must apply when authorizing sterilization upon petition of an incompetent person's parent or guardian. We keep in mind that the court is to determine whether to authorize sterilization when requested by the parents or guardian by finding the incompetent would so choose if competent. No sterilization is to be compelled on the basis of any State or parental interest.

In all cases, the parties must be given adequate notice of the proceedings, an opportunity to be heard in the trial court, and to pursue an appeal. Upon a guardian's petition for an order authorizing the sterilization of his or her ward, the court must appoint a guardian ad litem to represent the ward. The guardian ad litem is to be charged with the responsibility of zealously representing the ward, and must have full opportunity to meet with the ward, present proof, and cross-examine witnesses at the hearing. * * * This adversary posture will ensure that both sides of each issue which the court must consider are thoroughly aired before findings are made and a decision rendered.

In addition to the appointment of a guardian ad litem, the court may appoint independent medical and psychological experts for the purpose of examining the ward and reporting to the court. The experts should report, and the court make, findings regarding: (1) Whether the ward, despite being mentally retarded, is able to make an informed choice as to the need and desirability of sterilization. * * * (2) The physical ability of the ward to procreate. * * * (3) The possibility and effectiveness of less intrusive means of birth control. The court should find that all less drastic contraceptive methods, including supervision, education, and training are unworkable. * * * (4) The medical necessity, if any, for the procedure. A medical necessity could be supported by evidence that the possibility of pregnancy would threaten the physical or mental health of the person. (5) The nature and extent of the individual's disability. This inquiry should focus on the ability of the ward to care for a child, even with reasonable assistance, and the possibility that the ward may marry in the future and, with a spouse, be able to care for a child. * * * (6) The likelihood that the ward will engage in sexual activity likely to result in pregnancy. (7) The possibility of health risks, trauma, or psychological damage from the sterilization operation, as well as pregnancy or childbirth.

The court, to the extent possible, must also "elicit testimony from the incompetent concerning [his or] her understanding and desire for the proposed operation and its consequences." The judge, in his discretion, and the guardian ad litem in his recommendation, should attempt to ascertain the ward's actual preference for sterilization, parenthood, or other means of contraception. This inquiry is an important part of the substituted judgment determination. The result of the judge's exercise of discretion should be the same decision which would be made by the incompetent person, "but taking into account the present and future incompetency of the individual as one of the factors which would necessarily enter into the decision-making process of the competent person."

Additionally, the court must consider the ward's religious beliefs, if any. An individual might choose to refuse sterilization if the operation would be contrary to his or her religious beliefs. "If such a reason is proffered by or on behalf of an incompetent, the judge must evaluate it in the same manner and for the same purposes as any other reason: the question to be addressed is whether certain tenets or practices of the incompetent's faith would cause him [or her] individually to reject the specific [operation] proposed for him [or her] in [the] present circumstances." The Probate Court judge should also consider any special circumstances presented by the parties in favor of, or against, the proposed sterilization.

NOLAN, Justice (dissenting).

I dissent. Sterilization is a species of self mutilation which is almost always irreversible. Its effect is to deprive the sterilized person of her or his capacity to beget or bear a child. We do not deal here with what has been described as therapeutic sterilization in which as a secondary effect to an operative procedure which is necessary to save the life of a person such person is rendered sterile (*e.g.*, cancer of a reproductive organ may require its surgical removal).

The court today has decided that the probate judge has the power to divine the wishes of a severely mentally retarded woman who "currently functions at the level of a four year old" as to whether she should permit herself to be rendered forever incapable of conceiving and bearing a child. To say the least, this is an impossible task.

* * *

Questions and Comments

1. As of the mid-1970's, twenty-four states had eugenic sterilization statutes (a compilation of the states having such laws on the books as of 1975 is set out in Comment, *Eugenic Sterilization Statutes: A Constitutional Re-Evaluation*, 14 J. of Fam.L. 280, n. 2 (1975)). The current legal status of those laws is somewhat uncertain in spite of the 1927 U.S. Supreme Court decision which held that a state statute providing for the involuntary sterilization of "mental defectiveness" is a valid exercise in the state police power and is not repugnant to the due process clause of the Fourteenth Amendment. *See Buck v. Bell*, 274 U.S. 200, 47 S.Ct. 584, 71 L.Ed. 1000 (1927). Various commentators, however, have suggested that legal developments since *Bell* and particularly the "procreational privacy cases" [*e.g.*, *Griswold v. Connecticut*, 381 U.S. 479, 85 S.Ct. 1678, 14 L.Ed.2d 510 (1965); *Roe v. Wade*, 410 U.S. 113, 93 S.Ct. 705, 35 L.Ed.2d 147 (1973); and *Carey v. Population Services International*, 431 U.S. 678, 97 S.Ct. 2010, 52 L.Ed.2d 675 (1977)] either limit or have effectively reversed the holding of *Buck v. Bell*. *See* Burgdorf and Burgdorf, *The Wicked Witch is Almost Dead; Buck v. Bell and the Sterilization of Handicapped Persons;* 50 Temple L.Q. 995 (1977); Vukowtich, *The Dawning of the Brave New World—Legal, Ethical, and Social Issues of Eugenics*, 1971 U.Ill.L.F. 189 (1971); Note, *Eugenic Sterilization*, 13 J. of Fam.L. 344, 345 (1976). *See generally* Cynkar, *Buck v. Bell: "Felt Necessities" v. Fundamental Values*, 81 Col.L.Rev.

1418 (1981), a historical review of the social and legal developments leading to the decision of the Supreme Court in *Buck v. Bell.*

Nevertheless, as recently as 1976 the supreme court of one state, relying on *Buck v. Bell,* affirmed the power of states to adopt and administer appropriately drawn eugenic sterilization statutes. *See In re Moore,* 289 N.C. 95, 221 S.E.2d 307 (1976). As the *Moe* case illustrates, however, governmental power to compel sterilization of incompetent persons has received only restrictive approval by some courts reviewing such petitions. *See also In the Matter of A.W.,* 637 P.2d 366 (Colo.1981); *In the Matter of Grady,* 85 N.J. 235, 426 A.2d 467 (1981); *Guardianship of Hayes,* 93 Wn.2d 228, 608 P.2d 635 (1980).

2.   Where the issue has been raised, most courts have held that a guardian's general powers do not include the authority to consent to the nontherapeutic sterilization of the ward. In none of these cases, however, had the legislature expressly authorized the guardian to consent to nontherapeutic sterilization. Could a legislature give such authority to the guardian, or is an adversary hearing a constitutional requirement? Is the *Parham* case set out at p. 296 dispositive of this issue? Are there any considerations which might argue in favor of a more restrictive grant of authority to the guardian of an adult incompetent?

3.   There is a clear division among courts in the standard to be applied in these cases. Some courts, such as those in New York, apply the best-interest test. For instance, in *Sallmaier* the petition was granted on the basis of testimony by the court-appointed psychiatrist that pregnancy "would have a substantial likelihood of causing a psychiatric reaction in respondent." Courts in other states, however, require the application of the substituted judgment doctrine. In these jurisdictions the test is applicable even where the incompetent person has been retarded since birth. It is not altogether clear, however, how the presumed preference of the individual is to be discerned in these cases. *See Matter of Storar,* 52 N.Y.2d 363, 438 N.Y.S.2d 266, 420 N.E.2d 64 (1981); *In re Moe,* 385 Mass. 555, 432 N.E.2d 712 (1982). *See also Wentzel v. Montgomery General Hospital,* 293 Md. 685, 447 A.2d 1244 (1982), *cert. denied* 459 U.S. 1147, 103 S.Ct. 790, 74 L.Ed.2d 995 (1983).

4.   The application of either the best-interest test or the substituted judgment standard conceivably allows a court to approve sterilization any time the procedure is likely to be of *some* benefit to the incompetent individual. Such benefit might include the avoidance of trauma associated with delivery of a child, or the difficulty the ward might encounter in taking care of any children she might bear. A minority of courts have applied a more stringent standard, which allows the sterilization of an incompetent person only upon a finding that the procedure is medically essential "to preserve the life or physical or mental health of the incompetent person." *In the Matter of A.W.,* 637 P.2d 366, 375 (Colo. 1981). This restrictive approach has, however, been rejected by one court on the basis that it would infringe an incompetent person's right to self-determination as applied through the substituted judgment doctrine. *In the Matter of Moe,* 385 Mass. 555, 432 N.E.2d 712, 722 n. 10 (1982).

5.. While some courts have by way of *dictum* suggested that it is beyond the power of a guardian to authorize the performance of an abortion for an incompetent person, no reported case has to date expressly ruled on the issue. The related question of parental authority to *veto* a minor's decision to seek an abortion has been addressed by the Supreme Court in *Planned Parenthood of Central Missouri v. Danforth*, 428 U.S. 52, 96 S.Ct. 2831, 49 L.Ed.2d 788 (1976). See also, Comment, *Third Party Consent to Abortion Before and After: A Theoretical Analysis*, 15 J. of Fam.L. 508 (1976).

2. *Biomedical Intervention for the Benefit of Others*

In Re GUARDIANSHIP OF PESCINSKI

Supreme Court of Wisconsin, 1975.
67 Wis.2d 4, 226 N.W.2d 180.

WILKIE, Chief Justice.

Does a county court have the power to order an operation to be performed to remove a kidney of an incompetent ward, under guardianship of the person, and transfer it to a sister where the dire need of the transfer is established but where no consent has been given by the incompetent or his guardian *ad litem*, nor has any benefit to the ward been shown?

That is the issue presented on appeal here. The trial court held that it did not have that power and we agree. The appellant, Janice Pescinski Lausier, on her own petition, was appointed guardian of the person of her brother, the respondent, Richard Pescinski. In 1958, Richard was declared incompetent and was committed to Winnebago State Hospital. He has been a committed mental patient since that date, classified as a schizophrenic, chronic, catatonic type.

On January 31, 1974, Janice Pescinski Lausier petitioned for permission to Dr. H.M. Kauffman to conduct tests to determine whether Richard Pescinski was a suitable donor for a kidney transplant for the benefit of his sister, Elaine Jeske. Elaine had both kidneys surgically removed in 1970 because she was suffering from kidney failure diagnosed as chronic glomerulonephritis. In order to sustain her life, she was put on a dialysis machine, which functions as an artificial kidney. Because of the deterioration of Elaine, the petition contended that a kidney transplant was needed. Subsequent tests were completed establishing that Richard was a suitable donor, and a hearing was then held on the subject of whether permission should be granted to perform the transplant. The guardian *ad litem* would not give consent to the transplant and the county court held that it did not have the power to give consent for the operation.

At the time of the hearing Elaine was thirty-eight and her brother Richard was thirty-nine. Evidence was produced at the hearing that the other members of the Pescinski family had been ruled out as possible donors on the basis of either age or health. The father, aged seventy, and the mother, aged sixty-seven, were eliminated as possible donors by Dr. Kauffman because, as a matter of principle, he would not perform the operation on a donor over sixty. A similar rationale was applied by Dr. Kauffman as to all of the six minor children of Elaine, the doctor concluding that he "would not personally use their kidneys" as a matter of his "own moral conviction." Mrs. Jeske's sister, Mrs. Lausier, was excluded as a donor because she has diabetes. Another brother, Ralph Pescinski, testified that he was forty-three years old, had been married twenty years and had ten children, nine of whom remained at home. He is a dairy farmer and did not care to be a donor because there would be nobody to take over his farm and he felt he had a duty to his family to refuse. He further testified that he had a stomach disorder which required a special diet and had a rupture on his left side. He had been to see Dr. Capati at the Neillsville Clinic, who told him he should not get involved and that his family should come first.

The testimony showed that Richard was suffering from schizophrenia—catatonic type, and that while he was in contact with his environment there was marked indifference in his behavior. Dr. Hoffman, the medical director at the Good Samaritan Home, West Bend, Wisconsin, testified that in layman's terms Richard's mental disease was a flight from reality. He estimated Richard's mental capacity to be age twelve. No evidence in the record indicates that Richard consented to the transplant. Absent that consent, there is no question that the trial court's conclusion that it had no power to approve the operation must be sustained.

"A guardian of the person has the care of the ward's person and must look to the latter's health, education, and support." The guardian must act, if at all, "loyally in the best interests of his ward." There is absolutely no evidence here that any interests of the ward will be served by the transplant.

As far as the court's own power to authorize the operation, we are satisfied that the law in Wisconsin is clearly to the contrary. There is no statutory authority given the county court to authorize a kidney transplant or any other surgical procedure on a living person. We decline to adopt the concept of "substituted judgment" which was specifically approved by the Kentucky Court of Appeals in Strunk v. Strunk, 445 S.W.2d 145 (Ky.1969). In that case, the Kentucky court held a court of equity had the power to permit the removal of a kidney from an incompetent ward of the state upon the petition of his committee who was also his mother. Apparently a committee in Kentucky is like a guardian in this state. The Kentucky Court of Appeals authorized the operation based on the application of the doctrine of substituted judgment. However, the court also held that neither the committee nor the county court had the power to authorize the operation, in the absence of a showing that the life of the ward was in jeopardy—only the Court of Appeals had the power. In the instant case the county court had no power to authorize the procedure, and the question is whether this supreme court can by using the doctrine of substituted judgment.

As the dissenting opinion in Strunk v. Strunk points out, "substituted judgment" is nothing more than an application of the maxim that equity will speak for one who cannot speak for himself. Historically, the substituted judgment doctrine was used to allow gifts of the property of an incompetent. If applied literally, it would allow a trial court, or this court, to change the designation on a life insurance policy or make an election for an incompetent widow, without the requirement of a statute authorizing these acts and contrary to prior decisions of this court.

We conclude that the doctrine should not be adopted in this state.

We, therefore, must affirm the lower court's decision that it was without power to approve the operation, and we further decide that there is no such power in this court. An incompetent particularly should have his own interests protected. Certainly no advantage should be taken of him. In the absence of real consent on his part, and in a situation where no benefit to him has been established, we fail to find any authority for the county court, or this court, to approve this operation.

Order affirmed. No costs on this appeal.

DAY, Justice (dissenting).

I would reverse the decision in this case. The majority of the court holds that in the absence of a showing of "benefit" to the incompetent in this case or proof of consent on his part, the trial court and this court lack authority to authorize a kidney transplant operation to be performed on him to save the life of his sister. I disagree.

I think the court as a court of equity does have authority to permit the kidney transplant operation requested in the petition of the guardian of Richard Pescinski. I agree with the reasoning of the Court of Appeals of the state of Kentucky * * * That case involved the authorization of a transplant from a 27-year-old incompetent to his 28-year-old brother. The court in that case did find, based on the testimony of a psychiatrist, that while the incompetent had the mental age of six, it would be of benefit to him to keep his brother alive so that his brother could visit him on occasion; I would regard this as pretty thin soup on which to base a decision as to whether or not the donee is to be permitted to live. In the case before us, if the incompetent brother should happily recover from his mental illness, he would undoubtedly be happy to learn that the transplant of one of his kidneys to his sister saved her life. This at least would be a normal response and hence the transplant is not without benefit to him.

* * *

The majority opinion would forever condemn the incompetent to be always a receiver, a taker, but never a giver. For in holding that only those things which financially or physically benefit the incompetent may be done by the court, he is forever excluded from doing the decent thing, the charitable thing. The British courts have not so held. Two British cases cited in *Strunk* permitted the estate of an incompetent to provide a pension for a faithful servant in one instance and in another to help an indigent brother—this by the device known as "substituted judgment" where the court in effect does for the incompetent what it is sure he would do himself if he had the power to act. This approach gives the incompetent the benefit of the doubt, endows him with the finest qualities of his humanity, assumes the goodness of his nature instead of assuming the opposite.

The equities in this case favor taking the action which may save this mother's life.

3. Incompetent Persons as Research Subjects

The difference between the objectives motivating the inclusion of human subjects in research and the administration of innovative therapy raises significant obstacles to using incompetent persons in research. Innovative therapies employ experimental techniques to treat a patient's disorders. In research the *primary* purpose is the advancement of scientific knowledge, although the results ultimately may benefit the subject or members of the subject's class. The law has normally allowed *consenting* human subjects to participate in biomedical research, even when the research poses substantial risk to the subject. Society's acceptance of the individual's assumption of risk rests on the long-term benefits that may result from the medical discoveries or developments stemming from the research. Participation in research requires the same model of consent as is applicable to treatment. Thus, the research subject must be apprised of all known risks, and the individual's participation must be totally voluntary. *See generally Experiments and Research with Human Beings: Values and Conflicts* (Washington, D.C.: National Academy of Sciences, 1975), at 36–56.

By definition, incompetent persons are unable to give legally binding consent. Yet incompetent persons often suffer from mental disorders or abnormalities that are the legitimate subjects of scientific research. A blanket rule forbidding participation of anyone unable to give valid consent would, therefore, hinder the advancement of medical science. At the same time society has been reluctant to expressly countenance substituted consent in the research context. For instance, there are no reported legal decisions to date addressing the sufficiency of substituted consent where the incompetent ward is to be a research subject. However, some measure of regulation has been achieved by the passage of state laws regulating the conduct of research in institutions. These laws serve to place limits on all research involving institutionalized persons, including those who are incompetent. *E.g.*, Mass.Gen.Laws Ann. c. 111, § 70E (1979); N.Y. Pub.Health Law §§ 2440–2446 (McKinney 1977).

The participation of incompetent persons in research has also received the attention of federal agencies. The National Commission for the Protection of Human Subjects of Biomedical and Behavioral Research has proposed a set of guidelines regulating the conduct of research involving mentally infirm persons in all federally sponsored research institutions. Under the Commission's guidelines, a guardian could consent to an incompetent institutionalized subject's participation in nontherapeutic research, even if the research poses more than minimal risk to the subject. The guidelines define minimal risk as the "probability or magnitude of physical or psychological harm or discomfort that is normally encountered in daily life or in routine medical or psychological examination of normal persons." However, the guardian's consent would only be valid in research which might eventually lead to the amelioration of the subject's disorder or otherwise benefit the subject in the future. *Protection of Human Subjects: Research Involving Those Institutionalized as Mentally Infirm; Report and Recommendation for Public Comment*, 43 Fed.Reg. 11,328, 11,334 (proposed March 17, 1978). The proposed guidelines have yet to be adopted by the Department of Health and Human Services.

Questions and Comments

1. Some authorities have suggested third-party consent as a substitute for that of incompetent persons. The legal system has long employed third-party consent in the context of therapeutic intervention, but case law has not yet indicated what safeguards courts will find necessary to legitimize third-party consent to an incompetent person's participation in therapeutic research. One case that might have shed light on the conditions under which third party consent could be given is *Jobes v. Michigan Department of Mental Health*, Civil No. 74–004–130 DC (Cir. Ct., Wayne City, Mich.1973). Plaintiffs in *Jobes* brought suit to enjoin a state-authorized study that proposed to utilize behaviorally disturbed institutionalized minors. The research protocol contemplated the administration of a zinc supplement in the form of a commercially available vitamin preparation to a test group of children to determine whether there is a relationship between zinc deficiency and inadequate physical or intellectual development. Following commencement of the suit but before the initiation of the trial phase, the Michigan Department of Mental Health agreed to adhere to a proposed administrative rule that would have subjected the proposed research to a series of review requirements following consent by the parents or guardians. As a result, the case was set aside and a judgment never issued.

2. It has been suggested that third-party consent should be legally valid only if the research satisfies three specific conditions. First, the research must pose no more than minimal risk to the subject. Venopunc-

ture or small skin biopsies would probably constitute the maximum allowable physical intrusion under such a standard. Second, the researcher must show that there is no competent person or group of persons capable of serving the scientific design of the protocol, and that non-participation by incompetents would force abandonment of the study or greatly reduce its value. Third, the research must reasonably be expected to benefit the subject or the subject's class at some time in the future. Dickens, *Ethical Issues in Psychiatric Research*, 4 Int'l.J.L. & Psych. 288 (1981).

3. As noted in Chapter III, the distinction between nontherapeutic research and innovative therapy sometimes becomes blurred. Interventions initiated for research purposes may in time become therapeutically oriented. An example of the transformation that may occur is suggested by the research into the treatment of schizophrenia by hemodialysis.

Dialysis is a five hour procedure which involves drawing blood from a patient and circulating it through a machine in order to remove impurities. According to one expert, the procedure "often produces unpleasant psychological effects." "Dialysis for Schizophrenia? Doctors Debate Effects," *New York Times*, March 7, 1981, pg. 1, col. 1. As a result "depression and suicide are very common among renal dialysis recipients." *Id.* Among the possible side effects are the "risks of stroke, infection, and, in the case of equipment failure, death by loss of blood." *Id.*

The first account of hemodialysis experimentation involving schizophrenic patients appeared in a German medical journal in 1960. Since that time various research centers around the world have administered dialysis on an experimental basis. The National Institute of Mental Health, in fact, has recently financed two studies designed to determine the utility of this technique for various subtypes of schizophrenia. *Id.* Other facilities, however, are reported as having provided dialysis as a mode of *treatment* in spite of the fact that the technique is still experimental and poses significant risks for those undergoing the procedure.

Future research in this area will undoubtedly require the involvement of a cross section of schizophrenic subtypes. As a result, it is likely that research protocols will necessitate the inclusion of schizophrenic patients who are incompetent to give consent. Should the guardian have authority to give consent to the participation of an incompetent schizophrenic in such research? How immediate must the potential benefit to the research subject be to justify consent in the light of the risks currently associated with dialysis?

Chapter Eight

MENTAL HEALTH ISSUES AND THE CRIMINAL PROCESS

Table of Sections

I. OVERVIEW

Inevitably any rational system of criminal justice must involve some consideration of the mental state of individuals accused of criminal acts. The purposes underlying the evaluation of the mental status of the accused changes, depending on the particular stage of the criminal process involved.

Even before commencement of criminal proceedings, an examination of the mental condition of the accused may be called for to determine whether prosecution should be waived and civil commitment proceedings initiated. After prosecution for the crime is initiated, the mental competency of the defendant, as it pertains to his ability to participate meaningfully in his trial, may be questioned. Once a defendant is found competent to stand trial and his trial begins, the issue changes to a determination of whether or not the defendant can be held criminally responsible for his act. Here again the mental status of the defendant is in issue, for virtually all serious crimes require that the defendant must have intentionally, knowingly, or recklessly committed a certain act or produced a certain result. In addition, at least up to the present, most state and federal jurisdictions recognize the defense of insanity. Psychiatric opinion in the form of expert testimony is nearly always solicited to present such a defense most effectively.

Following the trial, the opinion of professionals in the mental health field may be sought for still other reasons. After a finding of not guilty by reason of insanity, psychiatric opinion may be obtained to determine whether or not the acquittee is currently mentally ill (a finding of not guilty by reason of insanity means only that the accused was found to be insane *at the time he committed the crime*), and, if so, whether or not his release would create an unreasonable risk of further dangerous or criminal behavior. If, on the other hand, the accused has been found guilty, then mental status indicators are often included in the presentence report used by the judge in determining the appropriate sentence for the criminal.

Since the criminal justice system has obviously made mental status issues a focal point of the decision-making process at many stages, why has the relationship between law and mental health professionals been so troubled? What are the specific points of disagreement that have increasingly led to calls for separation of legal and psychological issues and restrictions on the use of psychiatric evidence? One reason—relating specifically to the insanity defense—is the basic ideological incompatibility of law and psychiatry. The two systems have very different theories about individual responsibility and the basis for criminal liability. The nature of this conflict was described by the authors of a recent commentary on the insanity defense:

> The law tells us that if we commit illegal acts, we must be punished. But the law assumes that we have freely chosen to perform these acts. Psychiatry does not make any such assumption about free will or choice. Psychiatric theory is deterministic and assumes that behavior is caused, shaped, or determined by prior events—either immediate events or those in the distant past—or by

physiological states. For example, to the psychiatrist, an abused child is likely to become an abusive adult because he has learned from his parents that violent behavior is acceptable. He does not choose to abuse others. Or the psychiatrist may believe that chemical imbalances or chemical deficiencies within the brain will precipitate certain violent behaviors when certain external stimuli are present. In neither case could one be said to be "responsible" for the violent action in the sense that one chose it, for one does not (at least within the ordinary meaning of the word) choose either one's parents or one's brain chemistry.

W. Winslade and J. Ross, *The Insanity Plea,* 12–13 (New York: Charles Scribner's Sons, 1983). Thus, there is likely to arise an inherent conflict when psychiatry is called to address issues of criminal responsibility within the conceptual framework of the legal system.

A second source of conflict involves the allocation of decision-making responsibility when the mental status of the accused is subject to question. The legal system is committed to a model that allocates the determination of criminal responsibility to juries and judges. The issue of criminal responsibility is seen, under this model, as involving considerations beyond those that are purely medical or scientific. The ultimate questions are, thus, properly regarded as *not* entirely clinical, but rather ones that involve both legal and moral considerations. *United States v. Lyons,* 731 F.2d 243 (5th Cir.1984). The tendency of psychiatric experts to testify in terms of the ultimate issue rather than addressing the defendant's clinical symptomatology and behavioral patterns is seen as usurping the function of the jury and converting what should be moral/legal issues into clinical ones. Beyond this, critics contend that present limitations in the reliability of psychiatric judgments, coupled with vagueness in the standards that currently control the issue of responsibility, readily lead to capricious jury verdicts.

The variety of standards and procedural approaches that exist today in criminal trials involving the insanity defense is illustrative of the efforts of legislatures and courts to achieve an appropriate balance among competing policy interests. The nature of these interests and the manner in which the legal system has attempted to reconcile them when mental health issues are confronted in the criminal law process is the subject of this chapter.

II. COMPETENCY TO STAND TRIAL

A. INTRODUCTION

The notion that a mentally incompetent defendant may not be subjected to a criminal trial is deeply rooted in the common law. The common law rule was expounded by Blackstone:

If a man in his sound memory commits a capital offence, and before arraignment for it, he becomes mad, he ought not to be arraigned for it; because he is not able to plead to it with that advice and caution that he ought. And if, after he has pleaded, the prisoner becomes mad, he shall not be tried; for how can he make his defence?

4 W. Blackstone, Commentaries 24 (1769). This competency rule had a three-part rationale. First, it was an extension of the ban against trials *in absentia*. Second, the rule was deemed necessary to ensure against the conviction of innocent persons. Third, the trial of a mentally incompetent person was deemed to conflict with notions of common humanity.

In modern American law the common law rule has been elevated into a constitutional principle. *Drope v. Missouri*, 420 U.S. 162, 171–172, 95 S.Ct. 896, 903–904, 43 L.Ed.2d 103 (1975). The cornerstone of the Anglo-American criminal justice system is the entitlement of each litigant to an adequate hearing as embodied in the notion of due process. A necessary corollary of an adversary system, which emphasizes the role of the individual litigant, is the capacity of each party to participate meaningfully in the conduct of a trial. If the accused lacks the capacity to do so, his trial in such circumstances would deprive him of his entitlement to an adequate hearing. The requirement of competency is not subject to waiver by the defendant because:

> "[I]t is contradictory to argue that a defendant may be incompetent, and yet knowingly or intelligently 'waive' his right to have the court determine his capacity to stand trial.

Pate v. Robinson, 383 U.S. 375, 384, 86 S.Ct. 836, 841, 15 L.Ed.2d 815 (1966).

Notwithstanding the fact that the rule requiring competency on the part of a defendant in a criminal case is secured by the Constitution, the exact dimensions of this constitutional rule have not been clearly announced. The issues that have come to the forefront as courts have struggled to develop appropriate standards are considered in the section that follows.

B. THE MEANING OF COMPETENCY

1. Functional Elements of the Standard

Dusky v. United States, 362 U.S. 402, 80 S.Ct. 788, 4 L.Ed.2d 824 (1960), arose from the indictment of Milton Dusky on a charge of violating federal kidnapping statutes. At arraignment on motion on the defense attorney he was committed to the medical center of Springfield, Missouri, for examination to determine his competency to stand trial as provided in 18 U.S.C.A. § 4244. The defendant remained at the medical center for examination for four months. A. R. Matthews, *Mental Disability and the Criminal Law*, American Bar Foundation, 1970 [hereinafter cited as Matthews]. At the subsequent competency hearing the government psychiatric experts were of the unanimous opinion that Dusky was so mentally impaired by his mental illness that he could not adequately assist counsel in his defense. Haddox, Gross, and Pollack, *Mental Competency to Stand Trial While Under the Influence of Drugs*, 7 Loy.L.A.L.Rev. 425, 430–31 (1974). In spite of these findings the trial court found the defendant competent to stand trial. The trial court's holding was affirmed by the Eighth Circuit Court of Appeals which held that "how much mental capacity or alertness a defendant must have to be able to assist his counsel is a question of fact for the trial court [which] cannot be set aside on review unless clearly arbitrary or unwarranted." 271 F.2d 385, 397 (8th Cir.1959). The case was appealed to the U.S. Supreme Court. In an unusual action the brief of the Solicitor General argued in favor of a redetermination of the incompetency issue on the grounds that "[a] trial judge ought, at a minimum, [to] have other expert opinion before he undertakes to disregard the unanimous conclusion of disinterested experts." *Id.* at 430. The opinion of the Supreme Court follows:

DUSKY v. UNITED STATES
Supreme Court of the United States, 1960.
362 U.S. 402, 80 S.Ct. 788, 4 L.Ed.2d 824.

PER CURIAM.

The motion for leave to proceed *in forma pauperis* and the petition for a writ of certiorari are granted. Upon consideration of the entire record we agree with the Solicitor General that "the record in this case does not sufficiently support the findings of competency to stand trial," for to support those findings under 18 U.S.C.A. § 4244 the district judge "would need more information than this record presents." We also agree with the suggestion of the Solicitor General that it is not enough for the district judge to find that "the defendant [is] oriented to time and place and [has] some recollection of events," but that the "test must be whether he has sufficient present ability to consult with his lawyer with a reasonable degree of rational understanding—and whether he has a rational as well as factual understanding of the proceedings against him."

In view of the doubts and ambiguities regarding the legal significance of the psychiatric testimony in this case and the resulting difficulties of retrospectively determining the petitioner's competency as of more than a year ago, we reverse the judgment of the Court of Appeals affirming the judgment of conviction, and remand the case to the District Court for a new hearing to ascertain petitioner's present competency to stand trial, and for a new trial if petitioner is found competent.

It is so ordered.

Questions and Comments

1. Various state statutes have established standards that at least textually, are at variance, though not necessarily inconsistent, with the

Dusky test. But notwithstanding differences in statutory language, state courts generally adhere to the *Dusky* formulation. Moreover, it is likely that the Fourteenth Amendment due process clause obligates a competency test that incorporates at least the core elements of *Dusky*. The Supreme Court has quoted that standard in cases such as *Drope v. Missouri*, 420 U.S. 162, 170, 95 S.Ct. 896, 903, 43 L.Ed.2d 103 (1975), involving a state proceeding, though the Court had occasion to rule only on the procedure followed by the state court. *See also, United States ex rel. Curtis v. Zelker*, 466 F.2d 1092, 1095 n. 5 (2d Cir.1972).

2. The requirement that the defendant have the capacity to consult with his attorney has been broadly construed to include the "ability to confer intelligently, to testify coherently and to follow the evidence presented." *Martin v. Estelle*, 546 F.2d 177, 180 (5th Cir.1977). Thus, any substantial impairment that interferes with the defendant's ability either to communicate or to follow the proceedings with a "reasonable degree of rational understanding" will lead to a finding of incompetency. *Id.*

What specific functions are envisioned by the capacity of the accused to be able to consult with his lawyer with a "reasonable degree of rational understanding"? *Dusky v. United States, supra*, at 402. Among the questions that are typically asked by defense counsel are:

(1) Can the accused consult with you in a rational manner?

(2) Does he have a factual as well as a rational understanding of the proceedings?

(3) Can he communicate with you—not just talk but does he understand the defense or defenses?

(4) Does he understand his options of pleading guilty, not guilty, nolo contendere?

(5) Will he be able to help you in picking the jury?

(6) Will he be able to realistically follow the evidence?

(7) Will he be able to advise you during trial of anticipated adverse evidence?

(8) Can he assist you in locating witnesses?

(9) Does he understand he may take the stand?

(10) Is he agreeable to testifying and, if so, could he do so coherently?

The Insanity Defense: Hearings on S. 818, S. 1106, S. 1558, S. 2669, S. 2672, S. 2678, S. 2745 and S. 2780. Before the Senate Committee on the Judiciary, 97th Cong., 2nd Sess., p. 151 (1982) [hereinafter cited as Senate Insanity Defense Hearings]. (Prepared statement of Frank Maloney, Exhibit A). Would anything be gained if these elements, which define the capacity to rationally consult one's attorney, were explicitly stated as the standard governing competency? For instance, would it lead to more uniform and predictable results?

3. It has been suggested that the ability to consult meaningfully with counsel comprehends a capacity on the part of the defendant "to

remember the facts surrounding the occurrence of the alleged offense."
United States v. Wilson, 263 F.Supp. 528, 531 (1966). Consequently, a
defendant's inability to recall relevant events due to amnesia should, it
has been argued, lead to a determination of incompetency. For the most
part, however, courts have rejected this argument and have held that the
loss of memory due to amnesia unaccompanied by any other disorder is
not an adequate ground upon which to base a finding of incompetency.
See, United States v. Knohl, 379 F.2d 427 (2d Cir.1967); *United States
v. Stevens*, 461 F.2d 317 (7th Cir.1972); *Commonwealth v. Whitt*, 493
Pa. 572, 427 A.2d 623 (1981). But some courts have held that amnesia
may be the basis for a finding of incompetency where the defendant's
inability to recall events is deemed prejudicial to the construction of a
defense. Among the factors to be considered in determining prejudice is
whether the defendant is able, notwithstanding the amnesia, to reconstruct the "evidence relating to the crime and any reasonably possible
alibi." *See, Wilson v. United States*, 391 F.2d 460, 463–64 (D.C.Cir.
1968); *See also United States v. Swanson*, 572 F.2d 523 (5th Cir.1978).

4. *Dusky* established a second and independent requirement for
competency—that the defendant have a rational as well as a factual
understanding of the proceedings. This emphasis on "rationality" as an
ingredient of understanding undoubtedly signals a requirement of comprehension going beyond surface knowledge. *People v. Swallow*, 60
Misc.2d 171, 175, 301 N.Y.S.2d 798, 803 (1969). But the "rational"
understanding called for by *Dusky* means no more than some reasonable
degree of comprehension; an understanding without any impairment is
not required. Consequently, defendants who have some intellectual or
emotional disturbance preventing them from functioning at normal levels
of effectiveness can still meet the standard. Even the presence of a
psychosis is not necessarily controlling on the question of competency.
Feguer v. United States, 302 F.2d 214, 236 (8th Cir.1962). In the final
analysis, the dispositive issue is the degree of incapacity and its effect on
the accused's ability to "consult with counsel and understand the proceedings against him." *United States v. Swanson*, 572 F.2d 523, 526
(5th Cir.1978).

5. Although a defendant's incapacity may be attributable to physical
rather than mental or psychiatric causes, the federal statute and numerous state laws governing the determination of incompetency incorporate
the requirement that the defendant be "insane or otherwise *mentally*
incompetent" [emphasis added]. 18 U.S.C.A. § 4244. Notwithstanding
such restrictive language, it is unlikely that a finding of incompetency
could constitutionally be limited to persons suffering from a mental
disorder. Whenever the issue has arisen, courts have tended to ignore
the statutory restriction and have focused instead on the degree of
incapacitation. *People ex rel. Myers v. Briggs*, 46 Ill.2d 281, 263 N.E.2d
109 (1970). *See also Jackson v. Indiana*, 406 U.S. 715, 735–36, 92 S.Ct.
1845, 1856–57, 32 L.Ed.2d 435 (1972).

6. In determining competency the trier of fact (which most commonly will be a judge rather than a jury) is permitted to take into account
various types of evidence, including expert opinion and the testimony of

lay witnesses, which may include the defendant's attorney. *See, People v. Samuel*, 29 Cal.3d 489, 174 Cal.Rptr. 684, 629 P.2d 485 (1981), and *LeBron v. United States*, 229 F.2d 16 (1955). Additionally the trier of fact may consider his own impressions gathered from the defendant's appearance and demeanor during the proceedings. *United States ex rel. McGough v. Hewitt*, 528 F.2d 339, 344 (3d Cir.1975). Moreover, since the determination of competency involves the application of a legal standard, the trier of fact is not compelled to accept the medical expert's conclusions, though they may not be arbitrarily disregarded. For instance, in *People v. Samuel, supra*, the California Supreme Court held, in light of the undisputed expert testimony of five psychiatrists, that the defendant was incompetent to stand trial and the trial court had no basis to find the defendant competent.

2. *Legal Consequences of Drug-Induced Competency*

STATE v. JOJOLA

Court of Appeals, New Mexico, 1976.
89 N.M. 489, 553 P.2d 1296.

OPINION

WOOD, Chief Judge.

Defendant was convicted of two counts of aggravated sodomy. Section 40A–9–7, N.M.S.A.1953 (2d Repl. Vol. 6), subsequently repealed. He asserts that the trial court improperly admitted hearsay evidence to show that the offenses occurred on the date charged— "on or about the 1st day of February, 1975". We do not consider whether the evidence was inadmissible hearsay. The date of the offenses was established through testimony to which no objection was made and which was independent of the alleged hearsay evidence. The issues discussed are: (1) pre-indictment delay, and (2) medication of defendant.

*   *   *

[The court held that defendant's contention of prejudicial pre-trial delay was without merit.]

Medication of Defendant

Defendant had a long history of mental illness. An evidentiary hearing was held to determine defendant's competency to stand trial.

The evidence was that defendant was psychotic; that he suffered from a schizophrenia of the paranoid type with signs of being autistic. His paranoia was described as the type where defendant feels he is persecuted by just about everyone with whom he is in contact. "Autistic" was described as an exaggerated form of daydreaming, daydreaming to the point where one is completely detached from what is going on around one. There was evidence that defendant's condition was in a state of remission, being controlled by a dosage of Thorazine.

Thorazine was described as a type of phenothiazine medication. The effect of Thorazine was described as inhibiting or depressing the emotional part of the brain and allowing the cognitive part to come back into play. A person being dosed with Thorazine is sedated emotionally more than cognitively and would have the ability to make decisions and communicate with others.

The evidence was that defendant was competent to stand trial so long as he was medicated with Thorazine.

* * *

Defendant testified that he did not wish to go to trial while using Thorazine. His request was denied. He claims the trial court violated his right to due process of law in not permitting defendant to be tried when he was not under the influence of Thorazine. This due process claim has two parts: (1) the absolute right to be tried when not being medicated with Thorazine, and (2) the right not to be so tried because his trial demeanor was relevant to his theory of defense.

The inference from the record is that the Thorazine was administered to defendant by officials at the New Mexico State Hospital at Las Vegas. There is no evidence that defendant consented to taking Thorazine. The record is to the effect that the State had undertaken to control defendant's behavior by administering Thorazine.

In contending that he has an absolute right to be tried free from the influence of Thorazine, defendant relies on *State v. Maryott*, 6 Wash.App. 96, 492 P.2d 239 (1971). *Maryott* holds that the state had no right, without defendant's consent, to administer tranquilizing drugs to control a defendant's behavior during trial. Maryott was administered substantial doseages of Sparine, Librium and chloral hydrate by his jailers. "Expert testimony indicated the dosages administered would affect the thought, expression, manner and content of the person using the drugs." The decision in *Maryott* is based on freedom of thought, the right to appear in court with mental faculties unfettered and the state's action in controlling defendant's mental processes.

We do not agree that *Maryott* is controlling. There is no evidence that Thorazine affected defendant's thought processes or the contents of defendant's thoughts; the affirmative evidence is that Thorazine allows the cognitive part of the brain to come back into play. The expert witnesses declined to call Thorazine a mind altering drug. "Rather, Thorazine allows the mind to operate as it might were there not some organic or other type of illness affecting the mind." This difference in the facts makes *Maryott* inapplicable to this case.

In *State v. Hancock*, [247 Or. 21, 426 P.2d 872 (1967)] a physician's prescription for Valium was administered to defendant by county health authorities. In *Hancock*, as in this case, the medication was for the purpose of controlling defendant's emotions. Hancock claimed he was denied a fair trial because he was under the influence of tranquilizers which allegedly impaired his mental functions and ability to confront his accusers. The Oregon Court held there was no showing that the Valium impaired defendant's mental function in any way during his trial, and that defendant was not denied a fair trial.

The evidence in this case was that Thorazine enabled defendant to confer with his attorney and answer questions. "With this patient Thorazine brings him to the point that he does seem to me to be able to appreciate the charges, the consequences, the atmosphere of the courtroom, and why it is being done * * *." Thorazine enabled "the patient to relate in a realistic way, to see things as they really are." Defendant took the stand in his own defense. There is no claim that defendant was unable to comprehend or to fully participate in the trial proceedings.

The facts in this case are similar to those in *State v. Hancock, supra.* In the absence of evidence that defendant's thought processes or the contents of defendant's thoughts were affected by the Thorazine, we hold that defendant was not denied due process because the trial took place while he was being medicated with Thorazine.

In so holding, we have not overlooked the contention that all of the effects of Thorazine are unknown. The answer is that there was evidence as to the effects of Thorazine on this defendant, and that evidence does not show that defendant was denied due process because he was tried while taking Thorazine.

The evidence supports defendant's claim that his courtroom demeanor was affected by the Thorazine. He was sedated emotionally and had a calmer demeanor. Defendant asserts his demeanor was relevant to his theory of defense and therefore due process was violated because the jury saw only his altered demeanor during his trial.

Several cases hold that a due process question is presented if a defendant's demeanor is altered by medication and defendant's demeanor is relevant to any issue to be decided by the jury. There was a due process issue in *State v. Maryott*, supra, and *In Re Pray*, 133 Vt. 253, 336 A.2d 174 (1975) because of the insanity defense.

* * *

Once a due process issue exists, it must be determined whether due process has been violated. *State v. Gwaltney*, 77 Wash.2d 906, 468 P.2d 433 (1970) states: "The inability of a defendant to effectively express to a judge or jury his true emotional feelings on a subject is a fact that can be adequately explained to the trier of fact by either the defendant himself or by another witness. It is not a fact of which a judge or jury cannot be appropriately and effectively advised."

The jury was not informed that defendant had been sedated emotionally. A pretrial ruling of the trial court states: "[T]he defense can introduce any prior unusual behavior of the Defendant as evidence at the trial and, in addition, can introduce at trial as evidence the fact that he [is] using Thorazine and the effect that the drug medication has on the Defendant by expert testimony, unless the Court is persuaded to rule otherwise during trial proceedings."

Assuming that a due process issue existed in this case, there is nothing showing due process was in fact violated. Defendant was expressly given the opportunity to inform the jury as to the fact of Thorazine medication and its effect upon defendant. No effort was made to introduce such evidence, yet the record shows that defendant knew about the medication and its effect and had presented evidence on this issue prior to trial. Thus, even if a due process issue existed, there was no violation of due process.

Another answer to defendant's contention is that this record does not show a due process issue existed. In pretrial hearings, defendant contended that "it's going to be an important facet of the defense's theory that children in the neighborhood make up stories about Mr. Jojola"; that "a story made up by individuals got out of hand"; that when defendant takes the stand and appears normal "that is going to have an effect upon whether or not the jury would believe that indeed children would make up stories about a person such as this". This theory was not pursued at trial. There was no evidence about "made-up stories".

Defendant's claim that due process was violated because his demeanor was relevant to a defense theory is not supported by the record. Because the record does not show that the administration of Thorazine has affected defendant's defense or his right to a fair trial, we do not reach the question of what, if any, consequences result in a situation where the State involuntarily administers a medication.

The judgment and sentence are affirmed.

It is so ordered.

Questions and Comments

1. In the absence of a statutory prohibition, most state courts have followed the reasoning of the court in *State v. Jojola* to permit the trial of a defendant where competency is attained as a result of psychotropic medication. *See, e.g., State v. Stacy,* 556 S.W.2d 552 (Tenn.1977), and *People v. Parsons,* 82 Misc.2d 1090, 371 N.Y.S.2d 840 (1975). One court, however, has held that due process is violated when a defendant in a criminal trial is subjected to compelled medication. *State v. Maryott,* 6 Wn.App. 96, 492 P.2d 239 (1971). The holding was not based on the lack of trustworthiness of competency achieved by medication, but rather

because any *compelled* medication, which might effect the defendant's mental status, was deemed to violate the defendant's "freedom of thought."

As explained by the court in *Maryott*:

> When the state is allowed, during the time of trial, to administer drugs to a defendant, contrary to his will, it is able to affect the judgment and capacity of its own adversary. Our total legal tradition is contrary to this. Although drugs have not always been the subtle menace they now are in our society, action by the state which affected the reason of a defendant at the time of trial by other means was forbidden at an early time.

Id. at 241.

See also, In re Pray, 133 Vt. 253, 336 A.2d 174 (1975).

2. A minority of states have enacted *legislation* disallowing the trial of an *incompetent* defendant whose competency is obtained by the administration of antipsychotic medication. Winick, *Psychotropic Medication and Competency to Stand Trial*, 1977 A.F.R.J. 769, 772–775 (1977). States which impose this limitation by statute, moreover, generally extend the rule to defendants whose maintenance on psychotropic medication is voluntary. *Id.* at 772–773. The trend, however, is toward a repeal of these "automatic" bar statutes. *See, e.g.*, West's Fla.Stat. Ann. § 918.15(4)(a), Ohio Rev.Code § 2945.37.

3. The constitutional right of civilly committed patients to decline psychotropic medication has not been authoritatively resolved. See p. 444 *supra*. Would any constitutional restrictions on forced medication in the civil commitment context be *equally* applicable to the criminal trial process, where the purpose of the compelled medication is to restore the defendant's competency? Is the government interest in compelling medication the same in both situations? What if the defendant's attorney is convinced that a prompt trial would be in the defendant's interest? Should the attorney have the authority to waive any rights the defendant may have to be free from compelled medication?

4. As noted above, in most states a defendant can be forcibly medicated in order to restore and maintain his competency to stand trial. What problems does this raise for a defendant who, if brought to trial, would rely on the insanity defense? From the standpoint of the defendant, his overtly psychotic condition during the trial could enhance the credibility of his claim that he was "insane" at the time of the crime. Courts have split on whether a conviction obtained against a forcibly medicated defendant who has pleaded the defense of insanity may stand. Most states have not adopted a *per se* rule but will permit a conviction to stand where the defendant has had an opportunity to inform the jury of the medication and "its effect upon the defendant." *State v. Jojola, supra*, at 1300. *See also, State v. Law*, 270 S.C. 664, 244 S.E.2d 302 (1978).

Some courts, however, have held that the prejudice to the defendant cannot be cured by such a disclosure. One court, in reversing the conviction of a defendant who had been administered psychotropic medication, noted:

> The ability to present expert testimony describing the effect of medication on the defendant is not an adequate substitute. At best, such testimony would serve only to mitigate the unfair prejudice which may accrue to the defendant as a consequence of his controlled outward appearance. It cannot compensate for the positive value to the defendant's case of his own demeanor in an unmedicated condition. Moreover, "[i]f the state may administer tranquilizers to a defendant who objects, the state then is, in effect, permitted to determine what the jury will see or not see of the defendant's case by medically altering the attitude, appearance and demeanor of the defendant, when they are relevant to the jury's consideration of his mental condition." *State v. Maryott, supra* 6 Wash.App. at 102, 492 P.2d 239.

Commonwealth v. Louraine, 390 Mass. 28, 453 N.E.2d 437, 442 (1983).

5. Whether the medication was prejudicial to a defendant who has pleaded the insanity defense may depend in part on which insanity test is applied in that jurisdiction. As stated in *Commonwealth v. Louraine, supra*, at 444, n. 11:

> In *State v. Law*, 270 S.C. 664, 244 S.E.2d 302 (1978), the court held that the administration of psychotropic medication to the defendant during trial did not undermine his insanity defense. The case is distinguishable. Under South Carolina law, the defendant's sanity was judged by the M'Naghten test. *Id.* at 667, 244 S.E.2d 302. Under that test, the jury were asked to decide whether the defendant had the mental capacity to distinguish moral or legal right from moral or legal wrong, and to recognize the particular act charged as morally or legally wrong. *Id.* The test we have adopted is much broader and relieves the defendant of criminal responsibility if, at the time of the conduct, as a result of mental disease or defect, he lacked substantial capacity to conform his conduct to the requirements of the law. *Commonwealth v. McHoul*, 352 Mass. 544, 546–547, 226 N.E.2d 556 (1967). The defendant's demeanor is most relevant to this broader element of our test. Further, we adopted this broader test in part because it permitted a wider range of testimony to be received. *Id.* at 550, 226 N.E.2d 556.

C. DETERMINATION OF COMPETENCY: PROCEDURAL ASPECTS

1. Stage I: Initiating the Inquiry

In virtually all jurisdictions the adjudication of incompetency entails a three stage process. The first is essentially a pleading stage, involving a motion by either the defendant or prosecutor raising the issue. The issue may also be raised by the court on its motion. In fact, whenever "the evidence [presented] raises a 'bona fide' doubt as to the defendant's competence to stand trial, the trial court is under a constitutional obligation to raise the issue on its own motion and initiate a hearing." *Pate v. Robinson*, 383 U.S. 375, 385, 86 S.Ct. 836, 842, 15 L.Ed.2d 815 (1966). Once the question has been raised, neither the defendant nor his attorney can waive the issue and demand that the case be brought to trial. *Id.* at 384, 86 S.Ct. at 841.

Due process requires that the defendant be competent throughout the trial. *Drope v. Missouri*, 420 U.S. 162, 181, 95 S.Ct. 896, 908, 43 L.Ed.2d 103 (1975). As a consequence, an inquiry as to competency may be initiated at any point in the proceeding and in some jurisdictions even after trial and sentencing. The issue may also be raised for the first time in a federal *habeas corpus* action months or even years after the trial. *Clark v. Beto*, 359 F.2d 554 (5th Cir.1966); *United States v. Makris*, 535 F.2d 899, 904 (5th Cir.1976).

In most jurisdictions the initial motion raising the issue of competency automatically triggers a psychiatric examination. This examination usually is conducted by one or more experts who are appointed by the court and whose opinions are therefore regarded as impartial. Elsewhere the ordering of the examination is within the discretion of the judge. Unless there is sufficient evidence to raise a "bona fide doubt" as to the defendant's competency, the defendant has no constitutional right to a psychiatric examination. *Tyler v. Beto*, 391 F.2d 993, 997 (5th Cir.1968). The testimony of one lay witness to the effect that the defendant had been acting "peculiar" has been held to meet the test of "substantial doubt" requiring a psychiatric referral. *Id.*

2. Stage II: Preliminary Determination of Competency

The determination by the court of whether there are sufficient grounds to hold a formal hearing constitutes the second stage. As a practical matter, this determination is heavily influenced by the results of the psychiatric evaluation report. In the federal system, for instance, if the psychiatric report indicates that the defendant may be incompetent, a hearing on the question is mandatory. Aside from any statutory requirement that may mandate a hearing, the Constitution itself requires a hearing whenever sufficient evidence pointing to incompetency has been presented to the court. While the Supreme Court has declined to define the quantum of evidence that compels a hearing, it has held that a standard couched in terms of evidence raising a "bona fide doubt" satisfies constitutional requirements. *Drope v. Missouri*, 420 U.S. 162, 172–173, 95 S.Ct. 896, 904, 43 L.Ed.2d 103 (1975). Lower court decisions, in turn, have held that a "bona fide doubt" exists where there is any substantial evidence of incompetency. *Chavez v. United States*, 656 F.2d 512, 517–18 (9th Cir.1981). In deciding whether there is substantial evidence, the trial court must accept as true all evidence suggesting incompetency. It may reach the issue of credibility only after the actual adversary competency hearing.

3. Stage III: The Hearing

The determination of competency occurs at a separate and discrete hearing, which may take place either before, in the middle of, or after the guilt adjudication phase. The principal witness in this phase of the proceedings will usually be the psychiatric expert who conducted the initial mental status examination. Both the defendant and prosecutor may introduce additional evidence, including the testimony of lay or expert witnesses.

The hearing is adversary in nature, and the defendant has the right to be represented by counsel and to cross-examine adverse witnesses. The defendant, however, does not have the full range of procedural rights that pertain to the guilt adjudication stage of the trial. For instance, the defendant does not have a constitutional right to have the issue decided by a jury. In fact, it is generally the trial judge who makes the determination, though in some jurisdictions the court is empowered to submit the matter to a jury.

A second distinction pertains to the burden of proof, which in most jurisdictions is allocated to the defendant. Even when it rests with the prosecution, as it does in the federal system, it is the preponderance of the evidence standard rather than the beyond a reasonable doubt standard which governs. *United States v. Makris*, 535 F.2d 899, 906 (5th Cir.1976); *United States v. Digilio*, 538 F.2d 972, 988 (3d Cir.1976).

A final point of difference is the scope of the privilege against self-incrimination. The privilege has been held to apply in only limited form in the hearing to determine competency. For instance, the privilege may not be invoked by the defendant to bar the testimony of the examining psychiatrist when the testimony is directed to the issue of competency. *Estelle v. Smith*, 451 U.S. 454, 101 S.Ct. 1866, 68 L.Ed.2d 359 (1981).

Questions and Comments

1. Considerations related to trial strategy rather than competency itself may cause either the defendant or the prosecution to initiate a competency proceeding. For instance, in those jurisdictions that do not provide indigent defendants with funds to employ psychiatric experts to assist in the presentation of an insanity defense (*see* p. 602, *infra*), the defendant may use the incompetency hearing procedures as a means of obtaining a subsidized psychiatric evaluation for later use. *See* Matthews at 89–96.

Incompetency proceedings and the examination triggered by it may also be invoked by the *prosecution* for reasons unrelated to the issue of incompetency. As noted by the author of a comprehensive field study of the incompetency to stand trial procedures:

* * *

When a case shapes up from the start as a contested defense of insanity, the prosecution may raise the issue of competency to obtain testimony of psychiatric experts who tend to be prosecution-oriented (particularly if they are associated with a specialized forensic examination unit).

A. Matthews, *Mental Disability and the Criminal Law*, American Bar Foundation, pg. 89–96 (1970).

2. As noted in the text above, the privilege against self-incrimination does not bar the testimony of the examining psychiatrist when it concerns the issue of competency. However, the Fifth Amendment privilege may preclude the use of statements made by the defendant at the pre-trial competency assessment examination when those statements or any psychiatric assessments based on those statements, are used in a subsequent *sentencing hearing. See, Estelle v. Smith*, 451 U.S. 454, 101 S.Ct. 1866, 68 L.Ed.2d 359 (1981).

3. In contrast to the insanity defense issue, the competency of the defendant to stand trial is *not* a jury question in most states and in the federal system. *United States v. Maret*, 433 F.2d 1064, 1067 (8th Cir. 1970). Moreover, delegating the issue to the judge does not violate the defendant's Sixth Amendment right to a jury in criminal cases since the issue does not go to the guilt or innocence of the defendant. *People v. Samuel*, 29 Cal.3d 489, 174 Cal.Rptr. 684, 692, 629 P.2d 485 (1981). *See also*, Slavenko, *The Developing Law of Competency to Stand Trial*, 5 J.Psych. & L. 165, 168 (1977).

4. In some states, such as North Carolina, a court determination that there are sufficient grounds to have a formal hearing leads to the referral of the accused to a state diagnostic facility. *See* Ronald Roesch and Stephen L. Golding, *Competency to Stand Trial* (Urbana: Univ. of Ill. Press, 1980). It is not uncommon for individuals referred to evaluation facilities to be held in excess of 41 days. *Id.* at 142. *See also* Matthews at 82.

One study of individuals referred to this type of facility found that only 11 persons of a total sample of 151 defendants were determined by the facility to be incompetent. Roesch and Golding at 177. These findings led the authors of the study to suggest the establishment of local interdisciplinary screening panels (consisting of "representatives of both the legal and the mental health professionals"), which would be responsible for conducting a mental evaluation of all defendants. *Id.* at 205. The evaluation of the screening panel would, in turn, be presented to the judge hearing the case who would then determine whether more extensive evaluations were justified. *Id.* at 207.

5. A decision finding the accused competent is reviewable either by appeal in the event of the defendant's conviction or in a *habeas corpus* proceeding. It has been generally held that the competency determination is a question of fact which may not be set aside on appeal unless clearly erroneous. *United States v. Green*, 544 F.2d 138, 145 (3d Cir. 1976). A somewhat more searching standard of review has been applied by some courts on the basis that the question of competency involves a mixed question of law and fact having "direct constitutional implications." *United States v. Makris*, 535 F.2d 899, 907 (5th Cir.1976). *See*

also, People v. Samuel, 29 Cal.3d 489, 174 Cal.Rptr. 684, 692, 629 P.2d 485 (1981).

D. DISPOSITION FOLLOWING A FINDING OF INCOM-
PETENCY

It was traditionally the practice in most states to commit automatically a defendant found incompetent to stand trial. Moreover, the commitment would be indefinite; the defendant's release could only come about if he were restored to competency and brought to trial or if the charges were dismissed by the prosecutor. As a consequence, it was common for persons who neither had been convicted of a crime nor had been committed in accordance with the normal commitment procedures of the state to be incarcerated for extended periods in institutions for the criminally insane.

JACKSON v. INDIANA

Supreme Court of the United States, 1972.
406 U.S. 715, 92 S.Ct. 1845, 32 L.Ed.2d 435.

Mr. Justice BLACKMUN delivered the opinion of the Court.

We are here concerned with the constitutionality of certain aspects of Indiana's system for pretrial commitment of one accused of crime.

Petitioner, Theon Jackson, is a mentally defective deaf mute with a mental level of a pre-school child. He cannot read, write, or otherwise communicate except through limited sign language. In May 1968, at age 27, he was charged in the Criminal Court of Marion County, Indiana, with separate robberies of two women. The offenses were alleged to have occurred the preceding July. The first involved property (a purse and its contents) of the value of four dollars. The second concerned five dollars in money. The record sheds no light on these charges since, upon receipt of not-guilty pleas from Jackson, the trial court set in motion the Indiana procedures for determining his competency to stand trial.

As the statute requires, the court appointed two psychiatrists to examine Jackson. A competency hearing was subsequently held at which petitioner was represented by counsel. The court received the examining doctors' joint written report and oral testimony from them and from a deaf-school interpreter through whom they had attempted to communicate with petitioner. The report concluded that Jackson's almost non-existent communication skill, together with his lack of hearing and his mental deficiency, left him unable to understand the nature of the charges against him or to participate in his defense. One doctor testified that it was extremely unlikely that petitioner could ever learn to read or write and questioned whether petitioner even had the ability to develop any proficiency in sign language. He believed that the interpreter had not been able to communicate with petitioner to any great extent and testified that petitioner's "prognosis appears rather dim." The other doctor testified that even if Jackson were not a deaf mute, he would be incompetent to stand trial, and doubted whether petitioner had sufficient intelligence ever to develop the necessary communication skills. The interpreter testified that Indiana had no facilities that could help someone as badly off as Jackson to learn minimal communication skills.

On this evidence, the trial court found that Jackson "lack[ed] comprehension sufficient to make his defense," and ordered him committed to the Indiana Department of Mental Health until such time as that Department should certify to the court that "the defendant is sane."

Petitioner's counsel then filed a motion for a new trial, contending that there was no evidence that Jackson was "insane," or that he would ever attain a status which the court might regard as "sane" in the sense of competency to stand trial. * * * On appeal the Supreme Court of Indiana affirmed, with one judge dissenting. * * *

I. Indiana Commitment Procedures

Section 9–1706a contains both the procedural and substantive requirements for pretrial commitment of incompetent criminal defendants in Indiana. If at any time before submission of the case to the court or jury the trial judge has "reasonable ground" to believe the defendant "to be insane," [2] he must appoint two examining physicians and schedule a competency hearing. The hearing is to the court alone, without a jury. The examining physicians' testimony and "other evidence" may be adduced on the issue of incompetency. If the court finds the defendant "has not comprehension sufficient to understand the proceedings and make his defense," trial is delayed or continued and the defendant is remanded to the state department of mental health to be confined in an "appropriate psychiatric institution." The section further provides that "[w]henever the defendant shall become sane" the superintendent of the institution shall certify that fact to the court, and the court shall order him brought on to trial. The court may also make such an order *sua sponte*. There is no statutory provision for periodic review of the defendant's condition by either the court or mental health authorities. * * *

Petitioner's central contention is that the State, in seeking in effect to commit him to a mental institution indefinitely, should have been required to invoke the standards and procedures of Ind.Ann. Stat. § 22–1907, now Ind.Code 16–15–1–3 (1971), governing commitment of "feeble-minded" persons. * * * If the judge determines that the individual is indeed "feeble-minded," he enters an order of commitment and directs the clerk of the court to apply for the

---

2. The section refers at several points to the defendant's "sanity." This term is nowhere defined. In context, and in the absence of a contrary statutory construction by the state courts, it appears that the term is intended to be synonymous with competence to stand trial.

person's admission "to the superintendent of the institution for feeble-minded persons located in the district in which said county is situated." A person committed under this section may be released "at any time," provided that "in the judgment of the superintendent, the mental and physical condition of the patient justifies it." The statutes do not define either "feeble-mindedness" or "insanity" as used in § 22–1907. But a statute establishing a special institution for care of such persons, refers to the duty of the State to provide care for its citizens who are "feeble-minded, and are therefore unable properly to care for themselves." These provisions evidently afford the State a vehicle for commitment of persons in need of custodial care who are "not insane" and therefore do not qualify as "mentally ill" under the State's general involuntary civil commitment scheme.

Scant attention was paid this general civil commitment law by the Indiana courts in the present case. An understanding of it, however, is essential to a full airing of the equal protection claims raised by petitioner. Section 22–1201(1) defines a "mentally ill person" as one who

> "is afflicted with a psychiatric disorder which substantially impairs his mental health; and, because of such psychiatric disorder, requires care, treatment, training or detention in the interest of the welfare of such person or the welfare of others of the community in which such person resides."

Section 22–1201(2) defines a "psychiatric disorder" to be any mental illness or disease, including any mental deficiency, epilepsy, alcoholism, or drug addiction. Other sections specify procedures for involuntary commitment of "mentally ill" persons that are substantially similar to those for commitment of the feeble-minded. * * * An individual adjudged mentally ill under these sections is remanded to the department of mental health for assignment to an appropriate institution. Discharge is in the discretion of the superintendent of the particular institution to which the person is assigned. The individual, however, remains within the court's custody, and release can therefore be revoked upon a hearing.

II. EQUAL PROTECTION

Because the evidence established little likelihood of improvement in petitioner's condition he argues that commitment under § 9–1706a in his case amounted to a commitment for life. This deprived him of equal protection, he contends, because, absent the criminal charges pending against him, the State would have had to proceed under other statutes generally applicable to all other citizens: either the commitment procedures for feeble-minded persons, or those for mentally ill persons. * * *

In *Baxstrom v. Herold*, 383 U.S. 107, 86 S.Ct. 760, 15 L.Ed.2d 620 (1966), the Court held that a state prisoner civilly committed at the end of his prison sentence on the finding of a surrogate was denied equal protection when he was deprived of a jury trial that the State made generally available to all other persons civilly committed. Rejecting the State's argument that Baxstrom's conviction and sentence constituted adequate justification for the difference in procedures, the Court said that "there is no conceivable basis for distinguishing the commitment of a person who is nearing the end of a penal term from all other civil commitments." * * *

If criminal conviction and imposition of sentence are insufficient to justify less procedural and substantive protection against indefinite commitment than that generally available to all others, the mere filing of criminal charges surely cannot suffice. * * *

Respondent argues, however, that because the record fails to establish affirmatively that Jackson will never improve, his commitment "until sane" is not really an indeterminate one. It is only temporary, pending possible change in his condition. Thus, presumably, it cannot be judged against commitments under other state statutes that are truly indeterminate. * * *

Were the State's factual premise that Jackson's commitment is only temporary a valid one, this might well be a different case. But the record does not support that premise. One of the doctors testified that in his view Jackson would be unable to acquire the substantially improved communication skills that would be necessary for him to participate in any defense. The prognosis for petitioner's developing such skills, he testified, appeared "rather dim." In answer to a question whether Jackson would ever be able to comprehend the charges or participate in his defense, even after commitment and treatment, the doctor said, "I doubt it, I don't believe so." The other psychiatrist testified that even if Jackson were able to develop such skills, he would *still* be unable to comprehend the proceedings or aid counsel due to his mental deficiency. * * * There is nothing in the record that even points to any possibility that Jackson's present condition can be remedied at any future time. * * *

We note also that neither the Indiana statute nor state practice makes the likelihood of the defendant's improvement a relevant factor. The State did not seek to make any such showing, and the record clearly establishes that the chances of Jackson's ever meeting the competency standards of § 9–1706a are at best minimal, if not nonexistent. The record also rebuts any contention that the commitment could contribute to Jackson's improvement. Jackson's § 9–1706a commitment is permanent in practical effect.

We therefore must turn to the question whether, because of the pendency of the criminal charges that triggered the State's invocation of § 9–1706a, Jackson was deprived of substantial rights to which he would have been entitled under either of the other two state commitment statutes. *Baxstrom* held that the State cannot withhold from a few the procedural protections or the substantive requirements for commitment that are available to all others. In this case commitment procedures under all three statutes appear substantially similar: notice, examination by two doctors, and a full judicial hearing at which the individual is represented by counsel and can cross-examine witnesses and introduce evidence. Under each of the three statutes, the commitment determination is made by the court alone, and appellate review is available.

In contrast, however, what the State must show to commit a defendant under § 9–1706a, and the circumstances under which an individual so committed may be released, are substantially different from the standards under the other two statutes.

Under § 9–1706a, the State needed to show only Jackson's inability to stand trial. We are unable to say that, on the record before us, Indiana could have civilly committed him as mentally ill under § 22–1209 or committed him as feeble-minded under § 22–1907. The former requires at least (1) a showing of mental illness and (2) a showing that the individual is in need of "care, treatment, training or detention." Whether Jackson's mental deficiency would meet the first test is unclear; neither examining physician addressed himself to this. Furthermore, it is problematical whether commitment for "treatment" or "training" would be appropriate since the record establishes that none is available for Jackson's condition at any state institution. The record also fails to establish that Jackson is in need of custodial care or "detention." He has been employed at times, and there is no evidence that the care he long received at home has become inadequate. The statute appears to require an independent showing of dangerousness ("requires * * * detention in the interest of the welfare of such person or * * * others * * *"). Insofar as it may require such a showing, the pending criminal charges are insufficient to establish it, and no other supporting evidence was introduced. For the same reasons, we cannot say that this record would support a feeble-mindedness commitment under § 22–1907 on the ground that Jackson is "unable properly to care for [himself]."

More important, an individual committed as feeble-minded is eligible for release when his condition "justifies it," and an individual civilly committed as mentally ill when the "superintendent or administrator shall discharge such person *or* [when] cured of such illness." Thus, in either case release is appropriate when the individual no longer requires the custodial care or treatment or detention that occasioned the commitment, or when the department of mental health believes release would be in his best interests. The evidence available concerning Jackson's past employment and home care strongly suggests that under these standards he might be eligible for release at almost any time, even if he did not improve. On the other hand, by the terms of his present § 9–1706a commitment, he will not be entitled to release at all, absent an unlikely substantial change for the better in his condition.   * * *

As we noted above, we cannot conclude that pending criminal charges provide a greater justification for different treatment than conviction and sentence. Consequently, we hold that by subjecting Jackson to a more lenient commitment standard and to a more stringent standard of release than those generally applicable to all others not charged with offenses, and by thus condemning him in effect to permanent institutionalization without the showing required for commitment or the opportunity for release afforded by § 22–1209 or § 22–1907, Indiana deprived petitioner of equal protection of the laws under the Fourteenth Amendment.

III. DUE PROCESS

For reasons closely related to those discussed in Part II above, we also hold that Indiana's indefinite commitment of a criminal defendant solely on account of his incompetency to stand trial does not square with the Fourteenth Amendment's guarantee of due process.

A. *The Federal System.* In the federal criminal system, the constitutional issue posed here has not been encountered precisely because the federal statutes have been construed to require that a mentally incompetent defendant must also be found "dangerous" before he can be committed indefinitely. But the decisions have uniformly articulated the constitutional problems compelling this statutory interpretation. * * *

B. *The States.* Some States appear to commit indefinitely a defendant found incompetent to stand trial until he recovers competency. Other States require a finding of dangerousness to support such a commitment or provide forms of parole. New York has recently enacted legislation mandating release of incompetent defendants charged with misdemeanors after 90 days of commitment, and release and dismissal of charges against those accused of felonies after they have been committed for two-thirds of the maximum potential prison sentence. The practice of automatic commitment with release conditioned solely upon attainment of competence has been decried on both policy and constitutional grounds. Recommendations for changes made by commentators and study committees have included incorporation into pretrial commitment procedures of the equivalent of the federal "rule of reason," a requirement of a finding of dangerousness or of full-scale civil commitment, periodic review by court or mental health administrative personnel of the defendant's condition and progress, and provisions for ultimately dropping charges if the defendant does not improve. One source of this criticism is undoubtedly the empirical data available which tend to show that many defendants committed before trial are never tried, and that those defendants committed pursuant to ordinary civil proceedings are, on the average, released sooner than defendants automatically committed solely on account of their incapacity to stand trial. Related to these statistics are substantial doubts about whether the rationale for pretrial commitment—that care or treatment will aid the accused in attaining competency—is empirically valid given the state of most of our mental institutions. However, very few courts appear to have addressed the problem directly in the state context.

* * *

In a 1970 case virtually indistinguishable from the one before us, the Illinois Supreme Court granted relief to an illiterate deaf mute who had been indicted for murder four years previously but found incompetent to stand trial on account of his inability to communicate, and committed. *People ex rel. Myers v. Briggs*, 46 Ill.2d 281, 263 N.E.2d 109 (1970). The institution where petitioner was confined had determined, "[I]t now appears that [petitioner] will never acquire the necessary communication skills needed to participate and cooperate in his trial." Petitioner, however, was found to be functioning at a "nearly normal level of performance in areas other than communication." The State contended petitioner should not be released until his competency was restored. The Illinois Supreme Court disagreed. It held:

> "This court is of the opinion that this defendant, handicapped as he is and facing an indefinite commitment because of the pending indictment against him, should be given an opportunity to obtain a trial to determine whether or not he is guilty as charged or should be released."

C. *This Case.* * * *

The States have traditionally exercised broad power to commit persons found to be mentally ill. The substantive limitations on the exercise of this power and the procedures for invoking it vary drastically among the States. The particular fashion in which the power is exercised—for instance, through various forms of civil commitment, defective delinquency laws, sexual psychopath laws, commitment of persons acquitted by reason of insanity—reflects different combinations of distinct bases for commitment sought to be vindicated. The bases that have been articulated include dangerousness to self, dangerousness to others, and the need for care or treatment or training. Considering the number of persons affected, it is perhaps remarkable that the substantive constitutional limitations on this power have not been more frequently litigated.

We need not address these broad questions here. It is clear that Jackson's commitment rests on proceedings that did not purport to bring into play, indeed did not even consider relevant, *any* of the articulated bases for exercise of Indiana's power of indefinite commitment. The state statutes contain at least two alternative methods for invoking this power. But Jackson was not afforded any "formal commitment proceedings addressed to [his] ability to function in society," or to society's interest in his restraint, or to the State's ability to aid him in attaining competency through custodial care or compulsory treatment, the ostensible purpose of the commitment. At the least, due process requires that the nature and duration of commitment bear some reasonable relation to the purpose for which the individual is committed.

We hold, consequently, that a person charged by a State with a criminal offense who is committed solely on account of his incapacity to proceed to trial cannot be held more than the reasonable period of time necessary to determine whether there is a substantial probability that he will attain that capacity in the foreseeable future. If it is determined that this is not the case, then the State must either institute the customary civil commitment proceeding that would be required to commit indefinitely any other citizen, or release the defendant. Furthermore, even if it is determined that the defendant probably soon will be able to stand trial, his continued commitment must be justified by progress toward that goal. In light of differing state facilities and procedures and a lack of evidence in this record, we do not think it appropriate for us to attempt to prescribe arbitrary time limits. We note, however, that petitioner Jackson has now been confined for three and one-half years on a record that sufficiently establishes the lack of a substantial probability that he will ever be able to participate fully in a trial. * * *

* * *

Both courts and commentators have noted the desirability of permitting some proceedings to go forward despite the defendant's incompetency. For instance, § 4.06(3) of the Model Penal Code would permit an incompetent accused's attorney to contest any issue "susceptible of fair determination prior to trial and without the personal participation of the defendant." An alternative draft of § 4.06(4) of the Model Penal Code would also permit an evidentiary hearing at which certain defenses, not including lack of criminal responsibility, could be raised by defense counsel on the basis of which the court might quash the indictment. Some States have statutory provisions permitting pretrial motions to be made or even allowing the incompetent defendant a trial at which to establish his innocence, without permitting a conviction. We do not read this Court's previous decisions to preclude the States from allowing at a minimum, an incompetent defendant to raise certain defenses such as insufficiency of the indictment, or make certain pretrial motions through counsel. Of course, if the Indiana courts conclude that Jackson was almost certainly not capable of criminal responsibility when the offenses were committed, dismissal of the charges might be warranted. But even if this is not the case, Jackson may have other good defenses that could sustain dismissal or acquittal and that might now be asserted. We do not know if Indiana would approve procedures such as those mentioned here, but these possibilities will be open on remand.

Reversed and remanded.

Questions and Comments

1. Though *Jackson* does not preclude automatic commitment following a determination of incompetency, the Court cautioned that automatic commitment cannot exceed a "reasonable period of time necessary to determine whether there is a substantial probability that he will attain that capacity in the foreseeable future." *Id.* at 738, 92 S.Ct. at 1858. The Court imposed the additional condition that during this period of confinement the state must demonstrate "progress" in the attainment of competency, so that a defendant whose restoration to competency is not reasonably foreseeable must either be released or be subjected to "the customary civil commitment proceeding that would be required to commit indefinitely any other citizen." *Id.* at 738, 92 S.Ct. at 1858. The "reasonable" period of commitment authorized by the Supreme Court has been variously construed. Some states restrict the period of automatic commitment to twelve months. West's Fla.Stat.Ann.R.Crim.P. Rule 3.212[c]. Others permit confinement for up to three years or a period not exceeding the maximum sentence for the offense charged, whichever is shorter. West's Ann.Cal.Pen.Code § 1370(c)(1). The extent to which a state is free to enact commitment laws that differentiate in any way between incompetent defendants and others is open to question, though the laws of a number of states make such a distinction. *Conservatorship of Hofferber*, 28 Cal.3d 161, 167 Cal.Rptr. 854, 616 P.2d 836 (1980).

2. Because the statute of limitations is generally tolled during the period of incompetency, it is possible to bring a defendant to trial whenever competency is restored, even if a substantial period of time has elapsed. To prevent this result, it has been suggested that the Sixth Amendment's speedy trial guarantee should be applied to foreclose a trial where the delay has been substantial. *See United States v. Geelan*, 520 F.2d 585 (9th Cir.1975). In general, however, the mere passage of time has not been held to bar the trial of a defendant upon his restoration to competency. Of course, where the incompetency is permanent, the defendant can never be brought to trial.

3. A finding of incompetency does not preclude the adjudication of certain pretrial defenses, such as that the indictment is insufficient or that the charge is barred by the statute of limitations. *Jackson v. Indiana*, 406 U.S. 715, 741, 92 S.Ct. 1845, 1859, 32 L.Ed.2d 435 (1972). Nor does it bar the limited type of trial, authorized by some states, such as Massachusetts (Mass.Ann.Laws, Ch. 123, § 17(b)), at which the defendant is provided with an opportunity to "establish his innocence without permitting his conviction." *Id.* at 741, 92 S.Ct. at 1859. Typically, however, states which authorize a limited trial procedure do not permit the defendant to raise the defense of insanity.

4. The application of *Jackson* can leave a defendant in legal limbo. On the one hand, he is incompetent and therefore cannot be subject to a normal trial establishing his guilt or innocence. On the other hand, the individual may not meet civil commitment standards and therefore must be allowed to remain at liberty. The undesirability of leaving the matter

of responsibility unresolved as long as the person remains incompetent has led one commentator to suggest that the rules which preclude the trial of incompetent persons should be abandoned, since "the trial of the mentally disabled, would better achieve both justice and social protection than the presently spreading legislative compromises." Norval Morris, *Madness and the Criminal Law* (Chicago: Univ. of Chicago Press, 1982), p. 34. Most incompetent persons would, according to Professor Morris, not be prejudice, since "the competence of a defense rests more with the competence of the defense counsel than in any words by the accused * * *." *Id.* at 48. Moreover, in the exceptional case, "[w]here civil commitment is obvious and will clearly be for a protracted period * * *," the prosecutor, according to Professor Morris, should "abandon the criminal charge, and thus dispose of the specter of the unseemly criminal trial." *Id.* at 48.

III. THE INSANITY DEFENSE

A. PRELIMINARY OVERVIEW

1. Introduction

The insanity defense is distinct from the issue of competency in two significant respects. First, the time reference is different. While the issue of competency is concerned with the mental condition of the accused at the time of the trial, the focus of the insanity defense is on the mental condition of the defendant at the time of the alleged offense. Second, the standards used by the fact-finder to determine whether or not a person is incompetent or insane are also different. Competency standards are concerned with the ability of the accused to understand and participate in the defense of the charges brought against him. Although the standards for the determination of insanity vary somewhat, all focus on the defendant's capacity to be criminally responsible for his actions.

Historically, the insanity defense has represented society's belief that those who are sufficiently incapacitated because of mental illnesses should not be held criminally responsible for their acts. This belief reflects a view that the objectives of our criminal law system are not served by imposing sanctions upon persons whose actions are attributable to a severe mental disorder. To serve these objectives, legislatures, courts, and legal scholars have struggled throughout history to develop legal standards that can most accurately identify the small group of offenders who should be excused from criminal responsibility. These efforts have resulted in a variety of standards for determining legal insanity. There are presently some eighteen distinct "tests" of insanity in use in 11 federal and 50 state jurisdictions in the United States, each representing a jurisdiction's view as to the appropriate test to lead to the "correct" result when adjudicating criminal responsibility.

The history of the insanity defense and the differences in current insanity tests are discussed below. The mechanics of applying legal insanity standards are discussed in subsection C, where a minor portion of the more than 5500 pages of testimony from the John W. Hinckley trial are used to illustrate the application of the American Law Institute's substantial capacity test, currently applied in all federal courts and in approximately half of the states.

Differences in insanity tests do not account for all of the variations in the treatment of mentally ill offenders. One commentator has observed:

> The words of the insanity test are the merest beginning of a set of inquiries which moves from difficult problems of trial practice to fundamental questions about crime and responsibility at its narrowest, the defense can be appraised sensibly only if we know not only what its words signify but also what effect they have upon the evidence presented and the arguments made. There is little or nothing, for example, to tell us whether one rule is, or needs be, more restrictive of the admissibility of evidence than another; or whether one of them requires more evidence to carry the defense to a jury, or how lawyer and expert fare under each of the rules; or how jurors respond to each of them; or how often the defense might be pleaded but is not; or the differential consequences of conviction, on the one hand, and acquittal by reason of insanity on the other.

The Insanity Defense: Hearings on S. 818, S. 1106, S. 1558, S. 2669, S. 2672, S. 2678, S. 2745 and S. 2780. Before the Senate Committee on the Judiciary, 97th Cong., 2nd Sess., 315–19 (1982) [hereinafter cited as Senate Insanity Defense Hearings]. (Prepared statement of Abraham Halpern, M.D., Director of Psychiatry, United Hospital, Port Chester, N.Y.)

In short, procedural, evidentiary, and dispositional factors all play a significant role in the way particular insanity standards affect the function and define the purposes of the insanity defense in each jurisdiction. Procedural and evidentiary aspects of the insanity defense affect the availability of the defense in a particular case; the burden of meeting the standard that governs the defense; and the choice of evidentiary sources by which the validity of an insanity defense can be proven. These elements of the insanity defense are explored in detail in subsection B.

Finally, subsection D discusses the dispositional consequences of an acquittal by reason of insanity and the recent constitutional decisions bearing on this matter.

Questions and Comments

1. Most studies suggest that the insanity defense is raised in fewer than 2 percent of all felony prosecutions. The Insanity Defense Hearings, at 268. See also, Arthur Matthews, Jr., *Mental Disability and the Criminal Law* American Bar Foundation, 1970, pg. 25–31. These studies also indicate that even when the defense is pleaded it is only rarely successful in a contested jury trial. Id. Does this relatively low

incidence of its use support the observation of Professor Goldstein that while "the insanity defense has long dominated discussions about criminal law, it arises too rarely to deserve a place at the center of the stage."? A. Goldstein, *The Insanity Defense* (New Haven, Conn.: Yale Univ. Press 1967), 23.

The widespread interest in the insanity defense and the debate it has engendered may, to some extent, be the product of a popular misconception as to its frequency. According to one study, a group of college-aged respondents estimated that 37 percent of those indicted for felonies in that state pleaded not guilty by reason of insanity, and that of those who entered the defense, 44 percent were found not guilty by reason of insanity. This estimate contrasts sharply with the actual number of .5 percent (102 persons) who pleaded insanity, and only one who did so successfully. Robitscher, *In Defense of the Insanity Defense*, 31 Emory L.J. 9, 49–51 (1982).

2. "Recent statistics do indicate that the use of the insanity defense is increasing. In New York, for example, there were very few successful pleas of not guilty by reason of insanity during the 1960's. This number increased dramatically after 1971, when the New York law was changed to require civil hospitalization rather than hospitalization in an institution for the criminally insane. There was a 500% increase in insanity pleas from 1971 to 1976. In 1976 alone there were sixty-nine successful pleas of insanity for a total of 315 successful insanity pleas from 1971 to 1976.

It is similarly well established that the insanity defense is being utilized only in cases involving the most serious offenses. In New York, 148 of the 278 insanity pleas offered between 1965 and 1976 involved murder. A full 244 of the 278 pleas involved crimes against the person; only twenty-five of the pleas involved property offenses. Burglary, a frequent offense, accounted for only 2.5% of all insanity acquittals."

Robitscher, *In Defense of the Insanity Defense*, 31 Emory L.J. 9, 49–51 (1982). See also, Halpern, The Fiction of Legal Insanity and the Misuse of Psychiatry, 1 J. of Legal Medicine, 18, 47–48 (1980).

2. *Historical Foundations*

GRAY, THE INSANITY DEFENSE: HISTORICAL DEVELOPMENT AND CONTEMPORARY RELEVANCE

10 Amer.Crim.L.Rev. 555, 559 (1972).

Since the 12th century, the common law has recognized mental incapacity as a defense to criminal conduct. The modern tests for insanity, however, developed slowly and coevally with other defenses of incapacity as the law, both civil and criminal, moved from a concept of strict liability to one based on fault.

* * *

The use of insanity to excuse criminal conduct seems to have first appeared at the end of the reign of Henry III in the form of king's pardons granted to those he judged insane. These pardons became so frequent that they were ultimately granted as a matter of course if the situation so dictated. The courts later adopted insanity as a valid defense, and by the 16th century it was well-established in the criminal law.

Although it was held, even as late as 1724, that an accused must be totally deprived of reason for the insanity defense to apply, there were efforts to introduce partial insanity as a defense. At the end of the 17th century, Sir Mathew Hale, in his attempt to categorize the recognized defenses to criminal charges, developed in some detail the concept that partial insanity was sufficient to prove the absence of criminal intent. He proposed a rule whereby a person would not be held responsible if, at the time of the offense, his mental capacity was less than that of a child of 14 years. His test did not gain wide use, however, possibly because an understanding of the relationship between mental age and mental capacity had not yet developed in scientific circles. Furthermore, society at that time was not willing to accept the possibility of large scale exoneration of criminals on the ground of insanity, possibly because no alternative to imprisonment could be envisioned. The requirement of total insanity embodied in the traditional "wilde beeste" test therefore continued to prevail.

In 1800, *Hadfield's Case* added insane delusions to the "wilde beeste" [a] test as a basis for a finding of insanity. Hadfield, a soldier who had suffered severe head injuries in battle, attempted to assassinate the king in order to attain the martyr's death he believed to be his destiny. His delusion was held to be sufficient ground for acquittal. This defense, although not widely successful, led to acquittal in some cases. In 1840, for example, Edward Oxford, acting under a similar delusion, attempted to assassinate Queen Victoria and Prince Albert. He too was acquitted on the ground of insanity.

Three years later, the case of Daniel M'Naghten led to a substantial change in the legal rule used to determine insanity. M'Naghten had been found not guilty by reason of insanity of the murder of Sir Robert Peel's secretary, Edward Drummond. Lord Chief Justice Tindal had instructed the jury to decide whether, at the time of the crime, the defendant "had or had not the use of his understanding, so as to know that he was doing a wrong or wicked act." If he did not know that he was violating the law, he was to be acquitted; but if he was "in a sound state of mind," he was to be found guilty. When the verdict was rendered, however, the public and the Queen were so disturbed over the obvious ambiguities of the charge that the House of Lords was asked to define what constituted a sound mind and under what circumstances the insanity defense would apply in the future. Lord Tindal set out a double test, requiring that the defendant either not know what he was doing (total insanity) or not know that it was wrong.

---

a. Under this test, "A man, to be exempt from responsibility, must be totally deprived of his reason and memory, and must not know what he is doing, no more than an infant, or a wild beast."

* * *

The *M'Naghten* rule, later modified beyond recognition by experts and jurists alike, became the basic rule in the English and American courts for almost 100 years. The promulgation of the rule, heavily influenced by the American psychiatrist, Isaac Ray, marked the first instance in which the courts responded to the budding science of psychiatry. Its carefully drafted language made psychiatric testimony useful because it permitted the expert to formulate the relationship between criminal intent and mental state in a particular case. Furthermore, the rule allowed wide leeway in the definition of "disease of the mind" and yet prevented acquittals based solely on the presence of mental illness at the time of the crime.

* * *

It was not until *M'Naghten's Case* that the testimony of psychiatrists, as experts in the field of mental disease and deficiency, was accorded special status. For the first time they could offer an opinion concerning an event which they had not actually witnessed, but about which they might reconstruct information using their newly developed techniques.

Questions and Comments

1. "Insanity has been an acknowledged ground of acquittal in Anglo-American law at least since 1505. * * * In his treatise on The History of Pleas of the Crown, published posthumously in 1736, Lord Matthew Hale explained that the insanity defense was rooted in the fundamental moral assumptions of the criminal law * * *: 'man is naturally endowed with these two great faculties, understanding and liberty of will. * * * The consent of the will is that which renders human actions either commendable or culpable * * * and because the liberty or choice of will presupposes an act of understanding to know the thing or action chosen by the will, it follows that there there is a total defect of the understanding, there is no free act of the will.' " Myths and Realities: A Report on the National Commission on the Insanity Defense, 1983, p. 10.

2. The *M'Naghten* case, referred to in the article by Gray set out above, had a profound affect on the development of the insanity defense standard. Like the Hinckley case, *M'Naghten* involved the attempted assassination in 1843 of a major political figure, Sir Robert Peel's secretary. The following excerpts provide additional background:

> [Daniel] M'Naghten apparently believed that the tory government had singled him out for abuse. As he put it, "They follow and persecute me wherever I go * * * they do everything in their power to harass and persecute me; in fact they wish to murder me." As he considered his major persecutor to be the prime minister, he planned to shoot that governmental chief but instead killed his secretary.

Senate Insanity Defense Hearings, pg. 61.

After a plea of not guilty, and evidence having been offered of the shooting of Mr. Drummond and of his death and consequences thereof, Drummond then called witnesses to prove that he was not, at the time of the committing of the act, of a sound state of mind.

Chief Justice Tindal charged the jury as follows:

> The question to be determined, is whether at the time the act in question was committed, the prisoner had or had not the use of his understanding, so as to know that he was doing a wrong or wicked act. If the jurors should be of the opinion that the prisoner was not sensible, at the time he committed it, that he was violating the laws both of God and man, then he would be entitled to a verdict in his favor; but if, on the contrary, they were of the opinion that when he committed the act he was of a sound state of mind, the verdict must be against him.

McNaghten was found not guilty by reason of insanity.

Like the public excitement generated by the Hinckley case, the public excitement in England after the verdict caused the question of insanity as a defense to be debated by the House of Lords. The Lords submitted to the Law Lords of the House of Lords certain questions concerning the defense and particularly what type of definition should be accorded to it. In answer to some six questions the Law Lords defined the type of insanity as follows:

> To establish a defense on the ground of insanity, it must be clearly proved that, at the time of committing the act, the party accused was laboring under such a defect of reason from disease of the mind, as not to know the nature or quality of the act he was doing, or, if he did know it, that he did not know he was doing what was wrong.

Senate Insanity Defense Hearings, pg. 125–126.

3. During the 19th and early 20th centuries, the federal courts and some state courts added the "irresistible impulse" rule to the *M'Naghten* formula. Under this expanded form, the lack of power to control the act—due to mental disease—became an alternative to the requirement of lack of knowledge of the act's nature or wrongness. The courts that adopted this expanded *M'Naghten* test did so on the assumption that there are mental diseases which impair volition or self-control even while cognition remains unimpaired and that persons suffering from such diseases would not be acquitted under the original *M'Naghten* test.

Until the early 1950's *M'Naghten,* in one of its forms, remained the test in all U.S. jurisdiction except New Hampshire. Since 1870 the New Hampshire test has been based on the question of whether or not the offending act was a product of mental disease. In 1954 the District of Columbia Court of Appeals set out a rule that followed the New Hampshire test in most respects in *Durham v. United States,* 214 F.2d 862 (D.C.Cir.1954). This case marked the first modern break from the *M'Naghten* approach in the United States, and, although the *Durham* test itself was not adopted in any other jurisdiction, it marked the beginning of a series of significant and controversial changes in the prevailing tests of criminal insanity in the United States.

> At the very time *Durham* was decided, the concept of mental disease was being subjected to devastating attack. It emerged as a concept whose content is often affected by the ends for which a diagnosis is made. As a result, when questions arose as to whether psychopathy or neurosis or narcotics addiction were mental diseases, the disputes were strikingly reminiscent of those which had previously characterized trials under *M'Naghten.* Psychiatrists for the prosecution classified a given defendant's behavior as not psychotic and, for that reason, not the product of a mental disease. Those testifying for the defense urged that it was psychotic or the product of a lesser mental disorder which nevertheless qualified as mental disease.

Encyclopedia of Criminal Justice, 735 (S. Kadish ed. [New York: Free Press, 1983]).

The *Durham* test was subject to substantial and nearly constant criticism from the date of its introduction, chiefly because of the extreme latitude that the test gave to psychiatric experts and the testimony they gave.

The District of Columbia Circuit, the only circuit that adopted the *New Hampshire* "product" test as the standard for legal insanity, ultimately rejected that test and adopted the A.L.I. Substantial Capacity Test in *United States v. Brawner,* 471 F.2d 969 (D.C.Cir.1972).

3. *Contemporary Perspectives*

SENATE INSANITY DEFENSE HEARINGS
26–31 (statement of William French Smith, Attorney General
of the United States).

The insanity defense is of great concern even though the number of occasions in which the defense is successfully employed is not large. The manner in which the defense is defined involves policy decisions about the nature of criminal responsibility that are of basic importance to the criminal justice system. In addition, the defense tends to be raised in cases of considerable notoriety, which serves to influence, far beyond the numbers, the public's perception of the fairness and efficiency of the entire criminal justice process.

*   *   *

In our view, this model statement [the formulation proposed by the American Law Institute's model penal code] of the insanity defense contains two critical flaws. First, it undermines the basic concept of criminal responsibility by introducing motivation into the determination of guilt or innocence. Second, it invites the presentation of massive amounts of conflicting and irrelevant evidence by psychiatric experts.

Many have long questioned whether mental disease or defect should excuse a defendant from criminal responsibility. Congress has, by statute, defined the elements of all Federal offenses, including required mental elements or states of mind. Using murder as an example, Congress has said, in essence, that it is a crime intentionally to take the life of another human being. Ordinarily, under our law, the reason or motivation for such an act is irrelevant to guilt. For instance, the fact that a killing is politically motived—that the defendant genuinely believed that his act was morally justified because the victim was a bad man whose death would end injustice, be just recompense for past wrongs, or lead to a better social order—is clearly, and properly, viewed as irrelevant to his guilt or innocence. One would expect such an assassin to be found guilty. Motivation, if deemed to involve mitigating circumstances, would be taken into account only by the judge in sentencing.

Under the prevailing insanity test, however, an analogous situation can lead today to the opposite result: Acquittal. A defendant who intentionally killed another person could now be found not guilty by reason of insanity, for example, if some mental defect caused him to believe that God had ordered the murder because the victim was an agent of the devil, interfering with God's work.

Not only is this difference in outcome difficult to explain, indeed, in our judgment it is indefensible. A person who has intentionally killed another human being, or committed some other crime, should be held responsible for the act. Any mental disease or defect, like any other motivation, should be taken into account only at the time of sentencing.

The present insanity defense also frequently leads to a gross distortion of the trial process. Commonly, in a trial involving an insanity defense, the defendant's commission of the acts in question is conceded. The trial focuses on the issue of insanity. Both sides present an array of expert psychiatric witnesses who offer conflicting opinions on the defendant's sanity. Unfortunately for the jury—and society—the terms used in any statement of the scope of the defense—for example, the phrase "disease or defect"—are usually not defined and the experts themselves do not agree on their meaning. Moreover, the experts often do not agree even on the extent to which certain behavior patterns or mental disorders that have been labeled "inadequate personality," "abnormal personality," and "schizophrenia" actually impel a person to act in a certain way. In short, medical disagreement is implicit in the issue of whether a person could conform to the requirements of the law.

Since the experts disagree about both the meaning of the terms used to discuss the defendant's mental state and the effect of particular mental states on actions, it is small wonder that trials involving an insanity plea are arduous, expensive and worst of all, thoroughly confusing to the jury. Indeed, the disagreement of the supposed experts is perhaps so basic that it makes the jury's decision rationally impossible.

*   *   *

A. GOLDSTEIN, *THE INSANITY DEFENSE*

(Yale Univ. Press, New Haven, Conn. 1967) 223–26.

[E]liminating the insanity defense would remove from the criminal law and the public conscience the vitally important distinction between illness and evil, or would tuck it away in an administrative process. The man who wished to contest his responsibility before the public and his peers would no longer be able to do so. Instead, he would be approached entirely in social engineering terms: How has the human mechanism gone awry? What stresses does it place upon the society? How can the stresses be minimized and the mechanism put right?

This approach overlooks entirely the place of the concept of responsibility itself in keeping the mechanism in proper running order. That concept is more seriously threatened today than ever before.

*   *   *

In such a time, the insanity defense can play a part in reinforcing the sense of obligation or responsibility. Its emphasis on whether an offender is sick or bad helps to keep alive the almost forgotten drama of individual responsibility. Its weight is felt through the tremendous appeal it holds for the popular imagination, as that imagination is gripped by a dramatic trial and as the public at large identifies with the man in the dock. In this way, it becomes part of a complex of cultural forces that keep alive the moral lessons, and the myths, which are essential to the continued order of society. In short, even if we have misgivings about blaming a particular individual, because he has been shaped long ago by forces he may no longer be able to resist, the concept of "blame" may be necessary.

However much we may concentrate our attention on the individual, we rely implicitly upon the existence of a culture, and a value system, which will enable us to move the individual toward conformity or to a reasonable nonconformity. That value system, if it is to become fixed early enough, must be absorbed from parents. And it, in turn, is a reflection of the larger culture, absorbed slowly and subtly over generations, transmitted by parent to child through the child-rearing devices extant in a given society. The concept of "blame," and insanity which is its other side, is one of the ways in which the culture marks out the extremes beyond which nonconformity may not go. It is one of the complex of elements which train people so that it becomes almost intuitive not to steal or rape or kill. A society which did not set such limits would probably, in time, become a less law-abiding society. This is not to say that there is not a good deal of room for humanizing the criminal law, or the insanity defense, but only that it is essential that "blame" be retained as a spur to individual responsibility.

Finally, the heart of the distinction between conviction and acquittal by reason of insanity lies in the fact that the former represents official condemnation. Yet the acquittal is itself a sanction, bringing with it comparable stigma and the prospect of indeterminate detention. If the choice between the two sanctions is to be made in a way that will not only be acceptable to the larger community but will also serve the symbolic function we have noted, it is important that the decision be made by a democratically selected jury rather than by experts—because the public can identify with the former but not with the latter. It does not follow, however, that the decision regarding the type of facility to which a particular offender is to be sent need also be made by the jury. Once the distinction between "blame" and compassion has been made, decisions as to disposition should be made by those who are professionally qualified.

NORVAL MORRIS, *MADNESS AND THE CRIMINAL LAW*
(Chicago: Univ. of Chicago Press, 1982), pp. 61–64.

*   *   *

Hence we are brought to the central issue—the question of fairness, the sense that it is unjust and unfair to stigmatize the mentally ill as criminals and to punish them for their crimes. The criminal law exists to deter and to punish those who would or who do choose to do wrong. If they cannot exercise choice, they cannot be deterred and it is a moral outrage to punish them. The argument sounds powerful but its premise is weak.

Choice is neither present nor absent in the typical case where the insanity defense is currently pleaded; what is at issue is the degree of freedom of choice on a continuum from the hypothetically entirely rational to the hypothetically pathologically determined—in states of consciousness neither polar condition exists.

The moral issue sinks into the sands of reality. Certainly it is true that in a situation of total absence of choice it is outrageous to inflict punishment; but the frequency of such situations to the problems of criminal responsibility becomes an issue of fact in which tradition and clinical knowledge and practice are in conflict. The traditions of being possessed of evil spirits, of being bewitched, confront the practices of a mental health system which increasingly fashions therapeutic practices to hold patients responsible for their conduct. And suppose we took the moral argument seriously and eliminated responsibility in those situations where we thought there had been a substantial impairment of the capacity to choose between crime and no crime (I set aside problems of strict liability and of negligence for the time being). Would we not have to, as a matter of moral fairness, fashion a special defense of gross social adversity? The matter might be tested by asking which is the more criminogenic, psychosis or serious social deprivation?

*   *   *

[A]t first blush, it seems a perfectly legitimate correlational and, I submit, causal inquiry, whether psychosis, or any particular type of psychosis, is more closely related to criminal behavior than, say, being born to a one-parent family living on welfare in a black inner-city area. And there is no doubt of the empirical answer. Social adversity is grossly more potent in its pressure toward criminality, certainly toward all forms of violence and street crime as distinct from white-collar crime, than is any psychotic condition. As a factual matter, the exogenous pressures are very much stronger than the endogenous.

As a rational matter it is hard to see why one should be more responsible for what is done to one than for what one is. Yet major contributors to jurisprudence and criminal-law theory insist that it is necessary to maintain the denial of responsibility on grounds of mental illness to preserve the moral infrastructure of the criminal law. For many years I have struggled with this opinion by those whose work I deeply respect, yet I remain unpersuaded. Indeed, they really don't try to persuade, but rather affirm and reaffirm with vehemence and almost mystical sincerity the necessity of retaining the special defense of insanity as a moral prop to the entire criminal law.

And indeed I think that much of the discussion of the defense of insanity is the discussion of a myth rather than of a reality. It is no minor debating point that in fact we lack a defense of insanity as an operating tool of the criminal law other than in relation to a very few particularly heinous and heavily punished offenses. There is not an operating defense of insanity in relation to burglary or theft, or the broad sweep of index crimes generally; the plea of not guilty on the ground of insanity is rarely to be heard in city courts of first instance which handle the grist of the mill of the criminal law—though a great deal of pathology is to be seen in the parade of accused and convicted persons before these courts. As a practical matter we reserve this defense for a few sensational cases where it may be in the interest of the accused either to escape the possibility of capital punishment (though in cases where serious mental illness is present, the risk of execution is slight) or where the likely punishment is of a sufficient severity to make the indeterminate commitment of the accused a preferable alternative to a criminal conviction. Operationally the defense of insanity is a tribute, it seems to me, to our hypocrisy rather than to our morality.

P. JOHNSON, *REVIEW OF MADNESS AND THE CRIMINAL LAW*

50 U. of Chicago L.Rev. 1534, 1541–42 (1983).

It may be that our current insanity defense is too broad, especially in placing an unreasonable burden of proof on the prosecution, but to say this is in no way to deny that there is a residual category of persons whose mental disorientation is so severe that they are incapable of culpability.

Morris appears to concede the logic of this argument, but then attempts to answer it with a *reductio ad absurdum*. If we were to eliminate "responsibility in those situations where we thought there had been a substantial impairment of the capacity to choose between crime and no crime" then "as a matter of moral fairness" we should also allow a defense of "gross social adversity." This is said to follow because criminal behavior is less closely correlated with psychosis than with "being born to a one-parent family living on welfare in a black inner-city area." But this comparison is beside the point. We do not excuse psychotics because psychosis is highly correlated with crime, but because they are thought to lack the ability to make morally responsible choices. Six-year-old children hardly ever commit homicide, but when they do they are excused. The most severely disabled psychotics are probably *less* likely to commit criminal acts than those who are more nearly normal and hence more capable of effective action. The point is not that insanity causes crime, but rather that it prevents morally responsible choice.

Morris goes astray on this issue because he refuses to distinguish between the argument for having *some* insanity defense and the much less persuasive argument for having the kind of broad insanity defense with which we are currently saddled. A system of law based on a premise of moral responsibility needs to draw a line between those who are responsible and those who are not.

* * *

No one argues that small children have sufficient moral understanding to have criminal responsibility. Whether and to what extent psychotics should be held responsible is more controversial, but I judge that most people would consider that at least some extremely disoriented persons, in addition to the severely mentally retarded, are no more responsible than children.

Questions and Comments

1. Both Attorney General Smith and Professor Morris while advocating abolition of the insanity defense, would permit psychiatric testimony to be used to show lack of *mens rea*. The implications of this proposal are considered in greater detail at pp. 677–685 *infra*.

2. The insanity defense and whether it should be retained, and in what form, has over the years been the subject of extensive comment by a wide number of authorities. Some of the leading commentators on each side are listed in Morris, *Madness and the Criminal Law*, at p. 61, n. 60. *See also*, M. Moore, *Law and Psychiatry* (Cambridge: Cambridge Univ. Press, 1984), p. 217–245.

B. PROCEDURAL AND EVIDENTIARY ASPECTS

1. Overview of Insanity Defense Procedures

a. When the Insanity Issue Is Introduced

The insanity defense involves complex evidentiary questions and requires careful preparation of expert witnesses, and lack of notice can substantially prejudice the prosecutor's case. Consequently, the statutes of a large number of states require a defendant to state before the trial that he plans to assert the insanity defense. They are intended to prevent the interposition of the insanity defense unexpectedly at trial when the prosecution has not prepared evidence to meet it.

Disregard of the statutory requirement of advance notice can result in a forfeiture of the use of the insanity defense at trial. This drastic result is tempered, however, by additional statutory language or judicial interpretation generally providing that it is within the trial judge's discretion to allow the insanity defense to be asserted if the defendant can show good cause as to why the plea was not timely entered. A liberal view of "good cause"—which considers the difficulties many defendants have in obtaining counsel, in investigating their cases fully before trial, and in having their choices clearly explained to them—is common, as it is generally agreed that the insanity defense should not be denied to defendants because of inadequate procedures or lawyers.

Those states which place no obligation upon the defendant to specifically plead the insanity defense in advance are careful not to force the prosecutor into an untenable position. Thus, a prosecutor who learns of the defendant's intended use of the insanity defense in the defendant's opening statement in court will almost always be granted a continuance (a delay in the trial proceedings) by the court to prepare his rebuttal evidence. Those states which require pretrial notice often assert in support of that requirement the purpose of avoiding the waste of judicial resources of time and money caused by such continuances.

The prosecutor also has several pretrial devices available to him by which he can learn the nature of the defendant's defense:

> First, he has the results of the police investigation, often supplemented by his own. This may turn up circumstances surrounding the crime, or a psychiatric history, which will alert him to the prospect of an insanity defense. If he wishes to pursue the matter further, he may use the grand jury's subpoena power to examine all those who might have knowledge of the defendant and his crime, except perhaps the defendant himself. And finally, if he is willing to assert that the accused may not be competent to stand trial, he will ordinarily be able to persuade the court to order a psychiatric examination. Indeed, since the accused is often unrepresented, or represented in name only,

at these early stages, he may consent to an examination and make a court order unnecessary.

The results of such examinations, though ostensibly addressed to the competency question, will tell the prosecutor a great deal about whether an insanity defense may be in the offing. Even if he does not learn of the defense through his own initiative, the prosecutor may learn of it through that of the defendant. This may occur during the "plea bargain" stage as the defendant, in hope of advantage to himself, may try to persuade the prosecutor that he has defenses which will make the prosecutor's task a difficult one. Or it may become apparent when the defendant, lacking the resources to develop an adequate defense, asks the court before trial to appoint a psychiatrist to examine him.

A. Goldstein, *The Insanity Defense* (New Haven, Conn.: Yale Univ. Press 1967), 107–108.

b. Who May Raise the Insanity Issue

Most defendants facing a charge of serious crime will assert all available defenses, including the insanity defense. But occasionally a defendant with substantial grounds to claim the insanity defense chooses not to assert it. Courts respond to this decision in two ways: some courts accept the defendant's refusal; others may impose the defense over the defendant's objections.

The traditional approach to the issue of whether to impose the insanity defense over the defendant's objection is reflected in *Whalem v. United States*, 346 F.2d 812 (D.C.Cir.1965), cert. denied 382 U.S. 862, 86 S.Ct. 124, 15 L.Ed.2d 100 (1965). In that case the trial court had declined to impose the insanity defense against the defendant's will. Although on appeal the circuit court upheld this decision, holding that the court had not abused its discretion in refusing to impose the defense, it warned that "when there is sufficient questions as to the defendant's mental responsibility at the time of the crime, that issue must become part of the case." *Id.* at 817. As the court stated in a portion of its opinion:

One of the major foundations for the structure of the criminal law is the concept of responsibility, and the law is clear that one whose acts would otherwise be criminal has committed no crime at all if because of incapacity due to age or mental condition he is not responsible for those acts. If he does not know what he is doing or cannot control his conduct or his acts are the product of a mental disease or defect, he is morally blameless and not criminally responsible. The judgment of society and the law in this respect is tested in any given case by an inquiry into the sanity of the accused. In other words, the legal definition of insanity in a criminal case is a codification of the moral judgment of society as respects a man's criminal responsibility; and if a man is insane in the eyes of the law, he is blameless in the eyes of society and is not subject to punishment in the criminal courts. * * * We believe then that, in the pursuit of justice, a trial judge must have the discretion to impose an unwanted defense on a defendant and the consequent additional burden of proof on the Government prosecutor.

At 818–819.

Recently a different approach to the questions of an involuntary insanity plea has been taken in several jurisdictions. In *Frendak v. United States*, 408 A.2d 364 (D.C.App.1979), the District of Columbia Court of Appeals overruled the trial judge's decision to impose the insanity defense. The court held that, when a defendant has acted *intelligently* and *voluntarily*, the trial court must defer to his or her decision to waive the insanity defense. A "voluntary" choice, according to the *Frendak* court, is one in the absence of legal coercion. The "intelligent" portion of the court's test means that the defendant must be both fully informed of the alternatives available and able to comprehend the consequences of failing to assert the defense. *Id.* at 380.

In support of its deference to the defendant's choice of his own defenses, the *Frendak* court noted that a defendant may have compelling reasons to avoid the insanity plea:

> * * * First, a defendant may fear that an insanity acquittal will result in the institution of commitment proceedings which lead to confinement in a mental institution for a period longer than the potential jail sentence. * * * Although a judge may not automatically commit an accused to a mental institution if the judge, rather than the defendant, has raised the insanity defense, the state has a right to initiate civil commitment proceedings against an insanity acquittee. * * * The risk of civil commitment following a conviction could be substantial, especially if the crime involved violence.

> Second, the defendant may object to the quality of treatment or the type of confinement to which he or she may be subject in an institution for the mentally ill. If in need of psychiatric care, the individual may prefer the prospect of receiving whatever treatment is available in the prison. There are, moreover, "numerous restrictions and routines in a mental hospital which differ significantly from those in a prison."

> One commentator has written that hospitalization itself interferes with privacy, since the patient cannot shield himself from constant observation by both his fellow patients and the staff of the institution. Furthermore, patients in hospitals risk brutality at the hands of their fellow residents and even their attendants, and may be subject to life in an institution which is overcrowded, inadequately staffed, poorly maintained, and unsanitary.

> * * *

> Third, a defendant, with good reason, may choose to avoid the stigma of insanity. * * * Although an insanity acquittal officially absolves the defendant of all moral blame, in the eyes of many some element of responsibility may remain. Thus, the insanity acquittee

found to have committed criminal acts and labeled insane may well see oneself "twice cursed." In addition, many persons do not understand mental illness, and some have an irrational fear of the mentally ill. Thus, an individual once labeled insane may be socially ostracized and victimized by employment or educational discrimination.

Fourth, other collateral consequences of an insanity acquittal can also follow the defendant throughout life. In some states, an adjudication of insanity may affect a person's legal rights, for example, the right to vote or serve on a federal jury, and may even restrict his or her ability to obtain a driver's license. Such an adjudication also may adversely affect the defendant in any interaction with the legal system. For instance, it may be used to attack his or her capacity as a trial witness, or could be admissible in a criminal trial to attack the character of a defendant who has put his or her character in issue. Furthermore, the record of such an adjudication would surely be used in any subsequent proceeding for civil commitment.

Finally, a defendant also may oppose the imposition of an insanity defense because he or she views the crime as a political or religious protest which a finding of insanity would denigrate. * * * In any event, a defendant may choose to forego the defense because of a feeling that he or she is not insane, or that raising the defense would be equivalent to an admission of guilt.

at 376–377.

Courts continue to split on the issue of involuntary impositions of the insanity defense by the court with the majority following the *Whalem* view that the court may do so. The provision for a separate hearing on the issue of whether the defendant has the capacity to "intelligently and voluntarily" waive the assertion of the insanity defense in *Frendak* makes it clear that the trial court may still override the defendant's expressed wishes. *See e.g., State v. Khan*, 175 N.J.Super. 72, 417 A.2d 585 (1980).

Questions and Comments

1. The U.S. Supreme Court has not expressly ruled on the issues discussed above. In *Lynch v. Overholser*, 366 U.S. 958, 81 S.Ct. 1936, 6 L.Ed.2d 1252 (1961), the Supreme Court based its reversal of a lower court decision, which had imposed an insanity defense and a resulting commitment to a mental institution on a defendant who did not raise the defense, on statutory interpretation grounds. Finding that the statutory grant of power to the court to order the commitment of persons acquitted by reason of insanity applied only to cases where the defendant affirmatively relied on that defense, the court found it unnecessary to deal with the issues of whether the defendant was deprived of liberty without due process of law or of other constitutional claims concerning the fairness of the lower court proceedings.

2. The *Whalem* decision was based on the proposition that society has a duty to protect the morally blameless from punishment. In an earlier case *Tatum v. United States*, 190 F.2d 612 (D.C.Cir.1951), the

same court held that the prosecution could raise the insanity defense over the defendant's objections. Can you think of reasons, other than the proposition stated in *Whalem,* why the prosecution would want to interpose the insanity defense? In connection with the question, remember that insanity acquittals frequently lead to the commitment of the defendant to a mental hospital. Should the prosecution's motive for interposing the defense have any effect on the court's decision to allow the interposition? Would an inquiry into the prosecution's motive be proper in states requiring mandatory commitment of insanity acquittees?

3. Judge Bazelan in the *Wright* opinion recognized the dangers of imposing the insanity defense on a defendant whose irrational behavior closely resembles a lawful expression of political or religious belief. The Soviet Union's use of psychiatry and criminal process as a means of repressing political dissent has caused worldwide concern, and psychiatric abuses there have been the subject of recent hearings by the Sub-Committee on Human Rights of the House of Representatives. *See,* Abuse of Psychiatry in the Soviet Union, Hearings Before the Subcommittee on Human Rights and International Organizations of the Committee on Foreign Affairs and the Commission on Security and Cooperation in Europe, House of Representatives, 98th Cong., 1st Sess. (1983).

2. Evidentiary Issues

a. Allocation of the Evidentiary Burden

i. Burden of Proof

The allocation of the burden of proof between the defendant and the prosecution has a significant effect on the end result of the criminal trial—the jury's verdict. In no area of the criminal law is this generalization more valid than in cases involving the insanity defense. In the *Hinckley* case, for example, the prosecution had the burden of persuading the jurors beyond a reasonable doubt that the defendant was sane. Hinckley's lawyers achieved an acquittal merely by raising a reasonable doubt as to the defendant's sanity. Because the question of his sanity was closely contested, a shifting of the burden of proof to the defense might well have led to a guilty verdict. The following discussion briefly summarizes the major evidentiary issues.

The burden of proof in all criminal cases has two aspects: (1) the production of evidence; and (2) persuasion. Both the prosecution and the defendant normally must meet some burden of production. To satisfy its burden of production the prosecution must produce evidence of all the elements of the crime charged, that is, that the crime was committed and that the defendant committed it or is legally accountable for its commission. The defense, on the other hand, must produce evidence in support of his affirmative defenses (e.g., insanity, intoxication, self-defense, coercion). If the prosecution fails to satisfy its burden of production, the defendant becomes entitled to a directed verdict of not guilty. *See*, LaFave and Scott, *Criminal Law* (St. Paul, Minn.: West Co., 1972), 46–50.

When a defendant is tried on a criminal charge, the presumption is that the defendant was sane. "The presumption of sanity, standing in the place of evidence where no question is raised about the issue, takes care of the prosecutor's burden of proving sanity." *Mims v. United States*, 375 F.2d 135, 140 (5th Cir.1967). The presumption is based on the common sense notion that most persons are legally sane. Moreover, without that presumption, sanity would become a necessary element of proof in every criminal trial and an unnecessary burden on the prosecution, since a defendant's sanity is not generally at issue. The presumption of sanity is rebuttable, and all jurisdictions place the burden of producing *some* evidence of insanity on the defendant. The amount of evidence necessary to satisfy the defendant's burden of production varies among jurisdictions. Psychiatric testimony is not mandated; lay testimony is regarded as sufficient to satisfy the burden of production, even when the witness is not especially familiar with the accused and testifies in broad generalizations. *See*, Goldstein, *The Insanity Defense, supra*, p. 113. In *Clark v. United States*, 104 U.S.App.D.C. 27, 259 F.2d 184 (1958), a statement by the accused that he "must have been insane" was sufficient to satisfy the defendant's burden of producing "some evidence" of insanity.

Once the defendant has rebutted the presumption of sanity, the jury must consider whether the defendant's mental illness should relieve the defendant of responsibility on his criminal act. There is significant disagreement as to whether the prosecution or the defense must satisfy the burden of persuasion as to the defense of insanity. Currently the laws in about half of the states treat sanity as an element of the criminal offense once the defendant raises the issue of insanity. Accordingly, these jurisdictions place the burden of persuasion entirely on the prosecution, which must prove that the defendant was sane beyond a reasonable doubt when he committed the criminal offense.

The remaining jurisdictions treat insanity strictly as an affirmative defense for which the defendant must bear the burden of persuasion. In most of these jurisdictions the defendant can satisfy this burden by proving his insanity with a preponderance of the evidence. This standard of proof that requires the defendant to show that it was more likely than not that he was insane is much less rigorous than the traditional "beyond a reasonable doubt" standard in criminal cases. States which place this burden upon the defendant stress that the prosecution is not relieved of the constitutional requirement to prove each element of the crime since insanity is viewed as an affirmative defense rather than an element of a criminal act. The Supreme Court has also upheld a state statute placing an even more rigorous burden upon the defendant. In *Leland v. Oregon*, 343

U.S. 790, 72 S.Ct. 1002, 96 L.Ed. 1302 (1952), the court upheld a statute that required the defendant to prove his affirmative defense of insanity beyond a reasonable doubt. The constitutional permissibility of shifting the burden of proving insanity to the defendant has been reaffirmed in recent years by both federal and state courts. *See, Riviera v. Delaware,* 427 U.S. 877 (1976); *Patterson v. New York,* 432 U.S. 197, 97 S.Ct. 2319, 53 L.Ed.2d 281 (1977); *Howze v. Marshall,* 716 F.2d 396 (6th Cir.1983), cert. denied ___ U.S. ___, 104 S.Ct. 1015, 79 L.Ed.2d 245 (1984).

The 1982 acquittal of John Hinckley of the attempted assassination of President Reagan prompted congressional re-examination of the rules governing the insanity defense at the federal level. *See,* The Insanity Defense: Hearings on S. 818, S. 1106, S. 1558, S. 2669, S. 2672, S. 2678, S. 2745 and S. 2780. Before the Senate Committee on the Judiciary, 97th Cong., 2nd Sess. (1982); Limiting the Insanity Defense: Hearings on S. 818, S. 1106, S. 1558, S. 1995, S. 2572, S. 2658, and S. 2669. Before the Subcommittee on Criminal Law of the Committee on the Judiciary, 97th Cong., 2nd Sess. (1982); Reform of the Federal Insanity Defense: Hearings. Before the Subcommittee on Criminal Justice of the Committee on the Judiciary House of Representatives, 98th Cong., 1st Sess. (1983). Particular criticism was directed at the requirement which imposed upon the prosecution the burden of proving the defendant's sanity beyond a reasonable doubt. Following extensive hearings, Congress enacted and the president signed into law the Insanity Defense Reform Act of 1984. Pub.L.No. 98–473, § 402(a) (to be codified at 18 U.S.C.A. § 20). The Act introduced radical changes in the rules governing the insanity defense including a change in the allocation of the evidentiary burden. Under section 20(b) the *defendant* in all federal cases has the burden of establishing his insanity by "clear and convincing evidence."

Questions and Comments

1. The new federal provision which requires the defendant to prove his insanity by "clear and convincing" evidence would seem to be immune from constitutional attack so long as the Supreme Court adheres to *Leland v. Oregon,* 343 U.S. 790, 72 S.Ct. 1002, 96 L.Ed. 1302 (1952). However, special steps may be required by trial courts to ensure that shifting the burden of proving insanity to the defendant does not, as a practical matter, lessen the constitutionally imposed burden on the prosecution to prove beyond a reasonable doubt all elements of the crime (including *mens rea*). In this connection, consider the comments of Mr. Justice Rehnquist in his concurrence in *Mullaney v. Wilbur,* 421 U.S. 684, 95 S.Ct. 1881, 44 L.Ed.2d 508 (1975):

> The Court noted in *Leland* that the issue of insanity as a defense to a criminal charge was considered by the jury only after it had found that all elements of the offense, including the *mens rea,* if any, required by state law, had been proved beyond a reasonable doubt.

Although as the state court's instructions in *Leland* recognized, evidence relevant to insanity as defined by state law may also be relevant to whether the required *mens rea* was present, the existence or nonexistence of legal insanity bears no necessary relationship to the existence or nonexistence of the required mental elements of the crime. For this reason, Oregon's placement of the burden of proof of insanity on Leland, unlike Maine's redefinition of homicide in the instant case, did not effect an unconstitutional shift in the State's traditional burden of proof beyond a reasonable doubt of all necessary elements of the offense.

421 U.S. at 705–706, 95 S.Ct. at 1892–1893.

Does it follow from this consideration, i.e., maintaining the separateness of the *mens rea* issue and the insanity defense, that a defendant must, as a constitutional matter, be permitted to introduce psychiatric testimony rebutting the prosecution's evidence of *mens rea*? In this connection, see *Muench v. Israel*, at p. 675 *infra*.

ii. *The Insanity Defense Under a Bifurcated Procedure*

Several jurisdictions impose significant procedural changes in their criminal trial procedure when the insanity issue is involved. The result is generally a bifurcated trial procedure, which requires that the determination of a defendant's criminal responsibility be made in a separate proceeding from that in which the defendant's guilt or innocence is decided.

Under the bifurcated procedure adopted in several states including California, if the defendant combines a not guilty plea with an insanity plea, the court will proceed to try all issues other than insanity in the first phase of the trial—where the guilt or innocence of the crime charged is determined. In the "guilt phase," the jury operates under a conclusive presumption that the defendant was sane at the time of the act. A finding of not guilty serves to terminate any further proceedings and leads to the discharge of the defendant. If the jury finds the defendant guilty, then the court proceeds to try the issue of the defendant's sanity in the second, or "insanity," phase of the trial. This second phase may be tried before the same jury or a different one than used in the first phase as the court in its discretion sees fit. *See* West's Ann.Cal. Penal Code §§ 1016, 1026. Under the California system, if the defendant pleads only not guilty by reason of insanity, then it is presumed that the defendant has admitted the commission of the offense, and the court proceeds directly to the issue of insanity. *See* Louisell and Hazard, *Insanity as a Defense: The Bifurcated Trial*, 49 Cal.L.Rev. 805 (1961).

The bifurcated insanity trial has been justified on two different grounds. First, it constitutes a means of keeping out prejudicial and irrelevant psychiatric evaluations and other testimony not directly germane to the narrow issue of guilt or innocence. The California Commission for the Reform of Criminal Procedure, which justified the bifurcated trial on this basis when it recommended the adoption of the nation's first bifurcated trial statute in 1927, found that most of the evidence introduced by insanity defendants was not relevant to a determination of whether the defendant committed the offense. Instead, much of the defendant's evidence (*e.g.*, the defendant's traumatic childhood) often evoked undue juror sympathy and generally confused the jury. It was to prevent such evidence from influencing the jury's determination of the defendant's complicity in the criminal act, that the Commission recommended bifurcation. *See* Louisell and Hazard, 49 Cal.L.Rev. at 808–810.

In other states the bifurcated procedure was established to protect the defendant's constitutional right against self-incrimination. *State ex rel. La Follette v. Raskin*, 34 Wis.2d 607, 150 N.W.2d 318 (1967), is representative of this kind of decision. In *La Follette* the defendant had made an inculpatory statement during a compulsory pretrial psychiatric examination. Seeking to avoid the introduction of those statements as evidence at his trial, which could prejudice the jurors in their determination of his involvement in the alleged offense, the defendant requested separation of the issues of guilt and insanity. In accepting the defendant's contention, the Wisconsin Supreme Court ruled that a bifurcated trial was the most effective method of protecting the defendant's Fifth Amendment rights.

Jurisdictions that do not recognize the bifurcation procedure generally hold that the accused has no right, constitutional, statutory, or otherwise, to such a bifurcated procedure. As simply stated in *McKenzie v. Osborne*, 195 Mont. 26, 640 P.2d 368, 374 (1981), "[t]he petitioner offers no authority under our law that a defendant as a matter of constitutional law is entitled to a separate jury trial on the issue of insanity or diminished mental capacity to commit the crime charged." Some jurisdictions, however, have expressed or implied that, while bifurcation is not required as a general rule, it may be necessary under certain specified circumstances. In deciding whether the defendant's motion of bifurcation should be granted, these courts examine both defendant's insanity defense and his defense on the merits to determine whether both are bona fide defenses supported by facts and law. Bifurcation will be refused if either defense is found lacking. If both defenses are substantial, however, the court must then determine the likelihood that prejudice to the defendant would result if both defenses were presented in one trial proceeding. *State v. Boyd*, ___ W.Va. ___, 280 S.E.2d 669 (1981). These courts generally consider that the determination of a bifurcation procedure is a matter of judicial discretion. Such a decision is thus generally considered not reviewable on appeal.

Questions and Comments

1. Evidence of a defendant's mental illness is relevant in proving not only the defendant's insanity but also the defendant's diminished capacity. (Diminished capacity is treated more extensively in Part IV Section

C, *infra*). Elimination of all psychiatric evidence from the guilt phase of the trial can effectively deprive the defendant from using such evidence to challenge the presence of the *mens rea* (criminal intent) necessary for the commission of the alleged crime. Thus, the bifurcated trial often results in a conclusive presumption of *mens rea* because the defendant cannot rebut the inference of intent arising from commission of the criminal act. *See* LaFave and Scott, *Criminal Law*, (St. Paul, Minn.: West Co., 1972), 202–207. Attorneys for defendants have challenged the bifurcated insanity trial because the conclusive presumption of *mens rea* violates the well-established constitutional principle that the prosecution must prove beyond a reasonable doubt every fact necessary to constitute the alleged crime. *In re Winship*, 397 U.S. 358, 90 S.Ct. 1068, 25 L.Ed. 2d 368 (1970).

The Arizona Supreme Court in *State v. Shaw*, 106 Ariz. 103, 112–13, 471 P.2d 715, 724–25 (1970), agreed with the defendant's constitutional challenge to the state's bifurcation statute:

> Can this Court say that it is just to pass upon the guilt and innocence of a defendant without allowing all of the evidence available to determine whether he had the mental capacity to commit the crime? The bifurcated trial has been fraught with conflicts and difficulty of administration wherever its use has been attempted. As pointed out in the California Western Law Review, the courts in California have gradually picked away at its legal inconsistencies, and in doing this the objectives have been defeated by altering the rules of evidence to admit the very things the system was enacted to restrict from admission—namely, the admission of evidence of insanity at the first trial. Texas and Colorado have adopted a cumbersome double-trial on the same issues in order to comply with due process. To prohibit the introduction of any or all the evidence bearing on proof of insanity at the trial of guilt or innocence would deprive a defendant of the opportunity of rebutting intent, premeditation, and malice, because an insane person could have none. The first trial then would involve only proof that an act of a criminal nature had been committed, and that the defendant committed it. In effect, this gives rise to a presumption of intent, premeditation, or malice which runs counter to the common-law and constitutional concepts of criminal law. The second trial is limited solely to the question of legal insanity, the guilt of the defendant having already been determined. There is no provision, nor realistically could there be, to determine also intent, premeditation, or malice in reduction of the degree of the crime. Thus, the presumption raised in the first trial becomes an irrebuttable presumption. Such a presumption is in violation of due process. * * * For this Court to comply with due process, the statute would have to be interpreted as allowing admission of all the evidence at the first trial but to do this it emasculates the act in such a way that it would not be carrying out the purpose for which it was intended. The adoption of the reasonable interpretation of the act is a violation of due process, particularly since the lack of procedural due process adversely affects substantive rights to a fair trial.

*   *   *

We therefore accordingly hold that the [bifurcation statute] is in violation of due process as provided in our own State constitution and the Constitution of the United States. The procedure provided for prior to its adoption is hereby re-instated.

Other courts, however, have rejected challenges to the states' use of the bifurcated trial procedure and the resulting exclusion of psychiatric evidence at the initial guilt determination stage. *See, Muench v. Israel*, 715 F.2d 1124 (7th Cir.1983), which is discussed in greater detail at p. 675 *infra*.

2. Several other state supreme courts have struck down their bifurcation statutes for the reasons stated by the court in *State v. Shaw*. *See State* ex rel. *Boyd v. Green*, 355 So.2d 789 (Fla.1978); *Sanchez v. State*, 567 P.2d 270 (Wyo.1977). Besides California, Texas, and Colorado (mentioned in the *Shaw* opinion), other states with a bifurcated insanity trial are Maine (Mc.Rev.Stat.Ann. tit. 17–a §§ 9 (West Supp.1980)), Minnesota (Minn.Stat.Ann.R.Crim.P., Rule 20.02(b)(2)), and (Wisconsin Stats.Ann. 4697–4699). In Minnesota and Maine the defendant may waive the procedure. For a thorough discussion of the relationship between *mens rea* and insanity, *see* Note, *Mens Rea and Insanity*, 28 Mc.L.Rev. 500 (1976).

b. Meeting the Evidentiary Burden

i. Introduction

Although a great deal of attention has been paid to the differences between insanity tests in the various jurisdictions, in practical effect the quality of the evidence pertaining to the defendant's mental condition and the effectiveness of the presentation of this evidence to the jury are perhaps more determinative on the jury's ultimate verdict than the particular standard that the jury is called upon to apply. The following subsection focuses on evidentiary sources for establishing the defendant's sanity or insanity. In particular, the discussion focuses on the expert witness, almost always the single-most important evidentiary source at trial.

ii. Proof of Mental Status

a) Sources of Evidence

When the issue of insanity is raised as a defense in a criminal trial, the jury must determine, from all the testimony, lay and expert, two factors: (1) whether there existed the severity of mental disorder required to excuse the defendant; and (2) whether as a result the defendant was incapacitated to the extent required by the legal standard. The jury's determination of these questions is controlled by the evidence introduced by the parties.

The prevailing rule on the permissible sources of evidence was summarized in *Mims v. United States*, 375 F.2d 135, 143 (5th Cir. 1967):

> The sound rule is that the issue of insanity, when raised as a defense in a criminal case, should be determined by the jury from all the evidence, rather than from the opinions of experts alone, subject to the control that the court may always set aside an unreasonable verdict. The real value of expert testimony in these cases is "in the explanation of the disease and its dynamics, that is, how it occurred, developed, and affected the mental and emotional processes of the defendant; it does not lie in [the] mere expression of conclusion."

The expert witness has proven to be the most traditional source of opinion evidence on issues concerning the presence or absence of mental disease and the degree of incapacitation caused by mental abnormalities. The opinions of experts can be elicited in two ways. The expert's testimony can consist of his educated answers to hypothetical questions drawn from the facts of the case. Or the expert's testimony can be based on his own observations and examination of the defendant. To avoid conclusory testimony in the latter case, most jurisdictions require the expert to state the facts from which he bases his opinion so that the jury can judge its value independently.

The special knowledge possessed by mental health experts in the area of abnormal behavior and, more important, the perception of these witnesses as authority figures cause jurors to give greater credence to their testimony, thus making experts quite valuable as evidentiary sources. However, opinion evidence concerning the issue of insanity is not confined to that derived from expert testimony.

Since the issue of insanity is only in part a medical or scientific matter, lay testimony concerning the mental condition of the accused provides an additional source of evidence. In nearly all jurisdictions non-expert witnesses are permitted to give opinion testimony as to the sanity or insanity of a person whose mental condition is in question. However, to testify as to the question of insanity, the lay witness is usually required to show that he had adequate opportunities to observe the speech, manner, habits, or conduct of such person and to state the facts and circumstances upon which his opinion is based.

Finally, real evidence provides an additional source of evidence on issues of insanity. Photographs of a crime scene, weapons, clothing, and other items of physical evidence often may be used by either the prosecution or the defense to support their respective cases.

Limitations on expert testimony are treated in a later section (*see* p. 590 *infra*), but, in relation to the relative weights of evidence obtained from expert and from non-expert sources, some comments are warranted at this point. First, as one commentator has accurately observed: "The judiciary applies a liberal standard of usefulness [when considering the relevance of expert testimony]. The courts admit expert testimony whenever there is a material issue in a [case] involving the expert's particular skill or knowledge, and the expert possesses the kind of skill or knowledge that will assist the jury in arriving at an intelligent decision." R. Kwall, *The Use of Expert Services by Privately Retained Criminal Defense Lawyers*, 13 Loy. Univ.L.J. 1 (1981). In light of the liberal admittance standards it has often been stressed that the purpose of experts is to help the jurors understand and evaluate evidence or determine facts in issue, and not to take the role of decisionmaker or to determine facts in issue. The determination of whether the defendant is legally insane is not a clinical judgment and the evidence obtained from experts is properly only one source of the evidence considered by the jurors in making their ultimate determination. Courts have held that when the expert and lay testimony conflict it is within the province of the jury "to accept the lay testimony and reject the conclusions of the experts" even when the experts were unanimous. *Taylor v. State*, ___ Ind. ___, 440 N.E.2d 1109 (1982).

Questions and Comments

1. In order to rebut the defendant's insanity defense the prosecution ordinarily will need to introduce expert testimony to establish the defendant's sanity. Generally, an opinion of the prosecution's expert will, at least in part, need to be based on one or more psychiatric interviews with the defendant. Such interviews may be meaningless if the defendant does not cooperate or refuses altogether to submit to an examination. A failure of the defendant to cooperate can lead to one of several sanctions. Some courts have responded by refusing to allow the defendant to offer his own psychiatric evidence in support of the insanity defense. *See, Lee v. County Court*, 27 N.Y.2d 431, 318 N.Y.S.2d 705, 267 N.E.2d 452 (1971). A lack of cooperation may also result in instruction by the court to the jury "that the defendant has failed to cooperate and that the failure to cooperate should be considered by them in determining the merits of the defense." 27 N.Y.2d at 443–44, 318 N.Y.S.2d at 713–14.

Some commentators have argued that any court ordered psychiatric interview (whether by a psychiatrist appointed by the court or by one selected by the government) violates a defendant's Fifth Amendment privilege against self-incrimination. Also, it has been asserted that the defendant's Sixth Amendment guarantee of assistance of counsel is violated when his lawyer is excluded from the examination. Generally, these objections have been rejected primarily because of the "unreasonable and debilitating effect it would have upon society's conduct of a fair inquiry into the defendant's culpability." *United States v. Byers*, 740 F.2d 1104 (D.C.Cir.1984).

As a consequence, there is no bar to the admission of a defendant's statement during a compelled psychiatric examination where the testimony *pertains to the defendant's sanity*. *United States v. Byers*, at 1111, n. 8. However, a different rule applies when the defendant's statement is introduced not to establish the defendant's sanity but to prove commission of the offense, e.g., a confession by the defendant to the examining psychiatrist that he committed the act in question. Generally, the admission of such testimony will either be proscribed by statute or by the application of court rules designed to protect the defendant's Fifth Amendment rights.

2. As noted above, courts have invariably rejected the claim that the Fifth and Sixth Amendments entitle a defendant to have his attorney present during a court ordered clinical interview. It has been suggested that a fair accommodation of "Fifth Amendment values" could be achieved by the use of recordings (audio or video) of the psychiatric interview. *U.S. v. Byers*, 740 F.2d 1104, 1155 (D.C.Cir.1984) (Bazelon, J., dissenting). Such recording would, it has been asserted, "help ensure that overreaching does not take place and that the psychiatrist has not manipulated or intimidated the defendant in an *in-camera* interview." *Id.* Also, recording would "help inform the court's judgment regarding the voluntariness and reliability of the defendant's statement." *Id.* Others, however, have suggested that a recording of the examination would "prove disruptive or 'inhibiting' to the clinical interview". *Id.* at 1156. An extensive discussion of merits of requiring recording is found in *U.S. v. Byers*, 740 F.2d 1104 (D.C.Cir.1984), although the majority declined on procedural grounds to rule on the question.

b. *Qualifications for Expert Status*

When the issues in a criminal trial involve questions concerning the mental status of the defendant, psychiatrists, as noted in an earlier section, are the traditional source of expert opinion testimony. The qualifications for serving in that role, in the case of psychiatrists, are for the most part presumed. Physicians and surgeons who do not specialize in mental diseases may also be considered competent by most courts to testify as experts on insanity issues. Some jurisdictions, however, require physicians who are not psychiatrists to have special expertise in the treatment of mental diseases, making an exception only when the physician was the defendant's attending physician or, at least, had an opportunity to examine and treat the defendant in the past.

One additional caveat should be noted. Despite the fact that a particular physician, psychiatrist, or psychologist, is considered to be fully qualified to serve as an expert in an insanity trial, there may still be limits as to what he or she can testify to in terms of theoretical subjects. This issue is discussed in more detail in a later section defining the role of the expert witness.

The most current and still debated issue concerning qualifications for expert status in trials involving insanity issues pertains to the use of mental health professionals and personnel other than psychiatrists or sources of expert testimony on insanity issues.

STATE v. PORTIS

United States Court of Appeals, Seventh Circuit, 1976.
542 F.2d 414.

PELL, Circuit Judge.

Ronald Eugene Portis appeals from his conviction by a jury for robbery of a federally insured savings and loan association. At trial Portis did not controvert the evidence of Government witnesses about the events which had led to his indictment. He relied entirely on a claim of insanity. The issues on appeal are concerned with this claim.

Midday on September 3, 1975, Portis went to teller Grace Maria Mika's counter in the First Federal Savings and Loan Association, Chicago, Illinois. He was not wearing a mask and his eyes were glassy and bloodshot. He was carrying a transistor radio in his left hand. Portis mumbled something to the teller; she could not understand him. He then tossed a brown paper bag and a note over the counter and directed Mika to read the note. It said "It life or death 5000." The teller kicked the alarm and began placing money in the bag. While she was doing this, Portis instructed her not to touch anything until he was out the door and repeatedly told her to be a good girl. He spoke in a low monotone. The teller put $8,400 in the bag.

When the alarm was set off, an assistant vice-president of First Federal, Raymond Kennedy, was notified that a robbery was in progress. He observed Portis at Mika's station, walked over, and, as the defendant turned to leave, Kennedy grabbed him from behind, said "Come with me," and marched him toward a private office. Portis asked him, "Why don't you leave me alone and get your hands off of me?" A security guard, with gun drawn, came to Kennedy's assistance. Portis tried to shrug off Kennedy's grip but offered no other resistance. In a few minutes, agents of the Federal Bureau of Investigation came and arrested the defendant.

*   *   *

Portis asserts that the trial court "erred as a matter of law" in permitting Dr. Thomas White, a psychologist who testified on behalf of the Government, to express his opinion that Portis was legally sane at the time of the offense. Dr. White, the appellant contends, was not qualified to give an opinion on this important matter.

The record reveals the following. Dr. White has been awarded three degrees in psychology, a B.A., an M.A., and a Ph.D. He received the doctorate four months prior to Portis' trial. From August 1974 until July 1975, Dr. White held a one-year clinical internship at the internationally known Menninger Foundation, where he worked with patients in an outclinic. During this period, he also did some testing at the Federal Hospital for Prisoners in Springfield, Missouri; there, he worked closely with expert staff members. Before entering college, White had been trained by the Navy as a psychiatric technician and had worked for four years with persons suffering from psychiatric problems. He was, at the time of trial, a staff psychologist for the United States Bureau of Prisons at the Chicago Metropolitan Correctional Center, the first position he had held as a clinical psychologist. He had been at the Center for less than three months when he talked with and tested Portis. In November 1975, when Portis' trial took place, Dr. White was not a Diplomate of the American Board of Examiners in the Profession of Psychology nor could he have met the requirements established by the State of Illinois for certification as a psychologist. (Federal employees are not required to satisfy those criteria.)

In the Seventh Circuit, the test for insanity is based upon the definition formulated by the American Law Institute. Portis does not claim that all psychologists are incompetent to give an opinion whether a defendant's conduct resulted from "a mental disease or defect." He acknowledges that courts have held that certain clinical psychologists, by virtue of their training and experience, may be competent to give a medical opinion as to sanity. *See, e.g., United States v. Riggleman*, 411 F.2d 1190 (4th Cir.1969); *Jenkins v. United States*, 113 U.S.App.D.C. 300, 307 F.2d 637 (1962) (en banc).

In *Jenkins*, Judge Bazelon stated:

> We agree with the weight of authority * * * that some psychologists are qualified to render expert testimony in the field of mental disorder. * * * The test * * * is whether the opinion offered will be likely to aid the trier in the search for truth. In light of that purpose, it is hardly surprising that courts do not exclude all but the very best kind of witness. * * * The principle to be distilled from the cases is plain: if experience or training enables a proffered expert witness to form an opinion which would aid the jury, in the absence of some countervailing consideration, his testimony will be received.

Jenkins at 643–44 (footnote omitted). Judge Bazelon, for the court, held that the admissibility of a psychologist's opinion lay within the sound discretion of the trial court. "[T]he lack of a medical degree, and the lesser degree of responsibility for patient care which mental hospitals usually assign to psychologists, are not automatic disqualifications. Where relevant, these matters may be shown to affect the weight of their testimony, even though it be admitted in evidence." *Id.* at 646. At Portis' trial, the Court ruled that there was no legal barrier to the admissibility of Dr. White's testimony and that defense counsel's doubts regarding Dr. White's expertise were matters going to the weight to be accorded that testimony.

Portis points out that Judge Bazelon in *Jenkins* provided general guidelines for the exercise of discretion by a trial court and that concurring Judge Burger (now Chief Justice) recommended specific considerations. In the context of that case, it is understandable why the judges discussed at length possible criteria—not rigid criteria—

that would qualify a psychologist as an expert on a defendant's mental condition at the time of an offense.[a] The trial court in *Jenkins* had instructed the jury to disregard the testimony of three psychologists on the defendant's sanity at the time of the offense without scrutinizing the actual experience of the individuals and the probable probative value of their opinions. In the present case, the opinion of the psychologist was not excluded, and his *vita* shows that he fell within the middle range where an expert's credentials are not unquestionable but are sufficient that the court could, in the exercise of its discretion, permit the witness to state his opinion as an expert. *Contrast State v. Padilla*, 66 N.M. 289, 347 P.2d 312, 317–19 (1959), where the trial court erroneously accepted testimony from a psychologist who, unlike Dr. White, had no Ph.D., no post-graduate training, and no experience as an intern in a mental institution. Here, on both direct examination and cross-examination, counsel brought to the jury's attention the nature and extent of Dr. White's experience and education. Further, through the direct testimony of his expert witness Dr. Paull, a clinical psychologist, Portis criticized Dr. White's opinion and his alleged lack of adequate experience. The jury thus had all this information before it in determining the weight to be accorded Dr. White's opinion.

Questions and Comments

1. As late as 1980, Illinois remained one of the few states that put broad restrictions on the testimony of psychologists in cases involving insanity. An Illinois Appellate Court reaffirmed earlier precedent in *People v. Strange*, 81 Ill.App.3d 81, 36 Ill.Dec. 486, 400 N.E.2d 1066 (3rd Dist.1980) by stating:

> As we interpret the cases it is apparent that only a qualified psychiatrist, not a psychologist, could give an opinion as to the sanity of a defendant. In the instant case the testimony of the psychologist as to what tests were performed and the results thereof, was irrelevant unless it formed the basis for an opinion by a qualified psychiatrist of the mental ability of the defendant. Since it did not form such a basis the testimony was properly excluded.

However, in *People v. Free*, 94 Ill.2d 378, 69 Ill.Dec. 1, 447 N.E.2d 218 (1983), the Illinois Supreme Court has approved a more relaxed standard, which would allow a psychologist to express opinions as to the mental condition of the individual in accordance with recent statutory approval of more general testimony by psychologists. *See, e.g.*, Ill.Rev.Stat. ch. 38, par. 1005–2–5 (1983).

a. Rule 702 of the Federal Rules of Evidence, we note, speaks in broad terms:

If scientific, technical, or other specialized knowledge will assist the trier of fact to understand the evidence or to determine a fact in issue, a witness qualified as an expert by knowledge, skill, experience, training, or education, may testify thereto in the form of an opinion or otherwise.

2. In some cases, the testimony of a psychologist in an expert role is restricted to certain proscribed matters depending on their qualifications. In *Commonwealth v. Williams*, 270 Pa.Super. 27, 410 A.2d 880 (1979), a psychologist was held to have been properly precluded from testifying as to her opinion regarding whether the defendant understood the nature and quality of his acts and whether they were right and wrong in light of the psychologist's minimal experience with criminally accused patients. Her testimony concerning tests she administered to the accused six months prior to the offense, and the results of these tests, however, were properly admitted into evidence at trial.

3. Oregon has proved to be one of the more liberal jurisdictions with regard to psychologists serving as experts. In *State v. Walker*, 58 Or. App. 607, 649 P.2d 624 (1982), the Appellate Court ruled that the court below had the discretion to permit a *non-licensed* clinical psychologist to testify at a murder trial as to the defendant's mental state, ruling that the psychologist's lack of a license went, at most, to the weight of his testimony and not to its admission.

However, Oregon courts would not go so far as to admit the testimony of a psychiatric social worker. In *State v. Baucom*, 28 Or.App. 757, 561 P.2d 641 (1977), the court ruled that a psychiatric social worker, who counseled the defendant after the offense was not competent to give expert testimony because her work did not encompass making retrospective diagnoses of the existence of a mental disease or defect.

c) Limitations on the Use of Expert Witnesses

Once qualified to serve in the capacity of an expert, the expert witness is subject to additional rules that regulate his conduct as a witness. Concern about the proper scope of expert witness testimony has prompted courts in many jurisdictions to attempt remedial action to limit certain types of evidence and to control the manner in which testimony is given. The following materials illustrate some of these limitations on expert witness testimony.

WASHINGTON v. UNITED STATES

United States Court of Appeals, District of Columbia Circuit, 1967.
390 F.2d 444.

BAZELON, J.

* * *

We all agree that this court's limited role in supervising the verdict does not imply an equally limited role in supervising the evidence which is put before the jury. To the contrary, the jury's wide latitude in deciding the issue of responsibility *requires* that trial judges and appellate judges ensure that the jury base its decision on the behavioral data which are relevant to a determination of blameworthiness. We disagree, however, on the quality of the data in this case. Judge Robinson and I are deeply troubled by the persistent use of labels and by the paucity of meaningful information presented to the jury. Experience with the administration of the insanity defense has revealed that, despite the earnest efforts of witnesses, counsel and judges, these defects are a recurring problem.

* * *

[In the instant case] the jury was [repeatedly] diverted from evidence of the defendant's underlying mental and emotional difficulties by the emphasis on conclusory phrases.

* * *

The omission of significant underlying information was one defect in the testimony. Another was that the jury was often subjected to a confusing mass of abstract philosophical discussion and fruitless disputation between lawyer and witness about legal and psychiatric labels and jargon.

* * *

Even if these labels had meaning for the witnesses, the testimony was useless unless that meaning was communicated to the jury.

* * *

This kind of testimony does not give the jury a satisfactory basis for determining criminal responsibility. A proper adjudication requires that the jury be fully informed about the defendant's mental and emotional processes and, insofar as it affects these processes, his social situation. Of course, we cannot hope to obtain *all* the relevant information about a defendant. We cannot explore in full the effects of his genetic structure, his family relationships, his upbringing in slum or suburb. But within the limits imposed by the courtroom context and the level of scientific knowledge we should provide the jury with as much of this information as is reasonably available. We are not excused from doing what we can do simply because there are things we cannot do.

With the relevant information about defendant, and guided by the legal principles enunciated by the court, the jury must decide, in effect, whether or not the defendant is blameworthy. Undoubtedly, the decision is often painfully difficult, and perhaps its very difficulty accounts for the readiness with which we have encouraged the expert to decide the question. But our society has chosen not to give this decision to psychiatrists or to any other professional elite but rather to twelve lay representatives of the community. The choice was not made on a naive assumption that all jurors would be fully capable of dealing with these difficult questions or with the underlying information. Nonetheless, this decision, along with many equally difficult ones in other areas, ranging from negligence to antitrust, was given to a jury. As long as this is our system, we should try to make it work.

The trial judge should limit the psychiatrists' use of medical labels—schizophrenia, neurosis, etc. It would be undesirable, as well as difficult, to eliminate completely all medical labels, since they sometimes provide a convenient and meaningful method of communication. But the trial judge should ensure that their meaning is explained to the jury and, as much as possible, that they are explained in a way which relates their meaning to the defendant.

*   *   *

Questions and Comments

1. Much of the criticism directed at expert testimony in insanity defense trials followed the District of Columbia's adoption of the *Durham* "product" test. The *Washington* opinion represented an attempt to limit the role of psychiatric testimony to a description of the defendant's mental condition so as not to usurp the jury's function under the Durham rule—to make the determination that the defendant's criminal conduct was or was not a "product" of his mental illness. The guidelines set out by the *Washington* court were not a success, though, as experts continued to dominate insanity defense trials.

As one commentator observed, the broad scope of expert testimony was itself a "product" of the District of Columbia's definition of legal insanity under Durham:

> In 1972, the Court of Appeals for the District of Columbia abandoned the *Durham* rule entirely and adopted the American Law Institute's definition of legal insanity. One of the principal reasons for doing so was the problem that court had been having with the "product" portion of the *Durham* rule: Psychiatric witnesses came to substitute their own judgments of the responsibility of the accused for that of the jury, and to phrase their conclusions on that ultimate issue in terms of whether or not the criminal act was the *product* of disease.

> This illegitimate transfer to psychiatrists of the power to decide the meaning of a legal rule on criminal responsibility resulted directly from the assumption of the District of Columbia judges that mental illness, as used in the rule, was the same concept as that used in medicine.

M. Moore, *Law and Psychiatry*, 229–30 (New York: Cambridge Univ. Press, 1984).

2. In *Lampkins v. United States*, 401 A.2d 966 (D.C.App.1979), the District of Columbia Court of Appeals clarified its position on the proper scope of expert opinion evidence:

> In recent years, courts in this jurisdiction have relaxed the ultimate facts rule, holding that an expert may state a conclusion on such facts provided the conclusion is one that laymen could not draw. Thus, expert opinion testimony will not be excluded merely because it amounts to an opinion upon ultimate facts. *See, e.g., Casbarian v. District of Columbia*, D.C.Mun.App., 134 A.2d 488, 491 (1957) ("The real test is not that the expert opinion testimony would go to the very issue to be decided by the trier of fact, but whether the special knowledge or experience of the expert would aid the court or jury in determining the questions in issue"). As a practical matter, an exception to the ultimate issue rule exists where the helpfulness of the proffered expert opinion outweighs its prejudicial impact; to the

extent admission is necessary to aid the jury, an invasion of the jury's province will be tolerated. Nevertheless, we find objectionable questions which, in effect, submit the whole case to an expert witness for decision.

At 970.

3. Disagreement among experts on factual matters and interpretations of these facts occur in all fields, but it appears to be especially significant and troublesome in the area of mental health. *See,* Morse, *Failed Explanations and Criminal Responsibility: Experts and the Unconscious,* 68 Va.L.Rev. 971, 1055–56 (1982). Compare the following views on the capacities of psychiatrists serving as expert witnesses:

"The present insanity defense also frequently leads to a gross distortion of the trial process. Commonly, in a trial involving an insanity defense, the defendant's commission of the acts in question is conceded. The trial focuses on the issue of insanity. Both sides present an array of expert psychiatric witnesses who offer conflicting opinions on the defendant's sanity. Unfortunately for the jury—and society—the terms used in any statement of the scope of the defense—for example, the phrase 'disease or defect'—are usually not defined and the experts themselves do not agree on their meaning. Moreover, the experts often do not agree even on the extent to which certain behavior patterns or mental disorders that have been labeled 'inadequate personality,' 'abnormal personality,' and 'schizophrenia' actually impel a person to act in a certain way. In short, medical disagreement is implicit in the issue of whether a person could conform to the requirements of the law.

"Since the experts disagree about both the meaning of the terms used to discuss the defendant's mental state and the effect of particular mental states on actions, it is small wonder that trials involving an insanity plea are arduous, expensive and worst of all, thoroughly confusing to the jury. Indeed, the disagreement of the supposed experts is perhaps so basic that it makes the jury's decision rationally impossible."

Senate Insanity Defense Hearings, *supra,* at 28–29. (Statement of Attorney General William French Smith.) *See also,* Halpern, *The Insanity Defense: A Juridicial Anachronism,* 7 Psychiatric Annals 8 (1977) ("psychiatrists do not possess unique ability to determine the state of mind of a defendant long after the crime was committed"); Ennis and Litwack, *Psychiatry and the Presumption of Expertise: Flipping coins in the Courtroom,* 62 Cal.L.Rev. 693 (1974).

Despite the claims of the rabid antipsychiatry factionalists, psychiatry is becoming an increasingly refined field. The old saw that diagnostic reliability is no better than 50 percent (hence the phrase "flipping coins in the courtroom") is being pushed aside by studies that show high diagnostic reliability. Indeed, the severe mental illnesses such as schizophrenia now enjoy an interrater reliability of 80 to 95 percent thanks to the new diagnostic and statistical manual (DSM–III). A good review of reliability studies of psychiatric diagnoses was published by Grove and his colleagues in 1981. Furthermore, while the prediction of dangerousness continues to be a controversial area, several researchers, notably Monahan, have developed promising approaches.

* * *

[Moreover] similar "wars of the experts" occur in almost any area the law touches. Accountants, physicists, microbiologists, specialists of almost any discipline have been called at one time or another and displayed their disagreements in court. Orthopedic surgeons regularly testify in civil cases—one offering an opinion that a disability is nonexistent, the other offering the opinion that the disability is one hundred percent. All disciplines have disagreements, and the adversary process magnifies the controversies in an attempt to resolve them.

Senate Insanity Defense Hearings, *supra*, at pp. 64, 70. (Statement of Randolph A. Read.) *See also*, Myth and Realities, Hearing Transcripts of the National Commission on the Insanity Defense, 104 (Statement of Loren Roth, M.D.); Meehl, The Insanity Defense, Minnesota Psychologist, 11, 14 (Summ.1983).

UNITED STATES v. TORNIERO

United States District Court, District of Connecticut, 1983.
570 F.Supp. 721.

CABRANES, J.

By indictment filed September 23, 1982, the grand jury charged the defendant, John J. Torniero, with ten counts of transporting stolen goods in interstate commerce, in violation of 18 U.S.C. § 2314. On October 12, 1982, pursuant to Rule 12.2, Fed.R.Crim.P., the defendant filed a Notice to Rely upon the Defense of Insanity and a Notice of Intention to Introduce Expert Testimony Regarding Mental Disease or Defect Inconsistent with the Mental Element Required for the Offense Charged.

* * *

In seeking to rely on the insanity defense and to introduce expert testimony, the defendant argues that, at the time of the acts described in the indictment, he suffered from so-called "compulsive gambling disorder," as described in the Diagnostic and Statistical Manual of Mental Disorders (3d Ed., 1980) ("DSM III"), § 312.31 at 291–292, promulgated by the American Psychiatric Association ("APA"). An individual suffering from that disorder is characterized as one who is "chronically and progressively unable to resist impulses to gamble," *id.* at 292. The defendant contends that his compulsive gambling led to an accumulation of debts that, in turn, compelled his commission of the acts with which he is charged.

The practical effect of the defendant's notice of the introduction of expert testimony is to permit testimony on the defendant's behalf by psychiatrists, psychologists, and other mental health specialists, who would, under Article VII of the Federal Rules of Evidence, be permitted to offer professional opinions on the existence and effect of the condition from which the defendant claims to have suffered and to testify in response to hypothetical questions. Furthermore, by raising the issue of insanity, the defendant seeks to impose upon the Government the burden of proving beyond a reasonable doubt that the defendant was in fact sane at the time of the offenses with which he has been charged. When the insanity defense is properly before it, the jury is called upon to consider whether the defendant's mental state at the time of the alleged offense can be comprehended by the jury. The role of the psychiatrist in assisting that inquiry must be a limited one. From his experience with mental illness, the psychiatrist may be able to sharpen the jury's appreciation of the variety of mental conditions and the nature of the diseased or defective mind. Indeed, the psychiatrist may, in some cases, be better able than the defendant to describe the state of mind of the defendant at the relevant time.

* * *

The defendant in this case is not, of course, charged with gambling; he is charged with the interstate transportation of stolen goods. Nonetheless, the defend- [sic] of admission of expert testimony. First, he argues that compulsive gambling disorder is a mental disease, the result of which may be that the sufferer is unable to conform his conduct to the requirements of law. Thus, argues the defendant, a defense of insanity may be based on compulsive gambling disorder. Second, the defendant relies on cases holding that the question of whether a defendant suffers from a mental disease or defect is a question for the jury's determination and that, in aid of that determination, trial courts should liberally permit introduction of expert testimony.

The standard proposed by the defendant, however, is far too lax. It is questionable whether compulsive gambling disorder ought even to be the basis for an insanity defense when the offense charged is gambling. The defendant, though, would go much farther: he would have a putative disorder characterized chiefly by repetition of one kind of conduct become the basis for a conclusion that, in engaging in another kind of conduct, the defendant's mental state amounted to insanity. That relationship is too tenuous to warrant the introduction of expert witnesses.

This conclusion, which this court is not alone in reaching, is compelled by a recognition of the drastic expansion of the insanity defense threatened by the defendant's argument. Were the court to accept the defendant's proposed extension of the law, there would be no logical reason why alcohol or drug addiction would not form the basis for an insanity defense to any indictment, whether one for tax fraud, firearms possession, false statement, assault, kidnapping, or murder. The consequence of such a position would be an explosion in the amount of psychiatric testimony offered at criminal trials; it would also tend to redefine the criminal law as a system of therapy (biological or psychiatric) devoid of individual moral judgments. Just as this court has already declined to overturn the implicit assumptions of Congress and the Supreme Court by "abolishing" the insanity defense, it does not consider as an appropriate exercise of its authority the momentous expansion of the defense urged by this defendant.

During the course of hearings on the Government's *in limine* motion, considered along with the Government's motion to reconsider the law of insanity, the court has learned nothing that would suggest that the defendant, even if he could *potentially* assert a defense of insanity in response to a charge of illegal gambling, may *actually* assert that defense to the acts with which he is in fact charged in this case. Supposing that he was entirely unable to resist his impulse to gamble, it would follow only that he would have enormous debts. It would not then necessarily follow that his only recourse would be to the transportation of stolen goods. Indebtedness itself cannot be said to compel conduct. Unless the defendant could show that his insanity had a *direct* bearing on his commission of the acts with which he is charged, any psychiatric evidence he might seek to introduce would have to be excluded as irrelevant. The defendant has not offered to introduce expert testimony on compulsive gambling for the purpose of showing such a direct connection.

Under these circumstances, the court concludes that the defendant could enjoy no advantage from testimony regarding his compulsive gambling, except such impermissible leverage as he might obtain from jury confusion. To forestall such confusion, the court holds that the expert testimony proffered by the defendant shall be excluded.

Questions and Comments

1. *Torniero* illustrates a limitation on the use of expert testimony arising from the requirement that the evidence that is introduced in a trial must be relevant and germane to some issue in question. The *Torniero* court held that the defendant proposed expert testimony (that the defendant suffered from a "compulsive gambling disorder") was insufficiently related to the conduct (transportation of stolen goods) that formed the basis of the crime charged. Would the result have been the same if the criminal charge had involved the violation of federal gambling laws?

2. A further limitation on the admissibility of expert testimony arises from the general rule that such testimony is admissible only if the state of the pertinent act or scientific knowledge is sufficiently established to permit a reasonable opinion to be asserted on the issue in question. *McCormick on Evidence*, § 13 at 29–31 (E. Cleary, 2d ed. 1972).

The rule originated in *Frye v. United States*, 293 F. 1013 (D.C.Cir. 1923), and represents the most widely recognized standard that courts use to evaluate the admissibility of scientific evidence and its supporting expert testimony:

> Just when a scientific principle or discovery crosses the line between the experimental and demonstrable stages is difficult to define. Somewhere in this twilight zone the evidential force of the principle must be recognized, and while courts will go a long way in admitting expert testimony deduced from a well-recognized scientific principle or discovery, the thing from which the deduction is made must be *sufficiently established to have gained general acceptance in the particular field in which it belongs.* (emphasis added).

At 1014.

3. An issue involving the *Frye* standard arose in the Hinckley trial. The defense sought admission of CAT scans—computer reconstructed cross-section of the brain—as evidence on the issue of Hinckley's insanity. Defense counsel contended that Hinckley's scans, showing widened sulci (folds and ridges on the surface of the brain), constituted evidence of schizophrenia. In opposing admission of the expert testimony on this point the government argued that there was no reliable evidence that a CAT scan could aid diagnosis of schizophrenia, and further, that there was no proof of Hinckley's schizophrenia for a CAT scan to corroborate. Judge Barrington Parker initially ruled that the CAT scan evidence would not be admissable, but later changed his mind and let the defense present evidence relating Hinckley's CAT scan to the jury. *See* Caplan, *Annals of Law, The Insanity Defense*, The New Yorker, July 2, 1984, at 45, 64.

4. Whether a particular psychiatric theory may be testified to by an expert as being consistent with "the state of the pertinent art or scientific knowledge", *see* note 2 *supra*, may also arise in connection with issues other than the insanity defense. For instance, some defendants have sought to introduce expert testimony on "the behavior of women who have been subjected to sustained abuse from husbands or lovers is admissible to help establish claims of self-defense in murder cases." While the courts of some states have excluded testimony concerning the "battered women syndrome" other courts such as those in New Jersey, Washington, Maine, and Georgia have upheld the use of such testimony. *See, Use of Experts on Battering Is Upheld in Women's Trials*, New York Times, July 25, 1984, p. 1, col. 3.

5. Generally an expert retained by the *defense* to examine the defendant cannot be questioned by the *prosecution* unless the defense decides to call its expert as a witness at trial. Those jurisdictions applying this rule do so to protect the defendant's Sixth Amendment guarantee of effective assistance of counsel as well as the attorney-client privilege. There are some courts, however, which view an assertion of the insanity defense as a waiver of the attorney-client privilege as to communications between the client and his psychiatrist. For a more extensive development of this issue as well as case authority for both

views, see Chapter Four, Sec. II.D.3. The issue is included here only to describe, in brief, an additional limitation on expert witness testimony.

3. An Indigent's Right to Expert Witness Testimony

a. Current Practices

Although judicial opinions frequently state that expert testimony is not "essential" to raise the insanity defense, it is clear that a persuasive case is unlikely to be made on lay testimony alone.

> To persuade jurors that someone who behaves much as they do was insane at some prior date is incredibly difficult. In most cases, the defendant cannot possibly hope to succeed unless he can present an expert witness to bridge the gap between past unreason and present reason. This is particularly true because the prosecution will usually present its expert to describe as "normal" what defendant's laymen are characterizing as "abnormal"; the psychiatrist for the prosecution will be testifying, with a ring of authority which no layman can duplicate, that the defendant "knew right from wrong" or that he "knew the nature and quality of his act," or that he could control his conduct. In practical terms, a successful defense without expert testimony will be made only in cases so extreme, or so compelling in sympathy for the defendant, that the prosecutor is unlikely to bring them at all.

> * * *

> If an accused is to raise an effective insanity defense, it is clear that he will need the psychiatrist as a witness. He will need his aid in determining the kinds of testimony to be elicited, the specialists to be consulted, and the areas to be explored on cross-examination of opposing psychiatrists. And he may need him as a creative contributor to the development of the law.

A. Goldstein, *The Insanity Defense, supra,* p. 125–127.

Advances in science and technology and increased specialization in criminology have given the state an extensive array of investigators and experts whom the indigent's appointed counsel is ill-equipped to match. Unless the court supplies the indigent defendant with similar resources, the ability of the appointed counsel to prepare an adequate defense is seriously diminished. One commentator has gone so far as to argue that "[i]f the 'assistance' of the Sixth Amendment guarantee [right to assistance of counsel] is emphasized in conjunction with necessities of effective representation, then the concomitant services of experts and investigators must be supplied." Note, *The Indigent's Right to an Adequate Defense: Expert and Investigational Assistance in Criminal Proceedings,* 55 Cornell L.Rev. 632, 641 (1970). But the courts, fearful of costs, have not been enthusiastic in extending the representation rights of indigents. Cases such as that of John Hinckley, where the cost of the psychiatric experts for both sides was reputed to be in excess of $500,000, have undoubtedly contributed to this attitude. *See* Taylor, *Too Much Justice*, Harper's, Sept. 1982, at 56.

The first step toward providing the necessary extra assistance was embodied in the Federal Criminal Justice Act of 1964, which permitted federal courts to authorize counsel, upon request, to obtain necessary services on behalf of an indigent defendant at a cost not in excess of $300 for each person rendering such service. 18 U.S.C.A. § 3006A (1964). These congressionally authorized expenses were only authorized for services "necessary" to an adequate defense and most federal courts have interpreted this provision narrowly, by requiring proof that such additional services are absolutely necessary. The monetary restriction has also impaired the effectiveness of the act. In 1970 Congress removed the $300 limit and gave trial courts the authority to reimburse additional expenses, if they are found to be necessary. This change, however, has not led to any significant degree of liberalization in reimbursement amounts allowed by the courts. These limitations reflect the reluctance of the federal courts to give assistance beyond that of counsel. In *Christian v. United States*, 398 F.2d 517 (10th Cir.1968), the court declared that, although every criminal defendant financially unable to obtain counsel is entitled to the appointment of counsel at government expense, not every similarly situated defendant is entitled to appointment of an investigator or other expert service. However, authority to the contrary does exist. In *Hintz v. Beto*, 379 F.2d 937 (5th Cir.1967), the court stated that the right to have a psychiatrist appointed was a right cognate to effective assistance of counsel under the Sixth Amendment.

State courts in jurisdictions that have considered whether the state is required to furnish a psychiatrist in the absence of a statute so directing hold that it is not constitutionally required, and that granting such aid is entirely discretionary. The following case is an early illustration of such a view.

STATE v. CROSE

Supreme Court of Arizona, 1960.
88 Ariz. 389, 357 P.2d 136.

LESHER, Justice.

This appeal is from a judgment and sentence entered upon a jury verdict finding the defendant guilty of kidnapping, grand theft and aggravated battery.

The defendant was without means to employ an attorney. At his arraignment, the court appointed to represent the defendant his present counsel, who have conscientiously and ably served him through the trial and this appeal. Among his pleas to the charge was the plea of not guilty by reason of insanity. Prior to his trial defendant moved the court for an order appointing two qualified psychiatrists to examine him and aid him in the presentation of his defense of insanity. That motion was not made under Rule 250 of the Rules of Criminal Procedure, 17 A.R.S., but was specifically for the purpose of enabling defendant to prepare and present at the trial evidence relating to the question whether he was, under our law, criminally responsible for his acts. The motion was denied.

* * *

Respecting the first issue, defendant contends that the right to have medical experts appointed by the court, at the state's expense, to examine him and assist his defense, is an integral and essential part of his constitutionally-guaranteed right to counsel. He has cited us no authority to support that position, and our own independent investigation has disclosed none. That he has the right to counsel, and the right of private access to his counsel, is not in doubt. We know of nothing, however, either by constitution or by statute, requiring the state at its own expense to make available to the defendant, in addition to counsel, the full paraphernalia of defense. We have no doubt that court-appointed counsel in cases such as this often face grave difficulties in matching, on behalf of their clients, the resources available to the prosecution. It is also certainly true, as a practical matter, that the assistance of experts in advance of trial often lies at the very heart of a successful defense. Nevertheless, the constitutional right to counsel has never been construed to include such assistance. That right is one well known to our law. Its essential character is well understood. Those who sought to protect it by appropriate provision in our State Constitution made their intent and meaning clear. Right to "counsel" means, as it has always meant, the right to the services of an attorney, an officer of the court, appointed by the court to advise and assist the accused. Appellant, in urging that we here broaden the term "counsel" to include expert witnesses, misconstrues the function of this Court. That function in this case is only to interpret the constitutional provision; not to write it or re-write it. He asks us to construe it broadly—but we cannot "construe" it when merely reading it will alone suffice. We have no doubt that those who make the law could appropriately provide impecunious defendants with such assistance as was sought here, were it deemed practicable and in the public interest to do so. They have not done so. They were under no constitutional compulsion to do so. The denial of the motion was not error.

Questions and Comments

1. At least fourteen states have legislation providing for the reimbursement of trial preparation expenses, including investigators, lab analysis, and expert testimony. These statutes were adopted in response to the Federal Criminal Justice Act, and, while some of them are co-extensive with the federal act, others are more restrictive, paying for

expert and other services only in capital cases or only in cases in which persons are accused of murder, for example. *See* Ill.Rev.Stat. Ch. 38, § 113–3, 19 Pa.Stat. § 784. Courts in some jurisdictions simply refuse to exercise their discretion to provide additional assistance in any case on the grounds that the payment of investigator and expert witness fees is a matter for the legislature to determine, not the courts.

2. Even in states that refuse to provide any additional assistance, the indigent defendant may obtain additional expert testimony from mental health professionals who have treated the defendant during his lifetime by calling those people as witnesses. Compulsory process will then secure their attendance without the need for compensation by the defendant. However, as one commentator observed, the utility of this method of obtaining expert testimony may be limited:

> In the states which have no specialized procedure, and in the rest of the states as well, counsel may call as witnesses the persons who have dealt with the accused in the course of what is often an extensive psychiatric history. The accused may have been involved with school authorities, clinics, family service agencies, mental hospitals, and juvenile authorities, leaving behind him reports of psychiatrists, neurologists, clinical psychologists, and social workers. The authors of such reports need be paid no more than a nominal witness fee. In the case of the indigent, even that fee will often be paid by the state. When subpoenaed, these experts may be required to testify to the details of their relationship with the defendant, their test findings, their diagnoses, and the like. This testimony may, without more, persuade judge or jury to infer from the prior history that the accused was insane at the time of the crime.

> There will, however, be cases in which the time gap between the past condition and the crime is so great that a jury could not properly infer that the condition persisted. Expert testimony will be needed to show that the prior condition would ordinarily have persisted up to the time of the crime; or that the past condition, though not in itself sufficiently serious, would have deteriorated by the time of the crime.

*　*　*

> Clearly, the indigent accused supplied only with counsel and relying solely upon the general subpoena power is not in a position to present an effective insanity defense. Only if he has a substantial psychiatric history in the jurisdiction in which he is tried is he likely to be able to present psychiatric testimony. Even then, he may encounter problems in bringing the history up to date or in eliciting more generalized opinions. Moreover, he cannot expect any substantial commitment of time from a psychiatrist in preparing for trial.

A. Goldstein, *The Insanity Defense, supra,* p. 127–131.

While the statutes discussed above provide for the subsidization of expert services secured by the indigent's appointed counsel, the statutes more commonly grant the defendant access to a psychiatric expert appointed by the court. Typically these statutes allow the prosecution, the court, or the defendant himself to request the court to appoint a psychiatrist. The court-appointed expert—often termed the "impartial expert"—may also enter the trial when the issue of competency to stand trial is raised. In many cases, when the defendant lacks sufficient funds to pay for a psychiatric expert, and when state law does not provide for state reimbursement of such expenses, the defendant has no alternative but to rely on the court-appointed psychiatrist in order to have expert evidence relevant to his defense of insanity or incompetency.

This outcome, which forces the indigent to rely on a court-appointed expert, has been challenged on the grounds that it is unduly disadvantageous to an indigent defendant. The following subsection considers this issue in greater detail.

b. Emerging Issues: Denial of an Independent Expert

JOHNSON v. STATE
Court of Appeals of Maryland, 1982.
292 Md. 405, 439 A.2d 542.

DIGGES, Judge.

Lawrence Johnson was convicted, after removal of this criminal cause from Baltimore County, by a jury in the Circuit Court for Calvert County of first degree murder (both premeditated and in the commission of a felony), first degree rape, kidnapping, and use of a handgun during the commission of a felony or a crime of violence. The same jury subsequently sentenced Johnson to death for the murder. As is specified by the statute authorizing the sentence of death, we must, by this expedited appeal, scrutinize both the decision to execute the defendant as well as any claims of error properly presented by the parties. With the exception of the imposition of the death penalty, we sustain these convictions and sentences ordered, and remand this cause for a new hearing concerning the punishment to be given for the murder.

The sordid chronicle of this crime spree was related by the appellant, Lawrence Johnson, at trial. It began on the early morning of February 23, 1980, when he was suddenly awakened by a friend, Amos Batts, while perched on the couch at the home of his cousin, Dwayne Mayers. At the urging of Batts, Johnson followed his friend outside to a car being operated by the cousin. It soon became apparent to Johnson that Mayers and Batts had stolen the vehicle during the night and had abducted its owner, Betty Toulson, in the process. Although Johnson had earlier declined to participate when the other two decided to obtain some money through crime, the defendant this time joined them in the car with the victim. After a brief discussion, Mayers started the vehicle and drove around while the three men smoked "parsley flakes sprayed with some kind of embalming fluid." The victim remained silent throughout this journey "with her head down." Later, after driving to a remote area of

Baltimore County, Mayers stopped the car and asked whether his companions "wanted to have sex" with their prisoner. Mayers and the appellant eventually raped the woman on the back seat of her car. The trio then drove the victim to another location nearby where Mayers stripped Ms. Toulson of her coat and pocketbook. After discussing the problem presented by the victim's knowledge of their identities, Mayers returned to the automobile, removed a pistol from under the seat, and presented it to appellant with instructions to kill the woman. Johnson led her into the woods and complied with the directive. Ms. Toulson's snow-covered body was recovered five days later; she had received fatal shots in the head and chest.

Following his trial, convictions, and sentencing, Johnson, because he received the death penalty, appealed directly to this Court, where he presents numerous contentions concerning the conduct of trial on the issue of guilt as well as the murder sentencing proceeding.

* * *

Johnson initially contends that, following entry of his plea of not guilty by reason of insanity and his referral to a state hospital for a psychiatric examination, he was further entitled to appointment of a private psychiatrist of his own choosing at state expense to assist in his defense. The record reveals that, upon the filing of this plea, Judge Haile in the Circuit Court for Baltimore County ordered that Johnson be transferred to the Clifton T. Perkins state mental hospital for an evaluation. After a staff examination, the hospital issued the following report, over the signatures of its superintendent and clinical director:

> Mr. Johnson was admitted to the Clifton T. Perkins Hospital Center on June 16, 1980, and evaluated in accordance with your order of April 23, 1980.
>
> On June 19, 1980, Mr. Johnson was interviewed at a medical staff conference, where results of the multidisciplinary evaluation were examined. * * *
>
> It was the opinion of the psychiatrists present at the conference that:
>
> 1. The diagnosis is Antisocial Personality; Drug Abuse by History. (majority)
>
> 2. At the present time, Mr. Johnson is able to understand the nature and object of the proceedings against him and to assist in his own defense. (majority)
>
> 3. At the time of the alleged offense, Mr. Johnson was not suffering from a mental disorder which caused him to lack substantial capacity to appreciate the criminality of his conduct or to conform his conduct to the requirements of the law. (majority)
>
> Therefore, we are making arrangements to return Mr. Johnson to your custody.

The notation "majority" following each statement in the report resulted because Dr. Clermont, the clinical director of Perkins, declined to join, stating that he "did not arrive [at] a definite conclusion about the diagnosis and responsibility as the defendant was uncooperative with him during most of the interview."

Sometime later, Johnson's attorney, arguing that it was "crucial to the defense * * * that the defendant be evaluated by a privately retained psychiatrist in order to determine whether he was, in fact, sane at the time of the commission of the alleged crime," petitioned the court to appoint a private "independent psychiatrist" to further examine Johnson at the expense of the State. The trial judge denied Johnson's petition after noting that he had already been examined by the staff at Perkins hospital and that "the doctors practicing in the various institutions under the jurisdiction of the Department of Health and Mental Hygiene are 'independent psychiatrists' within the context in which that term is used in this case."

* * * Appellant now asserts that this refusal of his request for appointment of a private psychiatrist effectively denied him the rights to the assistance of counsel, due process of law, and the equal protection of law in violation of various State and Federal Constitutional guarantees. In making this argument, Johnson acknowledges that the judge before whom an accused has entered a plea of insanity has "full power and authority to order an examination of the mental condition of such person by the Department of Health and Mental Hygiene. * * *" Md.Code (1957, 1979 Repl.Vol., 1981 Cum. Supp.), Art. 59, § 25(b). Johnson also admits that "the Department is an impartial expert," but he goes further and asserts that, in addition to such neutral evaluation, an indigent accused is entitled to another psychiatric expert, this one of his own choosing, funded by the State, solely to assist with the defense.

Although there can be little doubt that an effective defense may sometimes require expert assistance, the issue as posed by appellant is a much narrower one. It solely concerns whether Maryland's statutory scheme providing for court appointment of a psychiatrist from the Department of Health and Mental Hygiene in cases involving a criminal defendant's asserted insanity or incompetency is inadequate and that the appointment of additional experts is constitutionally required.

Even though appellant doesn't specifically claim a right to a "psychiatric advocate," his position reduces to essentially that proposition; thus the words of Chief Justice Burger, speaking as a judge for the District of Columbia Circuit in *Proctor v. Harris*, 413 F.2d 383, 386 (D.C.Cir.1969), are particularly apropos here.

> From Appellant's posture, no psychiatrist can really "assist" him adequately unless he agrees with Appellant's position. Stripped of its verbiage Appellant's position is that he is entitled to a psychiatrist sufficiently sympathetic so that he will assist counsel in preparing his case favorably to his claims, and, accordingly, in structuring cross-

examination of the hospital doctors so as to neutralize their testimony.

Common sense dictates that there be some limit placed upon the right of indigents to the assistance of State-funded experts. This is not a case where the government has refused to provide psychiatric evaluation of a criminal accused who wishes to interpose an insanity defense, or where the resulting report is withheld from the defendant. Nor has appellant in this case produced evidence challenging the professional competence or impartiality of the psychiatrists at the Perkins Hospital. The doctors designated by the Department of Health and Mental Hygiene to examine Johnson are thus "not partisans of the prosecution, though their fee is paid by the State, any more than is assigned counsel for the defense beholden to the prosecution merely because he is * * * compensated by the State. Each is given a purely professional job to do—counsel to represent the defendant to the best of his ability, the designated psychiatrists impartially to examine into and report upon the mental condition of the accused." *McGarty v. O'Brien*, 188 F.2d 151, 155 (1st Cir.1951), *cert. denied*, 341 U.S. 928 (1951).

We are sensitive to the concerns of the defense attorney in this case faced with the task of undertaking to defend one who had voluntarily confessed to the crime in grim detail and where the state possessed overwhelming evidence of his client's participation in the criminal acts. Counsel indeed confronted a bleak prospect unless he could develop sufficient evidence of insanity to at least create a jury question. Certainly, in these circumstances the indigent accused is at a disadvantage when compared with the wealthy defendant who possesses unlimited resources for the marshalling of batteries of attorneys, investigators and experts. It cannot be seriously contended, however, that the State must precisely equalize the position of the penurious defendant and the wealthy one. Even in the case of the right to counsel, an indigent accused is neither entitled to several attorneys to represent him nor to select a particular attorney to be appointed. Here, Johnson was evaluated by a team of independent psychiatric experts, he was furnished with copies of the resulting reports prepared by the examiners, and he had the opportunity to subpoena and question at trial members of the examining team. Whatever the amount of required State assistance for the appointment of defense experts to enable the indigent to place the issue of insanity before the trial court, we need not determine here, for it is certain that once an accused is evaluated by state funded, impartial and competent psychiatrists, that constitutional duty, if any, ends. "[T]he State has no constitutional obligation to promote a battle between psychiatric experts 'by supplying defense counsel with funds wherewith to hunt around for other experts who may be willing, as witnesses for the defense, to offer the opinion that the accused is criminally insane' * * *." We have found no case which broadens constitutional principles this far and defendant has cited none.

Where an indigent accused has already received a competent psychiatric evaluation at state expense, either by the staff of a state institution, or by a private physician selected by the court, the cases throughout the country are in virtual unanimity and agree with our position upholding the denial of the indigent's request for an additional psychiatric expert of his own choosing compensated by the state.

Questions and Comments

1. On March 19, 1984, the Supreme Court granted certiorari in *Ake v. Oklahoma*, ___ U.S. ___, 104 S.Ct. 1591, 80 L.Ed.2d 123 (1984). Among the questions presented by the ruling of the Oklahoma Court of Appeals, 663 P.2d 1 (Okl.App.1983), is whether the state can constitutionally refuse to provide any opportunity for an indigent defendant to obtain expert psychiatric examination necessary to prepare and establish his insanity defense. In this case the defendant's sanity at the time of the offense was clearly seriously at issue. The court of appeals held that the state does not have such a responsibility, even in capital cases.

2. It has been argued that unless indigent defendants are provided with an independent expert, "their freedom and the conditions of their incarceration will turn on the opinions of psychiatrists employed by the government, and there will be little chance for the adversary process to expose conflicting expert views and disclose all the factual data a judge or jury needs to make an independent evaluation." Reisner and Semmel, *Abolishing the Insanity Defense: A Look at the Proposed Federal Criminal Code Reform Act in the Light of the Swedish Experience*, 62 Cal.L.Rev. 753, 787 (1974). Even if this contention is true, wouldn't the argument have to be balanced against other considerations such as the very substantial costs that would be incurred if the state had to provide an independent expert as well as the possible increased use of the insanity defense which might occur if independent experts were made available to all defendants.

3. It has been contended that the value of an independent expert is undermined where a *court-appointed* psychiatrist, who is clearly identified as such for the jury, is also allowed to testify. As noted by Professor Goldstein, "[t]he most important and dramatic feature of the procedure is the added credibility which accrues to the 'impartial' expert appointed by the court. Judge and jury tend to believe him. Prosecutors dismiss proceedings and defense counsel forego reliance on the insanity defense in accordance with his opinion. Indeed, advocates of the procedure rely heavily upon this very fact in arguing it is needed to correct the 'partisan' battle of the experts." Goldstein, *supra*, pp. 132–33. A study conducted in Ohio, where court-appointed psychiatrists are authorized, revealed that the jury rejected the findings of the state hospital staff in only 5 cases out of 1175. Guttmacher and Weihofen, *The Psychiatrist on the Witness Stand*, Bost.U.L.Rev. 287, 313 (1952). These authors concluded that the weight given to the "impartial" expert's opinion is so great that "lawyers have learned that it is usually hopeless to contest the hospital's findings." *Id.* at 314. Despite these concerns, the majority of the states make use of the court-appointed

psychiatric expert and reject the allegations that the procedure unfairly prejudices the defendant's case.

C. THE INSANITY DEFENSE STANDARD

1. Introduction

Once the jury has viewed the evidence presented by the prosecution and the defense, it must determine the ultimate issue of whether or not to hold the accused criminally responsible. To guide jurors in this determination, each jurisdiction has an insanity standard or test, and the jurors are instructed by the trial judge to apply the evidence to the standard and to decide by that measure whether or not the defendant's mental condition entitles his criminal behavior to be excused. In U.S. jurisdictions there are many different insanity tests (*see* note 1 *infra*), the most common test currently used, however, is the American Law Institute (A.L.I.) or Substantial Capacity Test. The A.L.I. test has been adopted, sometimes with substantial modifications, in 27 states and the District of Columbia, as well as in all circuits of the U.S. Courts of Appeal. The majority of these jurisdictions adopted the test through legislative means, although a few states introduced the A.L.I. test through judicial decision. *E.g.,* *Commonwealth v. McHoul,* 352 Mass. 544, 226 N.E.2d 556 (1967); *Graham v. State,* 547 S.W.2d 531 (Tenn.1977).

The text of the Substantial Capacity Test, as it appears in the A.L.I.'s Model Penal Code, follows:

Section 4.01   Mental Disease or Defect Excluding Responsibility

(1) A person is not responsible for criminal conduct if at the time of such conduct as a result of mental disease or defect he lacks substantial capacity either to appreciate the criminality [wrongfulness] of his conduct or to conform his conduct to the requirements of law.

(2) As used in this article, the terms "mental disease or defect" do not include an abnormality manifested only by repeated criminal or otherwise anti-social conduct.

The second part of the A.L.I. test was "designed to exclude from the concept of 'mental disease or defect' the case of the so-called 'psychopathic personality.'" Model Penal Code § 4.01, Comment (Tent.Draft No. 4, 1955). The comment states that psychopaths differ from normal persons only quantitatively and not qualitatively and that a considerable difference of opinion exists on whether psychopathy should be considered a disease. Much of the criticism of the A.L.I. Substantial Capacity Test has been directed at this part. Because of doubts about its soundness or effectiveness, some courts have adopted a modified form of the A.L.I. test, without this express exclusion. *See, e.g., United States v. Currens,* 290 F.2d 751 (3d Cir. 1961); *United States v. Smith,* 404 F.2d 720 (6th Cir.1968).

The A.L.I. test sets forth two necessary conditions before an acquittal by reason of insanity can occur. First, the defendant must suffer from a mental disease or defect. These terms are left undefined in the A.L.I. test as their interpretation was intended to be left to judicial decisions in each jurisdiction. Second, once the existence of a mental disease or defect has been established, a further two-pronged condition remains. If the jury finds that the defendant lacked *substantial* capacity in either area, the standards of the A.L.I. Substantial Capacity Test required his acquittal.

A comparison of the A.L.I. test with some of the insanity tests that preceded it highlights the problems and disputes associated with past standards. The A.L.I. Substantial Capacity Test rejected the *Durham* approach of excusing from criminal responsibility those whose unlawful act is the "product" of a mental disease or defect because of the ambiguity of the term "product." *See, Durham v. United States*, 94 U.S.App.D.C. 228, 214 F.2d 862 (1954). The A.L.I. formulation did not, however, totally reject the *M'Naghten* [a] or "irresistible impulse" [b] standards, but constituted a broader statement of their central concepts. A significant difference, though, was that where *M'Naghten* required a complete impairment of cognitive capacity and capacity for self control, the A.L.I. standard required only a lack of "substantial" capacity. This change was designed to temper the prohibitively strict requirements of the *M'Naghten* test.

In another modification, the A.L.I. test uses the word "appreciate" instead of "know," a term responsible for much of the criticism and misunderstanding of *M'Naghten*. *See*, LaFave and Scott, *Criminal Law* 276–277 (1972). The "conform his conduct" portion of the A.L.I. test avoids the implication, often derived from the "irresistible impulse" test, that the loss of volitional capacity can be reflected only in sudden or spontaneous acts as distinguished from those accompanied by brooding or reflection. Finally, the "criminality [wrongfulness]" wording provides flexibility in the A.L.I. standard that allows each jurisdiction adopting the test to choose what it views as the proper focus of the cognitive portion of the test, thus addressing another controversy that has surrounded the *M'Naghten* standard.

Questions and Comments

1. The variability that exists among the different jurisdictions as to their legal standards for insanity is still quite marked. The predominate test for insanity today is the American Law Institute's Substantial Capacity Test. The A.L.I. standard, as it was originally proposed, is the accepted test for insanity in 14 states and in all federal jurisdictions.

In 11 other states the A.L.I. test has also been adopted, but in modified form. Three of these states retain only the first part of the

a. To establish a defense on the grounds of insanity, it must be clearly proved that at the time of the committing of the act the party accused was laboring under such a defect of reason from disease of the mind as not to know the nature and quality of the act he was doing or if he did know it, that he did not know he was doing what was wrong.

b. See note 2 at p. 642 *supra*.

test as it was originally set out. The remaining eight states, while retaining the basic principles of the A.L.I. standard, have adopted differently worded or expanded or limited versions of the test.

The original *M'Naghten* formula remains the prevailing standard for insanity in 16 states, with three other states operating under slightly modified versions of the *M'Naghten* test.

Currently, the irresistible impulse provision supplements the insanity standards of four other states. Of these four states, three add the irresistible impulse provision to the *M'Naghten* standard, while one adds it to the appreciation of wrongfulness part of the A.L.I. test. See, Table on Current Tests for Insanity, Allocation of Burden and Quantum of Proof Within Federal Jurisdictions and the Several States Compiled by the American Bar Association's Standing Committee on Association Standards for Criminal Justice, November, 1982, cited in Britten and Bennett, *Adopt Guilty But Mentally Ill?—No!*, 15 Univ. of Toledo L.Rev. 203 (1983).

Of the remaining three states, New Hampshire operates under a test modeled on the *Durham* approach of defining legal insanity and remains the only jurisdiction to do so. Both Idaho and Montana have abolished the insanity defense as an affirmative defense and allow mental status evidence in only when it reaches a level capable of rebutting *mens rea* or criminal intent. *See* pp. 685–687 *infra.*

2. The A.L.I. standard has not gone uncriticized. Senior Circuit Judge David L. Bazelon of the District of Columbia Circuit, the author of the abandoned *Durham* Rule, has criticized the test in his reluctant concurrence to his circuit's adoption of the new test. *See, United States v. Brawner*, 471 F.2d 969 (D.C.Cir.1972). In comparing the A.L.I. test with the *Durham* standard, Judge Bazelon observed that causality was the essence of both tests and that only the language used to state it differs. Thus, whether causality is called "product" or "result," both tests encourage psychiatrists to testify in conclusory terms, preempting the role of the jury to determine guilt. As Judge Bazelon stated in his concurrence in *Brawner:*

> [In *Brawner*] the Court repeats precisely the mistake it correctly identifies in *Durham*: the articulation of a catch-phrase that facilitates conclusory expert testimony and that obscures the moral and legal overtones of the productivity question. Where a psychiatrist would formerly have testified that the act was not the "product" of the disease, he can now assert that the disease of the defendant does not entail as a "result" the kind of impairment that could have produced the act in question.

United States v. Brawner, 471 F.2d 969, 1027 (D.C.Cir.1972).

3. Whether juries are able to recognize distinctions among the various insanity tests has been the subject of considerable debate. Some believe that differences in the applicable legal standards do not have a significant effect on juries, either because juries do not understand the legal criteria or because they will, in any event, decide cases according to their own standards of justice. However, one study of jury behavior

concluded that, at the very least, juries recognize "the distinction between a clinical diagnosis and the application of a moral legal criterion, and that they understand it is the latter which they must use in deciding the case." R. Simon, *The Jury and the Defense of Insanity* (Boston: Little, Brown, & Company, 1967) p. 177.

However, even if juries are not responsive to differences in insanity defense standards, the use of one test rather than another is likely to materially affect the outcome of a case since it will govern the scope of psychiatric testimony that is admissible. In this connection, see *United States v. Torniero*, pp. 594–96 *supra* and the questions and comments that follow.

2. *Application of the Standard: An Illustrative Case*

a. *Background Profile of the Defendant*[a]

On 30 March 1981 President Ronald Reagan was scheduled to address a group of union leaders at the Washington Hilton Hotel. At about 1:45 p.m., approximately five minutes before the president's arrival, John Hinckley, Jr., reached the Hilton. He watched the president wave as he entered the hotel through the VIP entrance. He then positioned himself at the front of the press area and, mingling with the crowd, waited for the president to return. Emerging from the Hilton, President Reagan walked directly in front of the press area toward a waiting limousine. Hinckley drew a .22 caliber revolver from his pocket, assumed a crouching position, and fired all six rounds directly into the presidential entourage before he was subdued by Secret Service agents and bystanders.

One of the bullets ricochetted off the window of the limousine and struck the president in the chest, directly under his left arm. Also wounded in the attack were James Brady, the president's press secretary; Michael Delehanty, a local police officer; and Timothy McCarthy, a Secret Service agent. All four men survived their wounds, although Brady, who was struck in the head by one of the shots, suffered serious, permanent disability.

Over a 210-day period that began on 3 April 1981, government psychiatrists and psychologists conducted an extensive evaluation of Hinckley in preparation for the trial. This evaluation, subsequently joined in by psychiatric experts working for either the federal prosecutor or the defense counsel, consisted, in part, of interviews of the defendant, primarily about events of his life. This biographical information was crucial both in determining Hinckley's competence to stand trial and in the jury's determining Hinckley's criminal responsibility. Indeed, as is true of most trials in which the insanity defense is raised, the subject matter of the trial often became the defendant's life and the witnesses' impressions of it.

---

a. The information presented in this profile is based in part on statements made by John Hinckley to the evaluating psychiatrists and consequently is not, in every instance, subject to independent verification.

I.

No evidence suggests any abnormality in Hinckley's mental state or behavior prior to the age of eight or nine. Born in Ardmore, Oklahoma on May 29, 1955, he was the product of a normal pregnancy and delivery. Furthermore, Hinckley's blood line suggests no evidence of genetic abnormality. As an infant he walked slightly later than average but otherwise experienced normal growth and development.

Up to the age of fifteen or sixteen, Hinckley enjoyed a close relationship with the members of his family, which included his two parents, Jack and JoAnn; his brother Scott, seven years older than John; and his sister Diane, three years older than John. Their activities together, which included regular church attendance and annual vacations, were those of a typical, well-adjusted American family.

Hinckley grew up in an upper-middle-class environment. During his childhood he lived in a relatively luxurious home with a swimming pool located in an affluent suburb of Dallas, Texas. His parents sent him to summer camp, arranged for dancing lessons, and even bought him an electric guitar after he developed an interest in the Beatles. He excelled at grammar school sports, playing baseball, quarterbacking the school's football team, and starring on the basketball team.

About the only disturbing note—if it can even be called that—in this relatively idyllic childhood occurred when John was eight or nine. There is some evidence that his playmates perceived him as being unusually shy. But only in light of his introversion during adolescence is this evidence of any significance. Otherwise, there were no signs of maladaption during his early childhood.

II.

When John was in the sixth grade, the Hinckley family moved to Highland Park, an even more exclusive suburb of Dallas—a move which reflected Jack Hinckley's success as a petroleum engineer and entrepreneur. After the move John spent most of the year alone, unable to make friends in his new school. He overcame his shyness, however, when he entered a consolidated junior high school and was reunited with friends from his former grammar school. He was elected president of his homeroom in the seventh and eighth grades.

Yet after John entered high school, he gradually withdrew from the peer-group relationships that had been typical of his years in junior high. What emerges is a portrait of a boy who preferred to be alone and who seemed unable to establish lasting friendships, personality traits that continued into his early twenties. Usually John spent his time after school alone in his room, listening to Beatles' records, playing his guitar, or reading. This self-imposed solitude extended to the social activities of the family, prompting his father to make special efforts to establish a more meaningful relationship with him.

During high school Hinckley did occasionally go out with acquaintances, but by and large he established few friendships. Moreover, none of those friendships involved a sharing of his predominant interest during adolescence: the Beatles and their songs. Although he apparently developed a normal interest in girls, John never dated during his school days.

His academic record and extracurricular activities also reflect his seeming inability or unwillingness to become anything more than superficially involved with his immediate environment. His grades were slightly below average. His outside school activities were limited to management of the school's basketball team and membership in a few clubs; in marked contrast, his older brother and sister were extremely successful, both academically and socially.

III.

After Hinckley's graduation from high school in the spring of 1974, his parents moved to Evergreen, Colorado, a suburb of Denver; shortly thereafter John entered Texas Tech University in Lubbock. The structured environment of a college dormitory, where solitude was virtually impossible, at first brought John out of his shell. He established several friendships that continued throughout his freshman year, and, for the first and only time in his life, he shared his interest in music with others. He even played in a rock band. His interest in the business courses he took as a freshman was minimal, yet he attended classes and made passing grades.

During the summer and fall of 1974, however, he once again showed signs of withdrawal. Living in Dallas near the home of his sister and brother-in-law, he spent the summer sequestered in his one-room apartment, staring at the television. Lacking the motivation to return to school, he did not enroll for the fall term. But in response to parental pressures to return to college—pressure applied whenever John left school—he reenrolled in the spring of 1975.

Upon his return to the dormitory life, Hinckley failed to establish the friendships characteristic of his freshman year. Furthermore, his class attendance became increasingly sporadic. Hinckley's time became occupied by increasingly complicated fantasies.

At first John's daydreaming consisted of nothing more than imagining himself to be a famous singer-songwriter. But after he returned to Lubbock, John became preoccupied with a more disturbing fantasy, fueled by racist and right-wing literature he began reading, in which he became convinced that he had a leadership role in unifying adherents of right-wing ideology. John Hinckley gradually came to view himself as a special person, either marked for a special purpose or destined to perform a historic deed.

IV.

Hinckley attempted to realize his fantasy of becoming a famous musician in the spring of 1976, when he left school and traveled to Hollywood. His father told a friend at the time that John intended to "crash Hollywood."

In fact, Hinckley proved inept at setting up auditions with record producers—a frustrating and difficult task at best—and spent most of his time daydreaming in a rented room in the rough Selma Avenue area of Los Angeles. Despite his lack of success, and a growing discouragement about his abilities, Hinckley wrote a number of optimistic letters to his parents in an effort to retain their financial support.

Although Hinckley's stories of imminent success were merely pragmatic attempts to obtain money, his letters and behavior during his stay in Hollywood reveal not only his introversion and daydreaming but also a blurring of reality that borders on delusion. For example, Hinckley became preoccupied with the movie *Taxi Driver*, which he first saw in Los Angeles. It is difficult to overstate the effect of this film. Hinckley strongly identified with the film's main character, Travis Bickle, a loner angry with and alienated from society. Indeed, John began to imitate Bickle, buying an army jacket and boots like Bickle's. He also began keeping a diary, as Bickle had done.

It was in Hollywood that John fabricated his imaginary girlfriend Lynn, also patterned after a character in *Taxi Driver*. At first Lynn, whom he described as a wealthy, attractive actress, seems to have been created solely to persuade his parents to send him money, since his parents had always encouraged him to date. However, at some point during this period, he began to experience being with Lynn and entered their joint activities in his diary.

In contrast to his earlier optimistic letters, a letter Hinckley wrote shortly before leaving Hollywood revealed his own sense of failure. Although he added parenthetically that he was kidding, the letter contained Hinckley's first recorded threat of suicide after detailing his failure to secure a recording contract and a break-up with Lynn. In despair, he returned to Colorado in the fall of 1976, but went back to Hollywood in March of 1977, again failing to achieve success. After returning to Colorado, at his parents' urging, he subsequently enrolled in Texas Tech in April of 1977.

V.

Hinckley's first year at Texas Tech produced a B average and a place on the Dean's list. However, despite telling his parents that he was attending class—a condition for their financial support, Hinckley's class attendance dropped off markedly in the fall semester of the following year. The subsequent year and in the spring semester of 1979 he failed to enroll at all.

During this second period in Lubbock, Hinckley once again remained sequestered in his room for much of the time, watching television and cultivating his interest in reactionary ideology. In his German history class he authored papers on Hitler's *Mein Kampf* and on Auschwitz. He joined the American Socialist Party in March of 1978 and marched in a Nazi parade in St. Louis that same month. But in November of 1979, the party, apparently alarmed by Hinckley's letters to party leaders openly advocating the use of violence, refused to renew his membership. He also read several books on famous assassinations during this period: one about Lee Harvey Oswald and another about Robert Kennedy's murder, *RFK Must Die.*

Hinckley continued to view himself as destined for a position of leadership in the right-wing movement. This belief culminated in his attempt to form a national organization called the American Front, whose purpose was to alert white Protestants to the threat posed by minority groups. The organization was conceived as a sort of compromise between Republican conservatism and Nazism. Hinckley devoted considerable time and effort to the project, even producing a newsletter in September of 1979.

It must be noted that not all of Hinckley's endeavors were so unusual. In May of 1980 he wrote to his sister that he had formed a company called Listalot, to merchandise organizational membership lists (*i.e.,* the membership lists of country music fan clubs). Advertisements were taken out in such national publications as *People,* and at least initially John seemed certain he would succeed. But shortly thereafter he dropped the project, resigned to another failure. During this period he also resurrected the imaginary Lynn. For instance, in early 1979 Hinckley described his preparation for her arrival in Lubbock in a series of three detailed letters to his parents.

By the end of 1979, John Hinckley was finding it harder to escape reality. In an uncompleted draft of a letter to his parents written in November of 1979, he stated that things were not going well academically or financially; he was so depressed that he could not get out of bed in the morning. Life had not improved by Christmas: Hinckley spent the holiday alone, unable to face his family.

His depression led to suicidal thoughts. On January 2, 1980 Hinckley purchased a rifle to add to the .38 caliber revolver he had purchased earlier. Apparently he had put the revolver to his temple several times in November of 1979 and played Russian roulette with a single bullet in December. Pictures taken in May of 1980 show Hinckley with the revolver, reportedly empty, placed against his temple.

Realizing the seriousness of his depression and also experiencing some physical ailments, Hinckley sought professional help. At his parents' urging he returned to Colorado in early 1980 to be examined by three physicians. They could find no physical cause for the dizziness, head pain, and tingling of the extremities of which he complained and concluded that he was probably experiencing symptomatic expressions of anxiety and stress. Upon returning to Lubbock in May of 1980, Hinckley, still experiencing the same symptoms, sought out Dr. Rosen, a local physician, who also could find no physical basis for Hinckley's complaints. Dr. Rosen diagnosed his condition as a depressive reaction and prescribed Surmontil, an antidepressant. The drug did relieve Hinckley's anxiety but caused unpleasant side effects; Dr. Rosen then prescribed Valium, which provided limited relief.

John Hinckley went back to Evergreen in August and at his parents' request spoke with Dr. Benjamin, a psychologist. Jack and JoAnn Hinckley's hopes that Dr. Benjamin would convince their son that he needed to do something with his life were unfulfilled. John could not relate to Dr. Benjamin though the sessions did provide a basis for an interim understanding between John and his parents. Jack Hinckley agreed to provide his son with $3600 for the purpose of taking a writing course at Yale University. On 17 September 1980 Hinckley set out for New Haven on the first of a number of cross-country trips undertaken over the next six months, ending with his trip to Washington, D.C., in March of 1981.

VI.

Although a writing course like the one Hinckley had described to his parents was being offered at Yale, considerable evidence points to the conclusion that he went to New Haven solely to establish a relationship with Jodie Foster, one of the actresses in *Taxi Driver*. Hinckley had become increasingly obsessed with Foster ever since he had first seen *Taxi Driver*, in which Hinckley's role model Travis Bickle rescues Iris, the child-prostitute played by Foster, from her pimp. Hinckley's strong identification with Bickle led him to conclude that he, too, could prove his worth by gaining Foster's attention and affection, just as Bickle had done. In May of 1980 Hinckley read an article in *People* magazine which related Foster's plans to attend Yale in the fall. In August he watched several made-for-television movies in which she starred—movies which he believed had been placed on television solely to incite him to action. By the time he reached New Haven, his desire to see Foster and establish a relationship with her had become quite intense.

Hinckley made several attempts to contact Jodie Foster. He left cards at her door; he spoke with her roommate several times. On two occasions he did have telephone conversations with her, both of which he tape recorded. The tapes reveal that Foster rejected his polite but awkward advances and asked him not to call again. Deeply disappointed, Hinckley returned to Lubbock.

His reaction to this new setback shows how strong his identification with Travis Bickle had become. As did Bickle when rejected by a woman, Hinckley began to stalk the president of the United States. He added two .22 caliber pistols to his arsenal, giving him the same number of firearms that Bickle had owned—and left Lubbock for Washington, D.C. From there he flew to Columbus, Ohio, and then to Dayton, where President Jimmy Carter was to make a campaign appearance. Despite his success in getting close to the president, he simply could not muster the resolve to carry out the assassination.

After a sojourn to Lincoln, Nebraska, where he made a futile attempt to contact a leading figure in the Nazi movement, Hinckley followed the Carter campaign to Nashville, Tennessee. Again he found himself unable to kill the president. Moreover, the Nashville police apprehended him at the city's airport when a metal detector revealed the guns he had hidden in his suitcase. After Hinckley paid a fine, the police released him, not bothering to notify federal authorities.

A brief period of impulsive traveling followed, including trips to New Haven and New York, where he spent time picking up young prostitutes. By the middle of October Hinckley was back in Evergreen. Approximately one month had passed since he had left for New Haven.

VII.

Jack and JoAnn Hinckley had become increasingly concerned about their son's mental state. John confirmed their fears when shortly after his return he apparently attempted suicide by swallowing some twenty to twenty-five Surmontil tablets left over from Dr. Rosen's initial prescription. The occurrence caused Hinckley's parents to seek out Dr. Hopper, a local psychiatrist, who thereafter saw John on a regular basis until February of 1981. Dr. Hopper diagnosed Hinckley as suffering from anxiety neurosis, and his treatment focused on relieving that anxiety and its accompanying physical symptoms while reducing Hinckley's reliance on Valium. Biofeedback and other relaxation exercises were employed as part of the therapy.

Dr. Hopper did not consider his patient to be dangerous or in any way psychotic. Nevertheless, there is evidence that Hinckley kept his thoughts hidden from the psychiatrist and that Dr. Hopper did not delve deeply into Hinckley's innermost thoughts. For instance, on one occasion John did mention his interest in Jodie Foster, but neither he nor Dr. Hopper pursued the subject further although Hinckley's obsessive desire to possess the actress continued throughout his therapy with Dr. Hopper. Around this time Hinckley sent a letter to the FBI in which he threatened to kidnap Jodie Foster, prompting the FBI to assign an agent to guard her.

Hinckley's personal effects contained other evidence of the obsession and of some clearly delusional thinking. He evidently read a biography, entitled *The Fox*, whose leading character is a criminal who escapes prosecution by feigning mental illness, skyjacks a plane to New York, and then demands that certain people be brought to him. John copied a skyjacking note contained in the book, intending to use it to force President Reagan to resign and to have Jodie Foster brought to him. A postcard written to Foster in mid-February of

1981 was discovered between the pages of another book, *The Fan,* a story about a man who develops a psychotic fixation on a celebrity. The postcard, a photograph of President and Mrs. Reagan, contained a message promising Foster that one day she and Hinckley would occupy the White House together.

All of these disturbing themes are manifested in a sort of stream-of-consciousness monologue that Hinckley recorded on New Year's Eve of 1980. As usual, he notes, he is alone and afraid. The recent death of ex-Beatle John Lennon, one of his long-standing heroes, is lamented; Jodie Foster is proclaimed as the only thing that matters in his life. She must be protected from other men, even if this goal requires her death at Hinckley's hands. Yet at the same time he seems to be struggling to keep from harming her. Allusions are made to a death pact between himself and Foster and to his own suicide. There are expressions of apprehension about being able to make it through the coming year. Poetry written during this period explores similar themes: mental deterioration, suicide, alienation, and fantasized assassination that receives world-wide publicity.

The fear of losing his parents' love and support soon became another burden weighing on Hinckley's mind. As a result of the sessions with Dr. Hopper, John and his parents developed a plan that called for him to leave the family home and become self-supporting by the end of February. Though he made several half-hearted attempts at finding a job, he was ill prepared for independence as the deadline approached. Nevertheless, after his final session with Dr. Hopper on February 27, Hinckley kept his promise and left his parents' home for New York.

VIII.

After leaving Colorado, Hinckley spent the first week of March riding the bus back and forth between New York and New Haven, where he engaged in the now familiar ritual of leaving love notes for Jodie Foster. One note contained the following cryptic message: "Jodie, after tonight John Lennon and I will have a lot in common. It's all for you."

By March 7 John was back in Colorado. Hinckley's father at first resisted his son's request for airfare home but finally succumbed when confronted by John's vague threats of suicide. Still wishing to at least partially enforce the plan, Hinckley's father refused to allow his son access to the family home but did give him some cash. John spent the next two and a half weeks staying in different local motels. Then he decided to make one more last ditch attempt to sell his music in Hollywood.

On March 24, Hinckley flew to Los Angeles but failing in his attempt to contact record producers he departed by bus for Washington, D.C., intending to go from there to New Haven. After a three-day bus ride an exhausted John Hinckley arrived in Washington on

March 29, whereupon he checked into the Penn Central Hotel and tried to sleep. Unable to do so, he watched television and then dined at a fast-food restaurant before finally retiring to a restless night of sleep.

Hinckley awoke about 8:30 a.m., still somewhat fatigued, and went out for breakfast. After buying a newspaper, he returned to his hotel room and tried again to get some sleep, again without success. At about 11:30 a.m. he began to read the newspaper and came across President Reagan's itinerary for the day, which included the Hilton speech. It was at that point that Hinckley apparently decided to go to the Hilton and assassinate the president.

Hinckley showered, took some Valium to calm his nerves, and loaded his .22 caliber revolver with six Devastator bullets—deadly ammunition which explodes on impact with the skin. Travis Bickle had achieved a similar effect in *Taxi Driver* by carving crosses on the tops of his bullets. At about 12:45 p.m. he sat down to write a letter to Jodie Foster.

The letter provides some evidence of Hinckley's motive for the attack. Clearly in the minutes before he left for the Hilton his focus was on the actress and his own self-destruction. He described how he had repeatedly tried to gain her attention and affection but that time was running out. In order to win her respect and love, he was willing to give up his freedom or possibly even his life in the perpetration of what he called a "historic deed." Shortly after finishing the letter, John Hinckley concealed his weapon in the pocket of his raincoat and took a cab to the Hilton.

IX.

Immediately after the assassination attempt, federal agents transported Hinckley to a Washington police station. Early the next morning, Hinckley was taken to a heavily guarded federal district courtroom and charged with the attempted assassination of President Reagan. Federal agents then transported the defendant to the Marine Correctional Facility at Quantico, Virginia, where government psychiatrist, Dr. James Evans examined Hinckley to determine his competence to stand trial.

Later in the same week Federal District Judge William Bryant held a preliminary hearing to determine if there was probable cause to hold Hinckley over for indictment. After he had determined the existence of probable cause, the judge ordered Hinckley to submit to examinations by government psychiatrists for a ninety-day period following the hearing. The court later extended this period by an additional 110 days. Dr. Evans, the first psychiatrist to interview Hinckley after the assassination attempt, also testified at the preliminary hearing that Hinckley was competent to stand trial. Hinckley's appointed counsel made no attempt to challenge the competency determination, even though Dr. Evans's expert opinion was based on interviews with Hinckley that had occurred shortly after the shooting.

Following the preliminary hearing, federal officials transported Hinckley to the Federal Correctional Facility at Butner, North Carolina. On April 3 the first of hundreds of medical interviews with Hinckley was conducted by Dr. Sally Johnson, a psychiatrist affiliated with the Butner facility. Although Dr. Johnson was the prison psychiatrist principally involved in the initial evaluation, other psychiatrists affiliated with the Butner facility and a psychologist, Dr. Jim Hilkey, also evaluated Hinckley at this time.

In May of 1981 two more groups of psychiatrists began extensive examinations of the defendant. Drs. Park Dietz, Jonas Rappeport, James Cavanaugh, and Sally Johnson were retained by the U.S. district attorney's office to evaluate Hinckley and to testify as experts. Hinckley's defense counsel retained a team of three psychiatrists, Drs. David Bear, Thomas Goldman, and William Carpenter, and a psychologist, Dr. Ernest Prelinger; Judge Bryant permitted the defense psychiatrists to have equal access to the defendant at Butner. All three psychiatric teams conducted extensive physical examinations. The defense and prosecution teams also conducted interviews across the country with members of Hinckley's family and individuals who had been acquainted with Hinckley at various points in his life. All of the examinations were forensically oriented: The principal matter to be resolved was Hinckley's mental state at the time of the assassination attempt.

The prolonged mental health evaluations and Hinckley's suicide attempts in May and November of 1981 delayed the start of the trial. Shortly before the trial opened, defense counsel filed an insanity plea; however, the court and prosecution had been aware since the preliminary hearing that Hinckley intended to invoke the insanity defense. The trial finally opened on 27 April 1982, with Judge Barrington Parker presiding. The trial continued for almost two months. Because Hinckley's sanity was the only substantive issue to be determined, most of the evidence adduced was psychiatric testimony. Finally, on 21 June 1982 the jury returned a verdict of not guilty by reason of insanity. The following day Judge Parker committed Hinckley to St. Elizabeth's Hospital in Washington, D.C.

b. Proof and Rebuttal of the Elements of the Defense

The testimony set forth below was abstracted from the trial record of *U.S. v. Hinckley*, Criminal No. 81–306 tried in the District Court for the District of Columbia. The psychiatric testimony offered by the defense and prosecution take up approximately 4000 pages of the trial transcript. Excerpts from the testimony of three of the psychiatrists who testified in this case follows. While the testimony was in reference to the A.L.I. Model Penal Code Test (set out at p. 607 *supra*) the purpose of this extended example is to indicate the complexities involved in administering any test designed to shape the decision making process in the determination of criminal responsibility.

i. Mental Disease or Defect

a) Direct Examination of Defense Witness (William T. Carpenter, M.D.)

Q. Doctor, yesterday, before we started the chronological development of your exhaustive interview process, I asked you whether you had an opinion as to whether Mr. Hinckley had suffered from a mental disease on March 30, 1981. Do you recall that question?

A. Yes.

Q. And your answer was?

A. Yes, that I had formed an opinion.

Q. Now, would you tell us how you diagnose the defendant's mental illness, mental disease?

A. Yes.

MR. ADELMAN: Is this as of March 30, 1981?

MR. FULLER: Yes.

*   *   *

THE WITNESS: * * * I concluded then that on March 30th, and before, that he did have the following manifestations of mental illness, that he had blunted affect or restricted affect.

This process where he has an incapacity to have an ordinary emotional arousal that should be associated with events in life. Blunt affect is a critical importance because from the beginning of the descriptions of the major psychotic or major psychiatric illnesses the blunted affect has been one of the prime distinctions of the process of one of the psychotic illnesses, so that I concluded that he did have blunted affect and as a symptomatic expression of an illness process.

He also had what technically we would call an "autistic retreat from reality." The autistic refers to the process of pulling into your own inner mind and away from the outer reality * * *.

The third major symptom status that he had is the depression and the associated features, including the suicidal features that were present in Mr. Hinckley.

And the fourth—* * * [t]here was important illness derived manifestations of dysfunction and his ability to work and his ability to establish social bonds. And these were of a severe magnitude and help measure the impact of illness.

The diagnostic labels that I want to mention, as you say in psychiatry, in approaching diagnoses, there are two somewhat overlapping approaches and it may be important to mention both to you.

The American Psychiatric Association has recently accepted a revision in its diagnostic manual and this is called the Diagnostic and Statistical Manual. It is the third volume.

But it has the listing of the different categories of illness and the descriptions and criteria that go with these different categories and there are many different categories of illness.

This manual notices the fact that we cannot draw emphatically clear distinctions between different types of illnesses, that the manifestations of illnesses may overlap so we don't know exactly where to draw the dividing line.

We are better at drawing the dividing line as to whether illness is present or absent than precisely how to define each illness category. For that reason in this diagnostic manual that is used now in this psychiatrists are encouraged to make multiple diagnoses; that is, if a person meets criteria for a number of diagnoses.

So that Mr. Hinckley does meet either full or partial criteria for a large number of diagnoses listed in that manual. It is only useful to—for me to present in my diagnostic findings the way he fits into a couple of major categories.

The first category that I want to mention, it draws from a concept of schizophrenia, which is one of the major psychotic illnesses which was identified at the turn of the century and has usually lifetime implications in terms of the pattern of illness and the outcome of illness.

And conceptually linked to this are personality dysfunctions, that the term "schizotypal and schizoid personality" mean. To define these labels, "schizoid" refers to someone who is withdrawn from social contacts, aloof from them, a sense of the kind of tender feelings that are associated with tender feelings, usually implying a life-long pattern and may be used for a pattern of socialization and alienation.

The schizotypal personality is a very similar personality formation with the difference being that the person has either something eccentric or bizarre or their use of language gets—but some more severe symptoms than otherwise are similar.

And psychiatrists are directed if schizotypal features are there, to use that instead of the diagnosis of schizoid personality.

Mr. Hinckley did meet criteria for both schizotypal and schizoid. He also met criteria for schizophrenia. This is generally thought of as a more severe form of illness, but that has many of the same kinds of personality features, the development of illness is shown through the personality function that schizotypal and schizoid have.

And I would make, using the criteria of the Diagnostic and Statistical Manual, then from the American Psychiatric Association, a diagnosis of Mr. Hinckley of schizophrenia and would not use the label schizotypal and schizoid, because it is the same symptoms. If they are explained by schizophrenia, you would not resort to those.

Mr. Hinckley at this—to some extent on the point of view he had illness manifestation symptoms that meet the criteria for what is called a major affective disorder. For many years the two major severe psychiatric disorders were the schizophrenia and relating conditions and the manic depressive and related conditions.

Mr. Hinckley in his depression reached the criteria for major depressive disorder and, using DSM–III as a guide, one would make—I would make that diagnosis. The only reason to argue against making that diagnosis is if the presence of schizophrenia can potentially explain the disorder mood that he had, the depression that he had, one could account for the depressive components within the single diagnostic framework.

Those are the diagnoses that I would use in terms of DSM–III.

A more broadly used concept in the world for schizophrenia involves a concept which is called "process schizophrenia" and this term is the primary term that I have used in diagnosing Mr. Hinckley. This term is important because it implies a certain form of development of the illness, an illness that usually begins during adolescence or early adulthood. It has usually a slow development so that the first years in the illness will be the illness manifestation, begin with fairly subtle disorders and social functioning and in personality functioning, and it progresses to a more severe psychiatric disorder and psychotic disorder, and that is where the presence of the delusion and ideas of reference, this type of symptom comes in.

And in this concept people who have developed this disorder, in most instances they are persevering impairments in their health. It runs chronic on long-standing courses. So it is typically slow and gradual in development and once reaching the psychotic state, as the person continues to have continued dysfunction and a broad range of social and psychological measures.

Process schizophrenia, which is the diagnostic conclusion I have reached, is related both in concept and related in a genetic basis to the schizotypal and schizophrenic reference as well as overlapping with schizophrenia as defined in DSM–III so that the clinical diagnosis—that I concluded that the illness Mr. Hinckley had on and before March 30th is process schizophrenia.

[Excerpted from page 3295 through page 3304 of the trial transcript.]

b) Cross Examination by the Prosecution (Defense Witness, William T. Carpenter, M.D.)

*   *   *

Q. Now you testified Friday Mr. Hinckley had been suffering from what you called "process schizophrenia" from 1976, all the way back to 1976.

A. Well, expressing all the difficulties and pinpointing a beginning date for an illness, it began slowly and developed over time.

Q. But as best you can recall that is when he began to have—

A. I refer to '76 as when it began to reach the proportions that one could begin to consider schizophrenic illness present.

Q. In other words, you would have diagnosed him as process schizophrenic if you had seen him in 1976, from your testimony?

A. I don't know. That I would have if I had seen him. I don't know what I would have found out if I had seen him in 1976. Putting the development of the illness into a picture, you are always helped by subsequent developments. That is part of the very nature.

Q. All right.

A. And so when you find out that when symptoms have reached their greatest intensity in any illness, it helps you to interpret things that would be compatible with that illness as they developed earlier. It is like you went back to the earliest stages now that you know somebody had tuberculosis, if you had seen him when he had the first cough, you would have diagnosed it.

* * *

Q. Friday * * * [you testified that] * * * "his process schizophrenia did not become psychotic until 1976, right?" And you answered: "I think that would be the case." You still stick to that now?

A. Yes.

Q. And * * * your answer on the previous page to the same point, [was] "I don't think it was until about then," 1976, "that it developed to an intensity that it reached psychotic proportions." Right?

A. Right.

Q. Are you aware that Mr. Hinckley in the period of 1976 through 1980, was a student at Texas Tech University from time to time?

A. From time to time.

Q. Were you aware, then, as it comes to your attention, that during that period, '76 to '79, when he was there in certain courses he received As; did you learn that?

A. Yes.

Q. And he got some Bs.

A. Yes.

Q. And generally he kept a pretty good grade point average, right?

A. He had a lot of academic difficulty. He dropped a lot of courses because he was having difficulty with them. He had success in some courses.

Q. Well, Doctor, he got an A in writing, didn't he?

A. Yes.

Q. And he got this A in writing during this period you said he was suffering from process schizophrenia; right?

A. Yes.

Q. And you are aware, are you not, that in early 1977, he held a job at a place called Taylor's Supper Club in the Lakewood, Colorado area?

A. Yes, for about five months.

Q. Five months. And I take it you learned that he worked everyday at a busboy job there; right?

A. He didn't come to work quite everyday, but he did work fairly regularly during that period of time. Some absences.

Q. Right. And this is during a period of time when you say he suffered from process schizophrenia; right?

A. Yes.

Q. And you are also aware that in 1976, Mr. Hinckley traveled all by himself to California for several months; right?

A. Yes.

Q. And while he was there, he went trying to sell his songs; right?

A. Yes.

Q. And he also wrote a series of letters to his parents that you have identified on direct examination regarding the matter of Lynn; correct?

A. Right.

Q. And this is during a period of time when you say that Mr. Hinckley was a process schizophrenic; right?

A. Well, this is a time when I think it is beginning to develop its magnitude and it is this information from this very period of time that I would fit into that picture, yes.

Q. And then Mr. Hinckley got back from California all by himself in 1976; are you aware of that?

A. Oh, yes.

Q. I mean his parents didn't have to come out and bring him home in their car, did they?

A. Oh, certainly no.

Q. And this is during the time you said he was suffering from process schizophrenia; right?

A. Yes.

Q. You are aware in 1977, he spent a few weeks in California as well; right?

A. Yes.

Q. And again, he went out there by himself, did he not?

* * *

A. Yes.

Q. He didn't have any trouble getting out there. He didn't get lost in Arizona or run into the Grand Canyon, did he?

A. No.

Q. And while he was there he functioned pretty well, did he not?

A. Oh, no. He had impairments—you see, you may want to define "functioning" for me.

Q. He didn't get arrested by the police, he wasn't found walking around with no clothes on or anything of that sort while he was in California to 1977?

A. That's right and he never walked around without clothes.

[Excerpted from page 3517 through page 3524 of the trial transcript.]

c) Prosecution Rebuttal Testimony (Park Elliott Dietz, M.D.)

* * *

Q. All right. Now, let me ask you formally, if you determined whether at the time of the criminal conduct on March 30, 1981 the defendant Hinckley, as a result of mental disease or defect, lacked substantial capacity to conform his conduct to the requirements of the law?

A. I did make such a determination.

Q. What determination did you make?

A. That on March 30, 1981, as a result of mental disease or defect, Mr. Hinckley did not lack substantial capacity to conform his conduct to the requirements of the law.

* * *

Q. All right. Now, I take it you have some reasons for those conclusions?

A. Yes, I do.

Q. All right. Let's begin to discuss those this afternoon. Going back to part one, you have announced diagnosis of four mental disorders in Mr. Hinckley as of March 30, 1981. And you gave them certain labels, did you not?

A. Yes.

Q. Where did those labels come from?

A. Well, like other labels in medicine, these are derived from Greek and Latin words. These specific labels of mental disorder come from the official diagnostic system, the DSM–III.

Q. In each of the four instances that you mentioned were the diagnoses you announced from DSM–III?

A. Yes.

Q. All right. Now, in connection with DSM–III, can you tell us whether this book is designed for medical purposes or for legal purposes?

A. For medical purposes.

Q. And what do you mean by that?

A. I mean that this volume DSM–III is designed to allow physicians to make reliable diagnoses, to exchange information and know what they are talking about with one another, to be able to speak a common language. But that the diagnoses there do not automatically translate into anything legal and certain not into determination of criminal responsibility.

Q. And criminal responsibility to repeat has how many parts?

A. Depending on how one counts it, it would.

Q. As we have counted it, how many does it have?

A. Two.

Q. DSM–III deals with how many of those two parts?

A. One.

Q. Now, can you tell us, Doctor, with respect to the matter of mental disorders whether there is a range of mental disorders in DSM–III?

A. Yes, there is.

Q. Can you explain the range of mental disorders to the jury?

A. Well, DSM–III covers every conceivable sort of mental disorder from extremely serious to quite minor ones.

The types of disorders within the volume included such things as organic brain syndromes with psychosis, serious depressions with psychosis. Other serious disturbances of mood with psychosis.

It includes neuroses or what are now called anxiety disorders. It includes sorts of personality disorders that I've mentioned and will be talking more about. And it includes what we call situational stress disorders, when in a certain situation a person develops symptoms. For example, after a serious stressful incident.

It includes addictions of various kind. It even includes tobacco dependence disorder. It ranges from minor to serious. From longstanding to brief. It includes a whole host of conditions.

Q. Can you compare that range in some way to the range that we all might be familiar with in functional medicine?

A. Well, for just about any system of the body there is a range of disorders that can occur. People may, for example, have the sniffles or a cold which is an infection of the respiratory system. They [(sic)] may have more serious infection of the respiratory system like pneumonia and can have life threatening disorders of the respiratory system like pneumonia in a very old person or lung cancer or serious injuries to the lungs.

Q. Does that same range exist in mental disorders?

A. A similar range does.

Q. A similar range. Now, you have already mentioned, actually, certain psychotic disorders, correct?

A. Yes.

Q. And can you briefly describe those in terms of the range of mental disorders?

A. Well, the psychotic disorders, I think, all would agree, are the most serious of the mental disorders. There are many different ways to look at seriousness. I think it is fair to say that the disorders associated with psychoses at least while an individual is psychotic are the most serious.

Q. Going down the range, if you will, can you tell us the next general category of disorders?

A. Well, again, it depends on how one classifies it but there is a group of nonpsychotic mental disorders and, generally speaking, the nonpsychotic disorders are considerably less serious than psychotic. Nonpsychotic disorders that are less serious, for example, include the anxiety disorders and the personality disorders. There are other examples.

Q. All right. You mentioned personality disorders. Where do they fit on this spectrum?

A. On the nonpsychotic, less serious side.

Q. And further down or further along are there any other set of disorders that you would care to comment on?

A. Farther down.

Q. Along the range, along the spectrum?

A. Well, the organic mental disorders one associates with psychoses are further up toward the serious end.

Q. All right.

A. Many of the anxiety disorders are toward the less serious end.

Q. In Mr. Hinckley's case, did you find and determine that he had a psychotic disorder?

A. No.

Q. Did you find and determine that Mr. Hinckley had any organic disorder?

A. No.

Q. Now, where in the range do the disorders that you found in Mr. Hinckley, that is to say, the dysthymic disorder, the narcisstic and the schizoid disorder and mixed personality disorders, fall?

A. These are all within them, the dysthymic is an affective disorder and this is on the less serious side.

*   *   *

Q. Before I go any further, you are aware of a category in DSM–III called Schizophrenia; is that right?

A. Yes.

Q. Is Schizoid Personality the same as Schizophrenia?

A. No, it is not.

Q. All right, and briefly at this point could you explain your answer?

A. Schizophrenia is a serious mental disorder in which a patient will at least sometimes and frequently for long times be psychotic.

Schizoid Personality Disorder is a personality disorder. It is not a functional psychotic disorder, as we refer to Schizophrenia.

An individual whose problem is Schizoid Personality Disorder does not become psychotic as a result of it, and does not develop some of the symptoms so characteristic of Schizophrenia such as delusions and hallucinations.

Q. Dr. Dietz, in DSM–III, are Schizoid Personality and Schizophrenia in the same categories or in different categories?

A. They are in different chapters altogether.

Q. Now could you tell us a little bit about the nature of the Schizoid Personality Disorder?

A. Yes, I can. As I have mentioned, this, this is the lonely personality disorder. As a consequence of that, people who have the features of Schizoid Personality Disorder tend to do loner sorts of things. Many of these people, for example, will engage in occupations that don't require much interaction with other people.

For example, cowboys frequently don't have to interact much with others and that's the kind of thing that can appeal to someone who is Schizoid.

Computer operators may not have to interact too much with other people. Even librarians, forest rangers. Now, this is not to say that there is any problem with people who engage in these occupations. It's to say that these are occupations that one can do without having to interact much with others. And people perform beautifully at those kinds of professions if, even if they have this disorder. It's a way to, to be able to function well without having to run into the problem that individuals with these disorders run into when they try to interact with others.

Q. Would people with this Schizoid Personality Disorder function in everyday life without any difficulty?

A. I wouldn't say without any difficulty, but I would say they certainly function in everyday life in many ways. The one way that they are not likely to function, and this is part of the definition, is that they don't have friends.

Q. Can they hold jobs?

A. Yes.

Q. Can they go to school?

A. Yes.

Q. Can they travel?

A. Yes.

Q. Now Schizoid Personality, does that mean a person is out of contact with reality or psychotic?

A. No, it does not.

Q. Could you explain to the jury what you saw in Mr. Hinckley on March 30th, 1981, to indicate that he suffered from a Schizoid Personality Disorder on that day?

A. Well, I think there are really only two features that are known to have been present on that date in Mr. Hinckley, and the first of those is what we describe as emotional coldness and aloofness. That is, being, being cruel and unemotional, not becoming involved emotionally with other people.

Q. Does that mean a person is out of contact with reality?

A. No, no, but it may mean that they have trouble making friends.

Q. All right. What are the other characteristics?

A. Well, another one that I think was observable that day was indifference to the feelings of others. There are, one of the things we use to diagnose many of these mental disorders is to, to say that if there is, there are certain things that must not be present, if it's present, then we can't make this diagnosis, and one of those in Mr. Hinckley's case that was not present on March 30, and which we have to make sure wasn't present was no eccentricities of speech, behavior or thought, and there was nothing eccentric about his speech, behavior or his thought that day, and there were many observers I have interviewed to determine that.

*   *   *

[Excerpted from page 6388 through page 6411 of the trial transcript.]

d) Cross Examination by the Defense (Prosecution Witness, Park Elliott Dietz, M.D.)

BY MR. FULLER:

Q. Doctor Dietz, good afternoon.

A. Good afternoon, Mr. Fuller.

Q. Before we get into the substance of your testimony, I would like to extract an agreement I think we can reach, and that is that you share the view of other defense psychiatrists that Mr. Hinckley on March 30, 1981 was suffering from a mental disease? You do agree with that statement, do you not?

A. No, I do not.

Q. All right. Was it not your testimony on direct examination that Mr. Hinckley suffered a mental disease of dysthymic mental disorder?

A. No. I testified that Mr. Hinckley suffered in the past and indeed on March 30 from a mental disorder.

Q. Are you distinguishing between a mental disease and mental disorder?

A. Yes.

Q. I see.

Would you agree that on March 30, 1981 Mr. Hinckley had a mental illness in a broad sense?

A. I testified about a mental disorder, and I would have some difficulty agreeing with your statement that he suffered from a mental illness.

Q. All right, taking your term as a mental disorder, how do you distinguish that, sir, from a mental disease?

A. Well, a mental disorder is any of the diagnostic categories listed in DSM III, the guide book for mental disorders, and for the diagnosis of mental disorders. When one switches to the term mental disease or mental illness, one is suggesting that this is a sickness, that it has some kind of biological basis?

That is quite a difference.

Q. So it is your testimony that all of the descriptions of mental conditions in DSM III constitute mental disorders as compared or contrasted to mental diseases?

A. Yes, sir.

Q. Accepting your qualification, then, you will agree that on March 30, 1981 Mr. Hinckley suffered from a mental disorder?

A. Yes.

Q. And that the question before this Court and this jury would become as to the question of the severity of that disorder?

A. No, sir. The question before the jury is about his criminal responsibility.

*   *   *

[Excerpted from page 6388 through page 6411 of the trial transcript.]

Questions and Comments

1. A finding that the defendant has a "mental disease or defect" is a necessary condition for exculpation under the A.L.I. Model Penal Code Test. Significantly, though neither the Code nor the Commentary to the Code seek to define these terms. Does the inclusion of this element, in fact, provide any guidance to either the expert or the jury as to the type of abnormality which is required by the test? In this connection, consider the testimony, *supra*, of Dr. Carpenter, the defense psychiatrist, who concluded that Hinckley was suffering from "process schizophrenia," which, in turn, served to establish the presence of a mental disease.

On what basis did Dr. Carpenter establish the presence of process schizophrenia? How was he able to avoid the diagnostic conclusion of the prosecution expert that the clinical features pointed to a diagnosis of schizoid and schizotypical personality rather than schizophrenia? To what extent was the diagnosis of process schizophrenia impressionistic and tied to the basic diagnostic orientation of the clinician? If the diagnosis was, in fact, basically subjective, of what value is such expert opinion to the jury?

2. There was obviously sharp disagreement between the defense and prosecution experts whether Hinckley had a "mental disease" or only a "mental disorder." Does the jury's verdict suggest that it gave greater credibility to the defense testimony on this point? To what extent did the standard of proof, which placed on the prosecution the burden of proving sanity, influence the outcome and resolution of the mental disease issue? Is the adversary process effective in disclosing to jurors the limitations in the capacity of experts to ascertain the presence or absence of the "mental disease or defect" element?

3. If a legislature wanted to preclude defendants similar to Hinckley from qualifying for the insanity defense, would the addition of the word "severe" before mental disease serve to accomplish that goal? Such an addition to the insanity standard was the subject of a discussion during the deliberations of the Senate Committee on the Judiciary on the Insanity Defense. *See,* Senate Insanity Defense Hearings, p. 201.

ii. Capacity to Appreciate the Wrongfulness of Conduct

a) Testimony for the Defense (William T. Carpenter, M.D.)

Q. * * * Doctor, I believe I had asked you whether you had an opinion as to whether at the time of the shooting on March 30, 1981 the defendant, as a result of the mental disease you described, lacked the substantial capacity to appreciate the wrongfulness of his conduct.

* * *

A.   Yes.

Q.   Would you please tell us what that opinion is?

A.   Yes, that I do think that he had—lacked substantial capacity to appreciate the wrongfulness of his conduct.

Q.   Would you in your own terms elaborate on that and explain to the jury what you mean when you say he "lacked capacity to appreciate the wrongfulness of his conduct"?

A.   Yes.   In forming an opinion about his ability to appreciate wrongfulness, I tried to look at 3 components of that, the components in real life that are merged together, but found it useful to try to think of each separately.

The first was whether there was a purely intellectual understanding that what he did was illegal.   And it is my opinion on a purely intellectual level that he didn't know that he had that knowledge, that those were illegal acts.

The ability to reason that is implied in appreciation.   I think appreciation of wrongfulness would mean that a person had an ability to reason about it, to think about it, to understand the consequences, to draw inferences about the acts and their meaning.   And reasoning processes, which involve both the intellectual component and the emotional component.

It is part of what goes together in our reasoning about any issue. That in this regard I believe Mr. Hinckley lacked substantial capacity to appreciate.

The reason for this opinion is that it is an understanding of the very reasoning process he was going through in preparation for and in carrying out the facts, that in his own mind, his own reasoning, the predominant reasoning had to do with two major things, the first of which was the termination of his own existence; the second of which was to accomplish this union with Jodie Foster through death, after life, whatever.

But these were the major things that were dominating his reasoning about it.   The magnitude of importance to him in weighing and in his reasoning of accomplishing these aims was far greater than the magnitude of the events per se.   And in that regard it was not only his mind.   He was not able to—he was not reasoning about the legality issue itself.

On the more emotional side of appreciation, which would have to do with some—with the feelings, the emotional appreciation or understanding of the nature of the events, the consequences, he also had an impairment in that regard.   And the impairment there was that the emotional consequences of the acts that he conducted were in his experience solely in terms of the inner world he had constructed.

The meaning of this to the victims of the act was not on his mind. I don't mean to be crass about this, but in his mental state the effect of this on the President, on any other victims was trivial, that they— in his mental state they were bit players who were there in a way to help him to accomplish the two major roles and which his reasoning was taking place and were not in and of themselves important to this.

So that I do think that he had a purely intellectual appreciation that it was illegal.

Emotionally he could give no weight to that because other factors weighed far heavier in his emotional appreciation.

And as these two things come together in his reasoning process, his reasoning processes were dominated by the inner state—by the inner drives that he was trying to accomplish in terms of the ending of his own life and in terms of the culminating relationship with Jodie Foster.

It was on that basis that I concluded that he did lack substantial capacity to appreciate the wrongfulness of his acts.

Q. In considering his cognitive awareness, doctor, does that include an element of reason as well?

A. Well, the cognitive—the best analogy to that—

* * *

Q. Do you have the question in mind?

A. Yes. The cognitive part.

You see, reason is where the purely emotional and purely cognitive parts don't take place independent of each other. They come together and that is around the reasoning.

The cognitive part, just for clarity of thinking about it and analogy, that might help explain what I am thinking about there. If one were in a medical emergency, rushing someone to the hospital and you asked * * * "Are you aware that the speed you are going is breaking the law?" There would be a cognitive appreciation, but in their reasoning around what they are doing, because of the emotional importance of what is going on, this cognitive appreciation would not be having a major impact on their reasoning about what they are doing.

So in my view the purely intellectual and purely emotional doesn't exist independent of each other, but they come together in the reasoning.

And it is the impact on his reasoning that I have tried to describe predominantly in understanding his impairment in his ability to appreciate wrongfulness.

* * *

[Excerpted from page 3321 through page 3325 of the trial transcript.]

b) Prosecution Rebuttal Testimony (Prosecution Witness, Park Elliott Dietz, M.D.)

* * *

Q. [Dr. Dietz] can you tell us [of] some of the evidence that you have evaluated and set forth that indicates that Mr. Hinckley was on that day able to appreciate the wrongfulness of his conduct?

* * *

When he traveled to Dallas to purchase guns in October '80 after his arrest in Nashville, he was replacing his arsenal which had been confiscated by the police there. He made the decision to switch his target from President Carter to the President-elect Reagan after the November 4, 1980 election. He concealed successfully all of his stalking from his parents, from his brother, from his sister, from his brother-in-law and from Dr. Hopper, including hiding his weapons, hiding his ammunition and misleading them about his travels and his plans.

This concealment indicates that he appreciated the wrongfulness of his plans, of his stalking behavior throughout that entire time period and his further evidence of his appreciation of the wrongfulness on March 30, 1981.

Mind you, no single piece of evidence is determinative here. I am providing you with examples of kinds of evidence that, taken together, make up an opinion about his appreciation of wrongfulness on March 30th and these are examples of some of those pieces of evidence.

He purchased a highly concealable .38 caliber revolver the day after Reagan's inauguration. He indicated that he became interested in President Reagan's whereabouts in March of 1981 before he had even begun his trip to Washington, D.C. He said he had become interested in the President's whereabouts.

When we get closer to the events of March 30th his decision on that day to, as he put it, "check out the scene" and to see how close he could get at the Hilton Hotel indicates that his decision to go to the Hilton Hotel reflected his thoughts about committing assassination on that day.

He wanted to know how close he could get. Could he get within range? Could he get a clear shot?

He wrote a letter having made his decision to Jodie Foster and we discussed that day already in that letter to Jodie Foster, he indicated he was going to attempt to get Reagan and he indicates his knowledge that he could be killed by the Secret Service in the attempt.

That is an indication that he understood and appreciated the wrongfulness of his plans because the Secret Service might well shoot someone who attempted to kill the President.

His decision to load his revolver with exploding ammunition before he left room 312 at the Park Central Hotel, again decisionmaking reflecting a choice of the use of explodable bullets which would have maximum effect on the victim and understanding of the wrongfulness of his behavior and understanding of the damage that he might bring upon other people.

His concealment of his revolver in his right pocket because he shoots right-handed, a decision to have his revolver where he could quickly draw it and understanding that the purpose of taking the revolver with him was to shoot.

His waiting until he had a clear shot at the President before drawing his gun. He didn't draw his gun when the President first arrived at the Hilton Hotel, as I have indicated before, because he didn't have a clear shot of the presidential motorcade [sic] first arrived. The limousine was farther away and there was a curve in the wall between Mr. Hinckley and where the President entered the building.

His waiting until the President came within his accurate range before drawing his gun reflects an appreciate of the behavior he was about to engage in and it purpose, its purpose to shoot the President of the United States. [sic]

His reflection about his decision to draw the gun. I have referred before to his saying that he thought to himself "Should I?" reflecting on a moral decision he was to make.

And his decision to draw the gun at the very moment he did because of the circumstances which at that time favored successful assassination.

He viewed the situation as having poor security. He saw that the range was close and within the distance with which he was accurate, and at the precise moment that he chose to draw his revolver there was a diversion of attention from him. The Secret Service and the others in the presidential entourage looked the other way just as he was pulling the gun.

Finally, his decision to proceed to fire, thinking that others had seen him, as I have mentioned before, indicates his awareness that others seeing him was significant because others recognized that what he was doing and about to do were wrong.

These are examples of the evidence that he appreciated the wrongfulness on March 30.

Q And you say "examples." You have not exhausted the list, have you?

A No, I haven't.

*   *   *

[Excerpted from page 6587 through 6597 of the trial transcript.]

Questions and Comments

1. Dr. Carpenter, in his testimony at one point, conceded that Hinckley "had a purely intellectual appreciation that it was illegal." See p. 633 *supra*. Also, Dr. Thomas Goldman in testimony not included in these materials, testified "I think that at the moment Mr. Hinckley shot Mr. Reagan and the other people whom he shot, I don't think he had any substantial doubt about whether that was against the law." Trial Record at 4983. Nevertheless, both experts testified that Hinckley lacked "substantial capacity *   *   * to appreciate the criminality of his conduct," inasmuch as he didn't have an "affective" or "emotional" understanding of his conduct. This testimony was objected to by the prosecution, which contended that the "appreciate the criminality" language of the A.L.I. test refers only to cognitive or intellectual knowledge. Memorandum in Support of Motion to Exclude Evidence, Argument and Instructions Concerning "Emotional Appreciation" of Wrongfulness, (April 13, 1982). Evidence relating to emotional or volitional factors could, according to the prosecution, only be introduced with respect to the second part of the A.L.I. test, which asks "whether the defendant was without capacity to conform his conduct to the requirements of law." *Id.* This motion was never formally ruled upon.

While there is astonishing little case law on this point, most federal circuits do not limit expert testimony to the cognitive aspect of understanding. In part, this may be explained by the difficulty the courts would have in barring testimony dealing with emotional aspects as they relate to one prong of the A.L.I. test, but admitting such testimony to address the volitional part.

2. Once Drs. Carpenter and Goldman were accepted by the court as experts (*See*, p. 586 *supra*), was there any way except by the introduction of opposing testimony to effectively challenge the conclusions of the defense experts that Hinckley's condition prevented him from appreciating the criminality of his conduct? Recall in this connection that the conclusion that Hinckley lacked the ability to appreciate the criminality of his conduct was tied to the diagnosis of "process schizophrenia." Wouldn't a conclusion relating to Hinckley's inability to appreciate wrongfulness necessarily entail a challenge of the basic diagnosis?

3. Critics of the A.L.I. Model Penal Code Test who believe that its application leads to capricious results have proposed replacing the A.L.I. test with a *M'Naghten* type formulation. (As of 1981 some version of the *M'Naghten* defense was the test in about one-third of the states. See, Senate Insanity Defense Hearings, p. 2). *M'Naghten* in its original form provided:

    *   *   * To establish a defense on the grounds of insanity, it must be clearly proved that at the time of the committing of the act the party accused was laboring under such a defect of reason from disease of the mind as not to know the nature and quality of the act he was doing. If he did know it, that he did not know that he was doing what was wrong.

Is it likely that the Hinckley case would have been decided differently had the *M'Naghten* standard been applied? Would any of the psychiatric testimony pertaining to Hinckley's capacity to appreciate the criminality of his conduct be excluded and, therefore, not been before the jury?

iii.   Capacity to Conform [a]

a) Testimony for the Defense (Thomas Carl Goldman, M.D.)

Q. . . . I will now ask you, Doctor, whether on March 30, 1981, in your opinion, the defendant, as a result of the mental disease described, lacked substantial capacity to conform his conduct to the requirements of the law?

A. Yes.

Q. And what is that opinion, sir?

A. The opinion was that he did lack substantial capacity to conform to the requirements of the law. And the way in which his controls, that is, his behavioral controls, was impaired I think is indicated in a number of ways.

For one thing, I think I have demonstrated the chaotic jumping around aimless, pillar to post, desperate quality of his travels in the weeks and months preceding the final event, the sense of drivenness, the fact that he was under pressure internal impossibly, intolerable inner feeling states which he felt he had to get rid of. He felt he was on a roller coaster and he used that word and he felt he had to get off and he didn't know any way other than by ending it this way.

He had no choices. When you think about control I find it impossible to think about control without thinking about choice.

Now, Mr. Hinckley did not have any viable choices on March 30. Sitting here with the wisdom of hindsight and being outside his mind at that time, it is relatively easy for us to say, well, he could have done X, he could have done Y, he could have done Z. The fact is he had tried everything he had any reason to believe would help. He tried medicine. He tried psychiatry. He tried suicide. He tried magic, doing something magical with Jodie Foster. He struggled with that on and off. He went back to trying to get into treatment and it didn't work. Nothing worked and finally, the ultimate rejection of his being pushed out of his parental home was the thing that made him absolutely certain that there was no hope left.

There was no hope of his ever living a normal, reasonable, [life] being happy or not being miserable. That he felt that really he had

---

a. The Hinckley case was tried at a time when the test for insanity in the federal system made the defendant's inability to "conform his conduct to the requirements of the law" a basis for exculpation. This is no longer the case. See pg. 644, n. 6, *infra.*

to end it in some way. He didn't have any good choices, no choices that would be reasonable choices, no viable choices.

* * *

[Excerpted from page 4981 through page 4983 of the trial transcript.]

b) Cross Examination by the Prosecution (Thomas Carl Goldman, M.D.)

* * *

Q. Now, you have testified that on March 30th, * * * "That day Mr. Hinckley had a sense of drivenness," right?

A. Yes.

Q. "He was under pressure internal possibly," you say, "intolerable inner feeling states which he felt he had to get rid of," right?

A. Yes.

Q. You said he was on a roller-coaster, right?

A. Yes.

Q. You said he had no choices, no viable choices?

A. That is correct.

* * *

Q. Now, what was his sense of drivenness? What was driving him?

A. His feeling that he had to end—had to end the misery, that he had to do it somehow, that probably that it would involve death and that his plan as of the day that he arrived in Washington was to go to New Haven, thinking about going to New Haven.

That was still his intention and accosting Miss Foster and shooting her, shooting himself.

Q. What were these intolerable inner feelings that he felt he had to get rid of?

A. Feelings of hopelessness, feelings of rage.

Q. Rage?

A. Feelings of a sense that he was nothing, nobody, that he would never count, that he was a total failure, that he was forever cut off from any hope of ever being loved or ever being cared for, ever being supported, ever being nurtured.

He felt cut off from the human race.

Q. All right. And this sense of drivenness and this internal feelings he had to get rid of, when did that start in his mind, on the 30th day of March 1981?

A. Well, he had it—I think he had unformed intentions. I think he was in that state generally all the time on March 30th of 1981. I think that he hit upon a solution that came to him in a somewhat random way.

Q. Let's start then with the time he woke up, which was 8:30. Was he in that state of mind at that point?

A. He was at that point—the best that he has told me that I understand, he was intending to—thought he would probably go to New Haven. He didn't know exactly when he would go. He went out, got breakfast.

Q. My question is was he driven when he woke up at 8:30?

A. Yes.

Q. All right. That means he was driven when he went out to have breakfast?

A. Well, when I say, you know—when I say that he was driven, he didn't have to do what he was going to do immediately. He could do it—he had the general intention that he was going to do it pretty soon. He wasn't so driven that he couldn't stop for breakfast on that day.

Q. The stomach put some brakes on the drive, right?

A. At that moment, yes, sir. It wasn't inconsistent with what he was going to do, but he got some breakfast because he was hungry.

Q. After he ate, he was a block and a half from the White House as you know, correct?

A. Yes.

Q. But he wasn't so driven that he ran over to the White House with his gun and opened fire, was he?

A. That is true. I don't know that it's—I don't know that it's an accurate—I don't agree with your inference necessarily he wasn't so driven that the reason he didn't go to the White House with a gun is that he wasn't so driven. It's not clear that he thought that that was a reasonable plan. But—

Q. Well, I am exploring, but your claim in testimony that this man had an intolerable inner feeling which he had to get rid of?

A. Yes.

Q. But they weren't so pressing that he had to go to the White House in the morning to do it?

A. That's right. He was capable of some delay, and some formulation of possible consideration of some possible plans of ways to end it.

Q. Planning, correct?

A. Yes.

Q. Doctor, you pointed out in your report, page 12, "There was no doubt that he planned and premeditated a great deal."

A. That is correct.

Q. Now that refers not only to that particular day of March 30th, but before, correct?

A. That's right.

Q. So after breakfast then Mr. Hinckley—well, what did he do to your knowledge?

A. Came back, took a shower—I think he bought "The Star" on the way in back to his hotel, took a shower, looked at "The Star," saw the presidential schedule at that time.

Q. Was he driven when he got out of the shower to do what he eventually did?

A. I think that particularly driven quality intensified when he saw the schedule and saw that—at the time he experienced it as a possibility. He thought of it as "Let's go over and see what's happening."

This may be a way to end it all. That is what he reported to me, that he thought maybe this is a way to finish it.

Q. Well, it was a little more than that casual, "Let's go over and see what's happening." He decided to go over with a loaded .22 revolver, didn't he?

A. That is correct.

Q. And he decided to take it in his pocket so nobody could see it, didn't he?

A. Right.

Q. And he thought that out before he did, didn't he?

A. Yes, he thought he might be able to accomplish his end that very morning, that this was an opportunity to do that.

* * *

Q. And you are aware that he stood in the crowd as the President arrived at the hotel at 1:50?

A. That's correct.

Q. Yet he didn't shoot them.

A. That's correct.

Q. Was he driven at that point?

A. He was there under some sense of impulsion. He might have, but he controlled, he had enough control at that moment not to shoot him. His balance at that moment was in favor of not shooting although he had a sense that he might leave, he didn't know for sure what he was going to do, but he was clearly close to the point of attention.

Q. Now, Dr. Goldman, if he was on, had this sense of drivenness and had an intolerable feeling that he had to get rid of at 1:45 and 1:50 when Mr. Reagan was there, why didn't he shoot him?

A.   As in previous cases, he had some delay, he had some delay mechanism.   The amount of—always considered the possibility of not doing what he had set himself to do and he had at that moment, he had as I understand it, he had sufficient, he wasn't sure whether he would get a shot, whether he would get a shot again.   He wasn't sure how good an opportunity this was.   He didn't actually know—I think he—he wasn't sure in his own mind what he was going to do until President Reagan emerged.

* * *

Q.   You testified on yesterday and the day before at transcript 4892 Mr. Hinckley did not have any viable choices on March 30?

A.   That's correct.

Q.   Would you like to change that testimony in light of what I just brought to your attention?

A.   No.

Q.   And then were you aware that Mr. Hinckley waited in and about the hotel for 25 minutes while the President gave his speech?

A.   Yes, I'm aware that he waited.

Q.   And was he on this roller coaster and driven at that point?

A.   Yes.

Q.   Was he psychotic?

A.   Yes.

Q.   And you are aware, are you not, that Mr. Hinckley, during that period of time, was deciding what to do, turning over in his mind, if you will, whether to shoot the President or not.   Are you not aware of that?

* * *

A.   I asked—I asked him about that period and how he deliberated and he spoke about it in terms of should I leave, should I do it now and get it over with.   Should I leave and go to New Haven.   Should I simply get out of here.

Q.   You said deliberated, right?

A.   Well, he was aware, he was aware of the possibility that he might leave and not carry out the shooting.

Q.   I want to focus on that word "deliberating" that you used. You just said "deliberating," right?

A.   I said he considered that there were other possibilities.

Q.   Deliberation means considering options.

A.   It means being aware of options, right.

* * *

[Excerpted from page 5257 through page 5276 of the trial transcript.]

Questions and Comments

1. The purpose of the original "irresistible impulse" test and its relationship to *M'Naghten* is described by Abraham Goldstein in his incisive treatise on the insanity defense:

> This rule, broadly stated, tells jurors to acquit by reason of insanity if they find the defendant had a mental disease which kept him from controlling his conduct. They are to do so even if they conclude he knew what he was doing and that it was wrong. The lineage of this rule is at least as old as that of *M'Naghten*, with which it has often in the past competed for acceptance. In more recent times, however, it has been regarded as a supplement to *M'Naghten* and has rested on four assumptions: first, that there are mental diseases which impair volition or self-control, even while cognition remains relatively unimpaired; second, that the use of *M'Naghten* alone results in findings that persons suffering from such diseases are not insane; third, that the law should make the insanity defense available to persons who are unable to control their actions, just as it does to those who fit *M'Naghten;* fourth, no matter how broadly *M'Naghten* is construed, there will remain areas of serious disorder which it will not reach.

Abraham Goldstein, *The Insanity Defense* (New Haven: Yale Univ. Press, 1967).

2. A case decided in 1886 provides an early common law formulation of the "irresistible impulse" test as an adjunct to *M'Naghten*. After referring to the requirement that the defendant have a "disease of the mind," the court stated the questions in the following terms:

> Did he know right from wrong, as applied to the particular act in question? * * * If he did have such knowledge, he may nevertheless not be legally responsible if the two following conditions occur: (1) If, by reason of the duress of such mental disease, he had so far lost the *power to choose* between the right and wrong, and to avoid doing the act in question, as that his free agency was at the time destroyed; (2) and if, at the same time, the alleged crime was so connected with such mental disease, in the relation of cause and effect, as to have been the product of it *solely.* [emphasis added]

Parsons v. State, 81 Ala. 577, 2 So. 854, 866–67 (1886).

The capacity to conform portion of the Model Penal Code Test is basically a restatement of the irresistible impulse test with some refinements. First, it was not to be restricted to "sudden, spontaneous acts as distinguished from insane propulsions that are accompanied by brooding or reflection." A.L.I.'s Comments to § 4.01 of the Model Penal Code Tentative Draft # 4, p. 157. Second, by including the term "substantial" to modify the degree of volitional impairment required, the test would not be limited to conditions involving "total incapacity." As explained by the drafters:

> Nothing makes the inquiry into responsibility more unreal for the psychiatrist than limitation of the issue to some ultimate extreme of

total incapacity, when clinical experience reveals only a graded scale with marks along the way.

We think this difficulty can and must be met. The law must recognize that when there is no black and white it must content itself with different shades of gray. The draft, accordingly, does not demand *complete* impairment of capacity. It asks instead for *substantial* impairment. This is all, we think, that candid witnesses, called on to infer the nature of the situation at a time that they did not observe, can ever confidently say, even when they know that a disorder was extreme.

Id. at 158.

3. Dr. Thomas Goldman stated that in his opinion John Hinckley lacked the capacity to conform his behavior to the requirements of the law. Does the testimony disclose the basis upon which this conclusion rests? Was the conclusion linked to his diagnosis of simple schizophrenia, or did it have independent evidentiary support?

4. A recognized treatise on forensic psychiatry asserts "any psychiatrist, given sufficient time with the patient and an adequate history, can recognize a psychosis; and if the doctrine [irresistible impulse] be limited to psychotic impulses, there is no serious probative difficulty." Henry Davidson, *Forensic Psychiatry* (2nd ed., New York: Roland Press, 1965), at 19. Moreover, according to the treatise, when the issue involves "neurotic impulses,"

psychiatric science can still meet the challenge. The competent psychiatrist knows that a psychoneurosis is a way of life, not a transient reaction, and he looks for a neurotic history. He knows that in true compulsive neuroses, there is a typical pattern of mounting tension, internal conflict, abashed yielding to the impulse, brief relief from tension, subsequent recrimination, and guilt-feeling leading to more tension with a repetition of the cycle. The psychiatrist is suspicious of an irresistible impulse with no past history that began five minutes before the commission of the crime.

Id. at 19.

Does this suggest that Hinckley's history of not being able to conform to a normal lifestyle and engaging in impulsive acts was significant in the determination that he lacked normal volitional capacity? How can Hinckley and those diagnosed as unable to conform be distinguished from anyone who habitually has engaged in seriously impulsive criminal behavior?

5. At one time U.S. military courts utilized an insanity test that asked experts, among other questions, what would the defendant have done had a policeman been at his elbow? In the Hinckley case this was not a hypothetical question; a policeman was at the defendant's elbow. Should this be a significant factor in determining whether the impulse was irresistible? Is this simply another way of asking whether the behavior in question was non-deterrable? Should the fact that the behavior was not deterrable necessarily excuse the individual from responsibility?

6. In addition to shifting the burden of proving insanity to the defendant, the Insanity Defense Reform Act of 1984, Pub.L.No. 98–473, § 402(a) (to be codified at 18 U.S.C.A. § 20), eliminates the volitional prong of the A.L.I. Model Penal Code Test in all federal cases. As the hearings in the House and Senate make clear, these changes were in direct response to the verdict in the Hinckley case. *See*, The Insanity Defense: Hearings on S. 818, S. 1106, S. 1558, S. 2669, S. 2672, S. 2678, S. 2745 and S. 2780. Before the Senate Committee on the Judiciary, 97th Cong., 2nd Sess. (1982); Limiting the Insanity Defense: Hearings on S. 818, S. 1106, S. 1558, S. 1995, S. 2572, S. 2658, and S. 2669. Before the Subcommittee on Criminal Law of the Committee on the Judiciary, 97th Cong., 2nd Sess. (1982); Reform of the Federal Insanity Defense: Hearings. Before the Subcommittee on Criminal Justice of the Committee on the Judiciary House of Representatives, 98th Cong., 1st Sess. (1983).

Even before the Congressional Act, one federal circuit had, in the exercise of its discretionary powers, similarly abandoned the volitional prong of the standard after adhering to it for the better part of two decades. *United States v. Lyons*, 731 F.2d 243 (5th Cir.1984). In rejecting the volitional portion of the test the court held:

* * *

[W]e conclude that the volitional prong of the insanity defense—a lack of capacity to conform one's conduct to the requirements of the law—does not comport with current medical and scientific knowledge, which has retreated from its earlier, sanguine expectations. Consequently, we now hold that a person is not responsible for criminal conduct on the grounds of insanity only if at the time of that conduct, as a result of a mental disease or defect, he is unable to appreciate the wrongfulness of that conduct.

We do so for several reasons. First, as we have mentioned, a majority of psychiatrists now believe that they do not possess sufficient accurate scientific bases for measuring a person's capacity for self-control or for calibrating the impairment of that capacity. Bonnie, *The Moral Basis of the Insanity Defense*, 69 ABA J. 194, 196 (1983). "The line between an irresistible impulse and an impulse not resisted is probably no sharper than between twilight and dusk." *American Psychiatric Association Statement on the Insanity Defense*, 11 (1982) [APA Statement]. Indeed, Professor Bonnie states:

There is, in short, no objective basis for distinguishing between offenders who were undeterrable and those who were merely undeterred, between the impulse that was irresistible and the impulse not resisted, or between substantial impairment of capacity and some lesser impairment.

Bonnie, *supra*, at 196.

In addition, the risks of fabrication and "moral mistakes" in administering the insanity defense are greatest "when the experts and the jury are asked to speculate whether the defendant had the capacity to 'control' himself or whether he could have 'resisted' the criminal impulse." Bonnie, *supra*, at 196. Moreover, psychiatric testimony about volition is more likely to produce confusion for jurors than is psychiatric testimony concerning a defendant's appreciation of the wrongfulness of his act. APA Statement at 12. It appears, moreover, that there is considerable overlap between a psychotic person's inability to understand and his ability to control his behavior. Most psychotic persons who fail a volitional test would also fail a cognitive test, thus rendering the volitional test superfluous for them. *Id.* Finally, Supreme Court authority requires that such proof be made by the federal prosecutor beyond a reasonable doubt, an all but impossible task in view of the present murky state of medical knowledge. *Davis v. United States,* 160 U.S. 469, 16 S.Ct. 353, 40 L.Ed. 499 (1895).

One need not disbelieve in the existence of Angels in order to conclude that the present state of our knowledge regarding them is not such as to support confident conclusions about how many can dance on the head of a pin. In like vein, it may be that some day tools will be discovered with which reliable conclusions about human volition can be fashioned. It appears to be all but a certainty, however, that despite earlier hopes they do not lie in our hands today. When and if they do, it will be time to consider again to what degree the law should adopt the sort of conclusions that they produce. But until then, we see no prudent course for the law to follow but to treat all criminal impulses—including those not resisted—as resistible. To do otherwise in the present state of medical knowledge would be to cast the insanity defense adrift upon a sea of unfounded scientific speculation, with the palm awarded case by case to the most convincing advocate of that which is presently unknown—and may remain so, because unknowable.

*   *   *

Id. at 3596.

7. The volitional prong of the Model Penal Code Test has been singled out for particular criticism by some elements of the legal profession in recent years. For instance, the House of Delegates of the American Bar Association advocated deletion of the volitional prong of the A.L.I. Model Penal Code standards at its mid year meetings in February 1983. *See,* 32 Crim.L.Rep. (BNA) 2411–12 (February 16, 1983).

Opposition to the volitional part of the A.L.I. test is also developing among psychiatrists. An official statement on the insanity defense issued by the American Psychiatric Association, Statement on the Insanity Defense 6, 1982, noted:

> [M]any psychiatrists *   *   * believe that psychiatric information relevant to determining whether a defendant understood the nature of his act, and whether he appreciated its wrongfulness, is more reliable and has a stronger scientific basis than, for example, does psychiatric information relevant to whether a defendant was able to control his behavior.

Id. at 14.

This has led one commentator to conclude:

    * * * [P]sychiatrists have now decided that they prefer to testify under the classic *M'Naghten* standard, with its solely cognitive elements, rather than under the ALI test with its more "modern," volitional approach.

P. Johnson, *Review of Madness and the Criminal Law*, 50 U. of Chicago L.Rev. 1534, 1546 (1983).

    8. Is it arguable that the various reform efforts in recent years to bring the insanity defense in line with contemporary psychiatric theory have created unnecessary tensions and have led to a general disenchantment with psychiatry and particularly its use in the legal process? As noted (*see* note 2, *supra*) the Model Penal Code Test clearly represented an effort by law reform groups to move the insanity standard closer to contemporary psychiatric concepts. Adoption of the Model Penal Code Test, for instance, sought accommodation with modern psychiatric theory, which viewed behavior as a unitary phenomenon. Also the Model Penal Code Test intentionally left room for gradations of impairment, thus inviting a broader range of psychiatric testimony. Equally important was the creation of a separate category, which would excuse from responsibility those deemed unable to conform to the law, either as a result of an insane impulse or as a consequence of slow and insidious processes. Cases such as John Hinckley's suggest that the objective of the drafters of the Model Penal Code have been largely realized and that psychiatrists and other mental health professionals have been able to testify in fairly unrestrictive terms. The result, however, as suggested by the materials which follow, has been a growing perception on the part of the public that the insanity defense has been abused and that it all too often leads to unjust results. These perceptions, in turn, have lead to extreme proposals for the modifications of, if not abolition of, the insanity defense and restrictions on the use of psychiatric evidence. See, p. 677 *infra*.

    9. Since a jury need only render a general verdict of not guilty by reason of insanity, the actual basis of that verdict is not disclosed. Thus, in the Hinckley case whether the verdict rested on one prong of the A.L.I. insanity test rather than another is not ascertainable.

Some commentators believe that to the extent that the jury in the Hinckley trial was willing to adhere to the prevailing legal standard, the result was inevitable. One authority has written:

    "[T]he lawyers jousted for eight weeks of trial, examining and cross-examining expert witnesses who naturally gave conflicting and confusing testimony on whether Hinckley's obviously warped mentality amounted to legal insanity. The judge instructed the jury to return a verdict of not guilty unless they could agree "beyond a reasonable doubt" that Hinckley was sane. If taken literally, the instruction amounted to a directed verdict of not guilty, considering the deadlock of expert opinion and the difficulty of certifying the sanity of a young man who shot the President to impress a movie star. Juries usually ignore such unpopular legal standards, but the

Hinckley jury surprised everybody by taking the law seriously and finding him not guilty."

P. Johnson, *Review of Madness and the Criminal Law*, 50 U. of Chicago L.Rev. 1534, 1536 (1983).

Is Johnson's assertion that the verdict was compelled as a matter of law plausible? Would shifting the standard of proof, as is the practice in some states and now as a result of the newly enacted Insanity Defense Reform Act of 1984 in the federal system, give a jury leeway to reject the insanity defense in a case involving substantially the same evidentiary record?

D. DISPOSITION OF PERSONS ACQUITTED ON GROUNDS OF INSANITY

An acquittal on the grounds of insanity implies that the defendant has committed a criminal act but at the time of the act was not responsible because of mental illness or disease. It is not unusual though for a period of months or even years to have elapsed from the time of that act to the time of the acquittal. As a consequence, it has been argued that the state should not be able to institutionalize the acquitted defendant unless he is thereafter subject to normal civil commitment proceedings. Most states, however, provide for at least a temporary mandatory commitment period following acquittal to enable the state to assess the defendant's present mental condition and his potential for future dangerousness.

More controversial are those provisions which allow the acquittee to be committed under rules that are different, either substantively or procedurally, from those that apply to others facing civil commitment. Some states, for instance, authorize a lower standard of proof than is required in normal civil hearings, while others require the acquitted defendant to bear the burden of proving that he is not fit for commitment. *See*, Comment, *Criminal Commitment Following An Insanity Acquittal*, 94 Harv.L.R. 605, 606 n. 5 (1981). The provisions that subject the acquitted defendant to different standards have been justified as necessary to protect the society from the dangerously insane. The acquittee's proven unlawful behavior and mental illness at the time of the crime are said to give rise to the inference of continuing dangerousness and insanity. *See, Warren v. Harvey*, 632 F.2d 925 (2d Cir.1980), *cert. denied*, 449 U.S. 902, 101 S.Ct. 273, 66 L.Ed.2d 133 (1980).

Legal challenges to laws differentiating between insanity acquittees and regular civil committees have been based largely on the equal protection clause coupled with the Supreme Court decision in *Addington v. Texas*, which is set out at p. 409 *supra*. Some of these challenges have succeeded while others failed. Thus, until the Supreme Court's opinion in *Jones v. United States* (which follows), the permissibility of drawing any legal distinctions between insanity acquittees subject to commitment and those facing normal civil commitment remained largely unresolved.

JONES v. UNITED STATES

Supreme Court of the United States, 1983.
—— U.S. ——, 103 S.Ct. 3043, 77 L.Ed.2d 694.

Justice POWELL delivered the opinion of the Court.

The question presented is whether petitioner, who was committed to a mental hospital upon being acquitted of a criminal offense by reason of insanity, must be released because he has been hospitalized for a period longer than he might have served in prison had he been convicted.

I

In the District of Columbia a criminal defendant may be acquitted by reason of insanity if his insanity is "affirmatively established by a preponderance of the evidence." D.C.Code § 24-301(j) (1981). If he successfully invokes the insanity defense, he is committed to a mental hospital. § 24-301(d)(1).[2] The statute provides several ways of obtaining release. Within 50 days of commitment the acquittee is entitled to a judicial hearing to determine his eligibility for release, at which he has the burden of proving by a preponderance of the evidence that he is no longer mentally ill or dangerous. § 24-301(d) (2).[3] If he fails to meet this burden at the 50-day hearing, the committed acquittee subsequently may be released, with court approval, upon certification of his recovery by the hospital chief of service. § 24-301(e).[4] Alternatively, the acquittee is entitled to a

2. Section 24-301(d)(1) provides:

"If any person tried upon an indictment or information for an offense raises the defense of insanity and is acquitted solely on the ground that he was insane at the time of its commission, he shall be committed to a hospital for the mentally ill until such time as he is eligible for release pursuant to this subsection or subsection (e)."

Under this provision, automatic commitment is permissible only if the defendant himself raised the insanity defense.

3. * * * The statute does not specify the standard for determining release, but the District of Columbia Court of Appeals held in this case that, as in release proceedings under § 24-301(e) and § 21-545(b), the confined person must show that he is either no longer mentally ill or no longer dangerous to himself or others.

4. Section 24-301(e) provides in relevant part:

"Where any person has been confined in a hospital for the mentally ill pursuant to subsection (d) of this section, and the superintendent of such hospital certifies (1) that such person has recovered his sanity, (2) that, in the opinion of the superintendent, such person will not in the reasonable future be dangerous to himself or others, and (3) in the opinion of the superintendent, the person is entitled to unconditional release from the hospital, * * * such certificate shall be sufficient to authorize the court to order the unconditional release of the person so confined from further hospitalization * * * but the court in its discretion may, or upon the objection of the United States or the District of Columbia shall, after due notice, hold a hearing at which evidence as to the mental condition of the person so confined may be submitted, including the testimony of one or more psychiatrists from said hospital. The court shall weigh the evidence and, if the court

judicial hearing every six months at which he may establish by a preponderance of the evidence that he is entitled to release. § 24–301(k).[5]

Independent of its provision for the commitment of insanity acquittees, the District of Columbia also has adopted a civil-commitment procedure, under which an individual may be committed upon clear and convincing proof by the Government that he is mentally ill and likely to injure himself or others. § 21–545(b).[6] The individual may demand a jury in the civil-commitment proceeding. § 21–544. Once committed, a patient may be released at any time upon certification of recovery by the hospital chief of service. §§ 21–546, 21–548. Alternatively, the patient is entitled after the first 90 days, and subsequently at 6-month intervals, to request a judicial hearing at which he may gain his release by proving by a preponderance of the evidence that he is no longer mentally ill or dangerous.

II

On September 19, 1975, petitioner was arrested for attempting to steal a jacket from a department store. The next day he was arraigned in the District of Columbia Superior Court on a charge of attempted petit larceny, a misdemeanor punishable by a maximum prison sentence of one year. §§ 22–103, 22–2202. The court ordered petitioner committed to St. Elizabeths, a public hospital for the mentally ill, for a determination of his competency to stand trial. On March 2, 1976, a hospital psychologist submitted a report to the court stating that petitioner was competent to stand trial, that petitioner suffered from "Schizophrenia, paranoid type," and that petitioner's alleged offense was "the product of his mental disease." Record 51.

finds that such person has recovered his sanity and will not in the reasonable future be dangerous to himself or others, the court shall order such person unconditionally released from further confinement in said hospital. If the court does not so find, the court shall order such person returned to said hospital. * * * "

5. Section 24–301(k) provides in relevant part:

"(1) A person in custody or conditionally released from custody, pursuant to the provisions of this section, claiming the right to be released from custody, the right to any change in the conditions of his release, or other relief concerning his custody, may move the court having jurisdiction to order his release, to release him from custody, to change the conditions of his release, or to grant other relief. * * *

(3) * * * On all issues raised by his motion, the person shall have the burden of proof. If the court finds by a preponderance of the evidence that the person is entitled to his release from custody, either conditional or unconditional, a change in the conditions of his release, or other relief, the court shall enter such order as may appear appropriate. * * *

(5) A court shall not be required to entertain a 2nd or successive motion for relief under this section more often than once every 6 months. * * *

6. Section 21–545(b) provides in relevant part:

"If the court or jury finds that the person is mentally ill and, because of that illness, likely to injure himself or other persons if allowed to remain at liberty, the court may order his hospitalization for an indeterminate period, or order any other alternative course of treatment which the court believes will be in the best interests of the person or of the public."

The court ruled that petitioner was competent to stand trial. Petitioner subsequently decided to plead not guilty by reason of insanity. The Government did not contest the plea, and it entered into a stipulation of facts with petitioner. On March 12, 1976, the Superior Court found petitioner not guilty by reason of insanity and committed him to St. Elizabeths pursuant to § 24–301(d)(1).

On May 25, 1976, the court held the 50-day hearing required by § 24–301(d)(2)(A). A psychologist from St. Elizabeths testified on behalf of the Government that, in the opinion of the staff, petitioner continued to suffer from paranoid schizophrenia and that "because his illness is still quite active, he is still a danger to himself and to others." Transcript 9. Petitioner's counsel conducted a brief cross-examination, and presented no evidence. The court then found that "the defendant-patient is mentally ill and as a result of his mental illness, at this time, he constitutes a danger to himself or others." *Id.*, at 13. Petitioner was returned to St. Elizabeths. Petitioner obtained new counsel and, following some procedural confusion, a second release hearing was held on February 22, 1977. By that date petitioner had been hospitalized for more than one year, the maximum period he could have spent in prison if he had been convicted. On that basis he demanded that he be released unconditionally or recommitted pursuant to the civil-commitment standards in § 21–545(b), including a jury trial and proof by clear and convincing evidence of his mental illness and dangerousness. The Superior Court denied petitioner's request for a civil-commitment hearing, reaffirmed the findings made at the May 25, 1976, hearing, and continued petitioner's commitment to St. Elizabeths.

Petitioner appealed to the District of Columbia Court of Appeals. A panel of the court affirmed the Superior Court, 396 A.2d 183 (1978), but then granted rehearing and reversed, 411 A.2d 624 (1980). Finally, the court heard the case en banc and affirmed the judgment of the Superior Court. 432 A.2d 364 (1981). The Court of Appeals rejected the argument "that the length of the prison sentence [petitioner] might have received determines when he is entitled to release or civil commitment under Title 24 of the D.C.Code." *Id.*, at 368. It then held that the various statutory differences between civil commitment and commitment of insanity acquittees were justified under the equal protection component of the Fifth Amendment.

We granted certiorari, and now affirm.

III

It is clear that "commitment for any purpose constitutes a significant deprivation of liberty that requires due process protection." *Addington v. Texas*, 441 U.S. 418, 425 (1979). Therefore, a State must have "a constitutionally adequate purpose for the confinement." *O'Connor v. Donaldson*, 422 U.S. 563, 574 (1975). Congress has determined that a criminal defendant found not guilty by reason of insanity in the District of Columbia should be committed indefinitely to a mental institution for treatment and the protection of society. ("[T]he District of Columbia statutory scheme for commitment of insane criminals is * * * a regulatory, prophylactic statute, based on a legitimate governmental interest in protecting society and rehabilitating mental patients"). Petitioner does not contest the Government's authority to commit a mentally ill and dangerous person indefinitely to a mental institution, but rather contends that "the petitioner's trial was not a constitutionally adequate hearing to justify an indefinite commitment." Brief for Petitioner 14.

Petitioner's argument rests principally on *Addington v. Texas, supra,* in which the Court held that the Due Process Clause requires the Government in a civil-commitment proceeding to demonstrate by clear and convincing evidence that the individual is mentally ill and dangerous. Petitioner contends that these due process standards were not met in his case because the judgment of not guilty by reason of insanity did not constitute a finding of present mental illness and dangerousness and because it was established only by a preponderance of the evidence. Petitioner then concludes that the Government's only conceivably legitimate justification for automatic commitment is to ensure that insanity acquittees do not escape confinement entirely, and that this interest can justify commitment at most for a period equal to the maximum prison sentence the acquittee could have received if convicted. Because petitioner has been hospitalized for longer than the one year he might have served in prison, he asserts that he should be released unconditionally or recommitted under the District's civil-commitment procedures.

A

We turn first to the question whether the finding of insanity at the criminal trial is sufficiently probative of mental illness and dangerousness to justify commitment. A verdict of not guilty by reason of insanity establishes two facts: (i) the defendant committed an act that constitutes a criminal offense, and (ii) he committed the act because of mental illness. Congress has determined that these findings constitute an adequate basis for hospitalizing the acquittee as a dangerous and mentally ill person. We cannot say that it was unreasonable and therefore unconstitutional for Congress to make this determination.

The fact that a person has been found, beyond a reasonable doubt, to have committed a criminal act certainly indicates dangerousness.[12] Indeed, this concrete evidence generally may be at least as persuasive

12. The proof beyond a reasonable doubt that the acquittee committed a criminal act distinguishes this case from *Jackson v. Indiana,* 406 U.S. 715, 92 S.Ct. 1845, 32 L.Ed.2d 435 (1972), in which the Court held that a person found incompetent to stand trial could not be committed indefinitely solely on the basis of the finding of incompetency. In *Jackson* there never was any affirmative proof that the accused had committed criminal acts or otherwise was dangerous.

as any predictions about dangerousness that might be made in a civil-commitment proceeding. We do not agree with petitioner's suggestion that the requisite dangerousness is not established by proof that a person committed a non-violent crime against property. This Court never has held that "violence," however that term might be defined, is a prerequisite for a constitutional commitment.

Nor can we say that it was unreasonable for Congress to determine that the insanity acquittal supports an inference of continuing mental illness. It comports with common sense to conclude that someone whose mental illness was sufficient to lead him to commit a criminal act is likely to remain ill and in need of treatment. The precise evidentiary force of the insanity acquittal, of course, may vary from case to case, but the Due Process Clause does not require Congress to make classifications that fit every individual with the same degree of relevance. Because a hearing is provided within 50 days of the commitment, there is assurance that every acquittee has prompt opportunity to obtain release if he has recovered.

Petitioner also argues that, whatever the evidentiary value of the insanity acquittal, the Government lacks a legitimate reason for committing insanity acquittees automatically because it can introduce the insanity acquittal as evidence in a subsequent civil proceeding. This argument fails to consider the Government's strong interest in avoiding the need to conduct a *de novo* commitment hearing following every insanity acquittal—a hearing at which a jury trial may be demanded, § 21–544, and at which the Government bears the burden of proof by clear and convincing evidence. Instead of focusing on the critical question whether the acquittee has recovered, the new proceeding likely would have to relitigate much of the criminal trial. These problems accent the Government's important interest in automatic commitment. We therefore conclude that a finding of not guilty by reason of insanity is a sufficient foundation for commitment of an insanity acquittee for the purposes of treatment and the protection of society.

B

Petitioner next contends that his indefinite commitment is unconstitutional because the proof of his insanity was based only on a preponderance of the evidence, as compared to *Addington's* civil-commitment requirement of proof by clear and convincing evidence. In equating these situations, petitioner ignores important differences between the class of potential civil-commitment candidates and the class of insanity acquittees that justify differing standards of proof. The *Addington* Court expressed particular concern that members of the public could be confined on the basis of "some abnormal behavior which might be perceived by some as symptomatic of a mental or emotional disorder, but which is in fact within a range of conduct that is generally acceptable." 441 U.S., at 426–427, 99 S.Ct., at 1809–1810.

In view of this concern, the Court deemed it inappropriate to ask the individual "to share equally with society the risk of error." But since automatic commitment under § 24–301(d)(1) follows only if the *acquittee himself* advances insanity as a defense and proves that his criminal act was a product of his mental illness, there is good reason for diminished concern as to the risk of error. More important, the proof that he committed a criminal act as a result of mental illness eliminates the risk that he is being committed for mere "idiosyncratic behavior," *Addington*, 441 U.S., at 427, 99 S.Ct., at 1810. A criminal act by definition is not "within a range of conduct that is generally acceptable." *Id.*, at 426–427.

We therefore conclude that concerns critical to our decision in *Addington* are diminished or absent in the case of insanity acquittees. Accordingly, there is no reason for adopting the same standard of proof in both cases. "[D]ue process is flexible and calls for such procedural protections as the particular situation demands." *Morrissey v. Brewer*, 408 U.S. 471, 481 (1972). The preponderance of the evidence standard comports with due process for commitment of insanity acquittees.

C

The remaining question is whether petitioner nonetheless is entitled to his release because he has been hospitalized for a period longer than he could have been incarcerated if convicted. The Due Process Clause "requires that the nature and duration of commitment bear some reasonable relation to the purpose for which the individual is committed." *Jackson v. Indiana*, 406 U.S. 715 (1972). The purpose of commitment following an insanity acquittal, like that of civil commitment, is to treat the individual's mental illness and protect him and society from his potential dangerousness. The committed acquittee is entitled to release when he has recovered his sanity or is no longer dangerous. And because it is impossible to predict how long it will take for any given individual to recover—or indeed whether he ever will recover—Congress has chosen, as it has with respect to civil commitment, to leave the length of commitment indeterminate, subject to periodic review of the patient's suitability for release.

In light of the congressional purposes underlying commitment of insanity acquittees, we think petitioner clearly errs in contending that an acquittee's hypothetical maximum sentence provides the constitutional limit for his commitment. A particular sentence of incarceration is chosen to reflect society's view of the proper response to commission of a particular criminal offense, based on a variety of considerations such as retribution, deterrence, and rehabilitation.

* * *

Different considerations underlie commitment of an insanity acquittee. As he was not convicted, he may not be punished. His confinement rests on his continuing illness and dangerousness.

Thus, under the District of Columbia statute, no matter how serious the act committed by the acquittee, he may be released within 50 days of his acquittal if he has recovered. In contrast, one who committed a less serious act may be confined for a longer period if he remains ill and dangerous. There simply is no necessary correlation between severity of the offense and length of time necessary for recovery. The length of the acquittee's hypothetical criminal sentence therefore is irrelevant to the purposes of his commitment.

IV

We hold that when a criminal defendant establishes by a preponderance of the evidence that he is not guilty of a crime by reason of insanity, the Constitution permits the Government, on the basis of the insanity judgment, to confine him to a mental institution until such time as he has regained his sanity or is no longer a danger to himself or society. This holding accords with the widely and reasonably held view that insanity acquittees constitute a special class that should be treated differently from other candidates for commitment. We have observed before that "[w]hen Congress undertakes to act in areas fraught with medical and scientific uncertainties, legislative options must be especially broad and courts should be cautious not to rewrite legislation. * * *" *Marshall v. United States*, 414 U.S. 417, 427 (1974). This admonition has particular force in the context of legislative efforts to deal with the special problems raised by the insanity defense.

The judgment of the District of Columbia Court of Appeals is

Affirmed.

Justice BRENNAN, with whom Justice MARSHALL and Justice BLACKMUN join, dissenting.

* * *

The question before us is whether the fact that an individual has been found "not guilty by reason of insanity," by itself, provides a constitutionally adequate basis for involuntary, indefinite commitment to psychiatric hospitalization.

* * *

A

The obvious difference between insanity acquittees and other candidates for civil commitment is that, at least in the District of Columbia, an acquittal by reason of insanity implies a determination beyond a reasonable doubt that the defendant in fact committed the criminal act with which he was charged. Conceivably, the Government may have an interest in confining insanity acquittees to punish them for their criminal acts, but the Government disclaims any such interest, and the Court does not rely on it.

B

Instead of relying on a punishment rationale, the Court holds that a finding of insanity at a criminal trial "is sufficiently probative of mental illness and dangerousness to justify commitment." *Ante*, at 3049. First, it declares that "[t]he fact that a person has been found, beyond a reasonable doubt, to have committed a criminal act certainly indicates dangerousness." *Ibid.* Second, the Court decides that "[i]t comports with common sense to conclude that someone whose mental illness was sufficient to lead him to commit a criminal act is likely to remain ill and in need of treatment." *Id.*, at 3050. Despite their superficial appeal, these propositions cannot support the decision necessary to the Court's disposition of this case—that the Government may be excused from carrying the *Addington* burden of proof with respect to each of the *O'Connor* elements of mental illness and dangerousness in committing petitioner for an indefinite period.

* * * An acquittal by reason of insanity of a single, nonviolent misdemeanor is not a constitutionally adequate substitute for the due process protections of *Addington* and *O'Connor, i.e.*, proof by clear and convincing evidence of present mental illness or dangerousness, with the Government bearing the burden of persuasion.

A "not guilty by reason of insanity" verdict is backward-looking, focusing on one moment in the past, while commitment requires a judgment as to the present and future. In some jurisdictions, most notably in federal criminal trials, an acquittal by reason of insanity may mean only that a jury found a reasonable doubt as to a defendant's sanity and as to the causal relationship between his mental condition and his crime. * * * The question is whether—in light of the uncertainty about the relationship between petitioner's crime, his present dangerousness, and his present mental condition—the Government can force him for the rest of his life "to share equally with society the risk of error," 441 U.S., at 427, 99 S.Ct., at 1810.

It is worth examining what is known about the possibility of predicting dangerousness from *any* set of facts. Although a substantial body of research suggests that a consistent pattern of violent behavior may, from a purely statistical standpoint, indicate a certain likelihood of further violence in the future, mere statistical validity is far from perfect for purposes of predicting which individuals will be dangerous. * * * Research is practically nonexistent on the relationship of *non-violent* criminal behavior, such as petitioner's attempt to shoplift, to future dangerousness. We do not even know whether it is even statistically valid as a predictor of similar non-violent behavior, much less of behavior posing more serious risks to self and others.

Even if an insanity acquittee remains mentally ill, so long as he has not repeated the same act since his offense the passage of time diminishes the likelihood that he will repeat it. Furthermore, the *frequency* of prior violent behavior is an important element in any attempt to predict future violence. Finally, it cannot be gainsaid that some crimes are more indicative of dangerousness than others. Subject to the limits of *O'Connor*, a State may consider non-violent misdemeanors "dangerous," but there is room for doubt whether a single attempt to shoplift and a string of brutal murders are equally accurate and equally permanent predictors of dangerousness. As for mental illness, certainly some conditions that satisfy the "mental disease" element of the insanity defense do not persist for an extended period—thus the traditional inclusion of "temporary insanity" within the insanity defense.

In the final analysis, the Court disregards *Addington* not on the ground that the Government's interests in committing insanity acquittees are different from or stronger than its interests in committing criminals who happen to be mentally ill, or mentally ill individuals who have done violent, dangerous things, but on the theory that "there is good reason for diminished concern as to the risk of error" when a person is committed indefinitely on the basis of an insanity acquittal. See *ante*, at 3051.

The "risk of error" that, according to the Court, is diminished in this context subsumes two separate risks. First, the Court notes that in *Addington* we were concerned, at least in part, that individuals might be committed for mere idiosyncratic behavior, and it observes that criminal acts are outside the " 'range of conduct that is generally acceptable.' " *Ante*, at 3051, however, requires that a person be proved *dangerous*, not merely "unacceptable," before he may be subjected to the massive curtailment of individual freedom and autonomy that indefinite commitment entails. In *Addington* itself, the State had clearly proved by a preponderance of the evidence that the petitioner had engaged repeatedly in conduct far beyond the pale of acceptable behavior, yet we did not regard that level of proof as furnishing adequate protection for the individual interests at stake.

Second, the Court reasons that "[a] criminal defendant who successfully raises the insanity defense necessarily is stigmatized by the verdict itself," and therefore that committing him does not involve the same risk of stigmatization a civil commitment may entail. *Ante*, at 3051, n. 16. This is perhaps the Court's most cynical argument.

*   *   *

Avoiding stigma, is only one of the reasons for recognizing a liberty interest in avoiding involuntary commitment. We have repeatedly acknowledged that persons who have already been labeled as mentally ill nonetheless retain an interest in avoiding involuntary commitment. Other aspects of involuntary commitment affect them in far more immediate ways.

In many respects, confinement in a mental institution is even more intrusive than incarceration in a prison. Inmates of mental institutions, like prisoners, are deprived of unrestricted association with friends, family, and community; they must contend with locks, guards, and detailed regulation of their daily activities. In addition, a person who has been hospitalized involuntarily may to a significant extent lose the right enjoyed by others to withhold consent to medical treatment.

Therefore, I cannot agree with the Court that petitioner in this case has any less interest in procedural protections during the commitment process than the petitioners in *Addington*, *O'Connor*, or *Baxstrom*, and I cannot agree that the risks of error which an indefinite commitment following an insanity acquittal entails are sufficiently diminished to justify relieving the Government of the responsibilities defined in *Addington*.

*   *   *

C

The rationales on which the Court justifies § 24–301's departures from *Addington* at most support deferring *Addington's* due process protections—specifically, its requirement that the Government carry the burden of proof by clear and convincing evidence—for a limited period only, not indefinitely.

The maximum sentence for attempted petit larceny in the District of Columbia is one year. Beyond that period, petitioner should not have been kept in involuntary confinement unless he had been committed under the standards of *Addington* and *O'Connor*. Petitioner had been in custody for 17 months at the time of his February 1977 hearing, either in St. Elizabeths or in the District of Columbia Correctional Center. At that time he should have received the benefit of the *Addington* due process standards, and, because he did not, the findings at that hearing cannot provide constitutionally adequate support for his present commitment. I would therefore reverse the judgment of the District of Columbia Court of Appeals.

[The dissenting opinion of Mr. Justice Stevens is omitted.]

Questions and Comments

1. *Jones v. U.S.* represents the first time that the Supreme Court has passed on the constitutionality of commitment laws differentiating between those acquitted of a criminal charge on grounds of insanity and other civil committees. Those committed under the *regular* civil commitment statute of the District of Columbia were entitled to a jury trial and to have the burden of proof borne by the government to prove mental illness and dangerousness by clear and convincing evidence. Those acquitted on grounds of insanity, on the other hand, would be committed unless they could prove by a preponderance of the evidence that "they were no longer mentally ill or dangerous". 103 S.Ct. 3043, 3045, n. 3. The constitutionality of *certain* differentiations in the treatment of these two classes previously questioned by commentators, can now be considered authoritatively settled by the *Jones* decision.

2. Congressional passage of the Insanity Defense Reform Act of 1984, Pub.L.No. 98–473, § 403(a) (to be codified at 18 U.S.C.A. § 4243(a)), fills a gap which was the subject of longstanding concern by the Administration and members of Congress. Senate Insanity Defense Hearings, pg. 52. Previously, following a verdict of not guilty by reason of insanity, commitment in a federal case could only occur (except for the District of Columbia) if the individual was civilly commitable under state law and the process was initiated by federal or state authorities. As a result, an acquitted defendant who did not meet *state* civil commitment standards could not even be confined for an observational period and was "free to walk out of the courtroom." Hearing Transcript of the National Commission of the Insanity Defense, p. 28.

Under section 4243 of the 1984 Reform Act, any person found not guilty by reason of insanity in a federal proceeding will be "committed to a suitable facility until such time as he is eligible for release ∗   ∗   ∗" Eligibility for release, in turn, is determined at a judicial hearing where the acquitted person has the burden of proving "that his release would not create a substantial risk of bodily injury to another person or serious damage of property of another due to a present mental disease or defect." Section 4243(d). Moreover, the Act imposes a different burden of proof on the defendant depending on the nature of the crime of which he has been acquitted. Where the individual was found guilty of an offense "involving bodily injury to, or serious damage to the property of another person, or involving a substantial risk of such injury or damage," he must prove his eligibility for release by *"clear and convincing* evidence" (emphasis added). On the other hand, as to all other offenses, the individual only has the "burden of such proof by a *preponderance* of the evidence." *Id.* (emphasis added).

The provisions of the 1984 Reform Act which impose on acquitted defendants the burden of proving eligibility for release by a *preponderance* of the evidence conforms fully with the decision of the Supreme Court in *Jones v. U.S.* Does the *Jones* opinion also validate the provisions of the federal statute which, for certain classes of offenses, requires the defendant to prove his eligibility for release by *"clear and convincing* evidence."? Could Congress or a state enact legislation which would require the acquitted defendant to prove his eligibility for release *beyond a reasonable doubt*? Is it arguable that while it is rational to shift the burden to the defendant because of the likelihood that mental illness and dangerousness established by the acquittal is likely to continue, it is unreasonable to escalate the burden of proof to the *beyond a reasonable doubt* standard? In other words, does the acquittal by reason of insanity and the resulting inference of continued mental illness provide a sufficient foundation for the requirement that the defendant prove his recovery and non-dangerousness beyond a reasonable doubt? Similarly, does the clear and convincing evidence requirement of the federal statute meet the standard of reasonableness required by the Court in *Jones*?

3. It has been suggested that the *Jones* decision is destructive of the principle established by *Addington* set out at p. 409 *supra*.

The Supreme Court's conceptualization of continuing mental illness is disturbing because the Court's perceptions undoubtedly will be applied to civil commitments as well as insanity acquittals. In states that tie dangerousness to an overt act, the Court's interpretation might permit a presumption that dangerousness and mental illness continue to exist unless the defendant proves otherwise. The only significant difference between this situation and the insanity acquittal in the District of Columbia is the actual commission of a criminal act. Yet in many ways, the existence of a recent overt act of violence, which is required in a number of civil commitment statutes, constitutes a greater threat to society than a minor property crime such as shoplifting. As a result of the Court's interpretation, it would seem that any civil commitment statute that requires proof beyond a reasonable doubt (or perhaps even by clear and convincing evidence) that a criminal act had been committed (even a minor crime), and tied the act to a mental disorder would probably be sustainable given judicial deference to legislative opinion. It is even possible to read the language of the Supreme Court as supporting the idea that any kind of mental illness, where it is associated with a criminal act, violence or property damage, if proved, could form the basis for the presumption later that the need for confinement continued to exist. Because the need for treatment and dangerousness were sufficient to justify commitment, states could presume that the past mental illness and dangerous behavior by itself justified continued confinement.

7 Mental Disability Law Reporter, 293, 294 (1983).

4. Although *Jones* approved procedural practices for insanity acquittees different from those allowed under *Addington* for regular civil commitment, can the same latitude be allowed as to substantive law? In Illinois, for example, civil commitment requires that the mentally ill person be *imminently* dangerous, but commitment of insanity acquittees is authorized without a finding that the danger is *imminent*. Should *Jones* be read to preclude differences in standards such as those that prevail in Illinois?

5. It has been suggested that a hidden justification of the *Jones* decision may have been a hesitancy to completely excuse the insane from their acts:

By characterizing post-insanity-acquittal confinement as it did, the Court avoided confronting the difficult issues that underlie the long-standing controversy over the insanity defense. Given the invalidity of using a civil commitment rationale to uphold Jones' confinement, the sole possible justification remaining was punishment, a rationale on which the majority explicitly declined to rely. The refusal to concede that a portion of the motivation for indefinite confinement was punitive, though, allowed the Court to evade any explicit discussion of the degree to which insanity has an exculpatory effect on moral and legal guilt. Had the Court instead chosen to recognize and rely on punitive rationales for post-insanity-acquittal commitment, it would have had to acknowledge a major departure from the traditional foundation of the insanity defense: that individuals without knowledge or control of their actions are not morally culpable for them and therefore should not be held criminally responsible.

The Supreme Court, 1982 Term, 97 Harv.L.Rev. 4, 101–02 (1983). *See also*, Goldstein and Katz, *Abolish the Insanity Defense—Why Not?*, 72 Yale L.J. 855 (1963).

6. The release provisions challenged in *Jones*, are the same ones that would cover the release of John Hinckley. [While the Insanity Defense Reform Act of 1984 (see note 2, *supra*) establishes different insanity acquittal release provisions, these new provisions will presumably not apply to Hinckley whose original commitment was pursuant to the civil commitment code of the District of Columbia.] Thus, Hinckley could be released either after a hearing initiated by himself (commonly known as a "301 k release hearing") or on the basis of a petition initiated by the superintendent of the psychiatric facility where Hinckley is confined certifying that Hinckley "has recovered his sanity * * * [and] will not in the reasonable future be dangerous to himself or others." *Jones, supra*, at 3046 n. 4. In the instance of the former, Hinckley would have the burden of proving by preponderance of the evidence that "he is either no longer mentally ill or no longer dangerous to himself or others." *Jones, supra*, at 3046 n. 3.

Clearly, under both types of proceedings, the dispositive legal issue is the mental status of the confined individual and/or his propensity for dangerous conduct in the future. To what extent can the release decision in a case such as Hinckley's be resolved on the basis of the prevailing legal standards rather than other factors such as the attitude of the public? In this connection consider the following commentary:

> One who is as notorious as John Hinckley is held in custody to forestall public outrage, but it would not be easy to prove that he is really more likely to shoot anyone in the future than hundreds of other disturbed persons who have been released or that he is likely to benefit from further institutional treatment. That he may continue to harass the actress Jodie Foster or some substitute ideal figure is another matter, but we do not as a rule confine people to protect celebrities from unwanted attentions. It is difficult to avoid the conclusion that the primary reason Hinckley remains in custody is that most people think he is guilty of attempted murder regardless of the jury verdict.

P. Johnson, *Review of Madness and the Criminal Law*, 50 U. of Chicago L.Rev. 1534, 1539 (1983).

7.

Hinckley Tells Court 'I Am Ready Now' To Press for Release

New York Times, July 28, 1984, p. 2, col. 1.

> Washington, July 27—John W. Hinckley Jr., who shot and wounded President Reagan in March 1981, made an unannounced court

appearance today and said "I am ready now" to seek a "release hearing."

Speaking in a strong, clear voice, Mr. Hinckley stood before Federal District Judge Barrington D. Parker and said, "I have talked to some doctors and they want to back me up." He did not identify the doctors.

Courtroom observers understood Mr. Hinckley to be seeking complete freedom from St. Elizabeths Hospital, where he has been held since June 1982, when a jury found him not guilty by reason of insanity in the shootings of Mr. Reagan and three other men. Under a special act of Congress applicable only in the District of Columbia, Mr. Hinckley is entitled to be released from the mental hospital if he can prove that he is no longer dangerous to himself or others by reason of mental illness.

But Vincent J. Fuller, his lawyer, said in an interview after the hearing that he believed Mr. Hinckley would petition only for "some limited, supervised grounds privilege" at the hospital.

There were indications of some tension between the lawyer and his client. Mr. Hinckley said in a July 16 letter to Judge Parker that he might dismiss his attorneys, but he had not done so as of today. Mr. Fuller defended him successfully at his two-month trial in 1982.

Today Mr. Hinckley, 29 years old, told Judge Parker, who presided at Mr. Hinckley's trial, that he was not sure Mr. Fuller and Judith A. Miller, his other attorney, "are willing to represent me" at a release hearing. "I would like to proceed on my own" if they would not do so, he said.

While the prosecutors said little at the hearing, it is clear they would oppose any effort by Mr. Hinckley to win his freedom. Dr. William Prescott, superintendent of the hospital, said through a spokesman late today that staff doctors "are not prepared to indicate that Mr. Hinckley is ready for release."

What is the likelihood, in view of the burden of proof imposed on Hinckley under the D.C. statute, that he could prevail at a hearing if the petition is opposed by the institution on the ground that he has not regained his sanity? Wouldn't the basis for such an evaluation be the same as the one that permitted Hinckley to successfully plead the insanity defense, i.e., a clinical impression by mental health professionals?

8. Opposition to the Hinckley verdict was particularly pronounced in the Congress. See pp. 677–679 *infra*. St. Elizabeth's Hospital, where Hinckley is confined, is a public facility supported primarily by Congressional appropriations. Under these circumstances is it possible for the facility to deal with the Hinckley case in a detached manner? If such a problem exists, is it not a consequence of a verdict that was considered unjust by a significant segment of the public? Is it therefore arguable that, unless the standard governing the insanity defense leads to acceptable results, the system will be distorted to meet public expectations?

IV. ALTERNATIVE CRIMINAL LAW DISPOSITIONS OF THE MENTALLY DISORDERED OFFENDER

A. INTRODUCTION

As detailed in the preceding sections, mental disorder may be an issue in a criminal case either with respect to the capacity of the defendant to stand trial or in terms of a defense of insanity. The defendant's mental condition may also be pertinent in two other contexts. One is where a jurisdiction has adopted the use of a special verdict, guilty but mentally ill. Here proof of mental disorder will lead not to relief from criminal responsibility, as in the case of the insanity defense, but will affect the disposition of the case following conviction.

Second, the defendant's mental status at the time of the offense may be pertinent to the existence or lack thereof of the *mens rea* element of the offense charged. Depending on the severity of the disorder and the precise nature of the mental element of the crime charged, the defendant may be acquitted of that offense but convicted of some lesser offense (e.g., second-degree murder when the charge was first degree murder) not requiring the same mental element. But this is not inevitably the case. The defendant's conduct may be such that there exists no available lesser offense of which he could be convicted once the mental element of the crime charged has not been sufficiently proved (*e.g.*, a charge of theft, where intended to permanently deprive was not proved).

Recent efforts to abolish the affirmative defense of insanity have been coupled with proposals that would legislatively limit psychiatric testimony to the question of *mens rea*. The implications of these proposals are, therefore, best explored in connection with the doctrine of diminished responsibility which is treated in subsection C below. Before turning to the proposals which seek to abolish the insanity defense, consideration will be given to the guilty but mentally ill verdict which does not displace the insanity defense but merely provides an alternative mode of disposition.

B. GUILTY BUT MENTALLY ILL

TAYLOR v. STATE OF INDIANA

Supreme Court of Indiana, 1982.
—— Ind. ——, 440 N.E.2d 1109.

HUNTER, Justice.

A jury found the defendant, Ronald Taylor, guilty of murder, Ind. Code § 35–42–1–1 (Burns 1979 Repl.) and attempted murder, Ind. Code § 35–42–1–1, *supra*, and Ind.Code § 35–41–5–1 (Burns 1979 Repl.), and found that he was mentally ill at the time of the offenses. Ind.Code § 35–5–2–3(a)(4) (Burns 1981 Supp.). He was sentenced to concurrent terms of thirty years and twenty years for his respective crimes.

* * *

The record reveals that on September 7, 1980, Jeanette Taylor and her son-in-law, Colby Washington, were shot in their residence in Gary, Indiana. Taylor died of her gunshot wounds, while Washington, who had been shot five times, survived. The subsequent police investigation culminated in defendant's arrest and convictions for the crimes at issue.

* * *

Defendant * * * challenges the validity of Ind.Code § 35–5–2–3, *supra*,[a] maintaining it is unconstitutional on its face and as applied to the facts before us. Defined in the statute are the verdict alternatives available to the jury when a defense of insanity is interposed. The statute reads in pertinent part:

"Sec. 3. (a) In all cases in which the defense of insanity is interposed the jury (or the court if tried by it) shall find whether the defendant is:

"(1) guilty;

(2) not guilty;

(3) not responsible by reason of insanity at the time of the offense; or

(4) guilty but mentally ill at the time of the offense."

Ind.Code § 35–5–2–3, *supra*.

Defendant maintains the statute violates due process, equal protection, and the privileges and immunities guaranteed by our constitutions.

His constitutional claims share a common predicate: the definitions of "insanity" and "mentally ill" are so vague and susceptible to misinterpretation by persons of ordinary intelligence that the verdicts outlined in subsections "(a)(3)" and "(a)(4)" are one and the same. He argues that the vagueness of the statutory terms necessarily results in arbitrary and selective application of the two subsections; concomitantly, he argues that the terms "insanity" and "mentally ill" are so vague and overbroad that it denied him reasonable notice of the charge against him and subjected him to "the whim of the jury."

* * *

The legal definition of "insanity," as incorporated by reference in Ind.Code § 35–5–2–3(b), *supra*, is found at Ind.Code § 35–41–3–6 (Burns 1979 Repl.):

"Sec. 6. (a) A person is not responsible for having engaged in prohibited conduct if, as a result of mental disease or defect, he

a. The statute was repealed effective September 1, 1982, by Acts 1981, P.L. 298 § 10(c). The law was re-enacted substantially verbatim and is presently codified at Ind.Code § 35–36–2–1 *et seq.* (Burns 1982 Supp.). Acts 1981, P.L. 298 § 5.

lacked substantial capacity either to appreciate the wrongfulness of the conduct or to conform his conduct to the requirements of law.

"(b) 'Mental disease or defect' does not include an abnormality manifested only by repeated unlawful or antisocial conduct."

"Mentally ill," on the other hand, is defined in subsection "c" of Ind.Code § 35-5-2-3, *supra:*

"(c) 'Mentally ill' means having a psychiatric disorder which substantially disturbs a person's thinking, feeling, or behavior and impairs the person's ability to function. For the purpose of this section, 'mentally ill' includes having any mental retardation."

We reject the notion that the two definitions are so broad and vague that each describes the same mental condition.

Without question the conditions described by the legislature involve similar behavioral characteristics. A mental disease or defect which manifests itself in the volitional inability to conform one's conduct to the requirements of the law, or in the cognitive inability to appreciate the wrongfulness of particular conduct, constitutes "insanity," as the law recognizes and defines it. *People v. Sorna,* (1979) 88 Mich.App. 351, 276 N.W.2d 892. To that extent, of course, the terms "mentally ill" and "insanity" can be said to overlap.

This Court has long recognized, however, that the existence of a mental disease or deficiency does not *ipso facto* render a defendant legally insane. For purposes of criminal law, the focal point always has been whether any particular defendant acted with the intent and culpability for which the imposition of criminal penalties was justified. *Id.* That focus is perpetuated in the statutory definitions and verdict alternatives at issue.

* * *

[We do not] agree with defendant that the definitions employed by the legislature are so vague and overlapping that the trier of fact is bestowed with unlimited discretion in the application of the terms. Consequently, we reject defendant's equal protection and privileges and immunities arguments that the fact-finder's application of the definitions and alternative verdicts will result in an irrational classification between defendants found guilty but mentally ill and those found not responsible by reason of insanity. To be sure, the application of the terms to any particular defendant and factual context may be difficult. The same was true, of course, of the question which confronted juries when, prior to the existence of the "guilty but mentally ill" verdict, jurors were faced with only two alternatives: sane or insane.

Our legislature has now provided jurors with an alternative verdict, an intermediate ground, which embodies the circumstance long recognized in the law—the defendant who suffers from a mental illness or deficiency yet remains capable of appreciating right from wrong and conforming his conduct to the requirements of the law.

The "guilty but mentally ill" verdict serves the state's interest in securing convictions justly obtained and in obtaining treatment for those convicted defendants who suffer mental illness. The classification is thus one which is reasonably related to a legislative purpose, as is necessary to withstand an equal protection attack. Nor can it be said that the statutory definitions and alternative verdicts are not equally available to persons similarly situated; the application of the classifications rests on the evidence regarding any particular defendant's mental condition. There is no patent inequity to support an equal protection or privileges and immunities claim.

The appellate courts of Michigan, one of the few other jurisdictions which has established the "guilty but mentally ill" verdict, have also rejected constitutional arguments such as those put before us. In * * * [*People v. Sorna, supra.*] the Court of Appeals noted that the classification "guilty but mentally ill" represented the legislature's attempt to provide a solution " 'in a practical and troublesome area.' " *Id.*, 88 Mich.App. at 360, 276 N.E.2d at 896. The court continued:

> "The Legislature, in formulating M.C.L. § 768.36; M.S.A. § 28.1059, has established an intermediate category to deal with situations where a defendant's mental illness does not deprive him of substantial capacity sufficient to satisfy the insanity test but does warrant treatment in addition to incarceration. The fact that these distinctions may not appear clearcut does not warrant a finding of no rational basis to make them."

* * *

People v. Sorna, supra, 88 Mich.App. at 360–1, 276 N.W.2d at 896.

Like the court in *Sorna*, we have expressed our recognition that the question whether a particular defendant is not responsible by reason of insanity or guilty but mentally ill may not always be easily resolved. That fact, of course, does not render the legislature's definitions and verdicts invalid, for difficult factual questions may arise in any area of the law. Our legislature's attempt to ameliorate the problems which have plagued this troublesome area of law is commendable; in rejecting defendant's constitutional challenges to Ind.Code § 35–5–2–3, *supra*, we emphasize that courts and lawyers alike should strive to insure that jurors, in assessing the delicate factual question which confronts them, are equipped with an understanding of the terms "insanity" and "mentally ill," as well as the crucial distinction between the legislatively-defined concepts.

* * *

Judgment affirmed.

Questions and Comments

1. The guilty but mentally ill verdict option arises either as a result of the defendant's special pleading or occurs automatically when the defendant pleads the insanity defense. Therefore, the defendant who

does not place his mental status in issue runs no risk of being found guilty but mentally ill (GBMI).

2. Under the rule announced in *Taylor v. State* both the GBMI and the not guilty by reason of insanity verdicts require a mental disease or some similar finding. However, a verdict of guilty but mentally ill can be returned only if the mental illness does not negate both the defendant's ability to understand the unlawful nature of his conduct and his ability to conform his conduct to the requirements of the law.

3. The GBMI verdict did not exist prior to 1975, when Michigan became the first state to adopt such a statute. At least seven other states, following Michigan's example, have also added the GBMI classification. *See* Alaska Stat. 12–47–040; O.C.G.A. § 27–1503(a)(3) and (4); Ill.Rev.Stat., ch. 38, § 115–3(c); West's Ann.Ind.Code § 35–35–2–1; Ky. Rev.Stat. 504.120; N.M.Stat.Ann., § 31–9–3; Utah Code Ann., 77–35–21(a).

A proposal to adopt a GBMI alternative at the federal level was endorsed by the Attorney General's Task Force on Violent Crime. *See*, Senate Insanity Defense Hearings, pg. 32. The Justice Department, however, rejected this approach since it would not "eliminate confusing psychiatric testimony * * * [and could] serve to confuse the jury." *Id.* at 33.

4. Critics of the GBMI verdict have expressed concern over a jury's competence to make the finer psychiatric distinctions necessitated by the addition of such a verdict. Is the line between statutory definitions of mental illness and definitions of legal insanity sufficiently bright to avoid jury confusion? Is it arguable that, since the determination of criminal responsibility is as much a moral judgment as a medical one, there is little need for a standard that draws clear clinical lines?

5. Some states assist the jury in keeping mental illness and legal insanity separate by providing jurors with special verdict forms that require the jury to affirmatively find each element of the GBMI verdict, i.e., that the defendant committed the offense, that he was not legally insane, and that he was mentally ill at the time of the crime. *See* Ill.Rev. Stat., ch. 38, § 115–4(i); N.M.Stat.Ann., § 31–9–3(E).

6. Critics of the GBMI verdict contend that this alternative verdict invites the jury to evade the difficult task of distinguishing between those who are responsible and those who are not. Rather than make difficult choices, "[t]he jury can compromise." It may satisfy its desire for vengeance by convicting, while expressing sympathy for the defendant by tacking on the label "but mentally ill," without ever deciding whether the person should properly be held responsible—and punished—for his or her acts." Rubenstein, *Against "Guilty But Mentally Ill"*, New York Times, Aug. 5, 1982, p. 29, col. 3.

Fears that the GBMI verdict would diminish the effectiveness of the insanity defense are not borne out by the available empirical studies. A recent study by the Michigan Center for Forensic Psychiatry reveals that, in the five years prior to and following the adoption of the GBMI verdict, there was no significant difference in either the number of persons asserting the defense or the number of NGRI acquittals:

> What then has happened in Michigan pursuant to this new initiative? During the seven years prior to the advent of the "guilty but mentally ill" verdict, 279 persons were found not guilty by reason of insanity. During 1975, the year the new verdict was enacted, thirty-three persons were found not guilty by reason of insanity. The following year, thirty-two persons successfully asserted this defense. Between 1977–1980, approximately fifty-seven persons were acquitted by reason of insanity each year. The "guilty but mentally ill" verdict was successfully asserted by approximately eighty persons a year in Michigan between 1979 and 1981. Of these eighty persons, half were found to be mentally ill at the time of their admission to prison. Only half of this group need any special mental health program.

Morris, *The Criminal Responsibility of the Mentally Ill,* 33 Syracuse L.Rev., 477, 530 (1982). *See also* Project, *Evaluating Michigan's Guilty But Mentally Ill Verdict: An Empirical Study,* 16 U.Mich.J.L. Reform 77 (1982).

On the other hand, it has been reported that in Indiana the verdict has resulted in a "reduction in the practical number of entered pleas claiming not guilty by reason of insanity." Senate Insanity Defense Hearings, pg. 23 (statement of Senator Dan Quayle).

7. Defendants found GBMI are typically sentenced to prison terms comparable to those imposed on other persons found guilty of the same crime. In addition, an immediate psychiatric examination is often authorized to determine whether the defendant is currently mentally ill and, if so, whether psychiatric treatment would provide any significant benefit. In those cases where treatment is found necessary, it may be provided either at a penal institution or in a psychiatric facility. In contrast to the disposition of NGI defendants, a clinical finding that the defendant is no longer mentally ill does not result in his release. Since the defendant has been found guilty of the offense charged under the verdict, he must continue to serve the term of his sentence. Conversely, a defendant cannot be denied release at the end of his sentence because he is still mentally ill. Continued hospitalization requires full civil commitment proceedings. Should the defendant be eligible for probation or parole, the sentencing court or parole board is normally authorized to make continued psychiatric treatment a condition of the defendant's release.

The disposition phase that follows a GBMI verdict has led to various legal challenges. In a number of cases the challenges are based on objections to the transfer of a GBMI defendant to a mental health facility without benefit of a hearing to determine his present need for treatment. The Michigan Supreme Court considered this argument in *People v. McLeod,* 407 Mich. 632, 288 N.W.2d 909 (1980). The court held that a full commitment hearing was not required by due process to determine present need for treatment. Instead, the pre-sentencing examination required by the Michigan statute was found to be sufficient to satisfy due process. Because all states with GBMI statutes require a pre-sentencing examination, this due process challenge is unlikely to succeed elsewhere.

Other challenges have involved claims that GBMI statutes violate due process and the equal protection clause because they fail to guarantee that the defendant will receive treatment. One appellate court, which considered a defendant's right to treatment under such a statute, ruled that in view of the procedural rights afforded defendants at trial, GBMI convicts "enjoy no separate constitutional right to treatment for their mental health problems beyond the constitutional right to minimally adequate medical care which is applicable to all persons." *People v. Marshall*, 114 Ill.App.3d 217, 233, 70 Ill.Dec. 91, 102, 448 N.E.2d 969, 980 (1983).

In Michigan, a right to treatment under the State's GBMI statute was found by the judicial reading of such a right into the statute. *See, People v. McLeod, supra,* at 914.

C. MENS REA RELATED DEFENSES AS AN ALTERNATIVE TO THE INSANITY DEFENSE

1. *The Nature of the Mens Rea Defense*

The proposals to limit the insanity defense and particularly Title VII of Senate Bill 2572, which is discussed in greater detail in Subsection 2 *supra,* cannot be understood without some appreciation of the concept of *mens rea* and, more particularly, the difference between general and specific intent. All common law felonies and most legislatively created crimes require both the commission of an act and some prescribed state of mind. The common law termed this state of mind element *mens rea* (literally "guilty mind"). Most jurisdictions currently allow defendants to admit psychiatric evidence for the purpose of rebutting the prosecution's evidence that the defendant possessed the requisite *mens rea*. This defense has generally been referred to as diminished capacity, although the terms diminished or partial responsibility are also used.

The doctrine of diminished capacity and other "defenses" related to insufficiency of *mens rea* are distinguishable from the defense of insanity. Insanity is currently regarded as an affirmative defense relieving the defendant of responsibility for what would otherwise be a criminal act. Diminished capacity raises a reasonable doubt as to requisite *mens rea*, one of the essential elements of a crime. Theoretically, the absence of the *mens rea* element, due to the defendant's mental disorder, should lead to a finding that no crime has been committed and consequently serve as the basis for an acquittal separate and distinct from the insanity defense. As a practical matter, however, courts have generally resisted such extension of *mens rea* concept. Instead *mens rea* types of defenses, including that of diminished responsibility, have been largely confined to the crime of homicide. Here, proof of mental impairment has most commonly been used to negate a finding that the defendant was capable of premeditation or deliberation. The case which follows illustrates the application of the diminished capacity doctrine in this context.

COMMONWEALTH v. WALZACK

Supreme Court of Pennsylvania, 1976.
468 Pa. 210, 360 A.2d 914.

NIX, Justice.

Today we must decide whether psychiatric evidence is admissible to be evaluated by the jury when an accused offers it to negate the element of specific intent required for a conviction of murder of the first degree thereby reducing the crime to murder of the second degree. We are persuaded by the vast weight of authority that psychiatric evidence should be admissible for this purpose and, therefore, we hold that the learned court below erred in excluding the proffered testimony from the jury's consideration.

Prior to analyzing the specific facts of this case, it is necessary to clarify what we do not decide in today's opinion. First, appellant has not raised the defense of insanity and today's decision in no way affects the vitality of the M'Naghten test as the sole standard in this Commonwealth for determining criminal responsibility where the actor alleges mental illness or defect. Second, for reasons that will be discussed hereinafter, we do not view the position adopted today as inferentially accepting the irresistible impulse test which we have previously expressly rejected. Third, we do not here reach the question of the applicability of the principles announced herein to crimes requiring a specific intent other than murder of the first degree.

Appellant, Michael Walzack, was tried before a jury and convicted of murder of the first degree in the shooting death of one Ole Toasen. Following a penalty hearing, appellant was sentenced to life imprisonment. Post-trial motions for a new trial and in arrest of judgment were filed and denied and this direct appeal followed.

During the trial, the defense admitted the killing and attempted to establish its position through the testimony of appellant and a Dr. Willis. When called to the stand, the defense made an offer of proof indicating that the witness did not intend to contest appellant's sanity at the time of the incident, under the M'Naghten standard. The defense conceded that appellant was sane; that he could tell the difference between right and wrong and that he knew the nature and quality of his act. The single stated purpose in offering the witness was to demonstrate that as a result of a surgical procedure, a lobotomy, which appellant had undergone, he did not possess sufficient mental capacity to form the specific intent required for a conviction of murder of the first degree.[6] * * *

Appellant was charged with and convicted of murder of the first degree. The Legislature defined the elements of this crime as:

> "All murder which shall be perpetrated by means of poison, or by lying in wait, or by any other kind of *willful, deliberate and premeditated killing*, or which shall be committed in the perpetration of, or attempting to perpetrate any arson, rape, robbery, burglary, or kidnapping, shall be murder in the first degree." (Emphasis added).

Under this section the term "willful, deliberate and premeditated" describes the mental state that must accompany the act before a nonfelony murder can be murder of the first degree.

It is axiomatic that the Commonwealth must prove each element of a crime beyond a reasonable doubt. It is equally as clear that the requisite intent of an offense is one of the elements of the crime. Consequently, in the instant trial, it was incumbent upon the Commonwealth to prove beyond a reasonable doubt that appellant had the specific intent to kill to support the finding of murder of the first degree.

Any analysis of the admissibility of a particular type of evidence must start with a threshold inquiry as to its relevance and probative value. We have cited with approval the test for relevance propounded by two leading evidentiary authorities, Wigmore and McCormick. Wigmore defines relevance in terms of two axioms, "None but facts having rational probative value are admissible," and, "All facts having rational probative value are admissible, unless some specific rule forbids." 1 Wigmore, *Evidence* § 9–10 at 289–95 (3rd Ed.1940). McCormick suggests the following for determining relevance, " * * * [d]oes the evidence offered render the desired inference more probable than it would be without the evidence? * * * Relevant evidence then, is evidence that in some degree advances the inquiry, and thus has probative value, and is prima facie admissible." McCormick, *Evidence* § 185 at 437–38 (2nd Ed.1972).

In the instant case, appellant attempted to introduce expert testimony concerning his mental capacity to form the type of specific intent a conviction for murder of the first degree requires. This

---

6. While the offer was not as precise as it might have been, the reference to "diminishing the degree of responsibility of the Defendant for this crime" was sufficient to alert the trial judge of the intended purpose of the testimony. In this area, nomenclature has been a source of obfuscation. The concept has been referred to as partial responsibility, diminished responsibility and partial insanity. Probably, the most accurate label would be "diminished capacity" since the thrust of the doctrine relates to the accused's ability to perform a specified cognitive process.

"Although the terms 'partial' and 'diminished' responsibility are the common vehicles used by writers and courts to describe the theory we discuss today, they are highly misleading. They connote that the defendant is somehow not fully responsible for his actions. In actuality the defendant is fully responsible, but only for a crime which does not require the elements of premeditation and deliberation." * * *

testimony obviously would have "significantly advanced the inquiry" as to the presence or absence of an essential element of the crime. Thus, the exclusion of the proffered testimony cannot be based upon a lack of relevancy. Also, there is no basis for finding the tendered testimony incompetent for other reasons. Although early decisions in this jurisdiction can be found that express doubt as to the reliability of psychiatric testimony, our more recent decisions make clear that psychiatry has a legitimate scientific basis. While recognizing that psychiatry might well be less exact than some of the other medical disciplines we are nevertheless cognizant of the "tremendous advancements made in the field." * * *

We have long accepted psychiatric evidence on the issue of whether an accused is competent to stand trial. Similarly, we have long permitted psychiatric evidence under the M'Naghten test to determine whether an accused was insane at the time of the crime. More recently we have allowed psychiatric evidence for the purpose of determining whether an accused acted in the heat of passion when committing a homicide; whether an accused subjectively believed he was in imminent danger of death or serious bodily injury under his claim of self-defense; whether an accused was capable of making a detailed written confession; and, we have long accepted psychiatric evidence at the penalty stage of trial.

Having determined that psychiatric evidence possesses sufficient reliability for its admission for the purposes announced herein we must ascertain whether there are any policy reasons that might justify ruling it incompetent. Early opinions of this Court have suggested that acceptance of the doctrine of diminished capacity is tantamount to acceptance of the irresistible impulse test for insanity. We do not agree. The doctrines of diminished capacity and irresistible impulse involve entirely distinct considerations. Irresistible impulse is a test for insanity which is broader than the M'Naghten test. Under the irresistible impulse test a person may avoid criminal responsibility even though he is capable of distinguishing between right and wrong, and is fully aware of the nature and quality of his act provided he establishes that he was unable to refrain from acting. An accused offering evidence under the theory of diminished capacity *concedes general criminal liability.* The thrust of this doctrine is to challenge the capacity of the actor to possess a particular state of mind required by the legislature for the commission of a certain degree of the crime charged. * * *

[As] the Iowa Supreme Court stated:

We believe that failure to recognize there can be an unsoundness of mind of such a character as to negative a specific intent to commit a particular crime, is to ignore the great advancements which have been made in the field of psychiatry. The results which have been achieved confirm its growing reliability. We do not consider this position contradictory to our adherence to the right and wrong test of insanity. We do not pretend there are no mental disorders except those which qualify under this test, but rather limit the defense of insanity to the types of mental illness in which the defendant cannot comprehend the nature or consequences of his act. Weihofen in his text *Mental Disorder as a Criminal Defense* states that if we recognize the basic principle that a person should not be punished for a crime if he did not entertain the requisite state of mind, "there is no logical escape from the proposition that a person cannot be held guilty of a deliberate and premeditated killing which he did not deliberate and premeditate, and indeed was incapable of deliberating and premeditating. If, however, he was able to understand the nature of the act he was committing and if he intended to do that act, he should be held guilty of murder in the second degree or man-slaughter. There is no logic in the 'all or nothing' assumption underlying so many court opinions on the subject—that a person is either 'sane' and wholly responsible for all his acts, or 'insane' and wholly irresponsible."

Once it is determined that the proffered evidence was both relevant and competent, due process requires its admission. * * * It is inconsistent with fundamental principles of American jurisprudence to preclude an accused from offering relevant and competent evidence to dispute the charge against him. This, of course, includes any of the elements that comprise that charge.

Judgment of sentence reversed and a new trial awarded.

EAGEN, Justice (dissenting).

In *Commonwealth v. McCusker*, 448 Pa. 382, 292 A.2d 286 (1972), a majority of this Court overruled a multitude of prior decisions and held that psychiatric testimony is admissible at trial to aid the fact finder in determining if one who kills another did so in the heat of passion. Today a majority of the Court takes a further leap into the unknown and attributes to the science of psychiatry the ability to say with a reasonable degree of certainty that the instant killer, *who admittedly was sane and acted with malice and had the mental capacity to know what he was doing and to know what he was doing was wrong,* lacked the mental capacity to form a specific intent to kill. I dissented in *McCusker,* and I dissent here again.

The science of psychiatry has advanced materially in recent years and undoubtedly is now able to present reliable information as to human behavior in certain situations; however, the psychiatric testimony, here involved, is so patently devoid of reliability it should not receive judicial sanction.

Some psychiatrists will continue to dig up excuses for criminal behavior (as witness, the recent Hearst trial) even though some such "excuses" may border on the ridiculous and be totally lacking in scientific reliability. Unfortunately, some members of the judiciary will join them in accepting these excuses. * * *

The majority also states my position represents an expression of distrust of the judgment of the citizens of this Commonwealth. To the contrary, my trust in citizens serving as jurors has never and is not now waning. My concern is with submitting unreliable evidence to those jurors and thereby complicating their deliberations. I do not think jurors should have to evaluate evidence which has not been shown to be reliable. * * *

Questions and Comments

1. While the diminished capacity doctrine has been adopted by the majority of the states, a number of jurisdictions including Minesota have rejected the doctrine even to negative proof of specific intent. *See, e.g., Minnesota v. Bouwman*, 328 N.W.2d 703 (1982). In rejecting the doctrine of diminished responsibility the court made the following observations:

> In determining this issue it is essential that we differentiate between intent as a fact issue from the question of the mental capacity of the defendant. The state presents factual evidence as to the commission of the particular act the defendant has been charged with committing. Direct evidence as to the fact of intent is usually impossible because of the subjective nature of this element of the crime. What a person intends lies within the recesses of that individual person's mind. Yet, in determining this question, inquiry is made under an objective standard, namely, the standard that people operate within the broad boundaries of what is deemed normal or sane. To put it another way, the law presumes people, including the defendant standing trial, are responsible for their acts, *i.e.*, that they have the capacity to intend what they do.

> Within this ambit of normality or sanity, jurors, relying on their sensory perceptions, experiences in life, and their common sense, consider the manifestations of the defendant's conduct and determine if the defendant formed the specific intent to do what he did. The defendant has the right to offer evidence which disputes the physical facts upon which the inference of the fact of intent is sought to be established by the prosecution. However, psychiatric evidence is of no value at this part of the trial since it does not relate to the physical evidence upon which the jury is to determine the issue of intent. Rather, such expert testimony relates to the mental capacity of the defendant and is properly part of defendant's case wherein he must establish the defense of mental illness by the appropriate standard. Such psychiatric evidence relative to the state's obligation to establish the intent of the defendant is argumentative and of no probative value.

> When, however, the insanity defense is asserted, the inquiry shifts to a different dimension. The question becomes whether the defendant, even though he has manifested the specific intent to do the thing that he did, was laboring under such a defect of reason that he lacked the capacity to form the intent that was otherwise manifested.

The question becomes whether the defendant was acting outside the ambit of sanity and normality as delineated by the *M'Naghten* rule incorporated in Minn.Stat. § 611.026 (1980).

On this issue of capacity, expert psychiatric testimony has probative value. The inquiry is no longer on the direction the defendant's mind took but on how the defendant's mind worked. Here psychiatry can be of help.

There is a distinction, which society understands and accepts, between a verdict of "not guilty" and a verdict of "not guilty by reason of insanity." Because this is so, it is important that the inquiry at trial into the defendant's criminal responsibility for his acts proceeds in two stages, the first to determine intent and the second to determine capacity.

Also necessarily involved in answering the certified question [whether psychiatric evidence is admissable to negate *mens rea*] is the role of psychiatric evidence as it may relate to a lesser degree of guilt for the commission of a specific act—generally described as the doctrine of diminished responsibility. In *Bethea v. United States*, 365 A.2d 64, 83–92 (D.C.1976), the reasons for rejecting this concept are stated with clarity and logic and we adopt the reasoning of the District of Columbia Court of Appeals and its conclusion.

By contradicting the presumptions inherent in the doctrine of mens rea, the theory of diminished capacity inevitably opens the door to variable or sliding scales of criminal responsibility. * * * We should not lightly undertake such a revolutionary change in our criminal justice system.

328 N.W.2d at 705–706.

2. Those jurisdictions that reject the diminished capacity defense typically do so because of the intricacy of the distinctions it requires the jury to draw. As noted by one court, "theoretically the insanity concept operates as a bright line test separating the criminally responsible from the criminally irresponsible. The diminished capacity concept on the other hand posts a series of rather blurry lines representing gradations of culpability." *State v. Wilcox*, 70 Ohio St.2d 182, 436 N.E.2d 523 (1982). The *Wilcox* court expressed further concern that the "finely differentiated psychiatric concepts associated with diminished capacity demands a sophistication that jurors ordinarily have not developed." *Id.* Are these concerns legitimate in light of the widespread exposure of juries to psychiatric evidence in insanity defense cases? Are the distinctions required for diminished capacity significantly more complex than those involved in the various insanity defense tests?

3. Justice Wahl, dissenting in *State v. Bouwman*, discussed in note, *supra*, observed that "[t]he basic premise of criminal law is that without the necessary *mens rea*, or guilty mind, there can be no criminal liability." The Massachusetts Supreme Court in *Commonwealth v. Gould*, 380 Mass. 672, 405 N.E.2d 927 (1980), followed a similar premise to conclude that " 'a legal as well as logical incongruity' " would result if a defendant without the mental capacity to deliberate could be convicted

of deliberated, premeditated murder. Despite the rationality of the proposition that a defendant mentally incapable of forming the specific intent included in a crime is incapable of the commission of that crime, the right to present psychiatric evidence of mental capacity has not, as Justice Wahl suggests, been afforded independent constitutional protection. The U.S. Supreme Court, for instance, has twice dismissed, for lack of a substantial federal question, appeals based on a state court's denial of psychiatric testimony on the issue of intent. *Troche v. California*, 280 U.S. 524, 50 S.Ct. 87, 74 L.Ed. 592 (1929); *Coleman v. California*, 317 U.S. 596, 63 S.Ct. 162, 87 L.Ed. 487 (1942). In each case, California's practice of denying psychiatric evidence except on the issue of insanity was allowed, and no federal constitutional rights were found to be implicated. Similarly, in *Fisher v. United States*, 328 U.S. 463, 66 S.Ct. 1318, 90 L.Ed. 1382 (1946), the Supreme Court refused to overrule the District of Columbia's decision not to allow the consideration of the defendant's mental deficiency in determining if he was guilty in the first or second degree.

More recently, the Seventh Circuit made it clear that such constitutional protection exists only when the state itself has determined that psychiatric evidence is relevant and competent when the issue is the intent of the accused; *See Muench v. Israel*, 715 F.2d 1124 (7th Cir.1983). In upholding a Wisconsin court's decision to deny psychiatric testimony on the issue of intent in a first degree murder, the court provided the following rationale:

> Petitioners' argument regarding the materiality of the proffered psychiatric testimony is straightforward. Whether they actually committed their homicidal acts with the mental purpose of ending a human life was a fact in issue. Logically, their "capacity" to "form" that intention is a fact in issue, for if they lacked the capacity to form the intent, then they did not actually form that intent. Hence, their capacity to form an intent to kill is a fact in issue, and evidence standing for that proposition is material.

> It is naturally tautological that one who lacks the capacity to do something could not have done that something. Thus conceptualized, the process of cognition is described in essentially, physiological terms. "Forming" an "intention" can be likened to "performing" an "action," and just as evidence of a physical handicap which rendered a person incapable of performing a particular action would be material in a case where the person is accused of performing that action, it would logically seem that evidence of a mental handicap which rendered a person incapable of forming a particular intention would be material where the person is accused of forming that intention.

> If specific types of intentions were as discrete as particular types of actions; if one's mental abilities were as demonstrable as one's physical abilities; if the relationship between one's mental handicaps and a specific intent were as identifiable as the relationship between one's physical handicaps and a specific physical movement; and if one formed an intention the way one performs an action, the analogy would be compelling, but it is not.

The essential flaw in petitioners' argument is that the basic fact which they wish to establish is that they suffered from a personality disorder. It is not disputed that experts in psychology are competent to testify regarding that basic fact. What is the dispute—indeed, the entire debate over the doctrine of diminished capacity has as its focal point—is whether a personality disorder is probative of the defendant's capacity to form an intent to kill. Petitioners' experts contended that personality disorders rendered them unable to form such an intent. That is, their experts contended that the fact of their personality disorders was a material issue in their cases because the fact was probative of whether they were capable of entertaining a mental state in issue. In short, petitioners essentially maintain that the psychiatric testimony they proffered is relevant because their witnesses said so. The proposition does not survive its statement.

715 F.2d at 1143–1144.

4. Some jurisdictions have not had positive experiences in "controlling" the diminished capacity defense. The history of diminished capacity in California is particularly illustrative. The California Supreme Court during the 1950's and 1960's radically expanded the defense beyond its original role as a means of negativing specific intent. In *People v. Wolff*, 61 Cal.2d 795, 40 Cal.Rptr. 271, 394 P.2d 959 (1964), for example, the court recognized that the schizophrenic defendant was legally sane and had carefully planned the murder of his own mother. The court, however, reduced the degree of the defendant's offense from first to second degree murder. The California Supreme Court reasoned that the defendant, although capable of premeditation and deliberation, could not meaningfully evaluate and reflect on the consequences of his actions in the manner a mentally normal person could. Some critics have argued that *Wolff* effectively creates a type of partial insanity defense that although it does not permit complete acquittal, will permit a reduction in the severity of punishment. *See, e.g.,* Arenella, *The Diminished Capacity and Diminished Responsibility Defenses: Two Children of a Doomed Marriage,* 77 Colum.L.Rev. 827, 829–30 (1977).

California's diminished capacity defense took on absurd proportions in the case of *People v. White*, 117 Cal.App.3d 270, 172 Cal.Rptr. 612 (1981). The defendant White, a disgruntled former San Francisco city official shot and killed San Francisco Mayor George Moscone and Supervisor Harvey Milk while the two men sat at their desks in City Hall. White based his defense to these homicides on psychiatric evidence that his overconsumption of junk food, in combination with mental depression, prevented him from premeditating, deliberating, or harboring malice toward his victims. The press labeled White's novel theory "the Twinkie Defense." See Hager, *Twinkie Defense—It Proved to Be Right Recipe,* Los Angeles Times, May 23, 1979, at p. 1, col. 3. The jury acquitted White of first-degree murder and instead handed down a conviction of voluntary manslaughter. The verdict provoked riots in San Francisco and widespread criticism of the California judiciary's acceptance of novel psychiatric defenses. This criticism culminated in state legislation permitting the use of psychiatric evidence outside the context of the insanity defense solely to negate intent specifically required by statute. *West's Ann.Cal.Penal Code* § 28(a) (1982).

5. The limitation on the diminished capacity doctrine discussed in note 3, *supra* has been adopted where an affirmative defense of insanity was also available. As the materials in the following sections will make clear, the various proposals at both federal and state levels to restrict psychiatric defenses to the issue of *mens rea* would make this the exclusive channel for obtaining relief from criminal responsibility for those suffering from a mental disability. Thus, rather than supplementing the insanity defense, diminished capacity would serve as the only vehicle for the consideration of mental capacity issues. Consequently, the various policy reasons which have caused some courts to reject diminished capacity types of defenses would not, of course, have the same relevancy.

2. Efforts to Curb the Insanity Defense

a. Legislative Proposals

i. Proposed Changes in Federal Law

Speaking as a layman in law, I think I do speak as to the outrage that American citizens felt in the recent verdict in the Presidential assassination attempt in the trial of John W. Hinckley. It has caused a great expression of outrage and dismay. I think that for that reason we are thankful that you are working on this and I hope that something can be done in the very near future to make some corrections in our laws because I do believe the American people are registering their feelings of shock and disbelief concerning the decision of the jury in this case.

Senate Insanity Defense Hearings, p. 24 (statement of Senator Steven D. Symms).

The remarks of Senator Symms and that of others in the Senate underscore the enormous impact that the Hinckley verdict has had on the debate concerning the insanity defense. Clearly, Hinckley's acquittal on grounds of insanity served to coalesce and bring into focus the longstanding opposition to the defense. At the federal level it led to the introduction in the 97th Congress of several bills designed to modify or eliminate insanity as an affirmative defense. For example, Title VII of Senate Bill 2572 would have added the following provisions to Title 18 of the U.S. Criminal Code:

It shall be a defense to a prosecution under any Federal statute, that the defendant, as a result of mental disease or defect, lacked the state of mind required as an element of the offense charged. Mental disease or defect does not otherwise constitute a defense.

Senate Insanity Defense Hearings, pp. 9, 11, 29.

If enacted into law this provision would confine the use of psychiatric testimony in federal criminal cases to an adjudication of the *mens rea* issue. As explained by its sponsor:

Under S. 2572, the "insanity defense" (and I put that in quotes because strictly speaking there would be no "insanity defense" but only an argument by the defendant that the crime was not committed because one of its elements, namely *mens rea*, was absent) would be confined to legal issues. The complexity of modern psychological theory with its unknowns would be irrelevant, except to the degree that these theories might shed some light on whether the defendant demonstrated a *mens rea*. In the words of Chief Justice Burger, who commented while still a circuit judge: "No rule of law can possibly be sound or workable which is dependent on the terms of another discipline whose members are in profound disagreement about what those terms mean." *Campbell v. U.S.*, 307 F.2nd 597, 612 (1962). This bill makes contentions about the mental state of the defendant a question to be addressed within the legal terms of the state of mind requirements of any criminal offense.

Senate Insanity Defense Hearings, *supra*, 11 (Prepared statement of Senator Orrin G. Hatch).

While a number of other bills containing similar provisions were introduced in the Senate, it was the bill introduced by Senator Orrin Hatch that received the endorsement of the executive branch. Attorney General William French Smith, for instance, in testifying before the Senate committee asserted that this proposal "would best protect the public and promote efficiency." Senate Insanity Defense Hearings, pp. 26–29.

Others, both in and out of government, however, challenged the need for a radical change in the defense and questioned the timing of the Senate's proposed action. Concern was expressed over whether the anger and frustration that followed the Hinckley trial might not interfere with a dispassionate and rational consideration of the issues. See, Myths and Realities: A Report of the National Commission on the Insanity Defense, p. 5 (1983). Other commentators noted what they viewed as the shortcomings of the *mens rea* approach. In testifying before the committee Professor Richard Bonnie of the University of Virginia offered the following critique:

I would like to summarize the case against abolition of the insanity defense. In general, most of the bills before you would adopt this approach, and it has been recently enacted in Montana and Idaho. If the insanity defense were abolished, in my opinion, the law would not take adequate account of the incapacitating effects of severe mental illness. First, people who, in the Attorney General's words, who shoot people when they think they are shooting trees or squeeze a lemon when they think they are squeezing someone's neck do not really exist. And even if these conditions exist, individuals who make these perceptual mistakes might have the mens rea required for some criminal offenses because some criminal offenses actually require negligence or recklessness as the mens rea required in the rather than what we regard in a lay sense, as intentions or subjective beliefs.

Second, and this is the more serious problem, *mens rea* focuses only on conscious perceptions. It has no qualitative dimension. For this reason, the mens rea approach would ignore the realities of severe mental illness. Some mentally ill defendants, and by this I mean persons who were psychotic and grossly out of touch with reality, may very well be said to have intended to do what they did but, nonetheless, they may have been so severely disturbed that they were unable to appreciate the significance of their actions in any but a trivial way.

* * *

[A] criminal conviction signifying a societal judgment that [this class of] defendant deserves to be punished for what he did would offend the basic moral intuitions of the community. Judges and juries would then be forced either to return a verdict of conviction in such cases which they regard as morally obtuse or to acquit the defendant in defiance of the law. They should be spared such moral embarrassment.

Senate Insanity Defense Hearings, p. 258.

The Omnibus Crime Bill (S.2572), which included Title VII, the Insanity Defense Provision, was approved by the U.S. Senate's Committee on the Judiciary. However, on July 1, 1982, "under an unusual time agreement worked out by the senate leaders," the insanity provisions were deleted. *Congressional Quarterly Almanac*, 1982, p. 419. No further action was taken on the insanity defense issue during the 97th Congress.

Proposals for the abolition of the insanity defense in effect died with the passage of the Insanity Defense Reform Act of 1984. While this legislation significantly alters the rules which govern the administration of the defense in federal cases, it retains the insanity defense in its essential aspects.

Questions and Comments

1. To what extent would the application of the *mens rea* approach lead to results that are different than those obtained by the application of the Model Penal Code Test? The difference in result is perhaps best illustrated in the context of the following hypothetical fact situation:

"A man of about 50 years of age, he was indicted for second degree murder while armed. [Mr. A.] had never before even been charged with a significant criminal offense. One day he was seated in his car with his wife in an alley off 14th Street, N.W., in this city. He noticed a man, a harmless alcoholic who frequented, about 50 to 75 feet away. Mr. A became convinced that this man had a razor in his hand and that he was about to attack Mr. A and his wife, even though the man had done nothing whatsoever to justify this fear and was in fact unarmed. Mr. A, believing that his and his wife's lives depended on it, then shot the man to death. Mr. A, it turned out, was suffering from paranoid schizophrenia, a disease that was becoming progressively worse, and he sincerely believed that there was a plot against him involving powerful and ruthless drug dealers in the city. Mr. A was a skilled welder and mechanic, and he believed that these individuals wanted him to develop machinery that would duplicate tropical environments and permit the growing of narcotic-yielding plants in warehouses throughout Washington, D.C. Mr. A was convinced that these drug dealers knew that he would refuse on principle to participate in this scheme, and that they wanted to kill him in retaliation. When he saw the man in the alley, Mr. A believed that he was an assassin hired by his enemies, and Mr. A shot the man out of fear and rage.

* * *

It was beyond dispute that he suffered from a severe mental illness, and that illness prevented him from perceiving that his attack was in fact unprovoked and unjustified. Further, his illness substantially impaired his ability to control himself.

* * *

[Under the Model Penal Code Test, Mr. A. would, in all likelihood be found not guilty by reason of insanity.]

[H]ow would Mr. A have fared if the only question had been whether the mental elements of the offense were present? Mr. A, * * * would have to be convicted at least of manslaughter while armed (an offense carrying a possible penalty of life in prison under D.C. law) if not of murder. Mr. A deliberately shot and killed another human being—the essential elements of criminal homicide. Further, he had no viable self-defense (or defense of others) claim under D.C. law, because it was totally unreasonable to think that the victim posed an imminent threat of death or serious bodily harm to anyone. Mr. A's unreasonable belief to the contrary would, at most, have negated malice, an essential element of murder, and reduced the charge to manslaughter."

Senate Insanity Defense Hearings, pp. 216–217.

2. Opponents of the *mens rea* approach would presumably find the results obtained in the above hypothetical objectionable on two grounds. First, the conviction on charges of manslaughter of Mr. A, who, it could be argued, lacked comprehension of what he was doing, would be deemed unjust or irrational. *See* the comments of Professor Richard Bonnie, *supra.* See also, P. Johnson, *Review of Madness and the Criminal Law,* 50 U. of Chicago L.Rev. 1534, 1540 (1983). Further, a test limited to *mens rea* would in the view of its opponents lead to capricious results. In this connection consider the analysis of one critic:

Mr. A's case * * * reveals how a test that is limited to the mental elements of the offense can yield capricious results. For if Mr. A's delusions had been somewhat different, he could have escaped conviction even under an insanity standard limited to the elements of the offense. If, for example, he had believed that the man in the alley was in fact a robot sent after him by his enemies—rather than a paid assassin—Mr. A would have lacked the intent to kill a human being. Hence, he could not have been convicted even of voluntary manslaughter. Is it sensible to make guilt hinge in this way on the specific content of a person's insane delusions? I do not think so.

A question would also remain whether Mr. A, in this hypothetical variation of the actual facts of his case, could be convicted of involuntary manslaughter, on the theory that the killing was reckless even if it was not deliberate. Should the law deem him reckless in his belief that the man he shot was actually a robot? How indeed should the recklessness of a person suffering from such insane delusions be assessed?

An insanity standard that turned on the presence or absence of the mental elements of the offense would also entangle the courts in metaphysical conundrums not unlike the medieval puzzle of how many angels can dance on the head of a pin. Suppose an insane defendant had shot and killed a person, thinking that the victim was an alien from another planet. Did this defendant intend to kill a "human being?" What if the defendant thought his victim was a devil in human form? Or a human under demonic possession?

Instead of asking in all of these cases whether there was an intent to take "human" life, it is far more sensible I think to use the current test: whether the defendant's insane delusions substantially impaired his ability to recognize the quality of its act and its wrongfulness.

Senate Insanity Defense Hearings, pp. 218–219.

Does the application of the Model Penal Code Test lead to less capricious results? In this connection recall the issues raised in connection with the *Hinckley* case in Section III.C.2. *supra.*

3. Professional organizations in the legal-medical fields have adopted differing positions on the proposal to eliminate the insanity defense. The American Bar Association (ABA) and the American Psychiatric Association (APA), while favoring retention of the insanity defense, advocated either procedural or substantive modifications. *See* Wexler, *An Offense—Victim Approach to Insanity Defense Reform*, 26 Ariz. L.R. 17–19 (1984). In contrast to the ABA and the APA, the House of Delegates of the American Medical Association (AMA) supported the abolition of the special defense of insanity. *Id.*

4. Those favoring retention of the insanity defense have noted that opposition to it, at least in part, is a product of the public's misapprehension as to the frequency with which the offense is asserted. Available data suggests that the plea is raised in approximately one percent of all felony cases and that acquittals by reason of insanity are even rarer. Hearing Transcript of the National Commission on the Insanity Defense, p. 9. This contrasts with studies that have found that some groups in society, such as state legislatures, estimate the acquittal rate at 10

percent of all felony indictments. Committee on the Judiciary, Hearings on the Insanity Defense, p. 63.

On the other side, it has been argued that, while the insanity defense may not be statistically significant, "it probably has more of an effect than just a statistical analysis of the cases in which its raised would indicate." Hearing Transcript of the National Commission on the Insanity Defense, p. 27. This conclusion stems from the fact that "90 to 95 percent of criminal cases are resolved without a trial." *Id.* Accordingly, the rules governing the insanity defense are likely to influence the plea bargaining negotiations between the defendant and the prosecutor. Thus, in the view of the Justice Department, "the number of trials in which [the insanity defense is raised] wouldn't give a clear picture of the entire effect on the system." *Id.* at 27.

5. The current debate concerning the insanity defense presents an interesting illustration of how legal changes in one sector can have an unanticipated spillover effect in another area. The judicial and legislatively mandated changes in the civil commitment laws which began in the late 1960's resulted in a tightening of civil commitment standards. The application of these new standards to those acquitted on grounds of insanity resulted in fewer commitments of those in this class and the popular perception that the insanity defense allowed dangerous defendants to escape needed institutionalization. Moreover, the application of these new standards meant that, when commitment did occur, the period of confinement would be substantially less than it was in former years. Myths and Realities, Hearing Transcripts, at 74. Some commentators have suggested that an awareness of this fact on the part of defendants and their counsel explains, at least in part, the increased use of the not guilty by reason of insanity plea in states such as New York and Michigan. Senate Insanity Defense Hearings, p. 263 (statement of Richard Bonnie).

6. In adopting the Insanity Defense Reform Act of 1984, the Congress signaled its intent to retain the insanity defense in its essential aspects and thus rejected the proposals which called for its abolition. At the same time, Congress also implicitly rejected several other alternatives which had been proposed including the addition of a guilty but mentally ill verdict. Although advocated by the Attorney General's Task Force on Crime (Hearing Transcript of the National Commission on the Insanity Defense, pg. 24) this proposal was opposed by the administration on the grounds that this approach would not "eliminate confusing psychiatric testimony before a jury concerning a wide range of issues not directly related to the mental element required for the crime." Hearing Transcript of the National Commission of the Insanity Defense (Statement of Associate Attorney General Ruldolph Giuliani) p. 24.

The most far reaching of the proposals was that contained in S.1106, introduced by Senators Zorinksy and Thurmond, which would have eliminated the insanity defense and allowed only a "guilty but insane verdict" where the act was the product of a mental disorder.

Senate Insanity Defense Hearings, pp. 487–489.

S.1106 represented the most radical of the proposed insanity law revisions. First, unlike the guilty but mentally ill laws enacted by Michigan and other states, the "guilty but insane" verdict would *replace* rather than supplement the insanity defense. Further, and more significantly, S.1106 would effectively eliminate all psychiatric issues from the determination of *mens rea*. The constitutionality of this approach has been questioned. See, Senate Insanity Defense Hearings, pp. 6–7. Senator Orrin Hatch, for instance, in testifying on the various proposals to limit the insanity defense noted:

> The plea which the defendant would enter to invoke the defense in S.1106 would be "guilty but insane," instead of "not guilty only by reason of insanity," which I prefer. This misconstrues the nature of the *mens rea* defense. A crime is only a crime if all elements of its definition are present. If the defendant can show that he did not have the proper state of mind he did not commit that crime. It, therefore, makes no sense to call him guilty of a crime he did not, by its own terms, commit.

Senate Insanity Defense Hearings, p. 6.

What would be the basis for a constitutional challenge to this type of law were it to be enacted?

7. Questions have been raised as to whether the *mens rea* approach to criminal insanity would, as its proponents have contended, limit the range of psychiatric evidence that could be brought before the jury. *See*, Insanity Defense Hearings, at p. 41. Moreover, it has been suggested that, rather than limiting the grounds upon which relief from criminal liability may be granted, the *mens rea* approach might, in fact, expand the class of individuals who could be found not guilty by reason of insanity. These concerns were brought out in the questioning of Associate Attorney General Rudolph Giuliani by members of the Senate Judiciary Committee:

> Senator HEFLIN. Well, let me ask you about the mens rea, the state of mind that you are advocating. You defined it as being the required state of mind for the elements of the offense charged. And the word "elements of the offense charged" causes me a lot of concern. We will take several different crimes. The distinction between murder and manslaughter is malice. The distinction between first degree murder and second degree murder is premeditation. Those are states of mind. There are a quite large number of offenses, many different states of mind, and many different elements.
>
> In, for example, of receiving and concealing stolen goods, there is the element, depending on the statute, whether the person had knowledge that the article was stolen. Or in another instance in

some statutes, whether or not the accused had reason to believe that the article was stolen. All of those being states of mind.

We have recently adopted here in Congress a statute pertaining to CIA agents, the agent identity bill. This has, as I view it, at least four individual states of mind involved, one being proof that there be a course of a pattern of activities, and the second state of mind intended to identify and expose covert agents. A third state of mind is the requirement of the proof that there be reason to believe that such activities could impair or impede the foreign intelligence activities of the United States. Then it requires, of course, disclosure [sic] the identity; and then it has another state of mind: knowing that the information disclosed so identifies such individual and that the United States is taking affirmative measures to conceal such individuals classified intelligence.

Now, I am worried that the mens rea in the state of mind, where the burden of proof does not shift, will create a quagmire and will really give lawyers a field day in defending these cases. If you have to place the burden of proof on the Government to prove that there was premeditation, if there is an insanity issue that arises, this causes not a narrowing, but it seems to me to be causing a broadening of these—of the elements of insanity in its relationship to the specific crime that the accused may be charged.

Senate Insanity Defense Hearings, p. 37.

8. The following exchange between the chairman, Senator Strom Thurmond, and the witness, Associate Attorney General Giuliani, highlights the issue concerning the scope of psychiatric evidence which would be admissible under the *mens rea* approach:

The CHAIRMAN. Now, the Attorney General stated that you both view S.2572 to eliminate entirely the presentation at trial of confusing psychiatric testimony on the issue of the defendant's ability to control his behavior and the wrongfulness of his acts. However, if psychiatric testimony is still admissible to negate mens rea, won't the jury again be confronted with conflicting psychiatric testimony, what type of testimony would be admissible?

Mr. GIULIANI. The testimony that would be admissible would be solely limited to whether the person knew what he was doing at the time that he did it. There could no longer be testimony that ranged far afield, in our view, to include things such as irresistible impulses or voices talking to the person, or being unable to conform their conduct to the dictates of the law. It would focus on a very, very narrow issue, did the person know what he was doing. And in our view, at least of the insanity defenses that have been raised in the Federal courts in the last several years, 4 or 5 years, it is rare that a person is able to put in a defense, much less make out a defense, that he didn't know what he was doing. Usually, in the vast majority of cases, the insanity defense concerns what is really the second part of the test, not being able to conform conduct to the dictates of the law. That was the insanity defense principally in *Hinckley* and it is true in most of the others and psychiatrists will testify about the person operating under delusions and hearing voices and being compelled by irresistible impulses to commit the crime.

It is very rare that a psychiatrist will testify that the person had a mental age of 2 years, although he might be 30, or that the person thought he was shooting at an apple when, in fact, he was shooting at a human being. And that would narrow the scope of the testimony very, very dramatically, and we don't believe constitutionally there would be much room for avoiding that since that gets right down to the mental state required to commit the crime.

Senate Insanity Defense Hearings, p. 39.

9. Issues of a similar nature have been raised in connection with the *mens rea* legislation enacted by the State of Idaho. (The Idaho law is discussed in greater detail in subsection 2 below). Some have contended that the Idaho law, which has provisions nearly identical to those contained in S. 2572, could result in "a statutory construction which restores the insanity defense by judicial interpretation." Thomas, *Breaking the Stone Tablet: Criminal Law Without the Insanity Defense,* 19 Idaho L.R. 239 (1983). Could courts, for instance, construe the *mens rea* provisions to allow the inquiry of the *mens rea* "to be concerned with impairments in capacity to appreciate the wrongfulness of conduct or impairments of rationality, which affect motivation for committing a criminal offense"? *Id.* at 252. Stated another way, "[i]f one were to accept the proposition that *mens rea* means both the ability to understand the act and the ability to commit it in a morally blameworthy way, then the new enactment incorporates the old idea that ability to appreciate the wrongfulness of conduct is a proper inquiry for psychiatrists at trial." *Id.* Proponents of the Idaho legislation, however, are convinced that the wording of the statute and its legislative history would preclude such judicial expansion since "*mens rea* does not include any element of blameworthiness." Thomas, *Breaking the Stone Tablet: Criminal Law Without the Insanity Defense,* 19 Idaho L.Rev. 249, 252–253 (1983).

Is the analysis of Associate Attorney General Thomas convincing? Would it reasonably be possible for a court to construe the "awareness" requirement by *mens rea* as encompassing an emotional as well as an intellectual awareness? If so, is there any way that a legislature could prevent this result?

ii. *Legislative Initiatives at the State Level*

Although a number of states have considered laws abolishing the insanity defense, Montana and Idaho have become the first to adopt legislation eliminating insanity as an affirmative defense in criminal trials. Montana in 1979 and Idaho in 1982 enacted laws that, in the guilt determination stage of the trial, limit the admissibility of psychiatric evidence to the issue of whether the defendant possessed the requisite state of mind necessary to commit the crime alleged.

The Montana legislation deals with the insanity issue in the following manner:

* * *

During the guilt phase of the trial, the new law allowed admission of only one kind of evidence in support of an insanity defense— evidence that the defendant "did or did not have a state of mind which is an element of the offense." In other words, the State still bears the burden of proving every element of the crime beyond a reasonable doubt.

* * *

Taking a closer look, the new Montana law essentially provides that a psychiatric examination of the defendant will be conducted if the defendant or his counsel files a notice of intent to rely on a defense of mental disease or defect, or raises the issue of the defendant's fitness to proceed. If the defendant lacks the fitness to proceed, the court suspends the proceeding and seeks treatment for the defendant until his fitness is restored. Once fitness is determined, the defendant proceeds to trial to be found (1) "guilty;" (2) "not guilty;" (3) "not guilty by reason of mental state," *i.e.*, that because of a mental disease or defect the defendant could not have had a particular state of mind that is an essential element of the offense charged.

If the defendant is found not guilty he is discharged. If he is found guilty he may present evidence at his sentencing hearing concerning his ability to appreciate the wrongfulness of his conduct or to conform his conduct to the requirements of law. Taking this evidence into consideration the court may impose sentence, or it may commit him to the custody of the director of the Department of Institutions for placement in an appropriate institution. Under the third and final alternative, if the defendant is found not guilty by reason of lack of mental state, the court may: (1) release him unconditionally; (2) release him subject to conditions; (3) commit him to the custody of the superintendent of the state mental hospital for treatment until he may be released.

Senate Insanity Defense Hearings (Statement of John H. Maynard, Assistant Attorney General,) pp. 234–35.

The pertinent provisions of the Idaho statute provide that "mental condition shall not be a defense to any charge of criminal conduct." Idaho Code Chapter 18, § 207a (1982). This prohibition, however, is in turn qualified by the proviso that "[n]othing herein is intended to prevent the admission of expert evidence on the issues of *mens rea* or any state of mind which is an element of the offense, subject to the rules of evidence." Idaho Code Chapter 18, § 207c (1982). As noted by the Idaho solicitor general, who was instrumental in drafting the legislation, "[t]he most important effect of the statute is that mental illness becomes a simple evidentiary question instead of a principle of substantive law." Thomas, *Breaking the Stone Tablet: Criminal Law Without the Insanity Defense*, 19 Idaho L.R. 250 (1983).

Questions and Comments

1. Some have questioned whether Idaho's abolition enactment would, in fact, limit the scope of expert testimony that is admissible on the question of mental disorder. It has been suggested, for instance, that an expansive judicial construction of the statute might allow the introduction of evidence pertaining to the defendant's motive in committing a particular act. *See*, Wickham, *The Insanity Defense Is Alive and Well in Idaho*, 25 Advocate 4 (May 1982). In this connection reconsider the discussions in note 9 at p. 685 *supra*.

2. Maryland has by judicial construction eliminated the traditional not guilty by reason of insanity verdict. *Pouncey v. State*, 297 Md. 264, 465 A.2d 475 (1983). The consequence of a successful plea of insanity is the finding "guilty but insane." *Id*. at 475. The "guilty but mentally ill" finding means that no *criminal* sentence may be entered though "the defendant may be held in a mental institution until it is determined that release would not constitute a danger to the individual or to the person or property of another." *Id*. at 478.

In Maryland the defendant's mental incapacity can also lead to a finding of not guilty, however, apparently only in cases where the defendant is found to have lacked the necessary *mens rea*. *Id*. at 478.

b. *Legal Implications of the* Mens Rea *Approach*

The U.S. Supreme Court has never ruled on the existence of a constitutional right to assert the insanity defense, nor has the legitimacy of the recent Montana or Idaho statutes been constitutionally challenged. Three state supreme courts have had occasion to review statutes abolishing the insanity defense, however, and in each case the statute was found unconstitutional. In *State v. Strasburg*, 60 Wash. 106, 110 P. 1020 (1910), the Supreme Court of Washington reversed a first degree assault conviction because the defendant was denied the opportunity to assert a defense of insanity. The court held unconstitutional a statute that provided:

> It shall be no defense to a person charged with the commission of a crime that at the time of its commission he was unable, by virtue of his insanity, idiocy or imbecility, to comprehend the nature and quality of the act committed, or to understand that it was wrong; or that he was afflicted with a morbid propensity to commit prohibited acts; nor shall any testimony or other proof thereof be admitted in evidence.

110 P. 1020, 1021.

The Washington Supreme Court held that the statute violated its own state constitution's due process clause by relieving the government of its obligation to prove a substantive element of the offense charged: intent. The court also noted that the right to plead the insanity defense was considered a part of the right to jury trial at the time the Washington State Constitution was adopted, making it a substantive part of the due process guarantee.

A similar statute was found to violate the Mississippi Constitution in *Sinclair v. State*, 161 Miss. 142, 132 So. 581 (1931) (*per curiam*). As in *Strasberg*, the court found in *Sinclair* that the statute, which excluded evidence of insanity except for purposes of mitigation, violated due process because it relieved the government of the duty to prove intent. Judge Ethridge objected that the statute violated due process because, as applied to murder cases, it attempted "to enact by legislative fiat that insanity cannot destroy the mind so that it cannot form an intent * * *. In other words, it is equal to saying that malicious intent is obtained by legislative declaration merely; this, as has often been said by courts, cannot be done." 132 So. 581, 586 (Ethridge, J., concurring).

A third state court held a statute abolishing the insanity defense unconstitutional in *State v. Lange*, 168 La. 958, 123 So. 639 (1929). In *Lange*, the Louisiana Supreme Court considered a bifurcation statute that called for the insanity stage of criminal trials to be heard by a "Commission of Lunacy." The court held that the statute, which made the commission's determination of sanity final, violated the constitutional right to a jury trial. The court concluded that the right to a jury trial demands that " * * * where the offence itself is triable, under the Constitution, by jury, the accused has the constitutional right to have his defense of insanity tried by jury." 123 So. 639, 642.

Opponents to the abolition of the insanity defense argue that these state court decisions indicate that current attempts to abolish the defense will also be held unconstitutional. *See* Robitcher and Haynes, *In Defense of the Insanity Defense*, 31 Emory L.J. 9 (1982). The statutes that were held violative of due process in those cases are readily distinguishable, however, from the current attempts to substitute the *mens rea* standard of criminal responsibility for the insanity tests. The *mens rea* approach avoids the major objection to the foregoing statutes by permitting psychiatric evidence on the substantive issue of intent, thus maintaining the government's burden of proving every element of the crimes charged.

It has also been suggested that the insanity defense was fused with due process as a right which existed at common law at the time the U.S. Constitution was adopted. This argument, however, fails to take into account the fact that when the Constitution was originally adopted, and prior to the *M'Naghten* case in 1843, evidence of psychiatric experts was limited to issues of intent. Morris, *The Criminal Responsibility of the Mentally Ill*, 33 Syracuse L.Rev. 477, 500 (1982). Thus, the limitation of psychiatric evidence to the defendant's state of mind, as called for by either existing state or the proposed federal statutes, does not appear to violate constitutional requirements.

Attempts to extend the rationale of U.S. Supreme Court decisions in related areas to conclude that the court *will* find the insanity defense protected by the constitution are also unconvincing. Although the court held in *In re Winship*, 397 U.S. 358, 364, 90 S.Ct. 1068, 1072, 25 L.Ed.2d 368 (1970), that the due process clause "protects the accused against conviction except upon proof beyond a reasonable doubt of every fact necessary to constitute the crime with which he is charged," this requirement would seemingly not rule out the *mens rea* approach. As long as the government continues to bear the burden of proving that the defendant possessed the state of mind required by the offense charged, the limitation of psychiatric testimony to the issue of the defendant's state of mind appears to comport fully with this due process requirement. Similarly, when the court in *Davis v. United States*, 160 U.S. 469, 16 S.Ct. 353, 40 L.Ed. 499 (1895), ruled that in federal courts sanity must be proven beyond reasonable doubt as an element of every crime, it did not make sanity *per se* a constitutional issue. In *Leland v. Oregon*, 343 U.S. 790, 72 S.Ct. 1002, 96 L.Ed. 1302 (1952), the court upheld a rule requiring the *defendant* to prove insanity beyond a reasonable doubt, making clear that *Davis* merely established a rule for use in federal courts and should not be read as constitutional doctrine. 343 U.S. 790, 797, 72 S.Ct. 1002.

Another case often asserted as suggesting a constitutional right to assert the insanity defense is *Robinson v. California*, 370 U.S. 660, 82 S.Ct. 1417, 8 L.Ed.2d 758 (1962), in which the court held that a California statute making it a criminal offense to be addicted to narcotics violated the prohibition against cruel and unusual punishment because it made the "status" of narcotics addiction (characterized by the court as an "illness") a criminal offense. In dicta, the court stated:

> It is unlikely that any State at this moment in history would attempt to make it a criminal offense for a person to be mentally ill * * * [I]n light of contemporary human knowledge, a law which made a criminal offense of such a disease would doubtless be universally thought to be infliction of cruel and unusual punishment in violation of the Eighth and Fourteenth Amendments.

370 U.S. 660, 666, 82 S.Ct. 1417, 1420.

The likelihood that this language would support a constitutional right to the insanity defense is severely diminished by the decision in *Powell v. Texas*, 392 U.S. 514, 88 S.Ct. 2145, 20 L.Ed.2d 1254 (1968), where the court upheld a statute that made it a crime to appear drunk in a public place. Rejecting the argument that the statute made alcoholism a status offense in violation of *Robinson*, the Court observed that the defendant "was convicted not for being a chronic alcoholic, but for being in public while drunk." 392 U.S. 514, 532, 88 S.Ct. 2145, 2154. The court emphatically rejected the opportunity to rule on the constitutional adequacy of the Texas insanity test, which was also in question, observing that "[n]othing could be less fruitful than for this Court to be impelled into defining some sort of insanity defense in constitutional terms." 392 U.S. 514, 536, 88 S.Ct. 2145, 2156. *See also* Robitscher and Haynes, *supra,* at 58.

Index

References are to Pages

691

†